CRITICAL COMPANION TO

Ralph Waldo Emerson

CRITICAL COMPANION TO

Ralph Waldo Emerson

A Literary Reference to His Life and Work

TIFFANY K. WAYNE

Critical Companion to Ralph Waldo Emerson

Facts On File, Inc.
An imprint of Infobase Publishing
132 West 31st Street
New York NY 10001

Library of Congress Cataloging-in-Publication Data
Wayne, Tiffany K., 1968–
Critical companion to Ralph Waldo Emerson:
a literary reference to his life and work / Tiffany K. Wayne.
p. cm.
Includes bibliographical references and index.
ISBN 978-0-8160-7358-0 (acid-free paper) 1. Emerson, Ralph Waldo, 1803–1882—Handbooks, manuals, etc. 2. Authors, American—19th century—Biography—Handbooks, manuals, etc. I. Title.

PS1631.W37 2010
814'.3—dc22 2009024809

Facts On File books are available at special discounts when purchased in bulk quantities for businesses, associations, institutions, or sales promotions. Please call our Special Sales Department in New York at (212) 967-8800 or (800) 322-8755.

You can find Facts On File on the World Wide Web at http://www.factsonfile.com

Text design by Erika K. Arroyo
Composition by Hermitage Publishing Services
Cover printed by Sheridan Books, Inc., Ann Arbor, Mich.
Book printed and bound by Sheridan Books, Inc., Ann Arbor, Mich.
Date printed: July 2010
Printed in the United States of America

10 9 8 7 6 5 4 3 2 1

This book is printed on acid-free paper and contains 30 percent postconsumer recycled content.

Contents

ACKNOWLEDGMENTS

In July 2008 I had the privilege of participating in a special one-week National Endowment for the Humanities (NEH) Landmarks of American History workshop in Concord, Massachusetts. The goal of the workshop was to appreciate the power of place in American history, and indeed, I came away with a new perspective on Emerson's place in Concord that ultimately made this a better book. For the opportunity to look up from our books and revisit the literary past in a very real way, my first round of thanks goes to the historians and archivists, the curators and interpreters, who attend to Concord's living history on a daily basis—the staffs of the Concord Free Public Library, the Concord Museum, Orchard House, the Wayside, the Old Manse, Emerson House, the Thoreau Society and Walden Pond State Reservation, and the Minuteman National Historical Park. Thanks to your work, Ralph Waldo Emerson and friends are alive and well in 21st-century Massachusetts.

Special thanks to the directors of the NEH 2008 summer program in Concord—Geoff Grimes, Paul Benson, and Martha Holder—who created a positive and fruitful experience for all participants, and to David Berry, president of the Community College Humanities Association, for believing in the importance of this opportunity and showing up to tell us so. Finally, thank you to the teachers, scholars, colleagues, and now friends who shared their research, their passion, and their time with me while in Concord and Boston. In writing this book, I have returned again and again to our conversations about reading and teaching Emerson and the Transcendentalists.

My deepest gratitude goes to all of the contributors to the present volume for providing both depth and the necessary breadth to create this portrait of Emerson as lecturer and essayist, preacher and poet, family man, and citizen of Concord and the world. You allowed me—and now the reader—access to your collective decades of research, and your passion for Emerson convinced me again and again of the value of this volume. Special thanks, however, must go to Bill Scalia for his incredible insight into and analysis of so many of the poems, and to David A. Dilworth, idealist philosopher to my grounded historian, for his vast knowledge of the many intellectual influences on and legacies of Emerson, his willingness to always do "just one more" entry, and for reminding me, when I was overwhelmed and doubtful, that thinking and writing about Emerson on a daily basis was not such a bad job to have.

My sincerest thanks go to my editor, Jeff Soloway, for having enough faith in me to embark on a second project together and for entrusting the Emerson volume to me. He listened to every concern, suggestion, and excuse with professionalism, knowledge, and constant encouragement, skillfully guiding the direction of the book but always trusting my own (slow) process and vision. I must also acknowledge the staff of the Cabrillo College Library for their support of faculty research. Topsy Smalley, Stephanie Stainback, and Sylvia Winder located books, fulfilled interlibrary loan requests, and eagerly accepted my recommendations for additions to the library collection. Constance Manoli-Skocay of the Concord Free Public Library oversees a treasure trove of photographs related to Emerson and his circle and responded to all my 11th-hour needs—I only wish I could have used more of the images in the book. Thanks also to Heather Cole and Mary Haegert at the Houghton Library at Harvard University, Maria Powers at the Orchard House in Concord, and Mike Frederick and Jeff Cramer of the Thoreau Society and Thoreau Institute, for their timely assistance in locating and securing permissions of key photos. The behind-the-scenes staff of these institutions and others, such as the Library of Congress and the New York Public Library, made it possible for a researcher in northern California to access online the visual history of 19th-century New England at any time.

Lastly, I thank Ralph Waldo Emerson. I found in my subject constant inspiration for the work at hand, for he wrote often and thoughtfully on the scholar's task and on the act of writing—a side of Emerson acknowledged in Robert D. Richardson, Jr.'s recent gem of a book, *First We Read, Then We Write: Emerson on the Creative Process* (2009). Emerson became, to me, a guide not only for the writing life but for life in general. He was a philosopher of the work one is called to do (whatever it may be) and a poet concerned with the art of living. Reading Emerson raises more questions than answers, and, in his own words, all comes down to one question: "How shall I live?"

This book is dedicated to those with whom I live most closely. To Miles and Lillian, always inquisitive and wise beyond their years.

And to David Wayne, for seeing the same truths I see.

INTRODUCTION

More than 200 years after Ralph Waldo Emerson's birth in 1803, it is clear that he is still recognized as one of the nation's most important thinkers. For many, Emerson embodies certain American ideals, evidenced, for example, by the publication of a 2009 "keepsake edition" of President Barack Obama's inaugural address alongside writings by Abraham Lincoln and Ralph Waldo Emerson, noted as "two great thinkers and writers who have helped shape [Obama] politically, philosophically, and personally" (Barack Obama, *The Inaugural Address, 2009. Together with Abraham Lincoln's First and Second Inaugural Addresses and The Gettysburg Address and Ralph Waldo Emerson's Self-Reliance* [Penguin, 2009]). Emerson and his circle have also been the subjects of two recent acclaimed novels: Matthew Pearl's *The Dante Club* (2003) and Amy Belding Brown's *Mr. Emerson's Wife* (2005). We continue to hear Emerson's words everywhere, from television commercials to greeting cards—from "the shot heard 'round the world" to "a foolish consistency is the hobgoblin of little minds." If nothing else, Emerson stands as one of the most quotable American writers.

And yet the "real" Ralph Waldo Emerson remains an enigma. His most famous essays and poems—such as "Self-Reliance," the "Concord Hymn" poem, or *Nature*—are regularly taught in high school and college, but students are often unfamiliar with many of the other works produced in his more than 50-year career as a popular lecturer, essayist, and poet. Beyond the *idea* of self-reliance or of an appreciation of nature (the latter more often associated with his friend Henry David Thoreau's experiment at Walden Woods), few Americans could explain the core tenets of Transcendentalism, the 19th-century literary and philosophical movement with which Emerson became associated. While the core of Emerson's ideas—so often condensed to those perfect quotes and aphorisms—speak as timeless truths to so many, Transcendentalism remains a vaguely understood philosophy and a relatively specialized field of study.

This paradox began in Emerson's own lifetime. By the middle of the 19th century Emerson was an immensely popular lyceum lecturer, and by the time of his death in 1882 hundreds of young people and seekers were making the pilgrimage to see the Sage of Concord (unfortunately for Emerson, the stage from Boston made a stop right at his front gate). And yet many contemporaries who attended his lectures or read his essays (and undoubtedly many students since) found him extremely difficult to understand, even incomprehensible. A friend and fellow Unitarian minister, Cyrus Bartol, seems to have perfectly summed up the Emerson paradox in an 1847 review of Emerson's first volume of *Poems*. Bartol wrote: "The analysis of Emerson's writings is no short or easy task. . . ," and yet, "his works, on account of their peculiarity, if nothing else, will probably be among the most enduring of the present time."

Bartol was right, although mere "peculiarity" cannot explain the endurance of Emerson's name and ideas. As difficult as it sometimes is to dissect his language and thoughts, Emerson himself tried to help by noting that, in fact, throughout his works, he focused on one simple idea. He wrote in his journal of 1840: "In all my lectures, I have taught one doctrine, namely, the infinitude of the private man." In this theme he both reflected and created the new American spirit. What the Revolution created politically, Emerson and the Transcendentalists, the American romantics, promoted intellectually—that is, independence, self-sovereignty, the supreme rights of the individual. Our commitment to these ideals still holds, and so, then, does our interest in Emerson. For while he spoke in the language of abstractions—of philosophy and spirit, of nature and humanity—ultimately he wrote as an American living in a specific time and place, describing what it meant (and still means) to be an American.

It was through this lens "of the private man" that he approached all subjects, and no subject was beyond his view. His life's work was to collect his own impressions on history, science, power, politics, fate, poetry, heroes, nature, and the universe, as well as on the human experiences of childhood, friendship, love, marriage, death, and grief. He contemplated "great men" and the nature of genius, and then turned to consider with equal fervor and seriousness the flowers and the bees, or babies learning to talk. He was himself aware not merely of his personal influence (regarding which he would have been quite modest, as he only sought to encourage listeners or readers to cultivate their own thought) but of the great intellectual shifts of his time—shifts he, of course, helped bring about. He opened up our idea of the life of the mind, and in one of his last public appearances, delivered in 1880, he reflected of the century and the lifetime behind him, that "the mind had become aware of itself."

Emerson rejected the idea that an inward focus on the self, or "egotism," as critics charged, was undesirable and even harmful to society. As he wrote in "The American Scholar" (1837), "Our age is bewailed as the age of Introversion. Must that needs be evil?" The introspective philosopher of transcendence was always also a man of his times. He was a family man, a citizen of Concord, of Massachusetts, of New England, of the United States, and of the world. So it was that his town's history was also the history of his ancestors and of the founding of the nation, and so it was that an international event, the emancipation of African slaves in the British West Indies, sparked some of his earliest public pronouncements on the moral problem of slavery. Abstract principles must always apply to everyday life, and, in all of his works, his solution to the question of "the times" was always the same: self-trust, self-reliance.

And yet, Emerson did not think alone. Others around him were also beginning to ask new questions and seek new answers. Contemporaries as well as scholars since have struggled to define the term "Transcendentalism." (Readers are invited to explore the full range of the movement, beyond Emerson, by consulting my previous volume, also published by Facts On File, *Encyclopedia of Transcendentalism* [2006].) As the movement's leading spokesperson, Emerson himself was compelled to address the question directly in his lecture "The Transcendentalist," in which he provided perhaps the most simple and succinct definition, then or since. He defined the movement in both philosophical and historical terms, noting that "what is popularly called Transcendentalism among us, is Idealism; Idealism as it appears in 1842." He further defined idealism as, simply, the belief in the superiority of "intuitive thought"—in other words, self-trust.

While a good starting point, this was, precisely, the paradox of Transcendentalism: How did a belief in the power of the *individual* translate into a *social* movement? The fundamental belief in the right to self-development, in the integrity of the individual mind, had application to questions of equality and justice that dominated 19th-century political culture, from the right to vote to the right to an education, from labor reform to women's rights, from Indian removal to the atrocities of American slavery. The reality never quite lived up to the ideal. As Emerson maintained throughout his writings, however, society is made up of individuals, and so is only ever as good as those individuals make it. Emerson encourages us, as Mahatma Gandhi is credited with saying, to be the change we wish to see in the world. In all of his writings, Emerson only ever invited us into ourselves. To paraphrase Virginia Woolf reflecting on Emerson many years later, he could not be rejected, for to reject his ideas would be to reject ourselves.

HOW TO USE THIS BOOK

Emerson was not the only Transcendentalist, nor did all of his Transcendentalist colleagues agree with him. *Critical Companion to Ralph Waldo Emerson* offers a way to navigate the particulars of Emersonian Transcendentalism, its influences, its contexts, and its legacy. Part I of the book is a brief biography of Emerson, providing the necessary context for understanding how his personal, spiritual, and intellectual lives were blended and evolved over time. Not all of Emerson's works are considered in the biography; the reader should consult the following entries on individual works for a more thorough discussion of the influences and circumstances surrounding the writing and publication of specific essays or poems.

Part II presents entries on almost 140 of Emerson's most significant individual works, including more than 60 poems, many of which are often overlooked as important to his larger philosophical and literary project. Emerson left behind more than five decades of sermons, public addresses, lectures, essays, and poems. The present volume could not contain entries on every published work, but all works deemed most important by Emerson scholars (and regularly included in major anthologies of his writings) are included.

Each entry provides a brief introduction outlining the general theme of the piece and any known contextual information on the composition, delivery, and publication history. Emerson often published as essays lectures given some years earlier; in most cases, the date listed is the first date of publication. If the work was not published in his lifetime (or was published many years, even decades, later), the first date of composition is given. For entries on an essay or lecture, a synopsis follows the introductory material. The synopsis guides the reader through the work, while still retaining as many of Emerson's own words as possible, so that the reader will get a sense of his skilled use of language and metaphor to make his points. While Emerson's essays do not always follow a standard format or clear outline, the synopsis often reveals how his style as a writer (in both language and format) was to present the reader with a series of insights or examples that illuminated his main point, building outward through successive layers or, in his words, "circles."

Each entry also includes a critical commentary section that either synthesizes the prevailing scholarly interpretation or provides an original interpretation of each essay or poem. While finding consistency between entries, the reader will find different emphases in different entries. More often than not, this is not just a question of different disciplinary approaches by different scholarly contributors, but rather reflective of Emerson's own interests across topics and genres. In other words, some of his works lend themselves to more historically specific analyses (lectures on reform and antislavery, for example), while others to literary or religious themes, and still others to fleshing out his metaphysical inquiries as part of a longer intellectual-history trajectory.

The critical commentary section also makes connections to ideas and themes found in other essays, lectures, or poems, or even in his journals or correspondence. These intertextual references are especially helpful for understanding how Emerson worked as a writer, mining his journal musings for lines of poetry or for sparks of lectures that were then revised, expanded, and later (sometimes much later) published as more fully developed essays. Cross-references (indicated by SMALL CAPITAL LETTERS) are also made to the related entries, included in Part III. These are brief entries on people, places, publications, and events related to Transcendentalism, with the emphasis on their relationship to Emerson, either personally or intellectually. Readers are again directed to the Facts On File *Encyclopedia of Transcendentalism* for longer, more detailed information on these and other terms and individuals related to American Transcendentalism of the 19th century.

Finally, Part IV includes a chronology of Emerson's life and times and a bibliography of the most recent and significant secondary scholarship on Emerson and Transcendentalism and of original and collected volumes of Emerson's works. The best understanding of Emerson comes through reading his own words directly. It is the hope that readers will be inspired to seek out the original works and, in true Emersonian fashion, discover their own relationship to his ideas.

PART I

Biography

Ralph Waldo Emerson

(1803–1882)

Ralph Waldo Emerson spent a great amount of time reading, speaking, and writing about "great men" and about the purpose of biography and of history. Aware that a man's character was influenced by the time and place of his birth, Emerson also looked to great writers, thinkers, or leaders as "representative" of universal traits or characteristics possessed by all men, in all times. Of his own interest in writing biography (which culminated in his 1850 collection, *Representative Men*), he noted in his journal, "I would draw characters, not write lives." Emerson himself left a treasure trove of writings that reveal his own mind and character. But he was also a man of a specific time and place, and his ideas were shaped by his life experiences—domestic, local, national, and international—as a man of the 19th century.

Ralph Waldo Emerson was born in Boston, Massachusetts, on May 25, 1803, the fourth child of Ruth Haskins and the Reverend William Emerson. They would have four more children after Waldo, although three of the eight Emerson children would die in early childhood. Only the five middle boys survived to adulthood—William (b. 1801), Ralph Waldo (b. 1803), Edward Bliss (b. 1805), Robert Bulkeley (b. 1807), and Charles Chauncy (b. 1808). His father died when Waldo was only eight years old. On being a fatherless middle child, Emerson later reflected that "the advantage in education is always with those children who slip up into life without being objects of notice." Growing up, Waldo had neither the burdens and expectations of the oldest child nor, as he put it, the "pleasure, favor, and honor" bestowed upon the youngest. Of the surviving brothers, Robert Bulkeley was mentally impaired in a way that kept him perpetually childlike and requiring constant care and supervision. Throughout the rest of their lives, the other four brothers—William, Waldo, Edward, and Charles—were extremely close, helping each other financially, taking care of their mother, and advising one another on education and careers. Waldo ultimately outlived all of his siblings.

His mother was a religious woman who read and contemplated her spiritual life on a daily basis, teaching him the importance of religion as a personal and immanent experience. His father took a more formal theological approach to religion as a Unitarian minister, an intellectual and social leader in the community, and the author of a book of hymns and of a history of the Boston Church. Waldo Emerson would have few firsthand memories of his father, but the elder man left an imposing intellectual and religious legacy, an inheritance that Emerson would eventually reject.

Rev. William Emerson was himself the son of a minister (indeed, the Emerson ministerial legacy went back seven generations to the founding of Massachusetts Bay Colony in the 1630s). Emerson's grandfather, also named William Emerson, was a chaplain in George Washington's army, and his house in Concord (later known as the Old Manse) looked out across the North Bridge, where the British army advanced in April 1775, during

Reverend William Emerson, father of Ralph Waldo Emerson *(Originally published in* The Polyanthos, *1812)*

the opening battle of the Revolutionary War. He died the following year of camp fever.

The family Ralph Waldo Emerson was born into was not wealthy. What might have been a comfortable childhood among Boston's intellectual (if not economic) elite was disrupted with his father's death in 1811, which left his widow with six children to raise, all younger than 10. Part of his compensation as a minister had been a house and firewood, but without the minister, Ruth was left without a means of financial support. The church would provide a pension for a few more years, but she was forced to begin selling household belongings for cash, including her husband's library of more than 450 books.

Ruth Haskins Emerson never remarried; she depended on a network of extended family to raise and educate her sons. The Emerson children were tutored at home during the early years, but soon after his father's death, young Waldo entered the Boston Latin School, graduating in 1817 and then enrolling in Harvard College at the age of 14. He and three of his brothers would all eventually graduate from Harvard. Unlike most sons of the elite at Harvard, however, Emerson's family could not afford to pay all of his tuition and expenses, and he did without a lot of the extras that wealthier students enjoyed. He had to work to support himself through college, serving as assistant to the president his first year and later receiving a scholarship for boys from poor families.

Emerson was never a distinguished student at Harvard. He got through the curriculum of Greek, Latin, algebra, geometry, history, physical sciences, philosophy, logic, and language, all of which influenced his intellectual development, regardless of his performance in school. His junior year he entered an essay on Socrates for the Bowdoin Prize, which he did not win. Perhaps most important for his future career as a lecturer were the subjects of rhetoric and oratory and the influence of teachers such as Edward Channing. As with the religious heritage of his family, he would also eventually reject the institutional legacy of Harvard, coming to feel that what passed for an education at college actually prevented the acquisition of real knowledge about one's self.

Besides his formal studies, young Emerson developed extremely important habits as a voracious reader and keeper of journals. At Harvard he began to keep a reading list and notes on the books he read. By the time he graduated, his reading notes and early poetry show a remarkable departure from and expansion on the rationalist classical curriculum he had completed in school. His interests in poetry, in nature, in imagination, and in mythology showed the diverse intellectual and creative interests that paved the way to his later promotion of a personal spirituality and ethics of life. As his biographer Robert Richardson notes, Emerson emerged from Harvard asking not "What can I know?" but "How should I live?"

Arguably, the greatest intellectual influence on young Waldo was his paternal aunt, Mary Moody Emerson. Aunt Mary never married, and though she lived primarily in Maine, she visited her widowed sister-in-law and young nephews often and helped with their upbringing. She corresponded with all of her nephews throughout their lives, guiding their readings and offering religious instruction and advice. She disapproved of the Unitarianism of her late brother, William Emerson, and then of Waldo, but she expected at least one (if not all) of her nephews to enter the ministry; one by one, however, the Emerson brothers chose other paths. Mary Moody Emerson was self-educated, and Ralph Waldo Emerson spent years collecting, copying, and then rereading his aunt's letters and journals, which show her as the source of many of his later ideas. He called her "the best writer in Massachusetts," but as a woman of the late 18th and early 19th centuries, she had few, if any, opportunities for publication. In another era, she might have been a scholar or a minister herself.

After graduating from Harvard in 1821, at the age of 18, Emerson returned to Boston to live at home and teach at a girls' school with his older brother, William, for two years. But Waldo was soon profoundly disappointed with teaching as a vocation, reporting to a friend, blandly, "I teach school. I study neither law, nor medicine, or divinity, and write neither poetry nor prose." Fearing (at the tender age of 20) a life of "quiet mediocrity of talents and condition," he decided to consider a different path and began to pursue a rigorous course of independent studies. After contemplating a direction for his scholarly life and interests, as well as an outlet for his spiritual inquiries and his oratorical talents, by the spring of 1824 Emerson decided to pursue the ministry. He was encouraged in his studies by the great Unitarian leader William Ellery Channing, whom he met with weekly in preparation for entering Harvard's divinity program.

While Waldo pursued his studies, William wrote from Germany with news of a new school of biblical criticism. William's studies eventually discouraged him from pursuing the ministry himself, but Waldo continued on his path, combining his theological studies with readings on German philosophy, history, and criticism (including writings by Immanuel Kant) as recommended by William. Combined with the influence of his aunt Mary Moody Emerson on personal religious experience, Emerson was forming his own understanding of a transcendental idealism that included the idea that no knowledge (or authority) exists outside of the self.

Within weeks of entering Harvard Divinity School, Emerson suffered severe headaches and an inflammation of the eyes that required two surgeries and left him unable to read or study for several months. Whether due to physical illness, stress, or a subconscious conflict over pursuing the ministry, he had to put divinity school (and even his journal writing) on hold. In the fall of 1825 he returned briefly to teaching, but with both William and Edward turned to the law as a profession, Waldo was the family's (Aunt Mary's) last hope for a minister in the next generation. By late 1825 he was reading again, primarily Plato, whom he had been writing about when his eyes failed and who would inform his philosophy of "the divine unity" and of ideas (Plato's "forms") as the basis of reality. He was also reading Montaigne as a balance against Plato, a model for skepticism and for a theory of the self. Both Plato and Montaigne would remain with Emerson for decades.

In June 1826 he completed his first sermon, "Pray without Ceasing," which he preached in October in Waltham, Massachusetts. In his readings and studies, working on his first sermons during those months, Emerson was coming upon the ideas that would form the basis of his later Transcendentalism. From his first sermon on prayer—"All that can be done for you is nothing to what you can do for yourself"—to his realization shared with Aunt Mary that same year that we should "account every moment of the existence of the universe as a new creation, and all as a revelation proceeding each moment from the divinity to the mind of the observer," here are the ideas that would find their way a decade later into his foundational work *Nature* (1836), into the controversial "Divinity School Address" (1838), and into his inspiring essay "Self-Reliance" (1841).

Portrait of Ralph Waldo Emerson by Samuel Rowse, 1858 *(Library of Congress)*

Plagued by new lung problems, in late 1826 he sailed to South Carolina seeking the health benefits of a warmer climate. It was the first time he had traveled outside of New England. He was not satisfied with the southern climate, however, and after a month in South Carolina he continued on to Florida, which was not yet a state. The trip inspired a series of poems, written in the first of what would become his regular poetry notebooks. The highlight of the Florida trip, however, was that he met and boarded with Napoléon's nephew, a Florida slaveholder who also shared the same ship back to Charleston. He spent two months in Florida and returned in better health.

After returning from his southern trip, Emerson began traveling throughout Massachusetts and parts of New England as a guest preacher, but he was still unsure whether to pursue the ministry or life as a scholar and writer. In June 1827 he was rooming in Cambridge and preaching in his father's former pulpit, the First Church in Boston. His sermons in the Unitarian church were unexceptional in theme and delivery—he did what was expected, and just as in his readings, he was more interested in philosophy and literature than in doctrine and theology. His sermons were doing more to train Emerson as a public speaker than as a preacher.

In December 1827 Ralph Waldo Emerson met Ellen Tucker while he was preaching in Concord, New Hampshire. She was only 16 when they met—he was 24. She was a poet, and she was also already suffering from tuberculosis and had lost her brother to the disease less than two years earlier. Emerson returned to Boston but visited Ellen in New Hampshire whenever possible. In January 1829, just a few weeks after their engagement, he was voted in as minister at Second Church of Boston. His personal and professional lives were finally coming together. Preaching provided a regular salary for a young man engaged to be married; he started at $1,200 per year and was raised to $1,800 by July 1829. Ralph Waldo Emerson and Ellen Tucker were married on September 30, 1829, in New Hampshire. Ellen had been ill all summer, and Waldo wrote his brother Charles, before they were even married, that Ellen was "very skeptical about the length of her own life."

Like Emerson's own genealogy, the Second Church of Boston dated back to the 17th-century Puritans and had switched to Unitarianism in the early 19th century. Family, church, town, and national history were woven together, and in 1829 Waldo Emerson was ordained not only to the church but to his place in this larger history. The pressure only added to Emerson's reluctance over his chosen vocation; as the date for his first sermon as pastor approached, he wrote to his brother William about the pending "execution day." Emerson's strengths were in studying and in his eloquence as a preacher. These were important traits for a minister, although it was noted at the time that he made few references to actual scripture, Bible verses, in his sermons. He was less interested in ministering to the theological needs of the congregants and more interested in developing a personal theology. By 1830 he was already declaring that "every man makes his own religion, his own God," and that "each should hold his own nature in a reverential awe." That first full year of preaching he was also fine-tuning his personal style as a speaker and a writer that would define his eventual vocation as a lecturer and author, not as a minister or theologian.

By January 1831 Ellen was gravely ill. She died February 8, 1831, at the age of 19, after less than a year and a half of marriage. Waldo wrote to his Aunt Mary, "My angel is gone to heaven this morning and I am alone in the world and strangely happy." Presumably he was "happy" for Ellen to be released from her chronic pain. In his journal, the grief became a "miserable debility." He preached 12 days later on "an eagerness to the tomb as the only place of healing and peace." Emerson was only 27 years old when Ellen died, and her death was an important philosophical and spiritual turning point for him. Confronting love and mortality and grief were emotional and spiritual experiences that helped him—forced him—to define his beliefs and his faith in his self. He responded by relying more deeply on his self and on nature than on Christianity. Indeed, 1831 marks his first serious exploration of Eastern religion and philosophy in Hinduism and in the Bhagavad Gita. In particular, Emerson responded to the death of Ellen by confronting the inevitability of death head-on and by looking to nature (rather than to Christianity) for explanation and consolation.

Without Ellen, without the responsibility of a wife and home, Emerson now had a certain freedom from duty and began to loosen his bonds with the church. In the year after Ellen's death he began to see himself more clearly as a writer than as a preacher, declaring that "my own mind is the direct revelation I have from God." He began to sketch out ideas for a book that would become the core of *Nature* a few years later and began serious readings in science, botany, astronomy, and natural history. His writings were increasingly infused not only with analogies from nature but also with a freer more positive and enthusiastic tone. In his own words, he had developed a newfound "astonishment" with the world—the emergence of Emerson the idealist.

These readings and musings led quickly and decidedly to his break from the church. In the late spring of 1832 he drafted a letter to the church explaining that he would no longer be able to administer the communion or Lord's Supper. In his later sermon on the subject, he explained that he found no spiritual meaning in the ritual and felt it was a violation of his conscience to continue to offer it to others. The sermon effectively served as his resignation, which the church formally accepted in October 1832. Emerson's resignation was therefore not a loss of faith but rather a sign of his new faith in something besides religion—faith in his self. He confided in his journal that "in order to be a good minister, it was necessary to leave the ministry."

He was now free from the church and free from regular employment, as well as free from domestic responsibility. He left for his first trip abroad in December 1832. His nine-month tour included England, where he met William Wordsworth and Samuel Taylor Coleridge, whom he had read by now, and Scotland, where he met Thomas Carlyle, with whom he would form a lifelong friendship. With stops in Malta, Sicily, Naples, Rome, Venice, and Milan, he confronted firsthand the art, history, churches, and ruins of southern Europe. He went to Switzerland, where he revisited the intellectual history of 18th-century Geneva, and then on to Paris, which included the high point (intersecting with his recent intense interests in natural history and botany) of a visit to the Jardin des Plantes and the Cabinet of Natural History. The trip to Paris opened up new vocational considerations. He determined that "the Universe is a more amazing puzzle than ever," and declared, "I will be a naturalist." He subsequently became more focused on the relationship between humans and nature, and on nature as the key to understanding human life and the mind itself.

Emerson returned home from Europe in early October 1833, eager and energized to start a new life. Two days after arriving back in the United States, he lectured at the Boston Society of Natural History. His days in the church were not completely behind him as he agreed to some dates as a guest preacher in friends' congregations. He also secured dates as a lyceum lecturer, a new phenomenon in America and a perfect outlet for his oratorical skills. Inspired by his experiences in Paris, he quickly put together a lecture series, "The Uses of Natural History." He traveled between Boston and New Bedford, mainly, and other outlying towns to speak and preach. He was fine-tuning his ideas, and in early 1834 he determined that "the subject that needs most to be presented, developed, is the principle of Self-Reliance." Emerson had read an article on Coleridge and German philosophy written by his Divinity School colleague Frederic Henry Hedge. Hedge's article revealed an emerging perspective, a coalescing of interests and ideas, that would soon define the new Transcendentalist movement.

In February 1834 Emerson spoke as a guest preacher at the Plymouth, Massachusetts, congregation of Lydia (or "Lidian") Jackson. She was already 30 years old, never married, and Emerson was 31. Like Emerson, Lydia Jackson came from a long line of ministers going back to the founding of Plymouth colony and the Puritan church of John Cotton. As it turned out, Lydia Jackson had heard Emerson preach a few years earlier in Boston, around the time he married Ellen Tucker. It seemed that Waldo and Lydia were so intellectually compatible that a friend remarked of his sermon that Lydia was hearing her own ideas from the pulpit. He proposed nearly one year later and visited her whenever possible between speaking engagements. While biographers have noted that their courtship lacked the youthful ardor of his brief and tragic relationship with Ellen, the intellectual connection and compatibility were no less important or exciting to Emerson. She was, he noted, "so in love with what I love."

Rear view of the Old Manse, Concord, Massachusetts, the family home built by Ralph Waldo Emerson's grandfather in 1770 *(Photo by Daderot. Used under a Creative Commons license)*

Throughout his courtship with Lydia, he was still plagued by the problem of vocation. He was full of ideas; he was a prolific writer, a good speaker, and had developed a personal style or voice. He was also a meticulous journal keeper, and realizing these records could be a source of later inspiration, he began indexing his notebooks, which he would, indeed, mine for ideas for lectures and essays for years to come. By the mid-1830s he was also reading Goethe and Swedenborg and corresponding with Carlyle, had struck up a friendship with the Unitarian minister James Freeman Clarke, and, through Elizabeth Palmer Peabody, had also met the intriguing Bronson Alcott.

In October 1834 Emerson made a fateful move in terms of developing a new vocation and a new community—he moved to Concord to board with his step-grandfather, Ezra Ripley, at the Old Manse (his paternal grandmother, Phebe Bliss Emerson, had died in 1825). His brother Charles also lived with Emerson in Concord, as did his mother, Ruth, and his Aunt Mary came for an extended stay. Soon after his arrival, news came that his brother Edward had died in Puerto Rico of tuberculosis at the age of 29.

Emerson's room at the Old Manse was at the back of the house and overlooked the river and the North Bridge—the same room where Nathaniel and Sophia Hawthorne would later stay as newlyweds. From this upstairs room Emerson faced not only his family history but the history of Concord and of America as well. Even though he was a relatively new citizen of the town, his family had deep roots, and he was asked the following summer to give an address on Concord's 200th anniversary. It was from that upstairs room at the Old Manse that Emerson would begin to draft *Nature,* declaring in his journal that fall of 1834, "I believe in the existence of the material world as an expression of the spiritual or real."

When Ellen Tucker Emerson's estate was settled, Emerson came away with a substantial share, much to the dismay of her family, amounting to about $1,200 per year, the same he had made as a starting minister. If not wealthy, he had a secure income, and he was, besides his older brother, William, the most financially stable of his immediate family. He helped support his mother and his younger brothers, and he was soon able to purchase his own house in Concord. The home they called "Bush" was a large, square white house built only in 1828 and located near the town center; it faced the road that led to Cambridge-Boston, a two-and-a-half-hour trip by stage.

With an income now and a house, he married Lydia Jackson on September 14, 1835. He (and everyone else) began calling her "Lidian," and by all accounts she held her own among the Boston and Concord intellectuals soon congregating around her husband. She also read Swedenborg and was a friend of Elizabeth Palmer Peabody and Margaret Fuller, but she was more traditionally religious than her husband and would humorously reject some of the conceits of the new Transcendental philosophy.

By the time he met and married Lidian, Emerson was also paying more serious attention to writing poetry. While they were still courting, he told her, perhaps as an explanation for why he was no longer a salaried minister, "I am born a poet, of a low class without doubt yet a poet. That is my nature and vocation." Throughout his career Emerson defined himself as a "poet" in the broad sense of being a philosopher and translator of nature, not just a writer of verse. Some of his best nature poems are also his earliest, dating from the late 1830s, such as "The Rhodora," "The Snow-Storm," and "The Humble-Bee"—these were all composed during the earliest years of the Transcendentalist movement and in the same period and context as his writing of *Nature.*

In Concord, Emerson began to seriously consider lecturing as part of his vocation. In January 1835 he began a lecture series on biography for the Society for the Diffusion of Useful Knowledge at the Masonic Temple in Boston. He saw biographies of great men as "seeds," ideas planted in ourselves. He spoke on Swedenborg, Michelangelo, Luther, Milton, and Fox. The following winter, in the months after his marriage to Lidian, he gave a lecture series on English literature. He had also been talking of starting a magazine, in the tradition of

Lidian Jackson Emerson, Ralph Waldo Emerson's second wife and mother of his four children *(Concord Free Public Library)*

the European journals and magazines from England and Germany that he read when he could get them. That year, his friend James Freeman Clarke started a magazine called the *Western Messenger*, which published many of Emerson's poems as well as positive reviews of *Nature* when it was published the following year.

Late 1835 and early 1836 was therefore an important time for Emerson, not only vocationally and intellectually, but socially as well. The Emersons' home soon became the center of intellectual life in Concord. Bronson Alcott came to visit in October 1835—he was then running the Temple School in Boston with Elizabeth Peabody as his assistant and Margaret Fuller as a teacher, and Fuller soon also came to Concord to stay with the Emersons. Waldo and Lidian were then building rooms onto the house for Charles and his fiancée, Elizabeth Hoar, and Waldo and Charles were closer than ever. But Emerson was, unfortunately, away visiting his brother William in New York when Charles died in Concord in May 1836 at the age of only 28. He died of tuberculosis, the disease which had also taken Ellen Tucker Emerson and Edward Bliss Emerson at young ages. With the loss of his brother, this new circle of friends (Alcott, Fuller, Clarke, Peabody, the poet Caroline Sturgis [Tappan], and soon Henry David Thoreau) would make up a new inner circle at the Emerson home. Emerson's marriage and setting up house in Concord coincided with Transcendentalist stirrings in Boston among the Unitarian-Harvard establishment. Concord thus became, literally and symbolically, an alternative center of gathering for Transcendentalist outsiders. Emerson began to purposefully cultivate this community of friends, thinkers, and radicals in Concord.

In the winter of 1835–36, he was putting the finishing touches on *Nature,* the publication of which in September 1836 coincided with Harvard's bicentennial year celebration. On the very same day as the Harvard bicentennial dinner, several friends, including Emerson, his cousin George Ripley, and Frederic Henry Hedge, came up with the idea of the Transcendental Club, the first meeting for which was held a few days later in the Boston home of George and Sophia Ripley. These coinciding events in September 1836 symbolically bridged the two sides of Emerson—the Unitarian past and his Transcendentalist future.

The timing of *Nature* thus seemed to mark the end of Emerson's years of vocational doubts and philosophical strivings. But Emerson was part of a larger community and culture, and it was not coincidentally that his book appeared in a year in which other thinkers (most of them Emerson's close friends) were also rejecting institutional religion and forming new ideas about the "nature" of mankind. In 1836 the following works were also published: Orestes Brownson's *New Views of Christianity, Society, and the Church,* George Ripley's *Discourses on the Philosophy of Religion; Addressed to Doubters Who Wish to Believe,* Bronson Alcott's *Doctrine and Discipline of Human Culture,* and childhood friend William Henry Furness's *Remarks on the Four Gospels.* All of these works were either a direct challenge to or an attempt to reform liberal Christianity, especially of the Harvard-Unitarian type. By 1836, however, Emerson himself was less interested in engaging Christian doctrine directly (he had done that in 1832 with his resignation sermon "The Lord's Supper" and he would do it again in 1838 with the "Divinity School Address") and more interested in forming a new philosophy grounded in a firsthand experience of the natural world as the source of meaning, inspiration, and spiritual transformation.

The individuals who began meeting as the Transcendental Club in the fall of 1836 recognized that a new intellectual force was coalescing in the Boston-Cambridge area. Most of the major figures involved were male, and most had been trained at Harvard, many of them as Unitarian ministers; Bronson Alcott and, of course, women such as Fuller and Peabody were the notable exceptions among the early group. And yet, this seemingly socially and culturally homogenous group had diverse intellectual and spiritual concerns and commitments that made it difficult to call the Transcendental Club or this smattering of dense theological and philosophical publications a unified "movement." The Transcendental Club and the later *Dial* magazine (founded in 1840)—both of which Emerson was personally involved with—were the only institutional results of what was otherwise only a loosely collected group of "like-minded men and women," as Frederic Henry Hedge later explained. It was more accurately a current, or new wave of thought, and Emerson emerged as the most public—and therefore leading—voice.

By late 1836 Emerson was a published author and a popular lecturer and had a new community of friends and colleagues. He experienced another turning point in his personal life as well with the birth of his first child, Waldo, on October 31, 1836. Ralph Waldo and Lidian Emerson would eventually have four children—two sons (Waldo in 1836 and Edward Waldo, born in 1844) and two daughters (Ellen, born in 1839, and Edith, born in 1841). Emerson's letters to friends and his journal entries reveal a kindhearted father who saw his children as a blessing and delighted in every small accomplishment or childhood antic. Soon after Waldo's birth, Lidian noted that her husband was "a most attentive observer of nursery phenomena." Firstborn Waldo, especially, was the center of attention in a household of adults and the center of Emerson's world for the first few years of his life.

In December 1836 Emerson began a winter series of Boston lectures, "The Philosophy of History"—lectures that would form the basis of some of his later important essays such as "History," "The Over-Soul," and "Self-Reliance," among others. The lectures (and later essays) revealed a major coming together and articulation of the core of Emerson's Transcendentalism—of the relationship of each to the whole, and of individual experience as the source of universal knowledge.

He was also active in Concord and was asked to participate in two local public events. The first was the April 1836 dedication of a Revolutionary War monument at the North Bridge in Concord, for which he composed his now-famous "Concord Hymn." The dedication actually did not take place until the following summer, on July 4, 1837, at which time Emerson's poem was read and subsequently published in local papers. That same summer Emerson was asked to speak at Harvard's annual commencement ceremonies. On August 31, 1837, he delivered his address "The American Scholar" before the graduates and an audience of his former Harvard-Unitarian colleagues and professors. Emerson took the opportunity to apply his theory of self-education, and his call for breaking free from the rules of the past and of tradition, to the gathering at America's oldest institution of higher learning. The following day the Transcendental Club met at Emerson's house back in Concord.

Gaining a reputation as a thinker and a speaker, Emerson was never, as some contemporaries criticized, aloof from the social and political concerns of the era. In November 1837 the death of the antislavery editor Elijah Lovejoy in Illinois shook the entire North and prompted an abolitionist gathering in Concord, at which Emerson made some of his first public remarks against slavery. The following year he would speak at a meeting in Concord of those opposed to the U.S. policy of removing the Cherokee from their lands in Georgia. Concord was, in fact, a hotbed of reform sentiment, as was Emerson's own home. In September 1837, just a few months before Emerson spoke out on the Lovejoy incident, Lidian Emerson had met and had tea with traveling antislavery advocates, Sarah and Angelina Grimke, daughters of a South Carolina slaveholder who had published controversial "Appeals" to women to recognize it was their Christian duty to speak out against slavery. Cynthia Thoreau, mother of Henry David, was also active in women's antislavery groups in Concord.

Henry David Thoreau was among Harvard's graduates in the summer of 1837, although he did not attend Emerson's address. Thoreau left Cambridge and returned to his hometown of Concord that fall to take a teaching position. Thoreau was 14 years younger than Emerson, and the two had already met. Emerson had been called upon to examine Thoreau at Harvard a few years earlier and had, just the previous spring, written a letter on Thoreau's behalf in support of a scholarship plea. For his part, Thoreau was reading Emerson's *Nature* in early 1837, while still at Harvard. When Thoreau returned home in the fall of 1837, he became an immediate part of Emerson's inner circle of new friends. The friendship was mutually beneficial, but certainly served as a catalyst for Thoreau's direction as a writer; that fall it was Emerson who urged his younger friend to begin keeping a regular journal. Emerson obviously saw something in Thoreau, and Thoreau became a regular member of the Emerson household, befriending Lidian as well as the children and even living at the Emerson home on several occasions.

In January 1838 Emerson delivered a lecture (as part of his winter series) titled "Holiness," the core of which would reappear several months later in his address before the graduates of Harvard's Divinity School. Despite (or perhaps because of) some of the controversy already swirling about the Transcendentalists, and the radical call of the "American Scholar" address the previous summer, Emerson was chosen by the students themselves to speak to the Divinity School's small class of newly trained Unitarians. His speech on July 15, 1838, presented to this group of theology students, their families, and many of his own former professors, offered a radical theology of the self, a call for worship of nature rather than the old forms of "historical Christianity." One week later he addressed similar themes in his address "Literary Ethics" at Dartmouth College in New Hampshire.

By late August 1838, Emerson was under attack in the Unitarian press. The primary critic was again Andrews Norton, who had lashed out at the "infidelity" of the Transcendentalists in 1836 in a series of articles over the "miracles controversy." Now Norton focused specifically on Emerson, who had come to the Divinity School and launched "a general attack," in Norton's words, not only on "the Clergy" but on Christianity itself. Norton was not the only Unitarian who took, again in his own words, "a great offense" to Emerson's speech; others accused him of everything from benign incoherency to blasphemy and "foulest atheism." Still, some Unitarian colleagues responded in the spirit of intellectual and theological debate, and many of his Transcendentalist friends (notably George Ripley, Peabody, Convers Francis, and Theodore Parker) came to his defense.

Emerson was at first surprised, then dismayed, then bitter over the criticisms. Still, he chose not to publicly respond to Norton, letting his ideas speak for themselves and the debate play out in the press. Six years after his formal resignation from the church, he had now closed the door on his association with Harvard-Unitarianism. If anything, the experience of the "Divinity School Address" only confirmed for him the basic idea he had tried to convey of the problem of conformity to tradition and the need for, as he would develop in his next major work, self-reliance.

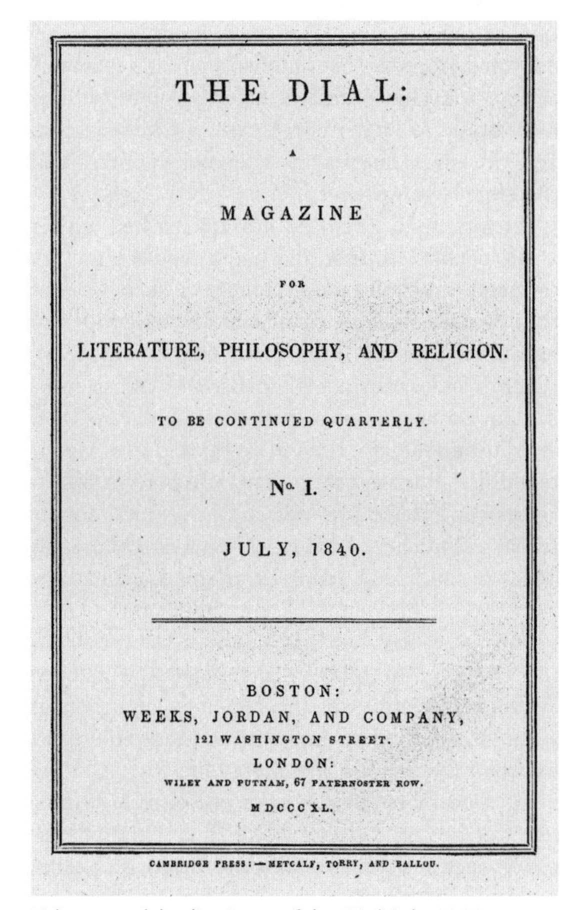
THE DIAL:

A

MAGAZINE

FOR

LITERATURE, PHILOSOPHY, AND RELIGION.

TO BE CONTINUED QUARTERLY.

No. I.

JULY, 1840.

BOSTON:
WEEKS, JORDAN, AND COMPANY,
121 WASHINGTON STREET.
LONDON:
WILEY AND PUTNAM, 67 PATERNOSTER ROW.
MDCCCXL.

CAMBRIDGE PRESS:—METCALF, TORRY, AND BALLOU.

Title page of the first issue of the *Dial,* July 1840 *(Concord Free Public Library)*

Contrary to his own fears, the public attacks following the "Divinity School Address" did nothing to diminish Emerson's continued success as a lecturer or his productivity as a writer. He had written a series of inspired poems, and his popular winter lecture series of the late 1830s and early 1840s would be mined for his first collection of *Essays,* published in 1841. By the time *Essays: First Series* was published, the Transcendental Club had ceased meeting, but the group had founded its own literary journal, the *Dial,* published by Elizabeth Palmer Peabody and edited first by Margaret Fuller and then, between 1842 and 1844, by Emerson. the *Dial* was founded as an important alternative forum for the Transcendentalist writers, many of whom were now shut out of or uninterested in the Unitarian papers. Fuller and Emerson were the most prolific contributors to the paper, publishing their own essays, poems, and literary reviews, but Emerson, especially, sought out new talent and genius in a host of young writers, reformers, and poets he published in the *Dial.*

The year after the *Dial* was founded, the Transcendentalist movement sparked another collective experiment: the utopian community at Brook Farm. In the spring of 1840 George Ripley left his pulpit and began plans to establish a community. That year Emerson as well was enthusiastic about the idea of an alternative learning community, a university or gathering place for lecturers and like-minded individuals, a sort of permanent year-round Transcendental Club. George and Sophia Ripley began operating Brook Farm in April 1841, in a somewhat different format than Emerson's envisioned university. It would be an educational venture that was also an experiment in communal living, a self-sufficient community in which residents lived and worked full time while also enjoying lectures, classes, and musical performances. Ripley no doubt expected Emerson to have a key role at Brook Farm. After weeks of agonizing, however, Emerson declined both participation and financial backing, stating his belief in individual reform over adherence to a communal structure. During its six-year existence, Brook Farm would attract many other Transcendentalists, reformers, and wanderers, as visitors, lecturers, or residents.

By 1841 the Emerson household itself was becoming an experiment in communal living. There was talk of the Alcott family moving in, but Abba Alcott dissuaded Bronson, her husband, from pursuing this offer. In April 1841, the same month the Ripleys began living at Brook Farm, Henry David Thoreau moved in with the Emersons. Margaret Fuller was a regular and extended visitor to the Emerson home throughout the early 1840s (a fact that caused some tension in the Emerson marriage), and in the summer of 1842 Emerson arranged for Nathaniel and Sophia Hawthorne to move into the Old Manse. In addition, facilitated in part by the opening of the Boston-to-Fitchburg rail service, which brought four trains a day through Concord, a steady stream of Harvard graduates and other young aspiring writers, thinkers, and idealists visited Brook Farm and Concord. Emerson turned no one away and, in fact, actively recruited new residents to Concord. Beyond just hosting these visitors and friends, the Emersons eventually (in 1846) turned their home into a boardinghouse, confining themselves to certain rooms and hiring a housekeeper to run the house.

In the fall of 1840 Emerson had written to Carlyle, "We are all a little wild here with numberless projects of social reform," and throughout the early 1840s he wrote (primarily for the *Dial*) numerous essays and thoughts on the reform impulse, on slavery, and on Fourierism and Brook Farm. In 1842 he helped send Bronson Alcott to England to visit reformers there; Alcott returned with Charles Lane, with whom he founded the short-lived communitarian experiment at Fruitlands in 1843.

Emerson was also busy with other ventures at the height of what Lidian would humorously refer to as these "transcendental times." He was editing the *Dial* and bringing out his *Essays,* and he was encouraging and facilitating the work of his new friends, all the while continuing a heavy schedule of lecturing and growing his family. His daughter Ellen, whom Lidian had graciously named after Emerson's first wife, Ellen Tucker, was born in February 1839, and Edith was born in late 1841. In October 1841 a traveling daguerreotypist came through Concord, and it was John Thoreau, Henry's brother, who suggested that five-year-old Waldo have his picture done. Just a few months later, tragedy struck. First, John Thoreau died suddenly of lockjaw, and for a few days, it was thought that Henry might have the disease as well. Henry recovered, but on January 24, 1842, young Waldo became ill with scarlet fever. Three short days later, the boy whom Emerson had once described as "handsome as Walden Pond at sunrise" was dead. Lidian's grief over the loss of their son caused her years of illness and depression; Emerson wrote of his grief in his letters to friends

Bush, the home of Ralph Waldo Emerson and Lidian Jackson Emerson in Concord, Massachusetts. Emerson's study was the downstairs front room on the right. *(Photo by Daderot. Used under a Creative Commons license)*

and family, and later in the essay "Experience" and in the poem "Threnody." In the immediate aftermath of Waldo's death, it was Lidian who revealed the depth of the loss to her husband; she wrote to a friend of Emerson, "How intensely his heart yearns over every memento of his boy I cannot express to you. Never was a greater hope disappointed—a more devoted love bereaved."

Emerson continued with his work and his commitments and by February 12 was in Providence, Rhode Island, lecturing again. In 1844 he published the last issue of the *Dial,* and later that year, he brought out his next volume, *Essays: Second Series.* That summer, Edward Waldo, the Emersons' last child, was born, and Emerson also had the opportunity to purchase his first bit of land near Walden Pond. He thought of building a "cabin" or a study out on the land for himself someday, but it was his friend Henry Thoreau who would famously launch his experiment in simple living on Emerson's land there the following summer.

The year 1844 was also a turning point in Emerson's antislavery voice. Reform activity was heating up among his circle of friends and across the nation over slavery in particular, but also over the Mexican War. In Concord, both Bronson Alcott and Henry Thoreau were arrested for refusal to pay taxes in support of an immoral government. Emerson did not necessarily approve—or, rather, did not see the effectiveness—of such actions, but he himself was speaking more forcefully than ever against slavery. In his August 1844 address on the anniversary of the emancipation of slaves in the British West Indies, he urged America to look to Britain as a model for making the transition from slavery to freedom.

Emerson was also writing and publishing more poetry, not only in the *Dial,* but to compile his first volume of *Poems,* published on Christmas Day, 1846. Covering several decades of poetic efforts and interests, the volume included a combination of now-famous nature poems (such as "The Humble-Bee," "The Rhodora," and "The Snow-Storm"); mystical complements to his philosophical essays, especially on the role of the poet ("Merlin," "Saadi," "The Sphinx," and "The World-Soul"); and contemporary and political pieces ("Concord Hymn" and "Ode, Inscribed to W. H. Channing"). It also included his poetic response to his son Waldo's death ("Threnody") and to the Divinity School controversy of several years earlier ("Uriel"). Emerson ended this most eventful and prolific decade by gathering together his most important prose works as well as some new lectures for the 1849 collection, *Nature; Addresses, and Lectures.*

In the midst of all this literary outpouring, Emerson returned to Europe for the second time, this time on an English lecture tour. When Emerson left Boston for England in October 1847, he did so as an immensely popular lecturer in the United States. In 1846 he had given more than 50 lectures, a pace he kept up throughout the 1850s, some years delivering as many as 80 lectures and covering an immense geographical region, outward from New England, throughout the Midwest and New York, as far west as California, and as far north as Canada. Having left the pulpit unsure of a vocational path and of finding an audience, he found it in the lyceum circuit. He was received in England as a renowned lecturer and essayist (each of his works having been published in English editions as well) and was able to draw great crowds in England of as many as 500 to 700 people. Lavish dinners were thrown in his honor, and he found that everyone had been reading the *Dial.* He gave 67 lectures in England and Scotland and met not only Carlyle and Wordsworth again but also Thackeray, Tennyson, Dickens, George Eliot, and numerous artists and scientists of the age.

It was a fruitful time for Emerson's thought. Like his earlier trip abroad some 15 years earlier, he was especially inspired by the natural sciences in Europe. Whereas the 1833 trip to the Jardin des Plantes in Paris had led to his decision to be a "naturalist" (and therefore to the writing of *Nature*), that line of thought was continued in his English lectures "Mind in the 19th Century" in the summer of 1848. These lectures were then repeated and revised over the next few decades, resulting in the "Natural History of Intellect" lectures of 1870–71. He was convinced that "the laws and powers of the intellect" may "be numbered and recorded as readily as the stamens of a plant or the vertebrae of a fish." It was a project, an idea, that occupied his mind for several decades. Most of his observations from the 1848 trip would end up in *English Traits* (published in 1856), and his English lectures were the foundation for later American versions, some eventually published in *Society and Solitude* in 1870.

Despite this productivity and success as a lecturer throughout the 1840s and 1850s, he had taken the trip to England partly because he felt restless and bored in Concord. He returned feeling even more out of place and lacking confidence about his own personal power and abilities. Upon his return this time, in particular, his relationship with Thoreau was becoming more strained, including an argument of some kind over the failure of Thoreau's *A Week on the Concord and Merrimack Rivers,* published in 1849. The two had philosophical and personal differences as well. Unlike Thoreau, Emerson traveled a great deal outside of Concord, and Thoreau did not always approve of Emerson's travels. Emerson's journal makes reference to Thoreau's "seductive" attempt to lure him (Emerson) "from the town to the woods," a trip that always ends in "want and madness." There may also have been tensions over Emerson's return home as head of household after a long absence, during which Thoreau had lived with and become dependent upon his friendship with Lidian. The friendship was, of course, reconciled, and by the time *Walden; or, Life in the Woods* was published in 1854, Emerson was Thoreau's most enthusiastic promoter.

In the early 1850s, however, Emerson was also establishing new or deeper friendships with men such as Ellery Channing (whom Emerson encouraged as another young Thoreauvian naturalist), Theodore Parker, Moncure Conway, Jones Very, and Bronson Alcott, who had returned to Concord in 1857 after living briefly in Boston and Connecticut. His mother and his younger brother, Robert Bulkeley, both died in the 1850s, leaving Emerson with only one surviving sibling, William, with whom he was especially close.

Margaret Fuller was no longer available, however, as she had left for Europe in 1846 to serve as a foreign correspondent for the *New York Tribune.* Fuller had met an Italian revolutionary named Giovanni Ossoli, with whom she had a son. In 1850 she decided to return to the United States with her new family, but their ship, loaded down with Italian marble, ran aground off the coast of Fire Island, New York, and sank on July 19, 1850. Fuller, Ossoli, and their infant son were all drowned. Emerson was devastated. He sent Henry Thoreau to the wreckage site to recover any of Fuller's belongings or manuscripts, but Thoreau returned empty-handed. Plans were soon made to collect Fuller's letters as well as reminiscences by friends, and Emerson joined with James Freeman Clarke and William Henry Channing to quickly edit the *Memoirs of Margaret Fuller Ossoli,* published in 1852.

It seems that Emerson wrote less in the 1850s, but in fact he was busier than ever. Besides his work on the *Memoirs,* his *Representative Men* was published in 1850, originating in lectures from the mid-1840s. Emerson had been reading works on Napoléon since early 1845 and that year began a lecture series, "Uses of Great Men." This interest in history and biography, and in the nature of genius, combined here, as biographer Richardson points out, with Emerson's "democratic belief in the fundamental equality of all persons." Many of his lectures of the early 1850s would end up in later projects, such as *The Conduct of Life* (published in 1860), and he also spent the early 1850s reworking his English lectures and journals for publication. He read extensively on English history, mythology, architecture, and landscape—reading that accounts for the long pause between the trip in 1847–48 and the publication of *English Traits* in 1856.

Emerson spent the 1850s raising his family, continuing his hectic lecturing schedule, and socializing in Concord and Boston. He was a founding member of the Saturday Club (begun in 1854), out of which grew the idea for the *Atlantic Monthly,* which was, from its founding in 1857 through the end of his life, an important forum for his essays and poems. Much of the poetry he wrote in the 1850s, including notable poems such as "Brahma" and "Days," was first published in the new *Atlantic Monthly* before being later collected for his second volume of poems, *May-Day and Other Pieces,* published in 1867. He was still thinking about the role of the poet in his new lecture of 1854 on poetry that would evolve into one of his most significant later essays, "Poetry and Imagination," which was not published until 1876. And in 1855, he received Walt Whitman's collection of poems, *Leaves of Grass,* famously responding to Whitman, "I find it the most extraordinary piece of wit and wisdom that America has yet contributed."

In the 1850s Emerson was increasingly pulled into the intense antislavery politics that would lead the nation to Civil War. Of particular concern to Emerson and other Northerners was the passage of the federal Fugitive Slave Law of 1850. Emerson was shocked along with many Northern abolitionists over the Fugitive Slave Law and, specifically, over Massachusetts senator Daniel Webster's support for its passage as part of a larger compromise with the South that included admitting California as a free state. Webster's betrayal was only made worse (and more personalized) by the high-profile cases of fugitive slaves in Boston, including the 1854 case of Anthony Burns. Emerson gave addresses on the Fugitive Slave Law in 1851 and 1854, repeating them in several cities. The Kansas-Nebraska Act brought further controversy over slavery in the territories and new states, and the decade ended with John Brown's raid on the federal arsenal at Harpers Ferry, Virginia, in October 1859. Several Bostonians, including friends of Emerson, had been involved in financing Brown's crusade, and both Emerson and Thoreau praised

Brown as a martyr after he was arrested and hung for treason. Emerson was also pulled, in the 1850s, briefly and reluctantly into women's rights, giving his one and only public address "Woman" at an 1855 convention in Boston.

Emerson's next collection of essays, *The Conduct of Life,* was published in 1860 and included the significant essays "Fate" and "Power." These were topics that occupied his mind in the aftermath of Fuller's death and have led many scholars to view the "later" Emerson as less idealistic, less optimistic, and more grounded in the limitations of this world. In many ways, however, Emerson's treatment of these themes is remarkably consistent with his foundational ideas, although here considered in new contexts and perhaps with a new realism. For better or worse, *The Conduct of Life* was ultimately one of his most popular works of the time, admired by and influencing writers of the post–Civil War era and the Gilded Age.

In the 1860s, of course, the nation was preoccupied with the Civil War, an issue that directly engaged Emerson as well. He delivered public addresses and published poems on slavery, on the Emancipation Proclamation, on President Lincoln, and on the Union Army—in particular, the all-black 54th Massachusetts regiment (the subject of Emerson's poem "Voluntaries") led by Bostonian Robert Gould Shaw, who was killed in battle in July 1863. Emerson's own son, Edward (who was turning 17 just as war broke out in 1861), talked of joining the Union Army. His parents were initially against it, not only for personal reasons, but because they were not supportive of the preservation of the Union as a justification for war. After the Emancipation Proclamation of 1863 (Emerson read his poem "Boston Hymn" to a packed crowd the day it went into effect), however, which indicated Lincoln's commitment to ending slavery, they reluctantly approved. By that time, however, Edward had changed his mind, and he entered Harvard medical school instead.

Death was everywhere in the 1860s, as the Civil War touched every town, every family. Concord's and Emerson's own greatest loss, however, was not due to the war but, once again, due to the pervasive presence of tuberculosis, which claimed Henry David Thoreau in May 1862, at the age of only 44. Emerson spoke at Thoreau's funeral, and the elegy was subsequently published in the *Atlantic Monthly* as "Thoreau," in which he wrote of his young friend, "The country knows not yet, or in the least part, how great a son it has lost." In between lecturing and his own publications, Emerson helped collect and edit Thoreau's writings for publication. Thoreau had only published a few essays and two full-length books—*A Week on the Concord and Merrimack Rivers* and *Walden*—in his lifetime. After Thoreau's death, Emerson, Thoreau's sister Sophia, and his friend H. G. O. Blake brought out several collections of Thoreau's letters, poems, and journals and essays, some in the *Atlantic Monthly* and then in collected volumes such as *Cape Cod, Maine Woods,* and *A Yankee in Canada.*

Already in his 60s, Emerson still kept an astonishingly busy lecture schedule throughout the decade. He gave more than 70 lectures in 1865 alone, including an elegy for Lincoln, and in 1867 he gave 80 lectures in 14 different states. His family was busy as well. In 1865 (the year Lincoln was assassinated and the Civil War ended), his daughter Edith married William Hathaway Forbes, and the following summer Emerson welcomed his first grandchild, Ralph Emerson Forbes. Emerson was working as well on a second volume of his own poems. It had been 20 years since the publication of *Poems,* though several new poems had been subsequently published in the *Atlantic Monthly.* The 1867 *May-Day and Other Pieces* focused on the theme of spring, of death and rebirth, and of renewal through nature. The war years had brought loss and renewal for the nation and for Emerson—in addition to the loss of Thoreau, his beloved aunt, Mary Moody Emerson, died on May 1, 1863.

Emerson also began a renewal in his relationship with Harvard College. It had been 30 years since he delivered the controversial "Divinity School Address," but in 1867 Emerson was asked to speak again at Harvard's commencement, paving the way for an invitation to present his course of lectures, "Natural History of Intellect," in 1870 and 1871. By the early 1870s, however, Emerson was aging, and his memory was less reliable and his senses less sharp, and, after the Harvard lectures, he would finally slow down on his journal writing and his public appearances. He collected some earlier lectures for the volume *Society and Solitude*, published in 1870, and he still gave nearly 30 more public lectures in the 1871 and 1872 seasons.

After his lecture course at Harvard ended, Emerson traveled to California with his son-in-law and his daughter Edith. He met John Muir in Yosemite, who described Emerson "as serene as a sequoia." Muir invited Emerson to camp out in the woods, but Emerson declined—he was nearly 70 years old.

He hardly had time to rest. In 1872, the year after he traveled to California, the Emersons awoke one night to a fire in their home. By the time it was put out by the neighbors and the Concord fire crew, significant fire and water damage to the home made it unlivable, although Emerson's downstairs front study had been spared. Friends and townspeople raised thousands of dollars to help the Emersons rebuild, and there was enough extra money to send Emerson away on a trip during the repairs. He and daughter Ellen left Boston in October 1872 for Europe, traveling to England (where they met with Emerson's son, Edward, who was studying medicine there), France, Italy, and on to Egypt. This time, he had no lecture dates. When Emerson and Ellen returned to Concord they were surprised to find school canceled and crowds gathered to welcome home the Sage of Concord. Emerson had become Concord's greatest pride and celebrity.

With Edith married (Edward also was married, in 1874) and Lidian aging (though still busy with her own interests), the elder daughter, Ellen, not only took over the housekeeping, but also became more involved in handling her father's career and affairs. Ellen never married and lived with her parents the

The Emerson family plot at Sleepy Hollow Cemetery, Concord, Massachusetts. Emerson's large memorial stone stands between those of his wife, Lidian, and daughter Ellen. *(Photo by Tiffany K. Wayne)*

remainder of their lives. She had worked closely with Emerson on the compilation of *May-Day* and had even more of a hand (along with his friend and literary executor, James Elliot Cabot) in organizing and publishing two more poetry volumes: *Parnassus,* a collection of Emerson's favorite poems by others was published in 1874, and his own final volume of *Selected Poems* appeared in 1876. They also brought out an 1876 essay collection, *Letters and Social Aims.*

Emerson's public appearances in the last years of his life were few and far between due to memory problems. In February 1880, Ellen Emerson and Cabot compiled a talk, "Historic Notes of Life and Letters in New England," which Emerson presented for his 100th lecture before the Concord Lyceum, an event that was noted in the newspapers. He attended some sessions of the Concord School of Philosophy and Literature, organized by Bronson Alcott in 1879 and held each summer at the Hillside Chapel, next door to Orchard House. He spoke at least once at the Concord School, in the summer of 1880. In February 1881 the death of his old friend Thomas Carlyle brought Emerson out for his final public address, a memorial talk on Carlyle at the Massachusetts Historical Society in Boston. It was recorded that Ellen sat nearby and mouthed the words to his talk for him to follow along.

The following year, in April 1882, he came down with a cold and subsequently developed pneumonia. Emerson left his study for the last time on April 21, 1882, and died six days later, upstairs in his home in Concord. The Concord School of Philosophy and Literature dedicated its 1882 summer session to "The Genius and Character of Emerson." Numerous friends, colleagues, and family members began publishing their correspondences and reminiscences, and the first biographies appeared before the decade was out.

The headlines immediately after his death read, "Concord's Irreparable Loss!" but the town and the nation, as well as students and philosophers and poets since, have kept Ralph Waldo Emerson alive. He speaks to each generation anew with his themes of self-education, resisting or questioning authority and received tradition, experimentation with genre, and of the creation of an American literature springing from our unique history and geography and peoples. Students of his life and writings will find inspiration in a man of curiosity about the world and of a voracious intellectual appetite—a man who once dreamed that he "ate the world" and lived his life in such a way as well—and a man with deep emotional commitments to family and friends.

Note: Information for this brief biography was drawn primarily from Robert D. Richardson, Jr., *Emerson: The Mind on Fire* (1995) and Phyllis Cole, *Mary Moody Emerson and the Origins of Transcendentalism: A Family History* (1998). Readers interested in more specific details about Emerson's life and family should consult these and the other fine biographical works and primary source collections listed in the master bibliography at the end of this volume.

PART II

Works A to Z

"Address at the Woman's Rights Convention" (1855)

See "WOMAN."

"The Adirondacs" (1867)

The 343-line blank-verse poem "The Adirondacs" was one of two long poems published in Emerson's 1867 collection, *MAY-DAY AND OTHER PIECES*, the other being the title poem, "MAY-DAY." "The Adirondacs" is part prose poem, part travelogue, recounting a trip to the Adirondack mountains of New York in August 1858. The Adirondack Club was formed by members of the SATURDAY CLUB and included Emerson, the HARVARD scientist Louis Agassiz, the editor JAMES RUSSELL LOWELL, and several others. Many of the men who made the trip were naturalists and scientists; others, like Emerson, were writers or intellectuals. Among them was the artist William Stillman, whose painting *Philosopher's Camp* reflected the makeup of their group, and their different relationships to nature, by portraying philosophers, outdoorsmen, and scientist-naturalists gathered together in the woods.

The poem is "Dedicated to My Fellow-Travellers in August, 1858," whom Emerson acknowledges as a "worthy crew." However, the poem does not identify the individual men, instead reflecting on humanity's intrusion into the wilderness and on the struggle between nature and civilization, both physically and spiritually. In the end, it is a Transcendentalist reflection on man's relationship with and, ultimately, triumph over nature.

CRITICAL COMMENTARY

Stanzas 1–6 detail the "ten men, ten guides" preparing for the journey and traces their exact route across lakes and into the mountains. Emerson names specific locations, but the deeper into the wilderness they go, more of the landscape is unnamed, unclaimed by men. Although the men travel together, it is an individual journey, "as each would hear the oracle alone." The travelers "wield the first axe these echoes ever heard," and they "cut" and "barked" the trees for their own use as lodging, poles, and firewood. Emerson takes on the role of naturalist, giving detailed physical descriptions of the landscape and cataloging the various types of trees. Nature, however, is also aware of their presence: "Welcome! the wood god murmured."

When discussing the travelers themselves, Emerson is amused that "ten scholars" are now happily lodging "like Sacs and Sioux" and acting like "boys again." He notes that there are no signs of civilization—no "polls," no "visitor," "no courier" (presaging the courier later on in the poem who brings news of the transatlantic cable), no business to be conducted, no concern even about the weather: "We were made freemen of the forest laws." In stanzas 7–10, Emerson shifts the focus from the travelers to a description of their guides, who possess all the skills necessary for the journey; with "a paddle . . . or an oar," a gun, and "strength and suppleness," the guides can perform all of the needed tasks. The travelers, in contrast, are "ye polished gentlemen!" They have "city airs" but find that in the wilderness "your rank is all reversed." It is the man who can row and catch dinner and tell time and direction who is "master" here. This is one of several instances in the poem where Emerson questions the abilities of the scholars compared with the men who spend more time in the wild.

Having established the superior skills of the guides, stanzas 11–12 describe what the scholars and scientists have to contribute to the expedition. "Two Doctors in the camp" keep busy collecting and "dissecting" specimens, from deer and fish to the "moth," while the "botanist" collects plant specimens. The men are so overtaken by the mountain air ("the Alpine element") and the beautiful views ("lofty pictures") that they feel removed from "the distant town" and become critical of civilization. They make plans to build "a spacious lodge" that they can bring their "sons" to in the future but wonder if their sons would even want to come.

The next two stanzas (13–14) reveal some of the hardships the campers encounter as "intruders" in nature. They even see nature differently. For example, where they once would have called out "spiteful names" to the bugs who bite them, they now "saluted them" for trying to protect the forest "from bold intrusion." Stanza 15 turns inward with reflections on the "sudden privacies" of each man—what "spiritual lessons" were learned from the "new sense" and "new knowledge" of being in nature. Watching the sky makes Emerson wonder whether there is any separation between self and nature: "The clouds are rich and dark, the air serene, / So like the soul of me, what if 'twere me?" The clouds remind him that "no day of life may lack romance," and the setting sun reminds him of death, which will call the "wanderer to his vaster home."

Stanzas 17–18 move back to the activities of the men by detailing the news that reaches them "of the wire-cable laid beneath the sea." Emerson sees the laying of the transatlantic cable in 1858 as a "glad miracle," not of nature, but of man's innovation, as "thought" can now travel along the same path as people. The poet is proud of "this feat of wit, this triumph of mankind" over nature: "The lightning has run masterless too long." Nature now serves humans, as our "messages" will be "shot through . . . the salt sea." Still, there is "a shade of discontent" as "the academicians" consider whether it is not merely the pursuit of "fortune" that has won out. After all, it was only "some lout" who discovered gold in California 10 years ago, and now "corporate sons of trade" (an interesting counterpoint to the earlier mention of "sons" of the philosophers) are "borrowing . . . the tools of science" for their own ends: "hand and head / Are ever rivals." In the end, he determines not to worry "who best entitled was" but rather acknowledges the benefit for all of humanity: "Enough that mankind eat, and are refreshed."

The final stanzas (19–20) reflect upon the end of the expedition. The men praise the experience but have no desire to give up their "books and arts and trained experiment"—they would not choose "Sioux" over "Agassiz." Surrounded by wilderness, the men are thrilled to hear piano music coming from "a log-cabin." The music has the power to tame nature, "the bear is kept at bay." This appreciation of culture eases his earlier doubts about the value of scholarly or artistic achievements in light of the advancements of trade and technology. The trip is now characterized not as a scientific expedition or spiritual journey but merely a "holiday," now over. The men's minds quickly turn to "intruding duties" and "the fires of home." Nature "almost" seems to "smile" at these men who now know more about her secrets: "As if one riddle of the Sphinx were guessed." The "riddle" of nature was a theme throughout his writings, and "The SPHINX" was the subject of its own poem in Emerson's earlier 1847 collection of *POEMS*.

FURTHER READING

Burkholder, Robert E. "(Re)visiting 'The Adirondacs': Emerson's Confrontation with Wild Nature." In *Emerson Bicentennial Essays*, edited by Ronald A. Bosco and Joel Myerson, 247–269. Boston: Massachusetts Historical Society / University of Virginia Press, 2006.

Sudol, Ronald A. "The Adirondacs" and "Technology." In *Emerson Centenary Essays*, edited by Joel Myerson, 173–179. Carbondale: Southern Illinois University Press, 1982.

"The American Scholar" (1837)

Originally published as "An Oration, Delivered before the Phi Beta Kappa Society, at Cambridge, August 31, 1837," Emerson's address to HARVARD COLLEGE graduates was reprinted in his 1849 collection, *NATURE; ADDRESSES, AND LECTURES*, as "The American Scholar." Emerson made two major calls to action in the address: to free American culture from its European past, and to free the individual American thinker from the bounds of society and tradition. Emerson identified promising signs of American intellectual life and themes emerging in the literature of his own time, but he felt that American genius had not yet fully emerged to its full potential.

The address posited a new role for the individual scholar as "Man Thinking," a way of being in the world rather than a profession. When Emerson delivered "The American Scholar" address, the Transcendentalist controversy and community were still in their beginning stages. He had made his break with the church and had been focused on building a career as a lecturer; "The American Scholar" was Emerson's chance to define himself against the institutions of Harvard and UNITARIANISM. Unlike the "DIVINITY SCHOOL ADDRESS," delivered a year later, his concerns here were less of a theological nature and more with a radical new understanding of education and with Emerson's own emerging sense of what it meant to be self-reliant.

SYNOPSIS

Emerson opens the address by acknowledging that the gathering itself—a Harvard graduation—is "a friendly sign of the survival of the love of letters amongst a people too busy to give to letters any more." But America is destined for more, and it is time for "the sluggard intellect of this continent" to "fill the postponed expectation of the world with something better than the exertions of mechanical skill." For Emerson, this is a turning point in history: "Our day of dependence, our long apprenticeship to the learning of other lands, draws to a close." There are peculiarly American "events, actions arise, that must be sung, that will sing themselves"; that is, that cannot find expression in European literary traditions.

Who, then, is the new "American Scholar"? In modern society men have come to be defined by their "functions" and have no relation to the whole, so that a man becomes a thing, "the farmer, instead of Man on the farm." The "attorney" is reduced to a "statute-book; the mechanic, a machine; the sailor, a rope of a ship." In this state of affairs, the scholar "tends to become a mere thinker," "the delegated intellect," rather than "Man Thinking." Instead, every man must be a student, every man a thinker. Emerson addresses separately each of "the main influences" on the human mind, the main sources of knowledge: nature, the past, and the practical world of action.

Part I

"The first in time and the first in importance of the influences upon the mind is that of nature." The question the scholar must ask, all men must ask, is "What is nature to him?" Nature is the "web of God . . . so entire, boundless." Nature moves "like rays, upward, downward, without centre, without circumference." When the human mind encounters nature, it goes through several steps. First, "classification begins"—our "unifying instinct" means that we approach nature scientifically. This is a necessary first step because our attempts at classification reveal "that these objects are not chaotic." Nature has laws, and in fact, we see that these are the same laws as "the human mind." Even a "school-boy" can have a "relation" and "sympathy" with nature. He sees that nature's "beauty is the beauty of his own mind. Its laws are the laws of his own mind." In this moment, Emerson is confident, "the ancient precept, 'Know thyself,' and the modern precept, 'Study nature,' become at last one maxim."

Part II

"The next great influence into the spirit of the scholar, is, the mind of the Past,—in whatever form, whether of literature, of art, of institutions." It may seem ironic that Emerson appeals to the past in an address that emphasizes the need for a break from tradition. But he points out that even books have their limitations: They may bring "life" and reveal "truth," but "each age . . . must write its own books." Books can do a "grave mischief" if we depend too much on past ages and past ideas. "Colleges are built on" reverence for books, but people come to rely too much upon the books rather than upon their own ideas: "Meek young men grow up in libraries, believing it is their duty to accept the views, which Cicero, which Locke, which Bacon, have given, forgetful that Cicero, Locke, and Bacon were only young men in libraries, when they wrote these books." A student becomes a "bookworm," taught only to "value books, as such; not as related to nature and the human constitution."

Emerson explains the "right use" of books as simply "to inspire." The reader must avoid becoming "a satellite instead of a system." We must realize that genius lies within us, a result of "the active soul," not the passive reader: "The book, the college, the school of art, the institution of any kind, stop with some past utterance of genius." Instead, true "genius looks forward" and comes from "solitude, inquest, and self-recovery." These are not methods or activities that colleges promote. Emerson here makes a radical statement to an audience with access to the world's literature and history: "Books are for the scholar's idle times." Only as "Man Thinking" can we "read God directly, the hour is too precious to be wasted in other men's transcripts of their readings." Colleges require a certain amount of "laborious reading," but education must do more than just impart the facts—it must "set the hearts of their youth on flame." We should only look to the past for guidance, not answers. It is not books themselves that we should praise, but what we find in "the best books" is insight into the universality of human nature, coming away "with the conviction, that one nature wrote and the same reads."

Part III

The final influence upon the scholar, or "Man Thinking," is the world of action. Some people have the idea "that the scholar should be a recluse," that he is uninterested in or unfit for work. This attitude leads "practical men" to "sneer at speculative men." This is why America has no public intellectuals—the clergy, for example, whom Emerson identifies as "more universally than any other class, the scholars of their day," are set apart from others in their work. But the scholar must have "action," and the man of action must be a thinker: "Only so much do I know, as I have lived." Knowledge and "power" come from a range of experiences, including "drudgery, calamity, exasperation, [and] want," which are "the raw material out of which the intellect moulds her splendid products." It is wrong to "shut myself out of this globe of action, and transplant an oak into a flower-pot, there to hunger and pine." Likewise, a scholar should not focus only on one subject, one task, and shut himself away from the world but rather seek experience through "intercourse with many men and women." Knowledge comes from living life, and "colleges and books only copy the language which the field and the work-yard made." Better than books is "living" itself.

Emerson then turns from "the education of the scholar by nature, by books, and by action" to a focus on the "duties" of "Man Thinking," which "may all be comprised in self-trust." The scholar is engaged in the "unpaid task of observation," so that he may guide and inspire others. The scholar forgoes "display and immediate fame" to work in private and in poverty for many years. The scholar knows nothing of "popular arts," "fashions," or "the religion of society." This leads to "virtual hostility" from society and self-doubt for the scholar. What is the reward, then, "the offset" for the scholar? He finds "consolation in exercising the highest functions of human nature." He creates "heroic sentiments, noble biographies, melodious verse, and the conclusions of history." He must therefore have "confidence in himself" and cannot be concerned about the world, which "of any moment is the merest appearance." By searching his own mind, the scholar searches the minds of all men: "The poet, in utter solitude remembering his spontaneous thoughts and recording them, is fond to have recorded that, which men in crowded cities find true for them also." What seems to be "privatest, secretest" is found to be "most public, and universally true." This pursuit, then, requires "self-trust": "The world is his, who can see through its pretension."

The scholar rejects the version of history offered by religion and tradition, the "mischievous notion that we are come late into nature; that the world was finished a long time ago." The scholar rejects the idea of creation as a single act, seeing instead that we create and change the world through ideas: "Not he is great who can alter matter, but he who can alter my state of mind." Emerson names great scientists as creators of new ideas and inspiration. Man has not only "been wronged" by this story, but "he has wronged himself" by lacking self-trust. "Men in history, men in the world of to-day are bugs, are spawn, and are called 'the mass' and 'the herd.'" Men have become content to look to one or two heroes rather than live for themselves. Aspiring only for "money or power," most men are not living, but merely "sleep-walking." Emerson calls for a "revolution" to be brought about by "the gradual domestication of the idea of Culture." That is, an American culture, "nearer . . . to the time and to this country." A search for an American scholar requires an understanding of history, and Emerson explains his view that "each individual passes through" the major periods or "epochs"—"the Classic . . . the Romantic, and now of the Reflective or Philosophical age." Who will be the scholar of this age, which some have labeled, negatively, as an age of "Introversion?" Emerson asks, "Must that needs be evil?" Is it wrong to want to understand ourselves? "Would we be blind? Do we fear lest we should outsee nature and God, and drink truth dry?" People glorify the past and tradition, when "this time, like all times, is a very good one, if we but know what to do with it."

He does find some "glimmer" of hope, some "auspicious signs of the coming days." First is that "the low, the common" have been "explored and poetized": "The literature of the poor, the feelings of the child, the philosophy of the street, the meaning of household life, are the topics of the time. It is a great stride." He goes on to catalog the sources of meaning in the everyday, in "the meal in the firkin; the milk in the pan; the ballad in the street; the news of the boat; the glance of the eye; the form and the gait of the body . . . the shop, the plough, and the leger."

The second "sign of our times" giving Emerson hope is American individualism, the idea of "man as a sovereign state." This is the path to "true union," to see that "the world is nothing, the man is all; in yourself is the law of all nature. . . . It is for you to know all, it is for you to dare all." His message to "the American Scholar" is that "we have listened too long to the courtly muses of Europe," a tradition that sees Americans as "timid, imitative, tame." But if the American scholar only relies upon "his instincts," trusts himself, "the huge world will come round to him." We are individuals, not bound by "party" or "section" or geography, as to "the north, or the south," and only when we are individuals, "a nation of men will for the first time exist."

CRITICAL COMMENTARY

"The American Scholar" is, first of all, a call for a break from European influence and tradition and toward a distinctly American intellectual and literary tradition, suited to American political, economic, and social life. This was a call Emerson would make in other addresses as well, most notably "LITERARY ETHICS" (1838) and "The YOUNG AMERICAN" (1844). Throughout his career, Emerson waited for the American scholar and American poet. This was not to deny the importance of the European influence; indeed, American Transcendentalism itself was a synthesis of various European influences, from SAMUEL TAYLOR COLERIDGE to IMMANUEL KANT to JOHANN WOLFGANG VON GOETHE. Likewise, when Emerson set out to identify his own catalog of *REPRESENTATIVE MEN* (1850) or to name his favorite poets in *PARNASSUS* (1874), nearly all of his subjects were from the ancient or European traditions.

In Emerson's terms, "Man Thinking" is a way of being rather than a specific role or job to fill; "every man" is a student of life, and the main sources of knowledge—nature, the past, and the practical world of action—are available to all. The question the scholar must ask is that which all men must ask: "What is nature to him?" This is Emerson's Transcendentalist question, and the answer is "always circular power returning into itself . . . so entire, so boundless." Emerson's use of circle imagery would be repeated throughout numerous other writings, including the essay "CIRCLES" (1841), and is one of his primary images of the soul and of the mind, itself "without centre, without circumference."

One of the core tenets of Emerson's Transcendentalism is summed up in "The American Scholar" in the philosophy that to know nature is to know thyself: "the ancient precept, 'Know thyself,' and the modern precept, 'Study nature,' become at last one maxim." Here he provides an outline of the thinker as scientist, intuiting and then classifying knowledge. He had established the relationship of knowledge and language to nature in his seminal work, *NATURE,* published just one year earlier, in September 1836. Emerson proposes a new way of "creative reading," that is, reading (books as well as nature) not just for the sake of knowledge but for the growth of one's own soul, and encourages the reader to be an "inventor" of his own ideas and his own future.

Emerson's words would be echoed in strikingly similar terms nearly 20 years later in HENRY DAVID THOREAU's *Walden; or, Life in the Woods* (1854): "Will you be a reader, a student merely, or a seer? Read your fate, see what is before you, and walk on into futurity." In *Walden*, however, Thoreau would more explicitly call for personal experience through nature rather than through books, announcing of his experiment in the woods, "I did not read books the first summer; I hoed beans." For Emerson, however, books (and the stories and histories and inspiring models of genius they contain), while best sought in "the scholar's idle times," were still useful tools of self-development, a theme he continued in his later essay "BOOKS" (1870).

Emerson urged the scholar to gain knowledge from experience and the active life: "Only so much do I know, as I have lived." The scholar must be of the world, and yet Emerson would return again and again to the practical conflict between thought and action, between self and society. This dilemma for the poet-scholar is at the center of the essays in SOCIETY AND SOLITUDE (1870) and in the poems "SAADI" (1842) and, in another sense, in "GIVE ALL TO LOVE" (1847) ("Friends, kindred, days, / Estate, good-fame, / Plans, credit and the Muse, / Nothing refuse"). Emerson's call to action in "The American Scholar" is not just an urging the scholar from his study but a recognition that one learns about oneself by stepping outside of oneself. "The world," for Emerson, is the "shadow of the soul, or *other me*," which will "make me acquainted with myself." Emerson placed great value on the everyday, extracting lessons not only from the simplest form of nature but from the mundane but authentic details of everyday experience; life is a "dictionary" and the knowledge in "colleges and books" is only a "copy" of that found in "the field and the work-yard."

Echoing the political revolution of the 1770s, which brought government to the people, Emerson calls for a "revolution" to be brought about by "the gradual domestication of the idea of Culture." As he would seek to do in *Representative Men* through the study of "great men," Emerson here brings the philosophical and literary to bear upon the common and accessible. He names "Goethe, Wordsworth, and Carlyle," as well as "Swedenborg," as geniuses for their idea "that things near are not less beautiful and wondrous than things remote."

Looking around in the late 1830s, Emerson finds two peculiarly American developments upon which to build this new culture: the literary interest in "the common" and the political belief in individualism. "The literature of the poor, the feelings of the child, the philosophy of the street, the meaning of household life, are the topics of the time. It is a great stride." Undoubtedly, this was what attracted him some years later to WALT WHITMAN, although Emerson never fully credited Whitman as being this American poet we were waiting for. Indeed, it was Emerson's words that would echo in Whitman; in "The American Scholar" Emerson values what is distinctly American and distinctly today: "I embrace the common, I explore and sit at the feet of the familiar, the low. Give me insight into to-day, and you may have the antique and future worlds." Emerson believed in American "events, actions arise, that must be sung, that will sing themselves," again, language that would inspire Whitman's own "Song of Myself" and songs of America.

Emerson ends the address with a political analogy that, delivered nearly 25 years before the Civil War, already spoke to his generation's rising political angst, emphasizing that "true union" comes from seeing "man as a sovereign state." As humans we are not bound by "party" or "section" or geography, as to "the north, or the south," and when we are fully realized as individuals, "a nation of men will for the first time exist." This is Emerson's call for a "revolution" in ideas and culture, a revolution that requires a different kind of break from Europe. This is why, in his 1884 biography of Emerson, OLIVER WENDELL HOLMES referred to "The American Scholar" as our "Intellectual Declaration of Independence."

FURTHER READING

Sacks, Kenneth. *Understanding Emerson: "The American Scholar" and His Struggle for Self-Reliance.* Princeton, N.J.: Princeton University Press, 2003.

"American Slavery" (1855)

"American Slavery" was delivered for the first time at a meeting of the Massachusetts Anti-Slavery Society in BOSTON on January 25, 1855. Emerson repeated it at antislavery meetings in Worcester, New York, Philadelphia, Rochester, and Syracuse during the winter of 1855. It was his third major speech protesting the Fugitive Slave Law. In his previous Fugitive Slave Law addresses of 1851 and 1854, Emerson had denounced the 1850 legislation, which forbade Northerners from aiding escaped slaves under penalty of law and ordered Northern marshals to participate in slave catching. Since the delivery of his March 1854 address, a new act had been passed in Congress allowing settlers in Kansas, a territory that had formerly been closed to slavery, to decide by referendum whether slavery would be tolerated. In Boston, another escaped slave, Anthony Burns, was captured and returned to slavery. These events generated intense debate in Massachusetts and were the backdrop to Emerson's decision to speak again on the subject. "American Slavery" was not published during his lifetime and was made available in print for the first time only recently in *Emerson's Antislavery Writings* (1995) and again in *The Later Lectures of Ralph Waldo Emerson* (2000) and *The Political Emerson* (2004).

SYNOPSIS

Emerson begins the lecture by admitting that the antislavery movement was one that he felt he did not have the "right qualifications" to effectively serve and therefore had left to others more gifted in speaking to political questions. Nonetheless, slavery was an exceptional issue that demanded the participation of everyone. Emerson argues that it would be "heaven" that would provide the solution to the problem, but that human will would be the means to the foreordained end.

Emerson declares that on this issue of slavery, one must "write with a red hot iron" to make any impression. He mentions that some Northern societies had invited Southern planters to the north to argue the case for slavery. Since the Southerners had refused the invitation, it was left to the Northerners to consider the question, "each as he could." When slavery was thought of not as an isolated issue but in relation to the broader American picture, Emerson finds it self-evident that the "advantages and superiorities" on which the country prided itself were negated and defeated by the "mortal disease" of slavery.

This disease had become "more malignant than ever" since the passage of the Fugitive Slave Law and other legislation that had spread the rule of slavery even into New England. It was found that "well-born, well-bred, well-grown men" in the North were willing to support and comply with this law. The disease would be fought and eventually purged by the health of the system. Nevertheless, to see slavery spread into the home of the Puritans and accepted by educated and industrious New Englanders "staggers our faith in progress." The blame for this is society's widespread skepticism, frivolity, and lack of faith. Those who would gladly devote their energies to high aims could find no channel to do so and eventually "fell into file," gave way to "the soft appliances of fashion," and were heartily congratulated by society for "settling down into sensible opinions and practices." Imagination and ideas were shunned. The "Party of Property" was in control and resisted progress. Everywhere was a worship of wealth and success and a "disbelief in principles." It was a period of darkness.

Yet, the law of compensation—of "smite and thou shalt smart"—was sure to intervene. When the Founding Fathers had agreed to a false system of representation and signed laws that preserved the institution of slavery, they secured a temporary union and prosperity. This was a "fatal" blunder and would be punished by a "great disaster." Man-made law was of no avail against original, higher law, which itself was a "transcript of natural right." In America, however, the lawmakers and even the judges were unwilling to look beyond the U.S. Constitution and speak for the eternal laws of love and justice. The effect of this was "to discredit government." Men disobey the government and turn instead for reason and truth to "private men who have brave hearts and minds" and to their own independent thoughts and resources.

Emerson encourages individual independence but makes it clear that he means not to "cripple but [to] exalt the social action." Southerners had encroached on the government to the point that it no longer represented liberty and freedom, but every wise American will realize that these are the very ideas or functions for which the country stands. It is "delicious to act with great masses to great aims." The end of slavery through negotiation is a "great task" for the people of America to accomplish, acting together to do what "one man" alone cannot. If the monetary cost will be high, then a way will be found to pay for it. All would gladly contribute to seeing slavery, an "accursed mountain of sorrow," banished permanently from the world.

CRITICAL COMMENTARY

In terms of philosophical content, Emerson's address on "American Slavery" is in most ways a development upon the themes and issues that characterized his earlier Fugitive Slave Law speeches. What is different about this speech is that here Emerson puts forward a practical strategy not only for overturning and invalidating the 1850 law but also for ending slavery altogether.

As in the "FUGITIVE SLAVE LAW" address of 1851, Emerson's chief ethical message in "American Slavery" hinges on the concept of compensation. This idea, that the universe was governed by laws that work toward justice, marked his earlier essays "COMPENSATION" (1841), "SPIRITUAL LAWS" (1841), and others before becoming an integral part of his antislavery rhetoric. There is a vision in this essay of a coming catastrophe. The Founding Fathers had chosen to sign the Constitution, which perpetuated and legitimated the slave system. Although it resulted in political union and prosperity, the crime committed against the slaves themselves would and must be balanced out. Unlike his 1851 "Fugitive Slave Law" address, however, Emerson proposes a way that the sin of slavery could be paid for—literally. Following the example set by the British in their 1833 Act of Emancipation, Emerson suggests that the United States could carry out a plan of compensated emancipation, ending slavery by repaying slaveholders for the loss of their "property" with public funds. Emerson recognized that the payment would not be easy and would demand sacrifice. In 1855, Emerson's suggestion that slavery should be abolished regardless of the cost to the nation's finances was extreme, even in New England. A few years later in the poem "BOSTON HYMN," written in the midst of the Civil War, Emerson moved to an even more radical abolitionist position, saying it would be wrong to "pay ransom to the owner / And fill the bag to the brim. / Who is the owner? The slave is owner, / And ever was. Pay him."

A striking feature of this address is Emerson's clear endorsement of the use of "social action" to solve a particular problem. This is effectually a reversal of the "moral suasion" paradigm to which he adhered in his early career, particularly before 1844. In essays such as "MAN THE REFORMER" (1841) and "SELF-RELIANCE" (1841), Emerson advised his audiences to concentrate on improving themselves before trying to improve society and to steer clear of "single issue" reform movements. In this lecture, in the section in which he extols "social action," Emerson seems to be making a deliberate reference to his well-known early works with the intention of conveying to his audiences that his opinions had changed. The issue of ending slavery, in Emerson's estimation, had reached a point where the active participation of all Americans had become necessary without further delay.

FURTHER READING

Collison, Gary. "Emerson and Antislavery." In *A Historical Guide to Ralph Waldo Emerson,* edited by Joel Myerson, 179–209. New York and Oxford: Oxford University Press, 2000.

Engstrom, Sallee Fox. *The Infinitude of the Private Man: Emerson's Presence in Western New York, 1851–1861.* New York: Peter Lang, 1997.

Gougeon, Len. *Virtue's Hero: Emerson, Antislavery and Reform.* Athens: University of Georgia Press, 1990.

Von Frank, Albert J. *The Trials of Anthony Burns: Freedom and Slavery in Emerson's Boston.* Cambridge, Mass.: Harvard University Press, 1998.

Daniel Robert Koch

"Art" (1841)

"Art" was first published in 1841 as the 12th and last essay in *ESSAYS: FIRST SERIES*. The essay originated as part of the lecture series "Philosophy of History" presented in BOSTON, in winter 1836–37. Emerson showed an interest in and enthusiasm for different forms of art throughout his life and writings. Before embarking on his career as a lecturer and writer, he spent much time during his first trip to Europe in 1833 visiting different galleries and architectural monuments. Emerson mentions in "Art" some of the details of this experience, one which contributed, in part, to shaping his own conclusions about the nature of art. In the essay "Art," Emerson presents his aesthetic intuitions primarily on the plastic arts and synthesizes them with various Transcendentalist themes, such as the value of the active creative life of the human soul, the relevance of the here and now, and the importance of common things and wild nature in the life of the individual.

SYNOPSIS

In the opening lines of the essay, Emerson says that the creative and "progressive" nature of the soul "appears in works both of the useful and the fine arts." The identification of these two forms of art is a "popular" one, and the latter (ostensibly the subject of the essay) is commonly believed to have as its aim the production of a "fairer creation"—as opposed to a mere "imitation"—of the things found in wild nature. The landscape painter, for example, is not to duplicate the "details, the prose of nature" but instead express "the spirit and the splendor" of nature: "the gloom of gloom, and the sunshine of sunshine." Works of art, as such, represent nature in a more perfect and refined form, just as the human being is said to exist as a contraction and "finer success" of the natural world.

Emerson next explains the importance of the historical setting of art. He says that all artists are conditioned by the cultural setting of their particular time and place, for "the artist must employ the symbols in use in his day and nation, to convey his enlarged sense to his fellow-men." No new work of art is absolutely original no matter how imaginative the mind of the artist, for each is "formed out of the old." The "Genius of the Hour" or the "spiritual character of a period" supersedes the "talent" of the individual artist and inevitably marks a great work, thereby giving it its "charm." Hence, historical works of art are observed to "denote the height of the human soul in that hour."

Following this, Emerson discusses a way in which art can serve to awaken the "dormant taste" of persons by educating them about the beautiful "immensity of the world." Emerson states that, given the "embarrassing variety" of the objects or "forms" of nature, the artist possesses the executive "power to detach, and to magnify by detaching" a single one, thus appointing it "for the time the deputy of the world." By a successive process of coronations each thing may take on an absolute worth until another replaces it "to be for their moment the top of the world." In its own moment, for example, a "squirrel leaping from bough to bough, and making the wood but one wide tree for his pleasure, fills the eye not less than a lion,—is beautiful, self-sufficing, and stands then and there for nature."

In light of this artistic method, Emerson deemphasizes the works of the fine arts, claiming that they lack a final value in themselves: "The office of painting and sculpture seems to be merely initial." Works of art serve to expand our perception and direct us to recognize the original source of things represented, which is nothing less than the wealth of living entities given in nature that are said to constitute an immense catalog or "eternal picture." Natural objects, as such, are praised as works of art themselves. In comparison to the inanimate forms of sculpture, for example, "there is no statue like this living man, with his infinite advantage over all ideal sculpture." In the face of the aboriginal greatness of nature, Emerson assails the fine arts: "Away with your nonsense of oil and easels, of marble and chisels: except to open your eyes to the masteries of eternal art, they are hypocritical rubbish."

Emerson next characterizes the works of the "highest art" by their quality of being "universally intelligible" to all of mankind. Their beauty resides in a "wonderful expression through stone, or canvas, or musical sound, of the deepest and simplest attributes" of human nature. This underlying principle or "moral nature" is likely missed by such a person as the "traveller who visits the Vatican" and gets lost in laboriously perusing the variety of available artifacts. The pedant who "studies the technical rules" of art overlooks the universal truth that each and all individuals "carry" within, and that is the foundation of the thoughts of the artist who looks to his own personal life experiences for inspiration. Emerson insists that artistic creation must not be restricted by theoretical rules, materials, or conventional and foreign standards of expression, since even the conditions of life of the common or financially impoverished individual "will serve as well as any other condition as the symbol of a thought which pours itself indifferently through all." Here Emerson recalls his own misconceptions, during his "younger days," of the great works of Italian painting and sculpture, and the subsequent destruction of these ideas upon seeing such works firsthand while visiting Europe. Rather than finding works that he imagined would appear as "foreign wonders," he found works that were surprisingly familiar, expressing the "old, eternal fact" he had already encountered back home, and thus proclaims "all traveling ridiculous as a treadmill."

Emerson neatly packages the different disciplines of the fine arts within the succinct definition: "Art is the need to create." He says that the "real value" of all the products of art is not that they exist as final statements but that they are "signs of power . . . tokens of the everlasting effort to produce"; what we praise is not the "actual result" but the aim or intent. Emerson further identifies the final end of art as "nothing less than the creation of man and nature," and its "highest effect . . . to make new artists." Given such defining qualities of art in general, the particular art of sculpture appears to us in the present age as a "childish carving" that has "long ago perished to any real effect." The essential shortcoming of this immature art form is that it is irrelevant to and detached from the ever-creative flow of nature, whereby "the statue will look cold and false before that new activity which needs to roll through all things." As he explains, "true art is never fixed, but always flowing."

Emerson concludes the essay by criticizing the art of "modern society." Being motivated by pleasure rather than love, it "makes the same effort which a sensual prosperity makes; namely, to detach the beautiful from the useful." Yet, this "division of beauty from use, the laws of nature do not permit." Hence, the abstract creation of modern society contrasts with nature and is a false and "sickly beauty." Such artists are presumptuous; they fail to recognize the beauty in nature and so "reject life as prosaic, and create a death which they call poetic." But, since in "nature, all is useful, all is beautiful," Emerson declares that "beauty must come back to the useful arts, and the distinction between the fine and the useful arts be forgotten." The artist is to acknowledge and revere the beauty of his own immediate and local surroundings, and to seek not an "economical" but a "divine use" in such things as "the railroad, the insurance office, the joint-stock company, our law . . . the galvanic battery, [and] the electric jar." In this way, "when science is learned in love, and its powers are wielded by love, they will appear the supplements and continuations of the material creation."

CRITICAL COMMENTARY

In the essay Emerson presents his philosophy of art. The poem introducing "Art" begins: "Give to barrows, trays, and pans / Grace and glimmer of romance." Apart from Emerson and other fellow Transcendentalists, it is undeniable that mention of a barrow is peculiar for most any discourse on art. In Emerson's essay our attention is directed away from the objects we customarily take to be works of art (paintings, sculptures, etc.) and directed toward the things of daily life and wild nature whose aesthetic value we tend to overlook: the landscape, farm, log hut, animal, and even the barrow. For Emersonian aesthetics, the leaping squirrel, "a dog, drawn by a master, or a litter of pigs, satisfies, and is a reality not less than the frescoes of Angelo." Emerson's fascination with the beauty of "natural forms" dates back biographically at least to his memorable experience in the Jardin des Plantes while visiting Paris in 1833, an experience he describes in his journal celebrating the cabinets of birds, fish, insects, minerals—in sum, the endless and "bewildering series of animated forms." The visit to Paris followed his travels in Italy, where he explored the country's collection of fine arts—an episode he characterizes in "Art" as a disenchanting experience. It was not that Emerson found no value in the halls of the Vatican and museums, but that he was, as characteristic of the father of Transcendentalism, concerned with the relevance art had for his own times and for his own person as a fellow partaking in the life of the Soul.

Emerson frames his naturalistic aesthetics by instructing that "we are immersed in beauty," for beauty is an essential property extending throughout the natural universe. This is the metaphysical foundation of Emerson's aesthetics, and an idea that he formulates elsewhere, such as in "The POET," where he says: "For the world is not painted, or adorned, but is from the beginning beautiful; and God has not made some beautiful things, but Beauty is the creator of the universe." That beauty is pre-established or inherent in nature is consonant with the Transcendentalist motif of divine immanence—a pantheistic cosmology whereby God and nature are one.

Given the pre-established beauty of the universe, Emerson conceives that rather than art creating or ordering a new and beautiful reality, it is the means of discovering or intuiting order and beauty. Beauty awaits the penetrating gaze of the artist, whose task is to *express* (rather than make) beauty. Yet, this is not to suggest that the artistic intent is to simply duplicate reality by presenting a mirror image of it. Emerson's remarks and example of the landscape painter, in the opening paragraph of the essay, prove that he does not have a realist conception of art. (Realism being the artistic style that creates a recognizable replication of its subject matter without idealization.) The work of art is not to imitate by artificial means (in stone, paint, etc.) the details of a particular scene or event in order to create a mere copy of nature (like a photograph). Rather, the project of the Emersonian artist is to suggest a higher standard of beauty, to produce a "fairer creation" by an attempt to express "the spirit and splendor" of things. This spirit is spoken by the language of natural symbols—a Transcendentalist idea Emerson formulates in his chapter "Language" in NATURE (1836)—and it is what the artist seeks to capture and contain within the boundary of a work of art. As such, Emerson's theory is that the work of art is a representation of an expression found in nature.

But, for Emerson, art does not begin only once the forms of nature are *re*-expressed. Nature is an "eternal picture" for the service it renders as a resource from which the artist chooses a particular subject matter for representing, yet this resource need not be filtered through the human will to constitute a "picture," that is, it need not be *re*-presented by the artist in order to *be* art. Simply put: Natural objects *are* works of art. Hence, Nature is a painter that "paints in the street with moving men and children, beggars, and fine ladies, draped in red, and green, and blue, and gray." Emerson presents in the poem "The SNOW-STORM" the same fascinating aestheticism of nature: He conceives of the snowstorm as an "artificer" that sculpts and leaves in its wake "astonished Art . . . The frolic architecture of the snow." With "Art," Emerson homogenizes the dualism between works of art as products of the human will and natural forms as products of wild nature, a tentative distinction he sketches in the "Introduction" of *Nature.*

Emerson dissolves not only the dichotomy between art and nature in "Art" but also the dichotomy contained between the useful (practical) and fine arts. Emerson opens the essay by noting the seemingly obvious and benign distinction between the arts, yet during the course of the essay, he moves to undermine the validity of this "popular distinction," claiming it to be false and the cause of the contemptible state of the arts in his day. In "nature, all is useful, all is beautiful." This first principle is unacknowledged by art that disobeys and disrespects the preordained beauty of the world. Its artists blindly "reject life as prosaic" and "fly to voluptuous reveries" by creating florid extravagances that awkwardly clash with the original forms and movements of those found in nature. From Emerson's poem "The Problem," we know that "art might obey, but not surpass" nature. The artist who denies nature denies in effect his own will, that is, his own "need to create," which exists as a part of the natural progressive flow of the cosmic "fountain of invention." The profane artist presented by Emerson in "Art" thus resembles the fractured and sickly academic criticized in "The AMERICAN SCHOLAR" as fallen from a state of natural perfection.

Emerson's declaration of his aesthetics in the final lines of "Art" is that "beauty must come back to the useful arts, and the distinction between the fine and the useful arts be forgotten." Mankind's "need to create" is to harmonize with that of the natural order, thus unifying as a single aesthetic process where "all is useful, all is beautiful." As such, even the so-called "useful arts" of commerce, technology, and science will come to realize their inherent and aboriginal beauty, as the "steamboat bridging the Atlantic between Old and New England, and arriving at its ports with the punctuality of a planet, is a step of man into harmony with nature" and "needs little to make it sublime."

In the chapter "Beauty" in *Nature,* Emerson says, "Thus is Art, a nature passed through the alembic of man. Thus in art, does nature work through the will of man filled with the beauty of her works." And thus in "Art" we see that the will of the artist is to operate in the "thoroughfare" of "new activity which needs to roll through all things," to share in the cosmic Power that creates in beauty all natural forms and common things . . . even the barrow.

FURTHER READING

Brodwin, Stanley. "Emerson's Version of Plotinus: The Flight to Beauty." *Journal of the History of Ideas* 35, no. 3 (1974): 477.

Hopkins, Vivian C. *Spires of Form: A Study of Emerson's Aesthetic Theory.* New York: Russell & Russell, 1965.

Nicholas Guardiano

"Art" (1847)

"Art" is a 28-line poem included as a motto to Ralph Waldo Emerson's essay "ART" in *ESSAYS: FIRST SERIES* (1841). The poem was also later included in *MAY-DAY AND OTHER PIECES* (1867) in a section titled "Elements," which republished several such essay epigraphs; it was reprinted in *SELECTED POEMS* (1876). The poem is composed of a series of rhyming couplets and, read in conjunction with the essay, explains Emerson's philosophy of and romantic aesthetic of art and artistic endeavor.

CRITICAL COMMENTARY

The poem opens by clearly stating that the purpose of art is to give the "grace and glimmer of romance" to everyday objects, revealing Emerson's romantic aesthetic of art as an idealized version of reality. Art, then, is not just painting and sculpture (the "high" arts), but there is beauty, as well as "the grace and glimmer of romance," to be found in the everyday objects of human life, such as "barrows, trays, and pans." Many human endeavours constitute "art," such as human society's attempts to beautify "the city's paved street" by planting flowers and installing "spouting fountains." Our "statue," our "park," our "ballad, flag, and festival" are all art in the sense that these efforts add beauty and meaning to the world around us. Additionally, art is a way we can honor our history, as well as connect to the present and envision the future: "The past restore, the day adorn, / And make to-morrow a new morn."

After identifying various alternative sources of art, the second half of the poem further explores the role of art in human life. Art plays a "cheerful part" by beautifying and adding meaning to our brief human existence: "Man on earth to acclimate, / And bend the exile to his fate." While the beginning of the poem was concerned with the human creation of art, the last stanza reminds us that art is not separate from nature and therefore not separate from life; it is "moulded of one element / With the days and firmament." While it is the "fate" of humans to have only a brief "exile" on earth, art gives us immortality; it allows us to "live on even terms with Time."

"Art" (1870)

Coming after "CIVILIZATION," "Art" appears as the third essay in *SOCIETY AND SOLITUDE.* Emerson delivered his first lecture on art in the "Principles and History of Art" series given in BOSTON in December 1836 as part of his course on the Philosophy of History. The present lecture first appeared as "Thoughts on Art" in the January 1841 issue of the *DIAL*. It contains some added passages from a lecture called "Art and Criticism" given in Boston in April 1859; and it is probable that he used it as the second lecture "Art" in the course on "Life and Literature" in Boston in April 1861. The 1870 essay reprises many of Emerson's early pronouncements on art and beauty in such essays as "ART," the concluding essay of *ESSAYS: FIRST SERIES* (1841), and "BEAUTY" in *THE CONDUCT OF LIFE* (1860), and has thematic relations with such poems as "The Problem," "EACH AND ALL," and "The RHODORA" (all collected in *POEMS*, 1847) and "NATURE" (from *MAY-DAY AND OTHER PIECES*, 1867).

SYNOPSIS

Emerson's central purpose in this essay is to show that art is not a production of the artist as an individual but a phenomenon of nature or the universal spirit. On the basis of this view, he expounds characterizations of both artistic creation and the reception and enjoyment of art to which the element of universality is essential.

The definition of art posited in this essay is founded on the view that the human mind, following the law of its nature, always seeks to express itself in words or action—seeks "the publication and embodiment of its thought." Such expression is sometimes unconscious or instinctual. When it is conscious, it is what Emerson defines as art. Art itself can be subdivided into two categories according to its ends: The useful and the fine arts aim, respectively, at pragmatic or utilitarian ends and at beauty. Emerson's examples of the useful arts include agriculture, building, navigation, and language.

Emerson says that an inquiry into art leads to the question "Who is the Artist?" His answer is based on the law that "the universal soul is the alone creator of the useful and the beautiful; therefore to make anything useful or beautiful, the individual must be submitted to the universal mind." While a thorough account of "the universal soul" lies beyond the scope of a discussion of art, Emerson's claims in this essay refer to a first principle or creative power that manifests itself through natural phenomena and in the inspired deeds and perceptions of men. Emerson sometimes refers to this as nature, the over-soul, or God.

In its application to the useful arts, the above law entails that "Art must be a complement to Nature, strictly subsidiary." In order to succeed, man's designs must strictly observe natural laws. For example, an architect's designs must take into account the strength of the available materials, the force of gravity, and the onslaught of the elements if they are to materialize and endure. Only within the narrow limits set by these constraints is the artist free to innovate. However, working within those limits allows us to draw on nature's boundless power, which far exceeds our own. Hydroelectric power or nuclear power offer even more striking examples of this than the use of steam and wind power known to Emerson and his contemporaries.

Emerson argues that the fine arts parallel the useful arts in that their greatest achievements are secured not by the faculties of individual artists but by the operation of the power of nature. He supports this, first, by trying to divorce the effect of art from the intentions and abilities of the artist. First, every fine art, like every useful art, depends to some extent on its material basis. Emerson suggests that the quality of that matter, independently of the form the artist imparts to it, accounts for some of the pleasure the work of art produces. "The pulsation of a stretched string or wire," for example, "gives the ear the pleasure of sweet sound, before yet the musician has enhanced this pleasure by concords and combinations." Second, the artist depends to some extent on the conventions that inform his work, ringing changes on established forms rather than innovating from the ground up. Finally, the effect of the artwork is conditioned by what Emerson calls "the adventitious"—its setting, context, or world. The aesthetic pleasure a temple inspires, for example, is "exalted by the beauty of sunlight, the play of the clouds, the landscape around its grouping with the houses, trees and towers in its vicinity." Emerson also suggests that we hesitate to credit "our best sense of any work of art" to the artist. From this intuition and the dependence of artwork on elements outside the author's control and intent, Emerson extrapolates that "the power of Nature predominates over the human will in all works of even the fine arts, in all that respects their material and external circumstances," producing "the best part" of every work.

Since he can accomplish little through his own personal talents, the best the artist can do is open himself to nature's influence, becoming a conduit for its action, an empty vessel for its light. This is accomplished when the artist "disindividualizes himself," surrendering his egotism and abstracting "everything individual" from his work. One corollary of this is the work's conformity to necessity; there is nothing capricious or arbitrary in it, since the idiosyncrasies and fancies of the artist qua individual are not involved in artistic creation. "Every work of art, in proportion to its excellence, partakes of the precision of fate: no room was there for choice, no play for fancy." Thus, according to Emerson, the work becomes a product of the universal soul or "the mind of humanity," and thus speaks to all men.

Because art and nature have this common root, Emerson thinks that studying art can enhance our perception of nature, that there is "a certain analogy" between natural and artistic beauty, and that appreciating art can induce religious states of mind. Moreover, because they emanate from the universal mind, "great works are always attuned to moral nature." Just as art and nature are affine, the different arts are also analogous for "they are the reappearance of one mind [the universal spirit], working in many materials to many temporary ends."

Finally, the essay undermines the dichotomy between the fine and useful arts. Beauty in nature, Emerson tells us, "depends forever on the necessary and the useful. . . . The most perfect form to answer an end is so far beautiful." The plumage of birds, for example, is beautiful because it is adaptive. In this connection, Emerson posits that art springs from and replicates objects of utilitarian use. Architecture, for example, originates as an idealization of primitive dwellings, while the Roman amphitheater echoes the shape of a crowd assembled to witness a brawl.

Since art is tied to our real needs, it can never be created capriciously. Emerson indicates that art languishes in his day because it does not answer to current needs. These, rather, are served by "popular institutions" such as insurance companies and telegraphs. Beauty, however, is never obsolete; these institutions "are preparing the soil of man for fairer flowers and fruits in another age."

CRITICAL COMMENTARY

This essay recapitulates many of Emerson's signature themes. The metaphysical ground for the argument developed here is the universal mind, an inexhaustible fountainhead of fresh ideas and perceptions common to all men. The most sustained exposition of this idea is found in "The OVER-SOUL" (1841). In "HISTORY" (1841), the universal mind serves as the basis for the perpetual relevance and intelligibility of the thoughts of every age; here, it is the basis of the congruence between the various arts and between art and nature. The depersonalization that this essay associates with the production and reception of art is tied to aesthetic experience throughout Emerson's works, most famously in the "transparent eyeball" passage in *NATURE* (1836). Likewise, the passivity Emerson prescribes to the artist who is open to nature is basically of a piece with his more general accounts of rapturous inspiration, such as in "The Over-Soul": "When I watch that flowing river, which, out of regions I see not, pours for a season its streams into me, I see that I am a pensioner; not a cause, but a surprised spectator of this ethereal water; that I desire and look up, and put myself in the attitude of reception, but from some alien energy the visions come."

Emerson had also noted the continuity between art created by nature and by humans in "The POET" (1844): "Readers of poetry see the factory-village, and the railway, and fancy that the poetry of the landscape is broken up by these; for these works of art are not yet consecrated in their reading. . . . Nature adopts them very fast into her vital circles, and the gliding train of cars she loves like her own." However, the essay on "Art" does offer a distinctive perspective. Technological innovation in Emerson is often connected to the "power" pole of the "fate-power" polarity, signifying man's power to shape his circumstances and environment. Here, too, Emerson develops the paradoxical thesis of the artist's active receptivity to nature.

The wealth of connections between art and major Emersonian themes may attest to an importance of beauty in Emerson's thought that is not always explicit. If so, it should come as no surprise that he turned again to art in the essay under discussion. The earlier "Art" of 1841 is also based on the premises of art's affinity or unity with nature and its provenance, which it also uses to argue against separation between art and life or between the fine and useful arts. The earlier essay upholds the universality of art, discrediting any essential difference between, for example, one nation's art and another's.

Roger Lopez

"Astraea" (1847)

"Astraea" was included in Emerson's 1847 collection *Poems* and reprinted in his *Selected Poems* of 1876. Astraea (which translates as "star maiden") was the Greek goddess of justice, daughter of Zeus and Themis. In astrology, she is identified with Virgo and with the scales of justice of Libra. According to son Edward Waldo Emerson in his centennial edition of the *Complete Works,* Emerson considered titling this poem "Know Thyself," which reflects a concern with internal balance or justice. Oliver Wendell Holmes used the same reference for his much-longer poem, "Astraea: The Balance of Illusions," which he read before the Phi Betta Kappa society at Yale in 1850.

CRITICAL COMMENTARY

Emerson's concept of justice is not specific to any one political system, as neither a "king" nor "sovereign states" can name a hero. He opens the poem declaring that we are our own "heralds," and we determine our own "rank" or importance in the world. We are all equal and "venerable" until we prove ourselves otherwise; that is, "until he write, where all eyes rest." Only then, when our characters are revealed through our actions, will we prove whether we are "slave" or "master." These are not labels that others can place up on us.

In the next section of the poem he reflects on the human interest in "Judgment and a judge." We must not look to some higher order for approval, neither "monarchs" nor "learned jurists," but rather look to those nearest to us, our "peers," and demand, "What am I? companion, say." The true "friend not hesitates" to tell us what they think. But Emerson is not speaking so much of validation as seeing ourselves in others. Our friends tell us about ourselves not necessarily directly "in word or letter," rather, we will see ourselves reflected in the opinions and characters of the friends we keep: "Each to each a looking-glass, / Reflects his figure that doth pass." In his essay "Friendship" (1841) a few years earlier, Emerson reflected on the purpose of friendship in bringing "two souls into one" and in facilitating "progress" of the individual soul. In "Astraea," friends influence one another in the smallest ways and gestures. This is the balance of friendship.

Still, our ultimate self-knowledge and self-worth come not from others but from nature. We are purer if we find ourselves "loved by stars and purest winds" and must ourselves be like a rock, "a granite ledge," strong within ourselves regardless of what others think. Like the sea, which "purges" and "purifies," so must we do to ourselves; as the sea, whose "depths reflect all forms," so with us. This ultimately looking within is necessary since those who judge us may not see our true selves: "Pure by impure is not seen."

Emerson refers to "Justice," represented by Astraea, as the only one who sees all of nature: "no sequestered grot, / Lone mountain tarn, or isle forgot." Unlike our friends or lawmakers, only nature contains all sides and thus provides perfect balance or harmony, or justice, a concept Emerson referred to by a different term in "Compensation" (1841).

"Bacchus" (1847)

"Bacchus" is a 65-line poem published in Emerson's 1847 collection *Poems* and reprinted in *Selected*

POEMS (1876). The poem reflects Emerson's interest in Persian literature and the poetry of Hafiz and Sa'di, the subject of his 1842 poem "SAADI." In 1846, around the same time "Bacchus" was published, Emerson copied a translation from Hafiz in his journal: "Come let us strew roses / And pour wine in the cup, / Break up the roof of heaven / And throw it into new forms." This stanza included imagery of the revelry or luxury that Bacchus represented and that Emerson then used in the poem (birds and roses). Emerson also repeated the imagery here of inspiration coming from the wine that would allow all truth and knowledge to open up, to be brought "into new forms," including the form of poetry. In "Bacchus" Emerson reflects upon the role of the poet-writer and the sources of inspiration for his work.

CRITICAL COMMENTARY

In the opening stanza the poet calls upon the god of wine and poetry to intoxicate the poet's imagination, not with actual wine, but with the wine of inspiration, "wine which never grew / In the belly of the grape." The image and language of intoxication as a source of poetry appears elsewhere in Emerson's writing. In the essay "CIRCLES," he spoke of the writer's "new wine of . . . imagination." In the later essay "Poetry and Imagination," he again invoked "celestial Bacchus," who could lure seekers of truth, those "hungry for Eloquence, hungry for poetry, starving for symbols," in "with the false wine of alcohol, or politics or of money." Finally, in his essay "The POET" he reflected on "the reason why bards love wine," meaning actual wine as well as other sources of intoxication such as "narcotics, coffee, tea, opium," and so on, and explained that these substances allowed the poet "passage out into free space," allowed the "abandonment to the nature of things" that poetry required. But Emerson, however, did not encourage such methods, and he warned that the feeling that comes from intoxication from these substances was "not an inspiration . . . but some counterfeit excitement and fury." As a poet he sought, and reflected upon in "Bacchus," a truer wine as source of inspiration, an "assimilation" with the flow of inspiration through the ages or, as one scholar has noted, to "become the wine."

The next section continues the image of the plant itself, invoking the "grapes," the "juice," and the "root." The root of this source of inspiration he seeks, however, goes deeper than the earth—it reaches to history and mythology. The "acrid juice," the wine, flows from the "Styx and Erebus." This mythological source is contrasted in the third longer stanza with the lack of sustenance from "ashes for bread" and "diluted wine," a reference to the Lord's Supper or Eucharist. Religion, in this comparison, offers an inferior, or at least limited, source of inspiration. The imagery of nature intervenes again, with the plant's "leaves" and reaching "tendrils," representing growth and curiosity. The product of this plant, the wine, is not like any other; it is universal inspiration, "everlasting," the original source ("form of forms"), and nourishes all ("blood of the world"). The inspiration from this source, in turn, allows the poet to be all and to understand all in nature. He is "assimilated" into nature, now understanding "the bird-language rightly spell, / And that which the roses say so well." The life-affirming "birds" and "roses" at the end of the stanza, images of spring and renewal, as well as the poet's relation to nature, again offer a counterpoint to the "ashes" and "diluted wine" of religion in the earlier stanza.

In the short fourth stanza, the "wine of wine" of the previous stanza does not come from an actual vine but still grows like a vine. It moves "up the horizon walls" and "like the Atlantic streams," moved by forces of nature. In the fifth stanza, this wine is sustenance, but true sustenance unlike, again, the "water and bread" of religion. This wine does not stand in as a symbol of a man (of Christ) but "is already man" and is "food which needs no transmuting." We are our own source of sustenance and inspiration.

In stanza 6, the inspiration from this wine allows the poet to know and understand all: the universe ("chaos"), science, the future ("kings unborn"), nature ("every crypt of every rock"). The poet thanks the wine "for all I know" and for allowing all barriers to knowledge and understanding to be opened. The poet discovers his inspiration and his memory, finding there is no distinction among past, present, and future. The "winds of remembering /

Of the ancient being blow" (a linguistic play on the "remembering wine" in the next and final stanza), breaking through "seeming-solid walls" so that all may "open and flow."

In the final stanza, memory is the inspiration—not personal memory, but memory of the universe, of our universal history. The poet calls upon Bacchus to pour "the remembering wine," to "retrieve the loss of men and mine!" and to bring back "the memory of ages quenched," the past, so that it seems new again, "again to shine." The imagery of the mind is also technological, as the mind has pictures imprinted upon it so the wine of memory and inspiration serves to "refresh the faded tints, / Recut the aged prints," and allow the poet not just to remember but to translate those images into writing, into poetry, to "write my old adventures with the pen."

"Beauty" (1860)

The poem "Beauty" represents the speaker's desire to find beauty in nature; this theme resonates throughout Emerson's prose and poetry and is foundational in his thought. The speaker of the poem "chases beauty everywhere" while recognizing the rhythms of nature (the "quaking earth," the ebbing and flowing seas, the "voice from centered and errant sphere"). The poem expresses Emerson's call for all to see the rhythm, the aesthetic beauty, in nature; for Emerson, this aesthetic is not merely formal but a part of our human constitution.

The first 10 and the last 16 lines of the poem were developed separately. The first section was drafted between May 1844 and March 1845. The couplet that became lines 15 and 16 was drafted between February 20 and May 11, 1858. The second section of the poem was drafted and joined to the first between 1858 and 1860. The poem was first published as the motto to the essay "BEAUTY" in *The* CONDUCT OF LIFE (1860); it was subsequently collected in MAY-DAY AND OTHER PIECES (1867), SELECTED POEMS (1876), and *Poems* (1884).

CRITICAL COMMENTARY

The poem is 26 lines long and is composed almost exclusively of rhymed couplets in iambic tetrameter. However, the poem contains a quatrain, distinguished by its *abcb* rhyme scheme, from lines 7 to 10. This variation is significant because it suggests that Emerson is calling our attention to this particular passage. In the quatrain, Emerson gives us four lines of action: The speaker throws stones into a lake to break the symmetry of the surface and to hear the accompanying sound. This is the only real "action" in the poem, in the sense of the speaker executing an action and observing (experiencing) results. The other images in the poem, while offering examples of the speaker's experiences of the rhythm of nature, give us images without the active participation of the speaker.

In terms of the poem's theme, the isolation of these four lines suggests that experience is not merely passive but requires the active participation of the speaker. In the lines preceding the closing couplet, Emerson makes us aware of the danger inherent in the speaker's condition: He searches for beauty only, and thus is the beauty (or truth) of nature lost on him: "Beauty chased he everywhere, / In flame, in storm, in clouds of air. / He smote the lake to feed his eye." This merely superficial appreciation of nature is also a theme in the poems "The RHODORA" or "EACH AND ALL." The poem's last two lines, the closing couplet, summarize the conceit of the speaker, who comes off as a mere sensualist: It is better to "die for Beauty than live for bread." Emerson's tone in the last couplet is critical of sensuality without deep connection.

Bill Scalia

"Beauty" (1860)

Emerson's essay "Beauty," published in *The* CONDUCT OF LIFE (1860), was first delivered as a lecture in 1855. The essay is not narrowly concerned with aesthetics per se but is rather part of his overall Transcendentalist affirmation of the creative imagination. Emerson featured the aesthetic dimension of experience in such essays as "ART" (1841), "The POET" (1844), and the essays "SHAKSPEARE; OR, THE POET" and "GOETHE; OR, THE WRITER" in *REPRESENTATIVE MEN* (1850). "Beauty" sets that idea in the broader idealism of his writings, which began with *NATURE* in 1836.

Like all the other essays in *The Conduct of Life,* "Beauty" blends metaphysical and humanistic emphases: "The question of Beauty takes us out of surfaces, to thinking of the foundations of things. Goethe said: 'The beautiful is a manifestation of secret laws of Nature, which, but for this appearance, had been forever concealed from us.'" Emerson adds that this power of aesthetic appreciation is the manifestation of "a deeper instinct" than the usual experience of only the surface of things.

SYNOPSIS

The essay begins with a critique of data-driven enterprises such as science and journalism. Our educational system, he says, churns up torrents of "facts," but does little to put such information in concrete relation to our own souls. The result, rather than expand our knowledge and appreciation of the world, is the opposite effect of keeping us at arm's length from nature and from an understanding of our relationship to it.

Emerson's thesis here is that our objectifying and classifying approach to knowledge fatally lacks a human side: "We should go to the ornithologist with a new feeling, if he could teach us what the social birds say, when they sit in the autumn council, talking together in the trees. The want of sympathy makes his record a dull dictionary. His result is a dead bird. The bird is not in its ounces and inches, but in its relations to Nature." Chemistry, also, "takes to pieces, but does not construct. . . . All our science lacks a human side." Man must realize his full powers, he says, and "must take Nature along with him, and emit light into all her recesses."

This deeper intimacy with nature is compromised not only by empirical science but also human frivolity and skepticism: "Men hold themselves cheap and vile; and yet a man is a fagot of thunderbolts. All the elements pour through his system: he is the flood of the flood, and fire of the fire; he feels the antipodes and the poles, as drops of his blood: they are extensions of his personality." Humans underestimate themselves and their abilities when, in fact, they possess the world.

Emerson then segues to a positive discourse concerning beauty in human life. There are the beauties of nature in general, of the human face and form, of manners, of the arts and intellectual methods, as well as the moral beauty of the soul, the path to "liberty and power." He does not mean to be superficial, though, as "we love any forms, however ugly, from which great qualities shine." This leads Emerson to enumerate some of the mysterious qualities of beauty. The first of these is its minimalist character: "We ascribe beauty to that which is simple; which has no superfluous parts." The beautiful always reveals that which is *essential;* its sheer simplicity invites us "to better health or more excellent action."

Emerson then details lessons concerning beauty that can be drawn from Greek and Gothic art as well as out of ancient mythology. The first is that all beauty must be *organic,* such that outside embellishment results in deformity: "It is the soundness of the bones that ultimates itself in a peach-bloom complexion: health of constitution that makes the sparkle and power of the eye." The animal world also reveals this lesson—"The cat and the deer cannot move or sit inelegantly"—as does every necessary action: "A man leading a horse to water, a farmer sowing seed, the labors of haymakers in the field, the carpenter building a ship, the smith at his forge, or whatever is useful labor, is becoming to the wise eye." This is compared to that which is done artificially or for show only: "But if it is done to be seen, it is mean."

Another lesson is that nothing has aesthetic interest that is "stark or bounded." Just as in the Greek story of Venus, "born of the foam of the sea," so it is throughout nature that "beauty is the moment of transition, as if the form were just ready to flow into other forms. . . . This is the charm of running water, sea-waves, the flight of birds, and the locomotion of animals." A third lesson is that "*beauty rides on a lion*" (italics in original). That is to say that the expression of beauty must be the result of perfectly organic economy. He gives two further examples from nature: "The cell of the bee is built at that angle which gives the most strength with the least wax; the bone or the quill of the bird gives the most alar strength, with the least weight." All the lessons of the structures of plants and animals are to this aesthetic effect. Great works of art, in which simplicity and truth merge, are similarly purged of every unnecessary element.

This accounts for the immortality of great works of art, which have the continued capacity to inspire as they draw the generations back and deeper into the laws of nature: "How many copies are there of the Belvedere Apollo, the Venus, the Psyche, the Warwick Vase, the Parthenon, and the Temple of Vesta? They are objects of tenderness to all." Such legacies of artistic intuition become paradigms of perfection and excellence in our consciousness. Their natural agreeableness to the human psyche serves also to weed out what is deformed and disagreeable.

For Emerson, nature is always a metaphor for and of the spirit: "The felicities of design in art, or in works of Nature, are shadows or forerunners of that beauty which reaches its perfection in the human form." Human beauty, he observes, "reaches its height in woman." "A beautiful woman is a practical poet," he says, "taming her savage mate, planting tenderness, hope, and Eloquence, in all whom she approaches." That man's idealization of feminine beauty is the height of human aesthetic consciousness, Emerson continues, is shown by the perpetual effort of nature to attain it. In various degrees we see through the imperfections of our own and other faces to the ideal type of the human species. Among the Greeks, a beautiful person was thought to enjoy "some secret favor of the immortal gods." "And yet . . . Beauty without grace is the hook without the bait. Beauty, without expression, tires."

Emerson ends the essay with the idea that beauty both requires and inspires imagination. Even if "things are pretty, graceful, rich, elegant, handsome," if they do not "speak to the imagination," they are "not yet beautiful." But beauty is not one distinct sensation, "not private, but universal." Beauty is that which has the "power to suggest relation to the whole world, and so lift the object out of a pitiful individuality."

A fundamental tenet of Emerson's writings is that the human imagination draws out the correspondences of things in nature, thereby showing "the convertibility of every thing into every other thing." He gives a somewhat humorous example: "I cry you mercy, good shoe-box! I did not know you were a jewel-case." Emerson perceives the symbolic character of any mundane fact beyond the scientific or journalistic description: "All beauty points at identity, and whatsoever thing does not express to me the sea and sky, day and night, is somewhat forbidden and wrong." Into every beautiful object there enters something immortal and divine, "disclosing its deep holdings in the frame of things."

CRITICAL COMMENTARY

"Beauty," together with "WORSHIP" and "ILLUSIONS," expresses the higher reaches of consciousness within Emerson's humanistic framework in *The Conduct of Life* (1860). All three essays refute the idea that Emerson's later writings lost the idealistic verve of his earlier writings. These essays exemplify the perennial influence of Plotinus and of the Hindus, the Buddhists, and the Persian poets on Emerson. Emerson's own governing principle in his texts, however, is PLATONIC—a comprehensive principle that encompasses the variety of things and reveals the interconnectedness of all things. In explaining that nature inspires us to seek the beauty of symmetry, he reprises the metaphor of his earlier essay "CIRCLES" (1841): "To this streaming or flowing belongs the beauty that all circular movement has; as, the circulation of waters, the circulation of the blood, the periodical motion of planets, the annual wave of vegetation, the action and reaction of Nature."

Emerson concludes that we do not understand the laws of nature's translation from the mundane to the beautiful. The spontaneity of beauty is immeasurable and divine, "hiding all wisdom and power in its calm sky." As well, beauty has a moral element; what begins in experiences progresses through "a climbing scale of culture, from the first agreeable sensations which a sparkling gem or a scarlet stain affords the eye, up to the ineffable mysteries of intellect and virtue." This ascent continues, "up to the perception of Plato, that globe and universe are rude and early expressions of an all-dissolving Unity,—the first stair on the scale to the temple of the Mind." This imagery was echoed in his poem "MERLIN" (1847), in which we "mount to Paradise / On the stairway of surprise."

Among the next generation of American philosophers, it was CHARLES SANDERS PEIRCE who, in his doctrine of aesthetics as the first science, developed Emerson's sense of the cosmical character of beauty and of the affinity of mind and nature. Peirce called this "Synechism," or the continuity of all things, combined with "agapism," or an ascendant evolution. For both Emerson and Peirce, scientific and poetic discoveries were two sides of the same coin of the human mind's power of penetration into the deeper harmonies of nature and beyond the ephemeral world of objective facts and information.

David A. Dilworth

"Behavior" (1860)

The essay "Behavior" was published in *The CONDUCT OF LIFE* (1860). Following other essays on social and moral qualities, such as "POWER," "WEALTH," and "CULTURE," Emerson here focuses on behavior, or manners. He had earlier included the essay "MANNERS" in *ESSAYS: SECOND SERIES* (1844). These later essays are all reflective of Emerson's expansion of his Transcendentalist individualism into a more pragmatic and ethically centered theory of social life. Taking up the subject of manners as having various social uses, such as convenience, power, and beauty, he ends the essay by recommending novels as providing insight into the subtleties of social intercourse.

Emerson's essay traces the "silent and subtile language" of "Manners; not *what,* but *how.* Life expresses." As is true for Emerson throughout nature, so it is that behavior or manners, the outward expressions of the body, reveal spiritual truths. Just as the poet translates the world of nature into symbols, so manners or behavior are a kind of poetry of the body, another aspect of nature as language, revealing the correspondences between moral and physical existence.

SYNOPSIS

Manners, Emerson declares, are not just simple deeds but actions in their aesthetic and moral dimensions: "There is always a best way of doing everything." Your manners are always under examination, deciding outcomes when you least realize it. Emerson first takes up "the minor morals" that simply make us agreeable to others; these manners "get people out of the quadruped state; to get them washed, clothed, and set up on end; to slough their animal husks and habits; compel them to be clean," and so on. Basic manners are the rudiments of civilized virtue that lay the foundation for more exquisite refinements.

"Bad behavior," on the other hand, "the laws cannot reach." Emerson here castigates the "rude, cynical, restless, and frivolous persons" in society, as well as self-pitiers. These, unfortunately, must be tolerated and are "social inflictions which the magistrate cannot cure or defend you from, and which must be entrusted to the restraining force of custom and proverbs, and familiar rules of behavior impressed on young people in their school-days."

However, the civil efficacy of manners reveals the balance between nurture and nature: "Manners are factitious, and grow out of circumstances as well as out of character." Emerson recognizes the relationship between circumstances and behavior—and develops a general character ethics seen throughout history: "If you look at the pictures of patricians and of peasants, of different periods and countries, you will see how well they match the same classes in our towns. . . . Broad lands and great interest not only arrive to such heads as can manage them, but form manners and power." On balance, however, Emerson's theory leans toward nature over nurture: "Manners are partly factitious, but mainly, there must be capacity for culture in the blood. Else all culture is vain."

After speaking of the civilizing aspect of manners in this general way, Emerson moves on to specific forms of moral and aesthetic expressiveness in the body and even specific parts of the body, chiefly that of the eyes. "Wise men," he observes, "read very sharply all your private history in your look and gait and behavior. . . . Men are like Geneva watches with crystal faces which expose the whole movement." Emerson adds that "the eye obeys exactly the action of the mind." Our body language, our expressions, and our "glance" are "not subject to the control of the will." The eyes are thus part of the universal language of nature, an "ocular dialectic" that "is understood all the world over." The conversation of the eyes is even more telling and trustworthy than that of the tongue: "You can read in the eyes of your companion, whether your argument hits him, though his tongue will not confess it." Likewise, "there is a look by which a man shows he is going to say a good thing, and a look when he has said it." The behavior of the eyes and of the face, in general, are visible signs not only of an individual's character and power but of universal character as well: "A man finds room in the few square inches of the face for the traits of all his ancestors; for the expression of all his history, and his wants."

In another respect, "fine manners need the support of fine manners in others." They reflect the degree of our social intelligence, as like attracts like. The reverse side is that we see through inferior characters who are merely bent on "mutual entertainment" or personal advantage: "Nature forever puts a premium on reality. What is done for effect, is seen to be done for effect; what is done for love, is felt to be done for love." These are expressions of Emerson's character ethics, which privileges nature over nurture in believing that humans can only ever act according to their individual natures, regardless of the social circumstances.

Emerson goes on to say that there are no "grammar-rules of this dialect," no instructions found in the writings of great men. These rules of behavior are "older than Sanskrit" and are the symbolic language of nature. Men take a "rapid knowledge, even before they speak, of each other's power and disposition. . . . men do not convince by their argument,—but by their personality." "Self-reliance," then, "is the basis of behavior," for we express ourselves in society as either pretension or "superficial culture," or as a means to our own "happiness."

Interestingly, this consideration of "behavior" forms a segue for Emerson's estimation of the relatively new importance of novels in his day. If "society is the stage on which manners are shown; novels are their literature," and he praises "the new importance of these books," which treat manners "more worthily." "Good novels" are like "good histories," in that they emphasize "the victories of character." Novelists thus "penetrate the surface" of human behavior and communicate the universal traits of the human soul: "The novels are as useful as Bibles, if they teach you the secret, that the best of life is conversation, and the greatest success is confidence, or perfect understanding between sincere people." Ultimately, "Nature alone inspires" good behavior or manners. The standards are high, as nature's "graces and felicities" are "not only unteachable, but undescribable." And "yet success is continually attained."

CRITICAL COMMENTARY

In "Behavior," Emerson explains that inborn character makes the man and indeed makes the circumstances, the events, and the destiny, as he also expresses it in "FATE," "Power," and numerous other writings. In literature and in life, "there is no beautifier of complexion, or form, or behavior, like the wish to scatter joy and not pain around us." In humorous mockery, Emerson writes: "If you have not slept, or if you have slept, or if you have headache, or sciatica, or leprosy, or thunder-stroke, I beseech you, by all the angels, to hold your peace, and not pollute the morning, to which all the housemates bring serene and pleasant thoughts, by corruption and groans." Such admonitions against the depressants and the naysayers of generous and cheerful living were ubiquitous in his writings.

Of note here is Emerson's depiction of our recognition of a person's good or bad manners as "a rapid knowledge." This recalls what the Scottish ENLIGHTENMENT philosopher David Hume called the principle of morals, namely "the quick sensibility" of instinctive moral estimation that cannot be traced to some higher rational rule. Hume in his *Enquiry Concerning the Principles of Morals* (1751) distinguished four classes of moral qualities to which the heart spontaneously responds: qualities useful to others, qualities useful to oneself, qualities agreeable to others, and qualities agreeable to oneself. Emerson's discussion also parallels centuries of Confucian teachings in China and Japan concerning the refinements of etiquette and ritual behavior.

These positive exhortations and negative admonitions concerning manners are part and parcel of Emerson's moral theory concerning the conduct of life. On these themes in his later writings Emerson pursued shades and nuances of personal and civilized behavior—and looked to the examples of the arts—to educate us beyond our normal ranges of insight into character. Manners are "the delicate question of culture" for which we usually only receive "negative rules" in the form of rules and admonitions. But Emerson wishes to look for "positive" guidance and "suggestion," and finds it in "Nature alone." As part of his Transcendentalist doctrine of the self-possessed individual, he argues that good manners form a part of one's personal genius.

David A. Dilworth

"Blight" (1844)

"Blight" is a 62-line, one-stanza poem that first appeared in the January 1844 issue of the Transcendentalist literary journal *The* DIAL under the title "The Times,—A Fragment." It was published as "Blight" in the 1847 collection POEMS.

"Blight" articulates Emerson's romantic view of nature, which was itself a rejection of Enlightenment-era rationalism and empiricism; that is, a rejection of the idea that one could objectively study nature and come to conclusions about nature outside of understanding man as part of nature. This right relationship with nature is therefore a core Transcendentalist theme explored throughout Emerson's other essays as well as other poems, most notably in "HAMATREYA" and "The WORLD-SOUL," which both contain similar critiques of humanity's misuse or misunderstanding of our relationship to the land. Emerson was not antiscience, however. In poems such as "The ADIRONDACS" he both sought personal meaning from his time spent in untamed wilderness and reflected on what a harmonious relationship between scientists and nature might look like. He concluded, in that poem at least, with a celebration of humanity's scientific innovation and even conquest of nature.

CRITICAL COMMENTARY

"Blight" opens with a statement that, in many ways, reflects Emerson's approach to all philosophy and inquiries and that he thus explored throughout his essays and lectures: "Give me truths; / For I am weary of the surfaces, And die of inanition." In all of his work Emerson sought to look beneath the surfaces, beneath the visible material world, to understand the "truths" of human experience. In "Blight," this statement has an edge of anger and is directed at humanity's treatment of and approach to nature.

After this opening statement, the next 15 lines are one long sentence detailing the source of all knowledge in the very basic facts of nature. The poet catalogs the various "herbs and simples of the wood," which "draw untold juices" and from which we can learn so much. He seeks a simple and interconnected relationship to nature, such as in the past, one in which "I could be a part / Of the round day, related to the sun / And planted world." He critiques his era's emphasis on a purely scientific view of nature and its materialism, comparing the "young scholars, who invade our hills" to earlier generations who recognized a relationship with nature. The relationship to nature has become one of "engineer" and scientist only, of interest in nature only at the level of "Latin names," by people who "love not the flower they pluck, and know it not." In the past, humans actually learned from nature in a way that united rather than separated us from nature. Emerson therefore warns against praising today's science as superior to "the old men" who "studied magic" or who studied "human fortunes in astronomy, / And an omnipotence in chemistry," for these practitioners understood the connections. They were "unitarians of the united world." Emerson makes the same argument in "HISTORY" (1841) that these pursuits may have been found to be scientifically faulty, but were steps in the right direction in terms of the quest for knowledge and looking to nature for answers.

Emerson describes our search for meaning in the universe—"Our eyes / Are armed"—but because we are not asking the right questions, we are missing the big picture, "we are strangers to the stars." For this reason, nature seems to be uncooperative to our quest. Nature has been injured by us, and "the injured elements say, 'Not in us;'" and only "stare" at us because we only "stare" at them: "And haughtily return us stare for stare." It is a standoff between man and nature because our methods and our motives are unpure and exploitative: "For we invade them impiously for gain; / We devastate them unreligiously." The terms used here of piety and religion indicate we are lacking a spiritual relationship with nature. Therefore, nature only gives what we ask, which is the minimum, and then pushes us away. There will be no "sweet affluence of love and song," no connection, no union between "man and earth," between "world beloved and lover."

Our desires are only "spoils and slaves." This is what we take from the earth, and this is what characterizes modern society. We are all "thieves and pirates of the universe," and the result is that we will "turn pale and starve." We will not be nourished by nature, and then, as a final insult, we turn "our sick eyes" to judge nature, complaining about the trees that also "look sick," complaining about inconveniences that affect our ability to make money: "the summer short, / Clouds shade the sun, which will not tan our hay." These are our own fault, however, as the natural process has been interrupted and "nothing thrives to reach its natural term." We have therefore created a vicious cycle of interdependence but disappointment in our relationship with nature.

The last 10 to 12 lines of the poem are heavy with images of "defeat," of life cut short, of waste and "wantonness." Nature, in turn, gives back little; nature is angry, "frugal," and "miserly." Is this a warning of environmental destruction, or also of spiritual destruction? In Emerson's Transcendentalist view, if nature has been harmed, then we have been harmed as well.

"Books" (1870)

"Books" began as a lecture that Emerson drafted in early 1847 and delivered for the first time in England during his 1847–48 lecture tour. The lecture, under the title "Reading," was used on numerous occasions throughout England and Scotland. It was first published in SOCIETY AND SOLITUDE (1870). Like other works in this later volume, "Books" has a somewhat disjointed feel, perhaps due to the difficulty Emerson experienced while reordering and revising his manuscripts in the early stage of his memory loss. The essay is intended as a practical guide to literature for students and general readers. In it, Emerson provides advice on how to get the most from literature and comments on the true value and the best use of books. Emerson's lifelong emphasis on the supreme value of "human culture," or the "upbuilding of man," finds expression here in the form of a treatise on why we read that is packaged together with a simple list of good books.

SYNOPSIS

Many books are bad, many are neutral. They "do nothing for us." Even the best are mere "records." Reading books does not necessarily lead to personal improvement. However, some books take on enormous importance in an individual's personal development, having as profound an influence as "parents and lovers and passionate experiences." Even in a small library one can have access to the learning and wisdom of the wisest men in the history of civilization. These books educate the moral vision, allowing one to see the world as a proud and positive place, and provide the basis for intellectual discernment and argument. Unfortunately, for every book that speaks to us, there are many more that will not. One who sifts through the many "false books" and finds "a few true ones which ma[ke] him happy and wise" does a good deed if he leaves future readers a guide to his findings.

Among the hundreds of thousands of printed volumes in the great libraries, there are only a few true books. Most of the works are mere "echoes" of a few great voices. For reading, the best method is a natural one. A reader should not plow through books mechanically and will profit more from

Emerson's study at his home in Concord, Massachusetts *(New York Public Library)*

profound study of great literature than from reading the works of "a crowd of mediocrities." A good student approaches texts "with the pilot of his own genius" and will profit from any material he reads. Luckily, "out of a million pages" written, only one is printed, and only the very best survive the decades and centuries. Thus, "old and famed books" promise a good return on time invested in reading. Reading the most recent "spawn of the press on the gossip of the hour" is all but a guaranteed waste of time. Emerson offers three practical rules to the reader: "1. Never read any book that is not a year old. 2. Never read any but famed books. 3. Never read any but what you like." Some books can enrich and inspire readers—Emerson lists a few he would recommend.

First are the Greeks: Homer, Herodotus, Aeschylus, Plato, and Plutarch are presented as the five whose work "we cannot spare." The final two are spoken of at length. Plato's works (a list of recommended segments is provided) contained all the signs and seeds of modernity. Plutarch's *Lives*, available in "cheap editions which make it as accessible as a newspaper," is essential reading as are his less well-known essays. These works, Emerson declares, "leave you stimulated . . . by philosophic sentiments, by the forms and behaviors of heroes," and by a detailed view of life and manners in Greece that stirs the imagination. For an outline of Greek history, Emerson recommends several scholarly and popular works. He also gives special mention to Plotinus, Poryphyry, and other NEOPLATONIC philosophers of the early centuries C.E. All good books can be read in translation, for true human insight is always translatable. There is little use in reading in the original language when a good translator has made it available in the "great metropolitan English speech." Emerson suggests some works on Roman history. For medieval literature he suggests Dante, the sonnets of Michelangelo, and a number of Scandinavian legends and epics. The richest English literature can be found in the great works of the 16th and 17th centuries by Shakespeare, Bacon, Milton, and others.

Transitioning from a chronological to a thematic focus, Emerson lists a number of the best autobiographies through history, the best works from the "table talk" genre, the best of the "vocabularies," or books of facts, and the most worthy "imaginative" works of fiction. This final category he deems of particular importance to the present age with its practical, unimaginative tendencies and material bias. Reading these works exercises the imagination and allows for regeneration of the moral soul. The novel is a promising but still imperfect literary form. Finally, the very best class of books is the "Bibles of the world, or the sacred books of each nation which express for each the supreme result of their experience." Emerson mentions the Hebrew and Greek scripture in the same sentence as the great works of the Zoroastrian, Hindu, Buddhist, Confucian, and other Eastern traditions. These books are all expressions of a shared "universal conscience." There are too many good books in the libraries to read them all, but Emerson suggests that in a "literary club," where each reads from the sections he likes best and reports to the others, all involved will be enriched.

CRITICAL COMMENTARY

The idea that animates "Books" is the one that Emerson had pronounced in "The AMERICAN SCHOLAR" in 1837. In that lecture he envisioned a "revolution" that would be wrought "by the gradual domestication of the idea of Culture." Emerson views books as tools that can assist in the great enterprise for which the world exists: "the upbuilding of a man." They are points of access to the "universal mind," which carry men beyond day-to-day understanding and practical thought and into the higher realm of universal reality, or reason.

Although the idea behind "Books" is essentially united to those of "The American Scholar," the difference between these two orations is due to the different types of audiences each was intended to reach. "The American Scholar" was delivered before the elite Phi Beta Kappa society at HARVARD COLLEGE. "Books," on the other hand, was a lecture that Emerson wrote in preparation for his 1847–48 British lecture tour and read repeatedly in the British Mechanics' Institutes for working-class audiences. "Books" is easier to follow than most of Emerson's works. The material seldom strays into abstraction. Nonetheless, Emerson was able to insert his philosophical outlook into what, at first appearance, seems to be a straightforward list of suggested readings.

As in "HISTORY" (1841) Emerson encourages a realistic view of what books and literary education are. They do not inherently provide anything; it is the motivations of the reader that determine the value of the reading experience. The principle that Emerson intends to transmit is a democratic one: He denies that one who has read more books will necessarily be superior to one who has read few. Reading does not always lead to moral improvement. Thus, the man who reads little has as much, if not more, right to a relationship with literature as one who has spent an idle career reading. The insistence that as much can be gained from a book in translation as from one in its original language is another encouragement to nonexpert readers to see through pedantry and to dig into the best books.

"Books" is the product of the tension that Emerson experienced between his love of literature and his dissatisfaction with the distance that exists between great ideas and noble action. He makes a powerful testimony for the value of reading but also discourages an unhealthy preoccupation with reading that, as he put it in "The American Scholar," can change the reader from "Man Thinking" to an ineffective "bookworm." He lists a number of "short-cuts" to the achievement of a good literary culture, including reading in translation, reading only the best books, and reading works "by proxy" through a club. Most importantly, Emerson advises readers to keep an open mind and to see reading not as a passive motion but as active exercise of the intellect and of the spirit.

FURTHER READING

Robinson, David M. *Apostle of Culture: Emerson as Preacher and Lecturer.* Philadelphia: University of Pennsylvania Press, 1982.

Scudder, Townsend. "Emerson's British Lecture Tour, 1847–1848: Part II: Emerson as a Lecturer and the Reception of the Lectures." *American Literature* 7, no. 2 (1935): 166–180.

Daniel Robert Koch

"Boston" (1876)

The poem "Boston" was read at Faneuil Hall on December 16, 1873, "on the Centennial Anniversary of the Destruction of the Tea in the Boston Harbor." The poem was published in the centennial year of the Declaration of Independence, first in the ATLANTIC MONTHLY in February 1876 and then collected in Emerson's *SELECTED POEMS* that same year; the poem was later included in *Sketches and Reminiscences of the Radical Club* (1880). His son EDWARD WALDO EMERSON later noted that, as early as 1842, Emerson planned to write "a verse or two to the praise of my native city," that included homage not only to "political and social institutions" but to the arts, education, and even the architecture as well. Some passages were penned as early as 1856 or 1857, at which time Emerson also had to confront the town of BOSTON's conflicted relationship to slavery. Some of the slavery stanzas were omitted after the Civil War as he prepared the poem for the Boston Tea Party centennial.

Although he was born in Boston and published the more well-known "BOSTON HYMN" (1863), Emerson was remembered as the poet of Concord, with his oft-cited "CONCORD HYMN." Both cities, of course, served important roles in the American Revolution, and both served, for Emerson, as models not only for all of America but for the world. In the poem "Boston," the city "can teach the lightning speech" (that is, the political rhetoric of revolution), "and round the globe your voices reach." The "voices" heard "round the globe" here contrast with the famous line from the "Concord Hymn" of "the shot heard round the world," situating Boston as the source of revolutionary ideas or "voices," compared with the military role of Concord.

CRITICAL COMMENTARY

"Boston" is prefaced by a Latin phrase, "*Sicut patribus, sit Deus nobis,*" or "God be with us, as he was with our fathers," the phrase from the official seal of the city of Boston. The first three stanzas situate Boston geographically ("Looking eastward from the farms" and located on the coast) and historically and economically (made up of men "stout and poor" who engaged in world trade, "sailed for bread to every shore"). Early Boston was admired by all as a model of the new world order: "The merchant was a man. / The world was made for honest trade." "The honest waves" brought the settlers to a new land, and with their call to "'Like us be free and bold!" Bostonians represented the spirit, hard work, and promise of the new American.

Throughout the poem Emerson returns to the imagery of the ocean. The "foaming seas" make possible Boston's role in world trade, but the oceans also represent the vast separation, both geographically and socially, between the "honest labor" of the colonists and "Old Europe" with its "palaces" and "lords." Stanzas 4 to 6 highlight these differences between the European and New World economic systems. Boston will be "a city of the poor," built by and led by regular people, with "no dukedoms to the few." The colonists "hold like rights . . . Equal on Sunday in the pew" (a reference to the practice of assigning church seating by class or gender) and "on Monday in the mall" or village. He describes a society that promotes "the noble craftsman," where "each honest man shall have his vote, / Each child shall have his school." While the reality of Emerson's vision of social and economic equality in colonial Massachusetts may be overstated (indeed, both universal male suffrage and public education were goals of the early 19th century), his purpose is to identify foundational virtues that would explain the later resistance movement. The revolutionary generation's commitment to equality and justice echoes in Emerson's own Civil War–era generation's continued struggle for these ideals: "a union then of honest men, / Or union never more again."

Although the imagery of the sea is present throughout the poem, the next two stanzas (7–8) turn explicitly to nature as representatives of Boston's virtue and appeal to "the feet of millions" who eventually come to that city—where now are "heated pavements" were once "wild rose and the barberry thorn." The city was/is surrounded by "fair rose the planted hills behind" and on the other side of "the western hills declined / The prairie stretched away."

Stanzas 9 to 12 look at other American cities and colonies arising at the same time. Whereas Boston was protected by its bay and gentler seas, the "rival cities" of "Penn's town, New York and Baltimore" arise "along the stormy coast," reflecting less the nature of their geography and more their inferior (according to Emerson) economic and social commitments. But Boston is not threatened by these other cities that lure more Europeans to America—"We greet you well, you Saxon men, / Up with your towns and stay!" There is plenty of "honest trade" for all to engage in, plenty of opportunities in trade or in farming—"Each street leads downward to the sea, / Or landward to the west." From Boston, all "roads lead everywhere to all."

The heart of the poem (stanzas 13 to 17) recounts the specific historical events that led to the American Revolution, including the Boston Tea Party, the anniversary of which is the original occasion of the poem. In stanza 13 all is well until King George decides that since Boston is "thriving well . . . You shall pay us a tax on tea." In George's view, "'Tis very small,—no load at all," but Boston responds, "Not so," and argues that it has already shouldered an economic burden by housing and paying governors appointed by the throne. The colonists would pay "millions for self-government, / But for tribute never a cent."

The next shipment of tea arrives, but "Indians seized the tea" and tossed it into, this time, "the laughing sea." The same sea that brought the colonists here and supports them through trade is again on their side. Emerson repeats the lines of an earlier stanza: "For what avail the plough or sail, / Or land or life, if freedom fail?" The lesson of the tea party is that Bostonians will not stray from their founding principles. Indeed, "the townsmen braved the English king" and "found friendship in the French" for their cause, their "patriot ring." Emerson again invokes the "bounteous seas that never fail!" which here bring news of the French from across the ocean, the "happy port that spied the sail / Which wafted Lafayette!" With a just cause and support of the French, "kings shook with fear" and "the little State" (the patriots) fought "to save / The rights of all mankind." It was not easy and much blood was shed—"Through good and ill the war-bolt hurled, / Till Freedom cheered and joy-bells rung." Again, it is nature in the form of the predictable sea ("returning day by day"), which economically supports the patriot cause and "restores the world-wide mart," preserving Boston's place as a center of trade.

The next two stanzas (20–21) remind every American, then, to "fold Boston in his heart" for its role, both militarily ("the blood of her hundred thousands") and philosophically/politically ("the wits of her wisest") in the revolution. Boston not only serves as a model to all of America but "round the globe your voices reach." The final two stanzas of the poem (22–23) repeat the lessons of the revolution that Boston gives to the world—that "each shall care for other, . . . / To the poor a noble brother, / To the good an equal friend"—lessons from history that Emerson explicitly presents to the current post–Civil War and still divided generation by repeating the opening phrase of the poem: "God With the Fathers, So With Us." The poem, then, is as much about America in 1876 as it is about Boston in either 1676 or 1776.

"Boston Hymn" (1863)

Emerson wrote the poem "Boston Hymn" during the Civil War to reflect upon President Lincoln's Emancipation Proclamation, which stated that, effective January 1, 1863, any slaves held in rebel or Confederate states would be freed. As Emerson noted in the subtitle, the poem was "Read in Music Hall, January 1, 1863" and was subsequently published in *Dwight's Journal of Music* in January 1863 (edited by JOHN SULLIVAN DWIGHT), in the *ATLANTIC MONTHLY* in February 1863, and reprinted in other publications throughout 1863 and 1864. "Boston Hymn" was later included in *MAY-DAY AND OTHER PIECES* (1867) as one of four poems that directly addressed slavery and the Civil War (along with "FREEDOM," "ODE SUNG IN THE TOWN HALL, CONCORD, JULY 4, 1857," and "VOLUNTARIES"); it was also included in Emerson's *SELECTED POEMS* (1876).

A few months earlier, Emerson had responded to news of Lincoln's plan with a speech in Boston called "The President's Proclamation" (subsequently published in the *Atlantic Monthly*). Privately, Emerson feared that the plan "seems to promise an extension of the war," and in his address, he acknowledged that, as the proclamation did not free any slaves in Union states, it would not have "any signal results on the negroes or on the rebel masters." Still, Emerson understood that the proclamation was symbolically important in identifying emancipation as the goal of the war and therefore "commits the country to this justice." Although "Boston Hymn" is ostensibly a celebration of the Emancipation Proclamation, it goes further in calling for a complete end to slavery and preservation of the Union as America's true destiny. "Boston Hymn" was one of the few poems Emerson wrote for a specific event and one he wrote specifically to be read aloud in public. The poem became instantly well known and oft-recited or sung.

CRITICAL COMMENTARY

"Boston Hymn" is made up of 22 four-line stanzas. The opening lines establish that "the Word" of emancipation has come, but it is not the word of Lincoln (who is never mentioned in the poem) but "the Word of the Lord," as the poem is written in the voice of God, who calls upon the United States to fulfill its own democratic promises. Emerson appeals to America's destiny by appealing to its spiritual founders, the "Pilgrims," who are waiting and watching. In this sense, the pilgrims could also be the slaves, whose lives hang in the political balance, or, indeed, the American people in general. "God said, I am tired of kings," and the connection between "Pilgrims" and "kings" invokes the original colonists and their ultimate struggle for independence. The destiny of the nation is directly tied to its history and to its predestined path toward freedom. God asks if the earth ("this ball") is truly made for "havoc and war," for the tyranny of the strong over "the weak and the poor"? He reminds us that tyrants can be "great" or "small," as slavery sees regular men exercising tyranny over others. But God is sending an "angel" named "Freedom" and implores America to "choose him to be your king."

The poem then shifts to a specific focus on the West, urging Americans to open up "pathways east and west," a reference to the existing tensions between North and South, and to the fact that the Civil War began as a result of fighting over whether the western territories should be slave or free. Emerson invokes the idea of manifest destiny: "I uncover the land / Which I hid of old time in the West, / As the sculptor uncovers the statue." God has provided open space, oceans, skies, forests: "I show Columbia, of the rocks / Which dip their foot in the seas / And soar to the air-borne flocks / Of clouds and boreal fleece." There is enough for everyone in America, enough for both Southerners and Northerners ("I will divide my goods") and enough for anyone who works hard ("none but Toil shall have").

Here Emerson captures perfectly the mid-19th century ideals of the West as not only the land of opportunity but the key to American democracy. In America there will be "never a noble, / No lineage counted great." It will be a representative "state," made up of "fishers and choppers and ploughmen," that is, common men. The 19th-century West, then, offered a second chance for America to fulfill its original promise. God has given nature to America for this use, urging us to "go, cut down trees" and "build me a wooden house"—that is, a church building, a simple and democratic religion in America. Again, the promise is not only democracy but equality, as the common people will meet in this land, young and old, "hireling and him that hires." The leaders will meet "in a pine state-house," which mirrors the "wooden house" built for worship. The imagery of "pine" and "wood" emphasizes the indigenous and simple or humble origins of American politics and religion. The leaders will be elected for "church and state and school," all of which shall be democratic institutions, and the leadership will rule according to the laws of nature—they will "govern the land and sea / And make just laws below the sun."

Emerson returns to the problem of slavery, declaring it is nature's law (and God's will) that all men be free. God will ultimately "unchain the slave," and the slave will be as free "as wind and wandering wave." It is God's (nature's) purpose that every person act according to their nature: "I cause from every creature / His proper good to flow." Slavery prevents this self-fulfillment and creates dependence for both slave and slaveholder. The violence and coercion required to keep slaves goes against nature's plan, and the slaveholder, who would "lay hands on another / To coin his labor and sweat," creates "eternal years in debt" for the victim's life that was robbed. His message to whites, even Northerners, is that to free the slaves is to free all of America: "To-day unbind the captive, / So only are ye unbound."

Connecting the spiritual dilemma of slavery to current political debates, Emerson argues that it would be wrong to "pay ransom to the owner," a proposal then circulating. This is impossible in Emerson's Transcendentalist terms since no one can ever truly own another person: "The slave is owner, / And ever was. Pay him." Instead, North, South, and West must all work to ensure "freedom's image and name." Again implicating even Northerners in the problem, he emphasizes that the issue is not confined to one region, and each can do its part: the North will "give him beauty," the South will give "honor . . . for his shame," and the West, symbolized in the poem by "Nevada," is a chance to begin anew, a place with freedom attached to it from the very beginning.

The poet is confident that "the dusky race" will rise out of "darkness long" and will burst forth with strength and speed. Again, slavery and freedom are issues for all of America, not just the South: It requires "East and West and North" together to "carry my purpose forth" (that is, God's purpose, as the poem is still in God's voice). Emerson encourages the nation "as snow-flakes" (a reference to the individuality of each person and the uniqueness of each region of the country) to come together and ensure that God's "will fulfilled shall be."

FURTHER READING

Cadava, Eduardo. "The Nature of War in Emerson's 'Boston Hymn.'" *Arizona Quarterly* 49, no. 3 (Autumn 1993): 21–58.

"Brahma" (1857)

The short 16-line poem "Brahma" was published in the first issue of the ATLANTIC MONTHLY (November 1857) and was later collected in MAY-DAY AND OTHER PIECES (1867) and SELECTED POEMS (1876). Emerson was fascinated by and indebted to Eastern religion and philosophy, as evidenced in other writings, including numerous poems and the 1858 essay "PERSIAN POETRY." Like other Transcendentalists, liberal Christians, and free religious advocates of the 19th century, he was interested in exploring comparative spiritual and philosophical themes in non-Christian religions. Beginning in the 1840s both Emerson and HENRY DAVID THOREAU read the Bhagavad Gita and the *Vishnu Purana,* and Emerson returned to these texts again and again in his journals, essays, and poetry. In his journal he copied out passages of the *Vishnu Purana* that would make their way into poems such as "HAMATREYA" and "Brahma." A longer draft of the poem was originally titled "Song of the Soul."

Brahma is one of the three main Hindu gods along with Vishnu and Shiva. Brahma represents creation, eternal truths, and the interconnectedness of all things in the universe, an idea similar to that developed by Emerson in "The OVER-SOUL" (1841). Everything is encompassed in Brahma, an idea and a paradox explored in the poem. This idea could be seen as comparable to the Christian idea of God, and in fact, in his edition of the *Complete Works,* EDWARD WALDO EMERSON relates the story that his father was "much amused when people found 'Brahma' puzzling" and said, simply, "If you tell them to say Jehovah instead of Brahma they will not feel any perplexity." Elsewhere, Emerson explained in the simplest terms that Brahma means "God everywhere."

CRITICAL COMMENTARY

The first stanza of the poem—"If the red slayer think he slays, / Or if the slain think he is slain, / They know not well the subtle ways / I keep, and pass, and turn again."—is effectively a rewrite of the original Hindu text: "What living creature slays or is slain? What living creature preserves or is preserved? Each is his own destroyer or preserver, as he follows evil or good." The theme of the poem is that Brahma is an eternal spirit, encompassing all things, and therefore has no beginning and no end, can neither slay nor be slain. The second stanza reiterates this idea that there is no beginning and no end, and therefore no separation between time, space, and knowledge, which are all interconnected: "Shadow and sunlight are the same." The "vanished gods" who appear to the poet refer to both religion and history, which are part of the past or tradition but yet are still drawn upon for knowledge and inspiration. The judgments of the world—"shame and fame"—mean nothing in the broader view of the eternity of the universe.

In stanza 3 this theme is expanded to include the interconnectedness between humans and the creative spirit of Brahma. The poet seeks to figure out who or what is Brahma, only to find that Brahma is the spirit of the poem itself: "I am the hymn the Brahmin sings." Here Emerson may be engaging in wordplay, as "the Brahmin" refers both to a person of high caste in Hindu culture and to Emerson himself as a 19th-century poet, as contemporaries had begun to refer to New England social and cultural elites as "Boston Brahmins." In that sense, Emerson is the Brahmin who "sings" or writes the poem; he is also both the one who asks questions and the question itself. His claim that "I am the doubter and the doubt" recalls the line in the poem "The SPHINX," "Thou art the unanswered question."

In the fourth and last stanza, "the strong gods," as well as the "sacred Seven" or holy people, "pine in vain" for the idea of a final resting place or "abode." All want to be with Brahma, but to be with Brahma is to embrace Brahma's spirit. Emerson points out that this spiritual union is available to everyone—to any "lover of the good"—and we should seek this state rather than the "heaven" of Western religion, which is exclusive and limited. The last line of the poem—"Find me, and turn thy back on heaven."—is a rejection of the Christian concept of "heaven" in favor of "the good," a concept that is both universal and based on personal meaning. In the poem's attention to the interconnectedness of all life, and therefore a promise of immortality, "Brahma" is Emerson's exploration of both life and death from a Hindu perspective.

FURTHER READING

Leland, Charles. "A Defense of 'Brahma.'" In *Critical Essays on Waldo Emerson,* edited by Robert Burkholder and Joel Myerson, 164–169. Boston: G.K. Hall and Co., 1983.

"Character" (1844)

Emerson's poem "Character" reasserts his view that the human experience is deeply connected with nature, that this harmony is perceivable to those who would seek it, and that this seeking is a fundamental part of the human condition. The poem also offers the idea of character as a kind of sacrament, both holy and human, by which a person speaks the correspondence between human and divine into existence. This theme suggests itself as early as the language section of *NATURE* (1836).

Emerson likely intended this poem for inclusion in a larger work titled "The Discontented Poet: a Masque," originating in notes and journal entries in late 1839, and probably first drafted between the fall of 1840 and the spring of 1842. During 1843 Emerson drafted several more fragments to be included in "The Discontented Poet," but the larger work, for whatever reason, never materialized. The various unused fragments of the project were discovered upon Emerson's death and were edited together by JAMES ELLIOT CABOT and retitled "The Poet," which was included in the posthumous edition *Poems* (1884).

Two manuscript drafts of "Character" were completed between 1841 and 1843. The poem first appears as the motto for the essay "CHARACTER" in *ESSAYS: SECOND SERIES* (1844) and was collected in *MAY-DAY AND OTHER PIECES* (1867) and *Poems* (1884), though the version edited by EDWARD WALDO EMERSON and printed in the later *Poems* has slight variations in the first six lines.

CRITICAL COMMENTARY

Early in the poem Emerson connects the speaker's faith with the stars, often his symbol for the divine. For Emerson, images of stars, the sun, planets, and the universe suggest nature in its largest physical sense as well as the abode of the Gods (in terms of classical mythology, as well as the Swedenborgian visions of heaven). Thus astronomy symbolically functions in Emerson as a link between the sacred and the physical.

The poem contains five sets of rhymed couplets (though the second couplet relies on a slant rhyme). The poem employs image and symbol resonances within the individual couplets. For example, "galaxy" rhymes imagistically with "eye," given the shape of galaxies (at least as known in Emerson's time). Also, in the next couplet, Emerson rhymes "sublime" with "time," suggesting a subtle effect of time on human experience.

In the final four lines Emerson offers the poem as sacrament, which, when offered in "words more soft than rain" (again the suggestion of nature in the sublime), reinstitutes the "Age of Gold," or the age of classical antiquity. For this poem, the "Age of Gold" suggests a time in which scientific determinism had yet to separate nature from spirit, and humans read nature as an expression of the divine. In the last couplet Emerson claims that this action on the part of the speaker wins reverence to the degree that it hides "all measure of the feat." The last image contains the common Emersonian view that the individual is lost in the expression, or perception, of the divine in nature. Also, however, Emerson employs a subtle play on words; if his poem is successful, it, too, will hide the measure of the metrical devices of the poem (the measure of the feet). Thus Emerson contains the theme of the poem within the operation of the poem itself; the poem is not merely a conveyor of images but is itself an invocation of the "Age of Gold."

Bill Scalia

"Character" (1844)

"Character" appears as the third piece in Emerson's *ESSAYS: SECOND SERIES* (1844). It focuses on the moral qualities of his new Transcendentalist image of man, continuing with the metaphysical framework laid out in the earlier essays "The OVER-SOUL" and "SELF-RELIANCE" and the binary model of nature in his essay "COMPENSATION," all of which appeared in *ESSAYS: FIRST SERIES* (1841). Variations on the theme of character were to also be conspicuous components of his later essays, such as those of *The CONDUCT OF LIFE* (1860).

SYNOPSIS

The essay begins by remarking on historical figures who generated an aura of "expectation that outran all their performance." "The largest part" of the "power" of great men comes from their "Character—a reserved force which acts directly by presence, and without means." It is part of the nature of a great man and cannot be taught or copied: "What others effect by talent or by Eloquence, this man accomplishes by some magnetism." Men of character "are often solitary" and "do not need society." Their character, in other words, is one of self-reliance.

But society needs such exemplary persons of original character, and Emerson undoes the assumptions of his readers by finding such men in politics and in trade. The people need more than talent or eloquence in their representatives; they need, "namely," someone with "the power to make his talent trusted." There is an analogous "motive force" in trade or business: "The habit of his mind is a reference to standards of natural equity and public advantage; and he inspires respect, and the wish to deal with him." The most prosperous men of trade act not as private agents but as nature's own appointed

"Minister[s] of Commerce." In all walks of life, the creative and successful person is "an agent and playfellow of the original laws of the world."

Emerson here says that "all individual natures stand in a scale, according to the purity of this element in them." Character is measured by a certain "resistance of circumstances." Emerson uses his principle of polarity in nature, of alternating and complementary forces, to explain that the "feeble" or "impure" person succumbs to "opinions, events, and persons," while "the hero sees that the event is ancillary: it must follow *him*." The man of character sees that the circumstance itself "has no power" outside of his perception and experience of it. "No change of circumstances can repair a defect of character," and "the soul of goodness" inserts its own "power and victory" into events.

In this context, Emerson explores the implication of his ethics of self-reliance. The limitations of a person of negative character reflects a narrowness of soul. On the other hand, "the face which [good] character wears to me is self-sufficingness." Character means "the impossibility of being displaced or overset." Such a self-sponsoring person is by nature a nonconformist, one who rejects the "frivolous" society. Conformity and the search for public approval are always indicators of dependent, not self-reliant, persons: "The wise man not only leaves out of his thought the many, but leaves out the few." In the central, or independent, man, thoughts and actions "announce the instant presence of supreme power."

Emerson goes on to reiterate another of his foundational tenets, namely that "in nature, there are no false valuations." "Character," Emerson concludes, "is nature in the highest form." It is the balance of nature, the heart of nonconformity. Unlike the sermons or creators of popular opinion that "teach that the laws fashion the citizen," it is nature that bestows character: "Nature keeps these sovereignties in her own hands." Therefore "she makes very light of gospels and prophets," who claim an "excess" of character; nature does not have "time to spare on any one." Character is unique, not emulated—"Nature never rhymes her children, nor makes two men alike"—and thus one can never "solve the problem of his character according to our prejudice, but only in his own high unprecedented way."

Here Emerson explicitly aligns his discourse on character with Confucian teaching: "I find it more credible, since it is anterior information, that one should *know heaven*, as the Chinese say, than that so many men should know the world. . . . He who confronts the gods, without any misgiving, knows heaven; he who waits a hundred ages until a sage comes, without doubting, knows men." But Emerson says we do not have to go back thousands of years for this perennial teaching. The modern equivalent is the advent of a true and noble friend, which aids "the progress of character": "there are persons, he cannot choose but remember, who gave a transcendant expansion to his thought, and kindled another life in his bosom." Emerson ends the essay on a prophetic, ameliorative note. While "history has been mean," and gives us too few examples of great character, the mind continues to imagine and demand "a force of character which will convert judge, jury, soldier, and king; which will rule animal and mineral virtues, and blend with the courses of sap, of rivers, of winds, of stars, and of moral agents."

CRITICAL COMMENTARY

The essay "Character" is one of many expressions of Emerson's character ethics. It joins the ranks of the greatest philosophical exponents of innate character found in Plato and Aristotle, the Confucian philosophers, and later the German idealists, such as IMMANUEL KANT. Emerson repeated here the basic terms of his wider moral worldview. A search for the "higher type" of character and its connection with nature consistently appeared in his earliest works and were carried forward into the later essays of *REPRESENTATIVE MEN* (1850), in "PLATO; OR, THE PHILOSOPHER," "SHAKSPEARE; OR THE POET," "GOETHE; OR, THE WRITER," "NAPOLEON; OR, THE MAN OF THE WORLD," and the others, several of whom are discussed here in "Character" as well. In *The Conduct of Life* (1860) the search for character is given a more pragmatic and ethical direction.

In essence, the solitary person of exceptional character is a pristine force of nature, one who "appears to share the life of things, and to be an expression of the same laws which control the tides and the sun, numbers and quantities." The "higher" active character also represents, then, evolutionary progress, the affinity of mankind's intellectual and moral nature with the nature of things.

Deep-seated in Emerson's idealism here is the Platonic principle of the Good and the Beautiful, refocused by Emerson as an immanent principle of nature and history. Emerson expanded on this view in his own tribute to Plato, the first subject of *Representative Men.* At the same time, a careful reading of the essay "Plato" suggests an autobiographical element, reflecting Emerson's self-consciousness of his own genius, notably his ability to see the relation of the particular to the whole, without which he could not have written his appreciation of Plato's intellectual and moral character. The philosopher John Dewey later provided a fitting epitaph for this entire subject when he wrote that "the final word of Emerson's philosophy, [is] the identity of Being, unqualified and immutable, with Character."

David A. Dilworth

"The Chartist's Complaint" (1857)

"The Chartist's Complaint" was published in the first issue of the ATLANTIC MONTHLY (November 1857). Its first draft goes back 10 years earlier, to March and April 1847, and Emerson conceived it as a companion to "DAYS," the draft of which dates to 1851. "The Chartist's Complaint" was originally titled "Janus" after its opening lines, but Emerson changed it to reference a near-contemporary agitation against privilege in England. Chartism took its name from the People's Charter, a bill drafted and published in 1838, aimed at equal electoral areas, universal suffrage, elimination of property qualifications, and the like. Its distinctive character was its working-class organization and objectives; as THOMAS CARLYLE put it, Chartism was "a knife and fork question." It took shape against the economic depression of 1837 and 1838, spreading around the country, eventually waning as a political and social movement with the upturn in prosperity of mid-Victorian Britain. Emerson's readers would have been familiar with this background of recent memory. The poem was collected in MAY-DAY AND OTHER PIECES (1867) and reappeared in the posthumous *Poems* (1884).

CRITICAL COMMENTARY

In the poem, a morally indignant laborer speaks the entire set of lines directly to the day—or Sun, which in the final line he equates with "harlot Day." The Chartist's accusation is that the day has "two faces, / Making one place two places." The first face is "by the humble farmer seen, / Chill and wet, unlighted, mean." This dreary place is "useful only, triste and damp," the sun's light only "serving for a labourer's lamp." But the same mists that dampen the laborer in his toils have "another side," serving as "the appanage of pride / Gracing the rich man's wood and lake, / His park where amber mornings break." The Chartist complains here of the Sun "treacherously" shedding its bright light to show the rich man's "planted isle where roses glow," the day's "mightiness" serving as "a sycophant to smug success." The Chartist even extends his accusation to the day's "sweet sky and ocean broad," asking if they too are "fine accomplices to fraud?" In view of this life's fatal maldistribution of wealth and enjoyment, he ends up cursing the sun in no Shakespearean terms: "O Sun! I curse thy cruel ray: / Back, back to chaos, harlot Day!"

In light of the relationship to "Days" ("the hypocritic Days" we mindlessly squander) and its companion essay, "WORKS AND DAYS" (1870), the reader of this poem has to ponder the general injustice of man's lot. This injustice of the day, sun, sky—or God—is linked to Emerson's rendering of the binary of FATE and POWER in the leading essay of *The* CONDUCT OF LIFE (1860) and in his overarching metaphysics of identity and metamorphosis. That the poem obliquely references the plight of the Negro slave, concerning which Emerson strenuously agitated at home in the time frame in which the poem was composed, is a plausible side-bar of interpretation. But the Chartist movement in England was a huge national affair, and in 1847–48 Emerson had just returned from a lecture tour in England and Scotland, where he lectured in many of the cities to which the Chartist movement had spread. His Chartist's moral indignation against the Sun, which shines equally on the just and the unjust, has a biblical ring, as well as resonating with the pathos of many similar lines in WALT WHITMAN.

David A. Dilworth

"Circles" (1841)

The essay "Circles" was published in *ESSAYS: FIRST SERIES* (1841) and, unlike many in that collection, was written as an essay and not first delivered as a lecture. Emerson relied on the image of the circle throughout his writings, whether as circumference, spheres, orbs, planets, the moon, or, as in the opening lines of the essay, "the eye" as "the first circle." The circular eyeball, especially, incorporated his philosophy of the interconnectedness of all things and of sight, or knowledge, bringing to mind his famous description of a firsthand experience in *NATURE* (1836): "Standing on the bare ground,—my head bathed by the blithe air, and uplifted into infinite space,—all mean egotism vanishes. I become a transparent eye-ball; I am nothing; I see all; the currents of the Universal Being circulate through me; I am part or particle of God."

SYNOPSIS

The opening verses to accompany the essay "Circles" are replete with circular or spherical images:

> Nature centers into balls,
> And her proud ephemerals,
> Fast to surface and outside,
> Scan the profile of the sphere;
> Knew they what that signified,
> A new genesis was here.

The essay opens with an explanation: "The eye is the first circle; the horizon which it forms is the second; and throughout nature this primary figure is repeated without end." Emerson sets up the circle, this "first of forms," as representative of "the circular or compensatory character of every human action." In a circle, the "centre was everywhere," a concept that describes not only human character but the very nature of God, of the universe, and even of knowledge: "Our life is an apprenticeship to the truth, that around every circle another can be drawn; that there is no end in nature, but every end is a beginning; that there is always another dawn risen on mid-noon, and under every deep a lower deep opens." This image of the circle, then, "this fact" from nature, is relevant to our lives in that it helps explain every action and "human power in every department."

Nature is "fluid," there is no "permanence." Therein lies the limitations or falsehood of a rationalist or empirical view of the world—"our globe" (another circle) is not "a mass of facts," but "a transparent law," the law of nature. Even human "culture" is not a fixed institution but only "the predominance of an idea" at any given moment. Indeed, the ideas produced by culture, whether as art or sculpture or architecture or technology, change over time; they "disappear" and are replaced by new ideas. Even cultural artifacts that appear to be permanent, such as a monument, were built with human hands powered by human thought and could be destroyed by such as well. So it is that the hand and the idea are stronger than the "tower of granite." Twice he states that "permanence is a word of degrees."

Like nature and like the universe, "the life of man is a self-evolving circle, which . . . rushes on all sides outwards to new and larger circles, and that without end." Human thoughts are propelled by the "force" of "truth" and create "circumstance" that is the social world. There are "immense and innumerable expansions" of the circle of human thought, but "there is no outside, no inclosing wall, no circumference to us." When we think we have come to an end of "the story," there is yet another "circle around the circle." Every "principle" in nature is part of "a bolder generalization," just as every day lived seems so important at the time but will become "abridged into a word." Everything we believe to be permanent today—our "creeds," "literature," "nations"—can be undone by the power of "the thought of to-morrow." Likewise, even we as humans are only "a suggestion" of the future potential of humanity: "Men walk as prophecies of the next age."

Emerson characterizes life as a "mysterious ladder," our ideas moving us ever-forward up "the steps" toward "power." He answers critics who say this is a "crass and material" view of human life, devoid of agency or even hope, "threatening to degrade thy theory of spirit," by explaining that the idea of circles removes any limitation on human actions, allowing us to pursue a higher level of thinking: "There are no fixtures to men, if we appeal to consciousness." "Every man supposes himself not to be fully understood," and this is good, for it means there is always an "unknown" element in human life, always "a greater possibility." This has implications for our relationships, though, for we are constantly seeking to be challenged and inspired: "Men cease to interest us when we find their limitations." "Conversation is a game of circles," for each thought builds upon the previous, sparking new ideas, we begin to see things in new "proportions"; our very "foundations" are shaken—when we come to "a perfect understanding" with another, then there is silence, so that is not the goal.

Their limitation is our limitation when we find that all thought is "expressions of one law," "one principle." Everything may be "turned," "revised and condemned," whether science, literature, religion, or "the very hopes of man," because everything is connected and "at the mercy of a new generalization." "Power" under this definition comes from "self-recovery," from resisting generalization and resisting stagnation. Just as Emerson spoke earlier of degrees of permanence in nature and in culture, so "there are degrees in idealism," that is, in our current philosophy. Idealism can be regarded "academically" (as a philosophy), as truth-seeking (such as in poetry), or as "ethical and practical" (that is, as a map for how to live one's life). Idealism is not a separate thing, however, but a recognition that what exists "at this hour" is related to "the ideas which have emerged" before, "as a tree bears its apples."

Unlike philosophy or abstract theorizing, "literature" is the "platform" by which we come to understand "our present life." It is a "base" or starting point, just as "the astronomer must have his diameter of the earth's orbit as a base to find the parallax of any star." Emerson is employing here not only a scientific metaphor but also another use of the image of the circle with "the earth's orbit." Because literature is important "we value the poet" (or *should* value the poet), as there is more knowledge, more "argument" and "wisdom" "in the sonnet or the play" than in scientific or religious texts. Poetry inspires more than these other sources because it relates directly to our view of ourselves: "I open my eye on my own possibilities" (again, Emerson utilizes the metaphor not only of vision but also of the circular eyeball).

Likewise, we should understand religion not "from the catechism" but from nature, "from the pastures, from a boat in the pond, from amidst the songs of wood-birds." Emerson's "system of concentric circles" returns to this theme of nature as symbolic. While the poet uses nature's symbolism to inspire, even the scientist or "naturalist" must look beyond the facts to find "the deeper law," the meaning in nature's forms and methods. Indeed, while the law of nature is "deeper" than the facts, it is also simple and its meaning accessible to all. It does not take a philosopher to decipher nature, for even "the poor and the low" have sayings that reflect nature's law: "'blessed be nothing,' and 'the worse things are, the better they are,' are proverbs which express the transcendentalism of common life."

What is good to one person may be bad to another, that is the balance in nature: "one man's beauty, another's ugliness; one man's wisdom, another's folly. . . ," and so on. This is because we live in different relations to "the same objects." One man may live according to a principle of "mathematics" (that is, relying upon logic), while another approaches the same problems as a matter of "character," each choosing a different course but arriving at the same ends. This struggle and then balance also takes place within the individual, for whom enough "divine moments" can ultimately override the bad, and vices are rendered meaningless by inspiration. Lest he be accused of condoning "our crimes" in the name of truth to ourselves, Emerson points out that no one should "set the least value on what I do, or the least discredit on what I do not, as if I pretended to settle any thing as true or false."

In the last part of the essay Emerson brings the reader back to the center of the circle. He steps back from "this incessant movement and progression" of human thought, of philosophy, of the universe, and places it in "contrast to some principle of fixture or stability in the soul." The soul is at the center of the circle, the source of new "knowledge and thought." The nature of the circle, however, of constant movement, is that the creation of that knowledge and thought is "in vain," for as soon as it appears, by the very act of its creation, it has already inspired to greater heights, to further knowledge and thought. As in nature so in human thought as "all things renew, germinate, and spring," the "incessant movement" of creation. Nature sheds the old in favor of the new just as we are constantly reaching beyond ourselves for something higher when "we converse with what is above us." In this way, "we do not grow old, but grow young." It is wrong to assume that we will reach a point when we stop growing, when we finally "know all" and can "renounce aspiration." Instead, we must always have "hope" and look upward for truth: "People wish to be settled; only as far as they are unsettled is there any hope for them."

While looking forward in this way, we can never know or anticipate "the power of to-morrow," we can only "be" today: "*so to be* is the sole inlet of *so to know*." To "be" in the present is also to let go of the past, "cast away . . . all my once hoarded knowledge." Knowledge is useful, therefore, for neither tomorrow nor yesterday, but only in the present. And it is "character" that gives us perspective on our current knowledge, that gives us the "power and courage to make a new road to new and better goals."

Emerson ends the essay with the idea that the goal of life is always "to draw a new circle." Only when we "forget ourselves" are we open to something new and surprising. This is why "dreams and drunkenness, the use of opium and alcohol" are so tempting as sources of inspiration and new ideas, as are "wild passions, as in gaming and war." These outside stimulants, though, are all "counterfeit" to the true source of genius within.

CRITICAL COMMENTARY

What is perhaps most striking about "Circles" is that it receives so little individual attention compared with other essays in the *First Series.* And yet, in the image of the circle, Emerson brings together the various concerns of his Transcendental philosophy—nature, human life and thought, culture, friendship, philosophy, poetry, inspiration, and the relationship between the self and society. These together make up what he terms the "transcendentalism of common life," the core idea of which is that each person must find their own truth. Indeed, perhaps because the image of the circle is so ubiquitous throughout his writings (Emerson humorously responds to "some reader" who will call him "O circular philosopher"), the essay does not stand apart as the source of this idea.

For Emerson, the circle is an image of unity and interconnectedness, between the material and the spiritual, between humans and nature, among the past, present, and future. The circle, like nature, has no beginning and no end, no boundaries: "There is no end in nature, but every end is a beginning." This is the opposite of a linear view of human life and of time. As he wrote in the poem "URIEL" (1847), "Line in Nature is not found, / Unit and Universe are round." In "The AMERICAN SCHOLAR" (1837), he described nature as a "web of God," its "circular power returning into itself . . . so entire, so boundless." The poet inspires more than the priest or teacher or even philosopher because poetry relates directly to our view of ourselves: "I open my eye on my own possibilities." Here Emerson again combines the image of the circle and of vision. In "COMPENSATION" (which appeared in the same volume with "Circles"), he defines "the true doctrine of omnipresence" as God appearing in even the smallest thing in nature: "The world globes itself in a drop of dew." In the later essay "BEAUTY" (1860), he defines "circular movement" as the most perfect (and therefore most beautiful) form of nature, such as is found in "the circulation of waters, the circulation of the blood, [and] the periodical motion of planets."

Throughout the essays in *First Series,* the never-ending circle was a favorite metaphor for human relationships, such as friendship and love. In the essay "LOVE," he mused that "the circle of the seasons are erotic odes and dances," and that love itself "enlarges its circles ever, like the pebble thrown into the pond, or the light proceeding from an orb." In "Circles" he discusses an always "unknown" element in human life, always "a greater possibility," that comes from our relationships with others, a theme he would explore in "FRIENDSHIP," again of the same volume.

The never-ending "unsettled" circle was also a key idea or image for other Transcendentalists, especially in poetry. Accused of moral relativism for rejecting the authority of doctrine or tradition in favor of the ever-widening circles of individual truth, Emerson responds "I unsettle all things. No facts to me are sacred; none are profane; I simply experiment, an endless seeker, with no Past at my back," presaging the language of WALT WHITMAN. MARGARET FULLER also used the image in understanding the interconnectedness of the male and the female, of past and present, of time and space, in her poem, "Double Triangle, Serpent and Rays": "Patient serpent, circle round / Till in death they life is found . . . / . . . And centered in the diamond Sun, / Time, eternity, are one."

Perhaps no other contemporaneous poet used the image more than EMILY DICKINSON, who used the term "circumference" in at least 17 different poems. Her use of the term was very similar to Emerson's, as an expression of both boundless possibility and limitation, especially for the poet. In "A Coffin is a Small Domain" the poet laments "Circumference without Relief— / Or Estimate—or End." Perhaps the most directly Emersonian use of the term was in her 1865 poem, "The Poets Light But Lamps," in which she reflected on how each age will interpret the poetry of the previous ages: "Each Age a Lens / Disseminating their / Circumference—." This was an idea strikingly similar to Emerson's in the "Circles" essay on men as the "prophecies of the next age" and on poems and literature as circular themselves and never definitive.

FURTHER READING

Von Frank, Albert J. "Essays: First Series (1841)." In *The Cambridge Companion to Ralph Waldo Emerson,* edited by Joel Porte and Saundra Morris, 106–120. New York: Cambridge University Press, 1999.

"Civilization" (1870)

"Civilization," the second essay in *SOCIETY AND SOLITUDE* (1870), originated in the lecture course "Life and Literature" delivered by Emerson in BOSTON in 1861. At the outbreak of the Civil War, Emerson reconfigured it under the title "Civilization at a Pinch," which he then further transformed as a lecture on "American Civilization" read before the Smithsonian Institution in Washington in January 1862. After the war he eliminated the local references, and the essay returned to the more general theme of the original lecture of 1861. The essay is conspicuous for Emerson's endorsement of the criteria of civilization discussed in Western ENLIGHTENMENT sources and can be read in tandem with another treatment of the subject in "Progress of Culture," an essay of 1867 (eventually appearing in *LETTERS AND SOCIAL AIMS* in 1876).

SYNOPSIS

Emerson begins by referring to Francois Guizot's *General History of Civilization in Europe* (1828). He says that Guizot did not succeed in defining the concept of "civilization," which is in fact better suggested by its negations. Civilization involves the advancement of mankind out of the rudest state—when men were "dwellers in caves, or on trees, or lived like the ape, a cannibal, an eater of pounded snails, worms, and offal." These are the characteristics of a barbarous people that has "no clothing, no alphabet, no marriage, no arts of peace, no abstract thought." He adds that we are still "complaisant" to call civilized certain of the Turk and Moorish nations, even though they have invented or imported many arts.

Civilization imports "a mysterious progress," though, since "in the brutes there is none; and in mankind to-day the savage tribes are gradually extinguished rather than civilized. The Indians of this country have not learned the white man's work; and in Africa the negro of to-day is the negro of Herodotus." The same is true of other races of the world that have not learned "the secret of cumulative power, of advancing on one's self." The Indian is "gloomy and distressed when urged to depart from his habits and traditions." The most advanced nations, he notes, are "always those who navigate the most." The sailor quickly acquires new powers in confronting the sea, "and the change of shores and populations clears his head of much nonsense of his wigwam."

Emerson then establishes a list of "the feats of liberty and wit" that have made the progressive epochs of history. He begins with the effects of a framed or stone house, which reflect the tranquillity, power, and refinement of the builder, and also shelter the frontiersman from the weather and the wilderness. Invention and arts are thereby facilitated; manners, social beauty, and delight follow: "'Tis wonderful how soon a piano gets into a log hut on the frontier. You would think they found it under a pine stump." Soon comes "a Latin grammar," "a hymn on Sunday," and then colleges and governments.

In a journal entry of 1854 Emerson wrote that his three tests of advanced civilization were roads, postal service, and the position of women. He expounds on each of these in the present essay. Thus, "when the Indian trail gets widened, graded and bridged to a good road," this opens the way for "a benefactor, . . . a missionary, a pacificator, a wealth-bringer, a makers of markets, a vent for industry." The postal service, with "its educating energy augmented by cheapness and guarded by a certain religious sentiment in mankind," comes as another measure of success. The right position of woman in the state is a crucial third barometer of civilized progress: "Place the sexes in right relations of mutual respect, and a severe morality gives that essential charm to woman which educates all that is delicate, poetic and self-sacrificing; breeds courtesy and learning, conversation and wit, in her rough mate; so that I have thought a sufficient measure of civilization is the influence of good women."

Emerson goes on to mention "the diffusion of knowledge, overrunning all the old barriers of caste, and, by the cheap press, bringing the university to every poor man's door in the newsboy's basket." The prodigious accomplishments of the latest steamers, whose equipment is "an abridgement and compend of a nation's arts," capable of controlling the forces of nature "in the wildest sea-mountains," elicit his applause, as does "the skill that pervades complex details" in "the man that maintains himself," as in "the chimney taught to burn its own smoke," and in analogous accomplishments of self-sufficiency on the farm.

Higher civilization is the result of a "highly complex organization," which, in contrast with the "bird and beast," allows mankind to enjoy "the absolute illumination we call Reason, and thereby true liberty." Climates, Emerson notes, may have something to do with this melioration: "The highest civility has never loved the hot zones. Wherever snow falls there is usually civil freedom." However, he adds that the genius of Egypt, India, Arabia, and Iceland proves that temperate climate is not the indispensable consideration for learning, philosophy, and art. The essential condition for the social education of man is a "deep morality," as "in the institutions of chivalry; or patriotism, as in the Spartan and Roman republics; or the enthusiasm of some religious sect which imputes its virtue to its dogma; or the cabalism or *esprit de corps* of a masonic or other association of friends."

Morality consists in "respecting in action catholic or universal ends." As exemplified in Kant's categorical imperative to act according to a universal rule of duty, civilization depends on the attraction of mankind to what is higher. But this imperative also extends to the use of our strength and power in the work of our hands, which depends upon "the aid of the elements." The carpenter, the farmer, and the courier are examples of agents of civilization who must work with the forces of gravity, the grains of woods, the lay of the land, the weather, and the waterways. Electricity has replaced "the horses; bad roads in spring; snowdrifts in winter; heats in summer." Instead, we find strength in "borrowing the might of the elements. The forces of steam, gravity, galvanism, light, magnets, wind, fire, serve us day by day and cost us nothing."

As the burgeoning handicrafts "borrow the natural elements, so all our social and political action leans on principles" in pursuit of "universal and catholic ends." Puny as man is, he borrows the omnipotence of great ideas, which instruct him to "work for those interests which the divinities honor and promote,—justice, love, freedom, knowledge, and utility." Consequently, "the true test of civilization is, not the census, nor the size and architecture of cities, nor the crops" of the countryside, nor a nation's technological prowess, "but the kind of man the country turns out." And here Emerson remarks on "how little government has to do with" the moral sentiments of individuals whose daily lives are "self-helped and self-directed"—"knots of men in purely natural societies, societies of trade, of kindred blood, of habitual hospitality, house and house, man acting on man by weight of opinion, of longer or better-directed industry; the refining influence of women, the invitation which experience and permanent causes open to youth and labor." In "the symmetry and force of their qualities,—I see what cubic values America has, and in these a better certificate of civilization, than great cities or enormous wealth."

"The vital refinements" to civilization, Emerson adds, "are the moral and intellectual steps." He names men such as Moses, the Buddha, the Greeks, Socrates, Jesus, John Huss, Savanarola, and Martin Luther who have motivated the progress of humanity: "In the presence of these agencies, it is frivolous to insist on the inventions of printing or gunpowder, of steampower, and gaslight, percussion caps, and rubber shoes," and the like—which are only "toys thrown off from that security, freedom and exhilaration which a healthy morality creates in society." Instead, "the popular measures of progress will ever be the arts and the laws."

Emerson concludes the essay by returning to the negative definition he advanced at the beginning. Any country that cannot meet the aforementioned tests of civilization—and he implies there are such—falls under the censure of barbarism. Such would be "a country where knowledge cannot be diffused without perils of mob-law and statute-law; where speech is not free; where the post office is violated, mail-bags opened, and letters tampered with; where public debts and private debts outside of the State are repudiated; where liberty is attacked in the primary institution of social life; where the position of the white woman is injuriously affected by the outlawry of the black woman; where the arts, such as they have, are all imported, having no indigenous life; where the laborer is not secured in the earnings of his own hands; where suffrage is not free or equal." Such "suicidal mischiefs" trump the natural "advantages of soil, climate, or coast" for any society.

CRITICAL COMMENTARY

The subtext of "Civilization" is Emerson's long-expressed declaration of stages of evolution in nature leading up to mankind, and of the historical progression of mankind to its present level of intellectual and moral advancement. In a number of other essays, the evolution of nature and history crucially attested to his objective idealism, in which the metaphysical concept of the affinity of the human mind and nature plays a prominent role. While squarely anchored in the romantic literary strain of Western modernity, these affirmations of his thought certify his reputation as a preeminent advocate of modern civilization.

"Civilization" and "SUCCESS" in *Society and Solitude,* and "Progress of Culture" in the later *Letters and Social Aims,* endorse these themes of the European Enlightenment, which produced a self-consciousness in the modernizing nations of the West with respect to contrasting primitive or "barbaric" conditions in other parts of the world. It should be noted, however, that the European Enlightenment had been affected by Eastern philosophical ideas imported in the 17th and 18th centuries by the Jesuit missionaries in China and disseminated by Leibniz, Wolff, Voltaire, Adam Smith, and others. Emerson took note of this greater legacy, not confined to China, but including many other strains of advanced culture, such as the Indian, Persian, and Arabic, as well as the legacies of intellectual and moral virtue couched in the works of the Greek philosophers—notably of Plato, Aristotle, and the Stoics.

The essay concentrates its focus on the degrees of civilized attainment in 19th-century American life. Emerson solidifies his thesis—as did his contemporary WALT WHITMAN, among others—by witnessing to the fact that the moral level of American civilization can be measured by the two historic breakthroughs of his own lifetime: the abolition of slavery and the emancipation of woman. All other progress and inventions rank behind these two major moral achievements: "Morality, and all the incidents of morality are essential; as, justice to the citizen, and personal liberty." And the highest goal of civilization, according to Emerson in this post–Civil War essay originally written in 1861, "is directed on securing the greatest good of the greatest number."

David A. Dilworth

"Compensation" (1834/1841)

Emerson wrote two poems under the title "Compensation." The first and shorter of the two, which begins "Why should I," was written in New York City in November 1834. The second, beginning "The wings of Time," was the motto to his important early essay "COMPENSATION" of *ESSAYS: FIRST SERIES* (1841), which featured the tension between opposites that became a defining concept in Emerson's prose and poetry, the moral principle of karmic reward or retribution.

CRITICAL COMMENTARY

The first poem consists of two quatrains, the subject of which prepares the ground for "The CHARTIST'S COMPLAINT," a poem that explores the subject of the sun's irrational way of shining equally on the just and the unjust. To the question "Why should he keep holiday, When other men have none?" Emerson can here only reply with the stark reasoning that "when these are gay, / I sit and mourn alone." This melancholy reply may have reflected his sadness at the news of his brother EDWARD BLISS EMERSON's death in Puerto Rico, which reached him in New York on October 18, 1834. Emerson continues this unrelieved stoical reflection in the next quatrain, which explains his current inability to speak as simply the reverse side of nature's inscrutable way of giving and taking away. Its pendulum swings so that "late I spoke to silent throngs, / And now their hour is come."

The later 1841 motto to the essay "Compensation" is less personal and topical. It also invokes the balance between opposites but in a more philosophical or cosmic manner: "The wings of Time are black and white," and "mountain tall and ocean deep / Trembling balance duly keep." The "feud of Want and Have" is seen in nature through the "changing moon and tidal wave." "Lonely Earth" itself is only a "supplemental asteroid, / Or compensatory spark."

The second stanza of this poem is humanistic, suggesting a more positive sense of polarity in nature and the universe: "Man's the elm, and Wealth the vine." Everything has the fullness of its own time, its place in the evolution of the universe: "There's no god dare wrong a worm." Puny man can thus be assured that "power to him who power exerts." Tied to his ethics of "SELF-RELIANCE" (also appearing in *Essays: First Series,* 1841), this is the law of karma—that is, of just reward for sincere, life-affirming efforts. Everyone has his or her share, and, for the deserving, "all that Nature made thy own, . . . / Will rive the hills and swim the sea, / And, like thy shadow, follow thee."

In the ensuing prose essay "Compensation," to which this second poem is annexed, Emerson wrote that "polarity, or action and reaction, we meet in every part of nature. . . . An inevitable dualism bisects nature, so that each thing is a half, and suggests another thing to make it whole; as, spirit, matter; man, woman; odd, even; subjective, objective; in, out; upper, under; motion, rest; yes, nay." He draws the moral lesson that "there is a crack in every thing God has made." He invokes "the ancient doctrine of Nemesis, who keeps watch in the universe and lets no offence go unchastised."

The two poems on "Compensation"—one personal and the other cosmical—address this law of karmic retribution that remained front and center in Emerson's writings. The later essays of *The CONDUCT OF LIFE* (1860) and *SOCIETY AND SOLITUDE*

(1870) would also depend on a dialectic of "fate" and "power," and the movement of his writings generally ascends from negative considerations of punishment and justice to positive affirmations of mankind's reward and place in the universe.

David A. Dilworth

"Compensation" (1841)

"Compensation" was published in Emerson's 1841 collection *ESSAYS: FIRST SERIES* and, unlike many of the other essays, did not originate as a separate lecture. Emerson's theory of "compensation" is that there is balance in nature, for every action a reaction, for every reward a cost, in every physical fact a spiritual lesson, and the essay illuminates those "correspondences." In the first line of the essay Emerson muses that this foundational idea has been with him for a long time: "Ever since I was a boy, I have wished to write a discourse on Compensation." As early as 1831 he wrote in his journal, "Is not the law of Compensation perfect? It holds, as far as we can see, different gifts to different individuals, but with a mortgage of responsibility on every one." A short poem titled "COMPENSATION" was published in his 1847 collection of *POEMS*, but this was different from the verses appearing as the prologue of the 1841 essay. In the opening poem he invokes the balance and duality within nature, within ourselves, and within the universe: "The wings of Time are black and white, / Pied with morning and with night. / Mountain tall and ocean deep / Trembling balance duly keep."

SYNOPSIS

In the opening lines of the essay Emerson establishes that the idea of "Compensation" is to him a central idea of life. It has application to all parts of life and is, in particular, ahead of what "the preachers taught"—it is an alternative to religious ideas about justice and punishment. Compensation is a "ray of divinity," a way to understand "the present action of the soul of this world, clean from all vestige of tradition." He makes an explicit reference to "a sermon at church" in which "the doctrine of the Last Judgment" was explained "in the ordinary manner"—that is, the belief "that judgment is not executed in this world" and that "compensation" for the actions of this life will be made "in the next life," in heaven or hell. Emerson is shocked to find that "no offence appeared to be taken by the congregation at this doctrine."

What is offensive to Emerson is the accepted idea "that the good are miserable in the present life" and that "the poor and despised" will not have their reward until the next life. This is a damaging lesson, according to Emerson, for it offers no insight into "the presence of the soul," setting up only an outward definition of justice. He reads the silence from the congregation on this doctrine, this "fallacy," not as agreement but as a lack of alternatives. His essay offers that alternative by drawing "the path of the law of Compensation."

First, he identifies the "inevitable dualism" of nature: "Polarity, or action and reaction, we meet in every part of nature; in darkness and light, in heat and cold; in the ebb and flow of waters; in male and female," and so on. In nature, "each thing is a half, and suggests another thing to make it whole." There is a balance or compensation throughout nature, as well as in "the mechanic forces" of "power" and "time." There are even advantages to "cold climate" and "barren soil." He continues with the analogy into other aspects of life, pointing out dualities such as sweet/sour, evil/good, pleasure/penalty, wit/folly, or gain/loss. "Nature hates monopolies and exceptions"; therefore, "there is always some levelling circumstance." Likewise, when it comes to human relations, it is no use to look at what others have and to be jealous: "The President has paid dear for his White House. It has commonly cost him all his peace, and the best of his manly attributes."

Throughout the essay Emerson repeats the idea that the parts make up the whole: "The world globes itself in a drop of dew. . . . So do we put our life into every act." This is "the true doctrine of omnipresence," that God appears in every thing. So it is in the "moral" universe—what is a "sentiment" within the individual is the basis of a larger "law." The law of compensation is the law of cause and effect; he again uses the analogy of nature, in which we see "the effect already blooms in the cause, the end preexists in the means, the fruit in the seed." Despite this truth, men tend to think (falsely) in parts, not in view of the whole. They focus on "the senses," on the needs of the body as separate from the needs of the soul. "The soul strives" for "all things," while the individual strives only for his own selfish needs. The true definition of greatness is "to possess" both sides of nature.

This "rebellion and separation" from nature is a "disease began in the will." In Christian terms, the will signals man's separation from God; in Emerson's terms, it is a separation from one's own soul. Despite this struggle, the idea of compensation permeates mankind's own thought, revealed in "fable," "history," and "proverbs." From the Greeks to ancient India, "mythology ends in the same ethics." In Western religion the idea manifests in the doctrine of "an eye for an eye; a tooth for a tooth; blood for blood," or the injunction to "give and it shall be given you." Emerson observes that these moral laws are "thus written, because it is thus in life"; that is, religion only reflects "the law of nature."

Every deed has a "benefit" as well as a "debt" or "tax" that must be paid. If there seems to be no negative aspect, no immediate justice, it is only "a postponement" of the inevitable. The same law applies to "labor": "Human labor . . . is one immense illustration of the perfect compensation of the universe." The law of labor is the "absolute balance of Give and Take, the doctrine that every thing has its price"; this law governs not only the "ledger" and "budgets of states" but the very "laws of light and darkness, in all the action and reaction of nature." He is not concerned only with negative actions and consequences, for "the law holds with equal sureness for all right action. Love, and you shall be loved."

Our negative characteristics or qualities can sometimes be "made useful," just as our positive or good points can sometimes harm us in the form of "pride" or other consequences. It is through these consequences and adversities that we become stronger and more self-reliant: When a man "is pushed, tormented, defeated, he has a chance to learn something; he has been put on his wits, on his manhood; he has gained facts; learns his ignorance; is cured of the insanity of conceit." That is why "a great man is always willing to be little."

Having explained the theory of compensation, Emerson emphasizes that "there is a deeper fact in the soul than compensation, to wit, its own nature. The soul is not a compensation, but a life. The soul is." The soul experiences only ways of "being," without "penalty" or "excess." Emerson lists these truths or "attributes," which know no limits in the soul: "virtue," "wisdom," "love," "knowledge," and "beauty." Rather than existing for these attributes, men are too concerned with what they will get, or what will be taken away; indeed, "the radical tragedy of nature seems to be the distinction of More and Less." Humans are too quick to define life in terms of these limits when, Emerson says, "life is a progress, and not a station."

We need only look at the lives of great men such as "Jesus and Shakespeare" to see that what makes them great are transcendent qualities accessible to all: "His virtue,—is not that mine? His wit,—if it cannot be made mine, it is not wit." They did not possess more or less "virtue" or "wit"; these qualities were only more pronounced. These can be ours as well if we stop "resting, not advancing, resisting, not cooperating with the divine expansion." It is a process of "growth," this striving for something greater than earthly gain. We are too tied to the "day by day": "We cannot part with our friends. We cannot let our angels go. We do not see that they only go out that archangels may come in." In this sense, then, our lives are governed by the law of compensation, for we have to give something up ("friends," the "day by day") to receive something greater in return.

The law of compensation does not always work immediately in our lives, and Emerson ends the essay with a consolation and reflection on how even the greatest losses may seem "unpaid" in the short term. We must be patient in expecting that somehow there will be gains "after long intervals of time": "A fever, a mutilation, a cruel disappointment, a loss of wealth, a loss of friends, seems at the moment unpaid loss, and unpayable. But the sure years reveal the deep remedial force that underlies all facts. The death of a dear friend, wife, brother, lover, which seemed nothing but privation, somewhat later assumes the aspect of a guide or genius; for it commonly operates revolutions in our way of life, terminates an epoch of infancy or of youth which was waiting to be closed, breaks up a wonted occupation, or a household, or style of living, and allows the formation of new ones more friendly to the growth of character." In the end, the law of compensation works so that all life experiences lead to "growth of character."

CRITICAL COMMENTARY

Emerson offers the theory of "Compensation" as a spiritual and moral alternative to religion. In contrast to learned tradition, compensation is a new "ray of divinity," it is "truth . . . revealed to us." Along with "SPIRITUAL LAWS," "Compensation" places Emerson's Transcendentalist philosophy in direct opposition to Christian beliefs. In Christianity, justice and punishment are imposed on humans by a supernatural god from above, outside of human or natural experience, but Emerson believes "men are better than this theology." In Emerson's terms, compensation works according to natural principles or laws and is revealed to humans, not through religious texts or supernatural revelation or coercion, but through a relationship with nature itself. The essay is Emerson's effort to bring this law to our attention and thus reveal the nature of our own character and actions in the world.

Emerson drew upon ancient mythology and on other religious or spiritual traditions to show that the idea of compensation appears in some form throughout human culture. He brings in the example of "that ancient doctrine of Nemesis . . . [who] lets no offence go unchastised," a reference he would make again in the poem "Merlin II," in which Nemesis "matches even with odd." Having rejected the Christian idea of judgment, Emerson's compensation is more similar to an Eastern spiritual concept in which "Every thing has two sides, a good and an evil." Whereas judgment tends toward an emphasis on punishment in Emerson's terms, evil is not a separate thing to be avoided but must be seen merely as an *absence of good.*

Acknowledging both sides leads to balance and harmony, and therefore optimism. The scholar Richard Geldard points out that, like the later "EXPERIENCE" (1844), the essay "Compensation" was Emerson's attempt to deal with grief and loss in his own life. Having experienced the early deaths of his first wife, his brothers, and, most devastatingly, his young son, Waldo, Emerson sought an explanation in the universality of nature rather than in the solitary focus on personal pain.

The essay is replete with examples of how "compensation" reveals the connection of all parts to the larger whole in nature. In the opening poem he uses astronomical imagery to characterize the earth itself, the planet, as not the end of creation, but as only a "supplemental asteroid, / Or compensatory spark." The earth itself is made of up various parts—trees and vines, worms and desert, hills and seas—that make up the whole, so that "the entire system of things gets represented in every particle." This is the main idea from Emerson's reading of EMANUEL SWEDENBORG and defines his entire approach to nature, from the writing of *NATURE* (1836) onward. In nature, as he writes in "Compensation," "no creatures are favorites, but a certain compensation balances every gift and every defect." Emerson would use this language of "gifts" and "defects" throughout his writings, in talking about nature as well as about human character. For example, the figures in *REPRESENTATIVE MEN* (1850), such as Plato, Swedenborg, Shakespeare, and others, each have gifts as well as defects or faults, attributes that make them not just great but human.

The law of compensation also applies to political life: "Things refuse to be mismanaged long." If unjust laws or taxes are instituted, such problems would eventually resolve themselves according to nature's laws. If there are imbalances in society, the problem is with the individuals in that society: "Every crime is punished, every virtue rewarded, every wrong redressed." This was Emerson's approach to political and social reform that he repeated in other instances as well, such as "NEW ENGLAND REFORMERS," "MAN THE REFORMER," and his addresses on women's rights and ABOLITIONISM. He explains that under the law of compensation, when we do harm to others, we harm ourselves:

"It is the whipper who is whipped and the tyrant who is undone." In his arguments against slavery, made in addresses such as "EMANCIPATION OF THE NEGROES IN THE BRITISH WEST INDIES" (1844), he argues that slavery will end when society realizes that slavery is as soul-killing for the slaveholder as it is for the slave.

Emerson would be criticized for his view that slavery would naturally work itself out according to the laws of nature, but he insisted here that "the doctrine of compensation is not the doctrine of indifferency." The essay on "Compensation" is not an explicit commentary on reform but is applicable to a range of human issues in its general critique of a focus only on "the solution of one problem" at a time, detached from the whole. For Emerson, social and political issues are not separate from issues of "the character" of individuals, and as might be expected, change must come from the individual in his or her striving for a right relationship to the whole. Emerson seeks only to make the reader aware of the larger system or laws governing nature, inspiring not indifference but hope and optimism in the eventual and eternal balance of the universe.

FURTHER READING

Geldard, Richard. *The Vision of Emerson.* London: Vega Publishing, 2003.

Von Frank, Albert J. "Essays: First Series (1841)." In *The Cambridge Companion to Ralph Waldo Emerson,* edited by Joel Porte and Saundra Morris, 106–120. New York: Cambridge University Press, 1999.

"Concord Hymn"

See "HYMN: SUNG AT THE COMPLETION OF THE CONCORD MONUMENT, APRIL 19, 1836."

The Conduct of Life (1860)

The Conduct of Life was published in 1860 and was composed of nine essays: "FATE," "POWER," "WEALTH," "CULTURE," "BEHAVIOR," "WORSHIP," "Considerations by the Way," "BEAUTY," and "ILLUSIONS." As with his earlier collections, most of the individual essays had been delivered as lectures in the 1850s; some previously had been published in the *ATLANTIC MONTHLY*. As early as 1824, when listing potential writing topics in his journal, he declared, "I propose to look philosophically at the conduct of life." While in some ways this was his objective throughout his work, to apply ideas to practical life, the specific focus on "the conduct of life" did not come full circle until the 1850s, by which time Emerson had become increasingly and explicitly concerned with issues of social and political reform and the ethical issues surrounding how to live one's life in society.

In *The Conduct of Life* Emerson attempted to reconcile what he termed in his journal as "the theory & practice of life"; or, as he stated in the opening lines of the essay "Power": "Life is a search after power." But he framed the volume with the essays "Fate" and "Illusions," both of which examine the limitations or the lack of power. Far from being an overly deterministic (or fatalistic) perspective, in Emerson's Transcendentalist terms, those limitations do not preclude seeking individual power on personal terms rather than based on society's expectations and definitions of power. He questions society's values from the perspective of individual development; for example, society sees wealth or beauty as sources of power, but Emerson approaches the topics not as external sources of power but as providing personal power as sources of "meaning" and knowledge: "Wealth is mental; wealth is moral." In Emerson's terms, wealth and beauty are spiritual rather than physical or economic values.

Likewise, culture, worship (or religious practice, which is antithetical to spirituality), and behavior are external values held by society and by which society judges individuals, but Emerson examines them instead as sources of alternative personal power. Emerson was concerned with the values and actions of his fellow citizens, but as he makes clear in the opening essay, "Fate," "we are incompetent to solve the times" and should focus instead on change within ourselves and on mapping our own lives. By 1860, when *The Conduct of Life* was published, Emerson had established a reputation as a radical in both theological and political issues. He rejected the dominant culture's views on religion, slavery, and most other issues; on the eve of the Civil War he had, like many Northerners, become convinced that political change was needed, but he was weary of efforts at institutional reform. *The Conduct of Life,* then, is not a call for social reform but a more optimistic call for spiritual reform of one's self; as he stated in "Fate," "the question of the times resolved itself into a practical question of the conduct of life. How shall I live?"

In this sense, then, *The Conduct of Life* seems to blend Emersonian self-reliance with HENRY DAVID THOREAU's call to "live deliberately" and a practical ethic of simple living, economy, hard work, and moral conscience as revealed in *Walden* and "Life without Principle." In some ways, Emerson's essays "Wealth" and "Culture," in particular, are a direct response to Thoreau's chapter titled "Economy" in *Walden,* and Emerson makes an explicitly similar appeal in "Culture," "to live coarsely, dress plainly, and lie hard." Like Thoreau, Emerson ultimately was concerned with the spiritual costs and implications of wealth, economy, worship, and other behaviors. The essays in *The Conduct of Life* each in some way address that concern.

FURTHER READING

Lopez, Michael. "*The Conduct of Life:* Emerson's Anatomy of Power." In *The Cambridge Companion to Ralph Waldo Emerson,* edited by Joel Porte and Saundra Morris, 243–366. New York: Cambridge University Press, 1999.

Robinson, David M. *Emerson and the Conduct of Life: Pragmatism and Ethical Purpose in the Later Work.* New York: Cambridge University Press, 1993.

"The Conservative" (1842)

"The Conservative" was delivered in BOSTON in December 1841 as part of the eight-lecture winter series "The Times." The essay was subsequently published in the *DIAL* (October 1842) and then later reprinted in *NATURE; ADDRESSES, AND LECTURES* (1849). After an "INTRODUCTORY LECTURE ON THE TIMES," "The Conservative" was the first lecture in the 1841 season, and one organized around the theme of different types or personalities, just as with "The POET," "The TRANSCENDENTALIST," "MAN THE REFORMER," "The YOUNG AMERICAN," "The AMERICAN SCHOLAR," and in his portraits in *REPRESENTATIVE MEN.* Throughout these works Emerson maintained that we should not hold the past up as a source of infallible truth but should be creating our own truths in the here and now; thus, his criticism of the conservative, who is "the upholder of the establishment."

As the biographer Gay Wilson Allen noted, and as current readers will surely agree, the essay serves as a reflection on and guide to "the slogans and positions of recent political campaigns." Of course, Emerson was not purely (or only) concerned with the actions of political parties. His larger Transcendentalist vision was to see these two opposing forces as representing different impulses in nature, indeed within each individual, and concluded that balance was needed. For, ultimately, when it comes to the question of "conservatism" versus "innovation," "in a true society, in a true man, both must combine."

SYNOPSIS

The state is divided into two parties, which Emerson terms "conservatism" and "innovation," but this is nothing new as these "have disputed the possession of the world ever since it was made. This quarrel is the subject of civil history." It is not only a "quarrel" between kings and nations and churches but a cultural and economic war, a struggle of applying "old usage and accommodation to new facts," and a conflict between "the rich and the poor." The cycle of history is such that "now one, now the other gets the day."

These two positions represent a conflict not particular to time or place but an "irreconcilable antagonism" throughout human history. Politics is only secondary, but the "opposition of Past and Future, of Memory and Hope, of the Understanding and the Reason" is eternal. Emerson recounts an "old fable" detailing the conflict between Saturn, who creates an oyster and, finding it satisfactory, focuses on only creating more oysters, while Uranus tires of oysters and calls for something new.

Saturn (the conservative) wishes to avoid "Night and Chaos," declaring, "I do what I have done; I hold what I have got." Uranus (the reformer) says change is inevitable, for the tide will come and the "pebbles and sea-foam" change the oysters. Emerson explains that "this may stand for the earliest account of a conversation on politics between a Conservative and a Radical. . . . Innovation is the salient energy; Conservatism the pause on the last movement."

Emerson declares: "There is always a certain meanness in the argument of conservatism, joined with a certain superiority of fact . . . Its fingers clutch the fact, and it will not open its eyes to see a better fact. The castle, which conservatism is set to defend, is the actual state of things, good and bad. The project of innovation is the best possible state of things." Conservatism resists change, and therefore must defend even "violence and vice." In this sense, conservatism focuses on "man's confessed limitations," while innovation or (Emerson now uses the term) "liberalism" focuses on possibility and "infinitude." Lastly, conservatism focuses on humans as members of *society*, while liberalism or reform focuses on the *individual:* "Conservatism goes for comfort, reform for truth."

Emerson is also critical of reform for its "antagonism," "egotism," and "hypocrisy." He characterizes these "metaphysical antagonists" as two parts of "an impossible whole." Nature gives its highest "approbation, namely, beauty," "to any action or emblem or actor . . . which combines these elements." Nature achieves balance through evolution, so that, "of all the ages, the present hour and circumstances is the cumulative result." And yet, men consider only "the nearest object," rather than "that which is best" about each side—namely, that conservatism "inspires reverence" for the "facts of universal experience," while reform "converses with possibilities."

Conservatism is limited in that it does not attempt to "transcend nature." For the conservative, "the existing world is not a dream . . . neither is it a disease," it is merely fact. The reformer's belief in "possibilities" is also a "sacred fact," however, and it matters not if their "schemes" are "feasible" or not. If it can be imagined, "it has life in it," and it is already true because it springs from "the powers of nature." The conservative's respect for the "ancestors" and tradition is a respect for history, for that which has worked in the past. In this sense, the reformer's viewpoint is "hypocrisy" because we all depend upon that past: "For as you cannot jump from the ground without using the resistance of the ground . . . so you are under the necessity of using the Actual order of things, in order to disuse it." The cycle of history is such that reform will lead to a "new" conservatism; there will always be "a jealousy of the newest." Each new generation will experiment with reform: "The youth, of course, is an innovator by the fact of his birth." We are born into an existing system of law and order, and then turn and question, "Is your law just?"

The reformer cannot accept the system of property that has "extended over the whole planet." Everything is claimed by "some man or corporation," and the reformer feels he was "*mis*sent to this earth, where all the seats were already taken." Emerson agrees that property ownership is a "disease" and a "lie," against the laws of nature: "Yonder sun in heaven you would pluck down from shining on the universe, and make him a property and privacy, if you could." The reformer criticizes this greed while the conservative praises "the industrious." It may be that not every individual owns property, but all have inherited the "substantial advantages" of "ancestral and national wealth."

Rather than focusing on "the supposed wrong which society has done you," the reformer should ask, instead, "how society got into this predicament." According to Emerson, "all men" are responsible for the state of society at any given time. Some may see society as "a foul compromise," but still every age manages to produce "many a poet, and prophet, and teacher of men." Neither the conservative nor the reformer gives enough credit to the individual: "The form is bad, but see you not how every personal character reacts on the form, and makes it new?" Conservatism concerns itself with a "cunning juggle in riches," when what humanity needs is "contemplation," "vigor," and "valor." Emerson turns, characteristically, to various figures in ancient and classical history for examples of these virtues, and even to "yonder peasant," who "carries a whole revolution of man and nature in his head, which shall be a sacred history to some future ages." Emerson pleads, "I want the necessity of supplying my own wants. All this costly culture of yours is not necessary. Greatness does not need it."

The problem with conservatism "when embodied in a party" is that "it hates principles." Conservatism prefers "acts" of "expediency" rather than "truth" or "right." The conservative accepts "sickness as a necessity" and only wishes to "organize" the sickness, not rid society of it: "Society has resolved itself into a Hospital Committee." Conservatism therefore takes a "low view of every part of human action and passion," and even "religion" becomes just another "lozenge for the sick." Religion and education are two important points for conservatism; they have "a market value" because through these the next generation is taught to be a part of the system, not challenge the system.

The final question is, "Which party on the whole has the highest claims on our sympathy?" Should we be among "the defenders of the old? or with the seekers of the new?" For Emerson, all questions lead back to the individual, as the answer is in "the private heart." He uses the analogy of war to explain the balance between positive and negative forces in society and in the individual; while war is destructive, it also brings forth "courage and resources." It is easy to say we "are honest men" when we are not tested. His question to both conservatives and reformers is, "How can your law further or hinder me in what I shall do to men?"

Having examined and criticized both viewpoints, Emerson ends in favor of reform or "innovation," which is a "hope" that "transcends all former experience." He emphasizes, however, that this hope comes not from "some celestial plant" (that is, it is not mere idealism) but from right "here on the wild crab of conservatism." We cannot completely disparage all that has come before, or those who would hang on to the old ways, because we have come from that same past. That idea alone is a source of hope because "it predicts that amidst a planet peopled with conservatives, one Reformer may yet be born."

CRITICAL COMMENTARY

In "The Conservative," Emerson laid out the theme for his entire series on "The Times"—that is, the relationship of the individual to society and of the present to this ongoing "opposition of Past and Future." As the conservative is an opposing force to the reformer, so Emerson introduces a host of binary forces or oppositions to characterize the times (all times) as an "irreconcilable antagonism" between "Memory and Hope," "Understanding and Reason," and "Fate" and "Wisdom." These antagonisms are featured throughout Emerson's Transcendentalism, for in determining our own character or nature, we are constantly pulled toward "two poles of nature."

Throughout his works, Emerson always sought to examine both sides of a question, so as to understand the natural laws behind the conflict or question. His idea of balance, or "COMPENSATION" (as explained in his 1841 essay), was that every force has an opposite and equal force in nature. To adhere too strongly to either position was an imbalance. Although he was clearly more critical of the conservative in this instance, for a too blind adherence to the past and traditions, here and elsewhere he was equally critical of the blind persistence and arrogance of the reformer.

The idealist (that is, the Transcendentalist) might disagree with the conservative that the world is not a dream, but would also surely disagree with the reformer that the world is diseased beyond repair. He challenges reformers—"You are welcome to try your experiments"—because any failure simply means that the experiment did not adhere to the laws of nature. Emerson's problem with reformers then is not their "hope" or their "innovation" but that they seek attention and reward rather than truth. This explains Emerson's point that to criticize the world is to criticize ourselves, for "the order of things is as good as the character of the population permits." He would make this same observation—that we are all implicated in the society we currently have, for better or worse—in his essays on reform, such as "Man the Reformer" (1841) and "NEW ENGLAND REFORMERS" (1844).

In "The Conservative," Emerson is particularly interested in the subject of religion, arguing that for the conservative, religion is only important as far as "tradition" and "a reliance on institutions" (which he harshly judges as "anything that will keep men amused, schools or churches . . . or what not") rather than a true spiritual endeavor. Religion itself, therefore, becomes degraded: "Religion among the low becomes low." This was a critique that formed the foundation of earlier works such as "The American Scholar" (1837) and the "DIVINITY SCHOOL ADDRESS" (1838).

"Courage" (1870)

Emerson first gave the lecture "Courage" in BOSTON in November 1859 in response to the abolitionist revolt of JOHN BROWN. Brown's small band had raided the federal weapons arsenal at Harpers Ferry, Virginia, on October 16, 1859; he was captured, tried, and quickly executed on December 2, 1859. Several Transcendentalists had conferred with Brown in the months prior to the rebellion, although Emerson did not personally know in advance of the Virginia plot. He delivered this lecture while Brown was under sentence, the first in a series of public lectures in defense of Brown, whom Emerson identified as "a new saint awaiting his martyrdom." HENRY DAVID THOREAU and other Transcendentalists also came forth to articulate the moral and religious significance of Brown's action.

In the next 11 years before its publication as an essay in *SOCIETY AND SOLITUDE* (1870), Emerson's original lecture underwent various revisions, eliminating specific references to, though still animated by his memory of, John Brown, while generalizing it into a larger philosophical tribute to courage.

SYNOPSIS

The essay begins by highlighting "three qualities which conspicuously attract the wonder and reverence of mankind." The first of these is "disinterestedness," or an ability to rise above "the ordinary bribes and influences of conduct." The second quality is "practical power," exemplified in the man of action who "argues down that adversary, moulds society to his purpose, and looks at all men as wax for his hands, takes command of them as the wind does of clouds." The third quality or "excellence" we admire is "courage," defined by Emerson as "the perfect will, which no terrors can shake, which is attracted by frowns or threats or hostile armies, nay, needs these to awake and fan its reserved energies into a pure flame." History affords only rare examples of this "pure article": "courage with eyes, courage with conduct, self-possession at the cannon's mouth, cheerfulness in lonely adherence to the right, is the endowment of elevated characters."

People praise courage through metaphors, likening "valor" to the strength of "lions, leopards, eagles and dragons." In actual fact, Emerson goes on to observe, man is a puny animal who "begins life helpless" in his mother's arms and gradually experiences "the terrors" of childhood and adult age. Modern man is protected by the "routine of safe industry," rarely called to the "rough experiences" required of "the Indian, the soldier, or the frontiersman." The result is that "we have no readiness for bad times." This was evident, Emerson notes, in "the late war" (the Civil War) in which "tender, amiable boys, who had never encountered any rougher play than a baseball match or a fishing excursion, were suddenly drawn up to face a bayonet charge or capture a battery."

Worse than this "pacific education" is the "cowardice" and "fear" society breeds. People retreat to the "protection" of "a house, a family, neighborhood and property." In reference to politics (and in an oblique reference to the execution of John Brown), he explains that society breeds "cowardice," which "shuts the eyes so that we cannot see the horse that is running away with us; worse, shuts the eyes of the mind and chills the heart." "Fear" and conformity create a situation in which "society is upside down, and its best men are thought too bad to live." Some of them, of course, proved courageous in spite of their poor preparation and upbringing.

"Knowledge, Use and Reason" can generally be regarded as "the antidote to fear" and cowardice. From childhood on, a person is presented with dangers, but "each surmounts the fear as fast as he precisely understands the peril, and learns the means of resistance." It is "knowledge that takes fear out of the heart . . . and use, which is knowledge in practice." It is our minds, our character, that create the situation, more than the circumstances. Just as "terror" is merely "ignorance surrendered to the imagination," so it is "they can conquer who believe they can." Whether it is "the veteran soldier," the "sailor," or the "hunter," each shows courage in the case of danger, because they have the confidence of experience—to a sailor, "a leak, a hurricane, or a waterspout is so much work, no more."

Courage, then, is nothing more than self-trust; it "consists in the conviction that the agents with whom you contend are not superior in strength or resources or spirit to you." It is "the right or healthy state of every man, when he is free to do that which is constitutional to him to do. It is . . . the instant performing of that which he ought." Courage is not confined to few actions or professions, but it is required in a variety of circumstances: "There is a courage of the cabinet as well as a courage of the field . . . a courage which enables one man to speak masterly to a hostile company, whilst another man who can easily face a cannon's mouth dares not open his own." Genius in any instance involves courage, and it is shown by "a master in architecture, in sculpture, in painting, or in poetry," or in "the beautiful voice at church [that] goes sounding on, and covers up in its volume, as in a cloak, all the defects of the choir."

He again directly memorializes "Captain John Brown, the hero of Kansas," who once said to Emerson that "for a settler in a new country, one good, believing, strong-minded man is worth a hundred, nay, a thousand men without character; and that the right men will give a permanent direction to the fortunes of a state." He reports that Brown believed that courage comes from conviction, that "'Tis the quiet, peaceable men, the men of principle, that make the best soldiers." The importance of someone like Brown is that courage is a "contagion": "Poetry and Eloquence catch the hint, and soar to a pitch unknown before." Even the men who arrested Brown now "ask leave to pay their respects to the prisoner." Everyone is moved by "the new breath" of courage, "except the old doting, nigh-dead politicians, whose heart the trumpet of resurrection could not wake." Emerson returns to the instinctive quality of courage, noting that "the charm of the best courages is that they are inventions, inspirations, flashes of geniuses." They are not out of character, though they may be out of place.

Again he makes reference to the martyrdom of John Brown: "A great aim aggrandizes the means. There is a persuasion in the soul of man that he is here for cause, that he was put down in this place by the Creator to do the work for which he inspires him, that thus he is an overmatch for all antagonists that could combine against him." Religious or spiritual courage, such as shown by Brown, "is always new, leads and surprises, and practice never comes up with it." He gives several other examples from the history of individuals who chose to endure "poverty, the prison, the rack, the fire, the hatred and execrations of our fellow men" for "a freedom that is ideal." The religious martyr (and he includes here Jesus, Paul, the Quakers, and the Puritan "Mrs. Hutchinson") is courageous because "he wishes to break every yoke all over the world which hinders his brother from acting after his own thought."

Emerson ends "Courage" with a series of observations that lie at the heart of his philosophy: "If you have no faith in beneficent power above you, but see only an adamantine fate coiling its folds about Nature and man, then reflect that the best use of fate is to teach us courage, if only because baseness cannot change the appointed fate." On the other hand, "if you accept your thoughts as inspirations from the Supreme Intelligence, obey them when they prescribe difficult duties, because they come only so long as they are used." Finally, if yours is an extreme skepticism, "then be brave, for there is one good opinion which must always be of consequence to you, namely, your own."

CRITICAL COMMENTARY

Emerson's essay ends on this note of having the courage of one's own convictions. He reprises his ethics of self-reliance, here specifically in reference to the moral heroism of John Brown and his small band, who sacrificed their lives to the cause of "the secular melioration of the planet." In both "SELF-RELIANCE" and "The OVER-SOUL," companion pieces from the earlier *ESSAYS: FIRST SERIES* (1841), he provided the ethical and metaphysical parameters in which he now memorializes Brown in this essay of 1870. Such later essays as "CIVILIZATION" (also in *Society and Solitude*) and "Progress of Culture" (in *LETTERS AND SOCIAL AIMS* [1876]) articulate variations on this theme, while continuing the theme of the binary or oppositional forces is addressed in "FATE" and "POWER," the key essays in *The CONDUCT OF LIFE* (1860).

The essay on "Courage" plays out these themes with particular emphasis on the instinctive force of moral valor and its affinity with the upward path of human history. A lament for the fate of Emerson's contemporary and personal acquaintance, John Brown, "Courage" also resonates with the affirmative conclusion of "THRENODY," Emerson's poem on the death of his young son Waldo, which ends with the sentiment of "the genius of the whole, / Ascendant in the private soul." In a more general sense, here he considers John Brown as hero and comes to the same conclusions he found in *REPRESENTATIVE MEN* (1850) and, specifically, in "USES OF GREAT MEN" (and even earlier in "HEROISM"); namely, that courage is not a special circumstance or "essence" that only some men are born with but is "the right or healthy state of every man, when he is free to do that which is constitutional to him to do. It is . . . the instant performing of that which he ought." Indeed, in "Courage," John Brown lurks as the "representative" reformer, or martyr. As with courage, wisdom is also a "contagion," and Emerson uses the same language in "Uses of Great Men": "There needs but one wise man in a company, and all are wise, so rapid is the contagion." We are inspired by the possibilities and actions of others to be wise or courageous ourselves.

David A. Dilworth

"Culture" (1860)

The poem "Culture" asks the question, "Can rulers or tutors" instruct us to recognize the "semigod" we await? For Emerson, the answer is no—we must be able to recognize the emissary of divine spirit intuitively. There should be within us a harmony with nature that allows us to perceive (from within) the divine without being "instructed" from the outside. The poem also offers the qualities necessary to perceive this "semigod" (and perhaps the qualities of the semigod itself), one who can recast the world in his own "mold." In the essay "The POET" (1844) this is a quality of the ideal poet Emerson regularly calls for: The poet forms the world to his mind, as opposed to forming his mind in response to the world. This suggests that truth is fundamental and perceivable intuitively, and that all humans have this in common. The poem is the motto for the essay "CULTURE" in *The CONDUCT OF LIFE* (1860) and was collected in *MAY-DAY AND OTHER PIECES* (1867) and *Poems* (1884).

CRITICAL COMMENTARY

The poem opens with a regular, rhymed couplet, asking a simple question: "Can rules or tutors educate / The semigod whom we await?" The couplet is set in iambic tetrameter, an ordered, regular verse form that Emerson often used. The verses that follow, however, are far from formalized. The remaining nine lines offer no set rhyme scheme or metrical pattern (though the last three lines form a rhymed tercet, and the grammatical break at the end of line eight serves to isolate the last three lines). In terms of form, the poem is broken into three sections: the opening couplet, followed by six irregular lines of description, summarized by a rhymed tercet that offers the basic quality of both perceiver of the semigod and the semigod itself.

This poem especially benefits from reading aloud in order to discern the more subtle rhythmic patterns present in the lines. For example, lines 5 to 8 might be read as hymn stanza (alternating lines of iambic tetrameter and trimeter). Emerson calls for us to be "musical"; if we are, we can recognize the subtlety of the rhythm, and sounds, in the lines. The *m* sounds in lines 3 and 4 offer a rolling rhythmic feel to these unmeasured, but not wholly irregular, lines ("He must be musical / Tremulous, impressional"). Also, the *f* sounds in line 10 ("Shall into Future fuse the Past") make this line a bit difficult to read, suggesting that the fusion of future into past will be a trial met only by the most intuitive poet (or reader). This is "gentle influence" indeed.

The closing tercet offers a familiar Emerson theme: The poet recasts the world according to his mind (the poet alone is capable of devising images to fit his unique perception of the world, while communicating that perception to everyone else), and the poet speaks the world into existence. This is the fusing of future into past, a view of the world that exists outside of time and outside of determinism, and speaks to a truth that we will recognize as truth—if we meet the qualifications set down by the poem.

Bill Scalia

"Culture" (1860)

Along with "POWER" and "WEALTH," the essay on "Culture" adds another angle to Emerson's many-sided configuration of human strengths and potential in *The* CONDUCT OF LIFE (1860). His polarity logic, ethics of self-reliance, and robust sense of affirmative life combine with acute observation of the actual affairs and manners of men. As usual, despite its local color, it reveals Emerson not as a sociologist or historian but as a philosopher of nature and man. The essay ranges from the topic of the moderating influence of culture on the inborn egotism of men to a consideration of the preeminence of education over politics, and from there to contrasting benefits of city and country environments for the soul's well-being. It also encompasses the theme of traveling, this time in a balanced account of its cultural effects. All the while it moves toward its culminating theme of nature aspiring to expression in the higher attainments of human culture, a theme he would return to in "CIVILIZATION" in *SOCIETY AND SOLITUDE* (1870) and in "Progress of Culture" in *LETTERS AND SOCIAL AIMS* (1876).

SYNOPSIS

Emerson begins "Culture" with a sustained critique of "egotism," which he notes is the inevitable effect of a "dominant talent." Such an egotism is inborn, nature's way of setting each individual uniquely in motion. Like sexual attraction, "nature has secured it against all hazards by immensely overloading the passion, at the risk of perpetual crime and disorder. So egotism has its roots in the cardinal necessity by which each individual persists to be that he is." The work of culture is to correct "this theory of success." It "reduces the inflammations of egotism by invoking the aid of other powers against the dominant talent, and by appealing to the rank of powers."

Culture works to produce a universality of outlook and a harmony of interests. And yet the majority of men remain "afflicted with a coldness and an incuriosity as soon as any object presents itself that is not connected with their self-love" or their own all too narrow and ephemeral "vital interests" and "causes"—such as "Tariff or Democracy, Whigism or Abolition, Temperance or Socialism." Such self-centered "illusions" are numerous (as he will also tell in the essay "ILLUSIONS" in the same volume). Culture is the "antidote" to such blinkered vision, working through "acquaintance with the world, with men of merit, with classes of society, with travel, with eminent persons, and with the high resources of philosophy, art, and religion: books, travel, society, solitude."

"Books, travel, society, solitude" provides an outline for the rest of the essay. Book learning enlarges a man's mind, in contrast to the run of "people who can never understand a trope, or any second or expanded sense given to your words, or any humor; but remain literalists." In this context he distinguishes education from politics, the latter "an after-work," "a poor patching," an attempt to remedy and repeal what should not have been enacted in the first place. Books or education, on the other hand, expand culture by putting at our disposal "the finest records" of human intelligence: "The best heads that ever existed, Pericles, Plato, Julius Caesar, Shakspeare, Goethe, Milton, were well-read, universally educated men, and quite too wise to undervalue letters." He says he is always happy to meet a man who recognizes the worth of Shakespeare or of Plato. The reason is that "this love does not consist with self-conceit."

He goes on to consider the pros and cons of traveling. The "restlessness" that takes the form of

Americans touring Europe takes its usual hit here. He is on the same page as Horace, who noted that *coelum non animam mutat qui transit mare currit:* A person brings his soul with him when he travels the broad ocean. Emerson says, "What is true anywhere is true everywhere. And let him go where he will, he can only find so much beauty or worth as he carries." But on the reverse side of this coin, there are some men who benefit from travel, and this consideration belongs to a just review of the possibilities of culture's benefits.

For example, by traveling we learn that "naturalists, discoverers, and sailors" are born to be such, while others are made to be "couriers, exchangers, envoys, missionaries, bearers of dispatches, or farmers and working-men." A sense of the wider world and varieties of men is provided in this way, and such a sense "is synonymous with all men's ideas of advantage and superiority." So it is that "a foreign country is a point of comparison, wherefrom to judge his own." Even at home, there is an aesthetic value to riding the railroads, which is "to unite the advantages of town and country life, neither of which we can spare" in a cultured outlook on life.

This preeminently 19th-century sense of enlarged experience by rail travel now becomes the segue for Emerson's comparison of the advantages of town and country life. In the city, he observes, there are "the swimming-schools, gymnasia, shooting-galleries, the opera, theatre, and panorama; the chemist's shops, the museum of natural history, the gallery of fine arts; the national orators, foreign travellers, the libraries, and his club." In the country, he can find "solitude and reading, manly labor, cheap living, and old shoes, moors for game, hills for geology, and groves for devotion." This is offset by "the want of good conversation," which is a positive aspect of culture. In the cities there is the stimulation of numbers, of the variety of "well-informed and superior people," who "keep each other up to any high point." "Especially women," Emerson adds, thrive on the cultural and social refinements afforded by the cities. But on the other side of the ledger, "cities degrade by magnifying trifles" and "petty comforts." The city dweller "has lost the lines of grandeur of the horizon, hills and plains, and with them, sobriety and elevation." In the city, "life is dragged down to a fracas of pitiful cares and disasters."

Emerson is critical of egotism and self-pity, here associated one-sidedly with city folk "who live to dine, who send for the doctor, who coddle and comfort themselves" in countless artifices: "Let these triflers put us out of conceit with petty comforts. To a man at work, the frost is but a color: the rain, the wind, he forgot them when he came in. Let us learn to live coarsely, dress plainly, and lie hard." So while "we can ill spare the commanding social benefits of cities," we must use them "cautiously." They will "yield their best values to him who can do without them. Keep the town for occasions, but the habits should be formed to retirement." Solitude (such as found in country living) is "the safeguard of mediocrity." "'In the morning—solitude;' said Pythagoras; that Nature may speak to the imagination, as she does never in company." He continues, "'Tis very certain that Plato, Plotinus, Archimedes, Hermes, Newton, Milton, Wordsworth, did not live in a crowd, but descended into it from time to time as benefactors."

Transcendentalist "periods and habits of solitude" are for Emerson the key to expansiveness of thought, and to the heights of the spiritual life of "the saint and poet." The latter are the exemplars of culture that most decisively modulate the shrill tones of egocentrism. But all the representative men of history manifest an intellectual quality in their outlook and in their action and for them "culture opens the sense of beauty." "A man is a beggar who only lives for the useful, and, however he may serve as a pin or rivet in the social machine, cannot be said to have arrived at self-possession. I suffer, every day, from the want of perception of beauty in people."

In the end, Emerson sets these thoughts on civilization within the framework of progressive evolution: "The fossil strata show us that Nature began with rudimental forms and rose to the more complex as fast as the earth was fit for their dwelling-place." He concludes that, "if one shall read the future of the race hinted in the organic effort of Nature to mount and meliorate, and the corresponding impulse to the Better in the human being, we shall dare affirm that there is nothing he will not overcome and convert, until at last culture shall absorb the chaos and gehenna. He will convert the Furies into Muses, and the hells into benefit."

CRITICAL COMMENTARY

The last-cited are the final words of the essay, which has ranged freely through general themes of the growth of the civilized mind that overcomes the narrowness of egotistic success, has endorsed the advantages of education through book learning and travel, and has considered the combined benefits of city and country living. In all this, Emerson combines his original ethics of the self-reliant individual with his polarity logic to frame a more comprehensive view of the powers and possibilities of human progress. Emerson was to ring further changes on this theme in two later essays, "Civilization" (in *Society and Solitude* [1870]) and "Progress of Culture" (in *Letters and Social Aims* [1876]).

In "POETRY AND IMAGINATION" (also published in *Letters and Social Aims*), he placed these considerations of cultural progress in the framework of his two metaphysical laws, identity and metamorphosis, and their attendant concept of the affinity of the human mind and nature's laws. He identified two forms of nature's metamorphosis or growth—"arrested" and "progressive." Arrested growth consists of the myriad of repetitions of nature along the horizontal axis of physical, chemical, vegetative, and animal (including human) processes. Progressive growth occurs on a vertical axis of evolutionary development, as exhibited by the advances in the paleontological records in the growth of the individual human mind. "Culture" and the other essays in *The Conduct of Life* exhibit a metaphysical framework that increasingly occupied his attention in his later-phase lectures and writings. In the *NATURAL HISTORY OF INTELLECT* (which began as a lecture in 1870, but was published posthumously in 1893), Emerson again celebrated the twin trajectories of the creative human imagination—namely poetry and science—as the open-ended agents of cultural progress.

David A. Dilworth

"Days" (1857)

"Days" was published (along with the poem "BRAHMA") in the very first issue of the *ATLANTIC MONTHLY* (November 1857) and was collected in *MAY-DAY AND OTHER PIECES* (1867) and *SELECTED POEMS* (1876). The poem was also included at the beginning of the essay "WORKS AND DAYS" in his 1870 collection, *SOCIETY AND SOLITUDE*. In "Days" Emerson reflected upon the passage of time, focusing on the smaller unit of the day rather than the seasons or the years that he did in other writings, such as the poem "TERMINUS," which looks at the span of an entire lifetime. As early as 1826, Emerson had recorded lines in his journal that showed his anxiety about making the best use of time: "My days roll by me like a train of dreams / A host of joyless undistinguished forms." Again, in 1847, he penned prose lines that would bear even more directly on the theme and language of the final poem: "The days come & go like muffled & veiled figures sent from a distant friendly party, but they say nothing, & if we do not use the gifts they bring, they carry them as silently away."

CRITICAL COMMENTARY

The 11-line poem is short, like a day itself, and yet Emerson acknowledges the immense gift contained in a single day, a gift of nature offered equally to each person. The challenge is to take the gift and to make each day count. The first line of the poem declares that the days are "hypocritic," that is, they make promises of unlimited potential but then are limited themselves. The days are "Daughters of Time," personified as female, with a mind and will of their own, but subordinate to (a smaller unit of) a larger sense of time. "Muffled and dumb," the days do not speak, but still they tease us with their possibilities. One of the ways the days trick us is by coming only one at a time, "marching single in an endless file." Their seemingly "endless file" lures us into the sense of the unlimited, while their "marching single" reveals the limits of a specific unit of time. The days "offer gifts" of nature in food from the "garden," "stars," and "sky." But it is up to the individual, each "after his will," to accept the gifts and to be active in our relationship with and use of the days.

In the second half of the poem (beginning with line 7), the poet appears. In the face of this bounty of the day that has just been described sits the poet, passively watching "the pomp" of nature's gifts from a distance. Rather than rush to accept these gifts of nature, of "kingdoms" and "sky," he sits in his "pleached garden," a shaded and protected domestic space that is less a sanctuary in this poem and more a confinement. Having begun the day with unlimited possibilities, he forgets all of the "morning wishes" or plans he had made and never ventures beyond that which is right in front of him, taking only "a few herbs and apples" rather than the "kingdoms" and "sky" offered to him.

Domestic concerns, especially, threatened interference with the best use of days, a theme that appears regularly in Emerson's writings. The poet-philosopher struggled with the use of the days and with maintaining a satisfactory level of productivity and appreciation as the days sped by. As the biographer Robert Richardson observed, "Emerson was haunted for most of his life by the sense that the days were slipping past him, one by one, in an irrevocable procession. He seldom thought he had made the fullest possible use of a day. He recorded the thought over and over, sometimes in verse, sometimes in prose."

In the end, "Days" is a reflection on the human dilemma of the passage of time, of the limited number of days available to us, but the call is still made to the individual to take charge, to exert "his will" over this inevitability. He expressed a similar idea in the essay "EXPERIENCE" (1844): "All our days are so unprofitable while they pass that 'tis wonderful where or when we ever got anything of this which we call wisdom, poetry, virtue. . . . Our life looks trivial and we shun to record it. . . . 'Tis the trick of nature thus to degrade to-day." Repeating the language of "muffled" days from the poem, in the essay on "Works and Days" (1870), he again reflected, "He only is rich who owns the day. . . . [The days] are of the least pre-tension and of the greatest capacity of anything that exists. They come and go like muffled and veiled figures, sent from a distant friendly party; but they say nothing, and if we do not use the gifts they bring, they carry them as silently away." In the poem, too soon "the Day / Turned and departed silent" and it is "too late" to take advantage of what that particular day, which will never appear again, had to offer. With little to show for the gift of time he had been given, even the day itself, in the last line of the poem, is full of "scorn," which has no match in the scorn the poet has for himself.

"Dirge" (1845)

In a letter written in 1844 before its first publication, Emerson explained that the poem "Dirge" "was composed or rather hummed by me one afternoon, years ago, as I walked in the woods & on the narrow plain through which our Concord River flows, not far from my grandfather's house, and remembered my brothers Edward & Charles. . . . At the time of this walk, I was thirty-five years old." First published in *The Gift,* an anthology of contemporary writers, in 1845, "Dirge" was included in both of Emerson's poetry collections, POEMS (1847) and SELECTED POEMS (1876). It was originally drafted in 1838; he added stanzas 1 and 2 between 1840 and 1844.

CRITICAL COMMENTARY

Stanza 1, which begins with the line "I reached the middle of the mount / Up which the incarnate soul must climb," recalls the opening lines of Dante's *Inferno: "Nel mezzo del cammin di nostra vita."* At this time in his life the poet "looked around" to those "with me who walked through space and time"; that is, his family of origin. In stanza 2, which begins with "Five rosy boys with morning light / Had leaped from one fair mother's arms," he memorializes his five brothers, John Clarke, WILLIAM EMERSON, EDWARD BLISS EMERSON, ROBERT BULKELEY EMERSON, and CHARLES CHAUNCY EMERSON; Emerson also had two sisters, both of whom died in infancy. Waldo had no clear memory of his oldest brother, John Clarke, who died at an early age; the "five rosy boys" of the poem more likely refer to himself and the four brothers he grew up with. Of these, Robert Bulkeley remained childish through life, and his two younger brothers, Edward and Charles, were both lost "in their prime": Edward died in 1834, and Charles two years later.

A precedent to his later poem "THRENODY," which lamented the death of his five-year-old son Waldo in 1842, "Dirge" of 1838 begins with the scene of Emerson wandering through a "lonely field" replete with the ghostly memory of his boyhood days when he played there with Edward and Charles. He eulogizes their memory in affecting words: "But they are gone,—the holy ones / Who trod with me this lovely vale; / The strong, star-bright companions / Are silent, low, and pale." Together there the brothers learned "the lore of time," as they "took this valley for their toy." Together as children the brothers had a direct connection to nature: "They coloured the horizon round; / Stars flamed and faded as they bade; / all echoes hearkened for their sound,— / They made the woodlands glad or mad." Emerson then hearkens to the "heavy tale divine" of a pine-warbler, who tells him that his two brothers "loved thee from their birth; / Their hands were pure, and pure their faith,— / There are no such hearts on earth." It is a unique individual experience of family—now remembrances of a "lonely man"—and yet tied to and acknowledged by nature in the form of the songbird. All three brothers, it goes on to sing, "drew one mother's milk," and they shared "a very tender history." Now, these sweet memories are gone with them; invoking a funeral, "the silent organ" of his own heart "loudest chants" this "requiem" of them.

David A. Dilworth

"Divinity School Address" (1838)

On July 15, 1838, Emerson presented *An Address Delivered Before the Senior Class in Divinity College, Cambridge* (1838), also known as the "Divinity School Address." In the speech, Emerson questioned the very foundations of Christian belief, the divinity of Christ, the role of the ministry, and indeed the necessity and desirability of theological education such as those the graduates had just received at HARVARD COLLEGE. The address sparked a round of harsh criticisms in the press that surprised Emerson, but to which he did not publicly respond. Many friends and colleagues publicly defended Emerson and his ideas, but by this time many Transcendentalists had made their own break from UNITARIANISM and from Harvard; Emerson did not speak again at Harvard until after the Civil War. The speech was immediately published as a pamphlet and was printed in England in 1844; it was included in the later collection, *NATURE; ADDRESSES, AND LECTURES* (1849).

SYNOPSIS

The opening lines of the address are a celebration of nature, of nature's bounty, and of life, including the famous first line, "In this refulgent summer, it has been a luxury to draw the breath of life." Emerson sets up his intention to draw inspiration not from religion but from living nature, where "the grass grows, the buds burst [and] The air is full of birds." Nature is the "mystery" (not God), the "stars" are "spiritual rays," "Man" is a "young child," and "his huge globe a toy." After laying out this extrasensory feast of nature, "one is constrained to respect the perfection of this world, in which our senses converse." No mention by name is made of God as the Creator, and so the implication is that nature is responsible for the "fruitful soils," the "navigable sea," the "mountains of metal and stone," the "forests," and "animals," as well as "the powers and path of light, heat, attraction, and life."

Emerson asks how are we are to understand this mystery. Again, there is not yet any direct mention of religion as a route to understanding, but instead "the mind opens, and reveals the laws which traverse the universe, and make things what they are." Knowledge, even of the deepest mysteries of nature, exists in the human mind. Nature's mysteries are not unknowable but only limited by our own minds and our lack of adequate time: "I would study, I would know, I would admire forever." It is this knowledge quest, this "human spirit in all ages," that is the tradition that Emerson honors, offering an alternative to religious tradition. This is our purpose in life, and we come to it either through "innocency" (that is, a childlike state) or through "intellectual perception."

Emerson defines "virtue" itself as "a reverence and delight in the presence of certain divine laws." It is the belief that life is not random, is not "foolish details," but is made up of "principles that astonish." These principles come from nature and "will not be written out on paper, or spoken by the tongue"; that is, are not found in religious texts or sermons. Likewise, "moral sentiment is an insight of the perfection of the laws of the soul." Again, this is very different from religious belief that understands morality as an outward motivation, obeying the law of God. Emerson explains instead an inward motivation that comes from the laws of nature. Morality, in this sense, is only acting according to nature's own system of rewards or punishments: "He who does a good deed, is instantly ennobled. He who does a mean deed, is by the action itself contracted."

This, Emerson explains, is the "intrinsic energy" in the universe, nature's way of "righting wrongs, correcting appearances, and bringing up facts to a harmony with thoughts." Thus, the law of the soul "becomes the law of society. . . . Thus of their own volition, souls proceed into heaven, into hell." Emerson offers here a radical reworking of the Christian concept of obedience and reward, of punishment and sin: "The perception of this law of laws awakens in the mind a sentiment which we call the religious sentiment, and which makes our highest happiness." While what he terms "religious sentiment" is divine, we must be careful of "deifying" it by locating it as something outside of ourselves. Deification leads to "worship" or "veneration," which leads to "superstition" and "sensuality." This desire for a sensual experience of religion is why Jesus is such an intriguing and necessary figure for so many people.

This law of moral sentiment is not embodied but is "an intuition. It cannot be received at second hand." He can only accept what "I must find true in me," not what someone else merely "announces." Once "the divine nature" is "attributed to one or two persons" (for example, Jesus), the human spirit becomes only as "an appendage" to the idea, rather than the idea itself. For Emerson, it is the "*indwelling* Supreme Spirit" within each man that must be worshipped: "Miracles, prophecy, poetry; the ideal life, the holy life, exist as ancient history merely."

The history of religion, specifically the history of the Christian church, provides many examples of what has been lost. He makes an appeal to the graduates, as new ministers, who are "now setting forth to teach." Christianity is of "great historical interest" because it is "the Cultus, or established worship of the civilized world." But the minister's task is not to teach this history as "the consolation of humanity" but of "pointing out two errors in its administration." He concedes that "Jesus Christ belonged to the true race of prophets": "Alone in history, he estimated that greatness of man" by understanding "that God incarnates himself in man." Unfortunately, this message has suffered from "distortion" ever since his time. Ministers and "churches" are more interested in "tropes" than in the "principles" and "truth" of his message. Jesus was only interested in "the law in us," not outward laws. For Emerson, Jesus was "a true man . . . the only soul in history who has appreciated the worth of a man."

Emerson returns to his points on the "defects of historical Christianity." The first problem is that it "corrupts all attempts to communicate religion." Christianity depends upon "ritual" more than "the doctrine of the soul." The church is built on "indolence and fear" and insists that "you must subordinate your nature to Christ's nature" and "accept our interpretations" rather than your own. Emerson, on the other hand, implores his listeners only to "obey thyself." In Christianity, "there is no longer a necessary reason for my being." He rejects "the divine bards" (that is, the writers and poets of the Bible) who "admonish me, that the gleams which flash across my mind, are not mine, but God's."

It seems "noble" that the Bible encourages us "to resist evil; to subdue the world," but this is not enough and is, in fact, harmful: "To aim to convert a man by miracles, is a profanation of the soul." Emerson appeals to the new ministers with his criteria for all great teachers or great men: "It is a low benefit to give me something; it is a high benefit to enable me to do somewhat of myself." The "vulgar tone of preaching" is an "injustice" to Jesus as well as to "the souls" one is trying to save.

"The second defect" of Christianity as it is taught is that "men have come to speak of the revelation as somewhat long ago given and done, as if God were dead." "Revelations," like "miracles," are spiritual concepts that are taught as historical events. Revelation is not, therefore, something that can be taught "from doctrines or books" but must come "through the soul." The preacher, in this sense, is up against "the spiritual limitation of the office." "The soul is not preached," and it is indeed "criminal" for anyone to try. Still, there is a need and role for ministers: "Preaching is the expression of the moral sentiment in application to the duties of life." The preacher may be a guide to practical questions, but it is not in churches that man is "made sensible that he is an infinite Soul; that the earth and heavens are passing into his mind." This understanding comes not from the words of the preacher but from nature, where "faith should blend with the light of rising and of setting suns, with the flying cloud, the singing bird, and the breath of flowers."

We go to church and we hear prayers, "which do not uplift, but smite and offend us." Emerson recounts attending church one winter day and being drawn to the outside scene in nature rather than the words of the preacher: "The snow storm was real; the preacher merely spectral." Nothing about the preacher or what he said was inspiring or connected to real life: "If he had ever lived and acted, we were none the wiser for it." Emerson urges these future preachers to bring themselves to the pulpit, to relate their faith to their own "experience," "to convert life into truth." Otherwise, he wonders why people should come to church at all: "It seemed as if their houses were very unentertaining, that they should prefer this thoughtless clamor."

Still, the listener may benefit even if the preacher is bad, because "there is poetic truth concealed in all the commonplaces of prayer and of sermons, and though foolishly spoken, they may be wisely heard." Most sermons contain ideas, but, unfortunately, those ideas are rarely made relevant to "the life and business of the people." Again, he reiterates that he does not entirely blame the preacher: "I know and honor the purity and strict conscience of numbers of the clergy." The problem is that even those good men rely upon a tradition "of the memory, and not out of the soul," upon the "usual" rather than the "necessary and eternal." For these reasons, fewer people go to church anymore, and Emerson sees this "loss of worship" as a tragedy. When "the eye of youth is not lighted by the hope of other worlds," then everything is affected: "Literature becomes frivolous. Science is cold . . . and when men die, we do not mention them."

Emerson's solution is that "redemption" is found in the soul, religion is found in humans: "Man is the wonderworker." Christianity is built upon a "falsehood," the idea "that the Bible is closed," out of "fear of degrading the character of Jesus by representing him as a man." God did not speak in the past, he speaks *now*. Religion is public and social, it relies upon "secondary knowledge, as St. Paul's, or George Fox's, or Swedenborg's," whereas God speaks directly to individuals through the soul.

Emerson then arrives at his recommendations: "Let me admonish you, first of all, to go alone . . . dare to love God without mediator or veil." His appeal to new preachers, especially, is to "cast behind you all conformity, and acquaint men at first hand with Deity." Do not be too concerned with tradition or duties, but be to your listeners yourself "a divine man; be to them thought and virtue." Be a preacher who inspires and draws out, rather than lectures. It does not matter how society measures or judges your position—"Society's praise can be cheaply secured"—it only matters your effect on others. "Influence" is greater than "fame." The "influx of the all-knowing Spirit" cannot be measured by human terms, and "the little shades and gradations of intelligence" that we call "wiser and wisest" are meaningless terms.

Having laid out the "evils of the church," the solution is clearly not just to create another church "with new rites and forms"; "Rather let the breath of new life be breathed by you through the forms already existing." Emerson may have rejected the church, but he does not expect these new preachers to leave the church. They can and should reinvigorate it with "new love, new faith, new sight." He identifies "the remedy" as "first, soul, and second, soul, and evermore, soul." Indeed, there are still some "inestimable advantages" to Christianity as a form, such as the setting aside of a "Sabbath, the jubilee of the whole world" as a time for acknowledging the spiritual. Indeed, even "the institution of preaching" is worth preserving, for "the speech of man to men" can be used to convey "the very truth, as your life and conscience teach it." He seeks only "the new Teacher" who can connect the "immortal sentences" of spiritual teachings to modern life and connects the laws of nature with the soul.

CRITICAL COMMENTARY

The "Divinity School Address" expanded upon many ideas Emerson had first introduced in *NATURE* two years earlier; namely, belief in a direct personal connection between the individual and God or nature. In this address before the graduating class of newly trained ministers, however, Emerson now singled out religion as an obstacle to, rather than facilitator of, this relationship. The address propelled Emerson and the new Transcendentalist movement into a public controversy and signaled the final step in his own break from both the church and Harvard. That break had begun several years earlier when Emerson resigned from the ministry after feeling that he could not, in good conscience, expect his congregants to participate in the ritual of the Lord's Supper (the topic of his 1832 sermon "The LORD'S SUPPER," that served as his resignation from the ministry and introduced many of the ideas he would expand upon for the "Divinity School Address"). Emerson felt that partaking of the Lord's Supper (or communion, in which congregants sample unleavened bread and wine or juice that represent, respectively, Christ's body and blood) was merely a tradition, devoid of any personal spiritual meaning to the participants.

In the intervening years, between his resignation in 1832 and the "Divinity School Address" in 1838, the conservative Unitarian establishment had engaged in a very public debate with Emerson and other Transcendentalists over the divinity of Christ and the proof (or lack of) for the miracles Christ performed in the New Testament. Emerson had been accused of atheism with the publication of *Nature* in 1836 (in which he called for "religion by revelation to us"), and other Transcendentalists had formulated public critiques of and broken ties with Unitarianism. Emerson's reputation, therefore, preceded him, and the Harvard graduates knew he was a controversial figure when they invited him to speak in 1838. Still, Harvard's divinity school was not quite prepared for his direct attack on not only Unitarianism but also Christianity in general and, indeed, Emerson's rejection of the need for ministers. Realizing that Emerson did not work alone, however, and was representative of a new current of thought, nine days after the speech ANDREWS NORTON published a condemnation of "The New School in Literature and Religion," which in turn prompted supporters and critics alike to join the debate. Emerson seemed surprised by and lamented the controversy in his journals and, ultimately, referred to it indirectly in the poem "URIEL," a parable of a fallen angel, cast out by the elite but ever-confident in his own self and ideas.

The "Divinity School Address" is, first and foremost, a radical plea for a spiritual life not dependent on organized religion. Throughout his writings, Emerson was willing to preserve the message of Christianity, just not the form. In Emerson's view, Jesus was a model of the Transcendentalist individual: "I am divine. Through me, God acts; through me, speaks. Would you see God, see me." The church taught the greatness of Jesus, rather than the greatness of all men that Emerson would celebrate throughout his writings. Belief in the divinity of Christ, and of Christ as a stand-in and savior for all of humanity, was the antithesis of Transcendentalism in its denial of the individual soul. As Emerson put it, in Christianity, "there is no longer a necessary reason for my being."

His later *REPRESENTATIVE MEN* (1850)—which, notably, did not include Jesus Christ—were "great men," not because they transcended the human experience, but because they represented it to others. What is perhaps most radical about the "Divinity School Address" is Emerson's appeal to the ministers to free themselves from the bounds of religion and be "a divine man," rather than merely study or worship one. As Emerson would write a few years later in "HISTORY" (1841), organized religion depends too much on "priestcraft," on dogma and rituals, all enforced by the ministers, who rule by "fear and obedience." Instead, in the "Divinity School Address," he defines the job of the minister as drawing out the best in others, making souls "wiser."

Emerson rejected the "miracles" of the Bible not only because they defied the laws of nature, but also because he believed in the everyday miracles in "man's life" and in nature as more worthy of our attention and "faith." Emerson's critique of Christianity in the "Divinity School Address" also centers on the idea that all that is to be known about religion has already happened and been recorded in the past—the idea of "historical Christianity," which taught "as if God were dead," something only to read about. This was the Transcendentalist critique of what Emerson referred to in his journal as "corpse-cold Unitarianism." The skepticism of the rational and scholarly Unitarians at Harvard had done away with the *spiritual* in religion; for Emerson, however, the spiritual (the "necessary and eternal") was never to be found in the stories of alleged supernatural occurrences recorded in the Bible centuries ago but in the living world of nature as experienced today, in this moment.

"Domestic Life" (1870)

As is the case for most of the chapters in Emerson's SOCIETY AND SOLITUDE (1870), "Domestic Life" was presented first as a lecture. Emerson had been lecturing on the subject of the home since his early career. During his 1847–48 British lecture tour, "Domestic Life" was his most oft-repeated and well-received lecture. The text that he used in Britain corresponds to that published in *Society and Solitude,* though it was clearly modified between 1848 and 1870. Like "BOOKS" in the same volume, the published version of "Domestic Life" is distractingly disorganized in parts. Nevertheless, the chapter is of high importance as the most thorough presentation of a theme that was central to Emerson's thought throughout his career. It is an uncompromisingly reformist piece that demands a total revision of social life and domestic values. It insists that personal development and human culture are the primary functions that the home, family, society, and state must serve.

SYNOPSIS

The essay begins with a portrait of an infant: a "puny struggler," whose "ignorance is more charming than all knowledge," comic, affecting, and utterly dependent on parental support. When he learns to use his fingers, he begins his study of "power, the lesson of his race." He demands better transportation than his legs can provide and effortlessly enlists adults to carry him on their shoulders. As the infant enters boyhood, everything that comes before his senses increases his knowledge and wonder.

For the man as well as for the child, the events of the home more than those of public life are the most personally important and affecting. The "spirit of the age" can be better seen in the dwelling places of men than in their state houses. By this logic, Emerson intends to test the hypothesis that the current age is characterized by "an increased consciousness of the soul." The economy of the home, and the property and possessions found therein, are all consistent with the character and the central idea of the occupier. Men should never buy anything that they do not want or that does not accord with their individual genius.

Prudence, convenience, and pleasure above all are the ideas that can be seen in the households of the present day. People arrange their homes "for low benefit"; the rich spend on unnecessary extravagances and for display, and the poor imitate them as far as they are able. The staggering number of challenges in domestic life can only be overcome by arranging the household to higher ends. It is better that the house be an environment in which affinity, repose, genial culture, and "innermost" beauty are to be found than that it be well-heated and stocked with "sweet bread." The presently prevailing "idea of domestic well-being" depends on wealth. It is understandable that people love wealth, which pays for "wheat and wool and household-stuff." In this sense, wealth is the "means of freedom and benefit." However, this does not mean that a good home should only be possible for those who possess wealth. The pursuit of wealth takes man from himself. If a man has little wealth, instead of simply giving him money, we should give him "manly encouragement" and access to his own nature. Genius and virtue are better than material wealth, and some of history's greatest heroes lived in poverty.

Instead of saying, "Give us wealth, and the good household shall exist," we should say, "Give us your labor, and the household begins." Rather than more money and material objects, what is truly needed is a total reform of social life and of the household. Perhaps a future generation will manage to spread labor equally among all members of society in such a way that all the essential work will be done in a few hours per day. What is clear now is that the change "must come with plain living and high thinking; it must break up caste," and result in each man doing the work or "vocation" for which he is most fit.

If we try for partial solutions without fixing the whole system "we shall soon give up in despair." We should proceed with high aims. The household must be built and garnished for "human culture." People with this aim see material wealth and poverty as of little significance compared with internal, moral qualities. Emerson honors a house that provides hospitality to strangers and travelers and is "simple to the verge of hardship" but where the "intellect is awake" and love and courtesy flow. In America, where state-funded education had brought taste and talent even into humble homes, this could be a reality. Boys in these humble households are held staunchly upright by "the iron band of poverty, of necessity, of austerity, which, excluding them from the sensual enjoyments which make other boys too early old, has . . . made them, despite themselves, reverers of the grand, the beautiful, and the good."

The household should be a place where refinement and mental enlargement can be achieved. The home should not be a showcase for fine objects—these should be housed in museums and libraries, which might one day be found in each town. If a love of beauty and the dignity of thought and action are present in a home, it will become an "esteemed Sanctuary." A "domestic conqueror," one who will "show men how to lead a clean, handsome, and heroic life," will be a true modern-day hero.

CRITICAL COMMENTARY

In "Domestic Life" Emerson describes two ways of conceptualizing the purpose of the home, one harmful and destructive, the other fundamental to the future progress of mankind. In a sense, "Domestic Life" seems to accord more with Emerson's early writings than with his later work, presumably due to its origins as a lecture in the 1830s and 1840s. His insistent critique of collecting excessive wealth, his hopeful vision of homes and communities where objects of culture would be shared, and his demand for a total reformation of public values are present in varying degrees in works from throughout his career, but bear particular resemblance to discourses in "MAN THE REFORMER" and "INTRODUCTORY LECTURE ON THE TIMES," both delivered in 1841.

Emerson takes issue with the idea that the present age is characterized by an increased focus on the spirit and the soul. He argues that in the home economics of the present age, one can easily see that the material spirit predominates. Instead of making the home a place where the intellect can be educated and the spirit improved, both the rich and the poor prioritize comfort and display. Emerson sees this focus on material well-being as having a poisonous impact. It accounts for the widely held belief that whatever is lacking in domestic contentment can be solved by gaining more wealth. In his analysis, the focus on wealth and material possession in the modern world creates a harmful misbalance. It distracts men and societies from reforming their home lives from the inside out.

A shortcoming of "Domestic Life" is that it ignores the realities of poverty. Emerson praises poverty, seeing a lack of riches as a factor that preserves humility and strengthens the moral sense. The type of poverty to which Emerson refers, however, is the type he experienced as a child in an educated family reduced by the early death of his father to dependence on local charity, or the principled poverty of friends such as BRONSON ALCOTT and HENRY DAVID THOREAU. He does not refer to the abject and systemic poverty of the lowest classes of society. Nevertheless, Emerson's central message in the lecture is about the dignity of the individual. His concern is with a society of excess. He urges his readers to reconsider the use of wealth, to be content with fewer material possessions, and to reorient their values from the pursuit of wealth to the pursuit of humility, human affection, and culture.

Some elements of this discourse are present in Emerson's writings in the 1850s and 1860s, though his later treatments reflect a decreased emphasis on the necessity of a complete reformation of society and its economic foundations. In the chapter "Wealth" in *ENGLISH TRAITS* (1856) Emerson looks at the accumulation of riches in England that resulted from its industrious, enterprising spirit as a sign of its success but adds a sharp critique to the discussion by showing that the pursuit of wealth had contributed to compromising England's moral integrity and creating horrible inequalities. In the essay on "WEALTH" in *The CONDUCT OF LIFE* (1860), Emerson concedes that "man must be a capitalist." There is no longer any insistence that virtue is in any way linked to poverty. However, the idea that wealth should not be wasted on mere comfort and show, but rather spent with high aims on tools and materials that will advance individual education and society as a whole, is upheld.

FURTHER READING

Newfield, Christopher. *The Emerson Effect: Individualism and Submission in America.* Chicago and London: University of Chicago Press, 1996.

Ryan, Barbara. "Emerson's 'Domestic and Social' Experiments: Service, Slavery, and the Unhired Man" *American Literature* 66, no. 3 (September 1994): 485–508.

Scudder, Townsend. "Emerson's British Lecture Tour, 1847–1848: Part II: Emerson as a Lecturer and the Reception of the Lectures." *American Literature* 7, no. 2 (1935): 166–180.

Daniel Robert Koch

"Each and All" (1839)

"Each and All" was first published in the Transcendentalist journal the *WESTERN MESSENGER* (February 1839) and was collected in *POEMS* (1847) and *SELECTED POEMS* (1876). The 51-line, one-stanza poem expresses Emersons's philosophy of the interconnectedness of all things in the universe. The poem took direct inspiration from a poem by the German idealist philosopher JOHANN WOLFGANG VON GOETHE titled "Eins und Alles," which was published as "One and All" in the *North American Review* in April 1839. Lines from Goethe's poem—"How yearns the solitary soul / To melt into the boundless whole"—are mirrored in the last line of Emerson's poem, where the poet announces, "I yielded myself to the perfect whole." Goethe's nature is constantly in action, "creating, changing," and "revolving." Likewise, but somewhat different in its focus on specificities, Emerson's nature is also vital and alive, and his poem abounds with the sights, smells, and sounds of nature.

In true Transcendentalist fashion, Emerson melded Goethe's idea of the relationship of the specific with the universal with his own personal experience of nature. One of the events recounted in the center of Emerson's poem is that of collecting seashells, an event that had been previously recorded in his journal and used in some lectures in 1834: "I remember when I was a boy going upon the beach and being charmed with the colors and forms of the shells. I picked many up and put them in my pocket. When I got home I could find nothing that I gathered—nothing but some dry, ugly mussel and snail shells. Thence I learned that Composition was more important than the beauty of individual forms to Effect. On the shore they lay wet and social, by the sea and under the sky." In the poem, this sense of loss is translated into a lesson about the wholeness of nature.

CRITICAL COMMENTARY

The title of Emerson's poem reflected the relationship between the individual (the "each") and the universal (the "all"). In the first section of the poem (lines 1–12), Emerson introduces the idea that all things in the universe are interconnected. This is a theme, of course, that flows throughout Emerson's writings. This interconnectedness is not always obvious in nature, and, indeed, one "little thinks" of the connection between the flowers on top of a hill and the cow in the fields below. People, as well, go about their daily tasks, one man not realizing that "tolling his bell at noon" has caused Napoléon to stop and reminisce. Finally, we do not know what influence one thing or one person might have upon another; we cannot know "what argument / Thy life to they neighbor's creed has lent." The poet reminds us, however, that, even if we fail to see the connections, "All are needed by each one."

In the next section of the poem (lines 13–28), Emerson explains that we cannot separate the various interrelated parts of nature, cannot take actions or beings out of context. The poem recounts specific instances when he attempted to do so, only to be drawn into a reflection on the whole. The first example is that of a bird, a "sparrow," whose song so entices Emerson that he brings the creature home. The bird still sings, but not as beautifully without the background of "the river and sky," which was the bird's true home. Indeed, he reflects that while the bird "sang to my ear," the river and sky equally "sang to my eye." The second example of this effect or realization of the particular within the context of the whole is Emerson's account of picking up some "delicate shells" from the seashore. Again, as with the beautiful sights of nature that frame the singing of the bird, it is the surrounding sounds of nature ("the bellowing of the savage sea") that attract Emerson to the beauty of the shell. The act of picking up the shells is the act of separating them from their natural context, from "the bubbles of the latest wave" and the "weeds and foam." He takes the shells home and finds that their features have changed—in contrast to the "bellowing" of the sea, the shells are now "poor, unsightly, noisome things." He determines that "their beauty" rested in their place "on the shore / With the sun and the sand and the wild uproar."

The next section (lines 29–36) gives a final example of how nature and beauty change when forced into different circumstances, this time through the example of women. What makes woman beautiful, or man most attracted to her, is her virginity, the "graceful maid," "mid the virgin train," her beauty "woven still by the snow-white choir." But when she is brought home and domesticated through marriage—"Like the bird from the woodlands to the cage"—she changes and loses her allure. She becomes, in the poet's disillusioned terms, "a gentle wife, but fairy none." The next three lines (lines 37–39) stand apart as a short personal reflection on growth. The poet addresses himself and reflects that, in his pursuit of the "truth," he has learned the lesson that it was not enough to seek to capture the beauty of the bird or the shell (or the woman) alone. Beauty is meaningless without context and substance, it is "the games of youth."

The last section of the poem (lines 40–51) takes Emerson's attention back to nature, but this time with the understanding that humans do not stand apart from nature. In this section he focuses on himself as he stands in, surrounded by, and as part of the sights, sounds, smells, and movement of nature: "beneath my feet / The ground-pine curled its pretty wreath," and "I inhaled the violet's breath." Nature is described as "around me" and "over me," "I saw," and "I heard." He can still appreciate beauty—"Beauty through my senses stole"—but, as is also the lesson of the poem "THE RHODORA" (also published in 1839), beauty is not the sole purpose. He now sees the interconnectedness of it all. At the end of "Each and All" he again sees and hears "the morning bird," but this time there is no thought of capturing it. The last line of the poem shows this final understanding: "I yielded myself to the perfect whole."

FURTHER READING

Dameron, J. Lasley. "Emerson's 'Each and All' and Goethe's 'Eins und Alles'" *English Studies* 67, no. 4 (August 1986): 327–330.

Miller, Norman. "Emerson's 'Each and All' Concept: A Reexamination." In *Critical Essays on Ralph Waldo Emerson,* edited by Robert Burkholder and Joel Myerson, 346–354. Boston: G.K. Hall and Co., 1983.

"Earth-Song"

See "HAMATREYA."

"Eloquence" (1870)

"Eloquence" in SOCIETY AND SOLITUDE (1870) originated in a lecture Emerson gave before the Boston Mercantile Library Association in February 1847. He delivered versions of it twice more in New England in 1847 and five times during his lecture tour of England in 1847–48. In 1850 he twice delivered it in New York and once in Ohio.

After leaving the ministry, which was the first outlet for his own natural eloquence, Emerson embarked on a career of public lectures on the lyceum circuits. Overall, between 1833 and 1881, he gave nearly 1,500 lectures, visiting hundreds of towns in more than 20 states and Canada. These tours, which lasted from November through March, involved arduous feats of traveling and endurance. He came to dread private hospitality, fearing to be assigned the unheated spare bedroom. "This climate and people," he wrote from Milwaukee one February, "are a new test for the wares of a man of letters. All his thin, watery matter freezes; 'tis only the smallest portion of alcohol that remains good."

In his lecture "Poetry and Eloquence," he argued that the best prose should be poetic, but the highest eloquence must *be* a poem. The overall effect of the essay "Eloquence" is Emerson's insistence on the moral qualities that are foundational to this civilized and civilizing art form on which he based his own career.

SYNOPSIS

Emerson opens his topic by saying that "every man is eloquent once in his life." Speakers' temperaments "differ in capacity of heat." One man, partaking in the excitement of conversation in the parlor, "boils with patty-pan ebullition"; another is "roused by a public debate"; others "by hot indignation," or "by revolutionary murmur," or "by the grandeur of sentences of absolute ideas," such as "the splendors and shades of Heaven or Hell." But "all this lust to speak" marks "the universal feeling of the energy of the engine, and the curiosity men feel to touch the springs." And so it is natural that "of all the musical instruments on which men play, a popular assembly is that which has the largest compass and variety, and out of which, by genius and study, the most wonderful effects can be drawn." And this is because an audience is not a simple aggregate of individuals, but "a social organism, which fills each member, in his own degree, and most of all the orator, as a jar in a battery is charged with the whole electricity of the battery."

The accomplished orator, Emerson notes, takes "sovereign possession of the audience" and plays "an assembly of men as a master on the keys of the piano." He is like "the 'Pied Piper of Hamelin,' whose music drew" followers "like the power of gravitation." This power requires "a great range of faculty and experience . . . such as Nature rarely organizes," so that ordinarily "we are forced to gather up the figure in fragments, here one talent and there another."

At a minimum, an orator must possess "a certain robust and radiant physical health." This "semi-animal exuberance" of a good orator serves to warm himself and his audience to the occasion—it is, "like a good stove, the first necessity in a cold house." "Climate and race" enter into this equation, explaining why a New Englander is naturally reserved in his narratives, while "a poor Irishwoman" is more enthusiastic in recounting hers. Southerners are more naturally eloquent, but neither Northerner nor Southerner, "nor the Irish, compare with the lively inhabitant of the south of Europe." Eloquence has riveted the attention of people of all ages and persuasions. "Improvisators" and "story-tellers" of earlier times performed "a controlling power over their audiences," but "these legends are only exaggerations of real occurrences, and every literature contains compliments to the art of the orator and the bard, from the Hebrew and Greek down to the Scottish Glenkindie."

Emerson here contrasts the higher *powers* of eloquence with a variety of oratory *skills* of "amusement" or salesmanship, such as "the petty lawyer's fluency," "the slanting art of journalists," "the mischievous member of Congress," and "the celebrated schoolmaster" who is "only one lesson ahead of the pupil." Such accomplishments are "only a degree higher than the coaxing of the auctioneer." They have their uses and conveniences to the practitioners, "but we may say of such collectively that the habit of oratory is apt to disqualify them for eloquence."

Coming to the positive side, genuine eloquence is "an example of the magic of personal ascendancy,—a total and resultant power, rare, because it requires a rich coincidence of powers, intellect, will, sympathy, organs and, over all, good fortune in the cause." We wish for such "a mind equal to any exigency." "Personal ascendancy" is not necessarily accompanied by "adequate talent for its expression," but when it is, "it seems first to become truly human, works actively in all directions, and supplies the imagination with fine materials."

Such a person of "substantial personality" must first of all have the "power of statement" in the form of the fact and "must . . . know how to tell it." This condition rules "a court of justice," in which "the audience are impartial," intent on determining the truth: "The statement of the fact, however, sinks before an eloquent statement of the law, which requires immeasurably higher powers, and is a rarest gift, being in all great masters one and the same thing ... some piece of common sense." Next to knowledge of the fact and application of the general law is "method, which constitutes the genius and efficiency of all remarkable men." Such men exhibit "some new principle of order"; their "higher style" "introduces beauty and magnificence" to the common affairs of this world, setting them apart and making others their followers. The great orator, then, must be a poet: "Condense some daily experience into a glowing symbol, and an audience is electrified."

However, "statement, method, imagery, selection, tenacity of memory, power of dealing with facts, of illuminating them, of sinking them by ridicule or by diversion of the mind, rapid generalization, humor, pathos" are only *sophistical* skills, still falling short of *true* eloquence—"and do often hinder a man's attainment of it." The sophist's talents "are too much for him, his horses run away with him." In contrast, the eloquent person is "a man who, in prosecuting great designs, has an absolute command of the means of representing his ideas, and uses them only to express these." He deals in statement of a truth "so broad and pungent" that his listener, however reluctantly, "cannot get away from it, but must either bend to it or die of it."

What distinguishes eloquence from the merely skilled speech "is the conviction, communicated by every word, that his mind is contemplating a whole." Add to this power "a certain regnant calmness," which "never utters a premature syllable, but keeps the flow of its means and method," so that "the orator stands before the people as a demoniacal power to whose miracles they have no key." Still, at bottom must be a "statement of fact." All other gifts and graces, powers of wit or learning, are beside the point, and are felt to be so by the audience.

In this context Emerson adds that reform, in particular "resistance to slavery," has created a new generation of orators: "Wild men, John Baptists, Hermit Peters, John Knoxes, utter savage sentiment of Nature in the heart of commercial capitals. They send us every year some piece of aboriginal strength, some tough oak-stick of a man who is not to be silenced or insulted or intimidated by a mob, because he is more mob than they." Such a man "has gone through the drill of Calvinism," so that he stands in the assembly "a purer bit of New England than any, and flings his sarcasms right and left."

"Eloquence," then, "is the best speech of the best soul." "The highest power" is reached "when a weak human hand touches, point by point, the eternal beams and rafters on which the whole structure of Nature and society is laid." Emerson here pointedly repudiates the paradigm of the Greek Sophist Isocrates, who taught the relativism and skepticism that makes the small great and the great small: "But I esteem this to be its perfection,—when the orator sees through all the masks to the eternal scale of truth, . . . thereby making the great great, and the small small, which is the true way to astonish and to reform mankind." All the great orators of the world have relied on a genuine virtue that secured their success.

CRITICAL COMMENTARY

The prefatory poem to this essay expresses the sentiment that the man "of soft persuasion," "upon whom the Muses smile," "can bring / Terror and beauty on their wing." It goes on to say of the inspiring speaker, that "in his every syllable / Lurketh nature veritable," so that before the listener's eye "swims the world in ecstacy, / The forest waves, the morning breaks, / The pastures sleep, ripple the lakes . . . / And life pulsates in rock or tree." Eloquence, then, is a form of intellectual and imaginative *power,* inspired by nature, as set within the framework of Emerson's previous volume, *The* CONDUCT OF LIFE (1860), and continuing on into *Society and Solitude.*

"Eloquence" occupies a key place within the framework of *Society and Solitude* of 1870. It is a companion piece to "CIVILIZATION," "COURAGE," and "SUCCESS" in featuring Emerson's foundational concept of the self-reliant, but socially efficacious, moral character. Insisting that true eloquence is grounded in the moral nature of things, it also carries on the work of the key essays of *The Conduct of Life,* which were dedicated to expressing the meliorative powers of the human mind. The eloquent man bears witness to the possibilities of ascending metamorphosis in human civilization, despite society's emphasis on money, political advantage, and other egocentric forms of life. As the carrier of nature's gifts of persuasion, he has the power to make a real difference in civilization. Though it is rare, eloquence is "the best speech of the best soul."

"Eloquence," then, is one of Emerson's powerful late-phase moral essays. It is also obliquely self-reflective of his dedication to the pursuit of philosophical truth through speaking in decades of travel and physical endurance on the lyceum circuits.

David A. Dilworth

"Emancipation of the Negroes in the British West Indies" (1844)

Although Emerson gave several public lectures on the topic of slavery during his lifetime, his *Address Delivered in the Court-House in Concord, Massachusetts, on 1st August, 1844, on the Anniversary of the Emancipation of the Negroes in the British West Indies* (Boston: James Munroe, 1844) was the only antislavery piece published during his lifetime. He gave another version of the speech the following year, on August 1, 1845. The address was also reported in newspapers at the time, and various versions of it appeared in later collected anthologies of Emerson's works.

Emerson was interested in the British case for lessons about the future of slavery and emancipation in the United States. He addresses both southern planters, who feared the economic and social consequences of emancipation, and northerners who had not taken a sufficient moral interest in the slaves. In the end, Emerson's speech is both a scathing critique of U.S. politics and an acknowledgment that emancipation was not merely a political issue but, rather, a question of "progress in human society."

SYNOPSIS

The first section of the address outlines the history of events leading to the emancipation of African slaves in the British colonies. Emerson marks the 10th anniversary of emancipation as a "day of reason," a time in which "clear light" can now be focused on the issue. He criticizes whites who would accept the "ruin of a race" in order to have the luxuries of life, but argues that whites could also benefit from emancipation, as it is ultimately "cheaper to pay wages than own the slave." Progress cannot be determined in economic terms alone, however, but must be defined as the "gain of truth and right." Rather than aiding progress, slavery actually degrades white civilization. Most whites do not realize this as they rarely (if ever) come face-to-face with the reality of slavery. If they did, it would offend the moral sense and fuel the public debate.

Emerson provides a detailed history of ABOLITIONISM in England beginning in the 1760s, when Quakers and others began to send missionaries who reported on conditions in the islands. Even though planters and other slave interests fought antislavery bills in England for years, at least the issue had been brought before the public, resulting in a boycott of slave-produced goods in 1791 and, finally, the ending of the international slave trade in 1807. Still, the slave trade continued, and reports of the brutal illegal trade fueled abolitionist sentiment in England. The Emancipation Act ending slavery throughout the British empire was effective August 1, 1834.

Emerson recounts how the black community was told about the Emancipation Act and how its members responded and "became men." While some whites feared violence, there was ultimately "no riot, no feasting," and the workers reported back to the fields after only one weekend of rest. Furthermore, 10 months after emancipation, the islands still reported no violence, no rebellion, and no fall in productivity. Emerson wants to convince whites that they will continue to prosper economically under emancipation. Despite the economic success of emancipation, oppression still existed because the government could not mandate against the custom of racism. Emerson disputes the argument that planters only want the economic benefits of slave labor, pointing out instead that there is a "love of power" involved.

In the next section of the address, Emerson take a more philosophical view. Each age thinks it is the best, the most civilized, but different qualities characterize each era. The current era is one of imitation, "cheap" and simple, and the United States has been an imitator of English economics and culture. Slavery fit into this system as Africans were seen as a less skilled and less market-oriented race. Since the actual trading was done far away, the focus has been not on the human beings involved but on the products of their labor, luxury items that seem to make life better, such as sugar, coffee, and tobacco. But Emerson argues the "laws of nature" and "moral sense" will ultimately prevail. Slavery produces inferior products and burdensome laws that make the planters themselves into "slaves," creating a white race "full of vices," an argument frequently made by American abolitionists at this time.

Having made implicit comparisons between England and the United States, Emerson now admits that it is the "painful comparisons" to New England that strike him most. He is personally disappointed in New England politicians who have "turned their backs on me," not just on the slave. Even in the supposedly "free" states, blacks are employed in low-paying jobs with "no law to save them" from being kidnapped, unjustly accused, and forced into slavery. Emerson argues that such acts are a disgrace to the Puritan legacy of morality, of history, and of democracy. Emerson asks whether the U.S. government can truly be called representative when it takes power from those it supposedly represents. He asks how congressmen can "sit dumb at their desks, and see their constituents captured and sold;—perhaps to gentlemen sitting by them in the hall?" While some fear "dangers to the Union" if they do not compromise with the South, in Emerson's view, the Union is already destroyed. Northern politicians have allowed the slaveholding "minority" to control them, rather than fulfilling the proper role of government, which is "to defend the weak and the poor."

Emerson then turns away from such "dark thoughts" and returns to the "bright aspects" of what is supposed to be this day of celebration. Emancipation in the British Empire is a "moral revolution" for all of humanity. It is not a revolution of heroes, of war, of insurrection, but a revolution created by the "plain means of plain men." All the great men of the age sided with justice on this issue, while those opposed were only controlled by money, vulgarity, "rage and stupidity." In the concluding section of the address, Emerson declares that emancipation is the beginning of "the civilization of the negro." He looks to nature, which has preserved African culture and humanity and therefore provides a lesson, since nature "only saves what is worth saving." In nature there is true equality since nature "deals with men after the same manner," with no attention to skin color: "If you have man, black or white is an insignificance." This is a matter of concern for all of humanity, for there will be no progress as long as Africans are enslaved.

Emerson ends his address on a hopeful note. While the slave may feel he has no friend and the abolitionist thinks no one else is listening, the truth is that the "noble wind of sentiment" will prevail. "There is progress in human society," Emerson offers, and "Intellect," "Right," "Power," and "Freedom" are all greater forces than oppression. "The First of August," the anniversary of British emancipation, is not just a celebration for one nation, but "a sign to the ages."

CRITICAL COMMENTARY

The 1844 speech was a shift toward Emerson taking a more public role against slavery in the United States. Although he had many friends and close family members active in the abolitionist cause, Emerson was reluctant to associate himself with any single reform issue. In the opening paragraph of his address, he acknowledges that he has no reputation as a social or political reformer: "I might well hesitate, coming from other studies, and without the smallest claim to be a special laborer in this work of humanity, to undertake to set this matter before you." Regardless, after 1844 the abolitionists believed they had an ally in Emerson. William Lloyd Garrison's paper, the *Liberator,* reported that "before we saw notice of this celebration, we were not aware that Mr. Emerson had sufficiently identified himself with the abolitionists, as a party, to receive such a distinguished token of our confidence."

After 1844, Emerson received regular requests to speak on the issue, and ultimately aligned himself with those against the Fugitive Slave Law of 1850 and in support of radical abolitionist JOHN BROWN in 1859. But while he would speak out on the legal and political crises of slavery in the coming years, his ultimate concern was the philosophical and moral implications. As he explained his concern about slavery in the "Emancipation in the British West Indies" address: "I am no lawyer, and cannot indicate the forms applicable to the case, but here is something which transcends all forms." Emerson argues that we should not "bow to" politicians, as they are not the great men of the age and do not affect the flow of human affairs. Instead, he retains faith that "what great masses of men wish done, will be done." This is an indictment of the American people, and even of abolitionists, who blame the government for slavery and look to the government for the solution.

FURTHER READING

Gougeon, Len. *Virtue's Hero: Emerson, Antislavery, and Reform.* Athens: University of Georgia Press, 1990.

Gougeon, Len, and Joel Myerson, eds. *Emerson's Antislavery Writings.* New Haven: Yale University Press, 1995.

English Traits (1856)

Before writing the main body of *English Traits,* Emerson visited England twice, once as a young man in 1833 and again as a renowned writer and lecturer during a severe economic crisis in 1847–48. Upon his return to the United States in late 1848, Emerson began working reflections on his personal experience and observations of England, along with descriptions of English character, English literature, and the English "national mind," into what would become the book's chapters. *English Traits* is an important indication of where Emerson's philosophical concerns lay as he entered the final stage of his career as a writer and orator. Emerson saw England as a symbol of power, in both practical and philosophical terms. His discourse on power in *English Traits* links his early fascination with the transformation of genius into results in the real world, to the philosophical speculations on the complex relationship between power and fate in his later works. *English Traits* reached publication after a long period of gestation in 1856, between REPRESENTATIVE MEN (1850) and *The* CONDUCT OF LIFE (1860). The book generated enormous interest and was a popular success.

SYNOPSIS

First Visit to England

The opening chapter begins with Emerson's description of his "first walk on English ground" in 1833. He had come wishing to meet some of the writers to whom he was most indebted and was able to see several of them. Emerson first describes his meetings in Italy with the American sculptor and art theorist Horatio Greenough and with the English writer Walter Savage Landor. He called upon SAMUEL TAYLOR COLERIDGE in London, THOMAS CARLYLE in Scotland, and WILLIAM WORDSWORTH in the Lake District. Emerson remarks that Coleridge first canceled their 12 o'clock meeting, as he was "still in bed." When they did meet, Coleridge ranted about the "quackery" of UNITARIANISM and made the visit "rather a spectacle than a conversation." Carlyle is described as a powerful and inquisitive interlocutor, disturbed by the pauperism and poverty in Britain and appreciative of the "huge machine" of London. Wordsworth was an elderly conservative poet with a "simple adherence to truth" but a narrow, "very English" mind.

Voyage to England

Emerson begins this chapter by explaining the background of his second trip to England in 1847–48. He had been invited to speak at some Mechanics' Institutions and, looking for a "change and tonic" in his life, decided to accept. A description of his sea journey across the Atlantic and a severe storm weathered in his ship follows. Emerson describes his sailing ship's weight, speed, and course and records stories and information he gleaned from conversations with the captain and crew. From these practical considerations Emerson drifts into a more speculative and symbolic mode. The sea becomes "an eternal cemetery" that could rise "steadily and insensibly" to swallow the fragile race of men. It is also capable of doing "private and local damage," and for this reason, Emerson wonders if any sane man could be a sailor. He learns a lesson about how men adapt to the seafaring life when he sees a stowaway boy forced into labor by the crew and finds out that "nine out of ten" sailors had started the same way. To counteract the dismal feeling produced by the sea, Emerson recommends study and reading. Finally, as the ship neared Britain, Emerson began to feel the "genius" of land.

Land

In "Land," Emerson describes England as a triumph of man over nature. The country had been converted from a "rude, uncongenial land" into a "paradise of comfort and plenty." The "long habitation of a powerful and ingenious race" had transformed the natural environment to make it serve man's needs. Emerson asks himself what accounts for England's power, success, and global influence. He defines England's influence as one that extends beyond territorial control and into the thoughts and aims of men everywhere. The direction of modern society in all parts of the globe toward practical, "utilitarian" laws and preferences shows, according to Emerson, that Turks, Russians, Chinese, Americans, and others had come under the influence of "the natural genius of the British mind."

Emerson proposes that England's dominance is explicable in part by its natural advantages. England's climate seldom sways to extremes and is naturally endowed with abundant supplies of water, stone, clay, coal, salt, iron, game, and fish. It is well positioned, "anchored to the side of Europe," close enough for trade and communication but also protected by the sea. Looking at England's advantages, Emerson imagines that nature "had held counsel with herself" and decided to give birth to a "new empire" that would eventually exert a broad, civil influence.

Race

The fourth chapter begins with a critique of a recently published book, *Races of Men* (1850) by Robert Knox, which argued that nations are temporary but that "races are imperishable." Emerson subtly rejects this argument by pointing out that it was not possible to define "where a race begins or ends" and suggesting that races should only be thought of in terms of their "ideal or metaphysical necessity." Emerson concedes that historically race had been "a controlling influence," which explains the preservation of certain characteristics in minority groups separated from their ethnic homelands. On the other hand, however, he suggests that civilization, religion, and other forces can "eat away the old traits" or, in other words, limit the controlling influence of race. Another fact that "threaten[s] to undermine" the doctrine of pure race is that races mix and evolve over the centuries. Emerson argues that the process of racial mixing is beneficial: "[T]he best nations are those most widely related; and navigation, as effecting a world-wide mixture, is the most potent advancer of nations." This belief, that in mixture there is strength, is the basis for Emerson's analysis of the English race and its rise to prominence. England has a "composite character."

Its language, laws, and intellectual character derive from a variety of sources. Its mixed tribal origins make it a "country of extremes" but also make its people "collectively a better race than any from which they are derived."

Before discussing the ancient tribes that combined to form the English tradition, Emerson first advises his readers (again showing that race cannot be used as an all-encompassing category) that not all Britons exhibit "English traits." Indeed, "the world's Englishman" is a particular type of cosmopolitan individual—English traits are found at last only in certain Londoners or in people "who come and go thither." As a caveat to his use of racial categories in the section that follows, Emerson admits that "the popular category" must sometimes be used "for convenience," but it should not be taken as "exact and final." He proceeds to describe the English race as a "trinity or quaternity" of Celtic, Scandinavian, Saxon, and Latin "bloods" and lists some enduring characteristics of each of these tribes.

The ancient Celts were learned and poetical. The German Saxons were tough and tenacious. The "Northmen" or Scandinavians were fierce raiders, hungry for individual wealth and acclaim. They were steady and substantial but barbaric and marked by a "singular turn for homicide." The Normans were a subgroup of Scandinavians who retained their Viking ferocity, greed, and penchant for thievery even after losing their language and acquiring new vices while residing in northern France. Emerson contends that the fierceness and brutality of the Northmen still lies not far beneath the surface of the English race and could be seen in the "manners of the lower class" and in England's still-current use of torture and flogging to punish criminals.

The chapter concludes with some observations of the English "union of qualities." English traits include the coexistence of extremes of courage and tenderness, strength in war and feats of culture and charity, manliness and femininity, beauty and ferocity, added to physical robustness, solid frames, and animal energy.

Ability

Most of the chapter "Ability" is given to an investigation into the "Scandinavian" parts of the English national character. Emerson first points out that both the Saxon and the Northmen were Scandinavian by blood, though in England, Norman and Saxon had very different significations. They represent the aristocratic and the democratic principle, respectively (Emerson warns that these terms are not scientific terms and are to be considered "a little mythically"). He provides a short history of Britain, focusing on the Saxons' ability to absorb and secure concessions from the Norman conquerors.

The "Gothic" Saxons are described as having a work mentality, a "taste for toil," which made later invaders feel as if they were surrounded by "goblin men with vast power of work and skilful production." By temperament they "resist every means employed to make [them] subservient to the will of others." They fight hard but fair, and think logically and practically. Within this logic is an inbuilt tendency toward justice. These traits are what have given the English the "leadership of the modern world." They are particularly suited to the industrial arts, business, and trade and are adept in modern warfare. They will not normally shed their blood for meaningless abstractions, but they will fight for their money and property and respect ideas that relate to them. Emerson sees the "supreme ability and cosmopolitan spirit" of the English as justifications of "their occupancy of the centre of habitable land."

Emerson devotes two final sections of the chapter to a discussion of English factitiousness and solidarity. Modern England is "factitious" or "artificial" in that, through works and arts, its people had overcome the limitations imposed by nature. Adeptness in trade made "oranges and pine-apples . . . as cheap in London as in the Mediterranean." The English have "trust in each other." Each Englishman, Emerson contends, "carries the English system in his brain" and knows his own part in it. With remarkable social cohesion, they march together "lockstep, foot after foot, file after file of heroes, ten thousand deep."

Manners

In "Manners," Emerson continues to describe English traits and behaviors, though with reduced emphasis on race and on connections between the present and the tribal past. He focuses on English "pluck." Emerson describes the English as firm, burly, vigorous, and direct. Industrialization had made "a terrible machine" of England, but mechanical power was matched by the human strength and stamina of the English. Their energy and character secure them against "desperate" political revolutions. The English are conventional, resistant to change, and deeply domestic in their affections. English domesticity is the "taproot" from which its empire grew, its ultimate end being "to guard the independence and privacy of their [own] homes." The conservativeness of the English mind translates in some Englishmen to a "wooden deadness," to "cold, repressive manners," a hatred of enthusiasm and "highflown expression." Dinner is "the capital institution." Nevertheless, English wit remains as good as any other nation's, partially due to the wide "range of nations from which London draws."

Truth

In "Truth" Emerson turns again to racial or tribal qualities, beginning the chapter by describing "German" (a term used more or less interchangeably with "Saxon," "Teutonic," and "Gothic" in *English Traits*) honesty, or "singleness of heart." Germanic "hereditary rectitude" combined with punctuality and preciseness produces "English truth and credit." The English deliver what they promise, and so does their government; it is on this sincerity that England's "practical power" rests. The English avoid exaggeration and pride themselves on keeping their word. Their truth is a love for reality as measured in wealth, power, hospitality, land, and durable assets. They are sturdy in their opinions and demand veracity in their leaders and public men. When abroad, they do not bend to foreign customs but carry on as at home. The English are stolid, plodding, and unable to keep secrets due to their natural openheartedness.

Character

This chapter begins by addressing the reputed moroseness of the English race. Emerson sees this reputation as the result of the inability of French travelers to understand that the English found their enjoyment not in singing and dancing or their "public diversions" but in their homes. He argues that the English are actually "cheerful and contented."

English character is epitomized by its "great range and variety" of propensities and proclivities. The English are both sweet and sour, of the earth and of the sea, good lovers and good haters. Generally, they are stout, obstinate, and headstrong; they enjoy sound sleep, butcher's meat, and being right. They have an excess of constitutional force, which accounts for their enterprise, their adventurous youth, and the rude behavior that they often display. However, Emerson contends, in the "deep traits of race" "the best stock in the world" can be found in England. The English character had room for warriors and clerks, for wisdom and folly, meanness and generosity, fierceness and "exquisite refinement." The English character gave birth to a superior brand of heroes and led naturally to their conquest of far-off peoples.

Emerson sees England's firmness as the stabilizing keystone of the modern world. Unlike the mutable French, the English stand durably for liberty and have the "personal force" to make freedom secure. The early histories of King Alfred and the Northmen show that the "genius of the English society, namely that private life is given the place of honor," had grown with the race. The "most British Briton" is private and cares nothing for public glories. The English "wish neither to command nor obey, but to be kings in their own houses," and their history shows that their inclination "for private independence" has endured despite the growth of their empire and continues to shape the laws, culture, and society of the nation and the commonwealth.

Cockayne

This short chapter provides some satire and comic relief but also contains a sharp critique of English vanity and conceitedness. In England, individual freedom is pushed "to folly" and taken by some to mean simply the right "to do as he pleases." The English dislike foreigners, are arrogant toward non-English people, and force their "island by-laws down the throat" of their colonies. The English are self-absorbed. Even this, however, is a key that explains the "secrets of their power and history." Their inflated self-esteem and their universal brag encourage a "manly bearing," forcing each to make the most of himself. Their excessive and "childish" national pride, however, is painted as an English vice.

Wealth

Having already pointed to the English obsession with material wealth, Emerson turns to a deeper investigation of its nature and significance. To be poor in England is a disgrace. The fruit of the worship of personal wealth is a prevalent acceptance of a "brutal political economy," in which there is no room for mercy to the poor. The English expect each to take care of himself. They work "three times as many hours" per year as other Europeans. Machines cause a rapid multiplication in population and wealth. The country has immense assets, open markets, comforts, splendor, and, unlike its neighbors, an apparent immunity to revolutions. Property is "the national life blood." Wealth has made "great and refined forces," such as education, the ability to travel, good society, and domestic well-being available for the private citizen. The ultimate source of English wealth, Emerson contends, is in their temperament and their "constitutionally fertile" nature.

Some paragraphs are devoted to the negative aspects of England's fabulous wealth. Working in the factories, repeating the same task day in and day out, the robust Saxon worker "degenerates" into a half-man, is robbed of his "strength, wit, and versatility." Trained to perform one task only, crowds of workers are "sacrificed like ant-hills" when suddenly their particular skill is no longer needed. The "division of labor" is ruining Englishmen's capacities to become "proper individuals, capable of thought and new choice." In this light, machinery and trade appear to be unmanageable and tyrannical. For all the new wealth generated, starvation, poverty, and grief amass unabated.

Aristocracy

Emerson points out that aristocracy still holds enormous meaning in England. Noble families all sprang from the "natural superiority," or adeptness in accumulating wealth and glory, of an ancestor. A characteristic of the British nobles is that they prefer life in their country homes to life in London or in the royal court. The English nobility share the values of the common people for domestic life and individual freedom, which, Emerson suggests, explains why unlike in France, popular anger and violence have never touched the British aristocracy. The loyalty of the English people is clearly with its aristocracy. Emerson contends that the aristocracy has been and continues to be useful as a model class. They set a standard of "good behavior" and "manners." They revolutionized British agriculture and were important "friends and patrons of genius and learning."

On the other hand, some aristocrats were clearly not models to be imitated. With wealth some grew "fat and wonton," copulating with prostitutes, gambling, cheating, and squandering fortunes. Most were guilty of "idleness." Hardworking middle-class Britons were rising to match or to surpass them in wealth, education, culture, and privilege. Emerson sees the old heraldry "perishing" and being replaced by a new working nobility that includes people "with titles and without."

Universities

The majority of this chapter is given to a discussion of the University of Oxford, including a description of Emerson's visit there in 1848 and remarks about its importance to England. Oxford was a conservative bastion of the Anglican Church and the old aristocracy. Emerson found it to be hundreds of years behind the times, with its gates "shut . . . against modern innovation," though full of ancient treasures. It was, in effect, a "little aristocracy in itself"—blessed with a long history and the loyalty of the nation, notable for producing great scholars, fit leaders, and model gentlemen, but being made obsolete by its idlers, profligate sons, spoiled fellows, exclusivity, and unbending conservatism. Nevertheless, Emerson hints in the chapter's final sentences that very good ideas were still coming from Oxford and Cambridge.

Religion

In this chapter, Emerson contrasts medieval and modern England. Medieval Britain is portrayed as a society in which Christianity was experienced in its "full heat." Religion inspired the tireless labor that was still visible in its ancient churches and Cathedrals and bent the English mind toward liberty, humanity, scholarship, and civilization. In the modern age, however, the spirit that powered the medieval church "has glided away into other activities," leaving "apes and players" to fill the seats of the great religious figures of the past. Religion has become false. The national church serves the gentry and not the poor. In modern England, spiritual genius is esteemed only if it is useful. Indeed, the English religion could no longer be called Christian. The church was unable to respond to recent German biblical scholarship. With a new wave questioning of the finality of the Gospels, the established church lay exposed as a hypocritical, theatrical, even pitiable institution. In a final paragraph, however, Emerson predicts that the true religious sentiment will survive the collapse of the church.

Literature

The key to the genius of English language is a mixture of the plain earthy masculinity of the Saxon element and the counterbalancing elegance and femininity of the Latin. England's greatest literature contains a blend of natural precision corresponding to Saxon "mental materialism" and "transcendental" spiritual perception, or "inspiration." English literature reached its apex in the age of Bacon, SHAKESPEARE, and Milton. Since then, the mixture had become one-sided: The inspirational, universal, and poetic had all but disappeared, drowned by the materialist, negative, "so-called scientific" element, due most of all to the influence of JOHN LOCKE. In 18th- and 19th-century English literature, Emerson finds merits in the work of Hallam, Coleridge, Carlyle, and others. Overall, however, the current situation is dismal. The English bias to "practical skill" had drained idealism, faith, and belief from the "national mind." Britain cares only for practicality and "material values." In this environment, English factitiousness takes on an appalling cast, ideals are laughed at, poetry degraded, the secret of beauty lost. The genius of Wordsworth is the great exception to this trend. To remedy the dismal situation, Emerson hopes that the influence of the East might balance and enlarge Britain's limited national mind. Another reason for hope is that the historical dialectic of conflict and resolution between the minority "perceptive class" and the majority "practical finality class" had traditionally been a constructive force, resulting in the production of English power.

The "Times"

The newspaper, and in particular the London *Times*, is portrayed in this chapter as the ultimate expression of the modern era. Its force rids England of feudal "incrustations" and drives it toward democratic social and political institutions. The *Times* had become a powerful institution in its own right, with a strong influence over the opinions of the nation. It seemed to have reporters in all corners of the world and yet had a consistent and confident tone, as if all its articles proceeded "from a single will." It is representative of the English national mind and echoes its arrogance and materialism but also its ability to comprehend present realities. The *Times* is good, but it could be better if it would guide "the public sentiment" to a higher morality. With its power, it could be a leading force in reform and even could play a role in the realization of the "dream of good men . . . an International Congress."

Stonehenge

This chapter briefly tells the story of Emerson's visit to Salisbury Plain with Carlyle in the summer of 1848. Emerson writes that while he understands that America would eventually become the "seat and centre of the British race" and that England would someday have to realize that it is old and can be strong "only in her children," he was nonetheless extremely impressed by the country's vitality and success. Emerson describes his awe at the ancient stone circle and at the nearby Gothic cathedral at Salisbury. When Emerson was asked whether he knew anyone with "an American idea," he responded by "opening up the dogma of no-government and non-resistance" but realized that among English gentlemen his idea would find no converts.

Personal

This chapter is partly a letter of thanks to the friends, generous hosts, and literary celebrities whom Emerson met during his 1847–48 British lecture tour. Much of the chapter is given to a description of his meeting with the aged Wordsworth in late February 1848. The poet was formulaically bigoted against the French, Scottish, and Irish, based on little but anecdotal evidence. Nevertheless, Harriet Martineau's tribute to his modesty and unpretentiousness is recorded along with Emerson's own high estimation of Wordsworth's early poetry.

Result

The final chapter in *English Traits* proper, "Result" provides a summary of the main points Emerson wishes to make about England. First, despite its distance from the ideal standard, England is the best of actual nations; London is the Rome of the present day. Second, unlike the Romans, the English are more domestic than public in their affections. In private, they are true. Third, in public affairs and in their worldview the English have a narrow and limited vision. They have an excessive attachment to property, and because of this they can be ungenerous and unjust. England does have an ugly side. Fourth, nevertheless, the English have also made real strides toward humanity, freedom, and civilization, though this does not excuse their unaccommodating nationalism.

Ultimately, one can say little about a nation beyond what is on the surface. Yet there is a deep inscrutable Englishness that exists and is the source from which so many detectable English traits derive. They had been brave and courageous, constructed a multifaceted society, and demonstrated a sober reserve while conquering the globe and "carrying the Saxon seed, with its instinct for liberty and law" with them as they went. However, the English mind had reached a state of "arrested development." Its universal vision had ceased to grow and was now limited to material reality only. It moved with a "tortoise's instinct," resisting all reform, but also able to resist pulls backwards. Harsh social inequalities still existed, a feudal holdover, but within this system, good men had been produced and had arrived at positions of power—indeed, England had "yielded more able men over five hundred years than any other nation," including America with its more democratic system. From England's great activity and its respect for the "sacredness of individuals," it had "over seven hundred years evolved the principles of freedom."

Speech at Manchester

The speech Emerson delivered at a gathering at the Manchester Athenaeum in November 1847 is included as an appendix to *English Traits*. Emerson prefaces the insertion by stating that the feelings expressed just after his arrival in England accorded well enough with the feeling of *English Traits*. In the speech itself, Emerson declares that what lures the American to come and study England is "the moral peculiarity of the Saxon race—its commanding sense of right and wrong." This trait is the justification for England's imperialism, its "aristocratic character," and its prowess in industry. Another interesting trait is the sense of loyalty that runs through all classes in England. Emerson alludes to the economic crash afflicting England in 1847–48 and recalls that in childhood he had been told that the English truly showed their greatness when facing adversity. He sees England responding to the crisis with energy rather than with despair and views this as a cause to exclaim, "All hail! Mother of nations, mother of heroes, with strength still equal to the time." He warns, however, that if England did lose courage and collapse in the crisis, he would return to Massachusetts and say that the "hope of mankind" must remain solely with the Americans.

CRITICAL COMMENTARY

The concept of power is central to *English Traits*. In Emerson's account, English power manifests itself in the nation's exceptional work and industrial capacities, in its literary and scientific achievements, its broad cultural influence, and, perhaps most of all, its expansive empire. Searching for the deepest sources of England's power, Emerson turns to a study of what is inside the minds and bodies of the English people, and what makes them different from others. From the mid-1840s onward, Emerson's thoughts on the topic of power related closely to the question of how one could convert interior character into real results in the external world. In his essay "EXPERIENCE" (1844), he declared that "the true romance which the world exists to realize will be the transformation of genius into practical power." Emerson saw England as a country that represented practical power above all others and examines its history in *English Traits* by working backward from its present prominence on the assumption that the result must have proceeded from internal causes in its constitutional makeup or its national "genius." This assumption, shared by many in Emerson's time, is a key to understanding the cause-and-effect linkages that Emerson draws between English traits and English power.

Emerson describes English power, actual and historical, in two senses. In the material world, the English had achieved the most productive economy, amassed the most wealth, implemented the most advanced machinery, and built the vastest empire in the modern era. This was partially a product of their bodily strength, their material mind-set, and their acquisitive nature. In another sense, the English had achieved unparalleled success in the realm of ideas. They produced the greatest literature, nurtured the best intellects, and exercised a positive moral and cultural influence throughout the world. This proceeded from the sincere faith and spiritual fires that burned in Christian Britain during the Middle Ages and lived on in the form of a sharp moral sense, a poetic spirit, and fidelity to truth. In Emerson's interpretation, England was able to overcome limitation and reach its golden age when these two modes of power were in full bloom.

However, Emerson is at pains to point out that since the age of Locke, the causes of the second aspect of England's greatness were being drowned out by the effects of the first. In "Wealth" and "Literature" Emerson argues that practicality and the determined pursuit of wealth—causes of England's greatness in one sense—had become so inflated in the English national mind as to push to the side and devalue all other spiritual and cultural pursuits. It led to the destruction of the balanced spirit and the deterioration of its once "universal" genius. Emerson's declaration that one side of the English genius had been "arrested" echoes the language of Robert Chambers in *Vestiges of the Natural History of Creation* (1844), an extremely popular pre-Darwinian book on evolution. Emerson was deeply interested in this book and met its author during his 1848 visit to Scotland. Chambers's theory of "arrested development" suggested that the progress or development of a race or species could slow to a halt in certain conditions. Emerson's allusion to the theory in *English Traits* adds force to his warning that if the balance were not recovered—if the predominance of the material over the intellectual-spiritual power continued into the future—England, unable to evolve, would swiftly decline and be overtaken by other nations.

The speculation on the causes of England's rise and its potential future decline foretells the complex relationship between human endeavor and collective destiny that Emerson described in *The Conduct of Life*. In *English Traits*, Emerson contends that, historically, harnessing power while keeping its moral and nonmoral elements in a fruitful balance had been England's key to progress and prosperity. *The Conduct of Life* universalizes this theme, suggesting that for all of humanity, the forces of fatal limitation are surmountable only by a combination of physical and moral power. The human race must use power to stave off the fatal forces of brute nature, stagnation, and barbarity and to advance toward a higher civilization.

FURTHER READING

Cole, Phyllis. "Emerson, England, and Fate." In *Emerson: Prophesy, Metamorphosis, and Influence,* edited by David Levin, 83–105. New York: Columbia University Press, 1975.

Gougeon, Len. "Emerson and the British: Challenging the Limits of Liberty." *REAL: Yearbook of Research in English and American Literature* 22 (2006): 179–213.

Nicoloff, Philip. *Emerson on Race and History: An Examination of English Traits.* New York: Columbia University Press, 1964.

Daniel Robert Koch

"Eros" (1844)

This six-line poem appeared in an early notebook with the title "Love" but was published as "Eros" in the DIAL (January 1844) and collected in POEMS

(1847). It was one of a series of love poems grouped together in *Poems,* including several specifically to Emerson's deceased first wife, Ellen Tucker Emerson: "GIVE ALL TO LOVE," "TO ELLEN, AT THE SOUTH," "THINE EYES STILL SHINED," and "INITIAL, DAEMONIC, AND CELESTIAL LOVE."

Eros was, of course, the Greek god of love, and the poem is a general reflection on the idea that "to love and be beloved" is the essence of the human condition, the entire "sense of the world." In this regard, it is fitting that Emerson created such a short poem to capture this essence, a variation on the idea of the haiku in Japanese tradition.

> The sense of the world is short,—
> Long and various the report,—
> To love and be beloved;
> Men and gods have not outlearned it;
> And, how oft soe'er they've turned it,
> 'Tis not to be improved.

But eros also refers to a specific type of love, in particular sexual love or desire or, more generally, the creative or life force. Emerson's poem works in both senses. In other poems and essays Emerson more fully explored different types of love, including friendship and marital love or union, such as in the essays "LOVE" and "FRIENDSHIP" (both of *ESSAYS: FIRST SERIES* [1841]).

Essays: First Series (1841)

Emerson's first major collection was titled, simply, *Essays* and was published in March 1841. In the five years between the publication of *NATURE* (1836) and the publication of this volume, Emerson had emerged at the center of the new Transcendentalist controversy within UNITARIANISM and had been publicly criticized for his remarks against religious and educational authority in the "DIVINITY SCHOOL ADDRESS" (1838). The 1841 *Essays* was a response to those various intellectual and theological challenges by presenting an alternative in a comprehensive new philosophy of the self. He hoped his work in *Nature,* as he explained to his friend THOMAS CARLYLE, would be seen "as an entering wedge . . . for something more worthy and significant," and it culminated five years later with the presentation in *Essays.*

As early as 1835, Emerson, after reading the great French essayist Michel de Montaigne (subject of his 1850 essay in *REPRESENTATIVE MEN*), acknowledged in his journal that he was anxious to put his own ideas into essay form, asking himself, "Where are your Essays. . . . Have you not thoughts & illustrations that are your own . . . the law of Compensation . . . the sublimity of Self-reliance?" Drawn from many of Emerson's subsequent and numerous lectures of the 1830s, *Essays* brings his ideas together in a systematic philosophy of individual experience as it related to universal themes and laws, in such essays as "HISTORY," "SELF-RELIANCE," "COMPENSATION," "SPIRITUAL LAWS," "LOVE," "FRIENDSHIP," "Prudence," "HEROISM," "The OVER-SOUL," "CIRCLES," "INTELLECT," and "ART." Except for Emerson's signature concepts of self-reliance and the over-soul, the individual essays are complex examinations intended to alter the reader's assumptions and previous knowledge about these otherwise familiar concepts. While Emerson was often (then and now) accused of lacking a system as a philosopher, *Essays,* in fact, introduces regular Transcendentalist themes that Emerson would take up again and again in his subsequent lectures, essays, and poems.

Emerson originally considered titling the collection "Forest Essays," directly connecting the pieces to his work in *Nature,* and all of the essays are, in some sense, expansions on the ideas first presented in *Nature.* Taken collectively, the essays are explorations of a single theme, laid out in the first sentence of the first essay, "History"—the idea that "there is one mind common to all individual men." The volume is an exploration of that idea, of finding the universal meaning in our individual (yet common) experiences and a rejection of materialism that sees no connection, no meaning, no trace of humanity in our individual experiences. Emerson's idealism restores meaning by revealing natural laws that govern history, friendship, love, intellect, and so on.

Essays went through both American and English editions, establishing Emerson's international reputation and leading to a successful English lecture tour in 1848. Reviews were mixed, from the criticism in the *New York Review* of such "a godless book" to the assessment in the *Boston Quarterly Review* (written by ORESTES AUGUSTUS BROWNSON) that the book would "take hold of the heart of the age, perhaps of the ages." His friend Carlyle's praise was even more effusive; upon reading *Essays,* he immediately wrote to Emerson to "persist, persist; you have much to say and to do. . . . You are a new era, my man, in your new huge country." Emerson's aunt, MARY MOODY EMERSON, was less impressed, characterizing the essays as a "strange medly of atheism and false independence." The popularity of the book led Emerson to revise the essays and republish them in an 1847 edition, now titled *Essays: First Series,* to place it in chronological relation to *ESSAYS: SECOND SERIES* (1844), which had been published in the intervening years.

FURTHER READING

Von Frank, Albert J. "Essays: First Series (1841)." In *The Cambridge Companion to Ralph Waldo Emerson,* edited by Joel Porte and Saundra Morris, 106–120. New York: Cambridge University Press, 1999.

Essays: Second Series (1844)

Essays: Second Series was published in October 1844 and was composed of eight essays and a recent lecture: "The POET," "EXPERIENCE," "CHARACTER," "MANNERS," "Gifts," "NATURE," "POLITICS," "NOMINALIST AND REALIST," and the lecture "NEW ENGLAND REFORMERS." Revised editions were also reprinted in 1850 and 1855, and again in 1876.

By the time *Essays: Second Series* appeared, Emerson was an established lecturer and author, and the volume was a greater publishing success than *ESSAYS: FIRST SERIES,* published three years earlier in 1841. The years between the two collections were one of Emerson's busiest and most prolific periods as a lecturer, essayist, and editor. During these years, Emerson was publishing in and co-editing the Transcendentalist literary journal the *DIAL,* which became a forum for experimental ideas and a showcase for new talent. By the early 1840s, Emerson had also been drawn more directly into conversations about political and social reform, most notably ABOLITIONISM, but also questions of UTOPIAN reform and women's rights. Emerson's personal life also underwent dramatic shifts during the years he was writing the *Essays;* his family grew to include four young children, he and his wife, LIDIAN JACKSON EMERSON, agonized over the death of young Waldo in 1842, and his home in CONCORD, MASSACHUSETTS, became a center of literary activity and intellectual community.

Within this context of reform movements and changes, Emerson's *Essays: First Series* helped establish the contours of his secular Transcendentalist philosophy, exploring the nature of power, of selfhood; but in *Second Series,* his inquiry takes a more practical turn, examining the relationship and development of that individual self within a more immediate social and political context. An early reviewer noted that, compared with the first volume of essays, *Second Series* was closer "to the experience of the mass of mankind."

Significantly, the first essay in the collection is "The Poet," which introduces Emerson's role in the interpretations offered throughout the other essays. The theme of the collection was the individual's relationship to the world of experience and politics, between the individual self and the daily world of society, the state, and others, and, in the larger sense, the individuals' relationship with or place within the universal; as he asked in the essay "Experience": "Where do we find ourselves?" There is throughout the essays a dualism between the individual or inner world and the outside world, between nominalist and realist, between nature and politics, between, as he noted in the essay "Character," the positive and negative: "Everything in nature is bi-polar, or has a positive and negative pole. There is a male and a female, a spirit and a fact, a north and a south."

In "Politics" he translated his Transcendentalist philosophy of the self to democratic individualism, declaring, "Of persons, all have equal rights, in virtue of being identical in nature." This simple yet radical view became the core of his other writings on politics in his time, from abolitionism to women's rights, reform issues that dominated his time and that he addressed again in the lecture "New England Reformers," published for the first time here. "New England Reformers" had been delivered as a lecture earlier that year, the same year that Emerson also ventured more forcefully into the antislavery debate with his address on "EMANCIPATION OF THE NEGROES IN THE BRITISH WEST INDIES." As scholar David Robinson points out, then, as a whole *Essays: Second Series* can be seen as a turning point for Emerson toward applying his philosophical tenets to the political, and "itself a formal representation of Emerson's emphasis on pragmatic alternatives to perceptual dilemmas."

FURTHER READING

Ellison, Julie. "Tears for Emerson: *Essays, Second Series*." In *The Cambridge Companion to Ralph Waldo Emerson,* edited by Joel Porte and Saundra Morris, 140–161. New York: Cambridge University Press, 1999.

Robinson, David. "'Here or Nowhere': *Essays: Second Series*." In *Emerson and the Conduct of Life: Pragmatism and Ethical Purpose in the Later Work.* New York: Cambridge University Press, 1993.

"Experience" (1844)

The poem "Experience" is, in one sense, an allegorical portrayal of a visionary experience. The speaker of the poem sees "the lords of life" pass by and address themselves to "little man." The poem offers a common Emerson refrain: Nature, "deep and kind," leads man into recognition of himself, and thus his race and God. Also, however, the poem (and the accompanying essay) is about loss, grief, and the value of life; Emerson wrote the poem just two years after his first son, Waldo, died at the age of five, on January 27, 1842. In this sense, the "little man" of line 14 is Waldo, whom Emerson sees as walking in the afterlife, among the gods.

The poem appears as the motto for "EXPERIENCE" in *ESSAYS: SECOND SERIES* (1844) and was collected in *MAY-DAY AND OTHER PIECES* (1867).

CRITICAL COMMENTARY

The poem opens with a line separated by a dash from the rest of the poem: "The lords of life, the lords of life." Emerson uses the dash both to set the line apart from the rest of the poem and to offer, by repetition, the theme and content: The poem is about the allegorical parade of these lords—"Use," "Surprise," "Surface," "Dream"—but is also about the "little man" as a "lord of life."

The poem breaks into three unmarked sections: the first line, which introduces the subject; lines 2–7, which offer a description of these "lords"—"Use and Surprise, / Surface and Dream, / Succession swift and spectral Wrong, / Temperament without a tongue"—as they pass "from East to West" (that is, from the rational, logical West to the intuitive, spiritual East); and lines 14–21, which offer a view of man's perception of this parade and its significance. In this last section, man, the least of all these "lords," is taken in hand by nature, who leads him into understanding.

The second section of this poem utilizes contradictions and paradoxical images to describe the shifting appearance of the lords of life between surface and dream; like and unlike. Emerson refers to these lords, in line 11, as "omnipresent without name." Emerson resolves these apparent contradictions by using an allegory to qualify the divine. Thus, in lines 17–21, nature takes man "by the hand" and comforts him. Also present in this poem is Emerson's tendency to resolve the poem's complication in a rhymed couplet. This last couplet, spoken by nature, answers man's "puzzled look" referred to in line 16: "Darling, never mind! / To-morrow they will wear another face, / The founder thou; these are thy race!" As in other poems in the *May-Day* collection in particular, Emerson suggests that we recognize our commonality by understanding that appearance is only surface. Emerson indeed would wish the reader to see below the surface to find that which is common in the race.

Bill Scalia

"Experience" (1844)

"Experience" is the second essay in Emerson's *ESSAYS: SECOND SERIES* (1844) and is in many ways a companion piece to the first essay in the volume,

"The POET," and to the earlier "SPIRITUAL LAWS" (1841). "Experience" is also infused with reflections on the death of Emerson's firstborn child, Waldo, at age five in 1842 (also the theme of the poem "THRENODY"). Emerson was surrounded by death, especially during his early life and career—not only the death of his young son but also of his father (in 1811), his first wife, Ellen Tucker Emerson (1831), and his brothers, EDWARD BLISS EMERSON (1834) and CHARLES CHAUNCY EMERSON (1836).

Waldo's death occurred at the peak of Emerson's idealistic phase and of his involvement in the new Transcendentalist movement, prompting a philosophical and spiritual crisis that tested Emerson's faith in his own ideas, in nature, and in life. In a letter to a friend after Waldo's death, he confessed, "I chiefly grieve that I cannot grieve." Some have read this note and the essay on "Experience" as a lack of feeling on Emerson's part, but his letters and journals reveal an extreme depth of feeling that resulted in emotional numbness: "Shall I ever dare to love any thing again. . . . Must every experience—those that promised to be dearest & most penetrative,—only kiss my cheek like the wind & pass away?" It was this philosophical dilemma—how to go on living and loving and find meaning in life—that is at the heart of the essay "Experience" and, indeed, of all of Emerson's work.

SYNOPSIS

Emerson begins the essay with the feeling that life seems random and confusing: "Where do we find ourselves? In a series, of which we do not know the extremes, and believe that it has none. We wake and find ourselves on a stair: there are stairs below us, which we seem to have ascended; there are stairs above us, many a one, which go upward and out of sight." Humans feel we are being moved through the universe by forces not of our own accord: "Ghostlike we glide through nature." We have no control over the passage of time, and the "unprofitable" days seem meaningless.

We begin to feel that "our life looks trivial, and we shun to record it." We can find nothing original, no inspiration: "How many individuals can we count in society? how many actions? how many opinions?" In "retrospect," most of our life is only "preparation" for greatness, and we see that "the pith of each man's genius contracts itself to a very few hours." As with individual lives, so it is with "the history of literature," which "is a sum of very few ideas, and of the very original tales,—all the rest being variation on these."

So starved for authentic experience are we that we even "court suffering, in the hope that here, at least, we shall find reality, sharp peaks and edges of truth." Here he directly mentions his own experience of grieving (or trying to grieve) the loss of his son: "The only thing grief has taught me, is to know how shallow it is." Grief only "plays about the surface" and can never truly reflect the depth of feeling and connection to the thing lost. "Grief too will make us idealists," in that it confirms "souls never touch their objects." He continues, "I grieve that grief can teach me nothing, nor carry me one step into real nature. . . . Nothing is left us now but death. . . . there at least is reality that will not dodge us."

Whereas death has a purpose in nature, grief does not. Emerson finds this "to be the most unhandsome part of our condition." Our relationship with nature is random and subjective. Even though "there are always sunsets, and there is always genius," ultimately "it depends on the mood of the man, whether he shall see the sunset or the fine poem." Emerson finds it "very mortifying" that human life is so dependent on factors beyond our control, on "fortune," "talent," or "imbecility." So many "young men" of "promise," either "die young . . . or if they live, they lose themselves in the crowd." The potentiality of any individual is thus "an optical illusion," showing promise "in the moment," but nothing to show after "the year" or "the lifetime."

Having reflected on the "illusoriness" of "ordinary life," he notes there is a "capital exception," and that is "temperament," which connects the individual self to nature: "On its own level, or in view of nature, temperament is final. . . . Given such an embryo, such a history must follow." This is not a very hopeful view of life; indeed, "on this platform, one lives in a sty of sensualism, and would soon come to suicide." Luckily, "the intellect, seeker of absolute truth, or the heart, lover of absolute good, intervenes for our succor," and "these higher powers" awaken us to something beyond ourselves. It is hard to underestimate "the pain this discovery causes us"—that "there is no adaptation or universal applicability in men, but each has his special talent."

So how does this idea relate to life? "What help from thought?" We don't need more "pedantries," "dialectics," and "criticism." He gives an example of theories of reform that have no practical application: "Our young people have thought and written much on labor and reform, and for all that they have written, neither the world nor themselves have got on a step." For example, at "Education-Farm" (a reference to the utopian community at BROOK FARM), "the noblest theory of life sat on the noblest figures of young men and maidens" who ultimately found themselves "quite powerless and melancholy." Their theory, it turned out, "would not rake or pitch a ton of hay; it would not rub down a horse."

Rather than formulating grand ideas, we should just focus on living our lives: "Do not craze yourself with thinking, but go about your business anywhere. Life is not intellectual or critical, but sturdy." "We live among surfaces, and the true art of life is to skate well on them." "Life itself is a mixture of power and form, and will not bear the least excess of either. To finish the moment, to find the journey's end in every step of the road, to live the greatest number of good hours, is wisdom."

We are in need of greater self-reliance and should not form our responses and emotions just for show. If the people around us "despise life," then "it is a great excess of politeness to look scornful and to cry for company . . . but leave me alone, and I should relish every hour and what it brought me." The person who "expects everything of the universe" will be "disappointed when anything is less than best." Instead, Emerson finds comfort in his immediate surroundings of "wife, babes, and mother, Concord and Boston, the dear old spiritual world, and even the dear old devil." These are "great gifts," neither abstract thoughts nor pure materialism or "sensation." Life is lived in this "mid-world": "Between these extremes is the equator of life, of thought, of spirit, of poetry,—a narrow belt."

Emerson advocates living life in "the strong present tense," tied to neither past nor future, but living fully in the moment. Let others debate and argue while you do your work and "heed thy private dream." If we look closely we will "see the artist, the orator, the poet, too near, and find their life no more excellent than that of mechanics or farmers." He gives as an example the fact that so many children read and enjoy art and draw, and yet they do not all become writers and artists. This does not mean their pursuits were wasted, as we all have talents we will not fulfill: "Every man is an impossibility, until he is born; every thing impossible, until we see a success." Society would have us believe that all that is needed is "manly resolution and adherence to the multiplication-tables" to "insure success." But the rules are constantly changing—"Life is a series of surprises, and would not be worth taking or keeping, if it were not"—and there is no steadfast formula: "The results of life are uncalculated and uncalculable."

Not everything is determined by human will, and this is why "the ancients . . . exalted Chance into a divinity." And yet life does have a purpose, and that is pursuit of "the Ideal," which is "journeying always with us." We access this ideal through self-development, "by persisting to read or to think." We thus can hope for "flashes of light . . . sudden discoveries of its profound beauty and repose, as if the clouds that covered it parted at intervals." The illumination of the mind or spirit comes like the illumination of nature—the clouds are parted, mountains revealed, meadows exposed, and shepherds celebrate—and Emerson is fulfilled by this promise of renewal: "And what a future it opens!"

Emerson brings order back to the chaos and despair of his earlier paragraphs, admitting, "If I have described life as a flux of moods, I must now add, that there is that in us which changes not." The one stable force in the universe is "the consciousness in each man," which connects the universal and the particular, the spiritual and the experiential. He rejects "Fortune, Minerva, Muse, Holy Ghost" as "quaint names, too narrow" to explain this phenomena, and different cultures throughout history have tried to turn "the metaphor" into "a national religion." He rejects any specific doctrine, declaring, "It is not what we believe concerning the immortality of the soul, or the like, but *the universal impulse to believe.*" This "impulse to believe . . . is the material circumstance"—the idea is the only reality. Through the "mighty Ideal" we gain "a new picture of life and duty" and "a doctrine of life which shall transcend any written record we have."

There was a time when "we lived in what we saw"—that is, the experience was all that mattered. We accepted on faith what we could not see or experience firsthand. But with "this new power" our vision is expanded: "Nature, art, persons, letters, religions,—objects, successively tumble in, and God is but one of its ideas." It is humans who created the idea of God and other "idolatries," but "people forget that it is the eye which makes the horizon." Jesus is great only because man made him great. But there can only be one great man, the self: "The soul is not twin-born, but the only begotten." Here Emerson combines the imagery of the newborn (or reborn) soul with the biblical language of Jesus as the "only begotten son" of God to explain that the individual soul is our divine and only self.

Emerson returns to the idea that there is no difference between thought and action: "There is no crime to the intellect." Our actions are outward expressions of our thoughts, therefore if you believe something to be good, it is good. We too often confuse "conscience" with "intellect": "Saints are sad, because they behold sin." The intellect understands sin has "no essence," it is only "less," the "absence of light." Whereas the conscience seeks to define and provide meaning, and therefore "must feel it as . . . essential evil." Sin and crime are subjective, manifestations only of the self: "As I am, so I see; use what language we will, we can never say anything but what we are." In this way, Emerson explains, we make our own world: "Thus inevitably does the universe wear our color."

The idea of subjectivity, of "self-trust" and "self-recoveries," is unlike "religion" in that it is affirmative; it builds rather than destroys. Self-trust "is not the slave of tears, contritions, and perturbations." Self-trust is ultimately faith in all humans: "I cannot dispose of other people's facts; but I possess such a key to my own, as persuades me against all their denials, that they also have a key to theirs." Nor does it claim "any completeness" of one's own self; self-trust means recognizing and accepting, that "I am a fragment, and this is a fragment of me."

Emerson is interested only in personal growth considered over the course of a lifetime and will not demand proof or "fruit" in "the instant month and year." This idealism accepts that one cannot have all the answers: "I am very content with knowing, if only I could know. . . . To know a little, would be worth the expense of this world." Thus Emerson is confident that "one day, I shall know the value and law of this discrepance" between the world of thought and the world of action, between the ideal and the experience. We must trust the process and accept the unknowable, having only "patience and patience" that the meaning will eventually become clear, that "we shall win at the last." We are too often deceived by "the element of time." We spend large amounts of time on the mundane things in life but need only an instant "to entertain a hope and an insight."

The essay ends on a triumphant note, confident that we will grow and be sustained through these brief fleeting moments of "hope" and "insight," of these sneak peeks behind the illusions of life: "Up again, old heart! . . . there is victory yet for all justice; and the true romance which the world exists to realize, will be the transformation of genius into practical power."

CRITICAL COMMENTARY

Emerson's solution to the problem of experience—to the "chasm," as he put it in the essay "MONTAIGNE; OR, THE SKEPTIC" (1850), "between the largest promise of ideal power, and the shabby experience"—is twofold. First, we must believe that the individual soul is defined by a few key moments of illumination, not by the totality of our mundane experiences; and, second, we must accept the difficulty of reaching these moments of insight at all. As a commentary upon Emerson's own experience of grieving the death of a loved one, "Experience" is ultimately a secular philosophical answer to the question of the meaning of life. The essay is also Emerson's clearest statement on subjective experience, and thus ultimately fits with his larger project of the self, as articulated most notably in "SELF-RELIANCE" (1841) and "Spiritual Laws."

Without the consolation of an afterlife, Emerson must find meaning in the here and now, not in a "secret cause" or "religion," but in nature. He redefines the "knowledge" that brings about "the Fall of Man" as the realization that we exist, that we will cease to exist, and that we cannot fully understand that existence. While he would elsewhere reject religious doctrine both generally ("DIVINITY SCHOOL ADDRESS" of 1838) and in the particular ("The LORD'S SUPPER" of 1832), here he makes one of his strongest statements of his philosophical idealism: "It is not what we believe concerning the immortality of the soul, or the like, but *the universal impulse to believe*." The philosopher WILLIAM JAMES was inspired by and later expanded on Emerson's premise here with his 1897 book, *The Will to Believe*. Emerson was ahead of his time in seeing a human psychological need for religion, and his Transcendental belief in "the mighty Ideal" provides the "divine answer" in self-trust.

"Experience" draws on imagery from Emerson's other prose and poetry. The opening lines were echoed in the poem "MERLIN" (1847), on life as our "mount to paradise / By the stairway of surprise." On our use of time he writes, "All our days are so unprofitable while they pass, that 'tis wonderful where or when we ever got anything of this which we call wisdom, poetry, virtue. We never got it on any dated calendar day." These lines are reminiscent of the poem "DAYS" (1857), whose "daughters of time" are a companion to the "lords of life" as forces defining human experience. Indeed, it is in these opening lines of "Experience" on the "unprofitable" days that Emerson sets up the main conclusion of the essay "The years teach much which the days never know."

As a companion to "Spiritual Laws" or "The Poet," the essay "Experience" urges us to trust the process of nature: "There is no need of struggles, convulsions, and despairs. . . . We interfere with the optimism of nature." At the end of the essay Emerson summarizes the main points of this journey: "Illusion, Temperament, Succession, Surface, Surprise, Reality, Subjectiveness,—these are the threads on the loom of time, these are the lords of life" (a phrase also used in the opening poem "EXPERIENCE"). The "lords of life" are different from the universal laws of "Spiritual Laws" or the other pieces in *ESSAYS: FIRST SERIES* (1841), such as "Self-Reliance" or "CIRCLES." If these other essays (including "The Poet," which focuses on the vocational self) present a more coherent system of identity, "Experience" acknowledges the divided self: "I am a fragment and this is a fragment of me." Emerson asks, "Where do we find ourselves?" and can only answer that "ghostlike we glide through nature." This is the language found in "NEW ENGLAND REFORMERS" in the same 1844 volume: "We are weary of gliding ghostlike through the world, which is itself so slight and unreal." If the "transparent eyeball" of *NATURE* sees all, the self of "Experience" now "know[s] better than to claim any completeness for my picture."

FURTHER READING

Ellison, Julie. "Tears for Emerson: *Essays, Second Series*." In *The Cambridge Companion to Ralph Waldo Emerson*, edited by Joel Porte and Saundra Morris, 140–161. New York: Cambridge University Press, 1999.

Francis, Richard Lee. "The Poet and Experience: *Essays: Second Series*." In *Emerson Centenary Essays*, edited by Joel Myerson, 93–106. Carbondale: Southern Illinois University Press, 1982.

O'Keefe, Richard R. "'Experience': Emerson on Death." *American Transcendental Quarterly* 9, no. 2 (June 1995): 119–129.

"Farming" (1870)

Ostensibly on a practical subject, "Farming," published in *SOCIETY AND SOLITUDE* (1870), actually contains many facets of Emerson's essential spiritual, moral, and aesthetic tenets. The fundamental law of nature and of Emerson is here again proclaimed: Do thy work. According to his son EDWARD WALDO EMERSON, the essay originated as a lecture called "The Man with the Hoe" delivered at the Middlesex Agricultural Society in 1858.

"Farming" is especially noteworthy for illustrating Emerson's sense of the interrelationship between man and nature. Its themes are echoed in WALT WHITMAN's paeans to the outdoor life and labor, such as "The Song of the Broad Axe," "A Song for Occupations," and "A Song of the Rolling Earth." As in Whitman's poems, Emerson's descriptions of mid-19th-century farm life stem from a world before industrialization. Horse, block and tackle, axes and two-man saws, makeshift ploughs, and the brawn of their backs were the standard equipment for clearing the lands and tilling the soil. But again as with Whitman, the essay is more than a historical document; it digs down into the soil to find the meaning of human existence.

SYNOPSIS

Emerson declares the farmer occupies the situation of mankind that stands nearest to God. God or nature is the first cause, and the farmer is the second cause: "The glory of the farmer is that, in the division of labors, it is his part to create. . . . He stands closest to Nature; he obtains from the earth the bread and the meat. . . . The first farmer was the first man." Mankind's respect for "the possession and use of land" is universal, and farming is the first calling of the human race.

Emerson adds to this opening accolade the beauty of nature, the tranquillity and innocence of the countryside, and its effects on the farmer's independence and pleasures, such as come from "the care of bees, of poultry, of sheep, of cows, the dairy, the care of hay, of fruits, of orchards and forests." In turn, these patient arts and skills seep into the character of the farmer, giving him strength and a plain dignity "like the face and manners of Nature herself." The essential dignity of the farmer consists in that he "represents" mankind as a producer, not a consumer. Emerson contrasts the active, season-driven, laborious life of the farmer with the idleness and vices of the towns.

The farmer's occupation is a reflection of his character: "This hard work will always be done by one kind of man." The "scheming speculators," the "soldiers," "professors," and "readers of Tennyson," he says, are not cut out for the work of the farms, which require "endurance—deep-chested, long-winded, tough, slow and sure." It is such a man who is chosen by nature herself and who is the "continuous benefactor" to mankind. As the farmer opens up arable land, drains swamps, builds durable houses, and constructs roads, walls, and fences, he bequeaths to civilization enduring fortunes that he himself cannot take with him to the grave. In terms of political economy, he is "the true abolitionist"—he is engaged in the work that will free mankind from the oppressive, less productive forms of slave, serf, and peasant labor in the fields.

It is the aboriginal forces of nature at the command of the farmer, not human labor: "Geology and Chemistry, the quarry of the air, the water of the brook, the lightning of the cloud, the castings of the worm, the plough of the frost." The farmer understands these energies, realizing that forces "long before he was born" have prepared the land for his work. Through science the farmer comprehends "the great circles in which nature works," the way that we depend on animals, who depend on plants, which "supply the oxygen for the animals to consume," which in turn supply the "carbon for the plants to absorb." The farmer, then, understands the idea of "*all for each and each for all.*"

Emerson continues using the language of science to explain the work of the farmer and its relation to all human work and thought. Just as "air is matter subdued by heat" and plants "burn, that is exhale and decompose their own bodies into the air and earth again," so it is that human beings "burn with internal fire of thought and affection." "Intellect is a fire: rash and pitiless it melts this wonderful bone-house which is called man." It is the farmer who faces this physics of fire on his own land and invents further transformations in the form of food and raw materials. Thus, while dependent upon the energies of physical nature, the farmer also engages with the creative power of his own thought, by circulating nature back into useful human commodities, based on patterns the farmer learns from nature itself.

Emerson remembers and celebrates the weary toils of the planters and harvesters since time immemorial. The progress of civilization, including the increase of its populations, has run parallel to the advances in agriculture. The farmer in his labors has thus carried forward the huge, cumulative effects of history. We today are still living off the fruits and meats of his cleared, demarcated lands. We drink wines whose provenance goes back a thousand years. This is why "the farmer stands well on the world." Indeed, his is an incomparable greater dignity than the inhabitants of "palaces."

Emerson ends the essay by explicitly drawing a moral lesson: "That uncorrupted behavior which we admire in animals and young children," he says, is to be found not only in the farmer, but also in "the hunter" or "the sailor," in any case "the man who lives in the presence of Nature." As distinguished from the "artificial" men and relationships of the cities, the farmer possesses a character, a "constitutional excellence," that comes not only through supplying our physical wants but also from being closest to nature.

CRITICAL COMMENTARY

In "Farming," Emerson draws a line between the farmer as active producer and the rest of society as passive consumers, reaffirming his ethics of self-reliance, work, and power through an original relation with nature. Throughout his works, Emerson establishes a polarity between mankind's spiritual and physical powers. His essays "FATE" and "POWER" in *The* CONDUCT OF LIFE (1860) were two of the strongest expressions of this dialectic that connects the spiritual progression of the soul with its rootedness in the earth's soil. The two powers intersect in the farmer's life even though working the land is actually a life of "continuous hard labor" with "small gains," such that we "must not paint the farmer in rose-color." As the farmer times himself to nature's calendar and temperament, he acquires the virtue of patience.

The compensatory advantage of this life of hard labor for the farmer is that "he is permanent." Emerson notes that, in his own town of CONCORD, "farms remain in the same families for seven and eight generations," with most of the farms still owned by descendants of "the first settlers (in 1635)." Indeed, those "first settlers" had included Emerson's own Concord ancestors, those who foolishly thought they ever held "possession" of the land, as he mused in the poem "HAMATREYA." Likewise, in *NATURE* (1836), Emerson notes that, looking over the Concord "landscape," he finds, "Miller owns this field, Locke that, and Manning the woodland beyond. But none of them owns the landscape. There is a property in the horizon which no man has, but he whose eye can integrate all the parts, that is, the poet. This is the best part of these men's farms, yet to this their warranty-deeds give no title."

We could speculate as to why Emerson included this essay on "Farming" in *Society and Solitude;* was it because the farmer, like the poet-philosopher, works mostly alone to produce something good for society—both of them constantly pulled between divine and earthly concerns and thus revealing vital aspects of their interrelationship? Is Emerson's writing like farming in that respect? Emerson does not explicitly make the comparison in this essay, and yet the farmer and the poet-philosopher are linked by his overarching ethos of self-reliance. He had already boldly asserted that nature underlies and enables human effort in his earliest addresses and lectures, including *Nature* (1836) and "SELF-RELIANCE" (1841). In "The AMERICAN SCHOLAR" (1837), he had declared that "the ancient, 'Know thyself,' and the modern precept, 'Study nature,' become at last one maxim." His later essays in *The Conduct of Life* (1860) also carried the keynote that "work is victory," and in "Self-Reliance," he urged, "Do your work, and I shall know you."

"Farming" obliquely comments on the "back to the land" ideology of Transcendentalist projects such as HENRY DAVID THOREAU's experiment at Walden and the UTOPIAN communities at BROOK FARM and Fruitlands. Thoreau's experiment in self-reliance included growing his own food, an activity he praises over reading books or other uses of time. As implied in his essay "WEALTH" in *The Conduct of Life* (1860), Emerson came to disagree with the "Arcadian fanaticism" of these efforts "to go upon the land, and unite farming to intellectual pursuits." Emerson's instinct and commitment to self-reliance repelled him from the communal scheme of Brook Farm, which he later parodied as "a perpetual picnic, a French Revolution in small, an Age of Reason in a patty-pan" in at least one context. The essay "Farming" therefore made the point that, unlike the commitment of the individual farmer, such communities in fact betrayed the separation between idea and execution. Emerson considered that the Brook Farmers were not, in fact, true farmers, in that their purpose was political and social, rather than seeking personal connection with nature.

David A. Dilworth

"Fate" (1860)

"Fate," to which Emerson gave pride of place as the first essay of *The* CONDUCT OF LIFE (1860), has sometimes been considered the culminating philosophical expression of his entire career. Together with such companion pieces as "EXPERIENCE," "WORSHIP," and "ILLUSIONS," it expresses the balanced wisdom of his later years in contrast to the more exuberant romanticism of his earlier essays of the 1830s and 1840s.

The frontispiece poem, which begins with "Delicate omens traced in air," keynotes this essay on the tension between *fate* (nature's laws of necessity) and *power* (of the human intellect and will) in human experience. The theme of *fate* implicates Emerson's sense of nature's "foresight" or "prevision" as to man's destiny. In the end he connects such musings on the mystical universal with the language of religious resignation and worship, in urging to "build an altar to the Blessed Unity . . . the necessity of beauty under which the universe lies." In the final analysis, the action of the human mind in response to the external pressures of nature underlie the principle of identity—what he earlier explained as the over-soul or as the unity of spiritual laws (both in essays of 1841). This principle accounts for the universal human discoveries of the poetic and scientific imagination—topics that continued to occupy Emerson into his late philosophical works, such as "POETRY AND IMAGINATION" and *NATURAL HISTORY OF INTELLECT*.

SYNOPSIS

The essay begins with a somewhat uncharacteristically chastened reflection: "We are incompetent to solve the times." True still to his Transcendentalist ethics of self-reliance, Emerson adds: "We can only obey our own polarity. . . . The riddle of the age has for each a private solution." But while we may seem constrained by and unable to reconcile the competing forces, "if we must accept Fate, we are not less compelled to affirm liberty, the significance of the individual, the grandeur of duty, the power of character. This is true, and that other is true."

Emerson first focuses on the reality of fate, that "Nature is no sentimentalist,—does not cosset or pamper us." He catalogs a host of terrible facts of the "rough and surly" world, which is "cold, inconsiderate of persons, tingles your blood, benumbs your feet, freezes a man like an apple. The diseases, the elements, fortune, gravity, lightning, respect no persons. The way of Providence is a little rude." Nature is full of "snake" and "spider," as is human nature: "These are in the system, and our habits are like theirs."

He goes on to spell out "the book of fate" with respect to physical, biological, and psychological forms, including the determinations of heredity and of geology. The earth "turns the gigantic pages,—leaf after leaf,—. . . . One leaf she lays down, a floor of granite; then a thousand ages, and a bed of slate; a thousand ages," and so on. These successive layers of "rude form" all lead toward the arrival of mankind, "her coming king." But humans are subject to the laws of evolution and time as well: "But when a race has lived its term, it comes no more again." One more deterministic feature that binds the human races, Emerson notes, has surfaced in "the new science of Statistics," which dictates that "in every million there will be an astronomer, a mathematician, a comic poet, a mystic." But in this context too there reigns the fatal law of compensation: "Famine, typhus, frost, war, suicide and effete races must be reckoned calculable parts of the system of the world." These are the necessities of nature, "which we call casual or fortuitous events."

In this framework fate seems "the vindicator" over human will or power: "We cannot trifle with this reality. . . . No picture of life can have any veracity that does not admit the odious facts." "A man's power is hemmed by a necessity" in nature, and even individual thought "must act according to its eternal laws . . . to its fundamental essence." Fate strikes a moral balance in nature, "levelling the high, lifting the low, levelling the high, lifting the low, requiring justice in man."

Characteristically, the essay now turns to the other side of the binary, that of human power, for "fate has its lord; limitation its limits." Emerson's idealism requires this balance or "compensation" in nature and in human consciousness: "For though Fate is immense, so is Power, which is the other fact in the dual world, immense. If Fate follows and limits Power, Power attends and antagonizes Fate." Fate may explain natural history, as he has just shown, "but there is more than natural history." Man cannot be explained merely as "order of nature, sack and sack, belly and members, link in a chain"; there is more to man, who is "a stupendous antagonism," bringing together "the poles of the Universe." Nature is made up of "elemental order" and of "thought," of "god and devil, mind and matter, king and conspirator, belt and spasm, riding peacefully together in the eye and brain of every man."

In this context Emerson insists that it is more "wholesome" for man to look optimistically to his practical power than to dwell on fate: "'Tis the best use of Fate to teach a fatal courage. . . . If you believe in Fate to your harm, believe it, at least, for your good." It is "the revelation of Thought" that gives man his "freedom" from fate. "We are as lawgivers; we speak for Nature; we prophesy and divine."

Notwithstanding the irreconcilable nature of fate, therefore, Emerson continues to valorize the active and positive self-reliant life: "A man speaking from insight affirms of himself what is true of the mind." The "intellect" is the source of our "organic power," and Emerson draws out the moral implication of this theory of *good karmic action:* "When souls reach a certain clearness of perception they accept a knowledge and motive above selfishness. A breath of will blows eternally through the universe of souls in the direction of the Right and Necessary."

Emerson's polarity logic having now swung full round, the essay culminates in a theme of the affinity of man's mind with nature's progressive evolution, of man's grappling with nature to harness her energies for human ends: "Steam was till the other day the devil which we dreaded." The world's brute and deadly forces, when intellectually mastered, provide great potential for human freedom from those forces. Overall, "the direction of the whole and of the parts is toward benefit, and in proportion to the health. Behind every individual closes organization; before him opens liberty,—the Better, the Best." But this ascending evolution, he warns, "pleases at a sufficient perspective." At closer range fate and freedom seem to be "sliding into one another" in any individual life, because "Nature is overlapped, interweaved and endless." The secret of the world is in understanding "the tie between person and event."

Moral conduct also suggests the relation of identity between each person and the world: "Person makes event, and event person." The role of fate may remain "hidden," but always "the soul contains the event that shall befall it." This aligns here, however, with Emerson's character ethics, for a man's "fortunes" (and presumably, therefore, his misfortunes) are "the fruit of his character." Aligned with his ethics of self-reliance, such a character ethics even becomes a method for evaluating the legacies of past history, for, he asks, what are the "'times,' 'the age,' . . . but a few profound persons and a few active persons who epitomize the times?"

Emerson ends "Fate" by dignifying this doctrine of moral and metaphysical participation as the essence of what he called, earlier in the essay, "the Blessed Unity" of the universe. He speaks of man's "double consciousness," in which, "when a man is the victim of his fate, . . . he is to rally his relation to the Universe, which his ruin benefits . . . [and] take sides with the Deity who secures universal benefit by his pain."

Here he writes: "Let us build altars to the Blessed Unity which holds nature and souls in perfect solution, and compels every atom to serve an universal end." He ends with a positive sense of trust in the process of nature, and of fate: "How idle," he continues, "to choose a random sparkle here or there, when the indwelling Necessity plants the rose of beauty on the row of chaos, and discloses the central intention of Nature to be harmony and joy."

CRITICAL COMMENTARY

Emerson's phrase "Blessed Unity" is an essentially paradoxical view of human life and fate. He began to express this paradox in "The TRAGIC," which combined the theme of the "House of Pain" of human existence with an overall affirmative attitude, setting the precedent for "Fate" and "EXPERIENCE," as well as several of his most personal poems, most notably "THRENODY," written after the death of his son Waldo in 1842, and the more mystical "BRAHMA." In "Fate," Emerson portrays the human person as the intersection of two inexhaustible "strong forces," both of which run off to infinite, though opposite, directions.

Among his philosophical precedents, Emerson here reprised IMMANUEL KANT's paradoxical duality of "the starry heavens above and the moral law within," itself a formulation of life's two most fundamental though contrary claims on human consciousness. For Kant, indeed, this led to his binary between the governing concepts of all philosophy, namely, of physical necessity and of moral freedom (these Kant would work out in his three "critiques," *Critique of Pure Reason* of 1791, *Critique of Practical Reason* of 1797, and *Critique of Judgment* of 1790).

Emerson's thought also reprises the NEOPLATONIC metaphysical framework in its own fashion, with one end of the ladder of creation stretching toward the infinitely bottomless depths of matter, with its patterns of cause and effect (nature "pardons no mistakes," as Heraclitus said), and the other end pointing upward into the immaterial realm of the spirit, the realms of truth, beauty, goodness, and oneness. There is no limit in either direction. Every individual then is "a dragging together of the poles of the Universe," as Emerson says in "Fate." A productive spiritual life is one in which one learns to "do one's work" in the setting of this battleground in the human heart. At the time, Emerson's existential focus on fate was at odds with Christian doctrine, as many critics noted. But, in the end, Emerson offers us an alternative theory of religious or spiritual resignation. Although the entire universe rises up to kill us, human beings have the dignity of knowing that the soul affirms the laws of nature. The ensuing essays in *The Conduct of Life,* which "Fate" opens, all continued to articulate the transformative power of the active, affirmative life.

In broader historical perspective, the philosophies of Taoism and Heraclitus, Hinduism and Buddhism, Stoicism, as well as Neoplatonism and the philosophy of the German idealists, are all effortlessly reenacted in Emerson's world-affirming perspective here. It is a literary ethics that at once supports a naturalistic pantheism, an objective idealism, and a metaphysical idea of oneness. These currents in Emerson's thought resurfaced in the creative expressions of the American Transcendentalist poetic tradition, as in WALT WHITMAN, EMILY DICKINSON, and, later, WALLACE STEVENS and others. A critique of Emerson's ultimately positive conclusions was found in HERMAN MELVILLE.

FURTHER READING

Arvin, Newton. "The House of Pain: Emerson and the Tragic Sense." *The Hudson Review* 12, no. 1 (Spring, 1959): 37–58.

Packer, Barbara. "History and Form in Emerson's 'Fate.'" In *Emerson Bicentennial Essays,* edited by Ronald A. Bosco and Joel Myerson, 432–452. Massachusetts Historical Society / University of Virginia Press, 2006.

Whicher, Stephen E. *Freedom and Fate: An Inner Life of Ralph Waldo Emerson.* 1953. Rev. ed., Philadelphia: University of Pennsylvania Press, 1971.

David A. Dilworth

"Fortune of the Republic" (1863)

Emerson first delivered "Fortune of the Republic" in BOSTON on December 1, 1863. Many years later, in 1878, he delivered a lecture by this title in Boston that was later published in *Miscellanies* (1884, 1904). This later lecture, however, was a synthetic piece, a combination of segments from various lectures, fabricated by Emerson's daughter ELLEN TUCKER EMERSON and his biographer and editor, JAMES ELLIOT CABOT. It bears little resemblance to the 1863 address, which was not published in its original presentation until 1995 in *Emerson's Antislavery Lectures.*

"Fortune of the Republic" was delivered repeatedly at a critical time in the Civil War. Despite major Union victories at Gettysburg and Vicksburg in July 1863, by December the war had become a virtual stalemate. With casualties reaching biblical proportions and no end in sight, war weariness began to take a toll on Northern resolve. Conservatives, led by Rep. Clement Vallandigham, Democrat from Ohio, were calling for a cessation of hostilities. These "Copperheads," as they were derisively called, favored a negotiated settlement that would include the re-establishment of the Union according to the status ante, with slavery left intact. Emerson was appalled at this prospect, which he saw as a potential moral catastrophe. He delivered "Fortune of the Republic" repeatedly throughout the winter season in an effort to support President Lincoln and to bolster Union resolve to carry the war through to victory, no matter what the cost.

SYNOPSIS

At the outset of his lecture, Emerson places the war in the context of a global struggle for universal human rights, the outcome of which will affect "the future of mankind." He then warns against allowing the "indifference" and "despair" of the moment to prompt a movement toward a "short and hasty peace, on any terms." He insists on the importance of continuing the struggle, to pursue it to its ideal ends, which would necessarily include the absolute destruction of the institution of slavery. One of the threats to achieving this end was the tacit support that Great Britain, the most powerful nation on earth at the time, was providing to the Confederacy. Emerson felt that the "rich, powerful, titled" elite in England sympathized with the rebels because they saw American democracy as a threat to their aristocratic institutions and also because of their economic interest in the cotton trade. "In sight of a commodity," Emerson says of England, "her religion, her morals are forgotten." He is particularly critical of British intellectuals, led by his friend THOMAS CARLYLE, who have supported this pernicious policy.

Emerson goes on to state that in the course of history, "there have been revolutions which were not in the interest of feudalism and barbarism, but in that of society." These were revolutions "in which a principle was involved." Among these, Emerson names the planting of Christianity, the establishment of free institutions in England, France, and America, and "the destruction of slavery" in most of the civilized world. He then alludes to the many improvements that have occurred since the Southerners were excluded from Congress. These include such measures as the Homestead Act (1862), which offered free land in the West to any citizen who wished to establish a farm there, and the Morrill Act (1862), which provided for the establishment of the first land-grant agricultural colleges and was a major step forward in public education. If the war is prosecuted to a successful conclusion, this progress will continue. "The next generation," says Emerson, "will vote for their children,—not a dame school, nor a Latin school, but a university, complete training in all the arts of peace and war, letters, science; all the useful and all the fine arts." The moral progress of the nation will also continue. As a result of Lincoln's Emancipation Proclamation, the nation has begun "to strike off the chains which snuffling hypocrites have bound on the weaker race." The notion that freedom, equality, and social justice were the birthright of *all* citizens, regardless of race, was beginning to take hold. Clearly, none of this could have happened were it not for the war.

The political progress of the nation has also been furthered by the war. Lincoln, a common man, has emerged as a true people's president, a virtual embodiment of the essential democratic concept that government should be of the people, by the people, and for the people. This ideal, Emerson insists, has been realized under Lincoln far more than "under previous administrations." By comparison, the politics of Europe remain "Feudal." In England, the "six demands of chartism" (a major reform movement) have still not been granted after

30 years of agitation, while "they have all been granted here to begin with," at least in the free states.

In light of all this progress for the republic, to cease hostilities now, to return to the dark ages of slavery and social injustice, would be truly tragic. "We [are] in the midst of a great revolution," says Emerson, "still enacting the sentiment of the Puritans. . . . we [are] passing out of old remainders of barbarism into pure Christianity and humanity,—into freedom of thought, of religion, of speech, of the press, of trade, of suffrage, or political right" as we work through "this tremendous ordeal." Emerson insists that American democracy is clearly becoming more liberal and progressive and that success must continue. "Humanity asks that a government shall not be ashamed to be tender and paternal; but that democratic institutions shall be more thoughtful for the interests of women,—for the training of children, for care of sick and unable persons and serious care of criminals, than was ever any the best government of the old world." The contrast between this vision of America and that of the slave oligarchs is profound. Emerson reminds would-be accommodationists that "'Tis vain to say that the war was avoidable by us, or, that both are in the wrong. The difference between the parties is eternal,—it is the difference of moral and immoral motive."

Emerson ends his address on a sober but optimistic note. America is now at a historic crossroad. The outcome of the war will determine the future course of democracy not only in America but in the world. He acknowledges that the sacrifices have been great, but so have the results. "Slavery is broken," he insists, "and, if we use our advantage, irretrievably. For such a gain . . . one generation might well be sacrificed,—perhaps it will be,—that this continent be purged, and a new era of equal rights dawn on the universe." He reminds his listeners that "the times are dark, but heroic" as the "war uplifts us into generous sentiments." His ultimate Transcendental vision is of a reborn America where all will "work for honest humanity, for the poor, for justice, genius, and the public good." At that point, this potentially great nation will at last become what it was destined to be, a "great charity of God to the human race."

CRITICAL COMMENTARY

Emerson's political philosophy devolved directly from his Transcendentalism. In his seminal essay, "The OVER-SOUL" (1841), Emerson asserts that all humanity share in that "Unity, that Over-Soul, within which every man's particular being is made one with all other." From this flows his belief in human equality, a "self-evident" truth articulated powerfully by the Founding Fathers. He deployed this Transcendentalist concept consistently in his 20-year struggle with slavery. It was impossible not to. "Democracy/Freedom," he recorded in an early journal entry, "has its root in the Sacred truth that every man hath in him the divine Reason." That is "the equality & the only equality of all men," and "because every man has within him somewhat really divine therefore slavery is the unpardonable outrage it is."

"Fortune of the Republic" is the culmination of Emerson's antislavery career. It is by far his most overtly political lecture. There were enormous national issues at stake when Emerson delivered this address. The future of democracy and the ideal of human equality would be determined by the outcome of the war. If Lincoln were not reelected, then the moral progress that the nation had made toward universal emancipation, social equality, and civil rights would be lost. At the outbreak of the war, Emerson was confident that it would ultimately prove to be the instrument of the nation's moral rebirth. In earlier addresses like "Civilization at a Pinch" (1861), "American Nationality" (1861), "Moral Forces" (1862), and "Emancipation" (1863), he had promoted the Transcendental values of universal freedom and equality that are prominent in "Fortune of the Republic." Emerson's sense of urgency and determination in the matter is reflected in the fact that he delivered this address no fewer than 14 consecutive times throughout New England and New York. Never before had he repeated a single lecture with such frequency. When Lincoln was eventually reelected in the fall of 1864, Emerson was elated. He saw it as a great triumph for all of humanity. In a letter to a friend he expressed "Joy of the Election," and added somewhat soberly, "Seldom in history was so much staked on a popular vote.—I suppose never in history." He no doubt felt a quiet satisfaction with the important role he had played in bringing about that Transcendental victory.

FURTHER READING

Emerson, Ralph Waldo. *The Later Lectures of Ralph Waldo Emerson.* Vol. 2. Edited by Ronald Bosco and Joel Myerson. Athens: University of Georgia Press, 2001.

Gougeon, Len. *Virtue's Hero: Emerson, Antislavery, and Reform.* Athens: University of Georgia Press, 1990.

———. "Historical Background." In *Emerson's Antislavery Writings,* edited by Len Gougeon and Joel Myerson, xi–lvi. New Haven, Conn.: Yale University Press, 1995.

Robinson, David M. *The Political Emerson: Essential Writings on Politics and Social Reform.* Boston: Beacon Press, 2004.

Len Gougeon

"Freedom" (1854)

On August 7, 1853, Julia Griffith wrote to Emerson for a contribution to a projected antislavery volume, intended to benefit the Rochester Antislavery Society; on October 24 he sent her the poem "Freedom." The poem was first published under the title "On Freedom" in *Autographs for Freedom,* edited by Griffith (1854), in a 22-line version. The poem was collected in MAY-DAY AND OTHER PIECES (1867), though for *May-Day* lines 21–22, "Counsel not with flesh and blood; / Loiter not for cloak or food," were added. The poem (the 24-line version) was also collected in *Poems* (1884).

Emerson's poem "Freedom" reflects his ongoing concern with ABOLITIONISM, as well as the poet's responsibility in effecting social change. "Freedom," as an abolition poem, reads comparably with "VOLUNTARIES" (in which Emerson sings the plight of abducted African natives); "BOSTON HYMN" (God's angel is "Freedom," which should be "king"); and "ODE, INSCRIBED TO W. H. CHANNING" (in which Emerson comments on "Freedom praised, but hid"). The poem offers a dialogue between a poet and his muse (or, abstractly, human and spirit), regarding the best way to free slaves. In this poem Emerson conceptualizes "freedom" not as determined by law but as a god, and thus accessible to (and a part of) everyone.

CRITICAL COMMENTARY

The first two couplets of this poem are set in dactylic tetrameter; that is, lines of four beats, with the accent at the beginning of the line and on the first beat in each foot (in this sense, "paean" should be read as two syllables). These four lines take on the rhythm of a march and suggest the strident attention and determination of the poet. Spirit's reply establishes the second section of the poem. In this section, Emerson ameliorates his own desire to effect abolition by abstracting freedom as a gift to all; that is, not an established practice dictated by men. In this way Emerson establishes freedom as a deity (enshrined on a mountain), and in terms of his own expressions of nature, it is present in every breath ("by heaving of the breast"). This expression calls to mind the Hebrew name for God: JHVH, *Yahweh,* or the sound of breathing, such that every breath is a prayer.

Emerson summarizes spirit's instruction to the poet in the last four lines of the poem: If you will know freedom's secret, do not look for it among humans. As stated earlier (line 17), freedom shines in the heart. If the poet will aid the cause of freedom, he must recognize the harmony of this god within his own heart, where the god "blends the starry fates with thine." The last lines of the poem echo this caution: "Right thou feelest, rush to do." Emerson privileges "feel" over "rush to do." Only by understanding the god "freedom" in the heart can the poet effectively sympathize with those who are not free. In this poem, Emerson calls again for common recognition, this time in terms of the god, freedom, which is a fundamental part of humanity, and which Emerson privileged both as a Transcendentalist (freedom as a gift to all from God) and as an abolitionist (freedom as social justice).

Bill Scalia

"Friendship" (1841)

The poem "Friendship" initially appeared in *ESSAYS: FIRST SERIES* (1841) as a motto, a set of verses expressing an ideal, to accompany his essay "FRIENDSHIP." It was published as a separate poem in the collection *MAY-DAY AND OTHER PIECES* (1867). However, the topic of ideal friendship is recorded in Emerson's journal as early as 1835, during a period when Emerson, MARGARET FULLER, CAROLINE STURGIS TAPPAN, and later, HENRY DAVID THOREAU, all wrote their thoughts on friendship and exchanged their journals, adding comments to one another's passages. Throughout his writings, Emerson argued that friendship depended on self-reliance, the shared soul, and the universality of thought. The duty of friendship, according to Emerson in the essay of that title, was to raise one's friend to a transcendent level of "loftiness": "I please my imagination more with a circle of godlike men and women, variously related to each other, and between whom subsists a lofty intelligence." This theme is prevalent in both the essay on "Friendship" and its related introductory poem.

CRITICAL COMMENTARY

The motto "Friendship" contains 20 lines of poetry divided into five four-line stanzas, with some lines rhyming. The first section describes a drop of "manly" blood being more powerful than the sea, and the "lover" being more constant than the uncertain world that "comes and goes." The word "manly" did not suggest sexism in the 19th century but rather strength, courage, and nobility of spirit. Furthermore, the word "lover" has also changed from its earlier definition as an affectionate or benevolent friend to its current sexual connotation.

In the second four-line section of the poem, the narrator is astonished that the friend has not "fled," as the narrator has thought, but has remained faithful and kind throughout the years, "like the daily sunrise." The strength and loyalty of the friend frees the narrator's "careful heart" in section 3, which intuitively knows that through the conduit of the ideal friend, nature is enhanced, "the sky is arched," and "the rose is red." Section 4 begins with the declaration that the friend has ennobled "all things" and causes them to transcend beyond the earth. The poem then progresses to the lines "The mill-round of our fate appears / A sun-path in thy worth." Emerson's language reflects the 19th-century usage of "mill" as either a verb, meaning to transform, or as a noun, meaning a circular motion. "Round" also suggests a circle, which, in Emerson's symbolism, often represents a genesis or new beginning. "Fate" on the other hand, in Emerson's writings, infers limits. "Sun-path" is the path of the sun that determines the length of days; however, a "sun–path" may also be a stream of light emanating from the sun, or a ray. Taken together, these images give another more literal meaning to "mill-round," as a road around a mill symbolizing the limits of worldly life compared to the light on the transcendent path to the sublime led by the ideal friend.

In the final segment of the poem, the message is revealed. The "nobleness" of the ideal friend has taught the narrator to overcome his "despair." The inspiration and energy of his "hidden life" of the mind are flourishing through the goodness and inspiration of the Transcendental friendship.

Barbara Downs Wojtusik

"Friendship" (1841)

"Friendship" was first published in 1841 in Emerson's *ESSAYS: FIRST SERIES.* Positioned in the volume between "LOVE" and "Prudence," "Friendship" is not widely considered to be one of Emerson's seminal works. It does, however, provide insight into Emerson's personal and intellectual connection to HENRY DAVID THOREAU. Although the essay does not name Thoreau specifically, at the time it was written Emerson was involved in influential and intense friendships not only with Thoreau but also with MARGARET FULLER, CAROLINE STURGIS TAPPAN, Samuel Gray Ward, Anna Barker, and AMOS BRONSON ALCOTT, each of whom was a constant presence in his life and in his journals throughout the 1830s and 1840s. It is therefore no surprise that Emerson was interested in developing a philosophy of friendship, as these years leading up to the essay's publication were his most social.

"Friendship," however, swings from pure enthusiasm over such new relationships to the inevitable disappointment when one becomes too enamored with one's friends. It concludes with a much more balanced understanding of the distinction between acquaintance and true friendship. It is this struggle to find balance between himself and the social realm that defines Emerson's Transcendentalist project. In other works of the same time period that are considered foundational to Emerson's thought, such as "The AMERICAN SCHOLAR" (1837) and "SELF-RELIANCE" (1841), there is a great focus on the power of one's own mind. If the main thrust of Emerson's Transcendentalism concerned this ultimate value of the individual, then the act of friendship was an attempt to locate that individual within the social world. "Friendship" is about seeing the difference between two people and bringing them together in a way that retains the individuality of each. When we look at the essay in this light, it becomes clear that "Friendship" shows Emerson struggling with issues that come up in several other areas of his work and themes that were fundamental to his Transcendentalism.

SYNOPSIS

Emerson begins "Friendship" in exuberance over the connection that we have with one another. This connection refers to our closest of friendships and also those that are much more casual. He notes that we feel warmth and kindness from and toward even those with whom we have very little actual contact. These relations that we have with one another "make the sweetness of life." The beginning of the essay accounts for the ways friendships enhance our lives, feeding our intellect and reminding us of all of the potential within the world. Our associations with one another sustain us: "Let the soul be assured that somewhere in the universe it should rejoin its friend, and it would be content and cheerful alone for a thousand years." Not only do our friendships bring us feelings of joy, they also give us access to the universal through the particular, as each friend "stands to us for humanity."

There is something magical specifically in making the acquaintance of new friends, an intoxication that comes from the pure potentiality that exists undisturbed in the beginning of a friendship. Hidden within the things that we have yet to discover about our new friend are qualities that—because they are not yet defined—seem almost superior to our own. We imagine that our new friend is perfection, that they will connect with us on a deeper level than anyone else, that their virtue will be unparalleled: "We over-estimate the conscience of our friend. His goodness seems better than our goodness, his nature finer."

Having exalted our friendships, Emerson then turns to some of the skepticism and disenchantment that can also be involved. Our tendencies to hold new acquaintances in such high regard in this beginning stage of connection leads to inevitable frustration. Emerson imagines that, in order to prevent this disappointment, we might write a letter to each potential friend explaining that, while we are searching for both our perfect match in our friend and also the perfection of humanity, we simultaneously know that this is impossible: "Friendship, like the immortality of the soul, is too good to be believed. The lover, beholding his maiden, half knows that she is not verily that which he worships; and in the golden hour of friendship, we are surprised with shades of suspicion and unbelief."

Emerson reminds us that while it may be a part of our *human* nature to seek the ultimate match in another soul, it is the nature of the world to show us that this is impossible. Predictably, over time our friend turns out to be something less than perfect, or our relationship turns out not to be a perfect match. This discontent in our relations is not confined to the other person but can also make itself manifest within our own desires. At one moment, we are ecstatic at the thought of our friend and want nothing more than their company, and in the next moment we find ourselves desperately needing our own solitude.

There is, though, something of greater worth in our friendships than this constant cycle of exaltation and disappointment. Emerson wants to consider a more substantial kind of relationship. Here the essay moves back into the exuberance that we saw in the beginning, but this time Emerson is a little bit more realistic in his joy it is not as feverish as we saw before. When friendships are real and true they provide perhaps a less intense emotion but a much more lasting one. When they are real, says Emerson, friendships are, "not glass threads or frostwork, but the solidest thing we know."

There are two necessary components that ensure authentic friendship: truth and tenderness. Emerson begins with truth, which in friendship is both a luxury and something to be honored and guarded. It is not always easy to be truthful in our friendships: "Every man alone is sincere. At the entrance of a second person, hypocrisy begins." The rules of society are such that we feel we should not always tell the truth, should not leave ourselves too vulnerable. Emerson tells the story of a man who let go of all of these societal boundaries and told the truth to every man he encountered, all the time, no matter the risk. For a while, this man became the least popular member of his community. Gradually though, people realized that what they lost in niceties, they gained in reliability. It is refreshing to know that when you ask someone a question, you will get the most honest answer. While this may seem radical, Emerson is stating that this kind of honesty and vulnerability is a demand of true friendship.

Tenderness, of equal importance in friendship, is quite simply about the feelings that we have toward one another. Friendship requires the expression of tenderness in acts, not only words. To say that we love a friend is not enough, we must *show* it by expressing tenderness, by being alongside our friend not only when it pleases us but, more importantly, when our friend needs us. Friendship, for Emerson, "is for aid and comfort through all the relations and passages of life and death."

While truth and tenderness are the pillars of authentic friendship, there are other aspects that are also important to facilitate and maintain this relationship. For example, for a more balanced exchange of thoughts, it is always better to have two people involved and not more. Further, friendship cannot occur when two people are not comfortable disagreeing and debating issues with each other. Friendship that rests on similarities alone will have no substance. As he says, friendship "requires an absolute running of two souls into one." And then, "there must be very two, before there can be very one." Unless there are two distinct individuals who mutually respect each other, this relation is impossible.

This mutual respect in friendship is necessary to ward off the ecstatic kind of friendship that Emerson spoke of in the beginning of the essay, the kind that tends to be short-lived. And the respect of difference and boundaries is not important only in conversation and debates; it also can prevent us from smothering our friends, or losing ourselves within them. Friends are not property, Emerson reminds us; they must be treated with respect and space. We cannot demand too much time or closeness from our friends. Our relationship should be based on a very simple give and take: "To my friend I write a letter, and from him I receive a letter. That seems to you a little. It suffices me."

Emerson emphasizes the importance of the balance between the inner self and the outer self in friendship, sometimes against our instincts and desires. The ideal balance is one that allows us to be able to cultivate the relationship both within ourselves, in understanding the ways in which our friend has influenced our minds and thoughts, as well as outside ourselves, in our active connection with that person. As he says, "I do then with my friends as I do with my books. I would have them where I can find them, but I seldom use them." For Emerson, attaining this balance allows him to "receive from them, not what they have, but what they are."

Emerson completes the essay urging us to open ourselves up truly to our friends, to be truthful and tender always, with no regard to whether we receive the same in return. If we are able to do these, we transcend both ourselves and the other person. The essay has moved from the description of the intensity and disappointment in our relationships with one another to the explanation of what is required to make sure this does not happen and to attain authentic friendship. Emerson ends the essay with a powerful statement: "The essence of friendship is entireness, a total magnanimity and trust. It must not surmise or provide for infirmity. It treats its object as a god, that it may deify both."

CRITICAL COMMENTARY

In order to understand "Friendship" within Emerson's entire catalog of thought, it is important to place its ideas within the context of his personal life as well as within his Transcendentalism. As with many of Emerson's essays, "Friendship" at first glance seems to hold a very simple idea, but this idea can be connected with Transcendentalist themes in more emblematic essays, such as "Self-Reliance," "The American Scholar," and "EXPERIENCE."

The time during which Emerson wrote this essay was his most social. As he began establishing himself as an influential member of the community in CONCORD, Emerson found himself surrounded by a new circle of friends. The essay is not just a listing or an appreciation of these friendships; rather, Emerson was grappling with a tension that he felt between himself and his newfound relationships. He expresses disappointment in his relationships with others but simultaneously feels thankful for the presence of his friends in his life, and also accounts for the boundaries that he feels need to be drawn between the social and the individual realms. Indeed, the most significant part of the essay is devoted to these tensions and the balance necessary to avoid them.

Emerson's journals reveal these personal reasons for this essay's conception. Margaret Fuller, one of Emerson's closest friends, chastised him several times for the way that he acted toward friends. She felt he was apathetic toward others, and, though this may have been the opposite of how he felt, she saw that he came off as distant and uncaring. In his journal on August 16, 1840, Emerson states: "I rode with Margaret to the plains. She taxed me, as often before, so now more explicitly, with inhospitality of Soul. She and C. [Caroline Sturgis Tappan] would gladly be my friends, yet our intercourse is not friendship. . . . They make no progress with me, but however often we have met, we still meet as strangers. They feel wronged in such relation." This accusation, made merely one year before the publication of "Friendship," was no doubt a catalyst for the essay, in which Emerson was not only outlining a philosophy of friendship for his readers but also defining the idea for himself and his specific circle of friends. He wanted to account for the way that he connected with others, so that it would give his friends a deeper understanding of why he may come off as apathetic, when really what he was trying to achieve was the balance required for the deepest kind of friendship possible.

Emerson's relationship with Henry David Thoreau was also certainly at work in this essay's conception. When Emerson writes about Thoreau in his journals, it is obvious that they had the kind of authentic relationship that Emerson describes in "Friendship," and that it is this relationship that Emerson had in mind when composing this section of the essay. Each pillar of authentic friendship is accounted for in his connection with Thoreau: They were very honest with each other, respectfully disagreeing with each other on many topics, providing lively conversation and debate, and certainly felt very deeply connected to each other.

Along with these personal reasons that might have caused Emerson to write "Friendship," the essay illuminates his Transcendental ideals. Emerson's Transcendentalism was concerned primarily with the power of one's own mind. As he explains in "Self-Reliance," "nothing is at last sacred but the integrity of your own mind." And in "The American Scholar" he argued that "in yourself is the law of all nature . . . in yourself slumbers the whole of Reason."

"Friendship" is also very much concerned with the balance between the individual and the world. This tension between self and society, and the struggle to find the balance, is at the center of many of Emerson's writings. In "Friendship," this struggle is reflected in the need for balance in one's relationships to other people, a theme also reflected in the essay "Experience," published in *ESSAYS: SECOND SERIES* (1844). In "Experience," widely thought to be a work of mourning following the death of Emerson's son Waldo, Emerson tries to avoid what he refers to as "the most unhandsome part of our condition"; that is, the human tendency to try to grasp hold of those things that we desire, rather than seeing each as one of many fleeting experiences to be lived through. As he eloquently explains in "Experience," "I take this evanescence and lubricity of all objects, which lets them slip through our fingers then when we clutch hardest, to be the most unhandsome part of our condition. Nature does not like to be observed, and likes that we should be her fools and playmates."

This echoes Emerson's words in the beginning of "Friendship," when he was detailing the inevitable disappointment when we become too infatuated, too optimistic about a new acquaintance. We want to hold on to our friends, we want to have a connection with them that is unlike any other, and yet, the more we try and get to this, the more it evades us and our friendships become shallow and untrue. His advice in "Friendship" is similar to that in "Experience": Appreciate things as they come to you, but do not try and grasp at them, for you will be left with nothing except disappointment. As he explains at the end of the essay, authentic friendship will enable you to focus on what you are, not what you have. In both essays, the overarching point is that no matter how much our instinct might rail against this fact, the world is to be lived in and through, not possessed or controlled.

FURTHER READING

McNulty, John Bard. "Emerson's Friends and the Essay on Friendship." *New England Quarterly* 19, No. 3 (September 1946): 390–394.

Smith, Harmon L. *My Friend, My Friend: The Story of Thoreau's Relationship with Emerson.* Amherst: University of Massachusetts Press, 1999.

Steele, Jeffrey. "Transcendental Friendship: Emerson, Fuller, and Thoreau." In *The Cambridge Companion to Ralph Waldo Emerson,* edited by Joel Porte and Saundra Morris, 121–139. New York: Cambridge University Press, 1999.

MaryCatherine Youmell

"From the Persian of Hafiz" (1847)

Emerson first read selections of the Persian poets in 1841; he wrote his poem "SAADI" for the Transcendentalist literary journal *The* DIAL 1842, and in the following year he read Saadi's *Gulistan.* After acquiring a copy of JOHANN WOLFGANG VON GOETHE's Hafiz-inspired poems, *East-West Diwan* in April 1846, Emerson entered his own translations, "From the Persian of Hafiz" and a companion piece, "Ghaselle," in his first collection *POEMS,* in 1847. At that time he read all the Persian poets more fully in the German anthology of Joseph Von Hammer-Purgstall, and he continued to read them to the end of his life.

Two of Emerson's most important poems, "BACCHUS" (1847) and "DAYS" (1857), were partially inspired by these readings of Persian poetry. In the *MAY-DAY AND OTHER PIECES* (1867) collection of poems, he included a quatrain titled "Hafiz": "Her passions the shy violet / From Hafiz never hides; / Love-longings of the raptured bird / The bird to him confides." He also included a section on translations of Persian poets in that volume. Numerous references to the Persian poets appear in such essays as "FATE," "POWER," and "ILLUSIONS" in *The* CONDUCT OF LIFE (1860), and even later in his career Emerson wrote a full essay, "PERSIAN POETRY," which was included in *LETTERS AND SOCIAL AIMS* of 1876.

CRITICAL COMMENTARY

In "Persian Poetry" Emerson regarded Hafiz and Saadi as his own ideal poets. He praised them for their expressive splendor, their freedom of thought and joyful affirmation that transcended religious fatalism, their sincerity and self-reliance, and their perception of beauty in nature and human life. He also cherished them for themes of the inspirational quality of woman, as well as the highest priority they placed on love and friendship, and their expression of the law of compensation. "Hafiz," he wrote, "praises wine, maidens, boys, birds, mornings, and music, to give vent to his immense hilarity and sympathy with every form of beauty and joy." In the same essay Emerson translated Hafiz's lines: "See how the roses burn! / Bring wine to quench the fire! / Alas! the flames come up with us, / We perish with desire"—the exquisite aestheticism of which he enfolded in his companion poem "Bacchus."

In "Bacchus" Emerson self-reflexively entwined his own poetic persona with that of Hafiz. His lines "Wine that is shed / Like the torrents of the sun / Up the horizon walls" connect Hafiz's wine of freedom with his sunshine of joy. Interlaced in many of Emerson's other poems, such as "The WORLD-SOUL," "WOODNOTES," and "MONADNOC," Hafiz's wine became a central metaphor for Emerson's own spiritual transcendence in *poesis*. As he wrote in "Bacchus," "Pour, Bacchus! The remembering wine, / Retrieve the loss of me and mine! / . . . A dazzling memory revive; / . . . And write my old adventures with the pen." In "POETRY AND IMAGINATION" (1876) he reprised the same sentiment of wine's inspirational intoxication when he wrote: "O celestial Bacchus! Drive them mad,—this multitude of vagabonds, hungry for Eloquence, hungry for poetry, starving for symbols, perishing for want of electricity."

The chronological companion to "Bacchus," "From the Persian of Hafiz" entirely concentrates on the trope of wine as the poet's self-conveyance into the dimension of Transcendental intuition. Hafiz begins by calling a servant-boy to "fetch the ruby wine / Which with sudden greatness fills us." "This philosophic stone" will "open / All the doors of luck and life." To the same servant-boy: "Bring me . . . the fire-water:—/ Drinks the lion, the woods burn; / Give it to me, that I may storm heaven . . . / Wine wherewith the Houris teach / Souls the ways of paradise!"

Hafiz-Emerson now sets these symbolic transformations in opposition to the cares and vices of the mundane world: "Give me wine to wash me clean / Of the weather-stains of cares, / See the countenance of luck." This celestial wine "increases life," in contrast to which "the world is all untrue." He counsels: "Be not certain of the world,—'Twill not spare to shed thy blood." "Desperate of the world's affair," he has thus come running to the wine house, in order "that I reason quite expunge," and "plant banners on the worlds," and "quench the sorrow-cinders."

To Hafiz-Emerson, a cup of this wine "imparts the sight / Of the five heaven-domes with nine steps." It signifies "purest love." This "toy of Daemons" "wake[s] the torpid heart." Hafiz's spiritual wine as a symbol of poetic inspiration expressed the essence of Emerson's Transcendentalism. A pervasive image in his writings, it also reverberated in FRIEDRICH NIETZSCHE's central image of the god Dionysius. Closer to home, it recurred in the poetry of WALT WHITMAN and of EMILY DICKINSON, who wrote her own rendition of Hafiz-Bacchus in her poem "I taste a liquor never brewed," which ends with her ingeniously delightful transformation of Emerson's Transcendentalist poetics: "Till Seraphs swing their snowy Hats— / And Saints—to windows run— / To see the little Tipler / Leaning against the—Sun!"

David A. Dilworth

"The Fugitive Slave Law" (1851)

"The Fugitive Slave Law" was delivered for the first time on May 3, 1851, in Emerson's hometown of CONCORD, MASSACHUSETTS. The lecture was given in response to the enforcement of a federal law passed as part of the Compromise of 1850. In the aftermath of Texas annexation and the Mexican War, Northern and Southern interests were sharply divided over the question of the expansion of slavery into newly won western territories. Some Southern states contemplated secession in reaction to the potential admission of California as a free state, which would tilt the balance of representative power in Washington toward the North. To offset this, it was proposed that other new territories in the southwest remain open to slavery and that demands for Northern cooperation in protecting existing slave property be addressed. The Fugitive Slave Act forbade Northerners from aiding escaped slaves and ordered Northern marshals to help catch runaway slaves under threat of fines and imprisonment.

Emerson was outraged over a series of arrests made in BOSTON in February 1851 in connection to the case of Shadrach Minkins, an escaped slave. Shadrach was arrested as a fugitive slave but was rescued from his captors by abolitionists who were subsequently persecuted under the law. "The Fugitive Slave Law" address, the first sharply pointed political speech of Emerson's career, was written in response to these events. After its initial delivery in Concord, he used the lecture on numerous occasions throughout the spring of 1851 as a stump speech in support of John Gorham Palfrey's unsuccessful run for U.S. Congress as a Free Soil candidate. It was published only decades later in the Centenary Edition (1903–04) of Emerson's *Complete Works,* compiled and edited by his son, EDWARD WALDO EMERSON. Recently edited versions are available in *Emerson's Antislavery Writings* (1995) and *The Later Lectures of Ralph Waldo Emerson* (2001). Although the speech is overtly political, Emerson employs the Transcendental theme of "compensation" to drive his argument and structure his discourse.

SYNOPSIS

Emerson begins the lecture by announcing that a sense of urgency, necessity, and duty compelled him to speak on the topic despite his distaste for political speeches: "There seems to be no option. The last year has forced us all into politics, and made it a paramount duty to seek what is often a duty to shun." He describes an ominous and oppressive atmosphere that "robs the landscape of beauty, and takes the sunshine out of every hour," and declares that those who had not already been affected by it soon would be. Emerson states that the sources of this general anxiety were the "late events in Massachusetts, and the behavior of Boston." Those who thought that no slave could be arrested in Boston had been proven wrong. Particularly disturbing was that the city of such importance to the American Revolution had become "spoiled by prosperity."

Emerson mentions the Shadrach Minkins case directly and refers to "Mr. Webster's treachery" early in the lecture. Daniel Webster, the Massachusetts senator whom Emerson once admired, was the "introducer and substantial author" of the 1850 legislation. Emerson's disgust with many Bostonians' support of Webster and acquiescent acceptance of the enforcement of the 1850 legislation is clearly evident. Clergymen, college professors, "brokers, insurers, lawyers, importers, manufacturers," and the press all seemed aligned in tacit support of the Fugitive Slave Law. The one benefit that Emerson attributes to the law is that it exposed the unreliability and hollowness of the cultural and political leadership and the insincerity of their celebration of America's revolutionary ideals and heritage. Emerson offered the failure of the "public mind" to grasp moral truth and react against injustice and the strength of "party ties" as explanations of how "humane people" could back the law and how Boston had become the slave catcher's "hound."

Emerson then turns to more philosophical language to explain ways in which the crisis illustrates "the divine laws." Emerson argues that it is in the order of the universe that evil deeds must be paid for. Northerners, in agreeing to the compromise, had "borrow[ed] the succour of the devil" to secure their own interests. The prosperity bought through this immoral agreement, however, would not prevent "natural retribution" from occurring. The devil "must have his fee." One way nature carries out retribution or compensation for corruption is to plague corrupted societies with hideous imperfections and calamities to accompany its advantages. Several paragraphs are devoted to illustrating five ways in which natural retribution for the Fugitive Slave Law would operate in America.

First, the "sentiment of duty" will contravene. An immoral law never stands long, even under tyrannical governments, because at the core of every human being there is virtue. The "primal sentiment of duty" makes "all men that are born . . . in proportion to their power of thought and their moral responsibility" the natural enemies of immoral law. After confessing this conviction, Emerson admits his bewilderment that "what must come at last" had not "come at first," or in other words, why the inevitable downfall of the law due to its incompatibility with "public morality" had not already caused "a banding of men against the authority of this statute." Emerson states that he had thought that "all men of all conditions had been made sharers of a certain experience," that they had once perceived the moral essence of the universe and that in thought they could return to this vision. This elevated "spiritual element" was the source of laws, which "draw their obligation only from their concurrence with it." He was surprised to find that American lawyers were nonetheless laughing over the concept of "Higher Law" despite the fact that the "great jurists" of history from Cicero to Jefferson all agreed that worldly laws, if not of accord with universal moral law, were void.

Second, "all the sentiments" would revolt against a law that "fines pity, and imprisons charity" and cause men, "as long as they have bowels," to disobey. The sentiments of indignation and pity are seen as built-in human features, provided by nature to defend the innocent from cruelty. Emerson emphasizes that men are ultimately children of nature and not of the human systems of law and government they are born into. Nothing short of "gagging the English language" and washing away the Ten Commandments would assure the success of the Fugitive Slave Law.

Third, previous written laws more attuned to the human sentiments, such as the 1807 statute forbidding enslavement of men in Africa, were incompatible with the 1850 law, which forbade a man from preventing re-enslavement. Fourth, "mischief" was sure to arise from a bad law as only "flagitious men" could be employed to enforce it. All men involved in the affair would be "contaminated" and lose the respect of the virtuous people. Statesmen and judges would be ranked among the turnkeys, hangmen, and informers. Fifth, the law would and already was causing a heightened interest in and attention to the problem of slavery. What was implemented in the name of "union" had brought "swords into the streets." It made the governors of the North—Webster first among them—into "white slaves," harnessed to the "chariot of the planters."

Taking discussion of Webster as his cue, Emerson segues from "ethical" into "political" considerations. He begins by remembering his own admiration for Webster as a powerful and intelligent orator. He was "the best head in Congress and the champion of the northern seaboard," but finally, in 1850, he became "the head of the slavery party." Emerson speculates that this was the result of Webster's obeisance to his "powerful animal nature." His mind works in full force only "when it stands for animal good; that is, for property." He is a "man of the past" who respects accumulated wealth. He respects the Constitution as a fixed law, but he is blind to the spirit from which it was born: "In 1776, he would, beyond all question, have been a refugee."

Emerson then turns his attention to the issue of "union" in America. He admits that the union of the American people is "a real thing"—an alliance of men with similar backgrounds, manners, and ideas living together in a country whose destiny is to be "great and liberal." Nevertheless, he asserts that within the union "there are really two nations, the north and the south," that are separated not only by slavery but also by "climate and temperament." This union must be sundered as soon as immoral law is ordained.

Finally, Emerson turns to the practical question, "What shall we do?" The duty of citizens of the nation and of the state is to first "abrogate this law, then proceed to confine slavery to slave states, and help them effectually to make an end of it." This must be done immediately as slave power "gives itself no holidays"—it had already expanded into Texas and was currently eyeing Cuba. Emerson is optimistic that America could emancipate its slaves peacefully and successfully: "Nothing is impracticable to this nation, which it shall set itself to do." However, even if the nation would not cooperate, "we must keep Massachusetts true." The state, though small, could be "the brain which turns about the behemoth." Slavery should not be allowed to be brought to Cape Cod and Berkshire. The Fugitive Slave Law "must be disobeyed." To conclude, Emerson encourages his audience to see that the uprightness of the few, along with private courage and obedience to higher law, can salvage an entire nation.

CRITICAL COMMENTARY

Unlike nearly all of Emerson's writings and orations before 1851, the central purpose of "The Fugitive Slave Law" is practical and political. It encourages active opposition to the law, denounces the Boston elite and particularly Daniel Webster for collaboration with slaveholders, and offers several concrete suggestions about how to react to the law.

The most direct precedents to "The Fugitive Slave Law" address in Emerson's work are his 1838 open letter to President Van Buren and his 1844 speech "EMANCIPATION OF THE NEGROES IN THE BRITISH WEST INDIES." The former was written to protest the forced removal of the Cherokee people from their homeland in the Southeast as a result of the Indian Removal Act of 1830. Like the "Fugitive Slave Law," the Van Buren letter denounces a law and policy of the U.S. government as immoral and fraudulent. In both pieces, Emerson included details that would appeal to any reader or listener's sense of humanity. In the 1838 letter he remarked that the government was contracting to put the Cherokee nation "into carts and boats, and drag them" from their farms into western wilderness against their will. In the 1851 speech he reminds listeners that, to obtain freedom, escaped slaves had risked "being shot, or burned alive, or cast into the sea, or starved to death, or suffocated in a wooden box" and conjures an image of a "poor black boy . . . in the recesses of a rice-swamp, or in the alleyways of Savannah" dreaming of freedom in the North only to find upon arrival all of Boston working as "his master's hound."

"The Fugitive Slave Law" is not merely a political tract but also a philosophical discourse constructed around several familiar themes in Emerson's Transcendentalism. In each of his antislavery writings the main emphasis is not on sentimentalist appeal but on philosophical argument hinging on the concepts of morality, higher law, and compensation. The letter to President Van Buren invokes the idea of the inevitable ultimate failure of laws that go against the "moral sentiment" and of a compensatory justice built into the universe: "However feeble the sufferer, and however great the oppressor, it is in the nature of things that the blow should recoil on the aggressor." For Emerson, the "moral sentiment" was more or less synonymous with reason, or the human faculty for direct perception of universal truth. Man-made laws and actions that went against the promptings of the "moral sentiment" also went against higher universal law. Although they may be temporarily successful, universal law would ultimately prevail. The 1841 essay "COMPENSATION" explains this concept more fully. This higher or universal law "writes the laws of cities and nations. It is in vain to plot or combine against it. Things refused to be mismanaged long. . . . Though no checks to a new evil appear, the checks exist, and will appear. If the government is cruel, the governor's life is not safe." In this sense, we can see that Emerson viewed his protest to Cherokee Removal and to the Fugitive Slave Law as rational responses to irrational laws.

"The Fugitive Slave Law" also holds a unique and important place in Emerson's antislavery writings. His speech "Emancipation of the Negroes in the British West Indies" in 1844 was the "Fugitive Slave Law" address's most important predecessor. Several themes connect these two discourses. In the 1844 speech Emerson had also combined sympathy-provoking detail about the demeaning and dehumanizing treatment of slaves with an insistence that a higher law or "blessed necessity" links moral action and human progress. Emerson's insistence that adherence to higher law is of greater importance than the preservation of the Union under immoral legislation in "The Fugitive Slave Law" address also has a precedent in the 1844 speech, in which he demanded that the government send federal troops to the South in order to find and release illegally re-enslaved free blacks, despite all "dangers to the Union."

Unlike earlier antislavery speeches that were delivered partly to commemorate the emancipation of slaves in British possessions and partly to encourage Americans to support similar measures in the United States, "The Fugitive Slave Law" was intended to convey a sense of immediate threat and crisis. It was the first speech in which Emerson suggests and even demands the breaking of a specific law. Emerson's harsh and acrimonious denunciation of a contemporary political figure, Daniel Webster, reflects a sense of betrayal and touches on a main message in the discourse: that through the 1850 statute, slavery had been made the law of the North as well as of the South. Emerson compares the cowardly actions of Webster and of the Bostonians of 1851 to those of the heroic revolutionary generation. These themes—the encouragement of civil disobedience and noncooperation with slave legislation, the unequivocal accusation of collaborators with slavery in government, and invocation of American revolutionary heritage—continued to shape Emerson's ABOLITIONISM throughout the 1850s, including a second address on the Fugitive Slave Law he gave in 1854.

FURTHER READING

Collison, Gary. "Emerson and Antislavery." In *A Historical Guide to Ralph Waldo Emerson,* edited by Joel Myerson, 179–209. New York and Oxford: Oxford University Press, 2000.

———. *Shadrach Minkins: From Fugitive Slave to Citizen.* Cambridge, Mass.: Harvard University Press, 1998.

Gougeon, Len. *Virtue's Hero: Emerson, Antislavery and Reform.* Athens: University of Georgia Press, 1990.

Petrulionis, Sandra. *To Set This World Right: The Antislavery Movement in Thoreau's Concord.* Ithaca, N.Y.: Cornell University Press, 2006.

Specq, François. "Emerson's Rhetoric of Empowerment in 'Address to the Citizens of Concord on the Fugitive Slave Law' (1851)." In *Ralph Waldo Emerson dans ses texts: rhétorique et philosophie,* edited by Philippe Jaworski and François Brunet, 115–129. Paris: Institut d'Études Anglophones, Université Paris VII, 2004.

Daniel Robert Koch

"Give All to Love" (1847)

The short six-stanza poem "Give All to Love" was included in Emerson's first collection, POEMS (1847), and reprinted in SELECTED POEMS (1876). The poem explores the tension between the individual self and the external demands of society, a regular theme for Emerson in other poems, such as "SAADI" (1842) and "DAYS" (1857), and in essays such as "FRIENDSHIP" (1841) and "DOMESTIC LIFE" (1870). In "Give All to Love," the poet considers not just the practical but also the spiritual demands of love, and advises to give as much of yourself as needed.

Emerson addressed the concept of love in other poems included in the 1847 volume of *Poems,* such as "EROS" and "INITIAL, DAEMONIC, AND CELESTIAL LOVE." In the essay "LOVE" he attempted an overall philosophy of love and in "COMPENSATION" (both collected in *ESSAYS: FIRST SERIES,* 1841), he uses language strikingly similar to the lines in "Give All to Love" to explain love as an eternal and balancing force in the universe: "We cannot part with our friends. We cannot let our angels go. We do not see that they only go out, that archangels may come in."

CRITICAL COMMENTARY

In the first stanza the poet implores us to "give all to love" and deny no one or no thing needing our attention: "Friends, kindred, days, / Estate, good-fame, / Plans, credit and the Muse, / Nothing refuse." The message is clear—answer whatever demands are made of you by the universe. In the second stanza, love is like the sun at its highest point—"It dives into noon"—but, again like the sun, love "is a god" that knows its limits, "knows its own path." You must trust love, which operates according to the laws of nature and therefore will not steer you wrong. Love knows its limits, which are virtually none ("the outlets of the sky"), and so it is we who impose artificial limits upon ourselves in our relations with others.

In the third stanza Emerson explains that, because love requires self-trust, it is not for the weak-souled, or the soul not interested in its own growth: "It was never for the mean; / It requireth courage stout. / Souls above doubt." Adhering to what Emerson elsewhere identified as the law of compensation, love "will reward," and those who love "shall return / More than they were." Love makes us better people. In the earlier essay "HEROISM" (1841), Emerson had made the same point, that if "done for love," our actions toward others will result in "compensations of the universe" in the form of growth of the individual soul. This sense of balance, of reward and growth from our relationships with others, then, explains how, in the fourth stanza, the poet can simultaneously advise to "leave all for love" and to remain always "free as an Arab / Of thy beloved."

This idea continues in the fifth stanza. While we should devote ourselves to those we love—"Cling with life to the maid"—we must still remember that they are also individuals on their own path and will inevitably have "a joy apart from thee." We cannot force love—"Free be she, fancy-free; / Nor thou detain her vesture's hem," lines similar to the maxim that if you love someone, you must set them free. The poet concludes with the sixth and final stanza, musing that if we have loved others as much as we love ourselves—"loved her as thyself, / As a self of purer clay" (that is, a more perfect human)—then we must accept and trust "her parting," which otherwise "dims the day." The imagery here is that of the sun, leaving or setting, which is also a reference to death. For Emerson, this might clearly be a reference to the death of his first wife, Ellen Tucker Emerson, though some scholars warn against too easily assuming a strictly biographical reference. But, given the numerous loves, friendships, and tragedies in Emerson's own life, one could also argue that his entire philosophical project was, in fact, to make the biographical universal, to relate individual experience to the universal human experience. In this sense, he often explicitly reflected upon and composed essays and poems with those personal contexts in mind.

The oft-quoted final lines of "Give All to Love"—"When half-gods go, / The gods arrive"—remind us that, when we give up superficialities and external motivations for love, then our true selves can be revealed. According to the scholar Len Gougeon, Emerson here defines romantic love as superficial or earthly and "only a stepping-stone to cosmic love."

FURTHER READING

Gougeon, Len. *Emerson and Eros: The Making of a Cultural Hero.* Albany: State University of New York Press, 2007.

"Goethe; or, the Writer" (1850)

"Goethe; or, the Writer" was the last essay in the volume of six biographical pieces included in Emerson's 1850 collection, *REPRESENTATIVE MEN.* It is said that, in all of his portraits of "great men," Emerson identified himself most with JOHANN WOLFGANG VON GOETHE, although Emerson's philosophy and view of himself as a writer ultimately drew in some sense from each of the individuals he chose to include. Of the figures chosen for *Representative Men,* Emerson had already read and written the most on Goethe and on William Shakespeare. He had lectured on Goethe and discussed him at length in the 1840 *DIAL* essay "Thoughts on Modern Literature."

Goethe stands apart, first of all, as a near contemporary; indeed, Emerson's older brother, WILLIAM EMERSON, had sought career advice from Goethe directly while a student in Germany. Secondly, Goethe came to have a central place in the development of American Transcendentalism in general, which drew extensively on German literature and philosophy, introduced in the United States through the English-language translations of THOMAS CARLYLE and of Transcendentalists such as JAMES FREEMAN CLARKE and MARGARET FULLER.

SYNOPSIS

Emerson opens the essay by explaining the role of the writer in society, which is "to report the doings of the miraculous spirit of life." The writer takes the facts and finds what is universal, the "characteristic experiences." Nature tells its own history through shadows, scratches, bones, and fossils; humans leave our marks in "memories" and in our influence upon others. The writer, however, does not just record the facts of nature but relates "experiences" in a "conversation" with the reader. The writer "believes that all that can be thought can be written," and he "finds new materials" in every experience, even "in calamity," in "rage and pain." In an ordinary man, relating such experiences might be "mere stenography," but "the speculative man, or scholar," must "see connection where the multitude see fragments." The writer's work is to understand and articulate "the frame of things."

The work of the writer is not just for individual purposes, however, as society desires and needs this class of men with "powers of expression" who can see through "the illusion" and bring "reason." Like all great men, the scholar or writer straddles the past, present, and future, standing with both "his contemporaries" and with "the ages." For this reason, he is often subject to "ridicule," at least "among superficial people." Emerson remarks that at the present time, there is more value placed on "public opinion" and "the practical man," obscuring the role of the scholar; the people favor "social order and comfort" over ideas.

Emerson warns, however, that "action" without "contemplation" puts men at risk of "loss of balance." It is dangerous for the "rite" or "covenant" to become more important than the "aspiration" or idea. He quotes from the "Hindoos . . . in their sacred books," who make the connection between "the speculative and the practical faculties" and believe that "great action must draw on the spiritual nature." Only "inferior persons" value action over speculation, and even "the leaders" we praise for their actions are guided by "real and admirable" ideas. For all of these reasons, "society has really no graver interest than the well-being of the literary class." Writers used to be the leaders of society and have influence, but if this position is no longer honored it is because the writer "does not honor himself." He has bowed to public opinion; he writes about government and law and writes novels rather than "sacred verse" and "epics."

In surveying "the list of men of literary genius in our age," Emerson finds that Goethe most closely represents "the powers and duties of the scholar or writer." Goethe mastered all disciplines in his writing: "histories, mythologies, philosophies, sciences, and national literatures." He created "elaborate forms" and "a philosophy of literature set in poetry." Goethe's writings are universal and encyclopedic, incorporating "the past and the present ages, and their religions, politics, and modes of thinking," all of which is "dissolved into archetypes and ideas." "Amid littleness and detail," Goethe "detected the Genius of life." Emerson goes so far as to declare that Goethe "has said the best things about nature that ever were said." Emerson emphasizes that "it is really of very little consequence what topic he writes upon," for in all things, Goethe shows "a certain gravitation towards truth."

For example, in *Faust,* Goethe takes on the idea of the devil as a representative, not literal, figure: "The Devil had played an important part in mythology in all times." Goethe's genius was to remake the Devil into a "real . . . modern . . . European . . . gentleman . . . in 1820." To do this he "stripped him of mythologic gear," changed his appearance, and created instead an image of someone "in every shade of coldness, selfishness, and unbelief," who "darkens over the human thought." What he created was a creature both more real and more terrifying, a creature who "was pure intellect, applied,—as always there is a tendency,—to the service of the senses" rather than (presumably) the service of the spirit.

Emerson's purpose here is not to analyze all of Goethe's work, which crosses several genres. Besides *Faust,* however, he comments upon "Wilhelm Meister," which "is a novel in every sense, the first of its kind," dealing as it does with "the spirit of life." This work contains "so many good hints for the conduct of life, so many unexpected glimpses into a higher sphere," which, according to Emerson, is not just a Goethean, but a German tendency, this "habitual reference to interior truth." Goethe, like the other great men in the volume, is representative of his nation and of the spirit of his times.

And yet, "talent alone can not make a writer. There must be a man behind the book." If there is a "truth to be declared," it is the writer's "calling" to get beneath the facts and reveal that truth. The "message" matters more than the style or method. It only "makes a great difference to the force of any sentence, whether there be a man behind it, or not." Writers for newspapers or journals have "no form," only a "shadow" hiding behind "some monied corporation" that sponsors their words. One can write about poetry "without any poetic taste or fire," and just because someone is considered to be a writer or a thinker does not mean "he holds heroic opinions."

But (as with the other great men included in the volume), there are also some limitations to Goethe. He will not appeal to all men because "he is incapable of a self-surrender to the moral sentiment." Some will prefer writers who are "purer" and will "touch the hearts" of readers. Some readers will also not fully appreciate that his was a quest for self-development, not accomplishment. Goethe asked "not for what he can accomplish, but for what can be accomplished in him." He wanted only "to know the history and destiny of man." Emerson concedes that to some Goethe will come across as "fragmentary"; if that is the case, it is only because "he knew too much." Unlike many geniuses, Goethe was a man of the world, not aloof or sickly or depressed: He "was entirely at home and happy in his century and the world." And yet, Goethe worked alone, steadily, from his own motivation, "with no external popularity or provocation."

In the end, "Goethe teaches . . . the equivalence of all times," that "the world is young." We are inspired by the breadth of his efforts to realize that "we too must write Bibles, to unite again the heavens and the earthly world."

CRITICAL COMMENTARY

Although each of the figures in *Representative Men* represents some characteristic of genius within every individual, Emerson saw himself (as a writer and scholar), perhaps more than any other, in Goethean terms. The very title of Goethe's autobiography—"Poetry and Truth Out of My Life"—spoke to Emerson's own Transcendentalist project of self-development and self-discovery. Emerson admires Goethe's ability to "see connection where the multitude see fragments"; indeed, this may be said to be Emerson's vision and achievement in his own work, to see unity in variety. Beyond his own associations, however, Goethe is regularly compared with the other "great men" of the volume, and the essay recalls Emerson's earlier call for intellectual independence in "The AMERICAN SCHOLAR" (1837). In "Goethe," Emerson determines that among "the list of men of literary genius in our age," only Goethe represents "the powers and duties of the scholar or writer." As with Emerson's other choices in *Representative Men,* the United States had yet to produce an equivalent writer to Goethe.

Throughout the essay on Goethe, Emerson makes comparisons, either directly or implicitly, with the figures in other essays in *Representative Men*—most notably, "SWEDENBORG; OR, THE MYSTIC" and "NAPOLEON; OR, THE MAN OF THE WORLD." His essay on Goethe's work and influence is most similar to his view of Emanuel Swedenborg. The representative writer and the mystic, respectively, seem to be engaged in the same project, as Goethe "has said the best things about nature that ever were said," and he credits Goethe with "the leading idea of modern botany," that is, "that a leaf, or the eye of a leaf, is the unit of botany, and that every part of the plant is only a transformed leaf to meet a new condition." Goethe's purpose as a writer, according to Emerson, was to understand and articulate "the frame of things," the same phrase Emerson uses to explain Swedenborg's project as a natural scientist. Perhaps the difference between the two is one of method and genre, as Emerson praises Goethe for more accessible writings, thus the central point of his genius. According to Emerson, Goethe "writes in the plainest and lowest tone," avoiding and despising "conjecture and . . . rhetoric."

The choice of Goethe as the representative writer was not just about his message but was related to the influence of German idealism on American Transcendentalism in the early 19th century. Emerson places Goethe within a specifically German philosophical tendency in the search for truth. This is in opposition to the American way of emphasizing service to the public, or to France, where "intellectual brilliancy" is admired "for its own sake"—that is, without requiring any insight into human condition or mind. It is only the Germans who ask, *"To what end?"* In this sense, then, Emerson acknowledges the German influence on American thought and philosophy: "Hence, almost all the valuable distinctions which are current in higher conversation have been derived to us from Germany." And Goethe is "the head and body of the German nation," speaking not from "talent" but from "truth." Emerson declares Goethe "the soul of his century," a designation he gives to each of his great men.

"Hamatreya" (1847)

"Hamatreya" appeared in Emerson's 1847 collection, *POEMS.* The poem is actually made up of two parts, as within "Hamatreya" is a second poem, "Earth-Song." In the poem Emerson brings Eastern spiritual themes to bear on Western ideas about land ownership and mortality and concludes that, while humans take pride in controlling and owning the land, in the end it is the earth that possesses humans, who are literally reincorporated into the land through death and burial.

In the 1840s Emerson was immersed in reading Hindu spiritual texts and poetry and, in particular, copied these lines from the *Vishnu Purana* into his journal: "I will repeat to you, Maitreya, the stanzas that were chanted by Earth." For the title of his own poem, "Hamatreya," Emerson seems to have combined the name "Maitreya" with the Greek word *hama* meaning "all together." The reference from the *Vishnu Purana* to "the stanzas chanted by the Earth" appears as the second part of Emerson's poem, "Earth-Song," which emphasizes that only nature, not humans, not the law that defines ownership, is immortal. In Hindu thought, however, even nature, the physical earth, is not eternal.

In the poem's title as well as in its themes, therefore, Emerson combined Eastern and Western meanings in the creation of a new idea in the poem, resulting in a neither purely Western nor purely Eastern perspective, but a new Transcendentalist reflection on humanity's relationship to nature. Themes from Emerson's readings in Hindu spiritual texts and poetry appeared in other writings, including poems such as "BRAHMA" and "BACCHUS."

CRITICAL COMMENTARY

The poem begins with a listing of the founders and early settlers of CONCORD, MASSACHUSETTS, included among them some of Emerson's own ancestors: "Bulkeley, Hunt, Willard, Hosmer, Meriam, Flint." These names represent claims of ownership over the land passed from one generation to the next, down to Emerson's own time and family. The men proclaim, "'Tis mine, my children's and my name's," the belief that they "possessed the land," which is the primary theme or conflict of the poem. These lines of Emerson's were inspired directly from the *Vishnu Purana* account of "kings" who declared, "'This earth is mine—it is my son's—it belongs to my dynasty,'" but who now "have all passed away."

In Emerson's poem, the men's relationship to the land is productive; they "toil" and the land produces food and items for human use—"Hay, corn, roots, hemp, flax, apples, wool and wood." They claim nature as their own—"my own trees!" and "my hill!"—but also believe that they have a reciprocal relationship with nature, that they "sympathize" with one another. In the last line of the first stanza it is not nature but man himself who determines this as the right relationship: "And, I affirm, my actions smack of the soil."

The second stanza sets up the argument between men who cultivate the land (thus claiming possession) and the earth itself. The men are mortal—"Asleep beneath their grounds"—but the earth lives on and laughs at the idea of "boastful boys" who are "proud of the earth which is not theirs." Emerson's now famous line that "earth laughs in flowers" was inspired by his readings, again, in the Hindu spiritual text *Vishnu Purana*, which reads: "Earth laughs, as if smiling with autumnal flowers, to behold her Kings unable to effect the subjugation of themselves." One of the main themes of the poem is the finality of death, and in this stanza the ground in which past generations lie will be plowed up by the next generation that stakes its own claim to the land: "Strangers, fond as they, their furrows plough." The reality is that humans, subject to fate and death, have no control; they may "steer the plough, but cannot steer their feet / Clear of the grave."

The second part of this stanza reflects on mankind's improvements to the land. Because they make changes to nature, men try to claim it as their own. "They added ridge to valley, brook to pond," drew boundaries around "their domain," designating a "pasture" or a "park," and had only their own needs in mind as they demanded "clay, lime, gravel, granite-ledge / And misty lowland, where to go for peat." It is nature's irony that, in the end, the earth is paid back in the form of the men themselves when they are buried: "Death, who adds / Him to his land." The poem them shifts to "Hear what the Earth says."

The next section of the poem is "Earth-Song," in five stanzas. "Earth-Song" provides a distinct shift in structure and therefore a shift in voice for the earth's response to the human perspective in the first poem. Here the earth echoes and challenges the men in their claims of ownership of the land, saying that the land is "mine, not yours." Responding to the men's view that their claim to the land lasts forever, the earth reminds them that "stars abide" or last forever and "the old sea" and "the shores" go on forever, but men do not go on forever: "But where are the old men?" The earth sees all, but immortal men "such have I never seen."

In the next stanza the earth mocks the men's belief that they can secure ownership of the earth through legal means. People try to cheat death through inheritance law, using "the lawyer's deed" to pass down the land "in tail," or down the line of heirs. Men declare their laws "without fail, / Forevermore." The earth responds in stanza 3 that this means nothing to nature's law. Men may make boundaries around the land, but the boundaries of human life are not permanent like these features. Those who inherit the land will themselves also eventually pass away "like the flood's foam," as will "the lawyers, and the laws, And the kingdom" itself. Nothing man creates is permanent in this sense.

In the fourth stanza the men tried to claim the earth, just because they worked it and legally defined it—"They called me theirs, / Who so controlled me;"—but the earth must ask, in the form of a riddle or paradox, "How am I theirs, / If they cannot hold me, / But I hold them?" The final four-line stanza of the poem is another shift in voice and in structure. This time, the man, the poet who "heard the Earth-song," is humbled in the face of nature and the reality of death: "When I heard the Earth-Song, / I was no longer brave; / My avarice cooled / Like lust in the chill of the grave."

"The Harp" (1876)

Emerson first published "The Harp" in *SELECTED POEMS* in 1876. Some of its lines appeared in his journals dating back to 1859 and 1861, and others appeared as part of the "MAY-DAY" poem in the *MAY-DAY AND OTHER PIECES* volume of 1867. The final version of "The Harp" was printed in the posthumous *Poems* of 1884. In 1859 Emerson worked on a never-published poem that recounts "the rippling of the pond under a gusty south wind," which "gives the like delight to the eye, as the fitful play of the same wind on the Aeolian harp to the ear." In an 1861 journal entry he inscribed a meditation on the Aeolian harp and the "delicious sensibility of youth," themes that became the principal motif of this poem. But "The Harp" ends with nostalgic and sobering reminiscences, indicating that it is a poem of old age.

In Homer, Aeolus is the god of the winds. An Aeolian harp was a simple stringed instrument from which sound is made by the currents of air. It consists of an open box of thin wood in which were stretched numerous strings of equal length, tuned in unison, and which was then placed in a window casement. This ancient wind chime excited Emerson's poetic imagination as a perfect symbol of nature's spontaneous musicality, comparable, for example, to the soft sounds of the wind in the pines in "WOODNOTES" and "MY GARDEN." The poem closely reverberates with "MAIDEN SPEECH OF THE AEOLIAN HARP," which was also first published in *Selected Poems.*

CRITICAL COMMENTARY

The poem appears to begin with a version of Emerson's symbolic representation of the transcendental poet who is associated with the wind harp: "One musician is sure, / His wisdom will not fail, / He has not tasted wine impure, / Nor bent to passion frail." But on closer inspection the "poet" in question is a wind harp itself—an Aeolian harp. In the poem, the wind harp's intrinsically musical nature is contrasted with the naysayers of life, who convert the joyful tones of life into inward wails. As well, this tuneful wind chime echoes "all the fables, And in their causes tells,— / Knows Nature's rarest moods, / Ever on her secret broods . . . / Knows the law of Night and Day, / And the heart of girl and boy, / The tragic and the gay . . . / What sea and land discoursing say / In sidereal years." It is one of the many disguises in which pantheistic nature, as expressed in "The SPHINX," "The WORLD-SOUL,"

"BRAHMA," and other poems, speaks its mystical riddles of identity in metamorphosis.

This opening stanza ends pointedly referring to "the children who have faith," in view of the fact that "only to children children sing," and "only to youth will spring be spring." The springtime ear of the poet listens in a register of metaphysical transparency. His "Aeolian harp" proves to have a "primeval memory," containing the old minstrels' tale of Merlin locked in a harp, as well as the other narratives of poetry and history in its "all-echoing shell"—indeed reverberating all the mysteries of the past and of the future, "the secrets of the earth, / And of the kinds that owe her birth." This all-echoing harp "speaks not of self that mystic tone, / But of the Overgods alone. / It trembles to the cosmic breath, . . . Obeying meek the primal Cause, / It is the tongue of mundane laws."

Gradually, however, Emerson shifts the focus from his metaphysical harp to "a boy" who transcends the best names in the history of poetry—Homer, Milton, Shakespeare, Collins, Byron, Wordsworth, Scott—none of whom can compete with the "the sights and voices ravishing / The boy on the hills in spring." This "boy," a composite memory of Emerson's own youth and loved ones recollected in tranquillity, alone has an ear for the tones and melodies of his wood harp. Such is the unique privilege of youth, who, when pacing through the oak forest, hears the "sharp queries of the sentry-bird, / The heavy grouses's sudden whir, / The rattle of the kingfisher"; or sees "bonfires of the harlot flies / In the lowland, when day dies; / Or marked, benighted and forlorn, / The first far signal-fire of morn." This youthful privilege is the real beginning of wisdom, Emerson muses, the origin of learning of the "threads of man at the humming-wheel"—namely, "the threads of life, and power, and pain"—as well as the "Delphian chord" of "how Nature to the soul is moored."

At this point the symbolic window casement in which the wood harp is placed beckons him to look forth "on the fields of youth." He sees "fair boys bestriding steeds" and knows "their forms in fancy weeds, / Long, long concealed by sundering fates, / Mates of my youth. . . ." Indeed, they are more than his mates, for in his reverie of poetic emotion they are "with grace, with genius, well attired." He expresses his joy for such "recoveries rare!" and thus "renewed," he breathes "Elysian air," recalling his "youth's glad mates in earliest bloom." But then, having sounded the note of "sundering fate," he implores the "obtrusive tomb" not to break his dream. Rather, he implores the spring to reconfirm the lesson of life-affirmation—the now painful lesson of "the grand recoil / Of life resurgent from the soil / Wherein was dropped the mortal spoil."

The poem thus reprises "the moody child and wildly wise" symbolism of the poet in the motto to his 1844 essay "The POET," as well as the same theme inscribed in many of his other poems that feature the poet's exhilarating recovery of the freshness of life in the innocence of childhood. (This is a romantic theme conspicuous in JOHANN WOLFGANG VON GOETHE, among others.) At the same time it seems to recapture personal memories tinged with sadness associated with the memory of his beloved son Waldo as lamented in "THRENODY" and also with nostalgic memories of playful companionship he enjoyed with his two brothers as recollected in "DIRGE" (both in *POEMS* [1847]). The overall music of his wood harp is life affirmative, but it also evokes old-age feelings that sober his mood in this instance.

David A. Dilworth

"Heroism" (1841)

Emerson's essay on "Heroism" appeared in the collection *ESSAYS: FIRST SERIES* (1841) but was first delivered as part of the "Human Culture" series given in BOSTON in 1837–38. The theme of heroism was of particular interest to Emerson as someone living through an age of reform and rebellion on a dramatic scale. Emerson was interested in turning to the past for examples of heroism as a universal human characteristic. He sought a different approach than his friend, THOMAS CARLYLE, who published his *On Heroes and Hero-Worship* around the same time. Emerson offered up his own answer to the question of what makes a hero, not only in his reflections in the essay on "Heroism," but also later in "USES OF GREAT MEN," the introduction to his biographical essays in *REPRESENTATIVE MEN* (1850). Emerson was interested in heroism as (in scholar Albert Von Frank's words) "the ultimate test of self-reliance." Regardless of whether the hero's actions were applauded or even recognized in his own time, his commitment to the self thus revealed a lesson for each of us and an inspiration to find the hero within ourselves.

SYNOPSIS

Emerson begins the essay by discussing the plays of the "English dramatists" and of ancient Athens, in which there are many examples of heroism in stock characters, as if it were an outward characteristic "as easily marked in the society of their age, as color is in our American population." In drama, one can recognize the hero by his manner of speaking, which "rises naturally into poetry." A survey of contemporary literature reveals that we no longer have such an idea of heroism as a type, though some poems and other pieces might have bits of "a certain noble music." Emerson determines that only Plutarch is worth reading in "the literature of Heroism," and we would learn more about human culture from Plutarch than from "books of political science, or of private economy."

On searching for heroes, he finds that no man is immune to "ferocity in nature" or to "violations of the laws of nature." We cannot overlook examples of suffering, of challenges, "the arming of the man"; we should not wish only for peace and be afraid to face war (that is, challenges build character). Emerson observes that it is "to this military attitude of the soul we give the name of Heroism." But the hero is not brave in a conventional sense; instead, he "advances to his own music." Because he acts on "the extreme of individual nature," the hero "is always right." This may mean that the hero sometimes goes against popular ideas and may be "in contradiction, for a time, to the voice of the great and the good." Heroism, by definition then, requires some action *against* what has been accepted and unchallenged: "Every heroic acts measures itself by its contempt of some external good." Heroism is a rejection of the status quo and therefore, ironically, puts the hero in antagonism with those around him. Emerson's important qualification here is the phrase "for a time." Indeed, "after some little time be past," history will show that the hero was right. So it is with so many "great men" who cannot be fully appreciated in their own time but become examples for later generations.

Again he restates that "self-trust is the essence of heroism." Heroism goes beyond the petty "littleness of common life," unconcerned with the immediate gratification of "health and wealth." It is "the little man" who spends his life worrying about his house, his health, "gossip," "a horse or a rifle," "sweet food and strong wine"—these are all distractions, "nonsense" for "the great soul." This is not to say that the hero is always isolated, outside of social relations. Indeed, what may seem trivial or "inconvenient," if "done for love," will result in "compensations of the universe" in the form of development of the individual soul. For example, if the hero practices "temperance," it must be only as a duty to his own "worthiness," not for the sake of "austerity" itself, and never for show or praise. It is of no concern to the true hero what anyone drinks or eats or smokes. Emerson's comments could be read as a response to the extremism of reformers who focus on people's actions rather than on their "virtue." "The heroic class," by contrast, is not concerned with "opinion," and therefore does not join in by signing "petitions" or "the show of sorrow." Reformers, then, are not the heroes of the age, as "the great will not condescend to take any thing too seriously."

Who are these heroes? We see all around us "young men" who seem destined for great things, who speak of great things and "throw contempt on our entire polity and social state." We expect revolutions, but instead "they enter an active profession" and are reduced "to the common size of man." So much is youthful energy and unfulfilled promise. Men have "ideal tendencies . . . but the tough world had its revenge." "Persistency," then, becomes one of the defining characteristics of heroism and what is lacking in these young men (and women) of his own time. He advises young people, "Do not weakly try to reconcile yourself with the world." "Adhere to our own act." This means recognizing the heroism within our own characters, as well as the "weakness or exposure" in ourselves. We must accept "the thought,—this is part of my constitution."

There are always heroes, because there are always "times of terror." Even though we say that this age is "somewhat better" and it is a better time to live than any before, that we have "more freedom" than ever before, there are still always "crises" the hero must confront. There is always a need for "champions and martyrs," because there will always be "persecution." He mentions the case of Elijah Lovejoy (an Illinois minister and antislavery editor who was murdered in November 1837), who died "for the rights of free speech and opinion"; that is, for something larger than himself. Lovejoy "died when it was better not to live." Paraphrasing Tennyson, Emerson reflects that the only peace will come in death: "Let them rave: / Thou art quiet in thy grave." Death is the only place "no enemy can follow us." We should be glad that Washington did not live to see "the meanness of our politics," the implication being that he was the ideal hero for his own time but would not have been suited to a later time. In the end, in Emerson's terms, death is "impossible," for we are all part of an "absolute and inextinguishable being."

CRITICAL COMMENTARY

In "Heroism," Emerson makes direct reference to his friend Thomas Carlyle, whose "natural taste for what is manly and daring in character, has suffered no heroic trait in his favorites to drop from his biographical and historical pictures." This is a criticism of Carlyle's failure to discern the "manly and daring" from true heroism. Indeed, of all of Emerson's writings on great or "representative" men, the biographical and historical are largely missing; Emerson instead emphasizes the universal aspects of heroic character. Influenced heavily by these discussions with Carlyle, as well as by reading Plutarch's biographies (alone worth reading, in Emerson's estimation, in "the literature of Heroism"), Emerson would create new theories of history, biography, and heroism, culminating in his 1850 project *Representative Men.* Emerson's representative men were those who inspired him personally and who contributed to a greater understanding beyond themselves; they were also often individuals not necessarily appreciated (even criticized) in their own time, such as those explored in "NAPOLEON; OR, THE MAN OF THE WORLD" and "SWEDENBORG; OR, THE MYTHIC."

This idea of heroes who speak to universal traits or truths, regardless of recognition in their own time, was important to Emerson as he observed those lauded as "heroes" in his own 19th century. He wondered if only history could determine the true heroes of the day. In "Heroism" he speaks directly to the reform impulse of his own time (such as in temperance or women's rights) in rejecting as heroes those who sacrifice or martyr themselves to a cause just for show, urging instead that we each "adhere to our own act." Self-reliance and following one's own truth are greater acts of heroism than trying to change the behavior of others. This was an individual philosophy of reform that motivated Emerson's other writings on reform, including ABOLITIONISM: the belief that only the self-development of individuals would bring about broader social change.

In one sense, all of Emerson's works developed from this core idea, the belief that heroism is universal and that we all should be heroes of our own lives. As he would write in his journal, "the world looks poor & mean so long as I think only of its great men; most of them of spotted reputation. But when I remember how many obscure persons I myself have seen possessing gifts that excited wonder, speculation, & delight in me . . . when I consider the absolute boundlessness of our capacity . . . [when] I recollect the charms of certain women, what poems are many private lives, each of which can fill our eye if we so will."

FURTHER READING

Bosco, Ronald. "'What poems are many private lives': Emerson Writing the American Plutarch." *Studies in the Literary Imagination* 27, no. 1 (Spring 1994): 103–129.

Von Frank, Albert J. "Essays: First Series (1841)." In *The Cambridge Companion to Ralph Waldo Emerson*, edited by Joel Porte and Saundra Morris, 106–120. New York: Cambridge, 1999.

"Heroism" (1847)

"Heroism" is a 10-line commentary on the distinction between false heroic attributes and that which Emerson considers to be authentic heroism. The poem asserts that heroism is a quality not of philosophers, mythic figures, or divines but of humans in the world, a theme he also explored in *REPRESENTATIVE MEN* (1850) and in the essay "HEROISM" itself. The poem "Heroism" was originally drafted in 1846–47, though some lines appear in journals as early as 1844; it appeared as the motto to the essay on "Heroism" in the 1847 edition of *ESSAYS: FIRST SERIES.* "Heroism" was reprinted in *MAY-DAY AND OTHER PIECES* (1867) and the posthumous *Poems* (1884).

CRITICAL COMMENTARY

The poem contains 10 lines of rhymed couplets and comprises three distinct sections, though this may not be clear because of the couplet pairings. The first section, lines 1–3, establishes the false hero: fat, drunk, a buffoon. The second section, lines 4–6, describes Jove: the idealized, mythological all-seeing father, just and vengeful. The third section, lines 7–10, contrasts these with the true hero, in between the vulgar and the ideal. The images in this last section play off the images in the first two sections for their contextual significance.

In the opening three lines, along with the insistent tone, Emerson uses descriptive nouns at the end of each line (where they have more weight): *knaves, slaves, buffoons.* These images set the terms of the contrast: While these nouns describe the earthly ("ruby wine," "sugar," "rose and vine–leaf"), Jove's festoons are "thunder-clouds." In the second section Emerson ends lines with *festoons, dread, head,* offering both a description of Jove and a contrast with lines 1–3. As in the poem "FREEDOM" (also published in *May-Day*), Emerson casts an abstract quality in the guise of a mythological figure. These images repeat throughout the poem and serve to heighten the contrast. The "ruby wine" and "sugar" of the first two lines becomes the "heart" the hero eats in 7–8; "rose and vine leaf" in line 3 opposes "thunder-clouds" in line 4 and "lightning-knotted" in line 5. Only two lines in the poem, lines 7 and 8, describe the hero directly.

The third section of the poem opposes the descriptions in the two sections, but Emerson uses this section to connect the human with the divine. If the false hero in lines 1–3 is contrasted with the ideal Jove in lines 4–6, the last four lines connect the ideal (Jove) with the real hero, who daily (note that the real hero is subject to time) eats his own *heart* (which is not sweet, opposing line 2). Emerson describes the quality of the hero in the poem's accompanying essay: "Heroism feels and never reasons, and therefore is always right; and although different breeding, different religion and greater intellectual activity would have modified or even reversed the particular action, yet for the hero that thing he does is the highest deed, and is not open to the censure of philosophers or divines."

Bill Scalia

"History" (1841)

"History" was included in Emerson's 1841 collection *ESSAYS: FIRST SERIES.* Although Emerson had already published his foundational essay *NATURE* in 1836, establishing him as the leader of a new school of thought, *Essays* now represented a more thorough exploration of Transcendentalist philosophy as applied to a variety of questions. In selecting "History" as the first essay (rather than even "SELF-RELIANCE," which comes second and which is more often identified as his seminal piece), Emerson uses his approach to the past to introduce many of the central themes of Transcendentalism that would be explored throughout the volume as well as in his other writings, such as the relationship between humans and nature, and between the individual and the universal.

In "History," Emerson connects the past, present, and future through the PLATONIC idea of a universal mind: "There is one mind common to all individual men. . . . Of the works of this mind, history is the record." The purpose of studying history is not to glorify the past but to understand our individual relationship to this universal mind. The essay "History" therefore establishes the core Transcendentalist idea of relating all inquiries back to individual experience.

SYNOPSIS

The brief verse that opens the essay "History" reveals Emerson's approach to studying individuals of the past:

> I am owner of the sphere,
> Of the seven stars and the solar year,
> Of Caesar's hand, and Plato's brain,
> Of Lord Christ's heart, and Shakspeare's strain.

The individual "I" is the proper study of history, and the "great men" named here (Caesar, Plato, Shakespeare) represent universal characteristics that we must cultivate in ourselves.

In the opening section of the essay, Emerson explains the idea of the "universal mind" and the belief that each individual possesses within him or herself all that has gone before: "Every man is an inlet to the same and to all of the same. . . . What Plato has thought, he may think; what a saint has felt, he may feel; what at any time has befallen any man, he can understand." Within each person is an "encyclopedia of facts" that makes up the entire history of the world, just as "the creation of a thousand forests is in one acorn." The universal mind "wrote" the story of the human past and now we "must read it" through our individual experience. As history is the record of the mind, literature is the record of universal "character." Readers are drawn to stories and poems on themes of education, justice, charity, friendship, and love, because these are characteristics we seek to develop within ourselves. Being universal, these characteristics are attainable by all. The student seeks out great men of the past, not in blind admiration, but in order to "find the lineaments he is forming" in his own self.

Emerson next addresses the question of education, of *how* to properly study history. The student must "read history actively and not passively; to esteem his own life the text." The goal of reading and writing history, just as in conversing with nature or appreciating art, is self-knowledge. When we read about some event in the past, such as the "victory of Napoleon," or "a Salem hanging of witches," we put ourselves there, "we aim to master intellectually the step, and reach the same height or the same degradation." This understanding we may then apply to current events, thus doing away with the false distinctions of time, what Emerson terms the "preposterous There or Then, and introduce in its place the Here and the Now."

Finding meaning in and from the past comes from an understanding of causation, more than specific facts. As in nature, causation in history reveals the unity between all things, while the details only show differences. Nature "casts the same thought into troops of forms, as a poet makes twenty fables with one moral." Within the individual egg is the "eternal unity" common to the entire species. So it is with history that "there are compositions of the same strain to be found in the books of all ages." Nature inspired the artists, poets, and architects that make up human history. The likeness of a cherub appeared in the clouds before the artist painted the image in a church, and the beauty of "the stained glass window" is only a copy of "the colors of the western sky seen through the bare and crossing branches of the forest." The inspiration is always greater than the final product: "The true poem is the poet's mind; the true ship is the ship-builder."

Past civilizations organized around "Nomadism" or "Agriculture" were not just stages of history but explain enduring characteristics of human society. Nomadism is the more "natural" way of organizing society, according to the season, weather, and needs of animals. In contrast, agriculture is the "domestication" of humans, and includes religion, the idea of private property, and a market-oriented society that requires the establishment of towns and eventually nations. These two "antagonistic" models also exist within the individual, manifested in our "love of adventure or the love of repose." Likewise, certain eras or themes of the past correspond to stages in our individual lives: "Every man passes personally through a Grecian period." We admire the Greek aesthetic because it represents a purer, more innocent state of human society and of the individual: "Our admiration of the antique is not the admiration of the old, but of the natural."

Ancient Greece represents for Emerson the "bodily" era of "perfection of the senses" and good health. He determines that "every man passes personally through a Grecian period." Greece represents an ideal of "incorrupt, sharply defined, and symmetrical features," unlike the 19th century's era of "modern cities," the chaos of which was reflected in modern art, "wherein the face is a confused blur of features." The Greeks, therefore, were not just an ancient civilization but a state of being that brings us closer to the "original circumstances" of nature.

The appeal of religion and fables in history is a desire by the individual to return to this more "natural" or childlike stage. Religious stories and mythologies are appealing because they "easily . . . domesticate themselves in the mind." Unfortunately, organized religion depends not on the simple "truths" it professes through stories but on what Emerson terms "priestcraft," or the external rules and "institutions" that instill "fear and obedience" in its followers. Mythology and fables, like history, reveal universal themes because they are produced from the universal "imagination" of humans. That is why there are so many similarities between the stories of different cultures. For example, a comparison of the Greek myths to Bible stories suggests "Prometheus is the Jesus of the old mythology." The riddle posed by this quest for both identity and universality may best be solved, not through religion, but through music, poetry, and "conversation with nature," which rely on truths about nature and humanity rather than on specific facts. Emerson declares that the old stories of fairies and elves "I find true in Concord."

In the concluding section of the essay, Emerson explains that nature itself has a history. Humans have no control over this history "of the external world," and yet we are "intertwined with the whole chain of organic and inorganic being." Humanity was created with a plan toward our development: "Does not the eye of the human embryo predict the light?" Emerson summarizes his main arguments of the essay: "Let it suffice that in the light of these two facts, namely, that the mind is One, and that nature is its correlative, history is to be read and written." If we understand human history in this larger context of universal experience based on our relationship to nature, "history no longer shall be a dull book. It shall walk incarnate in every just and wise man." The history of the world is distilled in the lifetime of a single individual. Most histories fail to reveal these connections between human society and nature, or even between our world and the world of the past: "I am ashamed to see what a shallow village tale our so-called History is." Emerson makes a call to look outside our own culture, our own nation, and our own traditions, for the greater understanding of human and natural history: "Broader and deeper we must write our annals . . . instead of this old chronology of selfishness and pride."

CRITICAL COMMENTARY

Emerson's essay "History" engages the Transcendentalist paradox of finding individual meaning within the universal facts that link all humankind together throughout time. Emerson's answer is that civilization, as well as each individual, goes "through the whole cycle of experience" revealed by the study of history. Emerson has no use for "heroes," only for what great men represent, the theme as well of his 1850 text REPRESENTATIVE MEN, in which he explained "that there is properly no history; only biography." Thus, it is not the biographical facts of men's lives that matter but the "genius and creative principle" of great men, great nations, or great ideas that we must seek out and relate to ourselves and to our own times. Each individual is to "live all history in his own person." Repeatedly throughout the essay, Emerson returns to the idea of history as a "riddle" (as well posed in his 1841 poem "The SPHINX") and to the need to translate facts into self-knowledge: "The Muse of history will utter oracles, as never to those who do not respect themselves."

Throughout the essay Emerson uses the analogy of nature, explaining that all of history is within each person, just as the forest is found in one acorn. It is not the "fact" of the individual acorn but the "unity" of all acorns that defines the forest. It is the role of the philosopher or poet to reveal this unity. In his essay "SWEDENBORG; OR, THE MYSTIC" (again, from *Representative Men*), Emerson explains that, while the naturalist may initially be concerned with only collecting and classifying objects, the philosopher looks to every rock, fossil, or fungus to reveal something about "the frame of things." Likewise, to look at the history, literature, architecture, art, or sculpture of a specific era is to see only different forms of the same genius. Just as "Nature is an endless combination and repetition of a very few laws," so with human history.

Emerson's discussion of how nature *inspires* humans through literature, art, architecture, or other forms is a foundational Transcendentalist and romantic theme that appears throughout his writings. In "History," a painter friend tells him "that nobody could draw a tree without in some sort becoming a tree." He relates the personal experience of seeing "a snow-drift along the sides of the stone wall which obviously gave the idea of the common architectural scroll to abut a tower." This imagery was repeated in his poem "The SNOW-STORM," published earlier the same year: "Come see the north wind's masonry . . . / . . . To mimic in slow structures, stone by stone, / Built in an age, the mad wind's night-work, / The frolic architecture of the snow." Emerson therefore shows by his own creative work the argument he makes in "History": that we should not just study the books or art or architecture of the past but "surround ourselves with the original circumstances," that is, with nature. We would do better to watch the snow than worship in the church, a scene he had in fact described in the "DIVINITY SCHOOL ADDRESS" (1838).

Religious stories and mythologies are also part of the story of the human past, and Emerson determines that, although there are many prophets, it is a "rare" voice that breaks through the external forms of religion and "discloses to us new facts in nature." Jesus might be an example of such a rare voice, but he stands apart as divine and therefore people "cannot unite him to history, or reconcile him with themselves." Rather than emphasizing his divinity, Jesus should be seen as a "great man," such as Socrates or Shakespeare. These are not Gods, but "gods among men"—again, the argument in the "Divinity School Address" being that all men are divine. In the essay "PLATO; OR, THE PHILOSOPHER" he celebrates the birth of the philosopher as leader of thought as a natural event, unlike the "voices heard in the sky" or the belief in "that infant man-child [as] the son of Apollo." The references here in multiple contexts were part of a larger debate within Transcendentalist-UNITARIANISM over the divinity of Christ and the nature of the "miracles." In *Nature* and other writings, of course, Emerson had rejected the belief in "miracles" as supernatural events, celebrating instead the miracle of everyday life.

Emerson's emphasis on our relationship to the natural world in "History" is an example of his use of the term to mean both human and natural history, as there was no separation between the two. "History" is a statement of his scientific naturalism—including his pre-Darwinian understanding of evolution and adaptation—as it is an interest in great men and great civilizations of the past. Emerson moves effortlessly between a discussion of ancient Greece as an evolutionary stage of civilization and of human life and the conclusion that "a man is a bundle of relations, a knot of roots, whose flower and fruitage is the world." The natural world becomes a landscape upon which human history is written; just as the explorer "needs a planet to shape his course upon," so "a gravitating solar system is already prophesied in the nature of Newton's mind."

Early in the essay Emerson explained that how one views the world and history is a reflection of individual character: "Everything the individual sees without him corresponds to his states of mind." We take knowledge and incorporate it to fit our own truths, to make it "intelligible" to ourselves. This thought and language he echoed in the essay on "EXPERIENCE" in the same volume: "Thus inevitably does the universe wear our color, and every object fall successively into the subject itself." In the end, history is not an objective record of the past but insight into the reader's own self and times.

FURTHER READING

O'Keefe, Richard R. "The Rats in the Wall: Animals in Emerson's 'History.'" *American Transcendental Quarterly* 10, no. 2 (June 1996): 111–121.

Von Frank, Albert J. "*Essays: First Series* (1841)." In *The Cambridge Companion to Ralph Waldo Emerson*, edited by Joel Porte and Saundra Morris, 106–120. New York: Cambridge University Press, 1999.

"The Humble-Bee" (1839)

"The Humble-Bee" is a six-stanza, 63-line poem first published in the Ohio-based Transcendentalist magazine the WESTERN MESSENGER in 1839 and included with some revisions in Emerson's 1847 collection *POEMS*. The image of the bee had long inspired Emerson, and he reflected in an earlier journal entry of a walk in the woods in which he "followed the fine humble-bee with rhymes and fancies fine." He mused that "the humble-bee and the pine warbler seem to me the proper objects of attention in these disastrous times." At the time of that journal entry, in 1837, Emerson was referring to a financial panic, but in the poem "The Humble-Bee" he extends this theme to compare humans, who are beset by the "fate and care" and "woe and want" of the world, with the bee, the "yellow-breeched philosopher," who sees only beauty and sweetness in nature. "The Humble-Bee" is a companion to Emerson's other "nature" poems of this period, including "The RHODORA" and "The SNOW-STORM."

CRITICAL COMMENTARY

"The Humble-Bee" presents not merely an escape into nature but a Transcendentalist critique of human values and priorities—a stepping back from the drive for wealth and power that leaves humans still in "woe and want," and a focus instead on the alternative philosophical perspective of the bee, who seeks out only the beautiful. The first stanza of the poem gives a sense of the action or movement of the "animated" bee, a "zig-zag steerer." The poet and the poem follow the "waving lines" of the bee and determine that there is enough action and adventure in following this small creature, no need to "sail for Porto Rique, / Far-off heats through seas to seek." Instead, Emerson determines that wherever the bee goes is exotic and adventure enough—"Where thou art is clime for me" and "I will follow thee alone," "singing over shrubs and vines."

While others may seek "far-off heats" in the south, in the second stanza Emerson is content to follow this "insect lover of the sun." The water or nautical imagery continues from the first stanza, where he compared those who sail "through seas" to southern islands with the bee who is "sailor of the atmosphere; / Swimmer through the waves of air." He implores the bee to "Wait . . . till I come / Within ear-shot of thy hum," so that the bee's lessons can be learned. Anything else, besides what the bee can teach by example, is in vain: "All without is martyrdom."

The third stanza again revisits the images of the "south wind" and the warmth of springtime, of "May days." But spring also brings a different kind of warmth, the "subtle heats" of love: "tints the human countenance / With a color of romance." Likewise, and in similar sexualized or procreative terms, the "subtle heats" of the bee pollinates the plants and creates new life in flowers: "turns the sod to violets." The difference is that the bee does it alone—"in sunny solitudes"—and that the bee provides not only the sights and smells of spring with flowers but the sounds of spring with its buzzing: "The green silence doest displace / With thy mellow, breezy bass."

In the fourth and fifth stanzas, the seasons are moving on, from springtime now into "hot midsummer." The "mellow breezy" sound of the bee in the previous stanza has become a "drowsy tune." The days of summer are "long," and unlike with the joy of watching the first sprouts of spring, in summer the "solid banks of flowers" are all grown in and in full bloom. Passing its life through these seasons, the bee does not have to deal with any negative or difficult aspects of nature, of life: "Aught unsavory or unclean, / Hath my insect never seen." The bee's brief life is filled only with flowers and tall green grasses, and Emerson lists them by name: "violets and bilberry bells, / Maple sap and daffodels," as well as "succory," "columbine," "scented fern, and agrimony, / Clover, catch fly, adders-tongue." Even the ordinary plants that humans take most for granted, that appear everywhere, commonplace, and perhaps even a nuisance, are of significance to the bee: "All was picture as he passed."

The last stanza names the bee as nature's true philosopher, "wiser far than human seer, / Yellow-breeched philosopher!" The bee's wisdom comes from looking only for the good in nature: "seeing only what is fair, / Sipping only what is sweet." The bee does not waste time with "fate and care" as humans do. At the end of the poem, the seasons shift again, toward fall or winter. The image of harvest reflects the philosophy of the bee: "Leave the chaff, and take the wheat." The winds have changed ("fierce north-western blast") and the bee's life is long over: "Thou already slumberest deep." The bee's life of pursuing beauty and creativity is contrasted with the troubles of human life we bring upon ourselves: "Want and woe which torture us, / Thy sleep makes ridiculous."

"Hymn: Sung at the Completion of the Concord Monument, April 19, 1836" (1847)

Emerson's "Hymn: Sung at the Completion of the Concord Monument, April 19, 1836" was written to commemorate the site of the first battle fought in the American Revolution, on April 19, 1775. The dedication of the Battle Monument was actually delayed until July 4, 1837, at which time Emerson was not in attendance and the hymn was sung by the townspeople. The poem was circulated as a broadside for the event and printed in local papers in the summer of 1837; it was collected in Emerson's POEMS (1847), with the full title, but appeared as "Concord Fight" in SELECTED POEMS (1876). It was not until after Emerson's death that the poem appeared for the first time by its most familiar title, as "Concord Hymn," in *Poems* (1884).

Emerson's own grandfather, the Reverend William Emerson, lived just near the bridge, in the OLD MANSE, when the battle was fought. Emerson would appear at the Old North Bridge on April 17, 1875, as a speaker at the battle's centennial celebration when Daniel Chester French's *Minute Man* statue was unveiled with lines from Emerson's poem inscribed at its base. Emerson's short poem follows a more traditional structure than most of his other verse and is made up of four stanzas of four lines each. It is one of Emerson's most well-known and oft-quoted poems and includes the famous line describing the first battle of the American Revolution as "the shot heard round the world."

CRITICAL COMMENTARY

The first stanza situates the reader "by the rude bridge that arched the flood." The bridge is "rude" or simply made, yet forceful, like the men who cross it in a flood of revolutionary fervor. Water imagery is used throughout the poem to represent the movement of men, of nature, and of time passing. The "flood" of events about to happen at the bridge will change the world, and the flood of time or history itself cannot be stopped; it is a force of nature. The men meet the British head-on, "their flag to April's breeze unfurled." They are defiant, raising their flag against the Crown. The date of the battle is in April 1775, but April also signifies spring, rebirth, a new era, and a new country about to be born, also signified by their possession of their own "flag," not the British flag. The "breeze" is another image from nature signifying movement or change.

Having established the location and the portent of change, the poem then focuses on the particular historical event: "Here once the embattled farmers stood," establishing that the British were launching an attack on hardworking and "embattled" colonists who had already endured years of British rule and exploitation. It is also significant that they are "farmers," as the colonial militia were, and not professional soldiers. It was only common men defending themselves who "fired the shot heard round the world." This famous line connects the battle site, the specific events of that day, with the ushering in of a new era. That first "shot" changed the course of history, as new ideas of freedom and revolution spread. The magnitude of the events, "heard around the world," is a striking comparison to the simple "farmers" gathered at this "rude bridge," all of which is a commentary on the American spirit

Daniel Chester French's *Minute Man* statue at Minute Man National Historical Park, Concord, Massachusetts. Erected in 1875 on the centennial of the first battle of the American Revolution, the statue bears an inscription on its base from the first stanza of Emerson's poem, "Concord Hymn":

By the rude bridge that arched the flood,
Their flag to April's breeze unfurled,
Here once the embattled farmers stood,
And fired the shot heard round the world.

(Photo by Dave Pape)

and the American political experiment that placed power in the hands of the people.

The next stanza is a broader reflection on the history that brings the farmer-soldiers to this point. Nature and time are again dominant themes of the poem, and in particular, British rule now belongs to the past, to history: "The foe long since in silence slept, / Alike the conqueror silent sleeps." The relationship between Britain and America will not remain silent for long, and the use of present tense, of peaceful times, presages events to come. History has brought them to this moment, the water imagery of the flood under the bridge appears again as the "dark stream" of history: "And Time the ruined bridge has swept / Down the dark stream which seaward creeps." Time has moved on since the Revolution, the poet reminding us of the date of commemoration at which he stands a generation later. The original bridge is long gone, as are the men who fought there. Time "seaward creeps," a reference to fate or nature pulling all waters in one direction. The forward march of history cannot be stopped.

In the third stanza the focus is on the present-day gathering, "on this green bank, by this soft stream," to raise this monument and remember the past. Again, the images of water and of springtime (the "green bank") tie in the themes of time and nature as witnesses. Whereas previously the water, like time, was rushing past like a "flood" or "dark stream" of the past, the water of the present is "soft" and reflective. Such a simple and gentle spot in nature contrasts with the significant and violent events that took place here, but the gentleness represents the redemption of the location. This line also again connects the simplicity of the Americans with the beauty of their land and the fact that, regardless of what took place here, nature continues on through her seasons.

They are gathered here for the purpose of erecting a monument—"We set to-day a votive stone"—as a promise to remember "that memory may their deed redeem." The monument is not just for the benefit of the present generation but to ensure that future generations will remember "when, like our sires, our sons are gone." The events of history connect the past, the present, and the future, represented in the poem as three generations—the "sires" of the revolutionary generation, the present generation of Emerson's time erecting this memorial, and "our sons" and beyond of the future. The human generations come and go, but the monument, made of "stone," and the "memory" will remain.

The final stanza addresses the spirit of the men who fought and the universal spirit that guided their actions: "spirit, that made those heroes dare." The men sacrificed their own lives for future generations—"to die, or leave their children free"—and for the nation. Emerson makes an appeal for the permanence of their memory and of the statue: "Bid Time and Nature gently spare." Throughout the poem, time and nature have been the two main forces moving history forward, and here Emerson asks that they be gentle on this memorial, "the shaft we raise to them and thee." Significantly, the memorial honors not only the men but "thee" as well, meaning the past and the forces of nature. While time and nature are impermanent, constantly changing, the actual stone monument (unlike the wooden bridge itself) is an attempt at permanency at this site, intended to stand up to the forces of both time and nature. The other "thee" to whom the monument is "raised" is the spirit, the ideas of liberty and freedom and revolution. Except for the preliminary shot fired, the poem never mentions the military battle itself but rather memorializes the larger significance of the world-changing events and ideas that the battle came to represent.

"Illusions" (1860)

"Illusions" has justly been celebrated as one of Emerson's most brilliant literary-philosophical essays. It was first published in the *ATLANTIC MONTHLY* (November 1857), but it is best known as the capping essay of *The CONDUCT OF LIFE* (1860). The sequence of final essays—"WORSHIP," "Considerations by the Way," "BEAUTY," and "Illusions"—was deliberately arranged by Emerson to have an ascendant trajectory, with "Illusions" ending with explicit reference to Hindu and NEOPLATONIC worldviews, which Emerson increasingly referenced as framing his own metaphysical views.

The long opening poem that prefaces "Illusions" keynotes the essay by juxtaposing "the endless imbroglio" of the world's appearances against the strength of the self-reliant, ascendant soul, as expressed in the final three lines: "Horsed on the Proteus, / Thou ridest to power, / And to endurance." The entire poem is another variation on Emerson's central binary of fate and power, as articulated in essays by the same names that frame the volume.

SYNOPSIS

"Illusions" opens with a scenario that provides a metaphor for the entire essay. Emerson describes at length his participation in a company exploring Mammoth Cave in Kentucky, in awe of the "theatrical trick" of natural forms and colors. This metaphor of Mammoth Cave's natural and man-made kaleidoscope is Emerson's idealistic theory of finding meaning in the mixing of nature and human perspective: "In admiring the sunset we do not yet deduct the rounding, coordinating, pictorial powers of the eye." In "Illusions" he explores this tenet with respect not only to the implicit reference to the appearances of perception in Plato's cave but also in reference to the human imagination and "deceptions of the senses." Emerson's descriptions of nature's and of life's illusions consistently reveal the imagination as simultaneously inspiring creativity and delusion: "The chapter of fascinations is very long. . . . Children, youths, adults and old men, all are led by one bawble or another."

Emerson parodies the scientist (standing for the false knowledge of "tuition") as "a sad-eyed boy" who comes in to the "charivari" but does not have imagination and strips things down "to one root." In another ironic respect he alludes to the fact that women, "more than all, are the element and kingdom of illusion. Being fascinated, they fascinate." He concludes that the realm "of affection" is one of "*mirage.*" Bad marriages, he cogently notes, are an especially notorious "trap." No one, however, is "exempt" from being a "fine madman" when it comes to the power of imagination. His last example is "the scholar in his library," who is always "the victim of any new page" or idea.

Emerson continues these observations by noting here that even our day-to-day lives are illusions, part of nature's larger theatrical game: "You play with jackstraws, balls, bowls, horse and gun, estates and politics; but there are finer games before you. Is not time a pretty toy?" What is more, "all this play and playground, this pompous history of illusory identities, are radiations from yourself,—yourself from whom the sun borrows its beams." Emerson's ability to detect illusion, to uncover the mask of perspective, allows him to both penetrate appearances and spiritually transcend them. His text consistently walks this fine line: "There are deceptions of the senses, deception of the passions, and the structural, beneficent illusions of sentiment and of the intellect. There is the illusion of love. . . . There is the illusion of time, which is very deep; who has disposed of it?" Generally, "the soul," in its "endless striving," does not even realize "itself in its own act." Our pretensions of material life, and even of self-hood, are only "yielding to a larger generalization." He thus sympathizes with the human condition, finding it "no wonder if our estimates are loose and floating. We must work and affirm, but we have no guess of the value of what we say or do."

"We cannot write the order of the variable winds. How can we penetrate the law of our shifting moods and susceptibility?" But the essay's opening poem has forecasted "power" and "endurance," and thus, characteristically, Emerson returns to his ethics from this binary of fate and power: "If life seems a succession of dreams, yet poetic justice is done in dreams also. The visions of good men are good; it is the undisciplined will that is whipped with bad thoughts and bad fortunes. When we break the laws, we lose our hold on the central reality"—the central reality that is our very own selves.

These observations also express Emerson's theory of ethics found in the karma or balance in nature: "In this kingdom of illusions . . . whatever games are played with us, we must play no games with ourselves, but deal in our privacy with the last honesty and truth. . . . Speak as you think, be what you are, pay your debts of all kinds." At the heart of these pronouncements we see the working of Emerson's twin metaphysical laws of identity and metamorphosis. "A man's reality," he goes on to say, "is the foundation of all friendship, religion, poetry and art." "Riches and poverty" are illusions, a "costume," our "employments" are only different "manipulations" of the same idea. It is only when "we transcend the circumstances continually and taste the real quality of existence" that we "see God" and "know the savor of nature."

In this context he significantly praises "the Greek philosophers Heraclitus and Xenophanes," and then especially "the Hindoos," as ones who have wrestled with the problem of our essential identity and of the illusory nature of variety: "The notion *'I am,'* and *'This is mine,'* which profoundly influence mankind, are but delusions of the mother of the world." Therefore the emphasis must be "in fixing one's fortune in absolute Nature." The message of the entire essay is summed up in the idea that "the intellect is stimulated by the statement of truth in a trope, and the will by clothing the laws of life in illusions. But the unities of Truth and of Right are not broken by the disguise."

The upbeat conviction of the opening poem becomes the culminating affirmation of the essay, turning the recognition of life's "magic" show into faith in a metaphysical identity behind the changes of things: "There is no chance and no anarchy in the universe. All is system and gradation. Every god is sitting in his sphere."

CRITICAL COMMENTARY

Emerson provided the essential interpretation of the opening passage on his fascination with Mammoth Cave when he wrote later in the essay: "The intellect is stimulated by the statement of truth in a trope, and the will by clothing the laws of life in illusions." The movement of the whole essay unfolds on the principle that life's ubiquitous illusions are to be seen—and seen through—as the "magic" of an underlying spiritual identity, the self. This was his reflection on the nature of things that formed the backbone of the volume *The Conduct of Life,* as well as his subsequent writings.

Emerson's later composite piece, "POETRY AND IMAGINATION" (included in *LETTERS AND SOCIAL AIMS* [1876]), had its provenance in this exploration of the creative imagination in "Illusions." (WALLACE STEVENS's essay "Imagination as Value" might be considered a legacy of Emerson's essay.) As Emerson here observes: "We live by our imaginations, by our admirations, by our sentiments.

The child walks amid heaps of illusions." Our pretensions as to the importance of material life was the theme of the "illusory" nature of property ownership (ownership in the earth) in Emerson's earlier poem "HAMATREYA" (1847). Emerson reprises here his alternative spirituality going back to his early writings in *NATURE* (1836), "DIVINITY SCHOOL ADDRESS" (1838), and other essays calling for an original spiritual relation to the universe. The establishment churches, he insists, are as well illusions: "Former men believed in magic, by which temples, cities and men were swallowed up, and all traces of them are now gone. We are coming on the secret of a magic which sweeps out of men's minds all vestige of theism and beliefs they and their fathers held and were framed upon." The preceding essay on "Worship" also set the stage for the same reflection here.

Emerson ends the essay with his own philosophy of self-reliance at the basis of metaphysical meaning, behind the illusions: "And when, by and by, for an instant, the air clears, and the cloud lifts a little, there are the gods still sitting around him on their thrones,—they alone with him alone." This final passage of "Illusions," which also retains the tone of the "Blessed Unity" passage of "FATE," has one of its best poetic resonances in the final segment of "THRENODY," which includes the lines on "the genius of the whole / Ascendant in the private soul." As the culminating essay of *The Conduct of Life* in 1860, "Illusions" caps the whole substantial volume of Emerson's mid-career with one of his most positive metaphysical affirmations in the face of the ubiquitous disruptions and deceptions of life.

David A. Dilworth

"Initial, Daemonic, and Celestial Love" (1847)

Although "Initial, Daemonic, and Celestial Love" appeared in *POEMS* in 1847, the thoughts within it revert to at least 1839. In the late 1830s and early 1840s, Emerson was involved in a round-robin of letters and journal entries with young friends, including Anna Barker, Samuel Gray Ward, MARGARET FULLER, and CAROLINE STURGIS TAPPAN. The root of their conversations was Emerson's attempt to establish and define an ideal friendship (and possibly to quell more intimate ones). The influence of these "thought exchanges" is evident in much of Emerson's Transcendental writing of that time, including "LOVE" and "FRIENDSHIP" (both published in *ESSAYS: FIRST SERIES* [1841]). In his 1845–46 lecture "Swedenborg" (later published in *REPRESENTATIVE MEN* [1850]), Emerson deals with EMANUAL SWEDENBORG's concept of "Conjugal Love," which is attuned to "Initial, Daemonic, and Celestial Love."

CRITICAL COMMENTARY

Emerson's poems are often short versions of the Transcendentalist themes he explores in his essays. This poem is actually composed of three separate poems or sections. "Initial Love" introduces love in the classical form of Cupid, the god of eroticism, who has evolved from the cherub to a predatory creature; a "boy, no more," he no longer does his mischief with his bow and arrow but entrances with his eyes, "which would bring back day if it were dark." All of his power is in his eyes, but most prominently, "They are his steeds . . . And they pounce on other eyes." His song of seduction is "love-love-love-love." Cupid is a "mystic and a cabalist" who uses his magical powers solely for pleasure and "intimacy." "Daemonic Love" relies heavily on Goethe's concept of demonology, an untamed, devious, mystical, unexplainable force often associated with the occult. Emerson, however, attributes these mysterious energies and phenomena to the wonders of nature and oneness with the universe. In "Daemonic Love," Emerson suggests a "daemonic" region between the base or initial level of the human spirit and the divine. The bonds of social man, "man's narrow path," must be transcended to unite with the "Highest Love who shines on all," a preview of "Celestial Love."

However, Cupid is soon reintroduced wearing "another face," that of the demon: "His nectar (drink of the Olympian gods) smacks of wine."

(Drink here is associated with the debauchery of Dionysus and the maenads, not the Transcendental elixir of inspiration desired in Emerson's poem "BACCHUS.") The demon does not unite but "builds a wall" around himself. He pursues the "beautiful" and the "fortunate." However, "his impatient looks devour / Oft the humble and the poor; / And seeing his eye glare, / They drop their few pale flowers, / Gathered with hope to please." Consequently, Jove, king of the gods, sees Cupid's behavior and destroys the imp's domain, hence opening the road to celestial love, the "pure realm" of Transcendentalism.

This lofty state is "where all form / In one only form dissolves." Here nature and the universe are unified with the source of the soul, "where unlike things are like; / Where good and ill, / And joy and moan / Melt into one." However, to reach celestial love, initial and daemonic love must be transcended. All aspects of common friendship, passion, demonstrativeness, social fetters, and romance must be left behind: "For this is Love's nobility— / Not to scatter bread and gold" but to offer simplicity, innocence, purity, and good counsel. "He that feeds men serveth few; / He serves all who dare be true."

Barbara Downs Wojtusik

"In Memoriam E.B.E." (1867)

Emerson composed this poem as a memorial to his brother EDWARD BLISS EMERSON, a lawyer, who died of tuberculosis on October 1, 1834. The poem is set in nine stanzas of no fixed length or meter, though rhyme does occur, and the lines have cadence, due to Emerson's reliance on regular meter. Exact dates for its composition are indeterminable, though Emerson may have started the poem as early as 1837. The poem went through much revision and verse additions between 1837 and 1867. Lines 92–96 of "In Memoriam" were published as the second motto to the essay "CHARACTER" in *ESSAYS: SECOND SERIES* (1844). The poem as a whole was first published in *MAY-DAY AND OTHER PIECES* (1867), and was reprinted in *Poems* (1884).

CRITICAL COMMENTARY

In stanza 1, the speaker recalls the Battle of Concord, mourning "not for those who perished here," rather the scene of the battle recalls to him his "brother of the brief but blazing star!" and, in stanza 3, "the living champion in the cause of the right." Edward Emerson executed his battle with law, rather than arms, "frowning down the evil-doer / Battling for the weak and poor"; Edward "gave the law which others took."

Emerson spends most of the poem contrasting these two kinds of soldiers: those who battle on the field and Edward, who battled in the courts. The first makes the second possible, though the law, if executed morally and justly, is no less heroic. In stanza 9, Emerson resolves the contrast:

> What matters how, or from what ground,
> The freed soul its Creator found?
> Alike thy memory embalms
> That orange-grove, that isle of palms,
> And these loved banks, whose oak-boughs bold
> Root in the blood of heroes old.

The sense of place is especially significant in this poem, in terms of both the Emerson family's history in CONCORD and the town's historical significance during the Revolutionary War, which Emerson spoke to in his earlier poem known as the "CONCORD HYMN." "The Briton's friendless grave" in line 14 refers to the spot where the first two British soldiers were slain in the first fire of the battle. In his later edition of the *Complete Works*, EDWARD WALDO EMERSON connects this spot to his father's childhood: "The Old North Bridge, across which the opening volleys of the Revolutionary War were fired in a battle whose field extended from the Musketaquid to the Charles River, was close behind the Manse built by Rev. William Emerson, the young patriot minister of Concord, and there his grandsons William, Ralph Waldo, Edward, and Charles had spent many pleasant days in boyhood." Thus, in "In Memoriam E.B.E.," Ralph Waldo Emerson connects the universal (the Revolutionary War) with the personal (his brother's death) to evoke a sense of justice and sacrifice inherent in the American ideal.

Bill Scalia

"Intellect" (1841)

One of the shorter pieces in *ESSAYS: FIRST SERIES* (1841), "Intellect" was an early exploration into a topic that culminated in Emerson's 1848 lectures on "Mind in the Nineteenth Century," first delivered in England and repeated in somewhat different form at HARVARD COLLEGE in 1870 and 1871. These lectures were collected by Emerson's literary executor, JAMES ELLIOT CABOT, and published after Emerson's death as *NATURAL HISTORY OF INTELLECT* (1893), a project never completed to Emerson's satisfaction. The 1841 version of "Intellect," however, cannot be read solely in terms of the later ongoing project, as it fits into Emerson's earliest efforts to define his own Transcendentalist idealism. In "Intellect" he explored the idea of the subjective mind that he had introduced in *NATURE* (1836) and the relation of the individual mind to the universal mind that he explored further in "The OVER-SOUL" and in "HISTORY" of the same volume.

SYNOPSIS

Emerson explains that "every substance" in nature has a negative or positive relationship to every other substance. For example, "water dissolves wood . . . air dissolves water," and so on; "the intellect," however, "dissolves fire, gravity, laws, method, and the subtlest unnamed relations of nature." Emerson's definition of genius comes from this understanding of the "nature" of intellect: "Intellect lies behind genius, which is intellect constructive." His goal in the essay is to "unfold in calm degrees a natural history of the intellect." He approaches the question scientifically, while acknowledging that intellect is a "transparent essence," beyond the natural world in that it has no boundaries: "Its vision is not like the vision of the eye, but is union with the things known."

The intellect encompasses all; it is "consideration of abstract truth . . . of time and place, of you and me, of profit and hurt." Yet, it is not personalized, for the intellect "separates the fact considered from you, from all local and personal reference, and discerns it as if it existed for its own sake." Instead, intellect "goes out of the individual, floats over its own personality, and regards it as a fact, and not as *I* and *mine*." It "reduces all things into a few principles." The facts of daily life cause us to feel "formed and bound" in nature, but the intellect allows us to see a "truth" beyond our human "destiny" precisely because it is "impersonal and immortal."

Intellect is, in one sense, the ability to philosophize, but it exists *before* philosophy: "Long prior to the age of reflection is the thinking of the mind." What begins in the unconscious becomes "reflection or conscious thought," and then "law." It is a *natural* progression of ideas: First comes an "instinct, then an opinion, then a knowledge, as the plant has root, bud, and fruit." The intellect is not, in other words, an act of human will: "What am I? What has my will done to make me that I am? Nothing." We are enamored of ideas, but in truth, "we do not determine what we will think. . . . We are the prisoners of ideas." The ideas come to us spontaneously, but only when we "recall" and make use of them does it become "Truth." The larger universal meaning may not be immediately apparent to our individual conscious minds: "Trust the instinct to the end, though you can render no reason. . . . It shall ripen into truth."

Although there are universal laws, still there are individual differences, for "each mind has its own method." "Do you think the porter and the cook have no anecdotes, no experiences, no wonders for you?" He warns against those who equate education with intelligence, arguing that it takes only "wit and culture" to inspire "curiosity" of the mind and not "the drill of school education." While every "healthy mind" has intuition or instinct, intellect demands a conscious decision to "sit down to consider an abstract truth." This is done "whilst we converse, whilst we read, [and] whilst we act"; it is active learning, and it is "the hardest task in the world." Sometimes we try too hard to find inspiration, and we think we need a change of venue, a quiet space, but all of this is too much effort; reflection requires effort, but thinking abides by "that law of nature" that regulates breathing and the heart beating.

The value of every thought (what Emerson terms "intellections") is not in "its present value," but in its role as "a lantern," which illuminates other "facts and thoughts." Readers of Plutarch, Shakespeare, or Cervantes will marvel, "Where did he get this? and think there was something divine in his life. But no; they have myriads of facts just as good, would they only get a lamp to ransack their attics withal." There are no men of "superior" wisdom, for "the difference between persons is not in wisdom, but in art." On the conscious level we may feel "we have nothing to write, nothing to infer." But as we age we see the larger meaning of our experience and find that our own personal "biography . . . is, in reality, nothing less than the miniature paraphrase of the hundred volumes of the Universal History."

Emerson distinguishes between "intellect receptive" (or "revelation") and "intellect constructive" (or "Genius")—it is the latter active form that "produces thoughts, sentences, poems, plans, designs, systems . . . the marriage of thought with nature." All minds can comprehend "good form" and beauty, but the painter or writer must go further and actually create something: "The world has a million writers . . . yet we can count all our good books." It is the role of the poet or artist to reveal "the truth" as "reflected to us from natural objects." Emerson concedes that not everyone will be a poet or a genius as "God offers to every mind its choice between truth and repose." Human will and "choice" then come in deciding to use the mind, while the person "in whom the love of repose predominates" accepts the first ideas they hear, the ideas "most like his father's"—that is, tradition. Those "in whom the love of truth predominates," on the other hand, "abstain from dogmatism" and must learn to live with "the inconvenience of suspense and imperfect opinion." This may set one apart from society but leads one to a truer *self.*

Emerson cautions that the search for truth requires one to be open and silent: "If I speak, I define, I confine, and am less." People too readily accept "a new doctrine"; instead, we should see great minds as only "one more bright star shining serenely in your heaven, and blending its light with all your day." Let not "fame and authority" be your criteria but your own judgment: "Entire self-reliance belongs to the intellect. . . . It must treat things, and books, and sovereign genius, as itself also a sovereign." Find and trust only in those ideas or thinkers that are most successful at "rendering back to you your consciousness."

Emerson himself therefore resists presenting yet another philosophy to choose from: "The gods shall settle their own quarrels." He seeks instead to inquire only of the "laws of the intellect" in an effort to understand the mind's relationship to philosophy; his is a history of intellect, not a history of philosophy. The lesson from nature is for each to "speak their own, whether there be any who understand it or not."

CRITICAL COMMENTARY

The essay on "Intellect" establishes Emerson's interest in the importance and process of thinking itself more than concern with *what* one thinks about. In other essays as well (such as "The AMERICAN SCHOLAR" in 1837) Emerson defined "intellect" as impersonal, but the act of thinking as highly personal and individualized. In his "Historic Notes of Life and Letters in New England" (written in 1867), he reflected that "The key to the period appeared to be that the mind had become aware of itself. Men grew reflective and intellectual. There was a new consciousness." He was, of course, the premier philosopher of the mind defining the very age he described.

In the opening lines of the essay Emerson describes intellect as a "transparent essence," separate from or beyond nature. In defining the "vision" of the mind as "not like the vision of the eye," Emerson clarifies that intellect does not work within the same natural laws that govern the physical body. Whereas the eyes look out upon the world from a specific point of self, the intellect "separates the fact considered from you, from all local and personal reference." The intellect is larger than the self in that it is the very "problem of existence," beyond "person or place." That is why, in the essay, Emerson emphasizes "spontaneous action," or the "intuitive principle"—thought before the intrusion of human will. In other words, Emerson's "intellect" is the idea of a subconscious mind: "In every man's mind, some images, words, and facts remain, without effort on his part to imprint them, which others forget, and afterwards these illustrate to him important laws." In "Intellect," Emerson's core Transcendentalist belief, as he would articulate again and again throughout his writings, is to trust nature by trusting your own mind.

Beyond intuition, however, intellect demands a conscious decision to "sit down to consider an abstract truth." This is the active learning and reading he demands in "The American Scholar" and in *Representative Men* (1850). We must not merely emulate great thinkers but use them to inspire the poet, writer, thinker, or artist within ourselves. In "Intellect" he urges us to see there is little difference between ourselves and Shakespeare, "only that he possessed a strange skill of using, of classifying, his facts, which we lacked." Likewise, in "The American Scholar," he admonishes "meek young men [who] grow up in libraries, believing it their duty to accept the views, which Cicero, which Locke, which Bacon, have given, forgetful that Cicero, Locke, and Bacon were only young men in libraries, when they wrote these books." Again here in "Intellect," he wryly warns against the enthusiasm "in this country" for "Swedenborg . . . Kant . . . Coleridge . . . Hegel or his interpreter Cousin"—all, of course, important influences on American Transcendentalism. Each of these, however, "is only a more or less awkward translator of things in your consciousness, which you have also your way of seeing, perhaps of denominating." Emerson presents the Transcendentalism of his own day not just as one more "philosophy of mind," but also as a philosophy of self-trust, through which to approach other thinkers and ideas.

FURTHER READING

Buell, Lawrence. *Emerson.* New York: Cambridge, 2003.

DeVoll, Matthew W. "Emerson and Dreams: Toward a Natural History of Intellect." *ATQ* 18, no. 2 (June 2004): 69–87.

Von Frank, Albert J. "Essays: First Series (1841)." In *The Cambridge Companion to Ralph Waldo Emerson,* edited by Joel Porte and Saundra Morris, 106–120. New York: Cambridge, 1999.

"Introductory Lecture on the Times" (1841)

Also referred to as "Lecture on the Times" or "The Times," Emerson delivered this opening address to his winter lecture series at the Masonic Temple in Boston on December 2, 1841, and later versions in Rhode Island and New York. The Boston series was titled "The Times" and included this introductory lecture followed by seven more lectures: "The Conservative," "The Poet," "The Transcendentalist," "Manners," "Character," "The Relation of Man to Nature," and "Prospects." The "Introductory Lecture" was subsequently published in the *Dial* (July 1842) and later collected in *Nature; Addresses, and Lectures* (1849). "The Conservative" and "The Transcendentalist" were also published as essays within the year, and their themes are echoed directly in the "Introductory Lecture." The lecture "The Poet," however, was different than the 1844 essay "The Poet" included in *Essays: Second Series;* the original 1841 lecture on "The Poet" was incorporated in part into the much later essay "Poetry and Imagination."

The lecture series on "The Times" was delivered at a turning point in Emerson's career. He had established himself as a successful lecturer and author with the publication of *Essays: First Series* (1841). With "The Times" he now turned to a more practical consideration of the philosophical tenets laid down in *Nature* (1836) and in the *Essays.* A few years later, in the essay "Fate" (1860), he had come to the conclusion that "the question of the times resolved itself into a practical question of the conduct of life. How shall I live? We are incompetent to solve the times. . . . We can only obey our own polarity."

SYNOPSIS

Emerson's goal in "The Times" is to connect "the present aspects of our social state, the Laws, Divinity, Natural Science, Agriculture, Art, Trade, Letters" with "their root in an invisible spiritual reality." He seeks to understand not only the "conspicuous facts of the day" but also the "reason" behind the facts and characteristics of the current age. Among

Ralph Waldo Emerson at the height of his career as a popular lecturer *(Concord Free Public Library)*

the topics he wishes to address are "the reason and influence of wealth," "the aspect of philosophy and religion, and the tendencies which have acquired the name of Transcendentalism in Old and New England," as well as "poetry, as the exponent and interpretation of these things" and "character as a social and political agent." He emphasizes that to speak of "the times" encompasses all of these themes but only in personal, immediate terms: "We talk of the world, but we mean a few men and women."

To understand the times, one must look to fellow humans not to government institutions or laws: "And so I find the Age walking about in happy and hopeful natures, in strong eyes, and pleasant thoughts, and think I read it nearer and truer so, than in the statute-book, or in the investments of capital, which rather celebrate with mournful music the obsequies of the last age." Rather, he looks to the smallest details of life ("the love-glance of a girl") or even to the fringes of society (the "fanatic" or "eccentric") to understand "that which shall constitute the times to come." He wants to create "a portrait gallery" of the times and capture people in their daily lives and expects to find "much to admire as well as to condemn" about the age. But we are not just "spectators of the pageant which the times exhibit: we are parties also." Whether we condemn or praise "the times," it is not separate from ourselves.

Emerson identifies "the party of the Past and the party of the Future" as two competing elements in all societies. First, there is "the innumerable multitude" who "accept the state and the church from the last generation" and work to maintain the status quo. On the other side is "the dissenter, the theorist," seeking "adventure" and change. In the current age, these are a "great army of martyrs" engaged in "projects for the reform of domestic, civil, literary, and ecclesiastical institutions." There are those engaged in "crusades" against "Negro slavery" and "Intemperance" and "the treatment of Indians," as well as reformers of government, education, and other institutions.

Regardless of the issue, the spirit of reform reveals much about "the conscience of the Age." Efforts to reform society exist because "our modes of living are not agreeable to our imagination." We seek the "beautiful and the just" in "nature, literature, science, childhood. . . . but not our own daily work." Reform is forward-looking in that it is the "hope" that "some distant age" will finally reflect "the thoughts of the mind." Reformers are the "conscience" of society, so that even if we disagree with them, we must still "allow and honor them." For Emerson, the problem is that reformers come to depend "on men, on multitudes, . . . on money, on party" rather than on principle. Reformers make the "mistake" of emphasizing only right action, when "we do not want actions, but men."

Young people are drawn to reform causes because they want to act, want to make a difference, and believe that they can do more by joining with others than alone. Emerson advises, instead, that we must "consent to solitude and inaction" and answer only to "the paramount duties of self-reliance." Reformers focus only on "outward circumstances," and he wonders whether anyone truly believes that if "every house had a Bible, and if every child was brought into the Sunday School, would the wounds of the world heal, and man be upright?" Likewise, the "slave-laws" of Georgia or Alabama exist "here on our north-eastern shores"; that is, that men's hearts in the North need to change just as much as the laws of the South, and yet reformers focus only on the latter.

The crisis of the age is not war or famine or religious fear, as in other times and places. The crisis of the age is an internal crisis, a "torment" of "Unbelief . . . Uncertainty": "We mistrust every step we take. We find it the worst thing about time, that we know not what to do with it." He characterizes this as "a too intellectual tendency": "It is not that men do not wish to act; they pine to be employed, but are paralyzed by the uncertainty what they should do." As a result, there is great thought but "so little action" and no real "conflict" or resolution. The "young American" grows up thinking, "'I want something which I never saw before;' and 'I wish I was not I.'" Still, there is hope in the fact that it is the striving for the ideal that produces this fear of not doing enough.

As his is an age characterized by this "love of greatness," it is also an age of "great mechanical invention" and "daring theories." The problem is that these outward accomplishments tell us nothing, for they are only "appearances"; inside us "lies that which is, that which lives, that which causes." He uses an analogy from nature, that of a "granite" mountain that "towers" above all else, most powerful and imposing, but "if we dig down, we find it below the superficial strata, so in all the details of our domestic or civil life, is hidden the elemental reality." Indeed, the granite (like "the grand men" and "leaders" of our time) does not stand alone but reaches down through and is supported by "a thousand formations and surfaces, under fertile soils, and grasses, and flowers, under well-manured, arable fields, and large towns and cities."

So it is that the signs of the times are seen not only in the great accomplishments but also in all the various aspects of daily social life, in our faces, our interactions, our "elections," our "juries," our politics and "histories" and "churches." It is in these places, these interactions, that we will find truth. We do not need grand inventions or great causes but need only look to "our immediate neighborhood": "For that reality let us stand: that let us serve, and for that speak." Having dedicated a lecture to the question of "The Times," he concludes that we should be concerned "not of to-day, not of the times, but of the Everlasting."

CRITICAL COMMENTARY

In the "Introductory Lecture on the Times" Emerson establishes a role for the philosopher as cultural critic: "Everything that is popular, it has been said, deserves the attention of the philosopher." So it was that, throughout his writings, he turned a critical and philosophical eye toward events, culture, and behavior in his own time. In "The Transcendentalist" of the same series, for example, he defines the movement not strictly in philosophical terms but in historical context as "Idealism as it appears in 1842." In 1848 he again picked up the theme of the "Spirit of the Times" for a lecture series, comparing his interest in the topic to his friend THOMAS CARLYLE's writing "The Present Age."

As Emerson explains in the opening paragraph, however, understanding the specifics of the present was the key to understanding the past, present, and universal: "The Times are the masquerade of the eternities." Even though only an "introduction" to the other lectures (and therefore often receiving less scholarly attention), it was as lengthy as other pieces and outlines important themes for the series and for Emerson's future writings. The lecture on the times also showed his willingness as a philosopher to engage contemporary politics and controversies, and indeed, he would address more directly political and social reform issues as the 1840s and 1850s progressed.

The lecture provides an introduction to Emerson's humanistic, rather than religious or abstract philosophical or even historical, view of the world. He places human beings at the center of the time, as "Thoughts" themselves, which "walk and speak, and look with eyes at me." The idea of humans as thought incarnate invokes a similar image as that of "Man Thinking" from "The AMERICAN SCHOLAR" (1838). Whereas the religious leader sees only the sin and downfall of humanity, and the historian will look only at the exterior accomplishments of society, Emerson wants the inside view—he wants to understand the times as humanity experiences and creates it.

Emerson's wide scope and frantic pace to create "a portrait gallery" of the times are reflected in his choice of imagery. Having dismissed "inventions" and achievements as the true markers of the times, he then makes a current technological reference in likening himself to "the Daguerreotypist" attempting to capture a moment. The reference is an apt one in terms of Emerson's favored imagery of seeing and of the eye; he invites, "let us set up our Camera also," and we shall see what humanity is up to. What he catalogs (in a manner similar to WALT WHITMAN) are people in a variety of occupations: the "agitator," "member of Congress," "college-professor," "editor," "priest," and "reformer," each contributes to what he calls "the general mind" of the times.

Emerson's search for the "invisible spiritual reality" at the foundation of present-day "Laws, Divinity, Natural Science, Agriculture, Art, Trade, Letters" is undeniably ambitious. Indeed, he would continue to address each of these individual themes in various later lectures and essays. Likewise, he spends a considerable amount of space in the introductory lecture discussing the reform impulse and the difference between "conservatism" and "reform," a dialectic he would explore in more depth in the essay "The Conservative." The "Introductory Lecture on the Times" serves as well as an introduction to Emersonian thought, showing him to be himself a philosopher of the times and of the everlasting.

Letters and Social Aims (1876)

Letters and Social Aims, with a publication date of 1876, was Emerson's final collection of essays to be published during his lifetime. The volume included the following 11 chapters or essays: "POETRY AND IMAGINATION," "Social Aims," "Eloquence," "Resources," "The Comic," "Quotation and Originality," "Progress of Culture," "PERSIAN POETRY," "Inspiration," "Greatness," and "Immortality."

Around 1870 Emerson had promised a volume of previously unpublished writings to a British publisher, but as the years wore on, his mental abilities faltered. As his daughter, ELLEN EMERSON, reported as early as 1872, "his memory is entirely gone." Ellen Emerson and JAMES ELLIOT CABOT agreed to work with Emerson to fulfill the publisher's request, but Cabot assured readers in the preface to a later edition of the volume that "there is nothing here that [Emerson] did not write, and he gave his full approval to whatever was done in the way of selection and arrangement." Still, Cabot was most likely the one responsible for piecing together essays out of fragments of other writings for *Letters and Social Aims*. Indeed, EDWARD WALDO EMERSON reported that his father had always insisted to Cabot that it was "your book."

Still, the volume included the significant later essay, "Poetry and Imagination," which had its roots as a lecture from the 1850s. This essay expanded upon Emerson's philosophical project (begun in his 1836 debut *NATURE*) of understanding the symbolic language of nature. In "Poetry and Imagination" he says, "A good symbol is the best argument . . . indeed Nature itself is a vast trope, and all particular natures are tropes." It is the task of the poet to interpret and re-present this language through writing: "Poetry is the only verity. . . . As a power, it is the perception of the symbolic character of things, and the treating them as representative."

FURTHER READING

Johnson, Glenn M. "Emerson's Essay 'Immortality': The Problem of Authorship." In *On Emerson: The*

Best from American Literature, edited by Edwin Harrison Cady and Louis J. Budd, 245–262. Durham, N.C.: Duke University Press, 1988.

Thomas, Joseph M. "Late Emerson: *Selected Poems* and the 'Emerson Factory.'" *ELH* 65, no. 4 (1998): 971–994.

"Literary Ethics" (1838)

First printed as a pamphlet, "An Oration delivered before the Literary Societies of Dartmouth College, July 24, 1838" was published with the title "Literary Ethics" in Emerson's 1849 collection, *NATURE; ADDRESSES, AND LECTURES.* Biographer Gay Allen calls "Literary Ethics" "a lower-keyed companion of the "DIVINITY SCHOOL ADDRESS," which Emerson had delivered at HARVARD COLLEGE just a little more than a week earlier (on July 15, 1838). In "Literary Ethics" Emerson focused on American literature, art, and culture, rather than on the disappointments of UNITARIAN theology. As Allen notes, the diagnosis was the same, a "fear of innovation, too much respect for authority, custom, and inherited opinion." "Literary Ethics" was also a restatement of themes Emerson had outlined the previous year in "The AMERICAN SCHOLAR" (1837) and in "Thoughts on Modern Literature" (1840). Even earlier, in *NATURE* (1836), he had written that ethics was "the practice of ideas, or the introduction of ideas into life." In "Literary Ethics" he meant to expound upon the ethics or practice of "the scholar's profession."

SYNOPSIS

Emerson begins by acknowledging the power of the scholar, who "by every thought he thinks, extends his dominion into the general mind of men." Yet our society has "a very different estimate of the scholar's profession," and this explains "the historical failure" of our American culture. We had a revolution in which "all feudal straps and bandages were snapped asunder," and yet American arts and culture lack the corresponding "grandeur" of our position. Americans show a preference for "antiquity," a dependence on the past rather than a propensity for "innovation" or "thought." In this atmosphere, the scholar may too easily "become a pedant," a man only of "schools" or "words," when the true "want of the times" is for a "doctrine of Literary Ethics."

Emerson sets out to identify "the resources, the subject, and the discipline of the scholar." The first resources available to the scholar are nature, "Time," and "the grand events of history." Yet, the scholar cannot interpret these resources and access truth if he is bound "to reigning schools, or to the wisdom of antiquity." Scholars must not be merely historians or chroniclers but also "the upholders and creators of our age." History gives us "Milton, Shakespeare, and Plato," but these are only "glorious manifestations of the mind," representatives of "the universal attributes of man." Unfortunately, "the youth, intoxicated with his admiration of a hero, fails to see, that it is only a projection of his own soul, which he admires." The scholar must reveal "the universal nature" in great men so that men of today may be inspired: "Be lord of a day, through wisdom and justice, and you can put up your history books."

Another resource available to the scholar is "the intellect of this country": "We have not heeded the invitation it holds out." We are too quick to assume "that all thought is already long ago adequately set down in books,—all imagination in poems." Emerson offers the alternative perspective that "all literature is yet to be written." For the American scholar, "his own conversation with nature is still unsung." Likewise with philosophy, which seems "conclusive," as if it is "all truth." In fact, philosophy is only an "observation" that "may open a new view of nature of and of man." This does not mean there is not value in the ideas of various philosophers—only that no one idea or system of thought should "exclude or forestall a new attempt," for "thought renews itself inexhaustibly every day."

Lastly, Emerson turns to the question of the scholar's "ambition and life." The scholar must "embrace solitude," depending only upon "his own estimate" and "his own praise," not that of others. If we are "hankering for the crowd, for display," then we are not able to think. He clarifies that he advocates not literal "insulation of place" but "independence of spirit." One needs the experience of society, but one need not participate in "its foolish routine, an indefinite multiplication of balls, concerts, rides, theatres." We claim we crave "muse and prophet . . . art and creation," yet we do not allow for those things in our "superficial existence": "out of our shallow and frivolous way of life, how can greatness ever grow?" We need "Silence, seclusion, austerity," not "fashionable or political saloons" and "newspapers."

Still, the scholar must engage "language,—the subtlest, strongest, and longest-lived of man's creations" by dealing with life directly: "He must work with men in houses, and not with their names in books." It is in our "houses," the routines of daily domestic life, that we learn "of love and hatred . . . sickness and pain . . . wooing and worshipping . . . disgrace and contempt." Rather than attempt to escape from life, the true scholar must live it: "Let him endeavor exactly, bravely, and cheerfully, to solve the problem of that life which is set before him." In addition to "toil and endurance," the scholar must be open to "inspiration"—this is the "twofold goodness" that all "great masters" possessed. "The man of genius" relies upon both hard work and inspiration, action and thought, "Reason" and "Common Sense." Too far "at either extreme" and "his philosophy will seem low and utilitarian; or it will appear too vague and indefinite for the uses of life."

Emerson wishes to counter the voices of those who would tell young people "the first duty is to get land and money, place and name." The scholar's quest is for nothing less than "Truth" and "Beauty." To give in to society's expectations, "then dies the man in you; then once more perish the buds of art, and poetry, and science, as they have died already in a thousand thousand men." Rather than seeking recognition by putting oneself on "display," "Be content with a little light, so it be your own. Explore, and explore . . . perpetual inquiry." For those who would argue that the scholar has no place, no employment, in modern society, he urges, "Make yourself necessary to the world, and mankind will give you bread."

Emerson ends the essay by emphasizing that he is not advocating that "the philosopher conceals his accomplishments, and hides his thoughts." Indeed, this is not possible: "Hides his thoughts! Hide the sun and moon. Thought is all light, and publishes itself to the universe. . . . It will flow out of your actions, your manners, and your face." The true scholar will find himself the recipient of "every sincere good that is in the soul," according "to the laws of that Nature."

CRITICAL COMMENTARY

In "Literary Ethics" (just as in "The American Scholar" and the "Divinity School Address" of the same period), Emerson calls for a cultural and intellectual break from the past to rival the political break made by the previous generation with the American Revolution. Emerson connects the state of American culture with that of the American individual who has not yet completed the break from Europe on questions of history, religion, philosophy, and art. Emerson speaks directly to America's Manifest Destiny, noting that, blessed by an immense landscape, nature is as yet "new and undescribed" in America. The "darkness" of the forest waits for illumination by our poets and writers; so it is for every individual, "his own conversation with nature is still unsung." He would echo this relationship between man, the nation, and nature in "The YOUNG AMERICAN" as well.

"Literary Ethics" is also concerned primarily with the role of history and of its relationship to the individual: "The whole value of history, of biography, is to increase my self-trust, by demonstrating what man can be and do." This was, of course, a foundational idea in "The American Scholar," as well as in the essays "HEROISM" and "HISTORY" (both, 1841) and in the later *REPRESENTATIVE MEN* (1850). Whereas history gives us perspective—"what high dogmas I had supposed were the rare and late fruit of a cumulate culture . . . were the prompt improvisations of the earliest inquirers"—biography inspires us with "the power of character." These are the only terms with which we should be concerned in our European or Western past.

As he would echo in "History," so in "Literary Ethics" he admires the "churches, literatures, and empires" of other nations or eras but only as records of what humans are capable of. Rather than worship the previous age, we must be "upholders and creators of our age" and "put our own interpretation on things." These words echo his call, not only in "The American Scholar" and "Divinity School Address," but even earlier in *Nature,* to pursue an "original relation to the universe." Our independence from history and tradition is just as important, spiritually, as independence from the religions and philosophies of the past.

Again, as in "The American Scholar," Emerson warns in "Literary Ethics" against scholarly solitude or asceticism, urging American artists to strive instead for a balance between self and society: "Think alone, and all places are friendly and sacred. The poets who have lived in cities have been hermits still." The balance between intellectual independence and social duties was a personal concern for Emerson throughout his life and one that he sought to resolve philosophically in numerous works, from poems such as "SAADI" to the essays in *The* CONDUCT OF LIFE (1860) and *SOCIETY AND SOLITUDE* (1870). In "Literary Ethics" he calls for the scholar to "study the uses of solitude and of society," but "not serve either"; a maxim he followed in his own life.

"The Lord's Supper" (1832)

"The Lord's Supper" was Emerson's most famous sermon and the only sermon published in his lifetime, reprinted in OCTAVIUS BROOKS FROTHINGHAM's history of *Transcendentalism in New England* (1876). It was included as the first piece in the Centenary Edition of the *Complete Works* (1903) edited by his son EDWARD WALDO EMERSON. Identified as "Sermon CLXII," it is also included in volume four of *The Complete Sermons of Ralph Waldo Emerson,* published in 1992.

Emerson was ordained a UNITARIAN minister in January 1829 and took a position at the Second Church in BOSTON. On September 9, 1832, he delivered a sermon as a request to the church to end the practice of the Lord's Supper, which served effectively as his resignation from the pulpit. The Lord's Supper, also known as Holy Communion or the Eucharist, is the ritual whereby the congregants eat unleavened bread and drink wine to symbolize, respectively, the body and blood of Christ. Emerson gave both theological and personal reasons to explain his inability to continue to lead this practice, a ritual that seemed to him devoid of any spiritual meaning and one that was carried out solely in the name of tradition.

Thus, six years before the "DIVINITY SCHOOL ADDRESS" (1838), Emerson was speaking publicly of the disconnect between the needs of the soul and the practices of the church. Nearly a decade before "SELF-RELIANCE" (1841), he asserts his core belief that what is true is that which speaks to the individual. While he undoubtedly cared about this particular issue as one of his formal ministerial duties, ultimately it seems he merely used the Lord's Supper to address his general dissatisfaction with ritual and tradition as sources of spiritual meaning.

SYNOPSIS

Emerson begins his sermon by noting that, "In the history of the Church," the Lord's Supper has often been a topic of "controversy": "There never has been any unanimity in the understanding of its nature nor any uniformity in the mode of celebrating it." He is not interested, however, in "the frivolous questions" that embroil so many churches over how to administer it or who should participate, nor in the theological questions of what, exactly, it signifies. He means to point out only that there is "the widest room for difference of opinion" on the issue. In this way Emerson softens his own critique, placing it in the context of longer and broader church debates. He proceeds to give his own opinion on the matter, which is twofold—first, "that Jesus did not intend to establish an institution for perpetual observance," and, second, "that it is not expedient to celebrate it as we do."

He goes directly to the four different gospel accounts ("Matthew, Mark, Luke and John") to support his point that there is no evidence or injunction from those closest to Christ indicating he expected

Christians to regularly participate in the rite. The closest proof is found in the gospel of Luke, in which Jesus says, "after relating the breaking of the bread . . . 'This do in remembrance of me' (22:15)." Still, Emerson interprets this phrase (which only appears in one of the gospels) only as "an affectionate expression" and one that was not "meant to impose a memorial feast upon the whole world."

Emerson places Christ's emphasis on the meal in context as a Passover feast enjoyed by all Jews at the time, and Christ's words ("This is my body which is broken for you. Take, Eat. This is my blood which is shed for you. Drink it."), Emerson believes, "are not extraordinary expressions from him . . . He always taught by parables and symbols." Jesus's method was "to spiritualize every occurrence." Furthermore, the Passover feast was not the only time he uttered those exact words, which Emerson sees as an explanation for why the other apostles do not mention the meal in this context. Emerson is more interested in Jesus's further clarification to his disciples that "the *words* that I speak to you, they are spirit and they are life"; that is, his words are the source of religion, not the action of participating in the feast.

Emerson wonders why the church has placed so much emphasis on the Lord's Supper while ignoring other practices, such as Jesus's act in washing the disciple's feet. He asserts that even if the early disciples decided to continue this ritual after Christ's death, that fact should not concern us. It makes sense for them "to remember their friend and repeat his words" because they had not yet fully grasped "the spiritual character of Christianity." The other New Testament source for the ritual is from Paul in I Corinthians, but Emerson argues that "A careful examination of that passage will not I think make that evidence so weighty as it seems." The passage is only a warning against "abuse" or "drunkenness" at the supper, not a mandate for "attendance." In other words, the reference in Corinthians proves only that the community was still holding such a feast, not that Christ had required it.

Emerson rejects an interpretation of Paul's words, "*I have received of the Lord,*" as "a miraculous communication," and he says Paul's words refer only to the accounts by the still-living apostles, who had literally "received" the Lord firsthand. If the early church did take Paul's words literally, Emerson can only fault this "prevalent error of the primitive Church"—that is, "the belief namely that the second coming of Christ would shortly occur, until which time, he tells them, this feast was to be kept." Emerson says that they did not yet understand that "his Second Coming was a spiritual kingdom," not a physical one. No one can know for sure "the purpose in the mind of Jesus," but we have no evidence that he expected the feast to be observed by Christians "in all times and all countries." Emerson summarizes his conclusion that the practice of the early disciples is now outdated: "I think it was good for them. I think it is not suited to this day. We do not take them for guides in other things. They were, as we know, obstinately attached to their Jewish prejudices. . . . On every subject we have learned to think differently."

Emerson then turns to another view, namely, those who would ask, "What harm doth it?" If the gospel evidence is unclear, why not administer and participate in communion anyway? "This is the question of Expediency." First of all, Emerson objects, believing it is wrong to celebrate it with "the claim of authority" from Jesus. Unable to make such a claim, he affirms that participation would have to be optional. Second, he argues, it does do harm to the spirit because it "tends to produce confusion in our views of the relation of the soul to God." He is speaking to Unitarians, who have an "old objection to the doctrine of the Trinity that the true worship was transferred from God to Christ," and yet, "Is not that the effect of the Lord's Supper?" Within Unitarianism, the practice makes no sense, for it requires the adherent "to clothe Jesus with an authority which he never claimed and which distracts the mind of the worshipper." He appeals to the "individual experience" of his listeners, who must admit, that when "the soul stands alone with God . . . Jesus is no more present to the mind than your brother or your child."

Lastly, Emerson objects to the very "*use of the elements*"—the bread and the wine—in the ritual. These particular food items may have meant something "in the East where it originated," but they are now "foreign and unsuited to affect us."

Furthermore, as part of his argument for a "living and operative" Christianity, he observes that New Englanders "are not accustomed to express our thoughts or emotions by symbolical actions." Thus, there is no connection in the heart between the ritual and the faith: "To eat bread is one thing; to love the precepts of Christ and resolve to obey them is quite another."

He gives his reasons why he cannot personally continue to administer the service: "This mode of commemorating Christ is not suitable to me . . . For I choose that my remembrances of him should be pleasing, affecting, religious." Far from doing no harm, he believes the ritual "is not consistent with the spirit of Christianity," which is "a moral system," not dependent upon "meat and drink." In fact, "Jesus came to take the load of ceremonies from the shoulders of men and substitute principles." Christ offered "to redeem us from a formal religion, and teach us to seek our well-being in the reformation of the soul."

In his view, the Lord's Supper has no connection with the meaning of Christianity: "What I revere and obey is . . . its boundless charity, its deep interior life, the rest it gives to my mind, the echo it returns to my thoughts, the perfect accord it makes with my reason, the persuasion and courage that come out of it to lead me upward and onward." True Christianity does not make meaningless demands of believers.

What Emerson wants is for "the church to drop the use of the elements and the claim of authority in the administration of this ordinance." Not surprisingly, the congregants have not agreed with their minister and he is therefore "compelled to consider whether it becomes me to administer it. I am clearly of the opinion that I ought not. . . . It is my desire, in the office of a Christian minister, to do nothing which I cannot do with my whole heart." He must thus announce that "I am about to resign into your hands that office which you have confided to me."

CRITICAL COMMENTARY

Delivered exactly four years before *NATURE* (published in September 1836), and six years before the controversial "Divinity School Address," the sermon known as "The Lord's Supper" was an important precursor to these coming statements that would define Emerson's Transcendentalist thought. Indeed, Edward Emerson later noted that "Mr. Emerson did not wish to have his sermons published. All that was worth saving in them, he said, would be found in the Essays." Of the early essays or addresses that followed, each served a different audience and led to a distinct shift in Emerson's thought and career. "The Lord's Supper" served as his formal resignation from the church; *Nature* not only established an alternative career for Emerson as a writer but also established the tenets of his Transcendentalist alternative of nature as a universal source of spiritual inspiration; and, finally, the "Divinity School Address" signaled his final break not only from the church but also from his broader Harvard-Unitarian connections, completing the vocational and spiritual break begun with "The Lord's Supper."

The 1832 sermon gives us a rare glimpse of Emerson the Unitarian, before he fully emerged as Emerson the Transcendentalist. Here is Emerson's distinct literary voice emerging but still speaking the language of the church as he reflects on the conflict between his position as minister and his own duty to himself. Here is the Emerson who declares for the last time, "I am so much a Unitarian as this, that I believe the human mind cannot admit but one God." He is speaking to his congregation as one of them, at the very moment he is breaking away.

As sincerely as Emerson seems to appreciate the "boundless charity" and "deep interior life" Christianity provides, this was his resignation speech and he would build a philosophy out of looking elsewhere (to nature and inward to the self) for such inspiration. He himself would have little future use for Christianity, and yet here he is urging his congregants toward a deeper and more personal Christianity of their own. While here he claims "Freedom is the essence of Christianity," in the subsequent "Divinity School Address" and in "Self-Reliance" he would define religion as the opposite of freedom. And although he would sometimes refer to Jesus Christ as a "divine man," as a man or as a philosopher Jesus Christ was never central to Emerson's secular Transcendentalism.

Here Emerson rejects any "miraculous communication" either between the disciples and Christ or between his 19th-century listeners and Christ. Even if the disciples required "miracles" for proof of Christ's divinity, such acts have no meaning if not witnessed firsthand: "if miracles may be said to have been its evidence to the first Christians they are not its evidence to us."

Emerson was not alone in rejecting the supernatural aspects of Christianity, as a "miracles controversy" soon threatened a split within Unitarianism. The Transcendentalists rejected the supernatural nature of Christ's miracles; in *Nature* Emerson called attention to "the miraculous in the common," asking, "What is a day? What is a year? What is summer? What is woman? What is a child? What is sleep? . . . These wonders are brought to our own door." Indeed, in "The Lord's Supper" he makes a statement that would provide the foundation for *Nature* just a few years later: "it is contrary to all experience to suppose that God should work a miracle to convey information that might be so easily got by natural means."

Likewise, in "The OVER-SOUL" (1841), he explains the completeness of awe-inspiring nature, which make the acts performed by Christ pale in comparison: "in the universal miracle, petty and particular miracles disappear." This worship of the miraculous in nature pervaded his prose and poetry, of course, most notably in a series of poems written in 1839, such as "The RHODORA," "The HUMBLE-BEE," and "The SNOW-STORM." In the latter, the snow replaces the coming of Christ in being "Announced by all the trumpets of the sky." This poem, in turn, was inspired by a passage in the "Divinity School Address" that contrasts the inspiration of the snow outside the church window with the dull preachings of the minister: "The snow storm was real; the preacher merely spectral." Emerson resigned from the ministry in 1832 in pursuit of the real.

FURTHER READING

Roberson, Susan L. *Emerson in His Sermons: A Man-made Self.* Columbia: University of Missouri Press, 1995.

"Love" (1841)

Emerson's essay "Love" originated as a lecture in the "Human Life" series in BOSTON in 1838–39 and was published in *ESSAYS: FIRST SERIES* (1841). Some scholars note that Emerson's vision of eros, or romantic love, was drawn from his brief, yet intense, relationship with his first wife, Ellen Tucker Emerson, and that his "mature philosophy" of a domesticated "impersonal" love reflected his longer-term marriage to LIDIAN JACKSON EMERSON. The biographical has its limitations, however, and serves only as a starting point for the greater philosophical inquiries. He himself privately noted of the essay "Love" that "I . . . have much more experience than I have written there, more than I will, more than I can write." Scholar Eric Selinger suggests that Emerson continued this conversation in the essay "EXPERIENCE" a few years later (1844).

Emerson's purpose in "Love" is to "attain to that inward view of the law, which shall describe a truth ever young and beautiful"; that is, to come to a philosophy of "Love," just as he does in this volume for other concepts or characteristics, such as "FRIENDSHIP" or "Prudence" or "HEROISM." Emerson wrote on the topic of love in his poems as well, including "EROS," "INITIAL, DAEMONIC, AND CELESTIAL LOVE," "GIVE ALL TO LOVE," "LOVE AND THOUGHT," and "TO ELLEN, AT THE SOUTH."

SYNOPSIS

Emerson opens the essay by acknowledging that the soul has "innumerable fulfillments" and "want," one of which is the "private and tender relation of one to one." Emerson places "love" at the center of our "domestic and civic relations" and at the center of our spiritual and emotional life as well; capable of "divine rage and enthusiasm" and of working "a revolution in his mind and body," love affects our actions, "senses," and "imagination." While many define love as the "throbbing experience" of the "youth and maid," he seeks a more "mature philosophy" of love, realizing that he will undoubtedly be charged with a lack of romantic feeling and "incur the imputation of unnecessary hardness and stoicism from those who compose the Court and

Parliament of Love." But while love may "begin with the young," it "forsakes not the old." Indeed, the universal "truth" of love defies age by keeping us "ever young and beautiful."

To get at these truths we must, as is often the case, give up "a too close and lingering adherence to facts." Love is forward-looking, a matter of "hope" and not "history." While our own lives may be "defaced and disfigured" (that is, marked by reality), our "imagination" is not. Love is a series of binaries or compensatory points, between hope and history, reality and the ideal, the "details" and the "plan," and between "experience" and "truth." The tensions between these various concepts explain our interest in the "personal relations" of others. Whether in society or in novels, we are drawn to the stories of romance and emotion for what they reveal about our own humanity: "All mankind love a lover." He returns again in reference to those in his circle who might think he, of all people, unfit to talk on this matter: "I have been told, that in some public discourses of mine my reverence for the intellect has made me unjustly cold to the personal relations." But he makes a distinction between "the power of love" that comes from nature and the negative "social instincts"; if he has been "cold" it is in reference to the latter, not the former.

Indeed, he sees love as responsible for "all things new." It awakens people to "music, poetry, and art," making "the moonlight" into "a pleasing fever," "stars" into "letters," and "the air coined into song." Because it encompasses the full range of emotions and experiences that makes us human, it is also, unfortunately, responsible for much "pain and fear." Love is therefore a defining element in nature and in man's relationship to nature; through love, "Nature grows conscious." Through the passion of love, "the tree sings," "the clouds have faces," and "the forests" and "flowers have grown intelligent." Love also changes the individual; it makes the weak strong, the coward brave. In giving love to others, we receive it back unto ourselves: "He is a new man, with new perceptions, new and keener purposes, and a religious solemnity of character and aims . . . *he* is a person; *he* is a soul." In essence, to love is to be fully human.

In trying to define the nature and power of love, it is "beauty" that initially inspires and attracts. But beauty is more "representative" than "personal"; the love object becomes "representative of all select things and virtues." Such virtue, such beauty, is not specific to "any relations of friendship or love known and described in society"; it is its own "quite other and unattainable sphere," it is "transcendent." Like music or poetry or art, beauty is most "beautiful when it begins to be incomprehensible." The "personal beauty" that inspires feelings of love toward another is, then, only a suggestion or an inspiration, "a story without an end." We cannot possess beauty anymore than we can possess or have a "right to . . . the firmament and the splendors of a sunset." "It is not you, but your radiance." The physical body, the "form," is only the outward "cause of the beauty." To focus on the body alone as the love object is "gross" and "misplaced," for the body is "unable to fulfil the promise which beauty holds out."

Emerson calls instead for a love between souls, beyond the "base affection" of physical attraction. He admits that this perspective is not new, it is what "the truly wise told us of love in all ages." But it bears reminding that love should be the quest for "a truer unfolding" than what society has made of marriage. Marriage is based too much on "sensualism" and on strict adherence to social roles. More than a mere social arrangement, love is "the procession of the soul from within outward," and marriage "the longing for harmony between the soul and the circumstance."

The first stage of love is "quite external stimulus" and leads to "fiery passion" and the sense that "the soul is wholly embodied, and the body is wholly ensouled." But the "delight" and "affection" does not last forever, nor is it the only experience of love: "Not always can flowers, pearls, poetry, protestations, nor even home in another heart, content the awful soul that dwells in clay." Love moves beyond the individuals involved "and aspires to vast and universal aims." The original attraction and "virtues" (beauty) may still be there, but "it is the nature and end of this relation, that they should represent the human race to each other." Time changes a "once flaming regard" for each other into "a thorough good understanding"; "the real marriage" is about "purification of the intellect and the heart." Marriage as an institution, however, works against this goal and such "purification" is rarely possible among those who "are shut up in one house . . . forty or fifty years."

Instead, our souls strive "for a love which knows not sex, nor person, nor partiality, but which seeks virtue and wisdom everywhere." In "the progress of the soul," however, we would not have our "happiness dependent on a person or persons." Love is about self-realization and any relationships we enter into will be "succeeded and supplanted only by what is more beautiful, and so on for ever."

CRITICAL COMMENTARY

Emerson's "Love" is a universal experience that feeds the needs of the individual body, mind, and soul. The 19th century brought a more romantic view of marriage as a spiritual and not just an economic union. Other writers of the era from NATHANIEL HAWTHORNE to WALT WHITMAN also struggled with the metaphysical aspects of romantic love. Feminist MARGARET FULLER, in her *Woman in the Nineteenth Century* (1845), advocated marriage as a spiritual union of souls. Emerson doubted whether such a union was truly possible, but his idea that the development of the individual soul must have primacy was echoed in Fuller's feminist critique that "We must have *units* before we can have *union*."

In "Love," Emerson worries that others will find him "cold" and unromantic for describing the end goal of marital love as "a thorough good understanding." At the time the essay was published, Ralph Waldo and Lidian Emerson had been married six years and were awaiting the birth of their third child. He was privately questioning the "permanence" of marital love and that same year wrote in his journal that "it is not in the plan or prospect of the soul, this fast union of one to one." The judgment of him around this time as "cold" by "the Court and Parliament of Love" was undoubtedly a reference to his female friends, in particular, Fuller and CAROLINE STURGIS TAPPAN, both of whom challenged Emerson intellectually and emotionally as he tried to define the parameters of these friendships with young unmarried women. As the married Emerson wrote playfully to Sturgis, "You & I should only be friends on imperial terms . . . I dare not engage my peace so far as to make you necessary to me." Much speculation has gone into the nature of his even more intense relationship with Fuller. In his journals, he expanded on a conversation in which he challenged her, "You would have me love you. What shall I love? Your body? The supposition disgusts you. What you have thought & said? Well, whilst you were thinking & saying them, but not now. I see no possibility of loving any thing but what now is, & is becoming; your courage, your enterprise, your budding affection, your opening thought, your prayer, I can love,—but what else?"

As early as 1827 love was the topic of a sermon in which he explained the idea that loving another leads us to a higher understanding, as we "expect perfection in the loved person, and from seeking perfection in the human friend were led to seek it in God." In his winter lecture series of 1838 Emerson delivered "The Heart," in which he again explained his idea that it is through love that we come to understand "the radical unity" of humanity and the "community of nature"; that is, that the personal leads to the universal. How to balance the needs of the self and relationships with others was a theme that engaged Emerson throughout his writings. In the poem, "Give All to Love," he urges the importance of remaining "Free . . . Of thy beloved." Indeed, in the final stanza of the poem, love is only one of the "half-gods" that inhibits the arrival of the true gods of self and of enlightenment. While attempting a secular philosophy of love, Emerson was simply reworking the biblical injunction against giving too much attention or worship to other persons or idols, to "half-gods."

In Emerson's Transcendentalist vision, it is not God's law but rather nature's law of the self that is broken if love for another becomes an obsession. In the end, "Love" is yet another of nature's routes to higher universal or spiritual laws. As he would write in the poem "Eros," love is the very meaning of human existence: "To love and be beloved; / Men and gods have not outlearned it; / And, how oft soe'er they've turned it, / Not to be improved."

FURTHER READING

Gougeon, Len. *Emerson and Eros: The Making of a Cultural Hero.* Albany: State University of New York Press, 2007.

Selinger, Eric Murphy. "'Too Pathetic, Too Pitiable': Emerson's Lessons in Love's Philosophy." *ESQ: A Journal of the American Renaissance* 40, no. 2 (1994): 139–182.

"Love and Thought" (1867)

Emerson's poem "Love and Thought" is an allegorical treatment of the inherent connection of Eros ("love") and Muse ("thought"). Emerson casts this pair as twins, which carries the suggestion that they are a reflection of each other; certainly in Emerson's thinking Eros and Muse are mutually dependent. Drafting dates for this poem are undetermined; it first appears in MAY-*DAY AND OTHER PIECES* (1867), was omitted from *Poems* (1884), but reinstated by EDWARD WALDO EMERSON and printed, with variations, in the *Complete Works* (1903–04).

CRITICAL COMMENTARY

The poem is composed of 10 lines set in rhymed couplets of iambic tetrameter, a favorite verse form of Emerson's. He describes the pair Eros ("Love") and Muse ("Thought") as "twins" and as "pilgrims"; in line 7 he states, "each for the other they were born." "Pilgrims" suggests that these twins are on a spiritual journey. Only in terms of the allegory—that is, by humanizing abstract ideas and conditions in order to portray their tensions dramatically—can Eros and Muse know "mortal grief." Thus, Emerson uses the allegory to describe both the nature of love and thought and the path they take through the world. The experience of love and thought in each life is personal, but Emerson utilizes the allegory to move the specific into the realm of common human awareness. In keeping with his prose writing on figurative language—that the poet uses figurative language to bring the truth of nature, and thus man, to the reader in a new relation—only in this way can we understand the relationship in human terms, and only in this way can we understand the spiritual truth behind the "fact" the allegory offers us.

Part of the problem with the poem is that the allegory is offered as a simple one-to-one relationship; usually Emerson's allegorical poems are more subtle, and they offer a greater degree of latitude in their symbolic images. "Love and Thought" seems like a poem that has not been fully realized, and it bears a resemblance to the poem "UNITY," the motto for the essay "The OVER-SOUL," included in *ESSAYS: FIRST SERIES* (1841). Lines 1–3 of "Unity" read: "Space is ample, east and west / But two cannot go abreast / Cannot travel it in two." "Love and Thought" is perhaps best read as a companion to "Unity," since the allegory in "Love and Thought" (which is not quite refined by Emerson's standards) is clarified by the images in the superior poem, "Unity."

Bill Scalia

"Maiden Speech of the Aeolian Harp" (1876)

Emerson's short 23-line poem, "Maiden Speech of the Aeolian Harp" was first published in *SELECTED POEMS* (1876) and was reprinted in the posthumous collection, *Poems* (1884). He had drafted a version of the poem as much as a decade earlier, for he presented it as a New Year's gift to his daughter, EDITH EMERSON, and her husband, William Forbes, on January 2, 1868.

An Aeolian harp is a simple slatted wood box, across which are several strings of equal length that vibrate and produce sound as air moves across them. The instrument was named for Aeolus, ancient Greek god of the wind. Emerson had an Aeolian harp in the western window of his study in his CONCORD home, "Bush." Upon entering Emerson's study, the lucky visitor, perchance, would be the glad recipient of an impromptu concert, if nature was convivial that day.

CRITICAL COMMENTARY

In his 1844 essay "NATURE" (published in *ESSAYS: SECOND SERIES*), Emerson speaks of the Aeolian harp as a "supernatural *tiralira*" that has the power to restore faith, not only in mythology, but also in life itself. A romantic spirit can hear the call of this harp, as there is some magical quality to a musical instrument that does not need lips or fingers to produce haunting melodies. The melodies of the Aeolian harp are produced by nature's musicians, the wind or breeze, and humans are enjoined to "Keep your lips or finger-tips / For flute or spinet's dancing chips." Gentler nonhuman "fingers" are desired to play this instrument: "Soft and softlier hold me, friends! / Thanks if your genial care / Unbind and give me to the air" (Lines 1–3). The Aeolian harp seemed to whisper back to Nature, "Give me to the atmosphere,— / Where is the wind, my brother,— where?" (Lines 8–9).

The mysteries of nature are revealed in the airy notes of the harp, which invites, "Lend me your ears, and I begin. / For gentle harp to gentle hearts / The secret of the world imparts;" (Lines 11–13). The harp speaks—and it is a "Maiden Speech," emphasizing its original source in nature—proudly announcing its transformative powers, including the ability to "mend the happiest days / And charm the anguish of the worst" (Lines 22–23).

In the late 18th and early 19th centuries, the Aeolian harp became a popular symbol in English romantic poetry, which, in turn, influenced Emerson. SAMUEL TAYLOR COLERIDGE extolled the magic of the instrument in his 1785 poem, "The Aeolian Harp," and Percy Bysshe Shelley pleaded in his 1819 poem, "Ode to the West Wind," to "Make me thy lyre, even as the forest is." The *Gentleman's Magazine and Historical Chronicle* of London printed an article in 1825 about "A Natural Eolian Lyre," found near the Black Forest, and which produced music by a "current of air ascending and descending . . . the tones of which are accompanied to the gurgling of the neighboring waterfall."

Interestingly, in "Nature," Emerson referenced "the Notch Mountains," which had a similar, naturally occurring Aeolian harp; he also noted that the wind effectively "converts all trees to wind-harps." Besides another poem, titled "The HARP" (also published in *Selected Poems*), Emerson made numerous references to the harp or "wind-harp" in his prose and poetry to symbolize the language of nature as well as the creation of art. He opens the earlier poem "MERLIN" (1847), addressing the poet, whose "trivial harp will never please / Or fill my craving ear." Poetry, instead, should come naturally, as music to the harp: "Its chords should ring as blows the breeze, / Free, peremptory, clear."

FURTHER READING

Cavanaugh, Cynthia A. "The Aeolian Harp: Beauty and Unity in the Poetry and Prose of Ralph Waldo Emerson." *Rocky Mountain Review* (Spring 2002): 25–35.

Hankins, Thomas L., and Robert J. Silverman. "The Aeolian Harp and the Romantic Quest of Nature." In *Instruments and the Imagination.* Princeton, N.J.: Princeton University Press, 1999.

Charlene Williams

"Manners" (1844)

The essay "Manners" was published as the fourth piece in Emerson's collection *ESSAYS: SECOND SERIES* (1844). The topic was presented as a lecture in "The Philosophy of History" series in BOSTON in the winter of 1836–37 and in the series "The Times" in the winter of 1841–42; another lecture on "Manners and Customs of New England" was given in New York around the same time. In *Essays: Second Series,* it is paired with "CHARACTER," which also deals with issues of personal and social power. There are two uses or understandings of the word "manners,"—as personal attitude or actions within polite society and, in the larger sense, as the customs or social rituals of a society or culture. Emerson speaks to both meanings of the word in the essay. The subject was also similar to that in "BEHAVIOR," an essay published several years later in *The CONDUCT OF LIFE* (1860).

SYNOPSIS

Emerson begins the essay by cataloging customs or "manners" from around the world, observing that "Half the world, it is said, knows not how the other half live." Some cultures have what Americans would consider crude or barbarous customs and, likewise, our "consumer" society might seem strange to others, this culture "where man . . . honors himself with architecture; writes laws . . . [and] colonizes every new-planted island." He points to the Western idea of "the gentleman," or a person of good "manners," as also a cultural and historical anomaly. Its relevance, "like the word Christian," is only to "the present and the few preceding centuries."

The idea of a "gentleman" is nothing but "a homage to personal and incommunicable properties." In trying to define what our society considers "the excellence of manners and social cultivation," no word seems to work—for example, we confuse "*fashion,* a word of narrow and often sinister meaning," with "the heroic character which the gentleman imports." Emerson humorously uses the language of nature to get at "the root of the matter," observing that when we speak of "courtesy, chivalry, fashion, and the like . . . the flower and fruit, not the grain of the tree, are contemplated." These words describe only an outward effect, not the true character of the thing. A true gentlemanly character is a matter of "personal force," regardless of station or fortune. Our language confuses the external position with internal "reality," "beauty" with "worth."

Emerson reading to his two youngest children, Edward and Edith *(Concord Free Public Library)*

Likewise, society cannot convey power onto someone simply through election. Power is an "original energy," coming from within: "The rulers of the world must be up to the work of the world." We think that money buys taste, but it is "a broad sympathy" that makes an effective and "popular" leader, whether in politics or in fashion. Manners are a way to "intimidate" when they become "a badge of social and civil distinctions." The false manners of aristocracy are concerned with "name," "distinction," and "cultivation," rather than with work. These concerns, however, do not have any "durability," and eventually they move out of fashion. This can be true of fashionable ideas as well: "We sometimes meet men under some strong moral influence, as, a patriotic, a literary, a religious movement, and feel that the moral sentiment rules man and nature . . . yet come from year to year, and see how permanent that is."

We cannot determine the appropriate manners for society and must rely only upon "our own sense of propriety." We "act" and "compliment" according to "ritual" when we should be motivated instead by "good sense and character": "speak or abstain, take wine or refuse it, stay or go, sit in a chair or sprawl with children on the floor, or stand on their head, or what else soever, in a new and aboriginal way: and that strong will is always in fashion." Some will attempt to set a standard for behavior, "but do not measure the importance of this class by their pretension, or imagine that a fop can be the dispenser of honor and shame."

We should ask ourselves "what is it that we seek" from others: "Is it your draperies, pictures, and decorations?" On the contrary, all anyone wants is to be understood. We hide behind "a fine house, fine books, conservatory, gardens," but these things prevent us from truly understanding one another. "Etiquette" is nothing but false manners, when "the first point of courtesy must always be truth." We tend toward "an excess of fellowship" in trying to impress others, when it is better to spend time alone: "Let us not be too much acquainted." It is neither necessary nor desirable to know too much of our "neighbor's needs." A person's character is not a matter of wealth or of "good-breeding" (as the aristocratic class would contend), but true manners are an innate "love of beauty," whereas "fashion is . . . relative."

Still, one cannot ignore what is popular, for there is "something necessary and excellent" in whatever people find important in life. Emerson, perhaps sarcastically, observes that "it is not to be supposed that men have agreed to be the dupes of anything preposterous." There is a "universality of the love of cultivated manners" but a "comic disparity" between the ideas of "justice, beauty, and benefit" and people of the "first circles," or fashionable class. Surely among "the purest circles of aristocracy in Europe" we will "find no gentleman, and no lady." We confuse being "courteous" (an action) with "courtesy" (a virtue). The "ambitious youth" seeks "the advantages which fashion values," but these "are of no use in the farm, in the forest, in the market, in war, in the nuptial society, in the literary or scientific circle, at sea, in friendship, in the heaven of thought or virtue."

Emerson ends the essay by conceding that "society and fashion" have their merits as well as problems. He recounts an ancient story of the gods puzzling over whether society is "fundamentally bad or good," only to conclude that society meets an observer's expectations of it: "If you called them bad, they would appear so; if you called them good, they would appear so."

CRITICAL COMMENTARY

"Manners" was a topic that interested Emerson in both cultural and historical contexts. He was concerned with manners as an attempt to modify the behavior of individuals, therefore forcing them to act against their natures. The person of good manners is confused in society as a good person. In the essay, Emerson, clearly in a controversial mood, compares the person of manners to "the word Christian"; that is, he suggests that to be a Christian in the eyes of society is not the same as to be Christ-like in one's heart.

The term "manners" appears in other works as well, most notably in *The Conduct of Life,* which takes as its main theme the question of how we live our lives. In the essay "Behavior" in that volume, he declares manners to be the "silent and subtle language" of nature: "Nature tells every secret once. Yes, but in man she tells it all the time, by form, attitude, gesture, mien, face, and parts of the face, and by the whole action of the machine. . . . What are [manners] but thought entering the hands and feet, controlling the movements of the body, the speech and behavior?" From "CULTURE" in the same collection he explores manners at the intersection of nature and social life: "Manners are factitious, and grow out of circumstances as well as out of character."

In his 1856 volume *ENGLISH TRAITS,* an entire section is dedicated to the "Manners" of the English, which he describes as "cold" and "repressive" due to the particularly harsh and conservative nature of English life. And still, the English place even more importance on "manners," on outward appearances, than other cultures. In "LITERARY ETHICS" (1838), Emerson laughs at the idea that we can hide our true natures behind social demands, declaring, "Hides his thoughts! Hide the sun and moon. Thought is all light, and publishes itself to the universe. . . . It will flow out of your actions, your manners, and your face."

While "Manners" seems a minor topic in light of Emerson's philosophical and political concerns in *Essays: Second Series,* the essay addresses a dilemma that pervades his writings, namely, that of reconciling our true natures with the need to live in society. For Emerson, manners are the outward sign of self-reliance, even as he concedes that we must all cooperate with social rules as long as there is no harm done to the self: "All that fashion demands is composure, and self-content."

Perhaps more significant is Emerson's position in "NEW ENGLAND REFORMERS," of the same volume, in which he characterizes the ideas of reformers as fashionable and temporary. While "friendship and association are fine," the danger of reform organizations or communities is their assault on the individual: "each finds that he cannot enter it, without some compromise." Indeed, much of the criticism in "Manners" seems directed at the fashionableness of reform. For example, he dismisses the "new chivalry in behalf of Woman's Rights," propelled not by a true sense of righting an injustice but by "the awkward consciousness of inferiority in the men"; that is, arguing for women's rights had become the socially desirable thing to do. This is not unlike his argument in his 1855 address "WOMAN," in which he laments that so few women actually support the cause.

Emerson's main point in "Manners" is to reject fashionable ideas or behaviors when they stem from societal dictates rather than from the motivations of the individual. As he would protest throughout his writings, it is always preferable to rely upon one's own judgment rather than seek to impress others: "In all things I would have the island of a man inviolate." This, of course, is the core of "SELF-RELIANCE" (1841), in which he also pointed out that people confuse the *display* of virtue with actually *having* virtue, when, for most people, virtues are only "spectacle," put on for the sake of society: "What I must do is all that concerns me, not what the people think."

FURTHER READING

Kateb, George. *Emerson and Self Reliance.* 1995. Reprint, Lanham, Md.: Rowman & Littlefield, 2002.

"Manners" (1860)

Emerson's poem "Manners" deals with the death, or at least the eternal sleep, of Endymion, who in Greek myth is the lover of the moon, Selene. She asked his father, Zeus, to grant him eternal life so that he would never leave her. Zeus placed Endymion in an eternal sleep, where Selene visited him every night. Thus Endymion is a symbol of eternal beauty and faithfulness. Emerson once again casts the ideal in terms of classical mythology; however, for Emerson myth has real significance since it represents the human search for truth in the world. Emerson may have had in mind John Keats's epic poem "Endymion" (1818), whose first line reads, "A thing of beauty is a joy forever."

The poem is set in 20 lines of hymn stanza, *abab* rhyme scheme, with subtle variations in the rhyme. A pencil draft of the poem, dated August 18, 1840, and titled "Manners," is found in Emerson's journals and is a versification of a prose passage written on the facing page. The poem was first published as the motto for the essay "BEHAVIOR" in *The* CONDUCT OF LIFE (1860); it was collected in MAY-DAY AND OTHER PIECES (1867) and reprinted in SELECTED POEMS (1876) and *Poems* (1884).

CRITICAL COMMENTARY

Son EDWARD WALDO EMERSON noted, "Mr. Emerson's notebooks are full of verses about the joyful Seyd (or Said) seeking beauty in Nature and man." "Manners" is one such poem. Endymion looks not at people but at their forms; he is looking at the truth in nature beyond the facts of nature, which is consistent with Emerson's thinking. Emerson also notes, in lines 10 and 11, that "The green grass is a looking-glass / Whereupon their traits are found." Thus Emerson turns the search for beauty into an inward (Christian) exploration, as opposed to the outward (classical) view of beauty.

The poem perfectly suits Emerson's essay "Behavior" in *The Conduct of Life.* For Emerson, manners ("Grace, Beauty, and Caprice," terms he capitalizes as idealizations) built this "golden portal," the ideal conduit for introspection. Emerson writes, "The visible carriage or action of the individual, as resulting from his organization and his will combined, we call manners." Conversely, "Bad behavior," Emerson writes, "the laws cannot reach." "Nature tells every secret once"; thus, if we are to maintain a "portal" to introspection, we must maintain the "silent and subtle language" of manners, "an element as unconcealable as fire."

Emerson employs variation in the meter of the poem in a way that ranks among his best work. Line 14, "So dances his heart in his breast," uses successive dactylic feet—the rhythm is repeated strong, weak, weak stresses—to give the line a rolling gait, serving the "dance" in the line. By opposition, lines

15 and 16, "Their tranquil mien bereaveth him / of wit, of words, of rest," utilizes single syllable words to communicate the tranquility, or steadiness, of the line.

Bill Scalia

"Man the Reformer" (1841)

"Man the Reformer," was "A Lecture read before the Mechanics' Apprentices' Library Association, Boston, January 25, 1841." Emerson's address was subsequently published in the *DIAL* (April 1841) and reprinted in *NATURE; ADDRESSES, AND LECTURES* (1849). Whereas the emphasis in his work to this date had been on defining the spiritual dimensions of Transcendentalism, after 1841 he spoke out on a variety of contemporary social and political issues, including ABOLITIONISM, UTOPIANISM, women's rights, and the reform impulse in general. "Man the Reformer" constitutes one of his earliest attempts to articulate a general philosophy of reform and to understand the reformer as a type or state of being, much like Man Thinking in "The AMERICAN SCHOLAR" (1837) address a few years earlier.

In "Man the Reformer," Emerson explains that true reform comes from within, from our relation to ourselves, and from our relations with others. Rather than trying to change the laws and political system, if we would just treat ourselves and others with respect, "it would operate in a day the greatest of all revolutions."

SYNOPSIS

Emerson opens the address by conceding that it is a noble impulse to seek "to cast aside all evil customs, timidities, and limitations" and wish to "make it easier for all who follow." The idea of reform is not new, but in this age of reform everything has become a target for change: "Christianity, the laws, commerce, schools, the farm, the laboratory; and not a kingdom, town, statute, rite, calling, man, or woman, but is threatened by the new spirit." Some of these attempts at reform are "extreme and speculative," and the reformers themselves "tend to idealism." The problem or "demon of reform" is that the ideas and methods of the reformer are the same used by "the broker, the attorney, the market-man."

It is not surprising that so many "virtuous young men" become reformers, as it is difficult to find "lucrative employments" in a society where "genius and virtue" are not economically rewarded; "nothing is left him but to begin the world anew." Emerson points out, however, that *everyone* is "implicated" in society as it exists; we all "eat and drink and wear perjury and fraud in a hundred commodities." Everyone benefits from the slave economy, from the plantation owners to the manufacturers to the merchants to the customers: "The sins of our trade belong to no class, to no individual. One plucks, one distributes, one eats." The entire system is run by "selfishness," "distrust," and "concealment." Only the reformer has "come forth" to act upon "the law of their nature" and try to change things.

The wrongs of slavery and of commerce can be traced to the "institution of property." Emerson defines property ownership as selfishness protected by law and custom. Even the man who wants to lead a simple life requires possession of some land, and therefore must have "a sort of concentration toward money," rather than toward love. Property requires "forming connections, by wives and children, by benefits and debts." Emerson concedes the limits of reform in this regard: "I see no instant prospect of a virtuous revolution"; and yet he cannot be against the idea that society would benefit if more young men turned away from "competition in the labors of commerce, of law, and of state" and more people were willing to suffer "a loss of some of the luxuries or conveniences of society." He does not believe this will ever happen, however, as there are too many "advantages which arise from the division of labor," including the necessity that "a man may select the fittest employment for his peculiar talent."

Emerson agrees that all men would benefit from participation in "manual labor," in "a farm or a mechanical craft." Even those who pursue "higher accomplishments . . . poetry and philosophy" should work with their hands, for inspiration and balance, for their "education." He laments that when he writes a check to the merchant for his supplies and food, it is the merchant and the farmer and even the slave who "have got the education, I only the commodity." We have become too dependent: "I feel some shame before my wood-chopper, my ploughman, and my cook, for they have some sort of self-sufficiency, they can contrive without my aid to bring the day and year round, but I depend on them, and have not earned by use a right to my arms and feet."

With inherited property, it is the first owner who has done all the work of acquiring and improving and maintaining the land, passing to his son only the finished property, not the "skill and experience." The property thus becomes a "master" over the son, who has only to worry about "walls and curtains, stoves and down beds, coaches, and men-servants and women-servants." He who inherits property spends all of his time protecting his "possessions" rather than using his wealth for the "helping of his friend . . . the worship of his God . . . the enlargement of his knowledge." That is why, Emerson concludes, "the whole interest of history lies in the fortunes of the poor," for we are more interested in those who have overcome obstacles to become self-sufficient, than the passive inheritors of wealth and power.

He does not mean to "insist that every man should be a farmer"; only that there is a "doctrine of the Farm" that says "that every man ought to stand in primary relations with the work of the world, ought to do it himself." Nor does this mean there is no place for "the learned professions, of the poet, the priest, the lawgiver, and men of study generally." "That class," who spends more energy on "intellectual exertion," should spend time in nature, if not in manual labor, then in "exercise, such as rambling in the fields, rowing, skating, hunting." Those who lead "the contemplative life" should avoid too many "privileges" and possessions and instead be "a pauper, if need be, celibate also."

What society needs is not reform, but "Economy": "It is for cake that we run in debt; 't is not the intellect, not the heart, not beauty, not worship, that costs so much." Economy, or frugality, does away with distractions, "that I may be serene and docile to what the mind shall speak." He admits it is unrealistic to give up all "advantages of civil society," or to expect to never "deal with any person whose whole manner of life is not clear and rational." We can only examine ourselves and ask "whether we have earned our bread to-day by the hearty contribution of our energies to the common benefit?"

The problem with reformers is that they look beyond "our daily employments, our households, and the institutions of property" and seek instead "to revise the whole of our social structure." Emerson believes man is "born" to be a "Reformer," "a Re-maker," "a restorer of truth and good," but we must focus on ourselves and our own actions; the reformer should first "renounce everything which is not true to him."

Americans are too "practical" for even faith in themselves, believing it impossible to "ever construct that heavenly society." It takes a "believer" to imagine this is not only "possible" but already exists in men of "principles." We need to recognize "love" as the most powerful influence "on our politics, on our modes of living." We spend money on "courts and prisons," rather than on fostering the "talents" and "hopes" of "the thief, and burglar," or the "laboring men and women": "Let our affection flow out to our fellows; it would operate in a day the greatest of all revolutions." The reformer should be a "mediator between the spiritual and actual world" and a man of virtue himself. Emerson ends the address again with a farming analogy: We harvest what we sow, and we must "be willing to sow the sun and the moon for seeds."

CRITICAL COMMENTARY

Always a keen critic and observer of the times, Emerson had told MARGARET FULLER just a few months earlier, in August 1840, that he wanted to see more on issues of reform in the pages of the *Dial:* "I wish we might court some of the good fanatics and publish chapters on every head in the whole Art of Living. I am just now turning my pen to scribble & copy on the subjects of 'Labor,' 'Farm,' 'Reform,' 'Domestic Life,' etc." Indeed, each of these subjects would find their way into his subsequent lectures and essays, always informed by the philosophical framework he established in "Man the Reformer."

Emerson concedes that society needs improvement; he wishes that life was "fair and poetic," but it is not. Emerson tries to take a broader view of the reformer's laments and presages the analysis and critique made by Karl Marx and Friedrich Engels in observing that as long as we have property ownership, grounded by preservation of the private family, we operate in a selfish mode that no surface reform will address. This is why the utopian or communitarian reformers, for example, whom Emerson often used as an example, focused on alternative family relations, including (in some instances) doing away with marriage. At the heart of all reforms (whether antislavery, women's rights, or utopian reform) lay a critique of the system of property ownership. The question of land ownership, of family and inheritance, was one that plagued Emerson personally and politically and which he addressed in other contexts, most notably in the poems "HAMATREYA" (1847) and "VOLUNTARIES" (1863).

By the early 1840s many of Emerson's closest friends had become directly involved in organizations and experiments for social and political reform. Specifically, "Man the Reformer" was penned as a response to the utopian reform experiment at BROOK FARM, which had been founded in 1841 and, by 1844, had been reorganized as a Fourierist phalanx. In the address he responded positively to the idea of community agriculture as a way to break with property ownership and inheritance and "put ourselves into primary relations with the soil and nature." He also noted the concept behind the ideas of CHARLES FOURIER, which was that each would do work according to his or her talent or inclination. While Emerson did not disagree with these concepts in principle, he still resisted the idea of forming communities around these ideas, fearing that eventually the ideas would rule, rather than individuals. Besides his dedicated addresses on abolitionism, a topic that engaged him frequently after 1844, he also explored the topic of reform in general in his "INTRODUCTORY LECTURE ON THE TIMES" and in "NEW ENGLAND REFORMERS."

Throughout, Emerson maintains this idea of an individual approach to reform—the need to change one's own life rather than seeking to change the minds and lives of others. There is no need to join an association; we need only pay attention to our own "modes of living," not those of others. Emerson's emphasis on "economy" in our own lives speaks to a larger question than just social reform. The question of how we should live our life serves as the impetus behind his later essays in *The CONDUCT OF LIFE* (1860); it was also the foundation of HENRY DAVID THOREAU's experiment in deliberate living and self-reliance that he recorded in *Walden; or, Life in the Woods* (1854), which included a chapter dedicated to "Economy."

"May-Day" (1867)

Emerson's long poem "May-Day" is a 31-stanza, 616-line celebration of the coming of spring, always for Emerson an expression of rebirth and a heightened awareness of nature. Rather than employ a single controlling metaphor or dramatic device, Emerson relies on Christian figures, classical allusions, pagan rites, and detailed observations on the passing of the season to show, from several perspectives, the significance of the first day of May. The poem has something of the feel of pagan May-pole revelry in its celebration of emotional and sensual experience.

The poem had its genesis in Emerson's journals as early as 1838, and six lines of the poem (from stanza 17) were used as the second motto for the 1846 edition of *NATURE.* A fair copy of about four-fifths of the poem can be found in Emerson's notebook, and they were probably begun in spring or summer 1864 or spring 1865. Emerson initially referred to the poem as "Spring," but it was published as the title poem, "May-Day," in *MAY-DAY AND OTHER PIECES,* Emerson's second book of verse, in 1867. The poem was reprinted, with significant alterations, rearrangement of verses, and the omission of 147 lines (by daughter ELLEN EMERSON and JAMES ELLIOT CABOT) in *SELECTED POEMS* (1876); most of the omitted lines were published separately under the title "The HARP" in the same book. Cabot made further changes (including restoration of the omitted lines and the addition of two new lines from Emerson's notebooks) for reprinting in *Poems* (1884), and this version of the poem was reprinted by EDWARD WALDO EMERSON for the poetry volume of his father's *Complete Works* (1903–04).

CRITICAL COMMENTARY

The poem relies principally on description and observation rather than on dramatic tension. Emerson was certainly interested in the passing of time at this late stage of his life (as is evidenced by one of his best late poems "TERMINUS," composed around the same period), and perhaps he felt more keenly the need to celebrate the coming of spring.

The poem consists of 31 largely self-contained stanzas, having no fixed form; they are unified somewhat by rhyme scheme or line length. Emerson does not benefit from experiments in free verse (as does WALT WHITMAN, for example), but his stanzas show an organic quality, mostly due to the maturity of his ear and his highly developed sense of rhythm. The "May-Day" stanzas evoke a felt sense of order that is hard to qualify, perhaps like Emerson's experience of spring itself. In the best of the stanzas, Emerson communicates by indirection, just as he required his "ideal poet" to read the spiritual truth of nature behind the *facts* of nature.

For example, in stanza 7, Emerson recalls the pain of winter:

> Eldest mason, Frost, had piled,
> With wicked ingenuity,
> Swift cathedrals in the wild;
> The piny hosts were sheeted ghosts
> In the star-lit minster aisled.

These lines certainly recall the great poem "The SNOW-STORM" (1841). Emerson furthers the images by connecting them to a larger context: the paralyzing, but beautiful, pain of the winter freeze. The internal rhyme of "ghosts" and "hosts" confirms this paradox, as does the image of the cold "cathedral" (an image of the orthodoxy Emerson opposed, as notably expressed in the "DIVINITY SCHOOL ADDRESS" [1838]). The coming of spring will thaw these cold cathedrals.

Later in the same stanza, Emerson writes, "But soft! A sultry morning breaks." The line, of course, is a nod to Emerson's representative poet, discussed in the essay "SHAKSPEARE; OR, THE POET," and references a passage in *Romeo and Juliet* in which Romeo sees significance, and poetry, behind every fact. The allusion references neither the poet nor the play but rather the emotions engendered by the particular passage. Later, in stanza 27, he will trot out a "parade of poets"—Homer, Milton, Shakespeare, Collins, Byron, Scott, WORDSWORTH—which seems like a collection of names only, without the evocation of particular genius (Emerson would later include works by Milton, Shakespeare, and Wordsworth in his edited volume of poetry, *PARNASSUS* [1874]).

Stanzas 24–27 form the "set piece" of the poem, the invocation of the muse, and also demonstrate Emerson's most controlled use of rhythm and symbol. Considering the lines of stanza 24 as quatrains, Emerson's lines show a variation of three-beat and four-beat lines. The lines do not alternate but occur in three-to-one patterns. In these groupings Emerson establishes a set rhythm, and he uses the odd line to vary the pattern. Emerson's "muse" has an organic rhythmic sensibility; nature is formal but subtle. Emerson writes, "The Muse of man is coy / Off courted will not come." Emerson's verse suggests the Muse evolving her own form, which (again) seems like a dance.

Stanzas 25 and 26 present something of a puzzle because of their brevity. Stanza 25 reads (in its entirety), "Who is the Bard thus magnified? / When did he sing, and where abide?" The "Bard" is described in the close of stanza 24 ("He renders all his lore / In numbers wild as dreams"). This bard seems to occupy a central place in the poem, and we are led to believe that this might be the tension of the poem. Stanza 26 settles (again, in its entirety) the question:

> Chief of song where poets feast
> Is the wind-harp which thou seest
> In the casement at my side.

The bard is the Aeolian harp, which Emerson will detail in stanza 27 (it is this stanza that makes up the core of the poem constructed by Cabot as "The Harp" for *Selected Poems*). Emerson, who writes in the essay "The POET," "I look in vain for the poet whom I describe," finds this poet in nature, *as* nature ("Sweet is art, but sweeter truth").

The opening of stanza 28 picks up the harp in stanza 27 and moves the poem forward:

> Not long ago, at eventide,
> It seemed, so listening, at my side
> A window rose, and, to say sooth,
> I looked forth on the fields of youth.

Thus Emerson moves from the abstract symbolism of stanza 27 (the wind as the breath of the muse, and truth) to the specific scene in stanza 28. The stanza describes a theme dear to Emerson, a return to youth (and innocence). So, while stanzas 24–27 center the muse (and recognize the Bard) in the poem, stanza 28 moves the poem into concrete territory, connecting the abstract with the actual.

"May-Day" also revisits another theme consistent in Emerson's writing, the language of nature. It might be said that, if Emerson has an ongoing "project," it is to find language to qualify the ways nature communicates. His aesthetic writing, including *Nature,* "The Poet," "POETRY AND IMAGINATION," "The New Poetry," and *REPRESENTATIVE MEN* all call for the poet who will be able to read the language of nature (which contains the paradox of making language do what language itself cannot do). In stanza 17 of "May-Day," Emerson includes two lines in particular that speak to this need: "The youth reads omens where he goes / and speaks all languages the rose." Only the youth, which for Emerson invokes innocence more than age, can understand nature at the most fundamental linguistic level, where "Words are signs of natural facts," and "All words are fossil poetry" (both quotes from *Nature,* 1836). In stanza 24 Emerson continues the idea:

> What the spangled meadow saith
> To the children who have faith;
> Only children to children sing,
> Only to youth will spring be spring.

And later, in stanza 29,

> Speaking by the tongues of flowers,
> By the ten-tongued laurel speaking,
> Singing by the oriole songs,
> Heart of bird the man's heart seeking

That nature has a language is firmly entrenched in Emerson's thought. Emerson's ideal condition for the poet (and for all) is to reunite us with nature and the divine, at its most basic level, without the need for the interface of metaphor or figurative language. This is not possible in reality, but Emerson is seeking the ideal, and we should remember that his own call is itself a metaphor—thus the circular logic of this complex problem.

"May-Day" ends with stanza 31 (the month of May has 31 days). While the previous stanzas observed no fixed form, varying in length from 62 lines (stanza 27) to two lines (stanza 25), stanza 31 closes the poem with a formality and order that is not found consistently elsewhere in the poem. The stanza contains 28 lines of rhymed couplets in iambic tetrameter, with very little variation, as though nature, with the arrival of spring, has found her best form; this is emphasized by the poem's last lines:

> Without halting, without rest,
> Lifting Better up to best;
> Planting seeds of knowledge pure,
> Through earth to ripen, through heaven
> endure.

Emerson realizes that some kind of form is necessary to lift chaos to order, and he closes the poem with the seeds of "knowledge pure," a knowledge that depends on both content and form; indeed, for Emerson, this is the fundamental connection, in innocence, of the two qualities necessary for the apprehension of truth.

Bill Scalia

May-Day and Other Pieces (1867)

May-Day and Other Pieces was Emerson's second collection of original poetry and was published 20 years after his first collection, *POEMS* (1847). His later volume, *SELECTED POEMS* (1876), included a handful of new poems, but it consisted mostly of previously published and revised poems, many of them originally appearing in *May-Day.* Several of the poems included in *May-Day* were themselves previously printed in publisher's anthologies of contemporary poets or in magazines such as the ATLANTIC MONTHLY. The volume collected together the long poems, "MAY-DAY" and "The ADIRONDACS"; Civil War poems such as "FREEDOM," "ODE SUNG IN THE TOWN HALL, CONCORD," "BOSTON HYMN," and "VOLUNTARIES"; and it included a mix of inspired and well-known pieces, such as "BRAHMA," "DAYS," "IN MEMORIAM E.B.E.," "LOVE AND THOUGHT," "MY GARDEN," "NATURE," "SEA-SHORE," "SOLUTION," "SONG OF NATURE," "TERMINUS," "The CHARTIST'S COMPLAINT," "The TITMOUSE," "TWO RIVERS," "UNA," and "WALDEINSAMKEIT," among others.

Additionally, *May-Day* included many poems that had originally appeared as epigraphs or mottoes (listed in *May-Day* under "Elements") to essays that had been published in *ESSAYS: FIRST SERIES* and *ESSAYS: SECOND SERIES* (1841 and 1844) or in *The CONDUCT OF LIFE* (1860), such as "ART," "BEAUTY," "CHARACTER," "CULTURE," "EXPERIENCE," "FRIENDSHIP," "HEROISM," "MANNERS," "POLITICS," "SPIRITUAL LAWS," "WORSHIP," and others. In all, *May-Day and Other Pieces* includes 44 main poems, plus a separate section of 30 different "Quatrains," or short 4-line poems, and a selection of "Translations."

The central or connecting theme of the poems in *May-Day,* as indicated by the title reference to springtime, is of renewal through nature. The volume has been characterized as overall much smoother and "less riddling" than the earlier collection *Poems.* The emphasis on the season of spring may also served as a reference to aging and the human life cycle. Not only "May-Day," but also poems such as "Days" and "Terminus," show Emerson (in his 60s at the time of publication) grappling with the idea of his own aging and mortality. This may also served as a more general commentary on the cycle of limitations and renewal in nature as well. Contemporary reviewer William Dean Howells wrote in the *Atlantic Monthly* (September 1867) that *May-Day* was "a succession of odes on Spring, celebrating now one aspect and now another . . . awaken[ing] the same emotions that the youth of the year stirs in us."

Literary scholar Saundra Morris has also pointed out that *May-Day,* published just after the end of the Civil War, should be read ". . . along with [HERMAN] MELVILLE's *Battle-Pieces* and [WALT] WHITMAN's *Drum-Taps* as part of the literary response to the war itself." Besides the four poems that specifically address the Civil War or the issue of slavery, others focus on more general themes of "camaraderie, reconciliation, and restoration," in nature so as in the life of the nation. Again, the imagery of spring invoked in so many of the poems could be read "as a trope for national renewal . . . [and] postwar healing," similar to the imagery in Whitman's "When Lilacs Last in the Dooryard Bloom'd," written in 1865 to mourn the death of Abraham Lincoln.

FURTHER READING

Morris, Saundra. "'Metre-Making' Arguments: Emerson's Poems." In *The Cambridge Companion to Ralph Waldo Emerson,* edited by Joel Porte and Saundra Morris, 218–242. New York: Cambridge University Press, 1999.

Memoirs of Margaret Fuller Ossoli (1852)

Ralph Waldo Emerson, with the prodding of WILLIAM HENRY CHANNING and JAMES FREEMAN CLARKE, responded to the death of MARGARET FULLER in 1850 by agreeing to compile a memoir of their friend. Emerson used letters and some of her writings as the foundation of his portions of *Memoirs of Margaret Fuller Ossoli* titled, "Visits to Concord" and "Boston Conversations." The first edition appeared in 1852. Emerson's contribution to the publication was met with contradicting reviews. Some saw Emerson's efforts as a sincere and honest tribute to Fuller; others criticized his writing as disjointed, tiresome, and pompous. Many questioned Margaret Fuller's character and lack of femininity. Regardless, *Memoirs of Margaret Fuller Ossoli* is valuable to the study of Emerson and of Transcendentalism.

SYNOPSIS

Emerson's parts in *Memoirs* consist mainly of random memories of Fuller interspersed with personal comments. The tone begins as a fireside conversation with Emerson reminiscing about people and events. In 1835 FREDERIC HENRY HEDGE loaned a copy of Fuller's translation of *Tasso,* a play by JOHANN WOLFGANG VON GOETHE, to Emerson. Soon afterward Margaret Fuller made her first visit to the Emerson home. Although she was attractively dressed, he was struck by her "extreme plainness." He was also disconcerted by her constant blinking, nasal voice, and overbearing personality. Emerson considered her bright but too satirical: "The men thought she carried too many guns, and the women did not like one who despised them." However, she soon won over her critics and established a following of admirers: "She wore this circle of friends, when I first knew her, as a necklace of diamonds about her neck. They were so much to each other, that Margaret seemed to represent them all, and to know her was to acquire a place with her." However, Emerson's tone falters. He views her friends as a chorus from a Greek tragedy, only repeating "the queen of the scene." She "disarms" them with her lack of "bookishness" and delights in conjuring "the German masters" for them. She was particularly interested in her friends' lives and lured them into "surprising confessions."

In "Visits to Concord," Emerson suggests that Fuller's gift for conversation is close to magical. Furthermore, she had a keen interest in "talismans, omens and coincidences" and closely identified with the goddess Leila, a symbol for the mysterious powers of women, whom she encountered in the works of German writer Novalis (Frederich von Hardenberg). The carbuncle, a red gemstone also associated with Leila, was Fuller's charm. She believed in fortune-telling and thought saints' days had mystical values. Rosicrucian, a movement dedicated to spiritual enlightenment, intrigued her. Fuller was fascinated by Goethe's "demonology." Emerson attributes this to her "temperament," which he finds "abnormal," and admits to never completely understanding her: "Her strength was not my strength,—her powers were a surprise."

Emerson finds further fault with Fuller by quoting her, "I now know all the people worth knowing in America and I find no intellect comparable to my own." Fuller had taught herself to read and translate several languages. Hence, much of her philosophy came from Italian poets Dante and Tasso, and from the Germans, "above all, Goethe." Emerson despairs that, although she related to the beauty of nature, she had a limited view of it: "She has never paid—and it is a little remarkable,—any attention to natural sciences." Fuller did no better with art. She had sympathy with the artist and was pleased by form and color but could not see "greatness." He also dismisses her letters in saying that they are "tainted with a mysticism" and colored by her personal judgments.

Emerson continues "Visits to Concord" by softening his remarks about Fuller, dubbing her "heroic." She was welcomed as a writer, teacher, and friend. Emerson sees her as courageous in her struggle to exist within the confines of 19th-century womanhood. He lauds her strength in caring for her family and praises her work with imprisoned women. In 1840, however, Emerson noted a change in Fuller, which he defines as a mystical experience of "ecstatic solitude." He found her letters of this period to be "pathetic," swaying between the desire for peace in the knowledge of the "absolute Centre" and the need for comfort from her friends.

Emerson concludes that Fuller's greatest talent lay in her conversations. His second section of the *Memoirs,* titled "Conversations in Boston," pays tribute to Fuller's art by reminiscing about her BOSTON days, including a compilation of notes and letters related to her. Fuller's Conversations ended in 1844, as does Emerson's account in the memoir.

CRITICAL COMMENTARY

Emerson's relationship with Margaret Fuller was challenging. He found her to be demanding but constant in her affection. Their friendship "was a war of temperaments, and could not be reconciled by words, but, after each party had explained to the uttermost, it was necessary to fall back on the grounds of agreement which remained, and leave the differences henceforward in respectful silence."

Friendship is a topic that Emerson deals with often in his writing. In his essay "FRIENDSHIP" (1841), Emerson elevates friends to a plane of spirituality, defining "real" friendships as recognition of the shared soul or "Over-Soul." His essay "The OVER-SOUL" (1841) establishes a basic tenet of Transcendentalism: that man, nature, and the divine are one. Every individual shares the common soul of nature and each other. The soul's progress is the ascension and return to its source: In "Friendship," Emerson asks, "Why insist on rash personal relations with your friend? Leave this touching and clawing. Let him be to me a spirit . . . universal and great as nature itself." Perhaps Fuller did not measure up to Emerson's vision of friendship. Perhaps she was too desirous of an earthly relationship. Clearly the "war of temperaments" between Emerson and Fuller affected their friendship.

Throughout *Memoirs* Emerson refers to Goethe's influence on Fuller, who herself admitted, "I am merely 'Germanico' and not 'transcendental.'" The problem with the Germanico for Emerson is "demonology," Goethe's insistence that there is a force within some individuals that relates to the power of nature. Emerson associated these mysteries to "spiritism," namely, omens, luck, and magic, which he found to be the antithesis of Transcendentalism. In "Arcana," a section of "Visits to Concord," Emerson refers to the paganism of Fuller and decries her seduction by the supernatural. He speaks in the same terms of talismans, omens, coincidences, and sortilege that appear in his lecture on "Demonology" (1839). In a section of *Memoirs* titled "Daemonology," Emerson explains that "Margaret held with certain tenets of fate, which always swayed her and which Goethe . . . had encouraged." In "FATE" (1860) Emerson declares that fate places limits on human will by accepting predestination and finality. However, the mind's emanation from the over-soul negates fate, "The right use of fate is to bring up our conduct to the loftiness of nature." Emerson quotes from Goethe's autobiography in his lecture "Demonology." To Goethe, demonology is similar to "chance" or "Providence." Emerson shares a fascination with the mysterious, but he feels that "read demonology and we are bewildered and perhaps a little besmirched." Alternatively, in Transcendentalism, the individual is the receptor of nature and is, therefore, omniscient, containing all knowledge. As Emerson concludes in "Demonology": "The whole world is an omen and a sign. Why look so wistfully in a corner? Man is the image of God." Emerson strongly opposed the mysticism that Fuller found attractive, declaring instead that "Life is an ecstasy."

FURTHER READING

Chevigny, Bell Gale. *The Woman and the Myth: Margaret Fuller's Life and Writing.* New York: The Feminist Press, 1976.

Cole, Phyllis. "The New Movement's Tide: Emerson and Women's Rights." In *Emerson Bicentennial Essays,* edited by Ronald A. Bosco and Joel Myerson. Boston: Massachusetts Historical Society, 2006.

Fuller, Margaret. *The Essential Margaret Fuller,* edited by Jeffrey Steele. New Brunswick, N.J.: Rutgers University Press, 1992.

Barbara Downs Wojtusik

"Merlin, I and II" (1847)

"Merlin" is a two-part poem first published in Emerson's 1847 collection POEMS, and it is one of his most widely read poems. The most popular association of the name Merlin is with the sorcerer or "kingly bard" of medieval legend, who, in turn, was based on stories of a sixth-century poet and prophet named Myrddin who was driven mad by society and fled to a life of solitude in the wilderness. In Emerson's journal, the poem was titled only "Merlin," but in the finished poem, the two parts, I and II, constitute a conversation or debate between different poetic ideals and even definitions of poetry. In both parts of the poem, the inspiration and final product of the poet both come from nature, whether as the "Artful thunder" of chaos in "Merlin I" or as the "Balance-loving Nature" in "Merlin II." In either sense, it is the poet who draws out meaning from nature, regardless of the final form the poetry takes. "Merlin I" (but not II) was included in Emerson's later collection, SELECTED POEMS (1876).

Emerson would address the role of the poet and the conflict between solitude and society for the poet in other contexts as well, including the poem "SAADI," also published in *Poems* and also an ideal or representative poet, and in essays on "The POET" (1844) and "POETRY AND IMAGINATION" (1876).

CRITICAL COMMENTARY

The voice in "Merlin I" is strong and forceful, as was the legend of poetry in the time of Myrddin. The voice, perhaps the same as in the poem "The SPHINX," instructs the poet to strike against expectations and forms to find his own voice, which "should ring as blows the breeze, / Free, peremptory, clear." The poet "Must smite the chords rudely and hard, As with hammer or with mace." The poem, itself, in which these lines are uttered, is one of forceful language, of poetry as "Artful thunder" and "supersolar blaze," but within a still predictable rhyme scheme; it is a voice of irony that declares the poet "shall not his brain encumber / With the coil of rhythm and number."

The language and form of the poem illustrate the struggle of the poet to break from form and from human expectations. The violence of "Merlin's blows" and "strokes of fate / Chiming with the forest tone" indicate that poetry occurs according to nature, not according to man's rules or forms. In seeking inspiration, in climbing the stairs to heaven, the poet must not be concerned with counting "compartments of the floors, / But mount to paradise / By the stairway of surprise." The poet's imagination and instinct must compete with the sounds and distractions of human activity, "the voice of orators," "the din of city arts," and "the cannonade of wars," the last of these a direct reference to the fighting that drove the sixth-century bard Myrddin to madness and escape.

The poet works as a chronicler of life and of nature in the form of "song's sweet influence." Emerson repeats the imagery of war and frenetic activity from the previous lines, but this time it is poetry that is "the tune whereto / Their pulses beat, / And march their feet." In one keynote passage, Emerson explains the power of poetry, of "Merlin's mighty line," over man and nature alike. Poetry has "Extremes of nature reconciled,— / Bereaved a tyrant of his will, / And made the lion mild." Poetry or "Songs" have calmed "the stormy air," and brought "poetic peace" and productivity to human life.

The true poet does not bother with simple or "weak" lines—"efficacious rhymes"—but waits for the highest inspiration, "the soaring orbit of the muse." Inspiration will take him beyond anything else—"from the nadir's floor / To the zenith's top can soar." Nor does the poet write for an audience or simply to amuse or to be published. Such reasons for poetry come from outside the poet, whereas the poet must be "self-moved" and must be ready for inspiration "sudden, at unawares."

The two distinct parts of the poem constitute a conversation between two ideals of the poet; indeed, between two sides of nature and of the poet himself. Whereas Part I emphasizes the power of inspiration and of breaking society's rules, Part II displays a gentler voice encouraging the poet to embrace balance and structure. In the *Complete Works* edition of his father's work, EDWARD WALDO EMERSON notes that "Merlin II" "well expressed [Ralph Waldo Emerson's] favorite idea of correspondence, universal rhyme and harmony in Nature, and compensation in life." This was a "favorite idea," of course, that would permeate Emerson's writing, most notably as the focus of the essay on "COMPENSATION" (1841) and in numerous nature poems as well.

"Merlin II" opens with the idea that poetry is above and beyond worldly concerns such as politics, or "the king's affairs." Poetry represents, or reflects, the reconciliation and symmetry of all things in "Balance-loving Nature," which "made all things in pairs." Indeed, the poem itself is a series of rhyming couplets and quatrains: "Hands to hands, and feet to feet, / In one body grooms and brides; / Eldest rite, two married sides / In every mortal meet." This symmetry, or unity, the poet translates into the language of love, whether self-love or conjugal, so that even "the animals are sick with love, / Lovesick with rhyme."

Like all things in nature, and like the lines of the poem, thoughts or ideas "come also hand in hand."

Ideas without complements are doomed to be "short-lived." Again using the language of marital or sexual union, Emerson compares these "solitary fancies" to "bachelors, / Or an ungiven maid," an unnatural state of being without a mate and without heirs. Poetry, like other pursuits such as "Trade and counting," depends on justice, on the sense of balance: "Justice is the rhyme of things." Even "Nemesis, / Who with even matches odd," provides a balance or compensation in nature. Again, in the essay on "Compensation," Emerson made reference to "the ancient doctrine of Nemesis, who keeps watch in the universe and lets no offence go unchastised." Nemesis, in the context of the poem, is the mythical counterpart to the rebellious voice of the Sphinx in "Merlin I"—the "subtle rhymes . . . In perfect and measure" compared to the "Artful thunder" of the first part. Nemesis "finishes the song," or the poem, "As the two twilights of the day / Fold us music-drunken in." The language of music, the finished song that ends the poem is, as Edward Emerson noted, similar to that in the poem, "WOODNOTES": "Come learn with me the fatal song / Which knits the world in music strong."

FURTHER READING

Morris, Saundra. "'Metre-Making' Arguments: Emerson's Poems." In *The Cambridge Companion to Ralph Waldo Emerson,* edited by Joel Porte and Saundra Morris. New York: Cambridge University Press, 1999.

"The Method of Nature" (1841)

"The Method of Nature, An Oration Delivered before the Society of the Adelphi, in Waterville College, Maine, August 11, 1841," was included in the 1849 collection, *NATURE; ADDRESSES, AND LECTURES.* It develops a number of key Emersonian themes, notably an interest in natural history, metamorphosis, the nature of intellect and genius, and the question of how to live one's life. "The Method of Nature" stands centrally among Emerson's texts dealing explicitly with the philosophy of nature, namely, his early lecture, "The USES OF NATURAL HISTORY" (1833); his first book, *NATURE* (1836); the essay "NATURE" (1844); and his late project, *NATURAL HISTORY OF INTELLECT.* It echoes a myriad of other essays and lectures in which the relationship between the mind (and intellect) and the physical world is foregrounded, such as "INTELLECT" (1841), "EXPERIENCE" (1844), "NOMINALIST AND REALIST" (1844), "SWEDENBORG; OR, THE MYSTIC" (1850), "GOETHE; OR, THE WRITER" (1850), "Powers of the Mind" (1858), and "FATE" (1860).

SYNOPSIS

"The Method of Nature" begins, as do many of Emerson's essays, with a diagnosis of contemporary American society. In this case, he finds it to have lost its fundamental connection to both itself and nature by becoming enchanted by technological progress and material success. Emerson writes: "We hear something too much of the results of machinery, commerce, and the useful arts. We are a puny and fickle folk. Avarice, hesitation, and following, are our diseases." This makes the work of scholars, whom Emerson celebrates as "the priests of that thought which establishes the foundations of the earth," ever more essential. Should they "neglect their posts," the "spiritual interest of the world" would be degraded; it would be "a common calamity." Although Emerson does not intend to wholly dismiss industrialization or its advances in practical thinking (indeed, he remarks: "I love the music of the water-wheel: I value the railway: I feel the pride which the sight of a ship inspires, I look on every craft as education"), he wants to remind us of the greater spiritual prerogative that moves beyond the workaday world of routine, commerce, and individual gain. To this end, Emerson concludes: "Let there be worse cotton and better men." Thus, as a "bringer of hope," the scholar's task is to open humanity's eyes to new capabilities for the greater good, to collective accomplishment.

For Emerson, to do so is to draw on the "power of the mind," not as "mortification," but as "life." Indeed, life and mind (and equally nature) are never static or still but always moving, shifting, and changing shape. As such, even the work of the great thinker is not "solid and secure" but given to flux. The scholar can at best push through surface strata but never penetrate depths of phenomena; he or she may temporarily exert an effect on the world, yet the world is always on the threshold awaiting a new, "more adequate interpreter." Intellect, likewise, "still asks that a man be born."

This relentless movement pushes Emerson further away from a notion of humanity as the single "end," or goal, of nature. He turns to a "study of the mind in nature, because we cannot steadily gaze on it in mind; as we explore the face of the sun in a pool, when our eyes cannot brook his direct splendors." This is not to ignore the place of humans in nature but to understand mind as a natural fact not intrinsically divorced from nature. Thus Emerson lays out his central task, namely, to "piously celebrate this hour by exploring the *method of nature.* Let us see *that,* as nearly as we can, and try how far it is transferable to the literary life." "Method" implies that nature will not be studied as a fixed, dead specimen to be classified or dissected but rather in its ongoing movement. However, even this movement confounds interpretation. As Emerson states in a key passage of the essay:

> The method of nature: who could ever analyze it? That rushing stream will not stop to be observed. We can never surprise it in a corner: never find the end of a thread: never tell where to set the first stone. . . . Every natural fact is an emanation, and that from which it emanates an emanation also, and from every emanation is a new emanation. If anything could stand still, it would be crushed and dissipated by the torrent it resisted, and if it were a mind it would be crazed: as insane persons are those who hold fast to one thought, and do not flow with the course of nature.

Here, Emerson draws explicitly on the Neoplatonic thought of Plotinus, who held that all nature continually flows (or "emanates") out from itself and thus could be traced to an original source or oneness. Nature is then metamorphic, perpetually becoming other than itself, or, as Emerson holds, "ecstatic." "Nature can only be conceived as existing to a universal and not to a particular end, to a universe of ends, and not to one,—a work of *ecstasy.*" Ecstasy (from the Greek *ek-stasis*) literally means "to stand outside itself" and as such is evocative of the outflowing "torrent" of nature.

Once Emerson has articulated ecstasy as his conception of the "genius or method of nature," he remarks, "let us go back to man." He does so primarily by tying this notion of ecstatic nature to genius: "Whilst a necessity so great caused the man to exist, his health and erectness consist in fidelity with which he transmits influences from the vast and universal to the point at which his genius can act." In turn, "health and greatness consist in his being the channel through which heaven flows to earth, in short, in the fulness in which an ecstatical state takes place in him." Like ecstatic nature, genius is pliant, receptive, and impersonal: "what strikes us in genius is that which belongs of right to every one." Genius does not "study where to stand," in order to best observe nature, rather "when genius comes the question is not where to stand in order to see, but for the light to come from within." Genius becomes a conduit through which universal power can circulate; it joins personal experience to an ecstatic impersonal nature. Genius is "finer love, a love impersonal, a love of the flower and perfection of things." In short, the "natural history of the soul" Emerson offers in "The Method of Nature" is a celebration of this joyous vision of nature in process, of the health, fullness, courage, hope, and exultation of human life.

CRITICAL COMMENTARY

The shift in Emerson's thinking in "The Method of Nature" toward an ecstatic vision of nature interweaves much of his philosophical reading at the time. It continues his uptake of German thought in terms of JOHANN WOLFGANG VON GOETHE's metamorphic idea of nature, romantic *Naturphilosophie,* and the idealism of IMMANUEL KANT and FRIEDRICH SCHELLING (the latter of whom famously held "mind is invisible nature, while nature is visible mind"). It allows these to merge with ideas drawn variously from his readings of Pythagoras, NEOPLATONISM (especially that of Plotinus), Zoroaster, and EMANUEL SWEDENBORG. This amounts to a "dynamic pantheism," which at many points verges on a mystical experience with the divinity of nature. Emerson's tone is jubilant, and he seeks to exemplify the ecstatic role of the scholar as "professor of the joyous science."

That "The Method of Nature" was delivered in close proximity to his "The TRANSCENDENTALIST" and "The CONSERVATIVE" begs comparison with these texts, which likewise deal with the problem of idealism and the relationship between philosophy and contemporary society. It marks a transition phase between Emerson's ESSAYS: *FIRST* SERIES, published earlier in 1841, and ESSAYS: *SECOND* SERIES, which would appear in 1844. "The Method of Nature" is in a sense the high point of Emerson's ecstatic Neoplatonism, which will then give way to the more sober idealism of "Experience," with its grounding realizations of personal grief and metaphysical doubt and its increased interest with the shifting surfaces of *this* world in which we find ourselves.

FURTHER READING

Robinson, David. "The Method of Nature and Emerson's Period of Crisis." In *Emerson Centenary Essays*, edited by Joel Myerson. Carbondale: Southern Illinois University Press, 1982.

Schelling, Friedrich Wilhelm Josef. *Ideas for a Philosophy of Nature.* Translated by Erol Harris and Peter Heath. Cambridge: Cambridge University Press, 1988.

Michael Jonik

"Mithridates" (1847)

Included in Emerson's 1847 volume *POEMS*, "Mithridates" is, at first reading, a most unusual, if not unsettling, poem. Emerson's tone and imagery in the poem are somewhat comical, delighting in an ironic use and juxtaposition of religious imagery and of scientific naturalism in the cataloging of plant and animal life. Emerson's earlier 1841 lecture, "The METHOD OF NATURE," sets an overall theoretical frame for the poem. The essay establishes the "cosmic" principle of Emerson's prose and poetry, which is his assertion of nature's richness, its incessant metamorphosis, its wholeness, order, and infinite distribution; in the poem, "Every thing is kin of mine." The ecstatic tone of the poem invokes a religious experience while it describes the life-affirming principle of the essay's "genius or method of Nature."

The poem invokes a spiritual principle that circulates through all things, a universal love and power. In his prose works Emerson repeatedly called for a new religion of immediate divinity, and the poem ultimately expresses this polarity between the hopefulness of Emerson's Transcendentalist naturalism and his rejection of a narrowly dogmatic Calvinist heritage.

CRITICAL COMMENTARY

"Mithridates" opens with an allusion to nature as the source of religious miracles in the phrase, "I cannot spare water or wine." The poem presents nature in the opening lines in a way that expresses Mithridates' ecstatic sense of sympathy with all things. But Mithridates does not separate the divine from the natural. He can spare nothing on this globe, he declares: "From the earth-poles to the Line [the equator], / All between that works or grows, / Every thing is kin of mine." "Water and wine" are no more miraculous than the "Tobacco-leaf, or poppy, or rose."

Mithridates VI was an ancient king of Pontus who is said to have became immune to poisons—the scourge of palace intrigues—by taking them in gradual dosages. In modern usage, *mithridate* refers to a substance once believed to be an antidote against all poisons. Emerson uses "mithridatic" as an adjective in his 1844 essay "The TRAGIC," in a sentence critically describing "low haggard sprites," or temperamentally depressant types, who feed on doom and gloom: "There are people who have an appetite for grief, pleasure is not strong enough and they crave pain, mithridatic stomachs which must be fed on poisoned bread, natures so doomed that no prosperity can soothe their ragged and dishevelled desolation."

In this poem, however, his meaning is quite to the contrary. He exploits Mithridates VI as a *persona* of his own self-image and teacher of the romantic sublime. His Mithridates is the poet-philosopher who joyously embraces the sheer variety of nature and whose Transcendentalist spirit, seeing the good even in the evil, is immune to the fatal contingencies of physical existence. It is a companion to the key line in "URIEL," "Evil will bless, and ice will burn." Of a piece with his essay "The Tragic," it is also an early version of the essays on "FATE" and "POWER" from *The* CONDUCT OF LIFE (1860), in which man "the causationist" remains the cosmic optimist, accepting the fatal decrees of nature while at the same time responding to nature's challenge to transform the frictions and resistances of physical existence for meliorating human purposes. The poems "BACCHUS," written at the same time, and "TWO RIVERS," published in 1858, are two natural companions to the sense of "positive power" expressed in "Mithridates."

With his sense of metaphysical identity, Mithridates enjoys a merry romp through the worlds of "sharp and slimy" rocks and minerals, trees and insects, fishes, birds, reptiles, and all the other larger animals of the sea and land, to engorge himself. As he says punningly, they will all "be my game." Carousing, he will outdo Bacchus himself, having "Ivy for my fillet band, / Blinding dog-wood in my hand, / Hemlock for my sherbet" and "prussic juice" (cyanide) for his desserts, as he swings "in the upas boughs" (a tall tree in Java whose bark produced a white milky poison), while "Vampyre-fanned."

This ostensibly disastrous but actually mirthful diet sets the stage for Emerson's Mithridates debunking the restrictive Calvinist heritage—"Too long shut in strait and few, / Thinly dieted on dew"—and he parodies the "reputed wrongs," "braggart rights," and "smug routine" of the received traditions.

The poem ends with two lines that were omitted when the poem was reprinted in *SELECTED POEMS* (1876), and thereafter in *Poems* (1884), but they nicely fit Emerson's bravado here: "Hither! Take me, use me, fill me, / Vein and artery, though ye kill me!" We know that Mithridates does not succumb to his diet of poisonous meats and juices. Rather, he converts them all into his soaring spirit. On its serious side, this is ultimately a religious poem, sublimely contrasting with the teachings of the deadening Christian heritage that Emerson, like Mithridates surrounded by his courtiers, had gradually and painfully overcome.

David A. Dilworth

"Monadnoc" (1847)

Emerson's poem "Monadnoc" grew out of and replaced an earlier one, "Wachusett," which featured a mountain in Massachusetts facing its neighbor, Mount Monadnock. "Mondanoc" was written between 1845 and 1846, first published in *POEMS* (1847), and reprinted in *SELECTED POEMS* (1876). In June 1846 Emerson noted in his journal that the poet "is there to see the type & truly interpret it; O mountain what would your highness say? Thou grand expressor of the present tense; of permanence . . . if the poet could only forget himself in his theme, be the tongue of the mountains, his egotism would subside and the firm line which he had drawn would remain like the names of discoverers of planets, written in the sky of letters which could never be obliterated." "Monadnoc" features the poet who transmits metaphysical truths from nature to mankind, breaking though the illusions of time-bound human existence. The poem echoes Emerson's worship of life and of nature that he articulated in such lectures and essays as *NATURE*, "EXPERIENCE," and "WORSHIP" and in such key poems as "BRAHMA," "HAMATREYA," and "The SPHINX."

CRITICAL COMMENTARY

This long poem begins with Mount Monadnock's call to the poet to attend its message: "Up!—If thou know'st who calls." The mountain bids him "Read the celestial sign!" urging him to give up being "a bookworm with sloth urbane," for "a greater spirit bids thee forth." Mount Monadnock exists "for bard, for lover, and for saint," and Emerson devotes several lines as a tribute to the natural beauty of this "Titan," with its ". . . wondrous craft of plant and stone / By eldest science done and shown!"

"Happy," Emerson exclaims, "whose home is here! / Fair fortunes to the mountaineer!" But in the ensuing verses he expresses disappointment in the squalid peasants and "mountain folk," not only unequal to but unaware of the magnificent beauty of this "proud" mountain. But having thus denounced the relationship of some humans to the mountain, Emerson turns and praises the "highland people" who engage in farming: "Sweat and seasons are their arts, / Their talismans are ploughs and carts." These "men of bone" represent a closer relationship to nature, their mountain existence more authentic than "the clergy and libraries, / Institutes and dictionaries." These "hardy" individuals are the true carriers of the "savage health, and sinews tough" of the mountain.

The mountain then welcomes Emerson, he who "wouldst be my companion," as a "gentle Pilgrim" who would know "the gamut old of Pan, / And how the hills began." The poet is ready to learn—"seest the smile of Reason beaming"—penetrating the secrets of nature: "The world was built in order, / And the atoms march in tune; / Rhymes the pipe, and Time the warder, / Cannot forget the sun, the moon. / Orb and atom forth they prance, when they hear from far the rune." Emerson then declares that it is mankind who occupies the superior place in creation: "But well I know, no mountain can / Measure with a perfect man." It is the poet and philosopher who inherits the earth: "Anchored fast for many an age, / I await the bard and sage." Resonating with his poem "BACCHUS," which employs the metaphor of wine for the inspiration of poetry, the mountain will shed "fountain-drop of spicier worth / Than all vintage of the earth."

Monadnock, representing what is permanent in nature and history, promises: "I will give my son to eat / Best of Pan's immortal meat; . . . / So the thoughts that he shall think / Shall not be forms of stars, but stars, / Nor pictures place, but Jove and Mars." But once again, Emerson balances this view of man as the inheritor of the earth with a critique of its current residents below, the commercial-minded man who lives in a "farm-furrowed, town-incrusted sphere, . . . / Cooped in a ship he cannot steer." He may climb the mountain but, Monadnock laments, will soon "forget me if he can." The townsmen see neither the poet nor the mountain, which transcends the boundaries of time: "Ages are thy days, / Thou grander expresser of the present tense, / And type of permanence!" Here Emerson expresses his central philosophy from the symbolic vantage point of the mountaintop: "Hither we bring / Our insect miseries to the rocks; / And the whole flight, with pestering wing, / Vanish and end their murmuring."

In the end, the mountain is both a "Complement of human kind" and a "barren mound." In its balanced presence in nature he teaches an important metaphysical lesson: "Shedding on all its snows and leaves, / One joy it joys, one grief it grieves." The ageless mountain, this "watchman tall," sees "our towns and races grow and fall" and reflects "the stable good / For which we all our lifetime grope." Emerson the poet figuratively climbs Mount Monadnock to bring back the "tablets blue, / The dancing Pleiads and eternal men," as he wrote in "Bacchus."

Here Emerson directly influenced WALLACE STEVENS's "Large Red Man Reading" (1948), which is devoted to the same theme of the poet descending the mountain with tablets of the imagination. Stevens's "Chocorua to Its Neighbor" (1943) is a longer version of the Transcendentalist mountain-poem, self-consciously echoing Emerson, with the mountain declaring that the overman-poet can achieve a sense of the sublime greater than the mountain's own commanding sense of reality.

David A. Dilworth

"Montaigne; or, the Skeptic" (1850)

"Montaigne" was the third of six essays included in Emerson's 1850 collection, *REPRESENTATIVE MEN*. As with each of the other essays, Emerson provides only a brief biographical overview of the thinker, devoting most of the essay not to Montaigne directly but rather to an exploration of the key ideas or concepts for which Montaigne stands. Emerson *makes use* of Montaigne, which is the goal or very definition of a "great man," as he outlined in the introductory essay to the volume, "USES OF GREAT MEN."

The *Essais* of Michele Eyquem de Montaigne (1533–92) were first published in 1580; upon reading Montaigne in 1825, Emerson mused, "it seemed to me as if I had written the book myself in some former life, so sincerely it spoke my thought and experience." By 1835, having left the ministry and embarked on a career as a writer, Emerson chastised himself in his journal, "When will you mend Montaigne? . . . Where are your Essays?" Emerson's *ESSAYS: FIRST SERIES* would appear just a few years later, in 1841, with a simple title that echoed Montaigne's *Essais*. Emerson greatly admired Montaigne's direct honest writing style that "shall smack of the earth and of real life." Even the simple one-word titles of Emerson's own *Essays* (such as "HISTORY," "LOVE," "FRIENDSHIP," "ART," and so on) are similar to Montaigne's essay titles on common topics of human interest. And yet, Montaigne is not the representative writer in *Representative Men* (for that, Emerson would turn to JOHANN WOLFGANG VON GOETHE) but the representative skeptic, a thinker taking a balanced look at life.

SYNOPSIS

Emerson begins the essay by explaining there are "two sides" to "every fact," "heads or tails." In philosophy, there are "sensation" and "morals," "Infinite and Finite," "Relative and Absolute," "Apparent and Real." So with people there are different "predispositions," such as between "the literary class" and those involved in "trade," politics, and labor. The first group tends to value "the superiority of ideas" but "undervalue the actual object," while "men of practical power" do not consider the "metaphysical causes" of their work.

Society cares more about property and "arithmetic," that is, counting money, whereas the world of "ideas" is inhabited by "young men, repudiated by the solid portion of society." Each side has its limitations, as the philosophers or "professors" "say more than is true," while the "men of the senses" only "weigh man by the pound." The "cynic" sees these divisions and forms "bitterness" about life, which seems to have no meaning; but "the skeptic" sees balance, for "human strength is not in extremes, but in avoiding extremes." The skeptic does not "rattle off theories of society, religion, and nature" but rather looks at all sides and admits there are "conflicting evidences": "Why pretend that life is so simple a game? . . . Why fancy that you have all the truth in your keeping?"

Emerson offers up marriage as a humorous example of a "practical question" that has no clear "solution," as "such as are in the institution wish to get out, and such as are out wish to get in." Likewise, "the state" is another unanswerable question, as is the church, or labor, or "any of the questions which touch mankind nearest." On these matters the skeptical position is not one of "unbelief; not at all of universal denying, nor of universal doubting," for that would be an extreme view. Skepticism, rather, advocates only "consideration" and is neither "too stark and stiff" nor "too thin and aerial." Any philosophy must be flexible and balanced, according to nature, ideas must fit "the form of man," "the soul of man."

Here Emerson finally introduces the biographical subject of his essay: "These qualities meet in the character of Montaigne." Placing Montaigne in historical and national context, he notes that Montaigne possessed a certain sense of humor, a "French freedom" that "runs into grossness." He warns that if you want "theology, and grammar, and metaphysics," you should read those "elsewhere." Instead, Montaigne touches on "every random topic," and his style is so straightforward and conversational that it hardly seems as if the book is "written."

For Emerson, the question is: Does Montaigne guide us as to "the conduct of life?" Humans are always seeking "Truth, or the connection between cause and effect." We want to see "that a thread runs through all things." We do not like a world that is "random and chaos" and want to see order and "sequence" in nature. "The wise skeptic is a bad citizen," because the skeptic questions our values and institutions and "penetrates the popular patriotism." The skeptic is never "the champion" of any one idea and never accepts the "easy interpretation" offered by "churches and school-books." The skeptic's mantra is always, "There are doubts."

Skepticism shows the way to a complete redefinition of wisdom: "Knowledge is the knowing that we can not know." Society values "earnestness" over intellect, and "lawgivers and saints" alike try to keep their "followers" from knowledge. But the questions are greater than the answers provided by any religion, as Emerson traces a chronology of religious belief and controversy from Catholicism to Puritanism to the UNITARIANISM of his own day: "What flutters the church of Rome, or of England, or of Geneva, or of Boston, may yet be very far from touching any principle of faith." We like to think that "we go forth austere, dedicated" to our "beliefs and unbeliefs," but the truth is that every "new experience gives a new turn to our thoughts" and our strongly held opinions can change when confronted with "a book, or a bust, or only the sound of a name." Our cherished ideas and beliefs are determined just as often by our "moods" and "dispositions" as by education or truth: "Is his belief in God and Duty no deeper than a stomach evidence?"

The second question for Emerson, then, is, if we have such a natural and individual relation to ideas, what can we learn from philosophy or history?: "Does the general voice of ages affirm any principle, or is no community of sentiment discoverable in distant times and places?" What he finds is that "fate, or Destiny, expresses the sense of mankind, in all ages." Our lives are determined by the laws of nature, illness, "climate," and "hereditary and constitutional habits." This may be our common experience as humans, but it still does not accept "the doctrine of the Illusionists," that is, that there is no free will, no reality, and that life is only a "performance." This doctrine or "rumor" notes that "Reason" and "the Law," which we hold to be so important, are only temporary and ultimately have little effect on our lives.

Emerson rejects such pessimism, these "diseases of thought," in favor of each person determining for himself the "reconciliation between the theory and practice of life." He affirms: Does not a man have "a right to insist on being convinced in his own way?" "Some minds are incapable of skepticism" and feel secure in their beliefs, but others have only a "parasite faith" in "something which is hid from themselves," that is, blind faith. Skeptics, those who cannot accept "doctrines" concerning "the hope of man, of the divine Providence, and of the immortality of the soul," "are always reckoned infidels, impracticable, fantastic, atheistic, and really men of no account." The skeptic is "content with just and unjust," recognizing that there is both "deity" and "law" in the world. It is "the tragedy of all souls" that there is such a "yawning gulf between the ambition of man and his power of performance." Nature limits our human "desire for the whole." Humans have "an appetite that could eat the solar system like a cake," but "the promise of ideal power" always comes up against "the shabby experience."

So man is forced to "generalize" and take the longer view—"to believe what the years and the centuries say against the hours." Instead, we should "look for the permanent in the mutable and fleeting." We should focus in the present and know that everything, no matter how small, has a purpose. Everything is "contained in the Eternal Cause."

CRITICAL COMMENTARY

Montaigne represents for Emerson his own philosophical inclination toward skepticism, or philosophical neutrality. In Emerson's writings this emerges as nature's law of balance, polarity, or "COMPENSATION." Those who strive for a definitive truth, whether in philosophy, religion, or even reform doctrine, go against nature, which allows for "fluxions and mobility." Indeed, as much as the essay is a critique of religion, institutions, and tradition (a critique he had made elsewhere, of course, such as in the "DIVINITY SCHOOL ADDRESS"), "Montaigne" is also an often overlooked political indictment of both reformers and the status quo. His critique of politicians and ministers who have "followers" rather than believers strikes the same tone as in the essay "The CONSERVATIVE," in which he chastises the extreme and doctrinaire positions of both conservatives and progressives or reformers.

As a philosopher, Emerson was not interested in doctrines but only in suggestions and opening up possibilities. In the earlier essay "CIRCLES" (1841), he positioned himself as a skeptic, a seeker, pleading, "let me remind the reader that I am only an experimenter. Do not set the least value on what I do, or the least discredit on what I do not, as if I pretended to settle any thing as true or false. I unsettle all things. No facts are to me sacred; none are profane; I simply experiment, an endless seeker, with no Past at my back." If these words seem to echo later, almost verbatim, in WALT WHITMAN (who would write in *Leaves of Grass,* "For I confront peace, security, and all the settled laws, / to unsettle them; / I am more resolute because all have denied me, than I / could ever have been had all accepted me"), it is because Whitman saw this in Emerson. In an 1880 review essay, Whitman wrote of Emerson, "He does not see or take one side, one presentation only or mainly, (as all the poets, or most of the fine writers anyhow)—he sees all sides. His final influence is to make his students cease to worship anything—almost cease to believe in anything, outside of themselves."

As with each of his *Representative Men,* Emerson sought to embody aspects of Montaigne, noting that the skeptic philosopher must be both "sufficiently related to the world" and also a "vigorous and original thinker." Here Emerson highlighted his own personal struggle throughout his life in finding that balance between solitude and social obligations and connections. This would be the theme of the later work "SOCIETY AND SOLITUDE" (1870) and, in terms of understanding the role of the poet, the guiding question of "SAADI" and other works. In this sense, then, Montaigne's skepticism provided an example for Emerson of translating philosophy into practical life, on "the conduct of life."

Through and inspired by Montaigne, Emerson approached the problem of balancing his project of self-reliance and original thinking with reliance upon the available intellectual tradition and texts. This was a project that defined the entire volume of essays on *Representative Men* and through which Emerson answered his own question; that is, to study the past and read the great thinkers, but only take what you can use and, ultimately, make it your own. Emerson takes from Montaigne the lesson "that there is no practical question on which any thing more than an approximate solution can be had." And yet Emerson ends the essay by finding skepticism too "superficial," favoring instead Transcendentalist idealism, a belief in defined (if not yet apparent) laws of nature and the universe: "I play with the miscellany of facts . . . but I know that they will presently appear to me in that order which makes skepticism impossible."

FURTHER READING

Marchi, Dudley M. "Emerson and Nietzsche: Between Innovation and Repetition." In *Montaigne among the Moderns: Receptions of the Essais.* Providence, R.I.: Berghahn Books, 1994.

O'Keefe, Richard R. "Emerson's 'Montaigne; or, the Skeptic': Biography as Autobiography." *Essays in Literature* 23, no. 2 (Fall 1996): 206–217.

"My Garden" (1866)

Emerson first published the poem "My Garden" in the *ATLANTIC MONTHLY* issue of December 1866. He collected it in *MAY-DAY AND OTHER PIECES* of the following year, 1867. Twenty years earlier Emerson had described his "garden" to THOMAS CARLYLE in a letter of May 14, 1846. The letter is now a prose legacy that allows for comparison with the poem, providing insight into how the Transcendentalist poet—featured for example in *NATURE* (1836), "The POET" (1841), and the near contemporary essay "POETRY AND IMAGINATION" (eventually published in *LETTERS AND SOCIAL AIMS* [1876])—transforms his material environment into spiritual reality, while exemplifying Emerson's related tenet of moral correspondences and affinities of man and nature.

CRITICAL COMMENTARY

Both the letter and the poem exemplify Emerson's method of directly engaging nature for the spiritual refreshment of the mind, a relationship that, in his own experience, "puts his woods in song." As Emerson describes it to Carlyle, his "garden" was in fact a wood-lot he purchased, part of a more than 40-acre piece of land bordering Walden Pond on the opposite side of Emerson's beloved pine grove where HENRY DAVID THOREAU lived for two years. Emerson's "garden" was actually situated atop a hill rising up to a rocky head 60 feet above the water's edge, a vantage point from which he could look out to Mount Monadnock, inspiration for the poem "MONADNOC," and other New Hampshire mountains.

In those May days of 1846—he wrote to Carlyle—he used to go thither "every afternoon, and cut with my hatchet an Indian path through the thicket all along the bold shore, and open the finest pictures." The road there from his house was nearly two miles, and in his walks through the woods over many years, sometimes accompanied by his children, Emerson composed verses, which gradually took the shape of two poems somewhat converging in content, "My Garden" and "Walden." Noteworthy in the former version are Emerson's strategy of contrasting his sylvan retreat with the commerce of the cities and the dreary lessons of the college halls, which, he says, cannot compare with the fresh lessons of the robins, and of the air and the wind streaming through their forest habitat. There "I walk in marble galleries, / I talk with kings the while."

In the more poetically sophisticated version of 1866 Emerson begins with a description of the forest ledge that was the site of "My Garden," citing certain aspects of its geological ancestry and the peculiarity of the neighboring Walden Pond's waters that "Play not in Nature's lawful web, They heed not the moon or solar tide,— / Five years elapses from flood to ebb." The physical cause of this phenomenon is traced to a hidden spring under Walden Pond. But here Emerson exploits this difference to turn it into a magical garden of the Muses, who, he says, came last in the train of Jove and all the other gods to this site. Keen poetical ears, he says, can still catch their syllables in the swaying hemlocks and the whispering grasses. As well, poetic ears can catch the tunes of Aeolian harps in the pines "ringing with the song of the Fates," and the voices of the distant chorus of "Infant Bacchus in the vine." The trick is to "copy in verse one chime / Of the wood-bell's peal and cry, / Write in a book the morning's prime, / Or match with words that tender sky."

Now metaphorically blending in his philosophical laws of identity and metamorphosis into the imagery of this enchanted, Muse-ical forest, Emerson exclaims: "Wonderful verse of the gods, / Of one import, of varied tone; / They chant the bliss of their abodes / To man imprisoned in his own." But these voices of the gods are not heard by secular ears. When the shadows fall on the lake and a whirlwind ripples its surface, it takes a poet to realize "meanings cleave to the lake, / Cannot be carried in book or urn." The final lines of the poem echo the same thought, as Emerson self-reflexively writes that these omens forecast the coming "of better men than live today," namely, those who would be able to translate the language of nature into poetry.

David A. Dilworth

"Napoleon; or, the Man of the World" (1850)

"Napoleon" is the fifth of Emerson's six essays in *REPRESENTATIVE MEN* (1850). Napoléon Bonaparte (1769–1821) (known as Napoléon I) loomed large in 19th-century politics and imaginations, whether as tyrant or as hero, as an icon of modern military power. Emerson had long been interested in not only the events of Napoléon's life and career but also in the character of the man himself. A very young Emerson had written a "poetical Essay" on Napoléon in 1815, the same year of the French emperor's defeat at Waterloo, and in 1823, he had listed "Bonaparte" in his journal as among "men of abilities without principle." Emerson undoubtedly read and was influenced by WILLIAM ELLERY CHANNING's criticism in "Remarks on the Life and Character of Napoléon Bonaparte" (published in the *Christian Examiner*, 1837–38), which was itself a review of Sir Walter Scott's three-volume biography. In 1838 Emerson had THOMAS CARLYLE's *The French Revolution* published in BOSTON. Emerson even had a personal encounter with the Bonaparte family, spending two months in the company of Napoléon's fascinating nephew during an 1827 sojourn in St. Augustine, Florida.

Emerson made repeated references to Napoléon in his journals and read dozens of memoirs and historical treatments by early 1845, when he chose the emperor for his first lecture in the series on "USES

OF GREAT MEN." Napoléon was probably the original individual figure who most inspired Emerson's idea to produce the collective biographical volume, *Representative Men*, a few years later.

SYNOPSIS

Emerson declares Napoléon to be one of the most well-known and "powerful" figures of the era because he represents "the middle class every where," with all of "their virtues and their vices." The defining characteristic of this group (and of Napoléon) is a focus on the "material" or "sensual," "subordinating all intellectual and spiritual forces into means to a material success." Napoléon was the "prophet" of "commerce, of money, and material power." He was "no hero, in the high sense," but his "position," "tastes," and "enjoyments" are "agreeable to the heart of every man in the 19th century."

So thorough was Napoléon's "adaptation to the mind of the masses around him," that he almost "ceases to have a private speech and opinion" about anything; he has become the mind of the 19th century. Napoléon was so thoroughly real, that "hypocrisy" and "sentiments" were not even necessary. He hated "ideologists," those who have a "desire of perfection." He was more interested in using "his hands and his head" and was "never weak and literary"; he was, in Emerson's terms, a "natural event," whose natural field of influence was "the art of war." Napoléon "respected the power of nature and fortune." "Inferior men" would take all the credit themselves, but Napoléon himself admitted, "I am the creature of circumstances."

Napoléon was also "a realist"—"He sees where the matter hinges." He was entirely self-sufficient—"His principal means are in himself. He asks counsel of no other." "History" gives many examples, "down to this day," of "kings and governors" who cannot lead, who "know not what they should do." Napoléon, however, was clear and decisive and thus "he inspires confidence and vigor" by his example. He did not just respond to "events," but he planned "policy." Some may say he was "bloodthirsty" and "cruel," but he was only removing "obstacles" to his goals. For example, he declared, "There shall be no Alps" and "built his perfect roads" despite the obstacles. He was a decision maker and yet, again, was only acting according to his "nature" as a leader and a conqueror: "He went to the edge of his possibility."

Emerson points out that Napoléon excelled in war, which would seem to make him exceptional; but, in fact, war is symbolic of life itself: "We are always in peril, always in a bad plight, just on the edge of destruction, and only to be saved by invention and courage." Emerson clarifies, however, that courage alone is not enough. Napoléon's actions were always also "the result of calculation." He was a master of "combinations" and "arithmetic," paying "attention . . . to the smallest particulars." It was these habits that were the true "gifts of nature," combined with the particular circumstances of his life, his "private and humble fortune," and his education. All of these combined to make Napoléon a "representative character."

As with Emerson's other great men, Napoléon was ultimately representative not because he "transcend[ed] the ordinary limits of human ability," but precisely because he was human; he "showed us how much may be accomplished by the mere force of such virtues as all men possess in less degrees." He was willing to discard "rules and customs" and follow his own mind. In Napoléon's time, people were limited in their belief "that there could be nothing new in war," just as in Emerson's time people believe that "nothing new can be undertaken in politics, or in church, or in letters, or in trade, or in farming." This is "the belief . . . that the world is used up." Napoléon is an example of someone who did not accept such limitations and knew no obstacles.

He also had, according to Emerson, a great intellectual curiosity and "capacity for speculation on general topics." He formed opinions that were "always original, and to the purpose." He asked such grand questions as "whether the planets were inhabited?" or "what was the age of the world?" and wondered about "the interpretation of dreams." He discussed "medicine" and "religion" with churchmen, philosophers, and "men of science." Still, he had "vices" as well as "virtues"; as everything in nature has two sides, so "the brilliant picture has its reverse." Napoléon's limitation was that he would not let "any stipulation or scruple" interfere with his "brilliant career." He lacked "truth and honesty," was "egotistic," and sought "fame" and "influence" as the route to "immortality."

Emerson ends the essay by reflecting that, if society is divided into "democrat and conservative . . . Bonaparte represents the Democrat, or the party of men of business, against the stationary or conservative party." These parties are not really opposites, however, but rather stages of society. Both are concerned with "property, which one endeavors to get, and the other to keep." Napoléon was "an experiment . . . of the powers of intellect without conscience." He had "vast talent and power," but, unfortunately, "It came to no result." Emerson repeats that Napoléon only acted according to his nature; if the experiment failed, it was only because he imposed "a sensual and selfish aim" upon it. Emerson compares him in this regard to CHARLES FOURIER, whose experiment will also fail, he predicts, since the only successful revolution will be one "which serves all men."

CRITICAL COMMENTARY

The essay on Napoléon seems, in some ways, to be the most paradoxical and conflicted in the volume. Although Emerson would point out the limitations of each of his *Representative Men,* in terms of the man himself, Napoléon's "virtues" and "vices" were perhaps the most difficult for Emerson to reconcile. Of the six individuals profiled in the collection, Napoléon was not only the most contemporary, but also the one with whom most readers would be familiar and about whom they surely had an opinion. Napoléon is also the least literary of the *Representative Men.* Unlike the others, he was neither a man of letters nor of ideas, in the philosophical sense, but rather a man of action; however, Emerson was interested in Napoléon's military and "official advices," which, he noted in his journal, were "literary and philosophical" in themselves.

What Emerson admires most is Napoléon's self-trust: "His principal means are in himself." Indeed, Emerson had Napoléon in mind several years earlier in the essay "SELF-RELIANCE" (1841), in which Emerson identifies a list of inventors and scientists, such as Benjamin Franklin, Galileo, and Columbus, all of whom made great achievements with the simplest tools of the times: "We reckoned the improvements of the art of war among the triumphs of science, and yet Napoléon conquered Europe by the bivouac [a temporary encampment], which consisted of falling back on naked valor, and disencumbering it of all aids." It was the character of the individual men, their ideas and commitment, which brought the success, not technological innovation.

Emerson both celebrates Napoléon and highlights his ruthlessness and selfishness, leading literary scholar Lawrence Buell to identify the essay on "Napoleon" as "an addendum to 'Self-Reliance' that . . . cautions against its single most characteristic abuse, overweening self-assertion." Buell sees Napoléon as "the Emersonian equivalent of *Moby-Dick's* Captain Ahab . . . an offbeat symbol of the new entrepreneur, the captain of industry." Emerson's Napoléon is an example of the problem of unrestrained extreme self-assertion—he is both "the incarnate Democrat" and "an imposter and a rogue"—the potential problem for 19th-century society in general. As Buell says, "To publish a deeply ambiguous essay like 'Napoléon' in the aftermath of failed revolution abroad and in the midst of increasing sectional division at home was to raise the questions: Is true democratic revolution possible?"

As with all of Emerson's great men, their lives and ideas infused his work and he returned to them again and again as examples. Emerson mentioned Napoléon in numerous essays and addresses, often in terms of power and history. In the earlier essay "HISTORY" (1841) he credits Napoléon with a definition of history that informed Emerson's thinking on the subject: "What is history," said Napoléon, "but a fable agreed upon?" The essay "Napoleon" shows an Emerson clearly engaged with the world of politics but also always interested in the whole man. He drew a surprisingly simple portrait of the contradictory impulses within Napoléon—which exist within any human—in the poem "EACH AND ALL" (1847), in which "that great Napoleon," upon hearing a familiar church bell, "Stops his horse, and lists with delight, / whilst his files sweep round you Alpine height." Napoléon was a "Man of the World," and yet, as Emerson emphasizes throughout, he was only always acting according to his nature. As Emerson said in "SPIRITUAL LAWS" (1841), "We impute deep-laid far-sighted plans to Caesar and Napoleon; but the best of their power was in nature, not in them."

It was important to Emerson to include this "thoroughly modern" man of the 19th century, who represented the "subordinating of all intellectual and spiritual forces into means to a material success." Napoléon Bonaparte was admittedly "no hero, in the high sense" but, rather, a cautionary tale for modern 19th-century man, a compensatory observation on the cost of success and of unrestrained power.

FURTHER READING

Buell, Lawrence. *Emerson.* Cambridge, Mass.: Harvard University Press, 2003.

Niemeyer, Mark. "Emerson's Napoleon; or, the French Emperor as (American) Democrat and Businessman." *Sources* 18, nos. 1–2 (Spring 2005): 29–41.

Natural History of Intellect (1893)

In many ways, the central focus of Emerson's later thinking is the project that came to be known as the "Natural History of Intellect." Emerson did not himself complete the text of *Natural History of Intellect*—it was rather compiled posthumously from manuscript sources, lecture notes, and previously published writings, first by his literary executor JAMES ELLIOT CABOT for the Riverside Edition of *The Works of Ralph Waldo Emerson* (1893), and subsequently reedited with additions by his son, EDWARD WALDO EMERSON, in the centenary edition of the *Complete Works* (1903–04). Emerson began delivering material devoted to the "Natural History of Intellect" in the series "Mind and Manners of the Nineteenth Century" (1848–49) and again for the "Natural Method of Mental Philosophy" (1858) and "Philosophy for the People" (1866) series. The material arguably found its fullest expression in the Harvard University Lectures delivered under the heading "Natural History of the Intellect" in the spring of 1870, which was repeated the following year. Thus, the project occupied Emerson for several decades, but in his own estimation, it was never brought to a satisfactory completion.

The 1893 version of the text drew extensively on these previous lectures and on years of journal entries. Despite lingering authorial and editorial questions, *Natural History of Intellect* thus marks one of the final articulations of Emerson's thought. It provocatively restates his lifelong philosophical interests in nature and natural science, and it reveals his thinking on everyday life and his adversity to systematic thinking—themes that occupied him since his earliest lectures and writings, such as in *NATURE,* "INTELLECT," "CIRCLES," "The METHOD OF NATURE," "FATE," *ENGLISH TRAITS, LETTERS AND SOCIAL AIMS,* and *SOCIETY AND SOLITUDE.* At the same time, it registers yet another shift for Emerson as a thinker, evidencing a persistent openness to new influences. To this end, and albeit incomplete, *Natural History of Intellect* stands as an important late statement of Emerson's ongoing intellectual development.

SYNOPSIS

The text of *Natural History of Intellect* is comprised of three sections: "Powers and Laws of Thought" (the title of which was added by Edward Emerson in 1903–04), "Instinct and Inspiration" (added by Edward from manuscript sources), and "Memory" (previously a stand-alone essay, also added by Edward in 1903–04). From the outset, Ralph Waldo Emerson's explicit interest is to enumerate the "laws and powers of the intellect" as "facts in a Natural History." In short, he seeks to provide a nomenclature for the "science of the mind" in the manner a naturalist would collect and classify natural facts or specimens—as a botanist, for example, might record the stamens and pistils of flowers. Yet since these powers and laws, as Emerson relates, occupy a "higher class of facts," they at once "have a deeper interest and lie higher and are nearer to the mysterious seat of power and creation." As a result, Emerson finds nature "always working" in every science, "in wholes and in every detail, after the laws of the human mind." This leads Emerson to a key reformulation of his idealism, namely, that "Intellect builds the universe and is the key to all it contains." Every creation is in rhythm with the methods and means of our mind, our thoughts find direct affinity, or a parallelism with natural facts: "every object in nature is a word to signify some fact in the mind." This posits the mind as both the instrument and the object of his enquiry.

Emerson is at pains to record the qualities of mind without imposing onto them a rigid, predetermined metaphysical system: "I cannot myself use that systematic form which is reckoned essential in treating the science of the mind . . . I might suggest that he who contents himself with dotting a fragmentary curve, recording only what facts he has observed, without attempting to arrange them within one outline, follows a system also." This "fragmentary curve" becomes tantamount to Emerson for a "New Metaphysics," albeit one whose work is not to create another detached abstract system but rather "anecdotes of the intellect," "a *Farmer's Almanac* of mental moods," a "true reporting" of the intellect's "play in natural action." This underscores Emerson's continued philosophical interest in the ordinary—of encountering things as wholes, where they lay, in their movement and multiplicity. This includes the "watching of the mind, in season and out of season," but he undertakes to do so as a poet might, not as the "cold and bereaving," "surgical" or "analytic" metaphysician.

Although he is skeptical of metaphysics, he does not pronounce its end but, rather, works to give it a revivified, or revivifying, form. "Metaphysics must be perpetually reinforced by life . . . My metaphysics are to the end of use." He wants to "domesticate" the laws of the "wonderful power" of the mind and nature. The poet is the most capable of this domestication, of molding a plastic form to suit it, of being its first instructor: "I think philosophy is still rude and elementary. It will one day be taught by poets. The poet is in the natural attitude; he is believing; the philosopher, after some struggle, having only reasons for believing." The poet draws on the source of action without the "obstructions" that practical, academic, or systematic forms impose, including the pretension of having a closed, unified system. Emerson's task, though more ambitious, is also more humble: "What I am now to attempt is simply some sketches or studies for such a picture; *Memoires pour servir* toward a Natural History of Intellect."

As such, Emerson further divides the task laid out in the opening section into three parts: (1) to speak of the "excellence" of the intellect as well as the "societal impediments" to its fullest realization; (2) to "treat the identity of the thought with Nature"; and (3) to "proceed to the fountains of thought in Instinct and Inspiration." The first of these deepens his description of intellect proper, thus providing an evocative picture of the fluid mind. Intellect is an "ethereal sea," before which "every human house has a water front"; thought finds us (as WILLIAM JAMES will soon similarly refer to consciousness) at the "bank of a river," whereby we "watch the endless flow of the stream, floating objects of all shapes, colors and natures"—we can merely run beside them a "little way along the bank." Along these lines Emerson asks, "Who has found the boundaries of human intelligence? Who has made a chart of its channel or approached the fountain of this wonderful Nile?" Likewise, intellect is a "science of degrees." It descends the "steep stair" from the "essence of Intellect pure" to our everyday "thoughts and intellections"; it detaches thoughts like earths and moons orbiting the "first mind." These "detached thoughts," the "perceptions of the soul," pass from mind to mind, they "incarnate themselves into action, to take body, only to carry forward the will which sent them out." "Nimble," they pass through the materials of the earth (wood and stone and iron), and the "ponderous instrumentalities" of the world (such as cities and nations, armies and institutions, laws and religions, men and ages of duration). This sets up an Emersonian genealogy of thought-movements, a series of metamorphoses through which each thought "buries it-self in the new thought of larger scope." (Restated later as the "every new thought modifies, interprets old problems.") This implies a dynamic "chain of being" of related thoughts, an animated natural classification of intellect.

This "appetite of the mind to arrange its phenomena" is further developed and "made useful" in Emerson's subsequent remarks on the identity, or unity, of nature and mind. Mind "reappears to us in our study of nature . . . therefore our own organization is a perpetual key, and a well-ordered mind brings to the study of every new fact or class of facts a certain divination of that which it shall find." Or later, "From whatever side we look at Nature we seem to be exploring the figure of a disguised man. How obvious is the momentum of our mental history!" Here, Emerson again relies on fluid analogies to describe the mind, with particular affinity to organic and botanical ones. This is most elaborately and elegantly stated in what is a central passage of the text:

> The idea of vegetation is irresistible in considering mental activity. Man seems a higher plant. What happens here in mankind is matched by what happens out there in the history of grass and wheat. This curious resemblance repeats, in the mental function, the germination, growth, state of melioration, crossings, blight, parasites, and in short all the accidents of the plant. Under every leaf is the bud of a new leaf, and not less under every thought is a newer thought. The plant absorbs much nourishment from the ground in order to repair its own waste by exhalation, and keep itself good. Increase its food and it becomes fertile.

Emerson's idea of mental activity in its relation to nature, and the type of "history" his natural history of the intellect entails, is thus one of organic growth and development. The mind is not merely receptive or wholly active but digestive: "A mind does not receive truth as a chest receives jewels that are put into it, but as the stomach takes up food into the system. It is no longer food, but flesh, and is assimilated. The appetite and the power of digestion measure our right to knowledge. . . . As soon as our accumulation overruns our invention or power to use, the evils of intellectual gluttony begin,—congestion of the brain, apoplexy and strangulation."

Emerson moves to consider the sources of our mental power (food for thought, presumably), which brings him to explore the "unknown country" of instinct and inspiration. He provides several definitions for each: instinct is "potential wit," "a taper, a spark in the great night," "the source of thought and feeling which acts on masses of men." Like intellect generally, instinct ascends by degrees, such that inspiration is its "power excited." Instinct begins "at the surface of the earth, and works for the necessities of the human being; then ascends step by step to suggestions which are when expressed the intellectual and moral laws"; instinct is "nature when it first becomes intelligent." Culture, rather than cultivating instinct, deadens it; thus, Emerson calls for a reinvigorated understanding of instinct and inspiration and, in so doing, details their relationship to perception, sensation, will, genius, aesthetics, science, and religion.

Section two, "Instinct and Inspiration," builds on these preceding definitions, and often repeats verbatim or with slight variation lines from the preceding section (not surprising as Edward Emerson added this section to the text based on manuscript sources). Emerson does, nonetheless, expand his thoughts on inspiration as excited instinct. Although it "remains a mystery," it is not so much sealed off to us as a fundamental source of the renewal of life. The inspired state is marked by its "incessant advance," the advance of perpetual novelty, of the invention of means, of the expansion and variation of thought, of its "recruitment" with "relations to all Nature." On this basis, Emerson celebrates those inceptual thinkers who, like the poet, move past the restrictions of personality: "Lord Bacon begins; Behmen begins; Goethe, Fourier, Schelling, Coleridge, they all begin." Or, later: "Divine energy never rests or repeats itself."

The text's final section, "Memory," describes yet another "primary and fundamental faculty" of the intellect, "the thread on which the beads of man are strung." Memory makes possible friends, family, home, history, and, as Emerson will remark later in the section, artistic creation, science, and writing, if not thought and intellect themselves. Memory "collects and recollects"—it allows for self-reference, for the distribution and differentiation of men, and for natural classification. Memory can take on a life of its own, for, like mind, it detaches itself, it "volunteers or refuses its informations at its will." Although memory is commonly celebrated as that which "holds past and present," Emerson is acutely attuned to its future orientation, linking it essentially to the novelty of inspiration: "The Past has new value every moment to the active mind." "Memory is not a pocket, but a living instructor, with a prophetic sense of the values which he guards; a guardian angel." In effect, the task of memory becomes just this—in his "metaphysics of use" memory is put to the service of the future. As Emerson concludes, "Memory is a presumption of a possession of the future. Now we are halves, we see the past but not the future, but in that day will the hemisphere complete itself and foresight be as perfect as aftersight."

CRITICAL COMMENTARY

The "science of the mind" Emerson develops in *Natural History of Intellect* embodies both culmination and a modification of much of his earlier thinking of the relationship between mind and nature, in terms of natural science, intellect, perception, memory, aesthetics, and religion. Emerson's explicit concern to treat the intellect as a natural fact deepens his project of writing, as he says in his 1858 lecture "Powers of the Mind" (and repeats here), "a metaphysics perpetually reinforced by life." It enables us to situate his often-repeated claim published in "SUCCESS," from his 1870 *Society and Solitude,* that: "Aristotle or Bacon or Kant propound some maxim which is the keynote of philosophy thenceforward. But I am more interested to know that when at last they have hurled out their grand word, it is only some familiar experience of every man in the street." This leads Emerson to use philosophical, natural historical, and literary sources in the way a poet might; he attempts to "write nature" according to the ideal of the "scientific poet" he found in JOHANN WOLFGANG VON GOETHE among others.

This marks his central concern with how to write his system, a concern that has added intellectual historical interest considering the growing influences of Hegelian philosophy, logic, and empiricism on American thought during the time of Emerson's later writing. GEORG WILHELM FRIEDRICH HEGEL could be said to embody the type of systematic philosophy Emerson resisted in the name of poetry, spontaneity, and intuition, though Emerson's work importantly intersected that of Hegel, whose philosophy of freedom, nature, and civil history Emerson often cites. Emerson devotes his "natural history" to understanding life and experience as we find it, to opening new, unrestrained—if incomplete—modes of thought.

The writing of *Natural History of Intellect,* as is true of Emerson's compositional practice generally, included the substantial honing of key passages in his journals and earlier published writings, as well as pretesting ideas in his lectures. Coupled with the fact that the text remained unfinished, and was subsequently restructured by James Elliot Cabot and Edward Emerson, the student of the work is presented with an array of editorial and critical difficulties. These difficulties, although they must be addressed, should not prohibit attention to Emerson's later project, especially given the importance that he attached to it for his career as a whole. One must then approach the *Natural History of Intellect* as a generative text, a still-sprouting seedbed of Emerson's later thought and, at the same time, as a marker of the contemporary philosophical concerns and questions that informed Edward and Cabot's reconstructions.

These difficulties aside, *Natural History of Intellect* reveals that, in his later years, Emerson, far from having completed his best work years before, was both still dynamically developing his own thought and actively invested in the intellectual work of his contemporaries. This gives us a clearer picture of Emerson's relationship to the thought currents of the late 19th century: Hegelianism, evolutionism, psychology, physics, and the emerging pragmatist philosophy, the proponents of which, like Emerson, were engaged in rewriting and reorienting the relationship of the mind and nature. Thus *Natural History of Intellect* stands as an enduring statement of Emerson's thought—and indeed one that has not yet received its due critical attention. To be sure, following the claim of Sampson Reed (American proponent of EMANUEL SWEDENBORG) that the mind is best understood by the fruits of its ongoing germination and development, Emerson's "later mind" still offers us a rich scholarly harvest.

FURTHER READING

Bosco, Ronald A. "His Lectures Were Poetry, His Teaching the Music of the Spheres: Annie Adams Fields and Francis Greenwood Peabody on Emerson's 'Natural History of the Intellect' University Lectures at Harvard in 1870." *Harvard Library Bulletin* 8, no. 2 (Summer 1997): 1–79.

Bosco, Ronald A., and Joel Myerson, eds. *The Later Lectures of Ralph Waldo Emerson.* Athens: University of Georgia Press, 2001.

DeVoll, Matthew W. "Emerson and Dreams: Toward a Natural History of Intellect." *ATQ* 18, no. 2 (June 2004): 69–87.

Levin, Jonathan. *The Poetics of Transition: Emerson, Pragmatism, and American Literary Modernism.* Durham, N.C.: Duke University Press, 1999.

Robinson, David M. *Emerson and the Conduct of Life: Pragmatism and Ethical Purpose in the Later Work.* New York: Cambridge University Press, 1993.

Michael Jonik

Nature (1836)

Nature is probably the work most often associated with Ralph Waldo Emerson and American Transcendentalism. *Nature* was published anonymously in 1836, the same year the TRANSCENDENTAL CLUB was formed and several other individuals also published texts associated with the movement. ORESTES BROWNSON's *New Views of Christianity, Society, and the Church,* GEORGE RIPLEY's *Discourses on the Philosophy of Religion; Addressed to Doubters Who Wish to Believe,* AMOS BRONSON ALCOTT's *Doctrine and Discipline of Human Culture,* and WILLIAM HENRY FURNESS's *Remarks on the Four Gospels* were all examples of the "new thought," which questioned traditional religion and sought a more authentic relationship to God. These UNITARIAN writers turned to nature as an alternative source of spiritual knowledge and came to remarkably similar conclusions, such as Furness's observation (in the context of questioning whether Christ's "miracles" were supernatural events) that "the existence of the merest atom, when we duly consider it, is an unspeakable miracle." Thus Emerson was not the only or even the most original voice in this new movement when he put forth the idea, as Ripley put it, that our "inward nature . . . is the source of more important and comprehensive ideas than any which the external senses suggest," and that this inner voice within each individual is "the inspiring voice of God."

In 1836 Emerson found himself at a crossroads in both his personal and his professional life. His first wife had died, he had resigned from the ministry, and he had traveled to Europe, where he met such key thinkers of the era as SAMUEL TAYLOR COLERIDGE and THOMAS CARLYLE. Emerson had probably begun to compose *Nature* on his

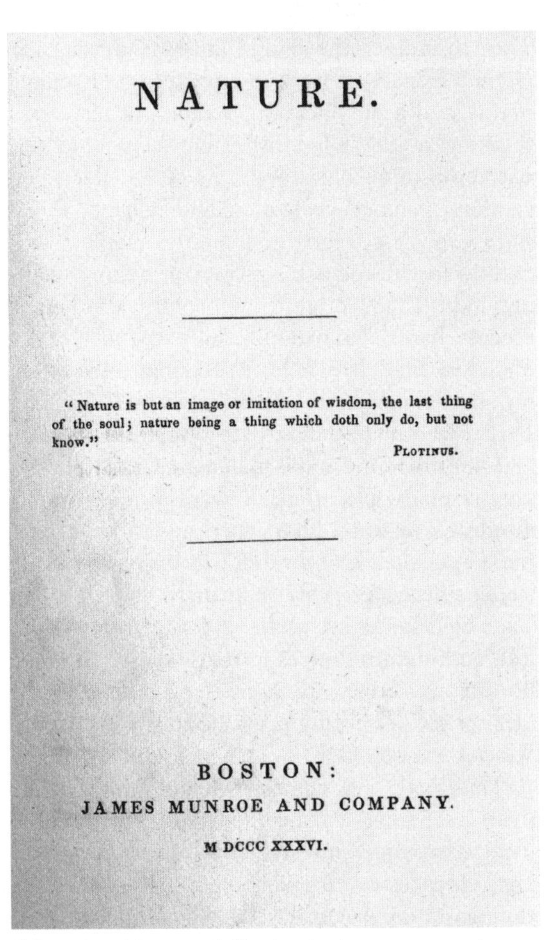

NATURE.

"Nature is but an image or imitation of wisdom, the last thing of the soul; nature being a thing which doth only do, but not know."

PLOTINUS.

BOSTON:
JAMES MUNROE AND COMPANY.
M DCCC XXXVI.

Title page of Emerson's first book, the anonymously published *Nature,* 1836 *(Concord Free Public Library)*

way home from this first trip abroad in 1833. By the time the book was published in 1836, he had embarked upon a new career as a lecturer and a writer. Although Emerson modestly explained to Carlyle that he hoped *Nature,* with its critique of organized religion in favor of a direct spiritual relationship with nature and with oneself, would at least be "an entering wedge . . . for something more worthy and significant," Carlyle recognized it as significant already, as "the Foundation and Ground-plan" for all of Emerson's thought.

Even though it was then common practice to publish books anonymously, the identity of the author became quickly known and the book sparked discussion in BOSTON and beyond. Samuel Osgood reviewed *Nature* positively for the *WESTERN MESSENGER* in the January 1837 issue, although he did take issue with Emerson's idealism: "We are unable to perceive the bearing of the writer's argument, in proof of Idealism, or to allow the advantage, which he claims for his theory. All his arguments, it seems to us, go to prove merely the superiority of mind over matter."

Nature is a short book (at only 95 pages one reviewer called it a "prose poem") and includes an introduction followed by eight brief thematic chapters that speak to various levels of human understanding of, and interaction with, nature. It was reprinted in 1849 along with several of Emerson's most important lectures given between 1837 and 1844, in *NATURE; ADDRESSES, AND LECTURES.* The book, *Nature,* is different from the essay on "NATURE" included in the 1844 collection, *ESSAYS: SECOND SERIES.*

SYNOPSIS

The introduction begins with Emerson's observation on society's backward-looking approach to knowledge: "Our age is retrospective. It builds the sepulchres of the fathers. It writes biographies, histories, and criticism." We must break our dependence on the books and thinkers of the past and develop instead "an original relation to the universe" and "a poetry and philosophy of insight and not of tradition." Emerson's confidence in the individual and in nature as the source of knowledge leads to his declaration that "we have no questions to ask which are unanswerable." Knowledge begins with a firsthand experience of nature, which we must then translate into some larger meaning: "He acts it as life, before he apprehends it as truth." Our main question in life should be, "to what end nature?" Thus, the "aim" of science and of life are the same: self-knowledge. Emerson explains what he means by "nature": "the universe is composed of Nature and the Soul. Strictly speaking, therefore, all that is separate from us . . . nature and art, all other men and my own body, must be ranked under this name, NATURE." So "nature" has two meanings, one "common" and one "philosophical," and he will explore both senses of the word.

1. "Nature"

In the first chapter Emerson explains that a true or "original" relationship to nature requires not only removing oneself from society but from our studies as well: "I am not solitary whilst I read and write, though nobody is with me. But if a man would be alone, let him look at the stars." Yet most people take nature for granted: "If the stars should appear one night in a thousand years, how would men believe and adore." The miracle of nature is all around. As children we appreciated the "simplicity" of nature; as adults we see its "wisdom." Regrettably, "few adult persons can see nature . . . At least they have a very superficial seeing." In nature, however, we will find "a perpetual youth."

A right relationship with nature also means an understanding of the relation of the parts to the whole. It is the difference between seeing individual farms owned by individual men and seeing "the landscape." It is "the poet" who "can integrate all the parts." Emerson provides the model, again in the language of truly "seeing" nature: "Standing on the bare ground,— my head bathed by the blithe air, and uplifted into infinite space,— all mean egotism vanishes. I become a transparent eye-ball; I am nothing; I see all; the currents of the Universal Being circulate through me; I am part or particle of God." In this experience, Emerson is aware of himself as simultaneously a small part of nature and an embodiment of the entire universe. The "inward and outward senses" are aligned in nature, which "always wears the colors of the spirit." Far from being a passive relationship of giving oneself up to nature, "the power to produce this delight, does not reside in nature, but in man, or in a harmony of both."

2. *"Commodity"*

The second chapter focuses on our use of nature, which provides us with raw materials and fulfills the basic needs of "our senses" with food, shelter, livelihood, and pleasure. We depend upon the "beasts, fire, water, stones, and corn." These are "low" uses of nature, only "temporary and mediate, not ultimate, like its service to the soul." Man takes for granted, and sometimes even complains with "childish petulance," all that nature gives him "on this green ball which floats him through the heavens." Beyond even the raw materials of nature that we use in daily life, nature also assists humans by providing the wind, sea, ice, rain, and plants that feed the animals, all part of the "endless circulations" we depend upon. Yet we still think we are superior to nature because through our "wit" we have been able to reproduce some of nature's work (such as replacing winds with "steam") or overcome some of nature's obstacles (conquering sea and overland travel). Emerson ends this briefest chapter by noting "the catalogue is endless," and yet it is not enough "that he may be fed, but that he may work."

3. *"Beauty"*

The third chapter examines "a nobler want" beyond our physical needs, that is, how nature inspires "the love of Beauty." Nature is filled with things that are beautiful "in and for themselves," and, again showing the interconnectedness of humans with nature, the human eye is perfectly suited for viewing the beauty of nature. He lists three aspects of nature's "Beauty." First, there are "natural forms," a beauty so "needful to man" that it almost seems like a commodity. Nature restores the mind and body, balances our attention to work, and gives us "a horizon" as a source of hope: "We are never tired, so long as we can see far enough." We can get from nature what we seek in philosophy—history, imagination, understanding, mysticism, and dreams. He challenges the utilitarian view that nature is beautiful only at certain times of the year, praising "winter scenery" as much as summer. Even the same spot changes not only with the seasons but also weekly, daily, even "every hour, a picture which was never seen before, and which shall never be seen again."

The second aspect of nature's "Beauty" is the "spiritual element," or the idea that beauty reflects virtue. Human actions are inspired by, and made more noble due to, the surrounding natural beauty; for example, the majestic scenery welcomed the early explorers. The third beautiful aspect of nature is as "an object of the intellect," inspiring "thought" and art; this is called aesthetics or "Taste." Beyond appreciation of art, there are those who, "not content with admiring, they seek to embody it in new forms. The creation of beauty is Art." Inspired by nature, humans create art, and art in turn "throws a light upon the mystery of humanity." Still, this is not "the last or highest expression" of nature.

4. *"Language"*

In this chapter Emerson explains how nature is a language available to humans and lists three ways in which "Nature is a vehicle of thought." First of all, the "outer" world of nature is a language of "inward creation." The words we use to explain ethics, thought, and emotion often come from the natural or physical world. For example, we say "head" when we mean "thought" or mind, and we say "heart" when we mean "emotion." Second, "natural facts are symbols of particular spiritual facts." For example, when we call someone a "lion" or a "fox," or describe someone as a "rock" or a "snake," we are attaching a moral quality to a natural form. "Light and darkness are our familiar expression for knowledge and ignorance," and analogies are made "between man's life and the seasons," between human life and the growth of a plant from seed to fruit. While it is the job of the poet-philosopher to illuminate these comparisons, it is also "free to be known by all men." Without this correspondence to human life, nature and science are just "dry catalogues of facts." Lastly, nature is a language of the mind as well: "Parts of speech are metaphors, because the whole of nature is a metaphor of the human mind." Nature is the language of "proverbs, . . . fables, parables, and allegories." When we understand nature "the universe becomes transparent," and we see the "higher laws." This has been the task of every philosopher and "genius since the world began," and he provides an intellectual history, from "the Egyptians" down to EMANUEL SWEDENBORG, of "each prophet" who "tries his fortune at reading her riddle." Behind the facts of nature is an "unconscious truth," which, once revealed, will be become "a part of the domain of knowledge."

5. *"Discipline"*

In this chapter Emerson uses both meanings of the word "discipline": that is, nature as a field of knowledge or study and nature as a model for morality. The "lessons" of nature are "unlimited," as nature educates "both the Understanding and the Reason," "Matter," and "Mind." In Emerson's use of the term (which he derives from IMMANUEL KANT) "Understanding" comes through measuring and classifying, through physical experience or "common sense." Through "Understanding" we comprehend nature's "laws"—this is the knowledge of "Agriculture, Astronomy, Zoology," the practical sciences. We then progress to "insight" as we are "impressed and even daunted by the immense Universe to be explored." This is the disciplining of our minds into nature's "Reason," a realization that objects in nature "reflect the conscience." Through nature comes "the laws of right and wrong," which "echo the Ten Commandments." Emerson shows how the Bible itself uses nature to explain morality, the "farm" as "gospel" with its stories of "the chaff and the wheat, weeds and plants, blight, rain, insects, sun." Unlike the Bible, however, the "variety" of nature suggests that there is no single morality or "truth" that applies to all humans: "Who can guess how much firmness the sea-beaten rock has taught the fisherman?" Nature "is like a great circle on a sphere, comprising all possible circles; which, however, may be drawn, and comprise it, in like manner . . . it has innumerable sides." Nature's lessons are both universal and particular, and these lessons are its most "public and universal function."

6. *"Idealism"*

In this key chapter Emerson defines his philosophy of "Idealism": that "the unspeakable but intelligible and practicable meaning of the world" is "conveyed to man" through "every object of sense," through nature. So "noble" is this as "the Final Cause of the Universe," that Emerson admits to even doubting "whether nature outwardly exists" at all, or whether it is only a series of "sensations" in the human mind. It does not matter to Emerson whether nature exists or it is only a manifestation of the mind, so long as the result is the same: "Be it what it may, it is ideal to me." "The effect of culture on the mind" may lead us to "regard nature as a phenomenon, not a substance." For example, "the rapid movement of the rail-road car" gives one a different view of the landscape than standing still. The difference in perspective challenges our view of nature as stable and man as changing, by suggesting the opposite, that is, that "the world is a spectacle, something in himself is stable."

Poetry also "communicates the same pleasure" of a new perspective. The poet "unfixes the land and the sea, makes them revolve around the axis of his primary thought. . . . The sensual man conforms thoughts to things; the poet conforms things to his thoughts. The one esteems nature as rooted and fast; the other, as fluid, and impresses his being thereon." The poet possesses not just "Reason," but "Imagination." Shakespeare possessed this power "of subordinating nature for the purposes of expression" and through his words was able "to dwarf the great, to magnify the small." But poets and philosophers differ in that the first has "beauty as his main end; the other Truth." Ideally, beauty reveals truth and truth reveals beauty, so these purposes are not entirely different, nor is the purpose of science, which is to understand the whole from "particulars." Emerson points out that, like poetry and philosophy, sciences such as physics and astronomy, in fact, rely less on "results of observation" and more on theory and formula. What Emerson terms "Intellectual science" then doubts "the existence of matter" since "Ideas" themselves become "objects of science" to be studied. He who pursues these questions will become "himself divine," "immortal," with the realization that even "time and space" are not fixed features of nature.

This inquiry into the nature of human existence itself leads Emerson to his last point in "Idealism," a discussion of "religion and ethics"—the first of these comes from humans, the second from nature. Religion goes too far in rejecting all things material, such as nature and the body, focusing instead on the supernatural. Ethics, on the other hand, does not require "the personality of God" nor does it require a repudiation of nature. For Emerson, ethics requires "a child's love" of nature. More than that, though, the idealist becomes part of nature: "I expand and live in the warm day like corn and melons . . . I only wish to indicate the true position of nature in regard to man." Whereas religion sees God acting upon the world, "Idealism sees the world in God." Whereas religion accepts the world "as it finds it," without question or inquiry, Idealism "beholds the whole circle" and thus inspires the soul. He ends this chapter with a harsh critique of religion as requiring man to be "a watcher more than a doer," creating passive rather than active souls.

7. *"Spirit"*

In this chapter Emerson explains that any "true theory of nature and of man" must be "progressive," it cannot have an "end" or "uses that are exhausted." He compares nature to Jesus, as both require us to be "devout . . . with bended head, and hands folded upon the breast." From nature, rather than from religion, we learn "the lesson of worship." As humans have found no way to describe or define God—"both language and thought desert us . . . That essence refuses to be recorded in propositions"—nature then stands in for God. Religion is not enough to understand "the whole circumference of man." Emerson proposes to "add some related thoughts" to the subject, organized into three questions that sum up his entire philosophical project: "What is matter? Whence is it? And Whereto?" or to what purpose.

His "ideal theory" is a way "to account for nature," and nature's answer to the question of God or "spirit" is that these do not exist outside of us, but they are rather all part of a "universal essence." The separate categories of God, nature, and man are imposed upon us, for "Who can set bounds to the possibilities of man?" Emerson argues that, through nature, "we learn that man has access to the entire mind of the Creator, is himself the creator in the finite." This truth "animates me to create my own world" rather than accept the world as it appears. And yet, we are still "strangers in nature" who have much to learn; for example, we do not yet understand the language of the animals, and there is still "discord" between the "noble landscape" and "laborers . . . digging in the field hard by." A pure relationship to the "Spirit" through nature remains an unattained ideal.

8. *"Prospects"*

Having worked through successive levels of understanding of humanity's relationship to nature, Emerson ends with the forward-looking "Prospects." Too much reliance upon "empirical science" can stand in the way and distract us with nature's "functions and processes," without "contemplation of the whole." The task of the naturalist is "continual self-recovery" rather than merely cataloging nature. The scientist must be content to guess rather than to know, to dream rather than to experiment. We have misunderstood "the problems to be solved" in nature: "It is not so pertinent to man to know all the individuals of the animal kingdom." It is more important to find patterns and "unity" in diversity. Thus we will find that humans are not separate from nature, but that humanity can be found "in every great and small thing, in every mountain stream, in every new law of color, fact of astronomy."

A purely scientific approach to nature is only "half-sight" and "man applies to nature but half his force," just as labor or work makes "but a half-man," feeding the body, not the mind or soul. There are a few examples in human history of man utilizing "his entire force," for example, in "the history of Jesus Christ . . . [in the] religious and political revolutions, and in the abolition of the Slave-trade; the miracles of enthusiasm, as those reported by Swedenborg . . . and the Shakers; . . . prayer; Eloquence; self-healing; and the wisdom of children." These are all examples of what humanity is capable of, "the exertions of a power which exists not in time or space." If individuals do not make "use of all their faculties," disharmony results: "The reason why the world lacks unity, and lies broken and in heaps, is, because man is disunited with himself." Exerting one's "entire force" requires only a right relationship with nature: "The invariable mark of wisdom is to see the miraculous in the common. What is a day? What is a year? What is summer? What is woman? What is a child? What is sleep?" These simple questions lead to greater ones: "What is truth? . . . What is good?" The answers to these questions are available to all who would ask. There is no difference between Caesar and a "cobbler" or a farmer and a scholar: "Every spirit builds itself a house; and beyond its house a world; and beyond its world, a heaven. Know then, that the world exists for you. . . . Build, therefore, your own world. As fast as you conform your life to the pure idea in your mind, that will unfold its great proportions."

CRITICAL COMMENTARY

The 1836 version of *Nature* opened with a verse from Plotinus, a NEOPLATONIC philosopher: "Nature is but an image or imitation of wisdom, the last thing of the soul; Nature being a thing which doth only do, but not know." The 1849 reprint in *Nature; Addresses, and Lectures* included instead this verse from Emerson:

> A subtle chain of countless rings
> The next unto the farthest brings;
> The eye reads omens where it goes,
> And speaks all languages the rose;
> And, striving to be man, the worm
> Mounts through all the spires of form.

This opening verse reveals Emerson's approach, in both philosophy and his writing, of starting from one point and moving outward. It also introduces many of the themes and images to follow in *Nature* and throughout his other writings, such as the circle and the eye to represent continuity and vision, the interconnectedness of all things in nature, and humanity as nature's highest "form." *Nature* is, according to biographer Robert Richardson, "a modern version of Plato, an American version of Kant." Emerson did not merely repeat, but he reworked these thinkers to create his own philosophy of idealism, what became known in the 19th century as Transcendentalism. Emphasizing the centrality of individual experience, Emerson presented *Nature* as his own personal conclusions, but in such a way that the reader could make them his or her own as well: "Know then, that the world exists for you . . . build, therefore your own world."

In calling for "an original relation to the universe" in the opening paragraphs of *Nature,* Emerson speaks to a particularly American concern about our relation to the past. Just as the United States was still defining itself in relation to its European past, Emerson himself struggled with breaking from the traditions of his ancestors, including from the church itself and from Christianity in general as a religion "revealed" to a past generation. Emerson seeks instead "a poetry and philosophy of insight" and self-trust, the theme of much of his later lectures and essays, from "The AMERICAN SCHOLAR" (1837), the "DIVINITY SCHOOL ADDRESS" (1838), "HISTORY" and "SELF-RELIANCE" from *ESSAYS: FIRST SERIES* (1841), "EXPERIENCE" and the other *ESSAYS: SECOND SERIES* (1844), and *REPRESENTATIVE MEN* (1850), in which he offers up a new history with examples of self-trusting "great men."

Emerson's self-trust meant trust in the entire universe: "we have no questions to ask which are unanswerable." This is a radical humanist statement against doctrinal religious belief, which he believed discouraged questions and, in fact, encouraged dependence. Emerson's call for "an original relation to the universe" is reflected in his famous first-person experience of literally becoming one with nature in the "transparent eye-ball" passage of *Nature.* This passage, this idea, was easily caricatured by colleague CHRISTOPHER PEARSE CRANCH in his drawing of Emerson as a walking eyeball with legs and, despite Emerson's emphasis that "all mean egotism vanishes . . . I am nothing," was criticized as the epitome of Transcendentalist individualism and self-absorption. Despite such criticisms, both the message of oneness with nature and the first-person stream of consciousness style defined a new literary genre as well as a new philosophy and would later be echoed in the works

"Standing on the bare ground,—my head bathed by the blithe air, & uplifted into infinite space,—all mean egotism vanishes. I become a transparent Eyeball." Nature, p. 13.

Christopher Pearse Cranch's caricature of the "transparent eyeball" passage from Emerson's *Nature* (*Houghton Library, Harvard University*)

of other writers of the era, such as in the poetry of Emily Dickinson or Walt Whitman.

Each of the chapters in *Nature* reveals a different use or relationship to nature, from utilitarian, or meeting our physical needs, toward "a nobler want," or more spiritual relationship to nature. Always, however, the physical and the spiritual are linked. The chapter "Beauty" introduces an aesthetic appreciation of nature and of nature's symbolism that he would return to in nature poems such as "The Rhodora" (in which he concludes, "Beauty is its own excuse for being"), "The Humble-Bee," "The Snow-Storm," and "Each and All." The imagery of seeing of the human eye, with its ability to appreciate beauty as art, is a recurring symbol of vision, of understanding, but also of roundness and continuity. The eye turns nature into "a well colored and shaded globe," and the landscape becomes "round and symmetrical," again representing unity and continuity within nature and between humans and nature. This is the circular symbolism of the interconnectedness of nature that he would develop more fully in the essay "Circles" (1841) and elsewhere.

Emerson's discussion in "Beauty" and of perspective, of truly seeing nature, leads to his organic or romantic aesthetic of art. The purpose of art is to further inspire by reflecting and re-creating nature's beauty: "A work of art is an abstract or epitome of the world. It is the result or the expression of nature, in miniature." Emerson would explore this theory in the essay "Art," in "History," and in poems such as "The Snow-Storm," in which nature's "frolic architecture" inspires human architecture. In *Nature,* it is human intervention, such as technology or what he terms "mechanical means," that changes our relationship to nature. For example, his discussion of the railroad, which has changed our perspective on the movement or stability of nature and thus our relationship to nature, is a theme he addressed in the poem "The Adirondacs" when he reports, joyfully, on the news that the transatlantic cable had been laid.

Although each person should form his or her own "original relation to the universe," just like the artist or the scientist or even technology, the poet-writer is another mediator between nature and humanity. The poet translates the observable "facts" of nature into "knowledge" about ourselves and the world. Nature is a mystery to be solved and "The Sphinx" (subject of a later poem) guards nature's secrets; the poet-philosopher is one who attempts to unlock the riddle. In the chapter on "Language" Emerson presents the idea that nature is a symbolic language. Indeed, this is a core idea of Emerson's Transcendentalist philosophy and of his own goal as a poet-philosopher, an idea he explored in the essay "The Poet" (1844) and that he especially saw manifested in the genius and craft of William Shakespeare. In *Nature,* Shakespeare possesses the power "of subordinating nature for the purposes of expression," and Emerson would later expand on this in his the essay, "SHAKSPEARE; OR, THE POET" (1850).

It is important to note that Emerson wants to make a comparison not only between idealism and materialism but also between "the ideal theory" and "the popular faith." What separated Emerson's *Nature* from that of his Transcendentalist colleagues (and made it more radical, if sometimes less accessible) was, first of all, that Emerson was not primarily concerned with theological debate within the churches. *Nature* was published inbetween his two primary statements on religion and Christianity—"The LORD'S SUPPER" (1832) and the "Divinity School Address" (1838). The former signaled his break from the church; the latter from organized religion completely. In these works, as in *Nature,* he offered an alternative theology of the self that did not depend upon the truths or untruths of what the Transcendentalist-Unitarians called "historical Christianity." If Christ's example had anything to offer as a spiritual or moral model, that was fine, but Emerson was not concerned with aligning his philosophical perspective with religious doctrine. He was more concerned with how to live and with what it meant to be human or, as he explained in *Nature,* "the laws of the world and the frame of things."

The chapter "Discipline" provides Emerson's clearest statement on nature as a source of moral guidance. He makes the humanist's argument that morality comes from within and that there are "natural," not biblical, reasons not to live ethically. Emerson's genius is in showing how the Bible, in fact, uses and relies upon the language of nature in parables, for example, not because nature is a simple language to understand, but because it is the first language and source of morality. Morality comes from studying nature, not religious texts, and ethics does not require what he calls "the personality of God," it only requires a right relationship with nature. This is a radical challenge not only to the necessity of the Bible but to the necessity of God, one he would return to in the "Divinity School Address" when he urged his listeners to be themselves "a divine man."

The chapter "Idealism" furthers his discussion of "religion and ethics," in which it is idealism (not God) that "beholds the whole circle." Idealism sees all things as related, unlike Christianity, which is passed down from "an aged creeping Past" to the next generation unchanged. Emerson's criticism is that religion accepts the world "as it finds it," without question or inquiry and, therefore, does nothing for the living soul. In a powerful conclusion, Emerson determines that everything about religion goes against philosophical and spiritual inquiry, which is the core of Emerson's philosophy and life-work. Religious belief requires passivity, not action, it "is a watcher more than a doer." Again, this would be the primary call to action of the "Divinity School Address" just two years later. In discussing nature as "Spirit," he was also working up to the idea he explored in the essay "The OVER-SOUL" (1841)—what he now termed in *Nature* as a "universal essence." It is not a distant or separate God-father who works upon the soul but our own responsibility to this "essence" and to ourselves that "animates me to create my own world through the purification of my soul."

Nature is thus a foundation for Emerson's Transcendentalist philosophy, which takes the supremacy of the individual mind and soul as both the starting point and the center of universal knowledge. In this formulation, nature is the source and language of that knowledge. This fact requires a radical reworking of the concept of "God" itself, in secular terms, as nature and as humanity itself. In the poem "The Adirondacs," Emerson reflects upon whether there is truly any separation between self and nature: "The clouds are rich and dark, the air serene, / So like the soul of me, what if 't were me?" Rather than seeing God's creation, the Transcendentalist-Idealist sees himself in nature. Emerson's new "ideal theory," as revealed in *Nature* of 1836, is that God is another word for knowledge, that this knowledge is accessible to all through nature, and that humanity's ethical imperative is toward individual self-development.

"Nature" (1844)

"Nature," the sixth essay of *ESSAYS: SECOND SERIES* (1844), reprises Emerson's seminal work *NATURE*

(1836), while carrying forward related themes of an earlier 1841 lecture "The METHOD OF NATURE." The earlier piece, "The Method of Nature," is primarily concerned with nature's infinitely creative manifestations. This later "Nature" of 1844 makes a distinction between "nature passive" (*"natura naturata"*)—expressed for the most part in terms of the sublime revelations of physical nature—and the inner life of the transforming or "Efficient Nature" (*"natura naturans"*). He continues this dualism or dual understanding of nature, explaining that "motion or change, and identity or rest, are the first and second secrets of nature," also understood as matter and spirit. Nature, he says, is "one stuff with its two ends, to serve up all her dream-like variety. Compound it as she will, star, sand, fire, water, tree, man, it is still one stuff, and betrays the same properties."

SYNOPSIS

The opening pages of "Nature" of 1844 begin with a reinscription of the Transcendentalist sense of the beauty of the terrestrial landscape that is comparable with the best passages in *Nature* of 1836: "There are days which occur in this climate, at almost any season of the year, wherein the world reaches its perfection, when the air, the heavenly bodies, and the earth, make a harmony, as if nature would indulge her offspring." Entering into nature on such days, man leaves all "custom" behind: "Here is sanctity which shames our religions, and reality which discredits our heroes. Here we find nature to be the circumstance which dwarfs every other circumstance, and judges like a god all men that come to her."

The "enchantments" of nature are not just beautiful, they "heal us," restoring balance between body and soul. Nature matches, or surpasses, "the music and pictures of the most ancient religion." He urges that we must "penetrate bodily this incredible beauty." There is nothing so wonderful in any particular landscape or horizon, Emerson adds, as the general "necessity of being beautiful." And yet men usually do not have the courage to confront nature's beauty directly. They go into nature with "the apology of some trivial necessity," using excuses such as going "to see a wood-lot, or to look at the crops, or to fetch a plant or a mineral," or to hunt or to fish. Such uses of nature are "barren and unworthy": "The fop of the fields is no better than his brother of Broadway." "Literature, poetry, science," these are the truer appreciations of nature: "Nature is loved by what is best in us." Emerson draws the lesson here that a person's search for the poetic and picturesque in nature is inseparable from his or her rejection of "false society." Our relationship with nature is evidence of "the presence or absence of the divine sentiments in man."

All the awesome beauty of nature falls under the two metaphysical rubrics of "Motion and Rest." The latter concept means that nature is in constant transition or "change." From plants to animals to humans there is a constant tendency to mutate into higher fulfillments. Even though things are constantly changing in nature, the human mind is capable of recognizing correspondences and analogies. Man "carries the world in his head, the whole astronomy and chemistry suspended in a thought." And "because the history of nature" is thus carried in our minds, man becomes "the prophet and discoverer of her secrets." Some people call this "common sense," but it is Emerson's principle of a "guiding identity" that "characterizes every law" in nature: "That famous aboriginal push propagates itself through all the balls of the system, and through every atom of every ball, through all the races of creatures, and through the history and performances of every individual." Thus every creature, every man or woman born into the world, is a unique and necessary manifestation of nature's exuberance; like the umbilical cord that ties the "babe" to the mother, so the soul of nature "circulates" in our blood.

Here Emerson crucially takes up another aspect of nature's constant change or motion, namely, her seeming chaos: "The appearance strikes the eye everywhere of an aimless society, of aimless nations." As in human life, the "woods and water" sometimes have "a failure to yield a present satisfaction." Nature fascinates and at the same time deceives. Even the poet experiences this disconnect, an "odd jealousy" in his inability to fully comprehend nature's secrets: "The pine-tree, the river, the bank of flowers before him, does not seem to be nature. Nature is still elsewhere." This ever-elusive characteristic of nature is repeated in the relations of men and women, between whom "there is always an absence, never a complete presence and satisfaction"—"She was heaven whilst he pursued her as a star: she cannot be heaven, if she stoops to such a one as he." Instead of an illusory identification with nature's effects, the wise person learns to feel the soul that "streams through us" and through the multiplicity and changes of nature. Thus, though we live in the "particulars" of daily life and of external nature, "we bring with us to every experiment the innate universal laws." Conversely, while these laws "exist in the mind as ideas," they find their manifestation "around us in nature forever embodied." Returning to the idea of nature as the source of our physical and mental health, he declares nature is "a present sanity to expose and cure the insanity of men."

In the end, Emerson comes back to his essential Transcendentalist theme that in mankind's modern technological progress in harnessing the outer forces of nature "nothing is gained: nature cannot be cheated." Rather, it is spiritual insight into nature's identity that brings advantage through self-knowledge. This identity of nature does not pertain to physical qualities but is purely qualitative: "It makes the whole and the particle its equal channel . . . and distils its essence into every drop of rain." But we do "not guess its essence, until after a long time."

CRITICAL COMMENTARY

The "long time" that passes before we divine the secret of the inner side, the *natura naturans,* of nature to which Emerson here alludes, signifies the transformation of the self achieved in the Transcendentalist perspective of the "transparent eyeball," the central image of the book, *Nature,* of 1836. In this later essay of 1844, he has reinscribed the perspective in terms of the transcendent soul that is armed against nature's and society's illusions and misconceptions. Here he carries forward his doctrine of "The OVER-SOUL" essay of 1841, and he anticipates its variants in "The SPHINX," "WOODNOTES," and "The WORLD-SOUL," all of *POEMS* of 1847. It is an early appearance of a persistent line of thinking to which Emerson returned on many occasions, perhaps most famously in his poem "BRAHMA" (1857) and in one of his greatest philosophical essays, "ILLUSIONS" (1860). The twin principles of rest and motion also make many appearances in Emerson's later writings, functioning as the basis of his radical affirmation of life in both *The CONDUCT OF LIFE* (1860) and *SOCIETY AND SOLITUDE* (1870), and of his declaration of the affinity of the human mind and the laws of nature in *Natural History of Intellect* (1893) and "POETRY AND IMAGINATION" (1876).

These Emersonian concepts also formed the provenance of CHARLES SANDERS PEIRCE, who, in his later-phase metaphysical generalizations explicitly acknowledged Emerson's influence on his thought—most notably in his "The Law of Mind" essay of 1892. Echoing Emerson, Peirce insisted that man divines something of the secret principles of the universe because his mind has developed as part of the universe and under the influence of the same secret principles. In Emerson's own "common sense" precedent in "Nature" of 1844: "Every known fact in natural science was divined by the presentiment of somebody, before it was actually verified." Emerson's view of nature is grounded in his idealism of finding meaning in our experience of the physical world.

David A. Dilworth

"Nature I" and "Nature II" (1867)

The poems "Nature I" and "Nature II" (not to be confused with the poem that opens the 1836 book *NATURE*) express common themes in Emerson's Transcendentalism, such as the coming of spring, constancy of spirit, and resistance to mere form. Emerson never tires of finding new expressions for these themes; it can be argued (indeed, as he did argue in *Nature*) that Emerson's ongoing project is to find a suitable kind of language to express the spiritual truth of nature.

Evidence for the first notes for "Nature I" exists as early as 1836; in December 1836 he delivered the lecture "Humanity of Science," a copy of which contains handwritten lines that appear in "Nature I." Other line versions and additions appear in his journals in 1846 and 1847. The draft for "Nature II" was written over a lecture copy of an address on the poet Robert Burns, delivered by Emerson in January 1859. "Nature I" and "Nature II" were first published together in the "Nature and Life" section of MAY-DAY AND OTHER PIECES (1867) and reprinted in *Poems* (1884).

CRITICAL COMMENTARY

"Nature I" contains two stanzas of 11 and 10 lines each; "Nature II" has 23 lines of rhymed couplets, a four-line stanza, and ends with a grouping of three rhymed lines (which accounts for the odd numbers of lines). "Nature I," stanza 1, opens the poem with a short, two-beat line (as opposed to the regular four-beat lines in the rest of the poem), perhaps as a way for Emerson to maintain the *aabb* rhyme scheme (and perhaps a sign of Emerson's weakening poetic powers at this stage of his life). After the opening line, the stanza, which is about the coming of spring and nature's intolerance of pretense, finds its most compelling expression in line 9: "But she dearly loves the poor." Emerson's use of the word "poor" emphasizes the humility of nature as he personifies it, while at the same time he comments ironically on the artificiality of "art and pains" of the "loud pretender." The line has no rhyme in the couplet scheme; it is the odd line out in the couplet stanza and thus draws attention to itself. The reversal marker "but" sets the line apart from the paired lines 1–8, and it is appropriate that this single line, stating nature's preference, is set aside to trigger the final couplet about nature's power to "strike the loud pretenders down." Stanza 2 of "Nature I" opens with "For," continuing the thought of the first stanza and answering the previous stanza's closing couplet. The stanza continues in a regular meter of four-beat lines. Emerson uses this form to demonstrate the steady rhythms of unimpeded nature.

"Nature II" is set in 23 lines, its couplet scheme interrupted by a quatrain (a group of four lines) and a tercet (three lines). This section, like the first, describes the subtle power of nature. But while "Nature I" considers "feats achieved before they're named," "Nature II" expresses the formative power of nature. This is best demonstrated in the quatrain (and thus set aside for our focused consideration), which is set apart by the rhyme scheme and "hymn stanza" form (alternating four-beat and three-beat lines, called "hymn stanza" because it is the most common lyric form of New England religious hymns). These lines call attention not only to nature's power but also to the poet's power: "And what they say they made to-day / they learned of oaks ands firs." Thus, Emerson's theory of genius (and poetry), namely, that, through the poet, we recognize the correspondence between heaven and earth, the human and the divine, and recognize nature as the metaphor for the mind of God.

Bill Scalia

Nature; Addresses, and Lectures (1849)

Nature; Addresses, and Lectures was published in 1849 as a collection of Emerson's previously published works; those that had not been included in either of his two volumes ESSAYS: FIRST SERIES (1841) and ESSAYS: SECOND SERIES (1844). This 1849 volume included the pamphlet NATURE, originally published anonymously in 1836, as well as nine of Emerson's most important public addresses given between 1837 and 1844, which had all been previously published either separately as pamphlets or in the pages of the DIAL literary magazine: "The AMERICAN SCHOLAR," "The DIVINITY SCHOOL ADDRESS," "LITERARY ETHICS," "The METHOD OF NATURE," "MAN THE REFORMER," "INTRODUCTORY LECTURE ON THE TIMES," "The CONSERVATIVE," "The TRANSCENDENTALIST," and "The YOUNG AMERICAN." Although published in 1849, the collection is established as volume I in the *Collected Works* because it begins chronologically with the 1836 *Nature*.

The years covered by these works, between the original publication of *Nature* in 1836 and the publication of *Essays: Second Series* in 1844, were extremely prolific and busy ones for Emerson. He had established a career for himself as a lecturer and had emerged as the unofficial spokesperson of the new Transcendentalist movement. The pieces collected together in the 1849 volume provide an overview of the emergence of Transcendentalism onto the national literary scene and, in fact, even within the brief time period covered, highlight several distinct phases of Emerson's career to that date—from his statement of the new philosophy in *Nature* to his challenges to and intellectual independence from the HARVARD and UNITARIAN establishments with "The American Scholar" and "Divinity School Address" to his emergence as an independent lecturer on "The Times" with the Addresses section of the volume focused on more current issues as related to individual and universal reform.

"New England Reformers" (1844)

Emerson's "New England Reformers, A Lecture read before the Society in Amory Hall, on Sunday, 3 March, 1844," was included at the end of his *ESSAYS: SECOND SERIES* (1844). The address was given in the mid-1840s, the peak of Emerson's direct engagement with reform movements as the decade was defined by both national and local excitement over ABOLITIONISM, FOURIERISM, and women's rights, as well as criticism (by 1846) of U.S. involvement in the Mexican War. In 1844 alone, in addition to "New England Reformers," Emerson gave three other major addresses on politics and reform: "The YOUNG AMERICAN," "POLITICS" (included in the same volume of essays), and "EMANCIPATION OF THE NEGROES IN THE BRITISH WEST INDIES."

Delivered in BOSTON before an audience of "nonresistance" or peace society members (organized and led by William Lloyd Garrison), "New England Reformers" is in some ways more forceful and more critical than some of Emerson's other more general statements on reform, such as "MAN THE REFORMER" and "The CONSERVATIVE" (both delivered in 1841). As in all of his writings on reform, Emerson does not deny the problems facing society; rather, he is critical of the methods of reformers and of single-issue platforms and organizations. He promotes instead a vision of comprehensive reform of the individual self as the path to improving society.

SYNOPSIS

In "New England Reformers," Emerson acknowledges that this is a generation and a region overcome by a "great activity of thought and experimenting," at least among the "middle" and "leading sections" of society. Religion is no longer confined to the church, but it has moved into "temperance and non-resistance societies, in movements of abolitionists and of socialists," calling "in question the authority of the Sabbath, of the priesthood, of the church." Some have focused on reforming agriculture, some on the market and money as "the cardinal evil," others on "diet," on technological advances, on animal rights, or on marriage. Emerson sees the humor in some of these extremes, such as the silliness of giving up yeast or refusing to use wheels, or of protecting the rights of insects and plowing the field oneself instead of using an ox.

He concedes that this "scrutiny of institutions and domestic life" has produced some positive results, such as "a tendency to the adoption of simpler methods, and an assertion of the sufficiency of the private man." The problem for Emerson is that the reform spirit that has characterized New England in the last 25 years has been "a gradual withdrawal" from the "spiritual facts" and dissent only for the sake of dissent: "This country is full of rebellion." When it comes to criticism of the market, Emerson agrees that "This whole business of Trade give me to pause and think, as it constitutes false relations between men," but only because we feel ourselves "relieved of any responsibility to behave well and nobly to that person whom I pay with money." The social relations of business have themselves become "commodity." The reformer worries about paying taxes to the government, but every day as a consumer, "I pay a destructive tax in my conformity."

Likewise, the problem with education is that people spend "ten or fifteen years" in an institution, after which they "do not know a thing." Education should focus on "truth and nature" rather than on "a memory of words." Educated people "do not know an edible root in the woods, we cannot tell our course by the stars, nor the hour of the day by the sun." Education should provide practical knowledge, and its goal should be self-sufficiency. Even the study of "dead languages" is only study for its own sake, separating the languages from their usefulness in science, mathematics, law, and theology. Students spend years learning Greek or Latin, and yet there are only "Four or five persons I have seen who read Plato."

Still, Emerson agrees with the "affirmative principles" of these "democratical" movements, which at least seek "to cast aside the superfluous" by developing a "growing trust in the private, self-supplied powers of the individual." The problem is that the reformer is "not himself renovated." It is wrong to assume there is only "one objection" to be made: "The wave of evil washes all our institutions alike." Reformers act as if they have "superiority to the institution," but no one lives outside of society and institutions are made up of individuals. It is wasted energy "to be irritable" and "waste all my time in attacks." Virtue exists in "a just and heroic soul," and virtuous individuals can be found anywhere, in the church, in the market, and in society.

Besides "partiality," Emerson identifies another problem with reform in its "reliance on Association," which assumes that individuals cannot change things unless joined together in "numbers." He mentions "three communities have already been formed in Massachusetts," and wonders whether those "who have energy" for such ventures might not find more fulfilled selves outside the community, where "compromise" is not required. Compromise and rules "dwarfs" the individual; conversely, he posits that those who are drawn to such communities are already those "of less faith," those who have "failed" and hope that, in banding together with others who failed, they will be strong. Emerson warns, "There can be no concert in two, where there is no concert in one." While he acknowledges "the interest these projects inspire," Emerson reiterates his basic point that "union must be inward. . . . The union is only perfect, when all the uniters are isolated."

Another problem Emerson sees is the general "want of faith" among reformers. Rather than actual ideas, reformers offer only "alleviations, diversion, opiates." The real "tragedy" of society is "limitation." The only "remedy" is that "Life must be lived on a higher plane." The reformer focuses only on "differences of opinion and character in men," instead of seeing commonalities: "we are all children of genius, the children of virtue." Reformers think that politics separates society, but Emerson asks, "Is not every man sometimes a radical in politics?" Emerson believes that "every man is a lover of truth." He believes that all men who go to the polling place "mean to vote right." This is a more optimistic view of humanity than that of the reformer, who believes that men must be forced to do the right thing. But if someone "refuses his assent to your opinion," it is not because they are wrong, but because they do not "accept you as a bringer of truth."

We must trust in the universe—"the good globe is faithful, and carries us securely through the celestial spaces . . . we need not interfere to help it on"—and worry only about ourselves—"our own orbit is all our task." There is no need to point out "the insufficiency of this or that teacher or experimenter," as eventually "he will have demonstrated his insufficiency to all men's eyes." Our life should be guided only by "the endeavor to realize our aspirations." Self-trust brings Emerson the confidence "that the future will be worthy of the past."

CRITICAL COMMENTARY

If Emerson was, by 1844, a friend to the abolitionist cause, it is difficult to tell from this address given before an audience of active reformers. But "New England Reformers" is also not specifically concerned with, and does not directly engage, the question of slavery. Rather, he singles out UTOPIANISM and education reform, issues that, by 1844, engaged not just New England in general but also many of his closest friends and fellow Transcendentalists.

His criticism of "association" is a direct reference to the nearby utopian communities at BROOK

FARM (founded by GEORGE RIPLEY in 1841) and Fruitlands (founded by BRONSON ALCOTT in 1843). His assessment that such communities attract those "of less faith" who have "failed" at other ventures, economic or domestic, are especially harsh words directed to these friends and other community members. Emerson had been invited to join Brook Farm and had agonized over how to tell Ripley he was not interested. In the end, his private answer to Ripley was consistent with his public message in all of his lectures and writings on reform: "I think that all I shall solidly do, I must do alone."

Emerson is not against "association," but only against association by individuals not themselves fully realized. His statement in "New England Reformers" that "union must be inward. . . . The union is only perfect, when all the uniters are isolated" applied to any social relation and was strikingly similar to that of MARGARET FULLER on marriage in her *Woman in the Nineteenth Century*, published the following year (1845): "Union is only possible to those who are units." Fuller and Emerson were deep in conversation about marriage, friendship, and "association" during this time period, and Fuller explicitly identifies her idea as originating from "a wise contemporary," undoubtedly a reference to Emerson.

Other aspects of "New England Reformers" also speak to Emerson's interactions with close friends at this time. He calls out the reformer who worries over paying taxes to the government, which would have included Bronson Alcott again, who was arrested for nonpayment of a poll tax in early 1843. Just two years after Emerson's address, HENRY DAVID THOREAU was also arrested and jailed for nonpayment of taxes in protest over the Mexican War. In "New England Reformers," Emerson points out the hypocrisy of refusing to give money to the government when, every day, we are consumers of goods that support the system reformers wish to change. Not only do such transactions cost us money, they also cost us part of ourselves: "I pay a destructive tax in my conformity."

Emerson's criticism of education reform, and his view of education in general, had been articulated a few years earlier in "The AMERICAN SCHOLAR" (1837). In "New England Reformers" he chastises the scholar who does not generate any new ideas, concerned only with "turning his gifts to a marketable use, and not to his own sustenance and growth." The political and social change reformers seek has its foundations in a change to our approach to education and "knowledge," which must always be "directed on action." The world wants change—"We are weary of gliding ghostlike through the world, which is itself so slight and unreal"—but radical action waits to be inspired by challenges to the "intellect," by "music" or by "poetry."

In "New England Reformers" Emerson articulates his Transcendentalist vision of universal reform that he would return to again and again. He affirms that rather than "some single improvement," what society needs is "a total regeneration." This will happen only through individual self-development and education. Reform, in this sense, was completely antithetical to his Transcendentalist idealism, for the reformers inherently *mistrust* human nature while Transcendentalism posits man as divine.

FURTHER READING

Garvey, T. Gregory, ed. *The Emerson Dilemma: Essays on Emerson and Social Reform.* Athens: University of Georgia Press, 2000.

"Nominalist and Realist" (1841)

The essay "Nominalist and Realist" was published in *ESSAYS: SECOND SERIES* (1844) and constitutes a straightforward application of Emerson's polarity logic, which he spelled out in the earlier essay "COMPENSATION" (1841). In this essay of 1844, the "Nominalist" stands for the person who champions the particularities of experience. The term "nominalism" already had a distinguished provenance in the writings of British empiricists, such as JOHN LOCKE, which Emerson is here contesting. To the nominalists, abstract concepts were only "general names, which have no basis in reality." Nominalists therefore rejected the PLATONIC, Aristotelian, and Scholastic traditions that found reality in universals; they embraced instead the hard facts of empiricism.

But in an unorthodox move of his own, Emerson co-opts the word "Realist" to stand for the opposite pole—for belief in what is general or universal as the source of knowledge. He provided the theoretical underpinnings for this in his contemporaneous doctrines of "The OVER-SOUL" and "SPIRITUAL LAWS," in the universal archetypes expressed by the classics of "HISTORY," and, at the basis of all these formulations, in his belief in the ever-ascending nature of the soul toward those universals.

SYNOPSIS

Emerson begins the essay by insisting: "I cannot often enough say, that a man is only a relative and representative nature." Each man is "a hint of the truth," but not yet the whole truth, which he only "inevitably suggests to us." A man rarely lives up to the "thought" or idea, rarely reaches his potential. The same is true of society, of political parties, and even of genius: "Our exaggeration of all fine characters arises from the fact, that we identify each in turn with the soul." We look for the universal in the individual but, in fact, the universal is transcendent: "there are no such men as we fable; no Jesus, or Pericles, nor Caesar, nor Angelo, nor Washington, such as we have made. . . . There is none without his foible. I verily believe if an angel should come to chant the chorus of the moral law, he would eat too much gingerbread, or take liberties with private letters, or do some precious atrocity." The ideal is rarely realized in the actual, for there is always contingency, accidents, the complication of circumstances and of human nature. This indictment applies not only to great men or public men but also to persons "who protect themselves by solitude, by courtesy, by satire, or by an acid worldly manner." These personalities are more like "concealing" aspects of their character and "want either love or self-reliance." We have "two sets of faculties, the particular and the catholic," and "thus we are very sensible" of the difference between the ideal (the "atmospheric influence" of humanity as a whole) and the real or possible (the "measurable properties"). He gives the example of the contradiction between the genius of a nation and its individual inhabitants: "England, strong, punctual, practical, well-spoken England, I should not find, if I should go to the island to seek it . . . not anywhere the Englishman who made the good speeches, combined the accurate engines, and did the bold and nervous deeds." The situation is even worse in America, where, "from the intellectual quickness of the race, the genius of the country is more splendid in its promise, and more slight in its performance." Given these contradictions and the choice between the ideal and the actual, Emerson urges, "Let us go for the universals"—these are the "essences" or "poetry" of life, balancing out "our proclivity to details."

By Emerson's own logic of compensation, however, this aspect of the human situation has its complementary upside; experience will "teach us a little reserve, and to dissuade a too sudden surrender to the brilliant qualities of persons." On the "Realist" side of the equation, then, "General ideas are essences. They are our gods: they round and ennoble the most partial and sordid way of living." This is seen in great "literature," which always seems to be "newly written," that is, conveying something universal hidden in the details. Likewise with "the day-laborer," who is looked down upon as the most mundane in society, but who, in fact, "is saturated with the laws of the world": "His measures are the hours, morning and night, solstice and equinox, geometry, astronomy, and all the lovely accidents of nature play through his mind." Labor, money, property, "laws and usages," these are general "essences" as well as public forms of life. As with literature, the market, and the assembly, all public business operates according to universal laws, "as if one man had made it all." The same wonder at the universal over the particular, Emerson confesses, he personally experienced in a recent performance of Handel's *Messiah:* "The genius of nature" was revealed through the music, despite "the littleness and incapableness of the performers."

Emerson's pendulum swings again toward the particulars of life, noting that, while it is true that "life will be simpler when we live at the centre, and flout the surfaces," the truth is that nature requires we live in and deal with the details of the everyday.

While people sometimes seem "like grass and trees, and it needs an effort to treat them as individuals," this is "rebellion" against nature: "Nature will not be Buddhist: she resents generalizing, and insults the philosopher in every moment with a million fresh particulars." Nature "will not remain orbed in a thought, but rushes into persons." Nature adds "personality" to the particularities of each person, and from many personalities creates a whole; ultimately, "the sanity of society is a balance of a thousand insanities."

Thus nature—"our economical mother"—distributes "genius and habit of mind" throughout society and, by "gathering up into some man every property in the universe," distributes her "power." She works through a constant recycling or recirculation of this power, so that "the rotation which whirls every leaf and pebble to the meridian, reaches to every gift of man, and we all take turns at the top."

Thus also on the "Nominalist" side is nature's debate within herself, for while nature "abhors mannerisms," it is also true that "it is so much easier to do what one has done before, than to do a new thing." The result is constant change or transformation in nature, for she "has set her heart on breaking up all styles and tricks." This counterbalances the human impulse to repetition as well, for "Each man, too, is a tyrant in tendency, because he would impose his ideas on others." This also explains "the immense benefit of party in politics." Without that antagonism, we would not be made aware of the "faults of character" in a politician: "Since we are all so stupid, what benefit that there should be two stupidities!" Parties, then, prevent "the consolidation of all men into a few men." We require "great genius" as stand-ins or "representatives" for our own potential and individual powers, not merely for the purpose of collecting "one star more in our constellation . . . one tree more in our grove." No individual contains the all (Emerson's warning against hero-worship): "If John was perfect, why are you and I alive?"

Here Emerson's comprehensive principle of the inexhaustible and spontaneous variety in nature surfaces to powerful effect as a celebration of the individual. "Why not a new man?" he inquires. Rather than putting old labels on new ideas, "Let it be a new way of living. Why have only two or three ways of life, and not thousands? Every man is wanted, and no man is wanted much." By understanding and appreciating the particulars, we will see the universals emerge: "What is best in each kind is an index of what should be the average of that thing." We hold too quickly and long to our ideas, not acknowledging that "there are other moods," and that our language is insufficient to reveal the depths of every person's mind. So it is that we seem "sincere" in "saying all that lies in the mind, and yet go away feeling that all is yet unsaid, from the incapacity of the parties to know each other, although they use the same words!" Nature designed this competition between thought and action.

CRITICAL COMMENTARY

In this essay Emerson strives for a balance in communicating how life is lived at the intersection of the two poles of individuality and universality: "Things are, and are not, at the same time. . . . All the universe over, there is but one thing, this old Two-Face, creator-creature, mind-matter, right-wrong, of which any proposition may be affirmed or denied." He presents in this essay the assertion that "every man" is both a "partialist" and a "universalist," and that life is one long effort to work out this "universal problem." Toward the end of the essay, Emerson sums up the Janus-faced predicament of the human soul as follows: "The end and the means, the gamester and the game,—life is made up of the intermixture and reaction of these two amicable powers. . . . We must reconcile the contradictions as we can." Emerson here asserts a philosophy of balancing compensations, of the parity between the particular and the general modes of consciousness. This he sets within his more general framework of an over-soul, of the wholeness of reality.

Emerson's "The TRANSCENDENTALIST" (1843) was a clear precedent for this essay. In it he wrote: "What is popularly called Transcendentalism among us, is Idealism; Idealism as it appears in 1842. As thinkers, mankind has ever been divided into two sects, Materialists and Idealists; the first class founding on experience, the second on consciousness; the first class beginning to think from the data of the senses, the second class perceive that the senses are not final." He goes on to prioritize the latter, when he explains: "These two modes of thinking are both natural, but the Idealist contends that his way of thinking is in higher nature." The Transcendentalist perspective is higher for resolving oppositions within an ultimate unity, identified as a "mind" or "spirit." In the same essay he calls this the "central Unity" of nature that "betrays its source in Universal Spirit."

In other contexts such as "The Over-Soul," "History," and "Spiritual Laws" (all of *ESSAYS: FIRST SERIES*), and "NATURE" (1844) and "The METHOD OF NATURE," Emerson was more strongly antinominalist. He rejected an exclusively empiricist or sensualist theory of human experience associated with the British philosophical tradition in authors such as Hobbes, Locke, Berkeley, and Hume. Among the American academic philosophers after Emerson, WILLIAM JAMES carried on this nominalist strain, while CHARLES SANDERS PEIRCE followed Emerson in rejecting it in favor of the endless ramifications and amplifications of nature and human intelligence.

In "Nominalist and Realist," Emerson argues that if we cannot always make "voluntary and conscious steps in the admirable science of universals," though there is no end of the "horizons" and "circumferences" of the soul, let us at least "see the parts wisely, and infer the genius of nature from the best particulars with a becoming charity." EMILY DICKINSON followed Emerson in featuring both the "circumference" and the precious particularities of her experience. WALT WHITMAN also followed Emerson's suit in these twin respects.

Emerson's poetry became a showcase of this central metaphysical polarity, as, for example, in "The SPHINX," "EACH AND ALL," "The WORLD-SOUL," "WOODNOTES," "MONADNOC," and "BRAHMA." Ultimately, Emerson teaches us that we have to learn to ride the alternating currents of our own moods and opinions, so as to win a larger sincerity with ourselves, with others, and the universe. Human existence itself calls for recognition of the relationship between the particular and the universal in the nature of things.

David A. Dilworth

"Ode, Inscribed to W. H. Channing" (1847)

Emerson's "Ode, Inscribed to W. H. Channing" was included in *POEMS* (1847), his first published collection of poetry. Like many of Emerson's poems, it began in his journal, in this case in passages dating as early as 1838. The poem was completed in 1846 as an address to abolitionist WILLIAM HENRY CHANNING on the issue of whether the North should separate from the slaveholding states of the South, an idea Emerson did not support. Many abolitionists were outraged over the Mexican War and the annexation of Texas by the United States, which would guarantee the spread of slavery into Western areas, an issue which prompted HENRY DAVID THOREAU to refuse to pay a poll tax, resulting in one night in jail and the inspiration for the essay on "Civil Disobedience" (1849).

"Ode, Inscribed to W. H. Channing" was one of several poems, including the later pieces on "FREEDOM" and "VOLUNTARIES," in which Emerson dealt directly with the questions of slavery, ABOLITIONISM, and civil war. Opposed to slavery in principle, Emerson feared the loss of personal power and influence for those who gave themselves over to reform organizations and political platforms. After the poem was written, however, Emerson was drawn more directly into the public slavery debate, and in the 1850s, he delivered a series of ever more forceful statements against slavery, such as the "FUGITIVE SLAVE LAW ADDRESS" (1851) and "AMERICAN SLAVERY" (1855).

CRITICAL COMMENTARY

The poem opens with Emerson's reluctance to leave his "buried thought" and enter into the political debate over slavery. He is reluctant to listen to either "the priest's cant, / Or statesman's rant," the church or the government, which were both under attack by radical abolitionists. Emerson finds politics all "trick," but he is torn because "the angry muse" will not let him ignore the issue.

In the third and fourth stanzas, the poet is impatient with Americans who see their growth and expansion as divine destiny, ignoring the fact that they win by wielding the "rifle" and "knife" against Mexico. Ill-gotten gains make a mockery of our high ideals. Northerners who "praise the freedom-loving mountaineer" and give our discoveries Indian names (the river "Contoocook!" and mountains of "Agiochook!") are nothing more than "jackals of the Negro-holder," supporting the spread of slavery.

The Contoocook River and Agiochook Mountains were both located in New Hampshire and, in the fifth stanza, Emerson makes a third reference to "the God who made New Hampshire." New Hampshire was significant in slavery politics of the 1840s as the home state of Daniel Webster (the Massachusetts senator who was criticized in 1850 for support of the Fugitive Slave Law) and because of the proslavery Democratic Party vote of New Hampshire in the 1844 presidential election (also seen as a betrayal of New England). In the poem, New Hampshire is "the lofty land" peopled "with little men." New Englanders are betraying their promise now nothing more than "small bat and wren," they are tiny creatures who make their homes in the mighty "oak" of America. The United States could come to war—"earth-fire cleave / The upheaved land, and bury the folk"—and "The southern crocodile would grieve"; that is, the politicians would cry fake or "crocodile" tears, showing no concern for the people who work the land. Using the language of death and burial, Emerson condemns our national ideals—"Virtue," "Right," and "Freedom" are only "Funeral Eloquence," words that are "praised, but hid" beneath "the coffin-lid."

In the seventh stanza he asks what good it would do to separate "The northland from the south? . . . / "Wherefore? to what good end?" He notes that, even with separation from the South, "Boston Bay and Bunker Hill / Would serve things still"; that is, that the commercial and financial centers of the Northeast would remain and the values of society would be the same. The reference to these proud sites of New England's revolutionary political history serves as another reminder that the North is also implicated in—and has an interest in—the slave system. Most people attend only to that which is important to their daily lives: "The horseman serves the horse, / . . . The merchant serves the purse, / . . . 'Tis the day of the chattel, / Web to weave, and corn to grind." But in all of this busy work we fail to see the larger problem, that our greed controls us: "Things are in the saddle, / And ride mankind."

In the ninth stanza Emerson makes perhaps one of his strongest statements on the workings of the U.S. economic and political system. He acknowledges that the government exists primarily to protect property, but that humans must answer to a higher law: "There are two laws discrete / Not reconciled,— / Law for man, and law for thing." This is a reference to the Constitution, which protects slaves as private property but makes no provisions for slaves as human beings. This is nothing less than a challenge to the Constitution itself, which puts Emerson on the side of radical abolitionists, who, as William Lloyd Garrison put it, would not be bound by the government's "covenant with death." Of the two laws, the "law for thing" is necessary for the economic and political functioning of society: it "builds town and fleet." But this law "doth the man unking," doing harm to our souls, our humanity.

Emerson is not against American expansion and growth: "'Tis fit the forest fall, / The steep be graded, / The mountain tunnelled, / . . . The orchard planted, / The steamer built." He celebrates this progress, including westward expansion ("The prairie granted"), a position he stated forcefully in "The YOUNG AMERICAN." But this progress cannot be made without regard for our own humanity: "Live for friendship, live for love." Our motivations and actions must be for "truth's and harmony's" sake, and the government will make laws accordingly: "The state may follow how it can." This is Emerson's approach to reform throughout his writings—that people must change before the laws can change.

In the 12th stanza he explains that when he speaks of the law of humanity or law of nature, he is not seeking a literal and direct relationship with nature. He does not call the "shopman to my sounding woods" or "the unwilling senator" to "ask votes of thrushes in the solitudes." He acknowledges "Every *one to his chosen work,*" and he is not asking that the laborer or the politician become philosophers. Different roles are all needed in society, and yet the laws that govern our actions are the same: "Wise and sure the issues are." It is only "foolish hands" that "mix and mar" the issues, risking our humanity in the process. There is a higher power, an "over-god" (a reference to his own idea expressed in "The OVER-SOUL") "who marries Right to Might." This higher force, this higher law, ultimately determines our human fate, not politicians. It is "The over-god, / Who marries Right to Might, / Who peoples, unpeoples,— / . . . who exterminates / Races by stronger races, / Black by white faces."

Nature is neither arbitrary nor cruel, and all is done in the name of progress for the human race; nature "Knows to bring honey / Out of the lion," a biblical reference to the story of Samson extracting honey out of the body of the lion he killed. Having seemingly justified the superiority of the white race as nature's law, Emerson explains that this does not preclude nature's plan to end slavery and to bring something better for humanity out of its destruction. Presaging a civil war (which is still more than a decade away from the publication of this poem), Emerson's final stanza speaks of this necessary destruction of society: The "last noble is ruined," the "last poet mute." And yet, from the ruins rises new hope, as some "for freedom strike and stand" and "the astonished Muse finds thousands at her side."

"Ode Sung in the Town Hall, Concord, July 4, 1857" (1857)

Emerson's 1857 "Ode" was written to be sung in the Town Hall in CONCORD, MASSACHUSETTS, specifically at a breakfast held on July 4 to raise money for improvements to the new cemetery at Sleepy Hollow. Emerson's poem deals with ABOLITIONISM, a movement in which he was active but about which he did not readily write. EDWARD WALDO EMERSON writes, "Mr. Emerson was reluctant to mount Pegasus to war against the enemies of freedom; but when it required him . . . to become a slave-hunter, he was stirred to plead her cause in verse." This poem, along with "BOSTON HYMN" and "ODE, INSCRIBED TO W. H. CHANNING," is an example of Emerson's abolitionist verse. The poem was published in *MAY-DAY AND OTHER PIECES* (1867) and reprinted in the Centenary Edition of Emerson's *Complete Works* (1903–04).

CRITICAL COMMENTARY

In Emerson's time, an ode was a poem of considerable length and intended to be sung, usually on the occasion of a significant state or royal ceremony. Emerson's "Ode," then, fits this description. It is an occasional poem and is composed in 10 hymn-form stanzas.

The poem describes not the Declaration of Independence, as we might expect given that it was written for the July 4 holiday, but the effect of the declaration. The poem is another kind of "declaration," of the *intent* of the Declaration of Independence. The poem was written in 1857, before the Civil War; the lines "Go put your creed into your deed / nor speak with double tongue" address the country as a whole, as a reminder to live the letter and spirit of the original Declaration of Independence.

We may read "He" in line 9 as God, but also as God-in-man. "He" made men free, and as the last stanza states:

> For He that worketh high and wise,
> Nor pauses in his plan,
> Will take the sun out of the skies
> Ere freedom out of man.

As is typical of Emerson's verse, the last stanza resolves the duality of God and God-in-man. God may have made man free, but it is up to us to preserve, and defend, that freedom.

Bill Scalia

"Ode to Beauty" (1843)

"Ode to Beauty" was first printed in the *DIAL* in October 1843, although Emerson penned some of its lines in his journal as early as 1836. He revised and added lines to the version collected in *POEMS* (1847) and then *SELECTED POEMS* (1876). Two of the added lines were also used as a motto to "The POET," published in *ESSAYS: SECOND SERIES* (1844). The theme of beauty loomed prominently in his inaugural work *NATURE* (1836) and continued throughout his career, for example in "The OVER-SOUL" (1841), "PLATO; OR, THE PHILOSOPHER" (1850), "BEAUTY" (1860), and "POETRY AND IMAGINATION" and "PERSIAN POETRY" (both in *LETTERS AND SOCIAL AIMS* [1876]). The early poem, "Ode to Beauty," in fact expresses a distinctly PLATONIC and NEOPLATONIC sense of beauty that pervaded much of his prose and poetic writing.

CRITICAL COMMENTARY

Expressed as a direct address "to Beauty," the poem features Emerson's Transcendental paradox that the beautiful is ever present and yet ever receding. Emerson traces beauty in nature, in human art, and in other deceptive forms, all of these working "in close conspiracy" to fill his heart and soul but elude his grasp. Beauty's elusive lure is pure and timeless: "Thou intimate stranger, / Thou latest and first!" he declares—reminiscent of St. Augustine's plaint in *The Confessions:* "Late have I loved Thee, O thou Beauty ever old and ever new!" Emerson complains of his thrall to beauty, "Sweet tyrant of all!" He laments that beauty provides only "false waters of thirst," leaving him in the condition that "New-born, we are melting / Into nature again." Beauty is a "lavish, lavish promiser," guilty of a "million painted forms." It colors and warms the various forms and changes within nature, "the frailest leaf, the mossy bark, / The acorn's cup, the rainbow's arc, / The swinging spider's silver line, / The ruby of the drop of wine, / The shining pebble of the pond." All these are only manifestations of beauty's "momentary play." The ubiquity of beauty permeates the sun and the sea, engulfing Emerson, drawing him on and yet flying ahead, so that paradoxically "As Fate refuses / To me the heart Fate for me choses." His "opulent soul" is "mingled from the generous whole," though in the end he is ever "self-betrayed."

Here Emerson turns to great works of human art (some of them oblique references to gifts received from MARGARET FULLER). He turns "the proud portfolios / Which hold the grand designs / Of Salvator, of Guercino, and Piranesi's lines." As well, he hears the lofty paeans of the masters of musical composition "who heard the starry music / And recount the numbers well," and the songs of the "Olympian bards who sung / Divine Ideas below, / Which always find us young, / And always keep us so." These, too, are the fleeting appearances of beauty "like the lightning through the storm." But always, it remains "somewhat not to be possessed, / Somewhat not to be caressed," an "eternal fugitive," "hovering over all that lives."

The poet is engrossed by beauty. It pursues him even in dreams. He dares not die "lest there I find the same deceiver / And be the sport of Fate forever." He ends with the plea: "Dread Power, but dear! If God thou be, Unmake me quite, or give thyself to me!" From beginning to end, the "Ode to Beauty" is Emerson's plaintive plea to beauty for access to its permanent but evanescent presence, a phenomenon examined in other poems as well, such as "The RHODORA" (1839) and "BEAUTY" (1867).

David A. Dilworth

"Old Age" (1870)

This essay, dating from a lecture in 1861, first appeared in the *ATLANTIC MONTHLY* of January 1862, before its publication in *SOCIETY AND SOLITUDE* (1870). "TERMINUS," a poem dating from the mid-1840s (and Emerson's early 40s), finalized in the 1850s, and first published in 1867 in *MAY-DAY AND OTHER PIECES*, shows Emerson already concerned with the issues of aging and mortality. "Old Age" is also intrinsically linked to "WORSHIP" of *The CONDUCT OF LIFE* (1860) and to "Immortality" of *LETTERS AND SOCIAL AIMS* (1876), both essays examining the theme of accumulated spiritual worth free of the egotism of self-centered religious cravings.

SYNOPSIS

Emerson begins this essay with a passing reference to Cicero's *De Senectute.* Like his reference to the title of Hesiod's ancient poem for his essay "WORKS AND DAYS," he characteristically says that the classic text does not exhaust the subject but "rather invites the attempt to add traits to the picture from our broad modern life." He folds this into the present consideration of old age in the form of analogy to the uniforms of military men, which Wellington once satirized as "masks . . . to hide cowards." "A like deception," Emerson muses, he has often detected "in the cloth shoe, wadded pelisse, wig, spectacles, and padded chair of Age." "Nature," as well, "lends herself to these illusions," adding "dim sight, deafness, cracked voice, snowy hair, short memory and sleep." But "these also are masks, and all is not Age that wears them." Signs of premature age can deceive as to a person's intellectual maturity: "Nature is full of freaks, and now puts an old head on young shoulders, and then a young heart beating under fourscore winters."

Ralph Waldo Emerson in old age *(Library of Congress)*

These outward signs of age, then, are "counterfeit and ridiculous," Emerson insists, and do not speak for "the essence of age," which is intellect and power. It is "time" that is "the seat of illusion," for the active mind "stretches an hour to a century and dwarfs an age to an hour." Time is a construct of social life, for "as long as one is alone by himself, he is not sensible of the inroads of time." For the "well-spent" life, the losses of age are only "what it can well spare—muscular strength, organic instincts, gross bulk, and works that belongs to these." Age or time does not change "the central wisdom, which was old in infancy, is young in fourscore years, and, dropping off obstructions, leaves the mind purified and wise." Indeed, without "the reflection of ourselves in the eyes of young people, we could not know that the century-clock had struck seventy instead of twenty." Society's view of age "is low, melancholy, and skeptical," considering only "sensuous experience." The verdict of youth is that "age is comely" only in certain situations, such as "in churches, in chairs of state and ceremony, in council-chambers, in courts of justice and historical societies." Age is also "becoming in the country" but not "in the rush and uproar of Broadway."

Emerson employs his logic of compensation in nature to reflect that "the cynical creed or lampoon of the market is refuted by the universal prayer for long life, which is the verdict of Nature and justified by all history." While there are examples of young men having achieved grand works—as in Alexander, Raphael, Shakespeare, Pascal, Burns, and Byron—"these are rare exceptions" to the rule that "Nature, in the main, vindicates her law." It is the law that "skill to do comes of doing; knowledge comes by eyes always open, and working hands; and there is no knowledge that is not power." "Almost all the good workmen," he concludes, "live long."

From these positive premises Emerson deduces certain benefits of age. The first of these is that it "has weathered the perilous capes and shoals in the sea whereon we sail, and the chief evil of life is taken away in removing the grounds of fear." Therefore, old age is nature's way of providing a reward in relief from life's turbulences. The "young animal" is presented with an "oversupply, of his wants" and desires; for example, "To insure the existence of the race, she reinforces the sexual instinct, at the risk of disorder, grief and pain." In later life, the "rabble of passions" that make youth "quite too tender, quite too hungry and irritable," is "replaced by nobler resources" and "grander motives."

Another laurel of age is the acquisition of insight into the vanity of worldly success. The mature person has met all the requirements of performance and can now rest on a fund of genuine accomplishments: "Every one is sensible of this cumulative advantage in living. All the good days behind him are sponsors, who speak for him when he is silent, pay for him when he has no money, introduce him where he has no letters, and work for him when he sleeps." Meanwhile, "The youth suffers not only from ungratified desires, but from powers untried and from a picture of a career which has as yet no outward reality." "What to the youth is only a guess or a hope," is enjoyed in later years as "results and morals." Consequently, the accomplished person is "serene," not feeling himself "pinched and wronged, but whose condition, in particular and in general, allows the utterance of his mind."

Yet another benefit of age is that "it sets its house in order, and finishes its works, which to every artist is a supreme pleasure." The condition of youth is one of "excess of sensibility, before which every object glitters and attracts." But time and "our instincts" make it so that we save up "innumerable experiences, that are yet of no visible value, and which we may keep for twice seven years before they shall be wanted." The day comes "when the hidden author of our story is found; when the brave speech returns straight to the hero who said it; when the admirable verse finds the poet to whom it belongs"; and, best of all, "when the lonely thought, which seemed so wise, yet half-wise, half-thought, because it cast no light abroad, is suddenly matched in our mind by its twin, by its sequence, or next related analogy; which gives it instantly radiating power, and justifies the superstitious instinct with which we have hoarded it."

The life of JOHANN WOLFGANG VON GOETHE, Emerson notes here, is an example of the completion of a life of discovery (both poetic and scientific) to the highest point: "Many of his works hung on the easel from youth to age, and received a stroke in every month or year. A literary astrologer, he never applied himself to any task but at the happy moment when all the stars consented." Goethe's genius was "patient," and he experienced the reward "which old men take in completing their secular affairs, rounding their estates, clearing their titles, reducing tangled interests to order, reconciling enmities and leaving all in the best posture for the future." There should be, Emerson adds, such "a proportion between the designs of a man and the length of his life."

As for immortality, "no whisper comes to us from the other side." Our immortality comes from "the moral sentiment" and "the working of intellect." Emerson concludes that "I have heard that whoever loves is in no condition old."

CRITICAL COMMENTARY

With these words Emerson's essay goes far beyond Cicero's disquisition on old age. As the final essay of *Society and Solitude*, Emerson's thoughts in "Old Age" resonate with the similar affirmations of the dignity of human life and destiny in "Worship" (1860) and in "Immortality" (1876). These are all the harvest of the spiritual wine for which Emerson longed for in the poem "BACCHUS" (1846). As well, these writings echo other expressions of his mature thinking, for example, in "ILLUSIONS" (1860) and "Works and Days" (1870), namely, reflection on moral integrity and spiritual attainment in light of "the illusions which cling to the element of time, and in which Nature delights." "Works and Days" spoke also of the "hypocritic," that is, masquerading, and fleeting days, a concept also used in the 1867 poem "DAYS."

"Old Age" develops the positive side of this coin. It focuses on possibilities of the soul's authentic achievements in this life, the enjoyment of its natural harvest in its golden years, in contrast with the undistinguished strivings of youth. Like several other essays (such as "PLATO; OR, THE PHILOSOPHER" and "GOETHE; OR, THE WRITER" from *REPRESENTATIVE MEN*), "Old Age" is transparently self-referential, written in the winter of Emerson's life when his physical powers were in natural decline though his philosophical mind remained as active as ever.

David A. Dilworth

"The Over-Soul" (1841)

The "Over-Soul" was one of Emerson's most celebrated essays, and the idea of an over-soul became the central symbol of American Transcendentalism. Published in *ESSAYS: FIRST SERIES* in 1841, the phrase encapsulated Emerson's youthful spiritual exuberance in this idea of an all-encompassing, as well as intimately indwelling, spirit of the universe. Later in his career—in such essays as "EXPERIENCE," "FATE," and "ILLUSIONS," as well as in many of his poems—he produced nuanced accounts of human life as at the intersection of two metaphysical dimensions, the "mid-point" between the realm of physical reality and the ideal, both overseen by the over-soul.

The basic thrust of "The Over-Soul" is to express the nature of a universal presence of identity, and for this Emerson drew upon several traditions. He seems to have taken the phrase from the Hindu concept of "Paramatma," translated as the "Supreme Soul" or "Supreme Spirit." But the over-soul is at once the all-embracing Law or Logos of Heraclitus, the idea of the good and the beautiful in Plato (see PLATONISM), the one and good beyond being in Plotinus (see NEOPLATONISM), the Tao of Taoism, the elemental Buddha of Eastern traditions, the omnipresent Judeo-Christian god, and the indwelling presence described by 18th-century mystic EMANUEL SWEDENBORG and Emerson's contemporary, German philosopher FRIEDRICH SCHELLING. Emerson rejects any one definition or tradition and accomplishes a synthesis of these timeless queries, while acknowledging that the question of the soul is so great as to never be fully resolved: "The philosophy of six thousand years has not searched the chambers and magazines of the soul."

The reader will find here Emerson's novel articulation of a full range of themes that appeared throughout his later writings. The paradoxical transcendence and yet immanence of the divine presence, the universe as the true and the beautiful, nature's moral correspondences, the intersection of time and eternity, the revelations of geniuses and prophets, the expanding circles of moral character, and the earthly attachments of our secular human consciousness are only some such themes that appear together here.

SYNOPSIS

The essay "The Over-Soul" straightforwardly begins by referring to the higher reality experienced in moments of spiritual intuition: "Our faith comes in moments; our vice is habitual. Yet there is a depth in those brief moments which constrains us to ascribe more reality to them than to all other experiences." The over-soul accounts for this felt sense of depth in our better moments: "I am constrained every moment to acknowledge a higher origin for events than the will I call mine."

All our aspirations for genuine truth and value have their ground in this encompassing wholeness: "The Supreme Critic on the errors of the past and the present, and the only prophet of that which must be, is that great nature in which we rest as the earth lies in the soft arms of the atmosphere, that Unity, that Over-Soul, within which every man's particular being is contained and made one with all other; that common heart." Empirically considered, we live our lives as a succession of events, divided into distinct parts or episodes. Meantime, within man is "the soul of the whole; the wise science; the universal beauty to which every part and particle is equally related; the eternal ONE."

Emerson's over-soul is both a receptive and a responsive power of, and to, our intuitive consciousness: "From within or from behind, a light shines through us upon things and makes us aware that we are nothing, but the light is all. A man is the façade of a temple wherein all wisdom and all good abide. . . . When it breathes through his intellect, it is genius; when it breathes through his will, it is virtue; when it flows through his affections, it is love."

The human soul, as Plotinus and the Eastern mystics also taught Emerson, drifts downward into the realms of sensuous experience or ascends upward into higher consciousness. Emerson's over-soul is the soul's "circle of circles" and its "pure nature," by which its higher aspirations of intellect, will, and affection are realized. Its presence thus allows the human soul to break through the limitations of earthly experience to realize its true nature in spiritual unity: "The soul circumscribes us on every hand. As I have said, it contradicts all experience. In like manner it abolishes time and space." He finds hope in this thought, which keeps us "young": "Some thoughts always find us young, and keep us so. Such a thought is the love of the universal and eternal beauty."

In this divine presence, "We come into a feeling of longevity. See how the deep divine thought reduces centuries and millenniums, and makes itself present through all ages." The soul exists outside of history, then, having no specific dates, nor persons: "The soul knows only the soul; the web of events is the flowing robe in which she is clothed." Instead, the encompassing and immanent over-soul is the "the law of growth," and thus of the human soul's own growth and change: "The soul's advances are not made by gradation . . . rather by ascension of state." Through the growth of the human soul or mind, "we see causes, and anticipate the universe, which is but a slow effect."

Emerson's over-soul is thus the universe's abiding wholeness, which manifests itself in individual acts of intuition and in the spontaneity of life and consciousness. But simultaneously it is the larger experience of man, which discovers "the identical nature appearing through all. Persons themselves acquaint us with the impersonal. . . . The third party or common nature is not social; it is impersonal; is God."

Although "there is a certain wisdom of humanity which is common to the greatest men with the lowest," the poets and prophets are the "best minds, who love truth for its own sake. They accept it thankfully everywhere, and do not label or stamp it with any man's name." From here Emerson returns once again to his basic binary of intuition versus tuition, or education, the latter being the primary source of knowledge for the pragmatic masses. While the soul has its true nature in unison with the over-soul, it, too, often plunges downward (as Plotinus said) into its lesser identities in the mundane world of everyday life.

The opposite of the soul's downward drift into the pragmatic, socioeconomic realm of time and space is the revelation gained through intuition. However fleeting, such intuition gives us glimpses into the embracing unity of the divine: "We distinguish the announcements of the soul, its manifestations of its own nature, by the term *Revelation*. These are always attended by the emotion of the sublime, whose communication is an influx of the divine mind into our mind." It thus happens that "by the necessity of our constitution a certain enthusiasm attends the individual's consciousness of that divine presence. The character and duration of this enthusiasm vary with the state of the individual, from an ecstasy and trance and prophetic inspiration,—which is its rarer appearance,—to the faintest glow of virtuous emotion, with which form it warms, like our household fires, all the families and associations of men, and makes society possible." The passage goes on to describe examples of revelation in various religious communities of his own time and, perhaps most importantly for Emerson, in the spiritual experience of Emanuel Swedenborg. He accepts the importance of enthusiasm and revelation in these accounts, while eschewing the organizational structures, rituals, and rules built up around them.

Emerson's new religious "doctrine" of the over-soul therefore presents the Transcendentalist emphasis on intuition as distinguished from the formalistic "understanding" of the established churches: "Revelation is the disclosure of the soul. The popular notion of a revelation is that it is a telling of fortunes. In past oracles of the soul the understanding seeks to find answers to sensual questions." There follows the famous passage in which Emerson says that Jesus never taught the immortality of the soul: "The moment the doctrine of the immortality is separately taught, man is already fallen. In the flowing of love, in the adoration of humility, there is no question of continuance. No inspired man ever asks this question or condescends to these evidences. For the soul is true to itself; and the man in whom it is shed abroad cannot wander from the present, which is infinite, to a future which would be finite." He adds, in condemnation of conservative church dogmas: "These questions which we lust to ask about the future are a confession of sin."

As noted above, it is the prophets and poets who are most open to moments of revelatory experience. Conversely, it is the over-soul that inspires the geniuses. This concept of the *poetic* genius itself has a *religious* connotation: "But genius is religious. It is a larger imbibing of the common heart. It is not anomalous, but more like and not less like other men. There is in all great poets a wisdom of humanity which is superior to any talents they exercise." The minds and hearts of the geniuses are inlets for our collective sense of higher graces flowing through civilization. Still, every person has his own unique resources as a potential mystic, prophet, or poet, if he only trusts his intuition: "When we have broken our god of tradition and ceased from our god of rhetoric, then may God fire the heart with his presence. . . . He has not the conviction, but the sight, that the best is the true, and may in that thought easily dismiss all particular uncertainties and fears, and adjourn to the sure revelation of time the solution of his private riddles." This is the core of Emerson's Transcendentalist ethics of self-reliance: "He must listen to himself, withdrawing himself from all the accents of other men's devotion." And this is the opposite of the established religions: "The faith that stands on authority is not faith. The reliance on authority measures the decline of religion, and the withdrawal of the soul."

In concluding the essay, Emerson sets the tone for his future essays: "Man will come to see that the world is a perennial miracle which the soul worketh, and be less astonished at particular wonders; he will learn that there is no profane history; that all history is sacred; that the universe is represented in an atom, in a moment of time. He will weave no longer a spotted life of shreds and patches, but he will live with a divine unity."

CRITICAL COMMENTARY

In the first paragraph of "The Over-Soul," Emerson admits, "I am constrained every moment to acknowledge a higher origin for events than the will I call mine." There is something beyond but inclusive of the self, a theme that ties together most of the pieces in *Essays: First Series*. "The Over-Soul" is in conversation not only with Emerson's earlier work on NATURE (1836) but also with all of the companion essays in *First Series*. The idea of the over-soul is the metaphysical correlate of Emerson's "transparent eyeball" announced in *Nature*: "I become a transparent eye-ball; I am nothing; I see all; the currents of the Universal Being circulate through me; I am part or particle of God."

In companion essays of 1841, such as "CIRCLES," he also inscribed a theory of the ever-expanding horizons of the visionary soul in its identity with a world-soul; and in "COMPENSATION" he boldly announced that there is "a crack in everything God has made," counterbalanced by his insistence here that there is no crack in the soul itself. Instead, the soul "returns" to its spiritual birthright through infinite expansions of its own essence of nature: "There is a deeper fact in the soul than compensation, to wit, its own nature. The soul is not a compensation, but a life. The soul *is*. . . . Essence, or God, is not a relation or a part, but the whole."

The connection between personal and universal wholeness inspired Emerson's optimistic idealism throughout his early essays and indeed the writings of his entire career. As he wrote in "SPIRITUAL LAWS" of the same volume: "A higher law than that of our will regulates events; our painful labors are unnecessary and fruitless; only in our easy, simple, spontaneous action are we strong." Or again: "God exists. There is a soul at the centre of nature and over the will of every man, so that none of us can wrong the universe." His thought is integrative rather than dualistic. Emerson's "divinity within" rejects (as he had explained in the "DIVINITY SCHOOL ADDRESS") the supernatural divinity of Christ and the immortality of the soul in the Christian understanding of a separation between the body and the soul, between earth and heaven, between nature and the divine; again, the main thrust of "Spiritual Laws" as well.

The soul's religious and poetic revelations reveal a unity between past, present, and future. Emerson drew out the implications of this position in the accompanying essay "HISTORY," the opening lines of which related the immortal works of genius to the contemporary mind: "There is one mind common to all individual men. Every man is an inlet to the same and to all of the same . . . Who hath access to this universal mind is a party to all that is or can be done, for this is the only and sovereign agent." Linked with these formulations is his insistence on the immediacy of nature, expressed as "the strong present tense" in the essay "Experience" (1844) and as a metaphysical reflection on nature in "SELF-RELIANCE": "These roses under my window make no reference to former roses or to better ones; they are for what they are; they exist with God to-day." Like the over-soul, nature, too, is the basis of intelligence, immortal, always present, and always available.

Emerson does not merely rework ancient philosophies, but he is intent on forming an original prose or poetic expression of his own central insights. His works (in this case, the various essays in *First Series*) are in conversation with each other, emphasizing the relationship between nature and an active moral character and development. Moral laws are revealed through the beauty and sublimity of nature and through a realization of the unity found in nature. "The Over-Soul" is thus one of Emerson's signature pieces, affirming a qualitative spiritual presence in the universe. This presence is sensed or mediated through a unified nature rather than through religious doctrine and belief in a humanlike God.

David A. Dilworth

Parnassus (1874)

Parnassus is a collection of nearly 700 poems by various authors selected by Emerson as those who interested and inspired him the most. The title refers to Mount Parnassus, which in Greek mythology was sacred to Apollo, the god of sun and music. Mount Parnassus was considered the center of the arts and the home of the Muses, the nine sisters responsible for inspiring genius in song and poetry. Conversely, *Le Parnasse contemporain*, 1866, was an anthology of poetry produced by French poets, contemporary to Emerson, who emphasized metrical form over emotion.

CRITICAL COMMENTARY

In the preface to *Parnassus*, Emerson explains his selection of poems by a combination of unknown and little-known, as well as famous, writers. The choices of poems are equally distributed among classic poetry and the "New Poetry" (a Transcendentalist concept of inspiration over form), but they are connected by those elements that Emerson considers essential. They must contain an "enormous force" in a few words, which convey great thoughts, a certain music, or a shared understanding. Emerson's selections, he states, are influenced by poems that contain history, sensibleness, and compelling language, or "magic of style." Some, he admits, are imperfect, but they all have truthfulness.

The poets chosen are those who know that the spiritual world is greater than the material, that "thought" is more important than form. The transcendent world is superior to the mundane, but all create "music." The music can be external or internal, it can be heard by all or strike a chord within the individual. Emerson defends some of the less sophisticated poems by noting that, "I know the peril of didactics to kill poetry." Poetry should not be dissected and analyzed, instead, it should be a shared experience. "There are two classes of poets," contends Emerson, namely, those who are poets through "education and practice," who are respected, and "poets by nature," who are loved. In the first category, Emerson includes several famous authors, but in the beloved group, the poets are determined by their attunement to Transcendentalism.

In his essay, "POETRY AND IMAGINATION" (published in *LETTERS AND SOCIAL AIMS* [1876]), Emerson discusses the genesis of poetry. Emerson considers poetry to be the "illustration of my thought," a personal and emotional response, a meaning made clear, a "spiritual truth." This "truth" is communicated from "God," the Supreme All, in "hints," which Emerson clarifies as "objects lying around us." "Genius," or the imagination, transfers and interprets the meaning of these symbols. "A happy symbol is a sort of evidence that your thought is just," Emerson explains, and "Poetry is the perpetual endeavor to express the spirit of the thing."

Emerson deals with the identification of the poet in the essay "The POET" (1844). The poet is "the man of Beauty." He uses the symbols of nature in his representation of all-man and awakens him to the unity of the universe. He is the interpreter of nature and can communicate nature's truth for he is "the Knower, the Doer and the Sayer. These stand respectively for the love of truth, for the love of good, and for the love of beauty." According to Emerson, poetry was written before time and is maintained through passionate and living thought. Thought and form are equal in time, but truth of thought existed before it was given form. "Genius" realizes truth and adds to it. The poet speaks "wildly," directed by nature, and he or she transcends through imagination into a higher plateau or ecstasy. However, much poetry, old and new, is conventional and ordinary, and only occasionally the poet offers truth in an original, beautiful manner. This is what charms Emerson.

In the preface to *Parnassus,* Chaucer garners considerable praise from Emerson; however, it is William Shakespeare who was Emerson's "representative" poet. In the essay, "SHAKSPEARE; OR, THE POET" of *REPRESENTATIVE MEN* (1850), Emerson defined "great men" as those who have imagination and are "meditative men of an intuitive habit of thought." According to Emerson, Shakespeare's power lay in his sympathy with humanity. He was able to transcend storytelling (Emerson notes that none of Shakespeare's tales were original) and to experiment wildly without bounds. In "Poetry and Imagination," Emerson says that Shakespeare observed human nature and used "whatever he found." Chaucer, too, is a "borrower," states Emerson, but all "originality is relative." The poet adds his genius and creates anew: "Translation gets its excellence by being translation on translation." Shakespeare is the superb poet because he communicates "to the Shakespeare in us." Our knowledge is intuitive but triggered by the poetic. A poet must have "cheerfulness, without which no man can be a poet,—for beauty is his aim." Great poets such as Shakespeare, Homer, Dante, and Chaucer knew the value of symbols as indicators of universal truth. Above all, the deciding factor for greatness is joy, for without cheerfulness beauty vanishes.

There are nearly 100 poems by Shakespeare in *Parnassus.* Some are sonnets but many are lines from his plays. Certainly Shakespeare is the epitome of poetic genius for Emerson, but what of the poets of the New World? In the preface to *Parnassus* Emerson comments on "the selections of American writers," which, due to the nation's young age, are "necessarily confined to the present (19th) century." Emerson's search for the "representative" poets of the new and evolving nation began in the 1830s. In "The AMERICAN SCHOLAR" (1837), Emerson emphasized the need for individualism, self-reliance and nurturing divine inspiration. More explicitly, in his essay, "Thoughts on Modern Literature," published in the October 1840 issue of the *DIAL,* Emerson pleaded for a poetry that reflects "steady, warm, autumnal light." It is not form, he suggests but "genius and suggestion of the whole" that identifies poetry. Modern literature should be varied, miscellaneous, and "breathe of the new morning" instead of exhaling the staleness of the "carcass of tradition." He urged adoption of the major tenets of Transcendentalism by calling for poetry that sees one nature in all things and relates the soul to the universe and infinity: ". . . small men introduce us always to themselves . . . [but] the great lead us to Nature."

The American selections of *Parnassus* are largely poems by writers associated with Transcendentalism and the *Dial,* notably, ELLERY CHANNING, HENRY DAVID THOREAU, Samuel Gray Ward, JONES VERY, and ELLEN STURGIS HOOPER. Indeed, the same issue of the *Dial* that includes "Thoughts on Modern Literature" contains an article by Emerson on "The New Poetry," which offered poems by Ellery Channing, nephew and namesake of the Reverend WILLIAM ELLERY CHANNING, as an example of the spirit of the new poetry. Emerson extols the virtue of producing poetry inspired by intuition rather than developed through contrived form: "These are proper Manuscript inspirations, honest, great, but crude. They have never been filled or decorated for the eye that studies surface."

Parnassus contains a combination of poems conceived by poets who are totally unheard of, little known poets, contemporaries of Emerson, and the infinitely famous. However, they are all linked according to Emerson by their imagination and music: "Poems may please by their talent and ingenuity; but, when they charm us, it is because they have this quality, for this is the union of nature with thought."

FURTHER READING

Myerson, Joel. *The New England Transcendentalists and the Dial: A History of the Magazine and Its Contributors*. Cranbury, N.J.: Associated University Press, 1980.

Barbara Downs Wojtusik

"Persian Poetry" (1876)

"Persian Poetry" was originally published in the ATLANTIC MONTHLY in 1858, but it was included later in the collection LETTERS AND SOCIAL AIMS (1876). The essay is an example of one of the pools of thought to which Emerson at times returned for fresh inspiration and renewed expressions of fundamental insights. It is the only theoretical expression of his interest in the Persian poets, but it clearly resonates with the poems, "BRAHMA," "HAMATREYA," "FROM THE PERSIAN OF HAFIZ," and "SAADI," as well as in numerous allusions in his prose writings. Inspired by his deep understanding of Hindu and Middle Eastern forms of spirituality, Emerson's writings reverberate with his own metaphysics of individual identity, which he saw as underlying cultural differences.

SYNOPSIS

Emerson begins by noting the introduction of writings of the "Persian Parnassus"—of Firdusi, Enweri, Nisami, Jelaleddin, Saadi, Hafiz, Jami, Ibn Jemin, Ferideddin Attar, and Omar Kyayyam—into the Western world of his day. These poets have broadened our field of vision, he says, but they also constitute a precious "record of intuitions which distribute facts, and are formulas which supersede all histories."

Eastern life and society, he adds, "stand in violent contrast with the multitudinous detail, the secular stability, and the vast average of comfort of Western nations." In contrast, "life in the East is fierce, short, hazardous, and in extremes. . . . The rich feed on fruits and game,—the poor, on a watermelon's peel. All or nothing is the genius of Oriental life." He suspects that the desert environment plays a crucial role: "The simoon, the mirage, the lion and the plague endanger it, and life hangs on the contingency of a skin of water more or less." Somehow, the temperament of the people agrees with this life in extremes, and "religion and poetry are all their civilization."

Emerson characterizes the religion of the East as teaching "an inexorable Destiny. It distinguishes only two days in each man's history,—his birthday, called *the Day of the Lot*, and the Day of Judgment." The only "virtues" in this system are "courage and absolute submission." On the other hand, under the crushing weight of this overarching religious determinism, "the Persians and the Arabs, with great leisure and few books, are exquisitely sensible to the pleasures of poetry." Citing the 19th-century Orientalist Austen Henry Layard, he appreciatively adds: "Poetry and flowers are the wine and spirits of the Arab: a couplet is equal to a bottle, and a rose to a dram, without the evil effect of either." He thus praises the themes and intuitions of the Persian mythologies, their poems and verses of sensual aestheticism such as the poem "by Adsched of Meru" on the "color, taste, and smell, smaragdus, sugar, and musk of a melon."

He then rates Hafiz, "the prince of Persian poets," as having mystical insights that "affords a deeper glance at Nature" than other poets. He appreciates the sheer variety, "audacity," and surprising intuition of his aestheticism: "See how the roses burn! / Bring wine to quench the fire! / Alas! The flames come up with us, / We perish with desire." "Harems and wine-shops," Emerson continues, are also sources of "observation" and inspiration for Hafiz, "whence to draw sometimes a deeper moral than regulated sober life affords."

Hafiz's poetry, he says, satisfies our hunger for poetry, for symbols of meaning. It opens the heart and the mind, while testifying to "his intellectual liberty" in the very midst of the pressures of "religions and politics." His poetry thus teaches Emerson's own central tenet that "the mind suffers no religion and no empire but its own." He tells his mistress that "not the dervish, or the monk, but the lover" has the true "spirit" of "the ascetic and the saint." It is "not their cowls and mummeries but her glances can impart to him the fire and virtue needful for such self-denial."

But again, neither erotic love nor wine debauch the poet: "Hafiz praises wine, roses, maidens, boys, birds, mornings, and music, to give vent to his immense hilarity and sympathy with every form of beauty and joy." He is the very model of Emerson's own Transcendentalist spirit: "It is the play of wit and the joy of song that he loves." With this obliquely self-referential nod to Hafiz's "joy of a supernal intelligence," Emerson cites a series of Hafiz's poems, the examination of each of which reveals that they share his own muse. He guides the reader through the joyful temper and tones of verses on the cedars, cypresses, palms, olive, and fig-trees and on the birds that inhabit them and the abundance of gardens. "The willows," he says, "bow themselves to every wind out of shame for their unfruitfulness." "Friendship," Emerson notes, is another "favorite topic of the Eastern poets," and at length, he also refers to Hafiz's poetry of love; he goes on to cite pages of poetry of erotic passion, which sometimes rises to a religious sentiment.

Concluding the essay, Emerson cites a number of poems illustrative of the work of other poets, including Nisami, Enweri, Ibn Jemin, and Ferideddin Attar. The latter's lengthy poem, "Bird Conversations," which was "written five hundred years ago," offers "a proof of the identity of mysticism in all periods."

CRITICAL COMMENTARY

Emerson's stature in his own time as a preeminent philosopher and popular lecturer made him one of the highest profile conduits of Eastern thought and poetry in his lifetime. In this he was personally impacted by the precedent of the Oriental poetry of JOHANN WOLFGANG VON GOETHE, who in his *Faust: Part Two* incorporated themes from *The Arabian Nights* and whose *Poems from the Parliament of West and East* (1814–18)—poems featuring Hafiz and his mistress Suleika—set a precedent for this literary cross-fertilization. Emerson had already begun to reconfigure these streams of influence in his own variations on Persian poetry, which, from the early 1840s—at the time of "The OVER-SOUL" and other expressions of Transcendentalist spirituality—constituted one of the sources of metaphysical thought to which he returned in the course of his career. Transparently self-referential, the essay illustrates the essential identification of Emerson with Hafiz (and the other Persian poets, especially Saadi). In *MAY-DAY AND OTHER PIECES* (1867), he included "Translations" of several Persian poems, including those of Hafiz.

"Persian Poetry" extols the poetry of Hafiz for its exuberant aestheticism and sensuous mysticism, the model of the joyful poet who presses the fatalities of natural and social existence into spiritual wine. Emerson dwells on Hafiz's ecstatic poetry of wine, evidently for its resonance with one of his best poems, "BACCHUS," which he composed earlier in his career after translating Hafiz in 1846 and reading the Persian poet Saadi, the subject of his 1842 poem "Saadi". In these earlier poems Emerson symbolized the relation of the poet to his art in the terms of "Pour me wine, but wine that never grew / In the belly of the grape." It is the Transcendentalist wine, the spiritual elixir of the imagination that lifts the poet into the region of aesthetic exhilaration: "Pour, Bacchus! The remembering wine; / Retrieve the loss of me and mine. / . . . A dazzling memory revive; / And write my old adventures with the pen." Emerson returned to this imagery of Bacchus in "Poetry and Imagination," also included in *Letters and Social Aims:* "O celestial Bacchus! Drive them mad,—this multitude of vagabonds, hungry for Eloquence, hungry for poetry, starving for symbols, perishing for want of electricity."

David A. Dilworth

"Plato; or, the Philosopher" (1850)

"Plato" is the first of the six biographical essays included in Emerson's 1850 text, *REPRESENTATIVE*

MEN and, as such, sets the stage for all other "great men" who are indebted to Plato, finding it "impossible to think, on certain levels, except through him." Emerson read and reread Plato (ca. 429–ca. 347 B.C.E.)—student of Socrates, philosopher, mathematician, and founder of the Academy in Athens—at different times in his life. He was not as concerned with reading Plato in the original Greek but read editions and translations brought out by his own 19th-century contemporaries. At the end of the "Plato" essay Emerson included a review of a new translation under "Plato: New Readings."

Emerson understood Plato, whose writings serve as the foundation of all Western thought, as belonging to each new generation, regardless of how many people actually read him. In his earlier essay "SPIRITUAL LAWS" (1841), he noted, "There are not in the world at any one time more than a dozen persons who read and understand Plato:—never enough to pay for an edition of his works; yet to every generation these come duly down, for the sake of these few persons, as if God brought them in his hand." The essay on "Plato" (as with each of his essays in *Representative Men*) was not so much about Plato the man, or even Plato's writings, as about the Platonic element in each of us, and, more to the point, a statement of the influence of PLATONISM in Emerson's own thought. Plato "honor[ed], at the same time, the ideal, or laws of the mind, and fate, or the order of nature." Indeed, this is the key point of Emerson's own Transcendentalism.

SYNOPSIS

Emerson declares Plato is the founder of all philosophy, literature, and wisdom: "Plato *is* philosophy, and philosophy, Plato." His writings are the "Bible of the learned," and he has his own school of thought, the "Platonists." Emerson lists a canon of international thinkers indebted to Plato, noting "his broad humanity transcends all sectional lines." Plato, "like every great man, consumed his own times," not in the sense of "plagiarism," but in synthesis. This ability to synthesize characterizes all great ideas and is what Emerson admires as most truthful: "Every book is a quotation . . . every man is a quotation from all his ancestors."

Emerson attempts to give some details of Plato's life, while observing that "great geniuses have the shortest biographies": "They lived in their writings." It is not even known if Plato had a "lover, wife, or children." Instead, Plato's biography is "interior" and important in terms of our "intellectual history." Struck by "the extreme modernness of his style and spirit," Emerson seeks to illuminate how Plato's ideas have "spread" into our own histories: "How Plato came thus to be Europe, and philosophy, and almost literature, is the problem for us to solve."

In our intellectual history, Plato is our childhood or "first period." As with childhood, his era was defined by learning to communicate: "If the tongue had not been framed for articulation, man would still be a beast in the forest." Without the proper language we miscommunicate and lament that no one understands us; we are left to "sigh and weep, write verses, and walk alone." We must constantly strive "to accuracy, to skill, to truth" in expressing our meaning and "converse" fully with the universe.

This same progression toward better communication can be traced in the "history of Europe . . . in philosophy." The early "masters" came up with mythologies and systems of ethics to communicate their ideas and beliefs; with Plato came the ability to "define": "This *defining* is philosophy." At "the base" of philosophy are the ideas of "1. Unity, or Identity; and, 2. Variety," or diversity. The mind searches for unity while recognizing the variety, the singular, within nature. Philosophy "separates" and "reconciles" these concepts, whereas religion "dwells in the conception of the fundamental Unity." The goal of religious belief is to "lose all being in one Being," to deny individuality. Religion thus teaches "ignorance" by promising "liberation from nature" into "heaven," or some other form of "resolution."

Emerson lists a series of binaries in nature—being/intellect, rest/motion, genius/talent, consciousness/definition, east/west—and argues that we always "adhere" to one idea or the other. Likewise, nations "correspond" to one side or the other—Asia or the East was founded on unity/institutions/fate, compared to Europe, which is characterized by creativity/culture/freedom. Plato's genius lay in bringing together the "energy" of both East and West—of both philosophy and religion—making Plato "a balanced soul." In his writings we find "abstract truth" laid out in "principles" and "absolutes." He showed the "two poles" of every argument without "partiality."

Other more "physical philosophers" (that is, materialists) have come up with theories of *how* the world works. But Plato asks the cause of the world—*why?* Plato said: "All things are for the sake of good, and it is the cause of everything beautiful." This is why we cannot understand Plato by reading about him in a "catalogue." He is "to be apprehended by an original mind in the exercise of its original power." Plato was always seeking out new information, while he also "adored that which cannot be numbered, or gauged, or known." Through Plato's example, philosophy became a "passion for reality" (rather than an escape from it), and philosophy is defined as nothing more than to "understand nature." Plato understood that "all things are symbolical." Even "love of the sexes" is symbolic: it is the "passion of the soul for . . . beauty."

Plato's model of four sections corresponds to Emerson's "four operations of the soul": "conjecture, faith, understanding, reason." But he finds a "defect of Plato in power"; he is literary, but he does not have the "authority" of "prophets and sermons of unlettered Arabs and Jews." To be fair, such a comparison cannot truly be made: "an oak is not an orange." Plato has the qualities nature gave him: "The qualities of sugar remain with sugar, and those of salt with salt."

Perhaps the only criticism to be made of Plato is that "he has not a system." He covers so many topics that he is open to interpretation, as a "theory of the world is a thing of shreds and patches." If we demand more of him, "we speak as boys," with "impatience." We can understand him only according to the "genius of our life," so that the defects are our own, not Plato's: "No power of genius has ever yet had the smallest success in explaining existence."

CRITICAL COMMENTARY

Plato, "like every great man," "absorbed" the great ideas of his time, and he was both a student and a teacher. Emerson sees the work of this representative philosopher in terms of absorption and then synthesis, which Emerson strove for in his own process. The philosopher is able to pick out the key ideas, or what Emerson terms "lustres," that other thinkers have to offer. Defining genius (not just of the philosopher) as the ability to synthesize is a point that recurs throughout Emerson's work, including in "The AMERICAN SCHOLAR" and in other essays of *Representative Men,* notably the introduction, "USES OF GREAT MEN." Plato's gift (and the role of the philosopher in general) lay in separating truth from opinions. His ability to do this made him a "balanced soul."

In "Plato" Emerson gives us his own definition of philosophy: "the account which the human mind gives to itself of the constitution of the world." The basic fact of philosophy is the relationship between "Unity, or Identity" and "Variety." This is the law of nature, and thus the law of philosophy, that the mind naturally searches for unity out of variety—the "one that shall be all." This is Emerson's Transcendentalist-idealist philosophy, in the idea of "The OVER-SOUL" (subject of his 1841 essay), or in "BRAHMA," the first cause. In "Plato," it is religion that is mere "speculation," whereas philosophy is based on the truth of nature.

Emerson uses "Plato," then, to explain the difference between philosophy and religion, namely, that while they both involve a search for a unifying concept, religion looks outside of nature for that source, to the *supernatural* for "resolution." Emerson remarks that no "voices," or "dreams," or other supernatural events are needed for understanding Plato's philosophy, an explicit reference to Jesus (or the core of any other religion) and perhaps another explanation for why Jesus Christ was not included as one of Emerson's "representative men." Plato (and therefore philosophy) precedes religion, looking for natural laws and finding no separation between humans and nature, between, as Emerson put it, "I and mind." Emerson's Transcendentalism, then, is the same—allowing for individuality (variety) within and reconciled (unity) with, not separate from, nature. Indeed, Plato is the original Transcendentalist—he "made transcendental distinctions," and his own philosophy constituted an example of "the wonderful synthesis so familiar in nature."

In his declaration that Plato's "argument and his sentence are . . . spherical," we see Emerson's self-identification with Plato as a Transcendentalist philosopher. In his essay "CIRCLES" (1841), in which he laid out his own "spherical" arguments, Emerson referred to himself as a "circular Philosopher." In the end, however, Emerson deems Plato "a great average man" with "a great common sense." All of Emerson's representative men are accessible, their ideas are democratic, and they speak to the greatness within each of us. So it is in Plato that "men see in him their own dreams and glimpses." He "builds a bridge" from his own time to ours. Socrates as well was, according to Emerson, "plain as a Quaker" with "a Franklin-like wisdom." Here Emerson connects the past and the present, with Franklin and the Quakers influencing the Greeks, rather than the other way around. Emerson thus makes Plato (and Socrates) into Americans, whereas it is Emerson who has been described as an "American Plato." If Plato's project is connecting the lived experience to the ideal, then perhaps it is more accurate to say, as biographer Robert Richardson points out, that "Plato is a Greek premonition of Emerson."

Poems (1847)

Actually released in late December 1846, *Poems* is usually attributed a publication date of 1847. It was Emerson's first collection of original poems—the first of only three volumes of his poetry published during his lifetime, followed by *MAY-DAY AND OTHER PIECES* 20 years later in 1867 and *SELECTED POEMS* in 1876. *Poems* includes 56 poems composed by Emerson between the early 1820s and the mid-1840s, including many of his best-known verses, such as "ASTRAEA," "BACCHUS," "BLIGHT," "DIRGE," "EACH AND ALL," "EROS," "FROM THE PERSIAN OF HAFIZ," "INITIAL, DAEMONIC, AND CELESTIAL LOVE," "GIVE ALL TO LOVE," "HAMATREYA," "The HUMBLE-BEE," "HYMN, SUNG AT THE COMPLETION OF THE CONCORD MONUMENT," "MERLIN," "MITHRIDATES," "MONADNOC," "ODE TO BEAUTY," "ODE, INSCRIBED TO W. H. CHANNING," "The RHODORA," "SAADI," "The SNOW-STORM," "The SPHINX," "THRENODY," "TO ELLEN," "URIEL," "WOODNOTES," and "The WORLD-SOUL." Several of the poems had previously appeared in newspapers such as *ATLANTIC MONTHLY*, the *WESTERN MESSENGER*, and the *DIAL*.

Poems offered up many of the Transcendentalist themes established in Emerson's preceding collections, *ESSAYS: FIRST SERIES* (1841) and *ESSAYS: SECOND SERIES* (1844). It established Emerson as a poet-philosopher breaking free of genre and of theme. His poems dealt with spiritual, but not religious, themes, a distinction noted by many of his colleagues and first reviewers. Even friend and fellow Transcendentalist MARGARET FULLER had noted that Emerson's poetry was "mostly philosophical, which is not the truest kind of poetry." Still, Fuller ranked Emerson as a poet, high "in melody, in subtle beauty of thought and expression."

Besides the themes of nature, love, spiritual laws, and politics that pervade the poems, Emerson was particularly concerned with the role of the poet himself and with establishing a theory of the language of poetry and of *poesis*, or the writing of poetry. As Emerson wrote in the essay, "The POET" (1844), "it is not metres, but a metre-making argument, that makes a poem,—a thought so passionate and alive, that, like the spirit of a plant or an animal, it has architecture of its own, and adorns nature with a new thing." The definition of poetry and the role of the poet in society were topics he explored not only in essays such as "The Poet" and "SHAKSPEARE; OR, THE POET" but also in specific poems from the volume, notably "Bacchus," "Merlin," "Saadi," and "The Sphinx."

FURTHER READING

Morris, Saundra. "'Metre-Making' Arguments: Emerson's Poems." In *The Cambridge Companion to Ralph Waldo Emerson*, edited by Joel Porte and Saundra Morris. New York: Cambridge University Press, 1999.

"The Poet" (1844)

"The Poet" is the first essay in Emerson's book *ESSAYS: SECOND SERIES*, published in October 1844.

In the three years that followed *ESSAYS: FIRST SERIES*, Emerson engaged in a series of lectures, developing material for his second book of essays. An unpublished lecture titled "The Poet," which Emerson delivered in BOSTON in the winter of 1841–42, provides much of the material for the essay "The Poet" as it appeared in 1844 (almost certainly the rest of "The Poet" lecture material appeared in the essay "POETRY AND IMAGINATION," in the book *LETTERS AND SOCIAL AIMS*, in 1876). Emerson had originally intended to finish a second essay on nature to tie the first and second volumes of *Essays* together thematically. As he had not been able to refine the second nature essay to his liking, the connecting essay, "The Poet," became the first essay of the new book.

The first motto poem for the essay is an unfinished Emerson poem (and thus relegated to the Appendix of the *Poems* volume of EDWARD WALDO EMERSON's *Collected Works*, appearing, with other unfinished verses, under the title "Fragments on the Poet and the Poetic Gift"). Emerson chose the second motto poem from his longer poem "ODE TO BEAUTY."

SYNOPSIS

The opening paragraph of Emerson's essay spells out the problem he wishes to confront: "There is no doctrine of forms in our philosophy. We were put into our bodies, as fire is put into a pan, to be carried about; but there is no accurate adjustment between the spirit and the organ." We are out of balance with nature; we are separated from God because we lack the ability to see past the surface of nature to its underlying, fundamental truth. This is the role of the poet: to enlighten us to "this hidden truth, that the fountains whence all this river of Time, and its creatures, floweth, are intrinsically ideal and beautiful." The poet, through use of language, image, and symbol, reconnects us to nature and to the divine, "for, as it is dislocation from the life of God, that makes things ugly, the poet . . . re-attaches things to nature."

The truth of nature, for Emerson, is not only divine but also is necessarily human, because "all men live by truth, and stand in need of expression." Thus, the poet reestablishes this truth by reading the truth of nature and returning it to us in language, image, and symbol. Thus, the poet's ability (his "science," to use Emerson's term) to do this is crucial; "By virtue of this science the poet is the namer, or language-maker, naming things sometimes after their appearance, sometimes after their essence, and giving to everyone its own name and not another's, thereby rejoicing the intellect, which delights in detachment or boundary." The poet recovers the essence of the truth and returns language to its origin. Emerson's idea is that all language was once a thing, or a deed; the separation of a word from its origin is the separation of language from truth: "The etymologist finds the deadest word to have been once a brilliant picture. Language is fossil poetry." And, later, "poetry was all written before time was." A recurring theme of the essay is the return to beauty and truth (which, according to Emerson's aesthetic, are equivalent), for "God has not made some beautiful things, but Beauty is the creator of the universe." The poet perceives this beauty (truth) and returns it to us (and us to it) by his skill.

The essay shifts at this point to a consideration of aesthetics, in particular to the relation between truth and form. For Emerson, a poem determines its own form, according to its own value and use. That is, the language dictates the poem. Thus, "For it is not metres but a metre-making argument, that makes a poem." The distinction is that which English poet SAMUEL TAYLOR COLERIDGE (a strong influence on Emerson) makes between mechanical form (like clay being shaped on a potter's wheel) and organic form (such as a pear growing on a tree). Emerson's claim rejects mechanical form ("metres") in favor of organicism (the "metre-making argument," or the truth behind the metre). Emerson writes, "the universe is the externization of the soul"; the metre-making argument is the truth of the soul, given expression as a new set of symbols, expressed in (or through) the universe.

Nature, according to Emerson, "offers all her creatures to [the poet] as a picture-language. . . . Things admit of being used as symbols, because nature is a symbol, in the whole, and in every part." Emerson envisions the symbol first, then the true word to inhabit the symbol. The poet "perceives that thought is multiform; that within the form of every creature is a force impelling it to ascend into a higher form." Man uses "the forms which express that life and so his speech flows with the flowing of nature." The "facts of animal economy," which Emerson lists as "sex, nutriment, gestation, birth, growth," all constitute symbols that connect the world to man and "impel" man to a higher form. Emerson's circles never close but spiral inevitably upward, toward "a new and higher fact"; that is, the truth "liberated" by the poet propels us beyond the superficial, to the fundamental truth. Thus, writes Emerson, "poets are . . . liberating gods."

In Emerson's view, language is temporary, but symbols are embodiments of eternal forms. *Symbol* is synonymous with *thought*. He writes: "The world being thus put under the mind for verb and noun, the poet is he who can articulate it. . . . We are symbols, and inhabit symbols; workmen, work, and tools, words and things, birth and death are all emblems; but we sympathize with the symbols, and, being infatuated with the economical uses of things, we do not know that they are thoughts." This process is made possible by Emerson's declaration of the symbol's significance: "For all symbols are fluxional; all language is vehicular and transitive, and is good, as ferries and horses are, for conveyance, not as farms and houses are, for homestead."

The poet can "see through the earth" and "turns the world to glass, and shows us all things in their right series and procession." Language is the vehicle available to the poet; it is the material at his disposal for communication. Language, in our common usage, is superficial, dead, separated from its original association by time and by dogmatic inflexibility. The value of language for the poet is its malleability and its transparency; thus the poet, through his insight and clarity of vision, may restore original associations of words and things, and may also use words to inhabit symbols, creating "new and higher facts." The *symbol* is the means by which the poet utilizes language and transforms thought into new, original thoughts.

Emerson's assertion that "poets are . . . liberating gods" refers to the ability of the poet to emancipate conventional associations of language and facts or, more precisely, facts as represented through language that has become deadened. Indeed, Emerson uses the terms "liberation," "emancipation," and "metamorphosis" frequently in describing the poet. This passage from the essay demonstrates in form and content Emerson's fervor: "If the imagination intoxicates the poet, it is not inactive in other men. The metamorphosis excites in the beholder an emotion of joy. The use of symbols has a certain power of emancipation and exhilaration for all men. We seem to be touched by a wand, which makes us dance and run about happily, like children." Emerson then proceeds, as he often does when caught in a fit of excitation, to cast off a list of examples across history; in this case, he fills out a single sentence of 300-plus words, even beginning with the qualification that "I will not now consider how much this makes the charm of algebra and mathematics." The first sentence of the next paragraph exactly frames the passage by repetition: "The poets are thus liberating gods."

Emerson's thesis is strengthened by the great wealth of examples from all disciplines from which he draws; the poet emancipates language from its staid associations with eternal forms, because of the poet's visual and perceptual abilities and because of his recognition of the fluidity of language, which makes this liberation initially possible. Thus the poet realizes that words are thoughts, that "poetry was all written before time was," and "by an ulterior intellectual perception, gives [thoughts] a power which makes their old use forgotten, and puts eyes, and a tongue, into every dumb and inanimate object" and "did not stop at the color, or the form, but read their meaning; neither may he rest in this meaning, but he makes the same objects exponents of his new thought."

But what are the prospects for poetry and the poet? Emerson finds hope in the more prosaic symbols of our own American experience; he writes, "See the power of national emblems. . . . The people fancy they hate poetry, and they are all poets and mystics!" However, he also writes, "I look in vain for the poet whom I describe. . . . Time yields us many gifts, but not yet the timely man, the new religion, the reconciler, whom all things await. . . . We have yet had no genius in America." We are able to be moved by symbols (as evidenced by the above claim), and Emerson, ever the optimist, writes, "Doubt not, O poet, but persist. Say, 'It is in me, and shall out.'" The representative is not an ideal but a real poet (the essay "SHAKSPEARE; OR, THE POET" presents Emerson's thoughts on the "representative poet"); for Emerson, the problem of America (as he claims in *NATURE*) is our lack of "original relation to the universe" or, as expressed in this essay, the lack of a representative American poet.

CRITICAL COMMENTARY

Emerson biographer Robert Richardson writes, "'The Poet' is arguably the best piece ever written on literature as literary process." Emerson's essays usually begin with an opening poem; "The Poet" begins with two, and both are significant in their form and in Emerson's juxtaposition of the poems. Emerson here is the theorist practicing his craft in the truest sense: The poems illustrate in fact what Emerson works to outline in theory. The first poem describes "A moody child and wildly wise / Pursued the game with joyful eyes." As is usual with Emerson, terms pertaining to vision have double and triple meanings; here, the child sees, and perceives, "Through worlds, and races, and terms, and times, / . . . musical order, and pairing rhymes." Emerson's faith in intuition over doctrine is suggested by the descriptive distinction between the "moody child" and his "joyful eyes." This is a fundamental component of Emerson's aesthetic: The eyes seek and recognize eternal form in the poet's mind. In other words, thought follows intuition, and intuition, in this sense, is associated with visual perception.

The second poem, taken from Emerson's own "Ode to Beauty," is a single, four-line stanza in regular, three-beat meter: "Olympian bards who sung / Divine ideas below, / Which always find us young, / And always keep us so." Line 3 suggests that the ideas, though sung in the past, still resonate and are thus timeless: Time, for the poet, is suspended in the presence of these divine ideas, yet line 4 suggests that time is secondary, an ordered concern of the mind, and not an eternal form; the ideas that find us young "always keeps us so." This idea is repeated from Emerson's 1841 essay "The OVER-SOUL": "Some thoughts always find us young and keep us so."

"The Poet" extends the purpose of the "DIVINITY SCHOOL ADDRESS" (1838) by establishing the poet, not the priest, as the minister of the Word. Emerson, through articulating the role and responsibility of the poet, redefined clerical responsibility in moral as well as aesthetic terms; "The Poet" affirms Emerson's shifting emphasis to the poet as the arbiter of spiritual significance for the self. He is able to do this on the basis of two principal tenets: that the poet is capable of liberating the Word from its dead associations, and that language itself is fluid. In the process of defining the poet's role, Emerson also articulates an aesthetic of organicism, one that will determine the limits of language and the power of perception.

We must be careful not to qualify Emerson's "poet" as merely a versifier, or a composer of lyric writing. For Emerson, the poet articulates the truth (a term Emerson equates with "beauty," "soul," or "nature") behind appearances. The poet, Emerson writes, "is representative. He stands among partial men for the complete man, and apprises us not of his wealth, but of the commonwealth." The term "representative," in Emerson's usage, suggests a *type* of poet, one who can speak for all people, while remaining part of the people (and thus is a representative symbol of God, who both is part of the soul and is outside the soul at the same time). In the opening essay of his book *REPRESENTATIVE MEN* (1850), Emerson writes, "The gods of fable are the shining moments of great men;" and later, "A man is a centre for nature, running out threads of relation through everything fluid and solid material and elemental." Thus is the poet "representative;" he stands among men (the center of the circle) and allows us, by relation, to find expression of the symbols we encounter. Emerson continues, in "The Poet," that "all men live by the truth, and stand in need of expression. . . . The man is only half himself, the other half is his expression." Thus is the poet the completion of man.

The work of the poet is defined by one of Emerson's key aphorisms: "Art is the path of the creator to his work." The scholar Joseph Slater refers to this as "an entire aesthetic in ten words," and the phrase helps to refine Emerson's central claims for the poet. On the surface this expression resembles a metaphor, but in fact these values are equivalent only in the sense that they all express a different perception of the phenomenon of nature. However, "path" does not rename, modify, qualify, or quantify the meaning of the term "art." Instead, the four nouns—"art," "path," "creator," and "work"—all require further elucidation. The *path* does not suggest a movement from one point to the next, or from one state of being to another. The *creator* is the poet, who does indeed create by his unique ability of perception of and unique combinations of language in order to liberate new, original meanings. Emerson writes:

> The poet is the sayer, the namer, and represents beauty. He is a sovereign, and stands on the centre. For the world is not painted, or adorned, but is from the beginning beautiful; and God has not made some beautiful things, but Beauty is the creator of the universe. Therefore the poet is not any permissive potentate, but is emperor in his own right.

The poet does not eschew form; in Emerson's determination, "it is a proof of the shallowness of the doctrine of beauty, as it lies in the minds of our amateurs, that men seem to have lost the perception of the instant dependence of form upon the soul." *Work* is the process of this perception, not its end result; the forms the poet observes, or perceives, are ever changing, and the poem's rendered symbols are, to use Emerson's term, "fluxional." The *path,* then, is also process: the process of intuition, possible in all humans but uniquely active in the poet. Thus, art is a means, not an end, and the significance of this means is the degree to which the poet reconnects us to the world. Emerson has removed, or at least defeated, time from his concept of the poet's work, so that his aesthetic has a quality of timelessness and also contains elements of form.

The most significant shape in Emerson's scheme is, of course, the circle. The 1841 essay "CIRCLES" begins:

> The eye is the first circle; the horizon which it forms is the second; and throughout nature this primary figure is repeated without end. It is the highest emblem in the cipher of the world. St. Augustine described the nature of God as a circle whose centre was everywhere, and its circumference nowhere. We are all our lifetime reading the copious sense of this first of forms.

Reading this "first of forms," or because "it is dislocation and detachment from the life of God, that makes all things ugly," requires of the poet a unique condition of seeing. Emerson calls for a poet who "re-attaches things to nature and the Whole,—reattaching even artificial things, and violations of nature, to nature, by a deeper insight,—disposes very easily of the most disagreeable facts." "Seeing" corresponds to the figure of the eye, and the eye to the circle, the "first of forms." Emerson's 10-word aesthetic statement—"Art is the path of the creator to his work"—may be applied to the physical model defined in "Circles":

> Eye = first circle / *Creator*
> Horizon = second circle / *Work*
> Repetition of the primal figure throughout nature / *the Path*

Art is the creator, the path, and the work in the sense of *process,* not product. Emerson's circles never quite close on themselves, which seems to suggest an evolution upward, as he expresses in this passage from "The Poet":

> But nature has a higher end, in the production of new individuals, than security, namely, *ascension,* or, the passage of the soul into higher forms. . . . The poet . . . resigns himself to his mood, and that thought which agitated him is expressed, but *alter idem,* in a manner totally new. The expression is organic, or, the new type which things take when liberated. As, in the sun, objects paint their images on the retina of the eye, so they, sharing the aspiration of the whole universe, tend to paint a far more delicate copy of their essence in his mind.

The spiraling form in nature is eternal; in language, the spiral pattern suggests the way in which words become distanced from their original associations. However, the spiral also implies a means by which the poet might realize the original relation of words to things by reattaching them in the opposite direction, in ways that recognize the passage of time (original associations of words with things) and transcend time (liberating words from static connections, making their symbolic possibilities eternal). The poet, then, must be able to recognize the spiral, "the circuit of things through forms," in nature. That is, first, the poet must have *sight*—physical sight, perception, and insight—to translate the forms of nature into the language of man. Emerson explains the qualifications and the process:

> This insight, which expresses itself by what is called Imagination, is a very high sort of seeing, which does not come by study, but by the intellect being where and what it sees, by sharing the path, or circuit of things through forms, and so making them translucid to others. The path of things is silent. Will they suffer a speaker to go with them? A spy they will not suffer; a lover, a poet, is the transcendency of their own nature,—him they will suffer. The condition of true naming, on the poet's part, is his resigning himself to the divine *aura* which breathes through forms, and accompanying that.

The "very high sort of seeing" Emerson describes here is the unique condition of seeing possessed by the poet, which combines sight, perception, and insight; but, it is important to recognize that Emerson emphasizes the visual, not only in a symbolic, but also in a very real sense, as essential to the poet and primary over all apparatuses of sensory input. The significance of sight is essential to the poet's task, by "sharing the path, or circuit of things through forms, and so making them translucid to others." The path is the art of the poet, in the nominal sense; in the active sense, the path is the conduit through which the poet communicates. Emerson's choice of the term *translucid* seems to express very precisely this intention. *Translucid* is a term Emerson construes as a noun to make use of the prefix "trans-," meaning through or across, and "lucid," meaning clear, bright, rational, or sane. Emerson wants to convey not only clarity of sight but also clarity through *forms*. The poet's role is that of "namer," but given the shifting quality of language (and the ability of language to change, in the hands of the poet, to create new symbols), making forms clear to others is the poet's role. Emerson uses the terms *words, language,* and *symbol* almost interchangeably, because in consideration of the distinction between symbol and language, the symbol is the key to understanding *form;* words inhabit symbols, and the quality of symbols is "fluxional." "All the facts of animal economy," writes Emerson, "are symbols of the passage of the world into the soul of man, to suffer there a change, and reappear a new and higher fact. He [the poet] uses forms according to the life, and not according to the form. This is true science."

In *Nature* (1836), and in later addresses (such as "The AMERICAN SCHOLAR" [1837] and the "Divinity School Address"), Emerson's thinking about the "ideal" poet contains a twofold strain: His progress toward the role of the poet, and not the priest, as the disseminator of truth and receiver of divine revelation often utilizes metaphor rather than direct language; also, Emerson's habit of using the oxymoronic phrase is obvious. But Emerson uses this style often to express ideas that *escape* the possibilities of language; he is interested in "nature" as ideal form, the mask upon which is imprinted the mind of God, but also nature as physical fact. And though HENRY JAMES, SR., referred to Emerson as the "man without a handle," Emerson the naturalist exists coincidentally with Emerson the idealist. "Language is fossil poetry" seems indeed the expression of an idealist, but this same writer penned the phrase "symbols are signs of natural facts," and the facts to which he refers are concrete. "America is a poem in our eyes," he writes in "The Poet," "its ample geography dazzles the imagination, and it will not wait long for meters." The expression of the forthcoming "meters" will be poetic, but the eyes and the geography are physical, concrete. The poet will communicate the forms behind the physical world we experience.

FURTHER READING

Francis, Richard Lee. "'The Poet' and 'Experience': *Essays: Second Series.*" In *Emerson Centenary Essays,* edited by Joel Myerson. Carbondale: Southern Illinois University Press, 1982.

Hopkins, Vivian. *Spires of Form: A Study of Emerson's Aesthetic Theory.* Cambridge, Mass.: Harvard University Press, 1951.

New, Elisa. *The Regenerate Lyric: Theology and Innovation in American Poetry.* Cambridge: Cambridge University Press, 1993.

Richardson, Robert D. *Emerson: The Mind on Fire: A Biography.* Berkeley: University of California Press, 1995.

Bill Scalia

"Poetry and Imagination" (1876)

Emerson's essay "Poetry and Imagination" was assembled from several lectures: "The Poet," a lecture delivered in 1841; "Poetry and Eloquence," delivered in 1847 and 1848 and "Poetry and English Poetry," delivered in 1854 (and which provides almost all of the introductory material for "Poetry and Imagination"). The essay was compiled by Emerson's daughter ELLEN EMERSON, along with JAMES ELLIOT CABOT, for inclusion in the book *LETTERS AND SOCIAL AIMS* (1876). Although it was Emerson's usual practice to compose short poetic epigrams for specific essays, this essay begins with a poem added by son EDWARD WALDO EMERSON for his Centenary Edition of *The Complete Works of Ralph Waldo Emerson,* 1903–04; the poem also appears as a completed stanza in section V of "Fragments on the Poet and Poetic Gifts" in the Centenary Edition volume *Poems.* (The epigram, probably composed in pieces between 1845 and 1851, was unpublished in Emerson's lifetime, and it is found in Emerson's poetry notebooks.)

Because the essay was assembled from lecture notes, it lacks the organization and development usually apparent in Emerson's prose writing. True, Emerson compiled his essays from journal and notebook entries, observations, and notes, but he worked and reworked this material to construct essays in his uniquely elliptical style. "Poetry and Imagination," divided into separate sections by topic ("Poetry"; "Imagination"; "Veracity"; "Creation"; "Melody, Rhyme, Form"; "Bards and *Trouveurs*"; "Morals"; "Transcendency"), lacks this quality; the essay seems more a collection of observations and pronouncements, without the aphoristic flair that marks the best of Emerson's prose. Still the essay is of interest, as it represents Emerson's continued thinking on the connection between the poet, the function of tropes in poetry, and the moral import of poetry.

SYNOPSIS

Emerson's essay begins with an introduction in which he lays the foundation for the essay to follow; he asserts the connections between thought and matter and claims that science "does not know its debt to imagination." In keeping with other work on the perception of truth through nature (*NATURE;* "The POET"; "CIRCLES"; "The METHOD OF NATURE"), Emerson writes, "there is one animal, one plant, one matter and one force. The laws of light and heat translate each other. . . ." Natural objects "out of connection, are not yet known"; "they are really part of a symmetrical universe, like words in a sentence, and if their true order is found, the poet can read their divine significance orderly as in a bible."

In the first section of the essay, "Poetry," Emerson discusses the significance of poetry and its uses to man. Following the introduction, Emerson distinguishes between two uses of facts: "the Primary use of a fact is low; the secondary use, as it is a figure or illustration of my thought, is the real worth." Thus, nature offers to us the truth of the world in symbols; he further writes, "I had rather have a good symbol of my thought, or a good analogy, than the suffrage of Kant or Plato." That is, the truth of nature is apparent in facts appearing as symbols; in that way, the individual facts of nature are given universal significance and cognizance. The poet is the "representative" who can read these symbols. Just how these symbols are read and reported, as well as their value, is the subject of the rest of the essay.

The next section, "Imagination," clarifies the importance of imagination: "While common sense looks at things or visible Nature as real and final facts, poetry, or the imagination which dictates it, is a second sight, looking through these, and using them as types or words for thoughts which they signify." Imagination is the means by which the poet sees through facts to their significance. However, Emerson makes a distinction between imagination and fancy; the distinction for Emerson is in the use of fancy (which is "superficial") for amusement; while the imagination is "a perception and affirming of a real relation between a thought and some material fact."

In the third section, "Veracity," Emerson claims that the poet may write only that which is true to him; the poet penetrates the surface to the truth (which comes from real experience), and thus possesses "second sight." Also, this expression has a religious dimension: "When [the poet] sings, the world listens with assurance that now a secret of God is to be spoken." Thus, "poetry is faith . . . [the poet] is a true re-commencer, or Adam in the garden again." This is especially important for America separated from its European influence (as Emerson called for in "The AMERICAN SCHOLAR" address): "American life storms about us daily, and is slow to find a tongue. This contemporary insight is transubstantiation, the conversion of daily bread into the holiest of symbols; and every man would be a poet if his intellectual digestion were perfect." Thus America is a new land, with a new experience of the world, and it requires its own poet; also, in keeping with Emerson's themes of nature as divine (and perhaps of America as the new relation of truth), this act of the poet is religious (because true, and vice versa), as well as fundamental.

The poet may have "second sight," but he must weld his imagination to the facts he experiences. This is the subject of the next section, "Creation." The poet must complete the "metamorphosis" of transmuting experience into the language of poetry, which Emerson refers to as "science." Creation is the third step of the poetic process—Imagination, Veracity, Creation—and concerns the practical aspects of the poet's work. But, as Emerson reminds us, poetry is a perception, dependant on "second sight": "Poetry begins, or all becomes poetry, when we look from the centre outward, and are using all as if the mind made it. That only can we see which we are, and which we make." Creation is that act of making.

The next two sections, "Melody, Rhyme, Form" and "Bards and *Trouveurs*," deal with the formal aspects of the poem: The poem must "pass into music and rhyme," since these aspects of poetry are most pleasing, and sympathetic, to us. Poetry must also be an end in itself, in that the poem dictates its own sense of rhythm and must "ask the fact for the form." This is one of Emerson's most well-known aesthetic statements, and rightly so; in these six words, Emerson determines the fundamental quality of all genuine poetic truths. The poet's words must be true to common experience. Emerson writes that, for the poet "his words are things, each the lucky sound that describe the fact." Thus, poetry has a form dictated by its own ends, and its veracity is in its use of words, which are sacramental.

The final two sections, "Morals" and "Transcendence," describe the ends and value of poetry, again in religious terms: "Poetry must be affirmative. It is the piety of the intellect. 'Thus saith the Lord,' should begin the song." The religious, for Emerson, as usual, is contained in nature: "The Muse shall be the counterpart of Nature, and equally rich. I find her not in books . . . every creation is omen of every other." "The supreme value of poetry," writes Emerson, "is to educate us to a height beyond itself . . . the subduing mankind to order and virtue."

Thus the essay moves from definition of thesis and terms ("Poetry") to a consideration of the fundamental aspects of the poet's task ("Imagination"; "Veracity"; "Creation") to the aesthetic workings of poetry ("Melody, Rhyme, Form"; "Bards and *Trouveurs*") to the value and necessity of poetry ("Morals"; "Transcendency"). Emerson writes, "The nature of things is flowing, a metamorphosis. The free spirit sympathizes not only with the actual form, but with the power of possible forms." The poet's task is in synthesis: freedom with precision; fact with form. The poet can thus lift us "to a platform where he looks beyond sense to moral and spiritual truth."

CRITICAL COMMENTARY

In the opening of the essay's "Poetry" section, Emerson states, "primary use of a fact is low; the secondary use, as it is a figure or illustration of my thought, is the real worth." The secondary use yields the "spiritual truth" of the fact. In the "Poetry" section Emerson emphasizes the necessity for tropes in language, especially poetic language. Emerson notes, "God himself does not speak prose, but communicates with us by hints, omens, inference, and dark resemblances in objects lying all around us." Emerson's interest in figurative language, as demonstrated in *Nature* (1836), "The Poet" (1844), and other works, is in how we read, and speak, nature. In "The Poet," Emerson states that only a uniquely perceptive mind will be able to recognize the resemblances between spiritual truth and the objects manifested in the world (thus keeping with Swedenborg's theory of correspondences; what is in heaven is real, and corresponding facts in the world merely illusion). For Emerson, the poet can see (perceive) the truth behind the fact and can speak it to us; thus, the necessity for symbols and figurative language. In "Poetry and Imagination," he writes, "a good symbol is the best argument, and is a missionary to persuade thousands."

Emerson also redefines the term "genius" in a way specific to this thought: "This term, when used with emphasis, implies imagination; use of symbols, figurative speech." Imagination allows the poet to infuse nature with symbols; this is significant because "Nature itself is a vast trope, and all particular natures are tropes." The poet himself is not necessarily a "genius," in the common use of the term, but makes use of genius, which is a twofold gift: the poet's ability to see beyond forms, and the ability to express the truth in figurative language in order to make the truth apprehensible for us. Genius is a conduit; under its influence the poet becomes a transitive figure, receiving truth and, according to his skill, using language to represent it to the world.

In "Imagination," Emerson writes, "poetry, or the imagination which dictates it, is a second sight, looking through these [facts of nature], and using them as types or words for thoughts which they signify." The "spiritual truth" Emerson refers to throughout "Poetry and Imagination" generates the facts of nature. The idea is common throughout Emerson's work: Nature is the generative, animating power in the world. While common sense uses words to describe the facts of objects, nature uses objects to express the truth of itself.

Also apparent in the "Imagination" section of the essay is Emerson's continued emphasis on sight. Even a casual reading of *Nature* (1836) suggests that sight, seeing, and vision are important terms for Emerson. Sight is both observation and perception: "common sense" observes; genius perceives the truth behind mere observation ("second sight"). Thus sight (recall the "transparent eyeball" image in *Nature*) becomes the most significant of senses. For Emerson's poet, the "I" of ego is dissolved in the "eye" of "second sight." In the "Imagination" section Emerson quotes Zoroaster: "poets are standing transporters, whose employment consists in speaking to the Father and to matter"; Emerson qualifies this by writing, "the world exists for thought: it is to make appear things which hide." Images exist in nature; the poet perceives the image and translates it to use. This, Emerson tells us, is EMANUEL SWEDENBORG's true value, "not his invention, but his extraordinary perception;—that he was necessitated so to see."

Reading nature is not merely an aesthetic exercise. First sight (observation) plus second sight (perception) "reads Nature to the end of delight and Moral use." Thus we are educated by nature; in an 1821 journal entry, Emerson writes, "Education is the drawing out of the soul." This is the moral value of poetry: The images we receive (through the poet's use of figurative language) correspond to the truth we already know in our soul, and we suddenly recognize something as true that we were not aware of before.

Emerson is careful in this section to distinguish the terms "Imagination" and "Fancy"; he follows SAMUEL TAYLOR COLERIDGE in his definition. As with Swedenborg, Coleridge's influence on Emerson's thinking is impossible to underestimate. In *Biographia Literaria* Coleridge defined imagination as being of two types, primary and secondary. Primary imagination, according to Coleridge, "I hold to be the living power and prime agents of all human perception, and as a repetition in the finite mind of the eternal act of creation in the infinite I AM." The secondary imagination is "an echo of the former," like primary imagination in kind but differing only in degree and mode of operation: "it dissolves, diffuses, dissipates, in order to re-create." Fancy, on the other hand, "has no other counters to play with, but fixities and densities. The fancy is indeed no other than a mode of memory emancipated from the order of time and space." This distinction is important to understanding Emerson's use of the term *imagination*; in "Poetry and Imagination" Emerson clarifies that fancy is merely ornamental, which has no moral value, while imagination is an integration of the poet's genius with spiritual truth.

Emerson treats the workings of poetry in the section "Melody, Rhyme, Form." Emerson emphasizes three principal ideas: Poetry preceded prose in human expression; we recognize rhythm and rhyme in the facts of nature by sight before they are given verbal expression; and rhythm and meter are organic, deriving from rhythms in the body and in nature. Here again, Emerson claims that poetry is the connection to the truth behind nature: we have poetry, in connection with the body and senses, before apprehension is possible.

But Emerson is not being merely analytical. The end of poetry is its moral import. Emerson writes, "Is not poetry the little chamber in the brain where is generated the explosive force which, by gentle shocks, sets in action the intellectual world?" The distinction Emerson draws is between *poetry* and *intellect.* Poetry is generative, when recognized as an expression of spiritual truth; intellect is the use of poetry, whether for social ends (Emerson was an outspoken abolitionist, as well as a champion of the French social reformer CHARLES FOURIER), politics (recall Emerson's definition of the perfect states in the poem "POLITICS"), or as a measure of our religious sensibilities. "Poetry," Emerson writes, "is the piety of the intellect. 'Thus saith the Lord' should begin the song."

However, Emerson seems skeptical about the existence of such poetry. In "The Poet," Emerson writes, "I look in vain for the poet whom I describe;" in "Poetry and Imagination," he writes, "Poems!—we have no poem." According to Emerson, "So many men are ill-born or ill-bred . . . that the doctrine is imperfectly received." Thus, "the grandeur of our life exists in spite of us." But Emerson, ever optimistic about the divine capabilities of man, closes the essay on an uplifting note: "Sooner or later that which is now life shall be poetry, and every fair and manly trait shall add a richer strain to the song."

Bill Scalia

"Politics" (1844)

Emerson's poem "Politics" emphasizes his belief in an America in which "the state is fluid" and in which "the only interest for the consideration of the State, is persons: that property will always follow persons; that the highest end of government is the culture of men," as he states in the essay "POLITICS." The poem first appears as the motto for the essay "Politics" in *ESSAYS: SECOND SERIES* (1844), and it was collected in *MAY-DAY AND OTHER PIECES* (1867).

CRITICAL COMMENTARY

EDWARD WALDO EMERSON, in the *Complete Works,* notes that "the motto is an example of the earlier poems of Emerson's second period, when . . . he felt that the strength of this thought would be lost in too much attention to melodious expression." Certainly "Politics" is a departure from Emerson's earlier verse, in that the lines are more compact, less regular, and more liberal in attention to the niceties of rhyme and meter.

The poem consists of 26 lines, mostly set in consistent three-beat lines, with the exception of the last two, which are lines of four beats, with a variation in the meter. Emerson freely uses metrical variation, rather than specific breaks, to divide the poem into sections (which will become common in his later poems). This is apparent as well in the rhyme scheme. Though the poem has no fixed stanzas, groups of lines are set apart by the *abba* rhyme scheme (allowing for slant rhymes); these breaks are further emphasized by his use of end-stopped lines.

Emerson utilizes figures from mythology such as Merlin (adviser to King Arthur) and Amphion (in Greek mythology, the son of Zeus) to give the poem a sense of both timelessness and context. Emerson uses mythic figures, specifically separated from their literary trappings, as expression of human characteristics. Here, Emerson applies this technique to the promise of the "perfect state."

Also characteristic of Emerson's later poems is his technique of breaking his shorter poems into two sections, defined by a centered group of lines that pointedly determines the poem's significance. Thus, the first half of the poem contains images and descriptions of mythic figures, and the second half describes the significance of those examples. The quatrain grouping of lines in "Politics" is interrupted by the couplet of lines 9 and 10. Clearly the lines are intended to be noticed; these two lines express Emerson's theme most directly: "Fear, Craft, and Avarice / Cannot rear a State." The poem deals, in a sense, with value and exchange: fleece / food, plow / wheat. The last four lines provide what for Emerson is the true balance for the perfect state:

> When the Church is social worth,
> When the state-house is the hearth,
> Then the perfect State is come,
> The republican at home.

The expression "is come" suggests an Advent and connects the "social worth" of the church with the practicality of the state-house. In these four lines Emerson details the specific qualifications for the state, thus using the mythic in the service of the specific and the politic.

Bill Scalia

"Politics" (1844)

Directly after the publication of *NATURE* in September 1836, Emerson began his first public lecture course, "The Philosophy of History," which included a first lecture "Politics" given on January 12, 1837. He offered the lecture again on January 1, 1840, as part of the series "The Present Age." Variations on this lecture were read in BOSTON, CONCORD, Providence, and New York, and they were finally honed into the essay "Politics" published in *ESSAYS: SECOND SERIES* (1844). He begins the essay by asserting that we are pre-political animals, and that the deeper base of our identity is our natural and moral individuality—this was to be his consistent theme from "SELF-RELIANCE" (1841) onward. A true politics, one that goes beyond "governments of force, where men are selfish," can be achieved only on the basis of exemplary individual characters, a theme he rearticulated in a companion essay, "CHARACTER," also of *Essays: Second Series,* and in many other contexts as well. One of the remarkable features of this networking of essays is its consistent theme of mankind's potential for higher planes of consciousness.

SYNOPSIS

Emerson begins with the historical observation that every political institution "was once the act of a single man": "In dealing with the State, we ought to remember that its institutions are not aboriginal, though they existed before we were born." Therefore, these institutions can be changed, they are "all alterable," and what "we may make as good; we may make better." While the "young citizen" thinks society and politics are "rooted like oak-trees to the centre," Emerson declares, "the old statesman knows that society is fluid; there are no such roots and centers." Accordingly, any man of "truth" or "will" may become the new center and pull all in his direction. Thus Emerson enunciates the democratic axiom "that the State must follow, and not lead the character and progress of the citizen . . . and that the form of government which prevails, is the expression of what cultivation exists in the population which permits it."

But in another respect, we are heirs to advances in political theory: "The history of the State sketches in coarse outline the progress of thought, and follows at a distance the delicacy of culture and of aspiration." He notes that the history of laws and revolutions, such as recently in America, has brought forth two progressive objects of political theory: one is the *equality of rights of all persons,* "in virtue of being identical in nature"; the other is *differential property rights.* As for the second, "One man owns his clothes, and another owns a county. This accident, depending, primarily, on the will and virtue of the parties, of which there is every degree, and, secondarily, on patrimony, falls unequally, and its rights, of course, are unequal."

"In the earliest society," principles concerning the rights of persons and of property fell into arbitrary patterns of acceptance and enforcement. "In modern times," these principles have been challenged as usages that "allowed the rich to encroach on the poor, and to keep them poor," combined with "an instinctive sense" that the whole idea of property "is injurious, and its influence on persons deteriorating and degrading." As a counter to these concerns, presumably, of reformers, Emerson offers that the only true concern "of the State, is persons: that property will always follow persons." Other than that, "the highest end of government is the culture of men: and if men can be educated, the institutions will share their improvement, and the moral sentiment will write the law of the land."

Emerson advocates a more direct connection between "persons and property" than inheritance: "Corn will not grow, unless it is planted and manured; but the farmer will not plant or hoe it, unless the chances are a hundred to one, that he will cut and harvest it." Emerson concludes that both persons and property "exert their power as steadily as matter its attraction." "A cent is the representative of a certain quantity of corn or other commodity. Its value is in the necessities of the animal man. It is so much warmth, so much bread, so much water, so much land. Though the law may do what it will with the owner of property, its just power will still attach to the cent." Reformers who argue against property ownership or for communal use of the land are not realistic. In this situation, "by a higher law, the property will, year after years, write every statute that respects property. The nonproprietor will be the scribe of the proprietor." The law will always respect property because "every man owns something, if it is only a cow, or a wheelbarrow, or his arms."

The same instinct that governs the law of property "determines the forms and methods of governing." Furthermore, these are distinct for each nation or society, for the government emerges from the particular "character and condition of the people." Emerson here judges that "the democratic form" is not intrinsically better than the "monarchical," which is deeply rooted in religious history and so is the right form for specific circumstances or times. It is simply that, in modern America, "democracy is better for us." Regardless of the "form" of government, there is the countervailing fact that "every actual State is corrupt." It is a "satire on government," including a democratic one, that "the word *politic*" itself "signifie[s] cunning, intimating that the State is a trick."

Political parties are a "benign necessity" imposed by nature. They are "founded on instinct" and "have nothing perverse in their origin." As parties only represent "interests" and "principles," "we might as wisely reprove the east wind, or the frost, as a political party." The problem is not the party itself, but when the party falls to "the bidding of some leader" or "personality." This is true of political parties as well as "parties of principle," such as "religious sects" or reform organizations such as the party of "universal suffrage, of abolition of slavery, of abolition of capital punishment."

In the politics of the state there is always such a balancing of opposite forces, "centripetal and centrifugal, . . . and each force by its own activity develops the other. Wild liberty develops iron conscience. Want of liberty, by strengthening law and decorum, stupefies conscience." It is only the soul itself that is whole and so, once again, Emerson's idealistic solution is not to trust self-interested persons but rather to "trust infinitely to the beneficent necessity which shines through all laws . . . an abstract of the codes of nations would be a transcript of the common conscience."

This is to go back to the foundational point that all governments have their origin in the moral identity of men: "Reason for one is seen to be reason for another, and for every other. . . . Every man finds a sanction for his simplest claims and deeds in decision of his own mind, which he calls Truth and Holiness, . . . and only in these." It is by virtue of such inner resources of truth, justice, and holiness that men presently act sanely in their "measuring of land, the apportionment of service, the protection of life and property." The baseline moral standard is that "every man's nature is a sufficient advertisement to him of the character of his fellows. My right and my wrong, is their right and their wrong." Therefore, for a time we can and do work together for common political ends.

But the pendulum swings to the opposite side when a person who is not sufficiently self-reliant attempts to guide the direction of another: "This undertaking for another, is the blunder which stands in colossal ugliness in the governments of the world." Emerson affirms: "A man who cannot be acquainted with me, taxes me; looking from afar at me, ordains that a part of my labor shall go to this or that whimsical end, not as I, but as he happens to fancy. Behold the consequence. Of all debts, men are least willing to pay the taxes. What a satire is this on government!"

With this further critical observation, Emerson consistently prioritizes the political value of private moral character and the fruits of individual labor: "Hence, the less government we have, the better,—the fewer laws, and the less confided power. The antidote to this abuse of formal Government is the influence of private character." In the broadest terms, moral political character brings forth "freedom, cultivation, intercourse, revolutions." The purpose of the state is "to educate the wise man; and with the appearance of the wise man the State expires." We think that modern society has reached a "meridian" of civilization when, in fact, Emerson remarks, "the influence of character is in its infancy." He goes on to condemn the "pompous" senators and presidents who have climbed to the top without the moral prerequisites.

CRITICAL COMMENTARY

Emerson concludes the essay by situating personal character as the keystone to politics. His ideal of "self-government," of self-reliance, provides the individual with "the rewards and penalties of his own constitution," and he is confident that these forces will "work with more energy than we believe."

If we go back to the earlier lecture versions of "Politics" dating from 1837 we see that Emerson blended in this published 1844 essay themes central to his entire career. His consistent position from the earlier lectures was that the less government we have the better. He articulated his theory of the great man of character whom he called "invulnerable," a "prophet" who transcends the opinion of the people, representing a Platonic Ideal—"this Idea of the all-sufficiency of private character." Thus Emerson declared that "the real government is ever this Theocracy," which is not just in the heart of the single individual but also in the hearts of all men, such that secular government and its politics are interferences. He concluded that character fulfills its own, whereas any benefit to others is merely contingent and not the effect contemplated by the doer. A great man, outside of politics, does not act out of any utilitarian calculation of good to be done but acts only according to his own character.

In "Politics" Emerson articulates a more balanced account, looking askance at, for example, the radical communitarian options being articulated in his own time, such as the rejection of private property by HENRY DAVID THOREAU and the utopian communities of BROOK FARM and Fruitlands. He notes that while "it is not easy to settle the equity of this question," he is conservatively inclined to see its resolution in our "natural defenses." That is to say, nature will solve the question of the protection of property rights and such communities can never say what is best for all men.

The essay on "Politics" complements, then, Emerson's view of reform politics and universal reform in other writings, such as in "The CONSERVATIVE." Here in "Politics" he posits a similar logic of compensation to balance the strong points of the democrat or reform party against the conservative party. As the pendulum of power swings naturally back and forth between them, they each fall prey to "personality" over "principle," and they each fall short. Neither, he says, has contributed "any benefit in science, art, or humanity, at all commensurate with the resources of the nation."

As is generally true of his various essays, Emerson's "Politics" alternates between expressions of a hardheaded skepticism and an open-ended optimistic idealism. The two ends blend together in his sense of the still untapped powers of the human soul. From around the time he published "Politics" in 1844 Emerson himself became increasingly involved in lectures and debates for ABOLITIONISM, most notably with the "FUGITIVE SLAVE LAW

ADDRESS" of 1851 and in speaking out about the JOHN BROWN case of 1860.

FURTHER READING

Shklar, Judith N. "Emerson and the Inhibitions of Democracy." *Political Theory* 18, no. 4 (November 1990): 601–614.

David A. Dilworth

"Power" (1860)

"Power" is the second essay in *The* CONDUCT OF LIFE of 1860, the companion to the opening essay on "FATE." Emerson delivered "Power" as a lecture on as many as seven occasions between the years 1851 and 1854. Beginning with *NATURE* (1836), in which he wrote that "Every spirit builds itself a house; and beyond its house a world; and beyond its world, a heaven," the theme of human potential stood at the heart of Emerson's philosophy. It received solid grounding in his ethics of "SELF-RELIANCE" ("Power and speed be hands and feet") and in his metaphysical symbolism of "The OVER-SOUL," the two celebrated companion pieces of his earlier volume *ESSAYS: FIRST SERIES* (1841). "Human power" is defined thereafter in the sense of intellectual, moral, and aesthetical potential as opposed to social and economic rewards. Now, in this later work of 1860 Emerson speaks of productive power in a more general sense, in which nature plays a role in the cause and effect of the "search after power."

SYNOPSIS

Emerson begins his discussion of the nature of "Power" by asking, "Who would set a limit to the influence of a human being?" Indeed, his purpose is not to explain the bounds of power, but rather, in effect, to enunciate the principle that "life is a search after power" and to combine it with Bacon's dictum that "knowledge is power." At the top end of this quest for power, the fully cultivated man is "the end to which nature works, and the education of the will is the flowering and result of all this geology and astronomy." Emerson's central concepts of self-reliance, compensation, the affinity of mind and nature, and life as an upward progression blend seamlessly together in this reflection.

The "vast majority of men," he opines, do not understand the most basic elements of nature because they "have no habit of self-reliance or original action." Successful persons, to the contrary, appear to have "constitutional traits" of "courage" to perform and to achieve to a high degree: "All power is of one kind, a sharing of the nature of the world. The mind that is parallel with the laws of nature will be in the current of events, and strong with their strength." But in human life, there is always a tension between good and bad forces: "This power, to be sure, is not clothed in satin. 'Tis the power of Lynch law, of soldiers and pirates; and it bullies the peaceable and loyal." He clarifies, however, "that all kinds of power usually emerge at the same time; good energy, and bad, power of mind, with physical health; the ecstasies of devotion, with the exasperations of debauchery."

It is nature's prodigious forces that are the "aboriginal source" of human power. "Recuperative forces," "buoyancy and resistance," and "*plus* health" are manifestations of such. Here Emerson highlights the fact that a "strong race or strong individual" historically emerges at the point of transition from "savage" man to culture: "In history, the great moment is, when the savage is just ceasing to be a savage, with all his hairy Pelasgic strength directed on his opening sense of beauty:—and you have Pericles and Phidias,—not yet passed over into the Corinthian civility." He continues to emphasize that "everything good in nature and the world is in that moment of transition, when the swarthy juices still flow plentifully from nature, but their astringency or acridity is got out by ethics and humanity." As in the case of Michelangelo, for example, "this aboriginal might gives a surprising pleasure when it appears under conditions of supreme refinement, as in the proficients in high art."

To this theory of the natural basis of ascending human achievement, Emerson appends specific instructions on how to harness our mental energies: "The first is, the stopping off decisively our miscellaneous activity, and concentrating our force on one or a few points." We must not commit ourselves to too many distractions: "You must elect your work; you shall take what your brain can, and drop all the rest. Only so, can that amount of vital force accumulate, which can make the step from knowing to doing." Concentration of forces, he asserts here, is the secret of power in politics, in war, in trade, in all management of human affairs.

A "second substitute for temperament" is discipline or "drill." Through "the power of use and routine . . . we spread the same amount of force over much time, instead of condensing it into a moment." Through active habit-forming we overcome "the frictions of nature" and achieve some mastery: "Six hours every day at the piano, only to give facility of touch; six hours a day at painting, only to give command of the odious materials, oil, ochres, and brushes." To master the "tools" through "thousands of manipulations" is "the power of the mechanic and the clerk" as well.

Emerson recognizes here that he is dealing for the most part with characterizations and criteria of worldly or "superficial" accomplishment. He refers readers to more "sublime considerations" in later "chapters on Culture and Worship." He is concerned here with enunciating a general philosophy of human accomplishment based on understanding the implications of natural causation: "If these forces and this husbandry are within reach of our will, and the laws of them can be read, we infer that all success, and all conceivable benefits for man, is also, first or last, within his reach, and has its own sublime economies by which it may be attained. . . . Success has no more eccentricity, than the gingham and muslin we weave in our mills." And indeed, Emerson continues, "when we go to the mill," we find "the machine is more moral than we": "Let a man dare go to a loom, and see if he be equal to it. Let machine confront machine, and see how they come out. The world-mill is more complex than the calico-mill, and the architect stooped less."

For Emerson, life's winners are those who transform nature into the self-reliant impulses of willpower and creative deed. He proclaims the gospel of the rugged and yet cultured, that is, self-cultivated, individual who masters the forces of nature in a universe that supports our efforts through cause and effect.

CRITICAL COMMENTARY

In his poem "MITHRIDATES" Emerson also featured the theme of this essay on "Power": "Health is good,—power, life, that resists disease, poison, and all enemies." Rejecting the pessimism of theologians and politicians, he believes that "recuperative force, buoyancy, and resistance" accompany the health of body and mind of the man or woman who embodies personal power and freedom, by drawing upon the ever-abundant resources of nature.

In historical perspective, Emerson's essay on "Power" presupposed the "social contract" framework of JOHN LOCKE's *Second Treatise of Government* (1690), with its principle of the necessity of man's labor. In Locke's words, "God hath commanded man to labor, and the penury of his condition required it of him. God and his reason commanded him to subdue the earth, i.e. improve it for the benefit of life, and therein lay out something upon it that was his own, his labour." Emerson's "POLITICS" of *ESSAYS: SECOND SERIES* (1844) already rang the changes on this political and economic premise, which was to anchor an ensuing 1851 lecture course, "The Conduct of Life," which included lectures on "Power," "Laws of Success," "Wealth," and "Economy," all of which he reworked into the published essays of *The Conduct of Life* in 1860.

Emerson's *REPRESENTATIVE MEN* of 1850 also featured paradigms of persons of power who contributed to human culture and to history, and thus of course to his own self-understanding in exemplary ways. Elsewhere Emerson's writings functioned as one of the most significant conduits of the ideas of JOHANN WOLFGANG VON GOETHE in American 19th-century intellectual life. The governing principle of all of Goethe's writings was "self-culture," which in turn keynoted Emerson's central theme of incessant striving and self-development. Emerson's "life is a search after power" directly echoed Goethe's account of *zum höchsten Dasein immerfort zu streben,* or the human spirit's effort "to strive on towards supreme existence."

Emerson's writings on man's active and productive nature set the direction for American

Pragmatism. WILLIAM JAMES was heir to Emerson's legacy of volitional individualism in such essays as "The Energies of Men," which stressed the strenuous life of the active person who pursues "pure experience." CHARLES SANDERS PEIRCE, a contemporary of James, inherited the Emersonian philosophy of human power and production in his own way. Peirce consciously acknowledged Emerson's idealistic naturalism in elaborating his master concept of synechism, which postulated the continuity and affinity of mind and nature in evolution. FRIEDRICH NIETZSCHE's central concepts of "health," "will to power," and "affirmation of life" also drew directly from Emerson's writings on human power.

FURTHER READING

Lopez, Michael. "The Conduct of Life: Emerson's Anatomy of Power." In *The Cambridge Companion to Ralph Waldo Emerson,* edited by Joel Porte and Saundra Morris. New York: Cambridge University Press, 1999.

David A. Dilworth

Representative Men (1850)

Emerson's 1850 volume *Representative Men* included an introductory lecture on the "USES OF GREAT MEN" and essays on six individual historical figures and the universal trait or position they represent: "PLATO; OR, THE PHILOSOPHER," "SWEDENBORG; OR, THE MYSTIC," "MONTAIGNE; OR, THE SKEPTIC," "SHAKSPEARE; OR, THE POET," "NAPOLEON; OR, THE MAN OF THE WORLD," and "GOETHE; OR, THE WRITER." The lecture series on which the collection is based began with an interest in Napoléon Bonaparte after Emerson had read several memoirs and historical treatments. Besides Napoléon, JOHANN WOLFGANG VON GOETHE was probably the figure Emerson had spent the most time reading and writing about by 1845, although Plato and Montaigne had also been his constant intellectual companions since his college days. The book was published in 1850, with a reprint in 1857, and revised editions in 1876 and 1879. EMILY DICKINSON famously described the volume as "a little Granite Book you can lean upon."

Each of the men included in the volume represented for Emerson a universal characteristic that transcended time and place. He had selected the final list for the 1845 lecture series, although his journal indicates that he had considered other names as lecture topics, including Jesus Christ, the poet Saadi, and the contemporary UTOPIAN socialist CHARLES FOURIER; he would write about each of these other figures in other contexts. Emerson did not strive for chronological coverage, skipping from ancient Greece to 16th-century England to several near-contemporaneous 18th- and 19th-century figures. Emerson did not select any fellow Americans for his list of representative writers and thinkers. Indeed, his volume in many ways, like "The AMERICAN SCHOLAR" address of 1837, was intended precisely to highlight his assessment that the United States had not yet produced its great poets or thinkers.

Emerson regularly looked to history for examples of the heroic that would illuminate universal laws and traits. He had delivered an early lecture series, "Biography," in 1835 with an interest in "the perfect sympathy that exists between like minds," and he intended to "hold these fellow minds as mirrors before ourselves to learn the deepest secret of our capacity." In addresses such as "The American Scholar" and "LITERARY ETHICS" (1838), he explored the larger question of the characteristics and influence of great men and great civilizations. He consistently warned against hero worship, reminding students in "The American Scholar" that great thinkers such as "Cicero, Locke, and Bacon were only young men in libraries, when they wrote these books."

Ultimately, *Representative Men* was a response to THOMAS CARLYLE's work *On Heroes, Hero Worship and the Heroic in History* (1841). What makes an individual "great," in Emerson's terms, was not their heroic exceptionalism but their accessibility and applicability to future generations. Emerson's interest in rethinking the uses of history, biography, and heroes extended to other works as well, most notably the essays "HISTORY" and "HEROISM," both from *ESSAYS: FIRST SERIES* (1841). In these works, as in *Representative Men,* Emerson emphasized the humanity and accessibility of great men by also addressing their limitations. Their humanity, flaws and all is what makes them great, and the extent to which each "must be related to us, and our life receive from him some promise of explanation."

FURTHER READING

Bosco, Ronald. "'What poems are many private lives': Emerson Writing the American Plutarch." *Studies in the Literary Imagination* 27, no. 1 (Spring 1994): 103–129.

"The Rhodora" (1839)

Emerson's short, 17-line poem, "The Rhodora," was first published in the Ohio literary magazine WESTERN MESSENGER in July 1839 and was later included, with some revisions, in POEMS (1847) and SELECTED POEMS (1876). The poem focuses on the romantic view of nature's relationship to man being both one of inspiration and one of beauty for its own sake. Emerson composed "The Rhodora" in 1834, by which time he was preparing his ideas for his seminal Transcendentalist work of 1836, NATURE. In *Nature,* Emerson explained, "Particular natural facts are symbols of particular spiritual facts. Nature is the symbol of spirit." In "The Rhodora," the natural facts surrounding the flower, and Emerson's interpretation of those facts, symbolize humanity's place in nature and the universe. In the poem, the flower exists purely for the sake of beauty. As he explained in the chapter on "Beauty" from *Nature,* "The world thus exists to the soul to satisfy the desire of beauty. This element I call an ultimate end . . . Beauty, in its largest and profoundest sense, is one expression for the universe."

CRITICAL COMMENTARY

The poem "The Rhodora" consists of only one stanza, beginning with a question, and then followed by four traditional rhymed quatrains. The first line asks the question that prompts the reflection in the poem: "On being asked, Whence is the flower?" As Emerson expressed in *Nature,* curiosity is the human condition, and his philosophy was based on the belief that "we have no questions . . . which are unanswerable . . . whatever curiosity the order of things has awakened in our minds, the order of things can satisfy." Where does the flower come from and for what purpose? These are the questions he seeks to answer in the poem.

The first quatrain names the elements referenced throughout the poem: wind, water, earth, and sky. The wind "pierced our solitudes," both announcing the coming of spring out of the "solitudes" of winter, and abruptly bringing the individual out of himself. But "*our* solitudes" indicates that the question concerns humanity in general, not just the individual poet. It is nature, the "sea-winds," which actively draws him out to discover the secrets of nature. The rhodora flourishes among humble surroundings, a "leafless" flower, hiding "in a damp nook" along "a sluggish brook." In this sense, the flower is like the poet himself who was hiding before being drawn out of his solitude. Emerson would have encountered almost identical imagery in the writings of German idealist JOHANN WOLFGANG VON GOETHE, who explained that knowledge comes from curiosity, as "at the smallest brook, I enquire when it comes and into what river it runs."

The next quatrain is full of color in describing the interaction between the flower and its surroundings. The flower's "purple petals" are a contrast to "the black water," and even the "red-bird" is less stunning next to "the flower that cheapens his array." Like the bird or the seashells in Emerson's poem "EACH AND ALL" (published in the same volume of *Poems*), the flower, no matter how beautiful, cannot be understood outside of its natural surroundings. The next quatrain returns to the original question, and Emerson marvels that "sages" might question the existence and purpose of a flower. Their view that the flower's "charm is wasted" indicates the limited materialist vision of those who see things only in terms of usefulness. Addressing the flower directly, the personification of nature here only highlights the difference between Emerson's relationship with nature and those who would ask such a question. Indeed, rather than directing his answer to the original inquirers, he urges the flower itself to "tell them, dear" what amounts to a clear statement of Transcendentalist-romantic aesthetics, pointing out that just as "eyes were made for seeing, / Then Beauty is its own excuse for being."

The final quatrain continues to address the flower directly. The poet does not understand why people would take the beauty of the "rival" rose for granted but question the rhodora. He himself "never thought to ask" why this particular flower was there. Indeed, his "simple ignorance" is a wry response to the supposed "sages" who do not have the understanding of nature that the poet possesses. The poem concludes with the realization that the existence of the flower is no different from the existence of humans; they are both part of nature: "The self-same Power that brought me there brought you." That "Power" was God or "The OVER-SOUL" or simply nature, emphasizing the affinity between man and nature. To question the flower's existence or purpose or beauty, then, is to question humanity's as well.

FURTHER READING

Tuerk, Richard. "Emerson and the Wasting of Beauty: 'The Rhodora.'" *ATQ* 4 (March 1990): 5–11.

"Saadi" (1842)

Emerson's long 8-stanza poem "Saadi" was first published in the *DIAL* magazine in October 1842 and was included, with some revisions, in *POEMS* (1847) and *SELECTED POEMS* (1876). The poem explores a theme that engaged Emerson in numerous contexts, namely, the question of the poet's role in society, and the poet's efforts to balance the need for solitude with life in society. Emerson referred to the piece as a "poem on poetical ethics," the theme of prose essays such as "LITERARY ETHICS" and "The POET."

Based on the 12th-century Persian poet Sa'di, "Saadi" was Emerson's model for the ideal poet and, indeed, his own alter ego. Emerson translated some of Sa'di's (whose name Emerson and others spelled variously as Saadi, Said, Seyd, or Seid) poetry into his journals, and his son EDWARD WALDO EMERSON noted that his father's fascination and identification with the solitary poet lends credence to the idea that "Saadi" "might be Emerson in Oriental mask." Emerson's interest in Eastern religion and mythology was evident as well in the poems "BRAHMA" and "FROM THE PERSIAN OF HAFIZ," and in the essay "PERSIAN POETRY" (1876), in which Emerson named Saadi as one of the "seven masters of the Persian Parnassus."

CRITICAL COMMENTARY

The first stanza contrasts society and solitude, with nature organizing itself into "groves" or "droves," "herds" or "flocks," and humans who "consort in camp and town"; but the poet is always an outsider who "dwells alone." This phrase describing the solitary poet is repeated as the final line in each of the first three sections: "But the poet dwells alone"; "Wise Saadi dwells alone"; and, finally, "Good Saadi dwells alone."

In the second stanza the poet's lyric voice comes from God; although he has been given this voice on behalf of humanity, it is God who "Straitly charged him, 'Sit aloof.'" The inspiration for poetry is sought by many, but comes to only a few; if too many "touch the string, / The harp is dumb." The poet stands apart: "Though there come a million / Wise Saadi dwells alone." In the third stanza, however, the poet does not (cannot) live apart from society: "Yet Saadi loved the race of men." The poet "wants them all" and requires readers to "give ear," to listen and to respond with emotions—to "Grow red with joy, and white with fear." Again, the poet may be surrounded by "ten" or by a "million," but still "Good Saadi dwells alone." He is in the world, but not of the world.

The fourth stanza continues this theme that the poet needs human society although they drain him. Society is likewise drawn to the illumination provided by the poet, to the "golden lamp" of "the man of truth." The poet exists for "those who need him most," the "simple maids and noble youth," and they "exhaust" him. Besides these who seek out the poet, the lone voice of the "critic" is admonished not to interrupt or "vex" the poet, for society needs him, this "cheerer of men's hearts."

The fifth stanza shifts to an emphasis on a different role of the poet—as singers of "Endless dirges," poets are "Sad-eyed Fakirs" (a phrase used twice in the poem). There is a poetic compensation, a balance found in nature, which Emerson notes with these lines: "Never in the blaze of light / Lose the shudder of midnight; / And at overflowing noon, / Hear wolves barking at the moon; / In the bower of dalliance sweet / Hear the far Avenger's feet." This is a warning to the poet that praise is not the true reward of poetry: "Drink not the Malaga of praise, / But do the deed thy fellows hate." The poet must make sacrifices—"compromise thy peaceful state"—and must tell the truth. Even painful experiences—"out of woe and out of crime"—reveal important truths and are routes to the "sublime." The fifth stanza, in particular, makes several references to the sun, an image of light and truth, as the poet "sat in the sun" and "Lighted each transparent word." Even though "woe and crime" are important experiences, in the end goodness reigns: "it seemeth not to me / That the high gods love tragedy."

In the sixth stanza, the muse guides Saadi to set himself apart from society, motivated not by "praise," "Or by thirst and appetite"; to avoid seeking "talents not thine own." In the quest for truth, the poet should not become involved in questions of doctrine: "Let theist, atheist, pantheist, / Define and wrangle how they list." The poet is both "Fierce conserver, fierce destroyer," and "joy-giver and enjoyer." The poet heeds only his inner voice and his true realm of influence in his poetry: "mind thy rhyme."

Stanza 7 continues this theme of the poet's distanced relationship to society. The "great world" goes on around him, "With war and trade, with camp and town." Presaging WALT WHITMAN's mode of cataloguing the daily activities of men, the poet observes: "A thousand men shall dig and eat, / At forge and furnace thousands sweat." The cycles of history and the world go on—"Oft shall war end, and peace return, / And cities rise where cities burn"—but through all these, "one man" emerges, the man "Who can turn the golden rhyme." The poet must let the world "manage how they may" and should "Heed thou only Saadi's lay" (a line repeated twice in the poem).

Emerson's line that the "Barefooted Dervish is not poor" brings to mind the same phrase used in another poem, "DAYS," with the dervish being Emerson's poetic equivalent to the mystic, standing between the physical and the spiritual worlds. The poet requires inspiration "So that what his eye hath seen / His tongue can paint, as bright, as keen." The poet's job is to take "what his tender heart hath felt" and translate it so that "With equal fire thy heart shall melt." This stanza emphasizes the fact that the poet is not looking for earthly fame or fortune, but that the poet's wealth comes from his inspiration, and then his ability to communicate what he has seen and felt to others.

Through his words the poet has "soft persuasion," but this is more powerful than "a storm-wind." The poet brings more "Terror and beauty" than anything in nature because nature is in his poetry: "In his every syllable / Lurketh nature veritable." Through the poet's words and images, "before the listener's eye / Swims the world in ecstasy, / The forest waves, the morning breaks, / The pastures sleep, ripple the lakes, / Leaves twinkle, flowers like persons be, / And life pulsates in rock or tree. / Saadi! so far thy words shall reach; / Suns rise and set in Saadi's speech."

In the final stanza the muse continues to speak to Saadi concerning the possession of different values from the majority of men: "Eat thou the bread which men refuse; / Flee from the goods which from thee flee; / Seek nothing; Fortune seeketh thee." Emerson uses images from nature to discourage Saadi from seeking only the beautiful and exotic, instead finding good in all things: "Wish not to fill the isles with eyes / To fetch thee birds of paradise; / On thine orchard's edge belong / All the brass of plume and song." In other words, poetry does not require embellishments to make it attractive, for the truth speaks for itself. The simplest, wisest poetry is "proverbs in the market-place;"—speaking to everyday life.

Finally, there is not just one path or source of inspiration. "The flood of truth" can be found behind "innumerable doors," namely, in our fellow human beings: "Those doors are men; the pariah kind / Admits thee to the perfect Mind." Again, "Seek not beyond thy cottage wall" for the inspiration "that can yield thee all." The original Saadi found inspiration even in scarcity and mundane life: "On the desert's yellow floor, / Listening to the gray-haired crones, / Foolish gossips, ancient drones." To the poet, these things "rise in stature / To the height of mighty nature."

In "SELF-RELIANCE" (1841) Emerson urged that "we must go alone" and not adopt "the faults" or "folly" of our friends and family. The world is "in conspiracy" against us, as against the poet, but we must have self-trust enough to resist: "No man can come near me but through my act."

"Sea-Shore" (1864)

Emerson's poem "Sea-Shore" utilizes the allegory of the sea ("spirit") reestablishing communication with pilgrim ("man"). Emerson emphasizes that the sea has never left, is eternal, and timeless; it is the man who wanders and returns. The poem is comprised of 50 lines, the opening four of which constitutes an opening quatrain (if we grant the slant rhyme between "come" and "home"). Though the poem breaks into three stanzas, there is no fixed stanza form. Emerson casts the lines in blank verse (unrhymed iambic pentameter), significant in that this line measure most closely approximates normal speech; this cadence ideally suits the sea's address to the pilgrim.

The source for this poem comes from a journal entry dated July 23, 1856, after a walk on the beach at Pigeon Cove, Cape Ann. The poem was first published in the journal the *Boatswain's Whistle,* October 18, 1864. It was collected, with revisions and the addition of two lines, in *MAY-DAY AND OTHER PIECES* (1867), *SELECTED POEMS* (1876), and *Poems* (1884).

CRITICAL COMMENTARY

The "Sea-Shore" poem offers an address by the sea, which stands symbolically for nature (and all that the term entails regarding the divine; as Emerson writes in the poem "WOODNOTES" [1847], "Once slept the world an egg of stone, / and pulse, and sound, and light was none; / And God said, "Throb!" and there was motion, / And the vast mass became vast ocean"). In the "Sea-Shore," the sea speaks to a pilgrim, who had wandered away and has returned to his source of inspiration; in this way the poem is similar to the poem "EACH AND ALL" (1847). The tone of "Sea-Shore" resembles God's answer to Job; however, the sea is perhaps more placid in its reminder to the pilgrim of the significance (and pervasiveness) of spirit. The image of waves in the poem, the harmony of nature with human rhythm, is further illustrated in the poem "Illusions," the motto for the essay "ILLUSIONS" in *The CONDUCT OF LIFE* (1860).

The theme is the danger of disunity, the separation of the physical self from the spiritual, and it is expressed in much of Emerson's work. Indeed, this emphasis on harmony between physical and spiritual existence runs throughout Emerson's thought, since, according to Emerson, this harmony is necessary for man to understand his connection to the universe (God) and experience its moral imperative. This, of course, allows the individual, and society, to reach its highest moral, intellectual, and spiritual state.

Bill Scalia

Selected Poems (1876)

Selected Poems was Emerson's third collection of poetry published during his lifetime and included several drawn from the previous volumes *POEMS* (1847) and *MAY-DAY AND OTHER PIECES* (1867). *Selected Poems* also included eight new, previously uncollected poems: "The HARP" (comprised of lines taken from the original "MAY-DAY" poem), "April," "WEALTH," "MAIDEN SPEECH OF THE AEOLIAN HARP," "Cupido," "The Nun's Aspiration," "Hymn, Sung at the Second Church, Boston, at the Ordination of Rev. Chandler Robbins," and "BOSTON." Some of these had been published in magazines or other venues, but most were previously unpublished.

Selected Poems has been a problem for scholars and students of Emerson's poetry because he significantly revised many of the previously published poems, reprinting them under the same titles. But the volume is also problematic because of Emerson's age at the time of publication (he was 73) and his declining mental health. By this period of his life, his friend and literary executor JAMES ELLIOT CABOT and daughter ELLEN EMERSON had taken over compilation and editing of his prose work and were actively involved in the publication of other works, such as *PARNASSUS* (1874), a collection of Emerson's favorite poems by other poets, and *LETTERS AND SOCIAL AIMS* (1876). During this time period Emerson also received assistance with his manuscripts from friends ELIZABETH HOAR, FRANKLIN BENJAMIN SANBORN, and JAMES RUSSELL LOWELL. Most scholars have therefore assumed that *Selected Poems* was also guided more by Cabot and Ellen Emerson than by Emerson himself.

Other scholars, however, now argue to the contrary, stating that *Selected Poems* "belonged to Emerson" more than any of these other later works, as the evidence shows he spent his own time carefully selecting and revising old poems and writing the new poems to include. For example, Ellen Emerson specifically noted in a letter to her sister EDITH EMERSON in September 1875, "Father is still at work on the new poems, and I am not helping." As scholar Joseph Thomas argues, Emerson remained more capable of and interested in completing the poetry project than in editing or writing prose in his later elderly years, making *Selected Poems* "his last full labor of love." The collection, therefore, perhaps deserves more attention from students and scholars than it has to date received.

Indeed, many of the poems included in the volume were not products of Emerson's later years, but they had been written by Emerson many years earlier and were previously published. It is now clear that he began selecting and revising poems for such a volume as early as 1865. His poems, even many of those published in his earlier collections, *Poems* and *May-Day,* were in fact always works-in-progress, fluid pieces that changed as his own identity as a poet changed.

FURTHER READING

Thomas, Joseph M. "Late Emerson: *Selected Poems* and the 'Emerson Factory.'" *ELH* 65, no. 4 (1998): 971–994.

"Self-Reliance" (1841)

Drawn from journals and lectures of the 1830s, Emerson's seminal essay on "Self-Reliance" was first published in *ESSAYS: FIRST SERIES* (1841). It has since become one of his most widely read essays, the foundational statement of Emerson's Transcendentalist philosophy and of American individualism in general. As Emerson later noted (in "Historic Notes of Life and Letters in New England") of his own 19th century, "The age tends to solitude," promoting "every one for himself; driven to find all his resources, hopes, rewards, society and deity within himself." Indeed, Emerson did more than anyone else to outline the philosophical imperative of "Self-Reliance." His essay opens with the Latin quote, "*Ne te quaesiveris extra,*" translated as "Do not seek outside yourself."

The idea of "Self-Reliance" is present throughout Emerson's thought and writing. The idea already formed the basis of his two earlier important addresses, "The AMERICAN SCHOLAR" in 1837 (which emphasized reliance on self rather than on books and history) and the "DIVINITY SCHOOL ADDRESS" of 1838 (with its call to finding divinity within rather than through religion). One therefore cannot speak of Emerson's philosophy, of American Transcendentalism, without the core idea of self-reliance. He himself wrote in his journal in April 1840: "In all my lectures I have taught one doctrine, the infinitude of the private man."

Emerson had lectured specifically on the topic of "Self-Reliance" as early as 1833, and in 1835 he listed "the sublimity of Self-Reliance" as one of his own "thoughts and illustrations" that he planned to more fully develop as a topic. In 1839 he had written in his journal, "Trust thyself. Every heart vibrates to that iron string." Nor is this simple message confined to one piece in his 1841 collection *Essays,* but it is intertwined throughout his expositions on "HISTORY," "LOVE," "FRIENDSHIP," "CIRCLES," "SPIRITUAL LAWS," and "The OVER-SOUL," as well as his later works.

SYNOPSIS

Emerson opens the essay "Self-Reliance" with an anecdote, recalling, "I read the other day some verses written by an eminent painter which were original and not conventional." This originality is, to him, the true "value" of an idea, "let the subject be what it may." This reflection in the opening lines supports the full force of his main argument for the essay: "To believe your own thought, to believe that what is true for you in your private heart is true for all men,—that is genius." He presents the Transcendentalist idea that every truth originates in and radiates outward from the human mind, so that "the inmost in due time becomes the outmost." We should look within and appreciate our own thought, rather than look to the thoughts of others: "A man should learn to detect and watch that gleam of light which flashes across his mind from within, more than the luster of the firmament of bards and sages. Yet he dismisses without notice his thought, because it is his." Education is not about "envy" or "imitation" but rather about self-discovery and self-acceptance. Knowledge is to be cultivated within ourselves, not derived from others. "Trust thyself." Trust the "transcendent destiny" of your own life.

Self-trust requires we return to the openness of childhood. Emerson watches the "oracles nature yields" in babies and children and wonders how and why we lose this "unaffected, unbiased, unbribable, unaffrighted innocence" we once held. Society requires conformity and thus requires we silence our authentic selves: "These are the voices which we hear in solitude, but they grow faint and inaudible as we enter into the world." The self-reliant person "must be a nonconformist" and must accept that "nothing is at last sacred but the integrity of your own mind." We must not accept others' definitions but determine the truth for ourselves: "He . . . must not be hindered by the name of goodness, but must explore if it be goodness . . . the only right is what is after my constitution, the only wrong what is against it." We cannot derive goodness or morality from "large societies and dead institutions." We must follow only what comes from within: "What I must do is all that concerns me, not what the people think."

Conformity and adherence to a "dead church" or to political parties are "screens" that hide "the impression of your character." It is not necessary to make such outward connections in an effort to prove your character; rather, simply, "do your work, and I shall know you." Religion is defined by conformity and unoriginality, the opposites of self-reliance: "If I know your sect, I anticipate your argument." The minister, in particular, is bound by sect, by "communities of opinion," and is not an independent man.

It is not just society that poses a risk to the self but limitations we impose upon ourselves. We are afraid of "self-trust" and adhere to our own "consistency" in the comfort of "our past act or word." We criticize change and contradiction, but "a foolish consistency is the hobgoblin of little minds, adored by little statesmen, philosophers, and divines. With consistency a great soul has simply nothing to do." It is better to speak different thoughts each day than to be consistent out of fear: "To be great is to be misunderstood."

We can only act in accordance with our nature and our false actions to please society to not reveal our true character: "Your conformity explains nothing." Instead, we are explained by a variety of seemingly unrelated "zigzag" actions throughout our lives: "The force of character is cumulative." If someone or something reminds you of someone else, it is not true or genuine, for "character" is unique and individual, and "reminds you of nothing else." Men of character are at "the centre of things" and "all history resolves itself very easily into the biography of a few stout & earnest persons."

Self-reliance means confidence in ourselves: "let a man then know his worth." Nothing is beneath you. Do not look at "a palace, a statue, or a costly book" and think it is greater than or "forbidding" to you; it *is* you, waiting for you to "take possession" and make your own "verdict" on it. Emerson believes that there is no difference in the lives of "great" men and "ordinary" men; whether "kingdom and lordship" or regular people doing a "common day's work . . . the things of life are the same to both." Your "private act to-day" is as important as their "renowned" acts of the past. The rights and honor due to kings and others is "the right of every man." Self-trust is the source "of genius, of virtue, and of life."

Emerson explains how self-trust relates to the idea of God, namely, that if there is a God, he would "communicate, not one thing, but all things." Truth and "divine spirit" are directly revealed, with no need for a mediator: "If, therefore, a man claims to know and speak of God, and carries you backward to the phraseology of some old mouldered nation in another country, in another world, believe him not." Why privilege the god of books rather than the god of direct experience? Why look to the past for something greater than yourself? "Is the acorn better than the oak?"

He answers his own question by declaring that humans are "timid and apologetic." We would quote someone else before trusting our own instincts and experiences. He uses the analogy of nature, which always trusts itself, making no reference to the past. The "full-blown flower" is the same essence as the "leafless root." Nature lives in the present and is "resolution of all into the . . . ONE"—"the ultimate fact." The power of nature derives from self-reliance, self-sufficiency—that which is not self-sufficient in nature will not survive.

Emerson then moves to a discussion of the relationship of the self to society. "We must go alone," being responsible only for ourselves. We need not adopt "the faults" or "folly" of our friends and family but must see that the world is "in conspiracy" against us with "trifles" and worries. We must have integrity enough to resist: "No man can come near me but through my act." We must obey only "the eternal law," not customs. This is not selfish, it is truth to self—"cannot sell my liberty and my power" to save feelings and friendships. Emerson urges to be "godlike" and be your own "doctrine, society, law." Society makes us "afraid" and "timorous," and the result is that most people "cannot satisfy their own wants." Everything we have in our lives—homes, relations, religion—"we have not chosen, but society has chosen for us." We wait for chance when instead we need "self-trust" and "new powers shall appear."

In the next section Emerson looks at four different aspects of social life and determines that "a greater self-reliance must work a revolution" in each of these areas. The first of these is religion, and the first problem with religion is the idea of prayer. Prayer is the opposite of self-reliance, for it "looks abroad" for guidance through "endless mazes of natural and supernatural." Prayer is, in fact, selfishness, and "as a means to effect a private end is meanness and theft." Prayer assumes separation from God "and not unity in nature and consciousness." If we were truly "one with God," there would be no need to "beg." Prayer comes from "discontent" and "regrets," which are the opposite of self-reliance: "As men's prayers are a disease of the will, so are their creeds a disease of the intellect." Religious beliefs originate in "some powerful mind," but when spread among "unbalanced minds," the idea becomes "idolized." The faithful soon look to "their master" to explain everything to them, blinded by this one idea to the true "million-orbed, million-colored" "immortal light" of the universe.

The second area Emerson addresses is American culture. "It is for want of self culture" that "educated Americans" have such a "fascination" with Europe and spend much time traveling abroad. Emerson challenges instead to see that "the soul is no traveler; the wise man stays at home." It is fine to travel and learn about the world, to spread "benevolence," but the individual must not expect to find something "greater than he knows." He will not "get somewhat which he does not carry" within himself and can never travel "away from" himself. It is easy to believe that happiness lies elsewhere, to believe that "at Rome, I can be intoxicated with beauty, and lose my sadness." But this is a problem within, and this person will find, no matter where he or she travels, "the stern fact, the sad self, unrelenting, identical, that I fled from."

The third (and related) area into which Emerson applies the question of self-culture is art. Travel and imitation of foreign culture are signs of "a deeper unsoundness." The American "intellect is vagabond" and imitation (in art, architecture, or furnishings) is "travelling of the mind." Americans should not focus on "the Past and the Distant" but realize that "beauty, convenience, grandeur of thought . . . [are] near to us." We need an American artist and mindset to appreciate America. The American artist must "never imitate," for no "master" can teach us about ourselves, which we will then have only "half possession" of. He notes that Shakespeare had no master.

Lastly, Emerson looks to the "spirit of society" itself and its relation to self-reliance. He concludes that "society never advances . . . for every thing that is given, something is taken." For example, the cost of "civilization" is loss of "aboriginal strength," technology replaces "skill," and religion replaces virtue. We only progress when we believe that "no greater men are now than ever were." Our science and art as it exists now would not be any greater education for great men centuries before: "Society is a wave. The wave moves onward, but the water of which it is composed does not." The main problem with society, Emerson warns, is "reliance on Property, including the reliance on governments which protect it,"—this reliance on property is "the want of self-reliance." We value and protect things and "institutions" and affiliations rather than who we are. We wait for "good days" to come from "Fortune" or "Chance," when, in fact, "nothing can bring you peace but yourself."

CRITICAL COMMENTARY

The essay "Self-Reliance" addresses both the meaning of self-reliance to the individual and the relationship of that self-reliant individual to society. It is a call to the individual to declare his or her independence from society, but throughout the essay, Emerson explains that self-reliance ultimately benefits society in several different ways. Self-reliance is not egotism but the foundation of a society made up of individuals who, in eschewing "consistency," questioning authority, and seeking authentic meaning in their lives, create a more perfect society. The idea of that perfect society manifests in terms that would echo throughout Emerson's prose and poetry, in particular in his call for a distinctly American culture ("The American Scholar") and in his writings on reform ("NEW ENGLAND REFORMERS" and his lectures on ABOLITIONISM).

In "Self-Reliance" Emerson emphasizes that self-trust means never imitating another and seeing instead the greatness within. "Character" is always unique and individual but also often "misunderstood." The idea of great men, of great character, and of misunderstood genius echoes throughout his later project, *REPRESENTATIVE MEN* (1850). His statement here in "Self-Reliance," that "all history resolves itself very easily into the biography of a few stout & earnest persons," is the companion piece to his exploration of this theme in the essay "HISTORY" (of the same 1841 volume) and seems to be the inspiration for the specific examples of Plato, Shakespeare, and the other representative minds, as discussed further in "USES OF GREAT MEN" (1850).

Beyond the development and self-trust of the individual, "Self-Reliance" constitutes a critique of the society, the institutions, that prevent the self-trust of the individual, namely religion, politics, and even philosophy. Against the "statesmen and philosophers and divines" who compete for our minds, he urges the individual to stand alone and "trust thyself." Institutions require conformity to rules, rituals, and tradition, and the "dead church" is perhaps the worst, as religion is defined by conformity and unoriginality. The minister, in particular, is bound by sect, by "communities of opinion," and is not an independent man. These thoughts echo his own reasons for leaving the ministry several years earlier, as explained in "The LORD'S SUPPER" (1832) and then generalized in his radical call in the "Divinity School Address" for each "to go alone; to refuse the good models, even those which are sacred in the imagination of men, and dare to love God without mediator or veil." Religion, in Emerson's view, is only the most blatant example of seeking something greater outside of oneself, and we should instead (as he urged in *NATURE* of 1836) seek "an original relation to the universe."

As with religion, so too with doctrines and methods of reformers. Emerson is emphatic, throughout his writings, that we cannot derive goodness or morality from doctrines, from "large societies and dead institutions," but we can only discern it from within. Thus, self-reliance is the basis of social change, for in building better individuals we build a better society. Emerson returned to this view of reform again and again throughout his writings, as those around him committed themselves to various causes related to antislavery, women's rights, UTOPIANISM, and education and labor reform. Emerson resisted joining organizations and in his general statements on reform (such as "New

England Reformers," "MAN THE REFORMER," and "The CONSERVATIVE") he resisted commitment to a single cause, arguing instead for universal reform and questioning the character and self-trust of the reformer, rather than the injustice of the issue at hand. He did address issues individually in essays such as "AMERICAN SLAVERY," "EMANCIPATION OF THE NEGROES IN THE BRITISH WEST INDIES," and "WOMAN," but in "Self-Reliance" he gives a clear and emphatic explanation for why he will not give money to every cause, instructing the earnest reformer to instead, "Go love thy infant; love thy wood-chopper: be good-natured and modest: have that grace; and never varnish your hard, uncharitable ambition with this incredible tenderness for black folk a thousand miles off. Thy love afar is spite at home."

In "Self-Reliance" Emerson defines nature (as he had as well in his 1836 book on *Nature*) as the "resolution of all into the ever-blessed ONE. Self-existence is the attribute of the Supreme Cause, and it constitutes the measure of good by the degree in which it enters into all lower forms." In this sense, then, "Self-Reliance" is the immediate personalized companion to his idea expressed in "The Over-Soul" of the same volume.

FURTHER READING

Buell, Lawrence. "Emersonian Self-Reliance in Theory and Practice." In *Emerson*, 59–106. Cambridge, Mass.: Belknap Press of Harvard University, 2003.

"Shakspeare; or, the Poet" (1850)

"Shakspeare; or, the Poet" was the fourth of six biographical essays included in Emerson's 1850 text, *REPRESENTATIVE MEN.* Although Emerson had admired the works of William Shakespeare (1564–1616) since college, and had lectured on Shakespeare in an 1835–36 series on English literature, the core of the essay for the 1850 volume was drawn from a lecture given in London in 1848. Many years later Shakespeare figured prominently in Emerson's selection of favorite verses and poets included in *PARNASSUS* (1874).

By the 1840s, there was a surge in literary and historical scholarship on Shakespeare, which informed Emerson's reading of (and continued return to) Shakespeare. The mid-19th century also saw the spread of theater as entertainment and the emergence of American playwrights producing Shakespeare's plays. Emerson (as reported in a reminiscence by Edwin Whipple in 1882) confessed that "while others are capable of being carried away by an actor of Shakspeare . . . whenever I visit the theatre to witness the performance of one of his dramas, I am carried away by the poet." (Note: the spelling of Shakespeare's name varied widely in historical and literary sources; Emerson usually spelled it without the "e" after the "k.")

Emerson's early views on Shakespeare have been identified by some scholars as "bardolatry." At least one contemporary, however, thought Emerson was too critical of Shakespeare; Emerson noted in his journal, "Henry Thoreau objected to my 'Shakspeare,' that the eulogy impoverished the race. Shakspeare ought to be praised, as the sun is, so that all shall be rejoiced." But Emerson was not interested in hero worship, declaring (as he did with each of his "great men") that what is most important about Shakespeare is "the Shakspeare in us."

SYNOPSIS

Emerson begins "Shakspeare" by repeating a point he addresses in each of the other essays in the volume: "Great men are more distinguished by range and extent, than by originality." To be a "genius" is to be already "indebted" to the ideas of others. Genius is moved by "the river of the thoughts and events" of the time. The genius works with "materials collected": "Men, nations, poets, artisans, women, all have worked for him, and he enters into their labors." Genius is "being altogether *receptive.*"

In 16th-century England, theater was the inexpensive form of "the people"; Emerson compares it to the "newspapers" of his own time. Many "stage-plays" were written and circulated as public property, altered and performed by different groups. In order to understand Shakespeare, then, we must take into account that there was an "audience and expectation" before he even began to write. Shakespeare admired these "old plays" and added to them. Thus, one can trace multiple voices and "rhythms" within the plays, while still identifying "unmistakable traits of Shakspeare's hand." Emerson points out that, in Shakespeare's day, "originality" was less important than it is today. Plays were not meant to be read but performed, and so the audience was "uncritical" of the writer who drew from other sources. In effect, then, playwrights were "librarians and historiographers, as well as poets." As well with Chaucer, who was "a huge borrower."

The influence of such writers comes from the extent to which their "borrowed thoughts . . . become our own." According to Emerson, "all originality is relative. Every thinker is retrospective" and every writer draws upon "friends, lovers, books, traditions, proverbs" for material. The Bible is the greatest example of a literary work "not made by one man, or at one time; but centuries and churches brought it to perfection." And the work continues on with new translations. Even within the Bible, the Lord's Prayer is an example of Christ taking previous lines from "the rabbinical forms" and restating them. This is true of most fables and tales, as well as with modern-day law, Emerson points out.

As with most geniuses, Shakespeare was not appreciated in his own time. People paid more attention to "every trifle" in the lives of the king and queen, ignoring this common man and playwright: "nobody suspected he was the poet of the human race." It was a prolific era and Shakespeare did not stand out; England in his day was like "Greece in the time of Pericles." It took more than a century before Shakespeare was recognized critically and "till now" for his influence on literature and history to be fully seen.

While "The Shakspeare Society" has spent time and money piecing together the details of his life, none of these "scraps of information" and "gossip" explains his genius or "imagination." No "file of accounts, or private letter" can explain "transcendent secrets." To understand Shakespeare, one must go directly to "the Sonnets": "What trait of his private mind has he hidden in his dramas?" In confronting his words directly, rather than being "the least known" person to us, Shakespeare becomes "the one person, in all modern history, known to us." Shakespeare's writings are so broad and so deep that he spoke on every point of concern to life—"of morals, of manners, of economy, of philosophy, of religion, of taste, of the conduct of life."

Whereas most would acknowledge Shakespeare as an important dramatist, perhaps "the best in the world," Emerson names him a great "poet and philosopher." Drama is just a "form," like a song or proverb or law, but the form is "immaterial" to the idea and the "universality of its application." Shakespeare "wrote the text of modern life" and "read the hearts of men and women." To be concerned with the form of the drama is "like making a question concerning the paper on which a king's message is written."

While his preferred form was drama, Shakespeare's subject is nothing less than "an omnipresent humanity," and thus his writings display "no discoverable egotism," whether in "farce, tragedy, narrative, and love-songs." As in nature, his details are perfect, no matter how small. The "single lines" of his plays or his sonnets are beautiful and meaningful each alone, and yet cannot be taken out of context from the whole. With Shakespeare, as with any poet, the "experience" comes first, then the thought, then the poem.

Another "trait" of a poet is that he must have "cheerfulness"—the ability to see and create beauty. The poet "delights in the world, in man, in woman, for the lovely light that sparkles from them." The "priest and prophet" take the same material from life as Shakespeare does, but they read it only as "duty," "obligation, a sadness . . . a pilgrim's progress . . . fall and curse . . . doomsdays and purgatorial and penal fires." Such are only "half-views of half-men." The world waits for a "poet-priest, a reconciler."

But while Shakespeare had no equal in "talent and mental power," his greatest fault, according to Emerson, was that he saw this beauty in humans and in nature and wasted it on "entertainments." Trifling away his talents on the "revels" of the theater was akin to having power over "the comets . . . or the planets and their moons," and turning them only into a "municipal fireworks" show. Shakespeare underestimated and therefore squandered his own genius: "it must even go into the world's history that the best poet led an obscure and profane life, using his genius for the public amusement."

CRITICAL COMMENTARY

Emerson looked to Shakespeare not as a source of entertainment but as his representative poet, a model and source of inspiration for all. Besides Napoléon Bonaparte, William Shakespeare was probably the figure in *Representative Men* that Emerson's 19th-century readers knew best and found most intriguing. He urges, however, to look beyond the "gossip" of history and go directly to the source. Likewise, in the essay "EXPERIENCE" (1844), Emerson questions this misplaced interest in great men, musing at "a collector" who purchased "an autograph of Shakspeare" for a large sum of money at auction, when "for nothing a school-boy can read Hamlet." Emerson encouraged this more direct, meaningful, and *democratic* access to great men.

Emerson was interested in the fact that, as he wrote in his journal in 1837, "Shakspeare was not a popular man in his day." Indeed, this seems to have been a defining trait of most of his "great men"—that they transcended their own times, that the world had not been ready for them, and that (certainly in the case of EMANUEL SWEDENBORG) their genius was still not fully appreciated. But this is especially true of the poet, as Emerson continued in his journal to reflect on Shakespeare: "He sat alone and walked alone, a visionary poet, and came with his piece, modest but discerning, to the players, and was too glad to get it received." This image of the solitary poet was echoed in Emerson's earlier poem "SAADI" (1842), in which the poet "dwells alone."

Of course, the lone poet is always building upon the work of others. Emerson cites figures on how many of Shakespeare's lines were "written by some author preceding" him, how many depended "on the foundation laid by his predecessors," and how many "were entirely his own." It is unlikely that "a single drama" was of Shakespeare's "absolute invention." Emerson takes time to detail these distinctions as his way of weighing in on the public debate then swirling over whether Shakespeare authored many of the plays attributed to him. While Emerson's essay challenges the importance or even definition of originality or authorship, he also posits Shakespeare as thoroughly unique in his genius and wisdom, asking in "SELF-RELIANCE" (1841), "Where is the master who could have taught Shakspeare?"

In positing such a popular figure as Shakespeare as the representative poet, Emerson sought a wider role for the poet in his own time. Just as Shakespeare wrote plays and sonnets, Emerson was himself building a career across genres as a writer of poetry and prose and as a lecturer to different types of audiences. Emerson, like Shakespeare, spoke to suit the audience and the times. On a lecture tour in Illinois in January 1856, he consoled himself with the idea of "Shakspeare, or Franklin, or Aesop, coming to Illinois." All of these were examples of writers who reached out to the masses with their plays, aphorisms, or fables. From these great men, Emerson learned the lesson that "he is no master who cannot vary his forms."

Emerson's essay on "Shakspeare" ultimately reveals less about Shakespeare and more about Emerson's view of the poet: "This power of expression, or of transferring the inmost truth of things into music and verse, makes him the type of the poet." This is the role of the poet that Emerson would explore in essays such as "The POET" (1841) and "POETRY AND IMAGINATION" (1876). When Emerson emphasizes Shakespeare as a poet rather than a dramatist, he remarks on the fact that the "single lines" of his plays can be extracted and have meaning on their own. Shakespeare took the universal and broke it down to the smallest unit, so that within each line the essence of the whole was still contained. Poetry thus reflects nature, as in Emerson's poem "EACH AND ALL" (1847) and, indeed, Emerson's example of Shakespeare speaks to his own pursuit as master of the sentence within his essays. It is this characteristic of the poet that makes both Shakespeare *and* Emerson imminently quotable.

FURTHER READING

Marovitz, Sanford E. "Emerson's Shakespeare: From Scorn to Apotheosis." In *Emerson Centenary Essays,* edited by Joel Myerson, 122–155. Carbondale: Southern Illinois University Press, 1982.

"The Snow-Storm" (1841)

Emerson's poem "The Snow-Storm" is a 28-line one-stanza poem first published in the January 1841 issue of the *DIAL* and collected in *POEMS* (1847) and *SELECTED POEMS* (1876). As early as 1832 he recorded in his journal imagery that would later appear in the poem, notably his desire, "Instead of lectures on Architecture" to "make a lecture on God's architecture, one of his beautiful works, a Day. I will draw a sketch of a winters day." In the poem, a snowstorm creates an architectural phenomenon to rival human efforts in art and writing, such as in the architecture of a poem.

CRITICAL COMMENTARY

The first part of the poem reports on the scene, detailing both the natural and the human worlds. The snow seems to come suddenly, and "the whited air" quickly covers "hill and woods, the river, and the heaven," as well as "veils the farmhouse." The snow hides what is beneath it, but also hidden indoors are the people affected by the storm. The poem reveals a domestic scene of "housemates" trapped inside "the farmhouse" during a winter storm, and "the sled and traveller stopped." Nature has an effect on human activities in the immediate, external sense, causing a forced "tumultuous privacy of storm."

The second part of the poem turns to a more spiritual or philosophical reflection on nature's effect on humans, as inspiration, anthropomorphizing nature as mason, the snow its medium drawn from "an unseen quarry evermore." Nature works through the night as the storm covers every "roof," "tree, or door" with "his wild work." The storm works in a "speeding," "fanciful," and "savage" way, seemingly chaotic, ". . . nought cares he / For number or proportion." The storm creates a more natural or organic form than mankind—seems to be even "mocking" humans—and refuses to be bound by style or rules. Nature's work is beautiful, one of hanging "wreaths" in "swan-like form." The "astonished Art" nature creates in one night will take humans "an age" of slow and deliberate work, "stone by stone." Even then, we can only "mimic" nature's work, "the frolic architecture of the snow."

Emerson used the image of the snowstorm in other writings; in the "DIVINITY SCHOOL ADDRESS" (1838) he compared the "merely spectral" minister to the "beautiful meteor of the snow" outside the window, a juxtaposition of religion as mediated by the minister compared to unmediated nature. In the essay on "HISTORY," also published in 1841, he made reference again to the snow as architectural inspiration, reflecting on seeing "a snow-drift along the sides of the stone wall which obviously gave the idea of the common architectural scroll to abut a tower." This is the image of nature's masonry he would call upon in the poem. JOHN GREENLEAF WHITTIER included lines from Emerson's "Snow-Storm" in the epigraph for his poem "Snow-bound" of 1865.

FURTHER READING

Morris, Saundra. 'Metre-Making' Arguments: Emerson's Poems." In *The Cambridge Companion to Ralph Waldo Emerson,* edited by Joel Porte and Saundra Morris. New York: Cambridge University Press, 1999.

Society and Solitude (1870)

Society and Solitude was published in 1870 and included 12 essays: "SOCIETY AND SOLITUDE," "CIVILIZATION," "ART," "ELOQUENCE," "DOMESTIC LIFE," "FARMING," "WORKS AND DAYS," "BOOKS," "Clubs," "COURAGE," "SUCCESS," and "OLD AGE." Like many of his essays throughout his career, most of these were revised from lectures Emerson had delivered in the previous decade. Seven of these had been previously published, in part or in their entirety, but five ("Works and Days," "Clubs," "Courage," "Success," and "Farming") were published here for the first time.

Ten years had passed between the publication of *The CONDUCT OF LIFE* (1860) and *Society and Solitude.* During those years the country had come through a devastating Civil War that ended with the abolition of slavery. In general, after 1860 Emerson turned to more pragmatic or social and political issues in his lectures and writing. The biggest political issue of his lifetime solved for now, by 1870 he was able to reflect even further on the relationship between the self and society, and on the balance between our inner moral selves and our outward social selves, a theme he had also addressed in the various essays in *The Conduct of Life* and in numerous other essays and poems.

Son EDWARD WALDO EMERSON noted in his Centenary Edition of *The Complete Works* that *Society and Solitude* reflects Emerson moving into old age and meditating on losses but also on his "delight" in family life, in children, and in grandchildren. Bringing his philosophical concerns to bear on everyday life, most of the essays deal in depth with some basic aspect of the individual's worldly experience. Friend THOMAS CARLYLE offered much praise for Emerson's later writings; in *Society and Solitude* he found "your old self here, and something more," and he commended Emerson for the "brevity, simplicity, softness, homely grace" of the essays.

"Society and Solitude" (1870)

Emerson's SOCIETY AND SOLITUDE came out in 1870, a decade after the publication of *The* CONDUCT OF LIFE (1860). While his preoccupation with the Civil War and its immediate aftermath accounts in part for the time between the two volumes, they are thematically continuous, addressing overlapping topics initially worked out in lectures of the 1850s. From "ILLUSIONS," the capping essay of *The Conduct of Life,* it is just a short step to "Society and Solitude," which keynotes the 1870 volume. Both essays refer to the illusory identities of the self-absorbed "mad crowd," in contrast to the self-reliant genius who sees through the charivari, understanding the causal laws of nature without self-delusion, thus enjoying his privileged aloneness with the gods. But Emerson in his later years has mellowed. In contrast with the individualistic flair of his earlier series of essays, "Society and Solitude" exemplifies his endeavor to reflect on matters of public participation and interest in such essays as "ART," "CIVILIZATION," "COURAGE," "SUCCESS," "FARMING," "OLD AGE," and the like.

SYNOPSIS

The essay takes its point of departure from one of Emerson's persistent themes, that of the individual genius. It begins on the negative side, with the disadvantages of the genius who, already oversensitized to the interventions of social life, pays a price for his solitary status. Nature works here by the law of compensation: "Nature protects her work. To the culture of the world an Archimedes, a Newton, is indispensable; so she guards them by a certain aridity. If these had been good fellows, fond of dancing, port and clubs, we should have had no Theory of the Sphere and no Principia." Here Emerson wryly dwells on the irony that there is "no remedy" for the "disease" of the genius's alienation from contemporary society, other than "habits of self-reliance that should go in practice to making the man independent of the human race, or else a religion of love."

The irony of this tension between society and solitude continues in the following: "We pray to be conventional. But the wary Heaven takes care you shall not be, if there is anything good in you. Dante was very bad company, and was never invited to dinner." Emerson goes on to mention Michelangelo and Columbus as other examples of geniuses out of sorts with their societies: "Columbus discovered no isle or key so lonely as himself." Yet each of these understood "the reason of his exclusion," namely, that their purpose was grand and that nature had assigned others to utilitarian tasks of the day: "But the necessity of solitude is deeper than we have said, and is organic." And so Emerson advises the geniuses of the ages: "Dear heart! Take it sadly home to thee,—there is no cooperation."

Emerson concludes this observation of the natural fate of genius on another wry note: "Such is the tragic necessity which strict science finds underneath our domestic and neighborly life, irresistibly driving each adult soul as with whips into the desert, and making our warm covenants sentimental and momentary." To rescue this observation from bleak negativity, he concludes on a more metaphysical note. The "ends of thought" achieved by the solitary geniuses "are deeper than can be told, and belong to the immensities and eternities. They reach down to that depth where society itself originates and disappears; where the question is, Which is first, man or men? Where the individual is lost in his source."

The essay now turns toward the other pole of the binary of society and solitude in saying that "this banishing to the rocks and echoes no metaphysics can make right or tolerable. This result is so against nature, such a half-view, that it must be corrected by a common sense and experience." Every man requires society, "or he will feel a certain bareness and poverty, as of a displaced and unfurnished member. He is to be dressed in arts and institutions, as well as in body garments."

In this context Emerson does not entirely compromise the solitary genius by society's civilizing effects, for he admits that "now and then a man exquisitely made can live alone, and must; but coop up most men and you undo them." But he goes on to feature the organic necessities of this side of the ledger—the nourishments of the soul that come in the streets and "the public square"—while estimating a man's contributions to the needs of society. Society, for its part, cannot do without cultivated men: "The benefits of affection are immense; and the one event which never loses its romance is the encounter with superior persons on terms allowing the happiest intercourse." To a lesser degree, "this genial heat is latent in all constitutions, and is disengaged only by the friction of society." The excitations of our "animal spirits" arise spontaneously from "health" and "social habit."

Emerson continues to move between the two poles of society and solitude. For he goes on to say that "the people are to be taken in very small doses. If solitude is proud, so is society vulgar. . . . We sink as easily as we rise, through sympathy." Our individual aims are high enough, but we compromise these in the face of the grosser aspects of social intercourse: "Men cannot afford to live together on their merits, and they adjust themselves by their demerits,—by their love of gossip, or by sheer endurance and animal good nature."

Once again, Emerson challenges the reader with insight into the ambivalences and self-deceptions of the human heart. His dialectic of the productive mind and the compromising crowd remains unresolved. Among other things, his message is that genuine intellectual intercourse cannot be forced: "Society exists by chemical affinity, and not otherwise." The remedy is once again his ethics of self-reliance by which one must continue uncorruptedly to live by his own lights, even in the assemblies of men and women that would impose their agendas on the individual heart. But given freedom of intercourse, humans will separate and group according to the natural "magnetic" principle of "each seeking his like."

CRITICAL COMMENTARY

Emerson rides this tension of solitude and society to a paradoxical, but still typically positive, end. We require solitude to nourish our "better consciousness," which we can then bring with us into the "street" and to the "palaces." But "society and solitude are deceptive names" until considered in individual terms. It is not the outward circumstance of estrangement or engagement but the readiness of benevolence and sympathy that influences our experiences of being alone or of being in society. A "sound mind" will accept society as the natural element in which its better thoughts are to be applied. We must thus keep our independence to nourish society.

"Society and Solitude" is vintage Emerson, another exploration of the themes of polarity in nature and of balancing the competing claims in life. A meaningful backdrop to this essay can be found in earlier essays on such related topics as "LOVE" and "FRIENDSHIP" (in *ESSAYS: SECOND SERIES* [1844]). The former of these features Emerson's sense of the stages of life through which earthly and heavenly loves pass. The latter focuses on the nature of enduring friendship. And yet the bottom line of this earlier essay is to prioritize the solitary, spiritually ascending self over attachment to friends, even the best of them: "I do with my friends as I do with my books. I would have them where I can find them, but I seldom use them. We must have society on our own terms, and admit or exclude it on the slightest cause." Emerson retained this essential commitment to self-reliance throughout his career.

The later writings of Emerson are considered, balanced expressions of his mature years. He presents the combined wisdom of "Society and Solitude" in its own ironic summation: "Here again, as so often, nature delights to put us between extreme antagonisms, and our safety is in the skill with which we keep the diagonal line. Solitude is impracticable, and society fatal. We must keep our head in the one and our hands in the other. The conditions are met, if we keep our independence, yet do not lose our sympathy. These wonderful horses need to be driven by fine hands." This image can, and should, be read as Emerson's own obliquely autobiographical statement.

David A. Dilworth

"Solution" (1867)

Emerson's poem "Solution" is an answer poem to the earlier poem "The Test," which had been published in the *ATLANTIC MONTHLY* in January 1861. Emerson had promised the editors an answer to "The Test," but perhaps because of difficulty with the poem, a complete draft was not finished until 1862 (Emerson composed four separate drafts, all with significant variations), and "Solution" first appeared in *MAY-DAY AND OTHER PIECES* (1867); it was reprinted in *Poems* (1884).

The poem contains five stanzas, each describing a thinker from whom Emerson drew inspiration (or considers to be "inspired," in the Latin sense of the term). These thinkers—Homer, Dante, Shakespeare, and Goethe—become representative of the mind under the influence of divine insight, a state produced not only by skill but also by harmony with nature (explored further in the essays, "SHAKSPEARE; OR, THE POET," "GOETHE; OR, THE WRITER," and "SWEDENBORG; OR, THE MYSTIC" in *REPRESENTATIVE MEN* [1850]).

CRITICAL COMMENTARY

The poem is spoken by the Muse; in Emerson's thought, this is genius, the spirit of the poet, which Emerson calls for in his writings on aesthetics ("The POET"; "POETRY AND IMAGINATION"). In the opening stanza, the eternal Muse narrates the rise of man, reflecting Emerson's own interest in evolution (recall the poem that opens *NATURE*: "Striving to be man, the worm / Mounts through all the spires of form"). In this poem the Muse first expresses itself through the "perfect Greek," Homer.

In stanza 3, the Muse moves from Greece (classical civilization) to Italy (Christian civilization) and sings through Dante. Here, the stanza refers specifically to the structure of the *Divine Comedy* (the "triple spheres"). Also, the line "Moulding to his will" recalls another of Emerson's qualifications for the ideal poet, who will shape the world to his will, rather than have his will shaped by the world. All of the thinkers in the poem accomplish this, through symbols and tropes.

In the third stanza the Muse moves to Elizabethan England, and to William Shakespeare. The fourth stanza finds the Muse in Sweden, with the philosopher and religious mystic EMANUEL SWEDENBORG ("the Swede Emanuel"). Swedenborg's theology regarding such ideas as divine revelation, the intimate connection between heaven and earth, and correspondences is key to Emerson's thought. In many ways Swedenborg represents for Emerson the complete thinker: Both a scientific mind and a spiritual mystic, Swedenborg represents the unity Emerson sought in the ideal man.

Stanza 5 moves from Sweden to Germany and to JOHANN WOLFGANG VON GOETHE, novelist, poet, playwright, and philosopher. Goethe's romanticism was well known to the Transcendentalists; the school of German romanticism (and the new Bible study inspired by it) was a significant influence on the Transcendentalists; and Emerson traveled to Germany personally to study scripture. In "newer days of war and trade, / Romance forgot and faith decayed," Goethe "Drew the firm lines of Fate and Life / And brought Olympian wisdom down" (the term "Olympian," a reference to Mount Olympus, connects us back to Homer), and "Stooping, his finger wrote in clay / The open secret of to-day" (the image recalls Christ writing in the dirt in the book of John, chapter 8).

The closing couplet summarizes this particular group of thinkers. Using the image of the flower ("unfolding petals five"), Emerson sees the Muse as the blossoming of genius in the world. The flower image also emphasizes the organic component of genius; inspired by God, genius is a product of human thought and divine insight.

Bill Scalia

"Song of Nature" (1861)

Emerson assembled the poem "Song of Nature" from fragments and notes in his journals over the course of several years. He sent a shorter version of the poem, which he titled "First of May," to his brother WILLIAM EMERSON in 1859. Encouraged by William's positive response, he added six additional quatrains and sent the poem to JAMES RUSSELL LOWELL, who published the poem, now titled "Song of Nature," in the *ATLANTIC MONTHLY* in January 1861. The poem was reprinted (with the Lowell-deleted stanza after line 64 restored) in *MAY-DAY AND OTHER PIECES* (1867), *SELECTED POEMS* (1876), and *Poems* (1884).

The speaker in this Emerson poem is nature herself, who seems to be calling for the ideal poet (or perhaps a "representative man"). The ideal poet will "speak" nature to the world, to bring us into harmony with the divine through figurative, poetic language. The search for the ideal poet was one of Emerson's long-term projects, which he describes in *NATURE* (1836), "The POET" (1844), and "POETRY AND IMAGINATION" (1876). In this poem he calls again for the poet, not in his aesthetic prose, but in the voice of nature.

CRITICAL COMMENTARY

The title of the poem refers not only to a song about nature but also a song sung *by* nature. In this sense, nature finds her own voice to call for the poet; thus, Emerson provides a different perspective on his own aesthetic description of the ideal poet.

The narrative voice of the poem represents the generating and animating voice of the universe (and, by extension, the soul, since for Emerson the universe is the extension of the soul). Emerson's typical description of the poet is carried out by describing our human need for a connection with nature; here, Emerson uses nature to describe its own need for human expression. Nature as speaker recalls a few examples—Jesus, Shakespeare—but is waiting for a poet for the contemporary age: "But he, the man-child glorious / where tarries he the while?"

The poem does contain a stubborn peculiarity, however. In stanza 17 Emerson refers clearly to Jesus and Shakespeare, but as to the two other unnamed poets, we can only surmise:

> One in a Judean manger,
> And on by Avon stream,
> One over against the mouths of the Nile,
> And one in the Academe.

EDWARD WALDO EMERSON writes, "Readers who wish nothing unresolved are much troubled by this verse, but Nature is not statistical or immediately intelligible. Like the gods, she 'says all things by indirection.'" Edward argues that "its [the stanza's] very ambiguity was probably intentional and makes it better harmonize with the preceding verse." Many readers believe the poem points to Egypt and to Moses, though Edward argues that Emerson more likely is referring to "one of the great Alexandrian Neo-platonists." As for the last poet, Italy is certainly "over against the mouths of the Nile," and Emerson may have been referencing classical Roman civilization, or the Italian Renaissance as a whole.

Bill Scalia

"The Sphinx" (1841)

One of Emerson's most popular poems and one of his personal favorites, "The Sphinx" was written in 1840 and published in the *DIAL* magazine of January 1841. Emerson chose it as the opening poem of his 1847 collection, *POEMS*, again in *SELECTED POEMS* (1876), and it held the same pride of position in *Poems* (1884). In preparing the centenary edition after his father's death, however, son EDWARD WALDO EMERSON rearranged the order, placing several other poems before "The Sphinx," justifying the decision with his belief that "The Sphinx has no doubt cut off, in the very portal, readers who would have found good and joyful works for themselves, had not her riddle been beyond their powers." This timid decision hardly took into consideration many other of Emerson's riddling poems in the collection—poems ringing changes on the same fundamental meaning as "The Sphinx"—which the reader would have had to penetrate, and with "good and joyful" results.

The poem is a long conversation between the Sphinx and the "cheerful" poet who has come to unravel her mysteries. As a meditation on the role of the poet and the secrets of nature, scholar Saundra Morris thus calls it a "threshold poem," which serves "to initiate volumes of poetry" by Emerson and others. Indeed, the Sphinx was a literary figure of special interest to Emerson's 19th-century contemporaries—HERMAN MELVILLE included a chapter on "The Sphynx" in *Moby-Dick* (1851) and Edgar Allan Poe published a short story titled "The Sphinx" (1846). Although the Sphinx is usually associated with death and struggle, including the inability to find poetic inspiration, in Emerson's poem the Sphinx is welcomed and praised: "'Say on, sweet Sphinx! thy dirges / Are pleasant songs to me.'"

CRITICAL COMMENTARY

"The Sphinx" is a poetic version of Emerson's basic philosophy articulated in such companion prose works as *NATURE* (1836), "The METHOD OF NATURE" (1841), and "NOMINALIST AND REALIST" (1844), as well as in many of his key poems such as "The WORLD-SOUL" and "WOODNOTES." In his journal of 1859, at a time when he wrote a companion metaphysical poem, "BRAHMA," Emerson declared that his philosophy centers on the two principles of identity or unity, and variety or change. In due course he applied this to the interpretation of the poem when he wrote: "I have often been asked the meaning of 'The Sphinx.' It is this—The perception of identity unites all things and explains one by another, and the most rare and strange is equally facile as the most common. But if the mind live only in particulars, and see only differences . . . then the world addresses to this mind a question it cannot answer, and each new fact tears it to pieces, and it is vanquished by the distracting variety."

In Emerson's celebrated poem of 132 lines and 17 stanzas, the Sphinx, in its ponderous stone fusion of human and animal forms, stands guard over his poetic collection, just as it stood at the entrance to the city of Thebes in the ancient mythology. The poem offers a series of riddling expressions of many-in-oneness with which she challenges humankind to unravel the mysteries of nature and the universe, including the existence and fate of humanity itself. The Sphinx says she "waited the seer" who would unfold "The fate of the man-child; / The meaning of man; / Known fruit of the unknown; / Daedalian plan." She then utters further paradoxes of the relationship between unity and variety in nature. In the fourth stanza, "The waves, unashamed, / In differences meet, / Play gladly with the breezes, / Old playfellows meet." In the fifth stanza, "Sea, earth, air, sound, silence, / Plant, quadruped, bird, / By one music enchanted, / One deity stirred." In the sixth stanza, she utters her riddle of the spiritual continuum of all things in a truly beautiful image: "The babe by its mother / Lies bathed in joy; / Glide its hours uncounted,— / The sun is its toy; / Shines the peace of all being, / Without cloud, in its eyes; / And the sun of the world / In soft miniature lies."

But receiving no responses, in caustic lines the Sphinx upbraids man as not up to the task—man who "crouches and blushes, / Absconds and conceals; / He creepeth and peepeth, / He palters and steals," and who in his infirmity, melancholy, and jealousy is "An oaf, an accomplice, / He poisons the ground." She laments mankind's "sadness and madness," asking "Who . . . has turned the man-child's head?"

Midway through the poem, a poet appears, responding to the Sphinx's challenge. "Aloud and cheerfully," he declares that the Sphinx's dirges conceal decipherable meanings: "Say on, sweet Sphinx! Thy dirges / Are pleasant songs to me / Deep love lieth under / These pictures of time: /

They fade in the light of / Their meaning sublime." The poet also speaks in the Sphinx's own language of paradox, revealing the secret of the good of evil in the universe and of other such mysteries of the relationship of the whole to the particular, of the spiritual to the physical, when "the soul sees the perfect, / Which his eyes seek in vain." The clairvoyant soul of the poet plunges deep into "the aye-rolling orbit / No goal will arrive"—that is, relies upon an affirmative intuition of the underlying unitary reality not visible to the eye. The untold heavenly sweetness of this vision draws him to new heights of insight: "Eterne alternation / Now follows, now flies; / And under pain, pleasure / —Under pleasure, pain lies. / Love works at the centre. / Heart heaving alway."

To these correct revelations of her deep secret "the old Sphinx bit her thick lip," declaring: "Who taught thee me to name? / I am thy spirit, yoke-fellow, / Of thine eye I am eyebeam." Emerson was to employ the same image of the "eyebeam" in many of his poems, and these all reprised his subjective perspective of "the transparent eyeball" that sees the sublime, as first announced in the opening pages of *Nature*. Here the Sphinx then announces that the poet has solved the riddle, that mankind is not only the answer to the riddle, but also the original riddle: "Thou art the unanswered question."

In the finale of the poem, the Sphinx is now constrained to disclose various other aspects of her riddle to the clairvoyant poet. For one, she notes that there is not a single answer to the riddle, for each individual must figure it out for himself or herself—as per Emerson's ethics of "SELF-RELIANCE" (1841) and his injunction for each person to "enjoy an original relation to the universe" (as he phrased it in *Nature*). In "HISTORY" (1841), he explained that "the human mind wrote history, and this must read it. The Sphinx must solve her own riddle. If the whole of history is in one man, it is all to be explained from individual experience." The Sphinx, then, is the universal reality, and each person must "take the quest through nature. / It through thousand natures ply." She is the "universal dame" that speaks through "a thousand voices," so that "Who telleth one of my meanings, / Is master of all I am."

Released now by the poet's clairvoyant spirit, the Sphinx, "crouched no more in stone," uprises merrily. Again, Emerson's eternal optimism, especially regarding nature's secrets, rewrites the ending for the Sphinx, which in traditional mythology is destroyed. In Emerson's hands, she ascends into nature: "She melted into purple cloud, / She silvered in the moon; / She spired into a yellow flame; / She flowered in blossoms red; / She flowed into a foaming wave; / She stood Monadnoc's head"—Emerson's brilliant metaphors of the Sphinx's final revelations of her true identity, invoking, not coincidentally, the same mountain of inspiration from his poem "MONADNOC."

The philosopher CHARLES SANDERS PEIRCE frequently quoted Emerson's line, "Of thine eye I am eyebeam," in his writings, and in a key work, "A Guess at the Riddle" (1887–88), he suggested that his own mature philosophical system was his own response to Emerson's poem "The Sphinx."

FURTHER READING

Morris, Saundra. "'Metre-Making'" Arguments: Emerson's Poems." In *The Cambridge Companion to Ralph Waldo Emerson*, edited by Joel Porte and Saundra Morris. New York: Cambridge University Press, 1999.

———. "The Threshold Poem, Emerson, and 'The Sphinx.'" *AL* 69 (1997): 547–570.

David A. Dilworth

"Spiritual Laws" (1841)

Emerson's essay on "Spiritual Laws" was included in ESSAYS: *FIRST SERIES* (1841) and, like the other essays in that volume, was drawn from lectures in the "Philosophy of History" series of 1836–37. "Spiritual Laws" was part of Emerson's project on defining the relationship of the individual to the whole and the implications for how we live our lives. In that sense, it is the companion essay to "EXPERIENCE" of ESSAYS: *SECOND SERIES* (1844) but also to his numerous writings on the role of "THE POET" (also 1844) and his general imperative to

"Do thy work." In "Spiritual Laws" he explains that "by doing his own work he unfolds himself." In the opening verse of the accompanying poem, "SPIRITUAL LAWS," he repeats this idea that while "Heaven" (or the universe) is both "House" and "architect" of our lives, we determine how we spend our days: "Sole and self-commanded works, / Fears not undermining days."

SYNOPSIS

Emerson opens the essay by explaining that life is made up of both "beauty" and "the tragic and terrible," and yet, in our "thought," the mind constructs a view of ourselves and our world that is generally positive: "The soul will not know either deformity or pain." While individuals may experience pain, the universe moves forward in a positive trajectory: "All loss, all pain, is particular. . . . For it is only the finite that has wrought and suffered; the infinite lies stretched in smiling repose."

So it is that the "difficulties" we experience we have brought upon ourselves, as a result of acting against the laws of nature. Our instinct does "not yield . . . any intellectual obstructions and doubts." Even "theological problems" are only intellectual exercises, which "never presented a practical difficulty to any man." The questions of "original sin, origin of evil, predestination, and the like" have no bearing on how we live our lives. They never vexed anyone "who did not go out of his way to seek them." Humans create doctrinal dilemmas and then confuse this with spiritual dilemmas: "It is quite another thing that he should be able to give account of his faith, and expound to another the theory of his self-union and freedom." What is needed is not religion but "self-knowledge," "strength and integrity in that which he is."

This "self-knowledge" comes from instinct and is actually impeded by what we call "education." We see morality and "virtue" as a "struggle," when we have an innate "moral nature," which is good. It therefore does not make sense to talk of virtue when "either God is there, or he is not there." Virtue is nothing more than "nature over will." This law is true in "practical life" as well: "There is less intention in history than we ascribe to it. We impute deep-laid, far-sighted plans to Caesar and Napoleon; but the best of their power was in nature, not in them." The lesson therefore is "that our life might be much easier and simpler than we make it; that the world might be a happier place than it is; that there is no need of struggles, convulsions, and despairs, of the wringing of the hands and the gnashing of the teeth; that we miscreate our own evils. . . . We interfere with the optimism of nature."

Difficulty arises when we expect conformity: "Our Sunday-schools, and churches, and pauper-societies are yokes to the neck." We make rules that apply to everyone and, yet, "Why should all virtue work in one and the same way?" Likewise with church: "why drag this dead weight of a Sunday-school over the whole Christendom? It is natural and beautiful that childhood should inquire. . . . Do not shut up the young people against their will in a pew, and force the children to ask them questions for an hour against their will."

Politics, church, education, all the "ponderous machinery" of society interferes with our true selves. Instead, "let us draw a lesson from nature," which always takes the simplest route to achieve the highest ends, and without struggle: "When the fruit is ripe, it falls. When the fruit is despatched, the leaf falls." We work too hard and worry that things are never complete, but this is the way of nature. As the soul is also "infused . . . into nature" it provides "guidance for each of us," if only we would listen: "Place yourself in the middle of the stream of power and wisdom . . . and you are without effort impelled to truth, to right, and a perfect contentment." If we would let nature guide us as individuals, then society as well "would organize itself, as do now the rose, and the air, and the sun."

What the world calls "choice" is actually intuition; we find "right or goodness" when we *choose* to listen to our inner selves. In this way we find our true work—whatever is "the state or circumstance desirable to my constitution" is "heaven." There is no "excuse" for blaming one's profession for one's actions, for a man is accountable "for the choice of his daily craft or profession." The "*calling*" is his "character." We choose that which comes most easily to us: "His ambition is exactly proportioned to his powers. The height of the pinnacle is determined by the breadth of the base." Nor should we find glory in the "outward signs" of our profession. A person who feels himself "extraordinary, and not in the roll of common men" is the very definition of "fanaticism"—nature shows "no respect of persons."

We must only do the work to which we are called, not adjust ourselves to the work that is put before us; when the latter happens, "then he is part of the machine he moves; the man is lost." Whatever the task, even "if the labor is mean," we must make it our own: "He must find in that an outlet for his character." When we underestimate work it is only because we underestimate mankind—we "do not perceive that any thing man can do may be divinely done." We look for "greatness . . . in some places or duties, in certain offices or occasion," when greatness may be in the most ordinary person or circumstance. Likewise, we call something "obscure" or "vulgar" only because the "poetry is not yet written" of that thing.

Our perspective comes from a subjective relation to the universe, with each selecting "what is fit for him" and rejecting "what is unfit." We are not always conscious of this "selecting principle" or of the meaning of our choices: "Those facts, words, persons, which dwell in his memory without his being able to say why, remain, because they have a relation to him not less real for being as yet unapprehended." Even if you do not yet understand, do not question or dismiss memories or interpretations of experiences: "They relate to your gift. Let them have their weight, and do not reject them. . . . What your heart thinks is great is great. The soul's emphasis is always right." The soul keeps no "secrets" and yet reliance upon intuition does not eliminate the role of human will. We must still have our minds "ripened" and eyes opened to receive these messages: "No man can learn what he has not preparation for learning, however near to his eyes the object."

Our dreams as well (the subconscious) are also a manifestation of the mind, they "are the sequel of our waking knowledge." Dreams are only as good or as evil as the dreamer: "The visions of the night bear some proportion to the visions of the day. Hideous dreams are exaggerations of the sins of the day." The same is true of our friends. A person is drawn to (or repelled by) another person, "according to their likeness or unlikeness to himself, truly seeking himself in his associates." Likewise, do we read books that reflect our own ideas back to ourselves; a single volume may be "a thousand books to a thousand persons." Such are "the eternal laws of mind," that "we can love nothing but nature." He uses the example of Plato, who is read by few and yet whose ideas are universal and therefore immortal. "There are not in the world at any one time more than a dozen persons who read and understand Plato," and yet "to every generation these come duly down, for the sake of these few persons, as if God brought them in his hand."

Emerson returns to the idea that we need not strive for virtue, neither is virtue rare: "Virtue is the adherence in action to the nature of things, and the nature of things makes it prevalent." We show our character whether we "act" or "sit still" or "sleep"; even "your silence answers very loud." "Faces never lie, it is said." "There is confession in the glances of our eyes; in our smiles; in salutations; and the grasp of hands." "Pretension" will not bring virtue or "greatness," only truth to ourselves can bring these things. "The lesson which these observations convey is, Be, and not seem."

The question of pretension and defining greatness returns Emerson again to the question of vocation. Society is based on "the worship of magnitude. We call the poet inactive, because he is not a president, a merchant, or a porter." But virtue and meaning are found not in the grand gesture but in everyday life, in the smallest insight: "The epochs of our life are not in the visible facts of our choice of a calling, our marriage, our acquisition of an office, and the like, but in a silent thought by the way-side as we walk; in a thought which revises our entire manner of life. . . . This revisal or correction is a constant force, which, as a tendency, reaches through our lifetime." What we call "action" is just "a trick of the senses." Action is not greater than thought, when "the ancestor of every action is a thought." To think is to seek a closer relationship with nature; "To think is to act."

Thus, he concludes, "Let me heed my duties" and not worry what others may think or do. Why praise great men when "my time should be as good as their time,—my facts, my net of relations, as good as theirs. . . . Rather let me do my work so well that other idlers, if they choose, may compare my texture with the texture of these and find it identical with the best." We, too, often "over-estimate" the work of others and "under-estimate" ourselves. Even menial work is "supreme and beautiful."

CRITICAL COMMENTARY

In "Spiritual Laws" Emerson comes to a similar conclusion as in the later essay "Experience," in that the first law of nature is one of affirmation. While individuals may experience pain, the soul of the universe does not: "All loss, all pain, is particular; the universe remains to the heart unhurt." Indeed, this is the realization in "Experience" that we live, we grieve, we die, but the universe goes on in an ever-upward "ascent." Everything man does is therefore "divine" because it is according to the laws and "optimism" of nature. If we call something "obscure" or "vulgar," it is not a fact of the thing or person but only our view of it. Instead, we must "make habitually a new estimate," change our perceptions. Emerson would come to this same conclusion in numerous other contexts, including the later essays on practical life in *The CONDUCT OF LIFE* (1860) and *SOCIETY AND SOLITUDE* (1870).

As in "Experience," so in "Spiritual Laws" he emphasizes that we have a subjective (or an "original" as he had phrased it in *NATURE* of 1836) relation to the universe. "A man is . . . a selecting principle," and what he chooses (or rejects) "determines for him the character of the universe." So in "Experience" he says that "the universe wears our color." We come to understand the universe not merely based on "facts" but on our own perceptions, which we often do not trust even though "the soul's emphasis is always right." While in "Spiritual Laws" he applies this law of self-trust to the question of selecting a vocation, in the later "Experience," this idea ultimately helps him to take grief as it comes to him, as an emotion, without being able to fully understand it. In both essays he comes to the same conclusions, as stated here in "Spiritual Laws," namely, "that our life might be much easier and simpler than we make it. . . . We interfere with the optimism of nature." Trusting ourselves and our own instincts *is* trusting nature.

As in "Experience" he also comes to the conclusion in "Spiritual Laws" that meaning will come not from the big decisions or events in our lives but from the rare and brief moments of "hope" and "insight." In "Spiritual Laws," after an extended discussion on this very question of "action" and "success," he determines that our vocation is not the source of meaning and understanding in our lives, so much as a "silent thought . . . which revises our entire manner of life."

While important as a meditation on work or vocation, "Spiritual Laws" also offers an alternative to religion, specifically to Christianity, in terms of a different source for universal laws and for practical guidance on life. As in "Experience" and in the earlier essay "COMPENSATION" (1841), "Spiritual Laws" emphasizes the complementary relationship between humans and nature, and the individual self as the source of higher laws. In a tone of religious exuberance (and in contrast to religious doctrines, which provide only confusion and fear), Emerson proclaims, "O my brothers, God exists. There is a soul at the centre of nature, and over the will of every man, so that none of us can wrong the universe." In this regard, "Spiritual Laws" had a profound effect on WILLIAM JAMES who, in his 1902 book, *Varieties of Religious Experience,* echoed an Emersonian definition of a subjective religion as "the feelings, acts, and experiences of individual men in their solitude, so far as they apprehend themselves to stand in relation to whatever they may consider the divine."

This is God in man, if only we have the self-trust to see it. Knowledge (including self-knowledge) does not come from religion (as he emphasized in the "DIVINITY SCHOOL ADDRESS"), nor does it come from "years of academical and professional education." Knowledge comes from our instinct and, in fact, what we call "education" actually works against our intuitions and therefore against truth; the conflict between intuition and "tuition" of "The AMERICAN SCHOLAR." Like the books for the scholar's "idle times" in "The American Scholar" address, so in "Spiritual Laws" he warns that we have a "preposterous use of books,—He knew not what to do, and so *he read*."

We need "Spiritual Laws" rather than society's laws, and here he advocates a turning away from the "ponderous machinery" of society and instead cultivating our "state of mind" through the "transcendentalism of common life" he spoke of in "CIRCLES" (1841). In "Spiritual Laws" he returns again to circular language in explaining the method of nature—"The circuit of the waters is mere falling"—and of the cosmic universe—"the globe, earth, moon, comet, sun, star, fall for ever and ever." Nature is "inexhaustible," but also "easy, simple, spontaneous," if only we would recognize it as such.

There is much in "Spiritual Laws" on the topic of reform, and he humorously includes his own association with the TRANSCENDENTAL CLUB as one of the activities we "fret and fume" over. Nature urges us away from "the caucus, or the bank, or the Abolition-convention, or the Temperance-meeting, or the Transcendental club" and "into the fields and woods." As in numerous other writings, Emerson urges that if we had a right relationship with nature and ourselves, then society as well "would organize itself, as do now the rose, and the air, and the sun." This was his general view of reform and reformers in writings such as "NEW ENGLAND REFORMERS," "MAN THE REFORMER," and "The CONSERVATIVE," among his numerous ABOLITIONIST writings.

FURTHER READING

Von Frank, Albert. "*Essays: First Series* (1841)." In *The Cambridge Companion to Ralph Waldo Emerson*, edited by Joel Porte and Saundra Morris, 106–120. New York: Cambridge University Press, 1999.

"Spiritual Laws" (1847)

Emerson's short poem "Spiritual Laws" uses the metaphor of heaven's construction to show how we, from the discarded hours of our lives, build our own salvation. The time we spend away from prayer and reverence reveals our true character; these hours are utilized, by the architect of heaven, to forge our salvation. Son EDWARD WALDO EMERSON noted that the poem is about "beneficent correspondence in Morals, as in Nature." "URIEL" and "BRAHMA" are two poems with similar themes. The poem went through several drafts in Emerson's notebooks, beginning in midsummer 1846. It originally appeared as the epigram for the essay "SPIRITUAL LAWS" in the 1847 edition of *ESSAYS: FIRST SERIES*. The poem was collected in *MAY-DAY AND OTHER PIECES* (1867), as well as in *Poems* (1884).

CRITICAL COMMENTARY

Formally, Emerson's poem breaks into three discrete sections. The first four lines are cast in iambic tetrameter, Emerson's preferred verse form. This section deals with the architect of heaven, and suggests the need for regular, standard form—"these eternal towers."

The second section, lines 5–8, utilizes an *abba* rhyme scheme setting these lines apart from the rhymed couplets of the opening four lines. Appropriately, since the section deals with our "sole and self-commanding works" (that is, not in accordance with divine architecture), these lines have no fixed meter; we might say they wander without fixed purpose.

The third section, lines 9–12, return to the regulation of the first section suggesting a more formal sense of order. This section describes how the "self-commanded works" of line 5 are forged (we may think of forging as both a shaping and a purifying power) into "Innocence." Thus, Emerson demonstrates the order of "living Heaven" contrasted with "self-commanded works" that "grows by decays," finally establishing a new order, echoing the "living Heaven" of line 1. Edward Emerson, in the *Complete Works* (1904), suggests that if Emerson had been in the habit of using italics, he might have italicized the word "living" in line 1, the emphasis being on the fact that heaven is alive. Indeed, in Emerson's verse-book draft, line 1 reads, "Heaven is alive."

Bill Scalia

"Success" (1870)

Emerson's essay "Success," appearing in *SOCIETY AND SOLITUDE* of 1870, grew out of a lecture given in Hartford, Connecticut, in December 1858, then presented as "The Law of Success" in a course in BOSTON in March 1859. It is a companion piece to "WORKS AND DAYS" of the 1870 volume in providing a critique of his era's unenlightened criteria of "success" measured by external works, in contrast with the true mettle and accomplishments of the spiritual life.

SYNOPSIS

The essay opens with Emerson's observation of 19th-century America's pride in its engineering feats and political prowess both at home and around the globe: "Our eyes run approvingly along the lengthened lines of railroad and telegraph. We have gone nearest to the Pole. We have discovered the Antarctic continent. We interfere in Central and South America, at Canton and in Japan; we are adding to an already enormous territory." This pride "is the way of the world; 't is the law of youth, and of unfolding strength." This focus on "success" is handed down through our histories, and yet Emerson demands a call for a moral critique of these assumptions:

> I don't know but we and our race elsewhere set a higher value on wealth, victory and coarse superiority of all kinds, than other men,—have less tranquility of mind, are less easily contented. The Saxon is taught from his infancy to wish to be first. The Norseman was a restless rider, fighter, freebooter. The ancient Norse ballads describe him as afflicted with this inextinguishable thirst for victory.

He goes on to portray the contemporary versions of external prowess as of merely "local convenience" but not adding to our spiritual stature. The greatest men of the world—Newton, Shakespeare, Alfred, Scipio, and Socrates—have managed not to want them. It is "the public" that "values inventions more than the inventor does." People are drawn to the windfall, the lucrative result; they flock to "the winning side," always wanting their "watches [to] go faster than their neighbors": "We are great by exclusion, grasping and egotism. Our success takes from all what it gives to one."

"Excellence," on an individual and on national and human levels, "is lost sight of in the hunger for sudden performance and praise":

> I hate this shallow Americanism which hopes to get rich by credit, to get knowledge by raps on midnight tables, to learn the economy of the mind by phrenology, or skill without study, or mastery without apprenticeship, or this sale of goods through pretending that they sell, or power through making believe you are powerful, or through a packed jury or caucus, bribery and "repeating" votes, or wealth by fraud.

Emerson's positive conviction is that each man is born with a special aptitude to do his unique work, but "it is rare to find a man who believes his own thought or who speaks that which he was created to say." Americans, he says, still "cannot shake from our shoes this dust of Europe and Asia." Unfortunately, "society is under a spell, every man is a borrower and a mimic, . . . and hence the depression of spirits, that furrow of care, said to mark every American brow."

The true sentiment of success appears in the homages we pay to beauty, such as through "music, poetry, and love," and as in the great works of "the greatest men,—Petrarch, Michel Angelo, and Shakspeare." Every "genius is measured by its skill" in revealing the secrets of human life. For this reason, "Every man has a history worth knowing," although this history, the "deep man there," is often "unknown hitherto to his neighbors." So it is "the great happiness of life" to discover these secrets, "to add to our high acquaintances." In truth, "the oracles are never silent," but "the receiver" must have "an open and noble temper."

Emerson concludes that the world-affirming mind is the shining trait of success: "The good mind chooses what is positive, what is advancing,—embraces the affirmative." "It is true that there is evil and good, night and day: but these are not equal. The day is great and final. The night is for the day, but the day is not for the night." At bottom truth and goodness are immortal demands of the soul. But these demands must have real effect and not just exist in the abstract: "Your theory is unimportant." What matters is "what new stock you can add to humanity, or how high you can carry life? A man is a man only as he makes life and nature happier to us."

We must and do indeed "apply this affirmative law to letters, to manners, to art, to the decoration of our houses," and so forth. The opposite, "the popular notion of success," is all "negative propositions." What is needed, in contrast, "is love. As much love, so much perception." Love includes love of self, or "the inner life," which "loves truth" and "right" but "makes no progress" in earthly terms of success: "This tranquil, well-founded, wide-seeing soul is no express-rider, no attorney, no magistrate." Emerson ends the essay with a quote from Euripides: "Zeus hates busybodies, and those who do too much."

CRITICAL COMMENTARY

"Success" was a midcareer expression of Emerson's ethics of spiritual self-sufficiency that dated back to its most famous statement in "SELF-RELIANCE" and in the companion essay "The OVER-SOUL" (both appearing in *ESSAYS: FIRST SERIES* [1841]). He applied this ethics to one's choice of vocation and work in more pragmatic and social contexts in *The CONDUCT OF LIFE* (1860) and in the companion essays of *Society and Solitude* (1870). In the latter volume, "Works and Days" and "FARMING," as well as "Success," articulate parallel themes of the illusions of external success in 19th-century American life. The essay "Success" draws the explicit moral lesson that such pretensions of accomplishment are rooted in social expectations and individual egotism—narrow, shallow, and anxiety-driven substitutes for the true "powers" of the human soul.

As in these other writings, self-trust is the secret of true success, and it consists in striving toward a true relationship to the universe, independent of external feats of performance. In "Success," he asks, "Is there no loving of knowledge, and of art, and of our design, for itself alone? Cannot we please ourselves with performing our work, or gaining truth and power, without being praised for it?" He thus reprises the fundamental tenets of the earlier essays and of *NATURE* (1836), in which he expressed the affinity of man's mind and nature. In "Success," he declares, "the fundamental fact in our metaphysical constitution is the correspondence of man to the world, so that every change in that writes a record in the mind. . . . and in the perfection of this correspondence or expressiveness, the health and force of man consists." This sentiment in turn continues the essential drift of "Works and Days," which teaches to receive the gifts of the day for their spiritual worth.

In "Success," he praises those who bring "music, poetry, and love" as "the greatest men," naming "Petrarch, Michel Angelo, and Shakspeare." From these he moves to acknowledge that we need not look to history alone for such examples, as "every man has a history worth knowing." It is "the great happiness of life" to learn these histories of our "neighbors," "to add to our high acquaintances." Emerson's exploration here of finding our definition of "Success" within ourselves as well as in others echoes his search for "great men" in *REPRESENTATIVE MEN* (1850).

A notable theme of "Success" is Emerson's rejection of pessimistic evaluations of life. This can be considered one of the central trajectories of his literary output, both prose and poetic. Even in his lectures and essays on the darker experiences in life, such as in "The TRAGIC," "EXPERIENCE," and "FATE," his affirmation of life prevails. His poetry as well—notably "THRENODY," "The WORLD-SOUL," "The HUMBLE-BEE," and "BACCHUS," to name only a few—celebrated the affirmation of the life through nature and thus defined true spiritual success.

David A. Dilworth

"Swedenborg; or, the Mystic" (1850)

"Swedenborg; or, the Mystic" was the second of six biographical essays included in Emerson's 1850 text, *REPRESENTATIVE MEN*. Emerson was introduced to the writings of the Swedish mystic and philosopher EMANUEL SWEDENBORG (1688–1772) through American Sampson Reed's book on Swedenborgian philosophy, *Observations on the Growth of the Mind* (1826). In 1834 Emerson sent a copy of *Observations* to THOMAS CARLYLE, summarizing the "many points of attraction" between Swedenborgianism and Emerson's belief in "the Natural World as strictly the symbol or exponent of the Spiritual, and part for part." Emerson lectured on Swedenborg in 1845 and during his 1847–48 lecture tour in England before publishing the lecture as part of *Representative Men.*

SYNOPSIS

Emerson begins the essay by setting Swedenborg apart from the other thinkers in *Representative Men,* from "poets" or "philosophers." Swedenborg belongs to a third class of men, those who "lead us into another region,—the world of morals, or of will." While reading Shakespeare may be a "refuge" from "the saints," in the end a "drama or poem" is only a "reply" to the moral questions. The questions themselves, which religion or philosophy seek to answer, are "Whence? What? and Whither?" The answers to these questions open "the doors of the universe" and require access to the "secrets" of nature "by some higher method than by experience." The philosopher "knows," but the mystic, like Swedenborg, "sees." Emerson uses different examples to show this idea of "intuition" as it exists in PLATONISM and in Hinduism or other religions as "transmigration" or reincarnation: "The ancients called it *ecstacy* . . . a getting out of their bodies to think."

According to Emerson, Swedenborg is the best "modern" example of a mystic or "visionary." Emerson gives a brief biographical overview of Swedenborg's "youth and training," his background as a scientist, engineer, metallurgist, and theologian, noting that he "anticipated much science of the 19th century" in his writings on astronomy, magnetism, chemistry, and anatomy. Emerson declares Swedenborg one of the "mastodons of literature," yet he was misunderstood in his own times. Like all great men, he both transcended his times and was also a product of his times; he "was born into an atmosphere of great ideas. 'Tis hard to say what was his own." Emerson details many of the advances in scientific and natural knowledge that characterized Europe of the 18th century—Gilbert, Descartes, Newton, Linnaeus, Leibnitz, LOCKE—and wonders, "What was left for a genius of the largest caliber, but to go over their ground, and verify and unite?" Ultimately, it "requires a long focal distance" to understand him, and Emerson seeks to provide that understanding by showing how "Swedenborg is systematic" in that he is "respective of the world in every sentence."

Emerson is particularly interested in Swedenborg's theory of "correspondence," which seeks relation between "all the parts" in nature and "the universality of each law." Swedenborg's "Identity-philosophy" declared that through knowledge of nature we get closer to God and that this knowledge is revealed "on successive planes." So, for example, the form of the snake is repeated in the form of the human spine, or the observation that every part of the body has an independent function and yet is related to the other. These repetitions in nature reveal that all scientific knowledge is related: "Astronomy . . . must come up into life to have its full value, and not remain there in globes and spaces. The globule of blood gyrates around its own axis in the human veins, as the planet in the sky; and the circles of intellect relate to those of the heavens."

Swedenborg sought "to put science and the soul, long estranged from each other, at one again"; his ideas therefore had both scientific and theological applications. Whatever is "too small" to see can be understood by looking at the larger picture, and that which is "too large" can be understood through the study of smaller "units." Through this method, Swedenborg was "so bold" as to believe he could "unlock the meaning of the world." Swedenborg sought to "elicit a spiritual truth" from every "physical truth" or fact of nature.

Again, Emerson concedes that this is an old idea, the spiritual lessons of nature are the foundation of "all poetry, in allegory, in fable, in the use of emblems, and in the structure of language." What Swedenborg did, however, was create a theory from this observation. Previously, "sciences, religions, philosophies" had operated as separate systems, but Swedenborg brought them together to understand the larger "frame of things." Swedenborg looked to nature to explain "the moral laws in their widest social aspects," but his efforts led others to view him as "an abnormal person," as someone who had conversations with "angels and spirits." Emerson notes that this is often the fate of people with new ideas, and he chooses instead to characterize Swedenborg as possessing "a deranged balance."

Even though he considered himself a Christian, Swedenborg saw the Bible stories as allegorical and worked at "extricating" the "universal sense" from them. His interest in the "correspondence between thoughts and things" was, for him, a "theologic" question, and history and science were part of this inquiry. The limitation of Swedenborg's system, according to Emerson, was that nature "is no literalist," and a single object could have multiple meanings or representations. The second problem with Swedenborg's system was the religious motivation in attempting to fix nature to specifically Christian purposes: "His theological bias thus fatally narrowed his interpretation of nature."

While critical of Swedenborg's bringing religion into nature, Emerson praises him for bringing nature into religion. Swedenborg advocated a religion for "every part of life," at a time when spiritual life for most people consisted of only "visits" to church only "three or four times" in their life—at birth, marriage, illness, and death. In contrast, Swedenborg's religion "accompanied him all day," having worked its way "into his thinking." Emerson applies to Swedenborg's thought and writings themselves a metaphor of nature, declaring his ideas and influence "immense . . . like the prairie, or the desert."

Emerson cautions the reader that Swedenborg's visions are "mystical, that is, as a quite arbitrary and accidental picture of the truth, not as the truth." Unfortunately, his "system of the world" relies too much on "the agency of 'the Lord,'" with less room for "spontaneity" or human "will." Emerson sees "theologic determination" as Swedenborg's "vice" and feels that, with Swedenborg, "we are always in a church." "The genius of Swedenborg" was "wasted," in Emerson's opinion, in trying to "reanimate and conserve" Christianity, which, Emerson feels, was "retiring from its prominence." Swedenborg would have done better to apply his system to a more universal "moral sentiment" that encompasses "innumerable christianities, humanities, divinities."

Whereas Swedenborg, in his Christian framework, talks of hell and of "sin," Emerson counsels that "no man can afford to waste his moments" worrying about such concepts. The spirit "deals in laws," that is, the laws of the natural rather than supernatural world. Emerson gives examples of how other thinkers and other religions—from Socrates to "the Hindoos," to the Quakers—define this spirit as a force *within* the individual, not outside of it, not in the realm of "ghosts and hobgoblins."

Swedenborg was a representative man, but a man influenced by the politics and religion of his own times; he "remains the Lutheran bishop's sons; his judgments are those of a Swedish polemic." Still, he possessed "a great nature," one that "invites us onward" and therefore opens up more possibilities than it closes. He "lived to purpose: he gave a verdict," and this is what Emerson most admires. Swedenborg's contribution was therefore twofold: As a scientist "he observed and published the laws of nature," and his "second passive service" was the effect his "trance of delight" could have on others, in that we, too, should be in such awe of nature.

CRITICAL COMMENTARY

Emanuel Swedenborg fit Emerson's definition of a "great" or "representative" man due to both his ability to synthesize and the universality of his ideas. These dual goals, in fact, defined Emerson's own identity and project as a writer. He compares Swedenborg's "varied and solid knowledge" with nature itself, with "one of those winter mornings when the air sparkles with crystals." "In exact antagonism to the skeptics," Swedenborg believed that greater wisdom made a man a greater "worshipper of the Deity." In other words, knowledge makes us more aware of the connection between all things, unlike the skeptic who says that knowledge makes us aware only of how much we do not know.

The main idea that Emerson took from Swedenborg—"that the physical world was purely symbolical of the spiritual world"—is an idea repeated throughout Emerson's own writings, in particular forming his earliest ideas in *NATURE* (1836). Although Emerson repeatedly criticizes Swedenborg for being confined to a Christian framework or understanding, in Swedenborg he found his own theology of nature, arguing that the reality of the wonders of nature should inspire us as much as the "miracles" religion takes in faith, again, a foundational point of *Nature*, as well as the "DIVINITY SCHOOL ADDRESS" (1838). Emerson credits Swedenborg for bringing nature into religion—"To the withered traditional church yielding dry catechisms, he let in nature again"—and for advocating a religion for "every part of life." In so much as humanity is a part of that miraculous nature, then the logical conclusion is that "God is the grand man," and Emerson draws from Swedenborg the idea that "Man, in his perfect form, is heaven." This is, again, the foundational argument of the "Divinity School Address" and other works (such as *Nature* and "EXPERIENCE") in which Emerson rejects any hint of the supernatural that sets God apart from man. Emerson finds Swedenborg's claim to "revelation" from God "a capital offence in so learned a categorist."

In the essay, Emerson remakes Swedenborg to fit the concerns of 19th-century America. Like the other great men, Swedenborg was ahead of his times; he "anticipated much science of the 19th century" and also anticipated, despite his own Christian beliefs, a move away from organized religion. In "The AMERICAN SCHOLAR" (1837), Emerson claims that, more than anyone else, it was Swedenborg who "pierced the emblematic or spiritual character of the visible, audible, tangible world." In these and other references, Emerson credits Swedenborg with nothing less than providing in his writings the roots of American Transcendentalism, and, indeed, with an American literary and cultural renaissance in general. In detailing Swedenborg's early biography, Emerson is particularly interested in how religious and scientific "genius" emerged from a man who began his work in "quarries and forges" and "ship-yards." This connection between physical and intellectual labor, between practical and spiritual pursuits, between nature and religion was the very definition of Emerson's own 19th-century democratic romanticism, concerns reflected in the literature of his contemporaries as well, such as EMILY DICKINSON or WALT WHITMAN.

"Terminus" (1867)

Emerson's poem "Terminus" was published in the *ATLANTIC MONTHLY* in January 1867 and appeared in his collection of poems *MAY-DAY AND OTHER PIECES* that same year. As early as the 1840s, however, Emerson penned prose lines in his journal about growing old that would resonate in the poem. The poem deals with the themes of the passage of time, of aging, and of making the best use of time and the days. Emerson struggled not only with his own aging and mortality but also with an extraordinary number of deaths of people close to him, many of whom died at a young age. In addition to the premature deaths of close friends in the prime of their lives, such as MARGARET FULLER and HENRY DAVID THOREAU, Emerson witnessed the deaths of his first wife, Ellen Tucker Emerson, at the age of 20, of his three younger brothers, EDWARD BLISS EMERSON, ROBERT BULKELEY EMERSON, and CHARLES CHAUNCY EMERSON, and, most difficult of all, his five-year-old son, Waldo.

It was in an earlier poem, "THRENODY" (1847), that he dealt directly with young Waldo's death, but themes of time, death, and renewal through nature appear in other writings as well. In the poem "HAMATREYA" (1847), the earth "laughs" at the idea that humans think they can own the land when, in fact, they are only on earth for a short period of time. In "Terminus," Emerson is reflecting not only on the deaths of those around him but on his own mortality and aging. He accepts that everything in nature has a cycle and that "it is time to be old, / To take in sail." Growing old, of course, was the true course in nature, one that could not be explained in the seemingly untimely and unfair deaths of younger people, especially Waldo.

CRITICAL COMMENTARY

"Terminus" is divided into two parts, the first, longer part (lines 1–33) is the voice of Terminus talking to the poet; the second, shorter part (lines 33–40) is the poet's response. In the first section of the poem, Terminus, identified in the poem as "the gods of bounds" or limits, is warning the individual to accept the passage of time and his own limitations. The first two lines seem to be an explicit acknowledgment of old age and mortality: "It is time to be old, / To take in sail." The poet recounts that Terminus "Came to me in his fatal rounds," a reference to Emerson's own theory of life as a series of concentric circles moving ever outward. In Emerson's 1841 essay "CIRCLES," he explained that "life is an apprenticeship to the truth that around every circle another can be drawn: that there is no end in nature, that every end is a beginning, that there is always another dawn risen on mid-noon, and under every deep a lower deep opens."

In the poem, Terminus's "fatal rounds" and the gods' injunction of "'No more! No farther shoot" implies a counterview to the never-ending circles of accepting ending points and limitations. The imagery of the tree implies not only physical roots, in being rooted to the earth, but also roots in the sense of family and ancestors and perhaps Emerson's efforts to move beyond his own roots, intellectually and philosophically. The next lines support this interpretation, as he moves beyond the physical limitation of time to address the limitations of thought as well, "Fancy departs: no more invent." He advises instead to "contract thy firmament," which could be read as a caution to pull back and focus on the reality of life at hand.

This idea of the need for focus and of decisiveness rather than speculation continues into the next section: "There's not enough for this and that, / Make thy option which of two." This seems to be a direct response to (and in direct contradiction to) Emersonian idealism and skepticism. The poem relies upon the terms of nature to describe the possibility of narrowing life down to the reality of details rather than the immensity of ideas—"Leave the many and hold the few"—while still acknowledging the gift of nature—"Not the less revere the Giver." Terminus could be seen as the voice of rationalism, of materialism, even of UNITARIANISM with the focus on a single "Giver," everything that Emerson and Transcendentalists were reacting against. But while the voice seems to want to pull Emerson away from idealism to an acceptance of life's passages—"Timely wise accept the terms"—it is not the voice of resignation. There is still room for human action and influence over the quality of life, and Terminus counsels to "Still plan and smile."

The next stanza addresses the question of ancestors, of the intellectual forefathers that Emerson was responding to as a Transcendentalist. It may be true that their ideas were wrong or limited and therefore there is reason to reject them: "Curse, if thou wilt, thy sires" who were "Bad husbands of their fires," that is, did not fully develop their own ideas. Perhaps they "Failed to bequeath" an adequate intellectual inheritance and instead left only "a legacy" of "Inconstant heat and nerveless reins," inspiring neither poetry ("Amid the Muses, left thee deaf and dumb") nor action ("Amid the gladiators, halt and numb"). Here Terminus acknowledges the immensity of Emerson's Transcendentalist effort; he has challenged the "gladiators" of thought and broken through tradition and sacred texts in search of something truer. This challenge to the ancestors was a topic Emerson had addressed in the poem "URIEL" (1847) in response to the harsh criticism (including banishment from HARVARD) in the wake of his 1838 "DIVINITY SCHOOL ADDRESS."

The last lines of the poem are set apart and shift to a first-person response to Terminus from the poet. The poet, like "the bird" in nature, accepts the direction the wind is blowing and prepares for "the storm of time," but he will not be blown along aimlessly. He will be active and will "man the rudder, reef the sail." He will take direction from nature now, just as he has done in the past: "Obey the voice at eve obeyed at prime." Trusting nature (and his inner voice), he has no fear of life, of aging, and knows he will be "unharmed"; in this sense, the poet rejects the idea of the passage of time as a limitation. In fact, the end point, "the port," is just as important as the journey. While some have read "Terminus" as an acceptance of human limitations and a softening of Emerson's idealism, it could also be seen as a Transcendentalist triumph of nature over human institutions and tradition, and as a reaffirmation that humans are a part of nature, not separate from or limited by it.

"Thine Eyes Still Shined" (1847)

A love poem, "Thine Eyes Still Shined" is a short (three stanzas of four lines each) poem written to Ralph Waldo Emerson's first wife, Ellen Tucker Emerson, sometime during their courtship or early marriage. The poem recounts a period during which they were separated and Emerson sees in nature various reminders of his love: "yon evening star," "the deep-eyed dew," and "the rosebud ripened to the rose," each reminds him of Ellen.

The poem was first published in the 1847 collection *POEMS*. It is one of several of Emerson's love poems and sits among those written specifically to Ellen that he included in *Poems*, along with "TO ELLEN, AT THE SOUTH" and "To Eva" (both of these had been previously published in the *DIAL*, in 1843). Other love poems included in this series in *Poems* were "GIVE ALL TO LOVE," "The Amulet," "EROS," and "INITIAL, DAEMONIC, AND CELESTIAL LOVE."

"Thoreau" (1862)

HENRY DAVID THOREAU died on May 6, 1862, in his native CONCORD, MASSACHUSETTS. Services were held at the First Parish Church, where Thoreau had delivered his "A Plea for Captain John Brown" just a few years earlier. BRONSON ALCOTT, superintendent of Concord's schools that year, canceled classes so that local children could attend the funeral, and Alcott read aloud passages from Thoreau's writing. (WILLIAM) ELLERY CHANNING wrote a hymn, and Ralph Waldo Emerson delivered the eulogy. Also in attendance was editor James T. Fields, who would publish four of Thoreau's essays posthumously, and who published Emerson's eulogy, "Thoreau," in the August 1862 issue of the *ATLANTIC MONTHLY*. The eulogy has since received mixed reviews as a portrayal of the man, but it is surely the single best biographical piece on Thoreau written by a contemporary. It must also be considered as an exploration of Emerson (and of Thoreau) as Transcendentalist.

SYNOPSIS

Emerson begins the essay with details of Thoreau's ancestry, birth, and education. After graduating from college, Thoreau went on to teach school, "which he soon renounced." Neither was he interested in running the family pencil business; having accomplished his goal of creating "a better pencil than was then in use," he explained to his friends "that he should never make another pencil. 'Why should I? I would not do again what I have done once.'" Instead, "he resumed his endless walks and miscellaneous studies, making every day some new acquaintance with Nature." Although "very studious of natural facts," Thoreau was not a scientist: "never speaking of zoology or botany . . . he was incurious of technical and textual science."

Emerson notes that it was a "rare decision to refuse all the accustomed paths" available to young men of his generation. Thoreau rejected "any narrow craft or profession, aiming at a much

Henry David Thoreau, 1856 *(The Thoreau Society and the Thoreau Institute at Walden Woods)*

more comprehensive calling, the art of living well." He did "drift into . . . the profession of land-surveyor," mostly due to "his intimate knowledge of the territory about Concord"—indeed he found the work "helped his studies of Nature." Thus did he secure "all the employment he wanted" to supply his "few wants."

Thoreau tackled "graver questions" than those of the surveyor: "He interrogated every custom, and wished to settle all his practice on an ideal foundation." In his attempt to reduce things to "simplest terms," "few lives contain so many renunciations." Here Emerson lists all the things Thoreau did *not* do in his life: "He was bred to no profession; he never married; he lived alone; he never went to church; he never voted; he refused to pay a tax to the State; he ate no flesh, he drank no wine, he never knew the use of tobacco; and, though a naturalist, he used neither trap nor gun." He was a "bachelor of thought and Nature," rejecting all niceties of society: "A fine house, dress, the manners and talk of highly cultivated people were all thrown away on him." This made it difficult for Thoreau, the "hermit and stoic," to fit in with society. And yet, because he was "a speaker and actor of truth," people were always interested in his opinions.

Here Emerson mentions the actions for which Thoreau would be best known: "In 1845 he built himself a small framed house on the shores of Walden Pond, and lived there two years alone, a life of labor and study. . . . As soon as he had exhausted the advantages of that solitude, he abandoned it." Thoreau was also jailed for one night when "he refused to pay his town tax." In these pursuits, "No opposition or ridicule had any weight with him. . . . It was of no consequence, if every one present held the opposite opinion."

Emerson determines that "no truer American existed than Thoreau." Thoreau loved his country, having once noted that, unlike in Europe, in "New England . . . We have not to lay the foundations of our houses on the ashes of a former civilization"—an interesting observation given Thoreau's critique of the effect of European-American settlement on native Americans, and given Emerson's earlier observation that Thoreau "much preferred a good Indian" to the society of his New England peers. Indeed, Emerson mentions Indians several times throughout the address, recalling that "Indian relics abound in Concord" and "these, and every circumstance touching the Indian, were important in his eyes."

There were other paradoxes in this man, "idealist as he was," who was "for abolition of slavery, abolition of tariffs, almost for abolition of government," and yet "equally opposed to every class of reformers." Thoreau held only "one man . . . with exceptional regard"—JOHN BROWN. Even when other abolitionists advised him against speaking publicly about Brown, Thoreau simply said, "'I did not send to you for advice, but to announce that I am to speak.'" He delivered an "earnest eulogy of the hero."

Unlike men "of abstract intellect" who seem uncomfortable in the material world of their bodies, "Mr. Thoreau was equipped with a most adapted and serviceable body. . . . His senses were acute, his frame well-knit and hardy, his hands strong and skilful in the use of tools." He used his eyes and hands to measure, assess, and "find his path in the woods at night." He could swim, run, skate, "and would probably outwalk most countrymen in a day's journey." It was the "relation of body to mind" that explained a correspondence between his physical and intellectual activity: "If shut up in the house, he did not write at all."

Thoreau "had a strong common sense": "He could plan a garden, or a house or a barn; would have been competent to lead a 'Pacific Exploring Expedition;' could give judicious counsel in the gravest private or public affairs." Emerson reflects on his own personal loss of this friend of 25 years whose judgment he trusted and who always seemed to be available to help with some project. Although always busy and "highly organized," Thoreau was "always ready for any excursion that promised well, or for conversation prolonged into late hours."

Thoreau had an "excellent wisdom" that drew people to him: "I have repeatedly known young men of sensibility converted in a moment to the belief that this was the man they were in search of, the man of men, who could tell them all they should do." Yet he often turned away visitors and "admiring friends," focusing on his larger mission: "Mr. Thoreau dedicated his genius with such entire love to the fields, hills, and waters of his native town, that he made them known and interesting to all reading Americans, and to people over the sea."

Emerson recounts some of his own walking excursions with Thoreau, observing his friend's method of chasing after a specimen or a bird call: "His interest in the flower or bird lay very deep in his mind, was connected with Nature,—and the meaning of Nature was never attempted to be defined by him." Thoreau had no interest in speaking before "the Natural History Society" because he knew his experience of nature would not mean the same to another person—he knew "that it is not the fact that imports, but the impression or effect of the fact on your mind." And yet his relationship with nature was still formed by culture—in another context, he might have been a great hunter, "but, restrained by his Massachusetts culture, he played out the game in this mild form of botany and ichthyology." He might have been a professor or member of a natural history academy, yet "these learned bodies" would have felt "the satire of his presence."

Among his townspeople, he was at first "an oddity," but they soon came to appreciate the "native authority" of "Mr. Thoreau." Still, Thoreau had a "dangerous frankness," so that even "his admirers called him 'that terrible Thoreau.'" Emerson himself felt Thoreau lived too much in "extremes": "I think the severity of his ideal interfered to deprive him of a healthy sufficiency of human society."

Finally, Emerson assesses Thoreau the writer: "His poetry might be bad or good; he no doubt wanted a lyric facility and technical skill; but he had the source of poetry in his spiritual perception." In the end, "his genius was better than his talent," although he "knew well how to throw a poetic veil over his experience." Emerson gives an example of "his mythical record" in *Walden,* saying "his riddles were worth the reading." And yet Emerson believes Thoreau was not called to lead the "contemplative life": "with his energy and practical ability he seemed born for great enterprise and for command; and I so much regret the loss of his rare powers of action, that I cannot help counting it a fault in him that he had no ambition." He repeats a phrase used earlier in the eulogy, noting that "instead of engineering for all America, he was captain of a huckleberry party." Emerson ends the eulogy with "a few sentences taken from his unpublished manuscripts, not only as records of his thought and feeling, but for their power of description and literary excellence." For example, "The bluebird carries the sky on his back." Or, "How can we expect a harvest of thought who have not had a seed-time of character?"

"Thoreau" ends on a poetic note, recalling a "plant called 'Life-Everlasting,' . . . which grows on the most inaccessible cliffs of the Tyrolese mountains": "Thoreau seemed to me living in the hope to gather this plant, which belonged to him of a right." His work was so grand "as to require longevity," which he was denied. "The country knows not yet, or in the least part, how great a son it has lost. It seems an injury that he should leave in the midst his broken task, which none else can finish,—a kind of indignity to so noble a soul, that it should depart out of Nature before yet he has been really shown to his peers for what he is."

CRITICAL COMMENTARY

Henry's sister, Sophia Thoreau, was the first to be unhappy with Emerson's eulogy, writing several months later to a friend that, "reading it for consolation as a stricken mourner, I felt somewhat disappointed. Henry never impressed me as the stoic Mr. E. represents him. I think Henry was a person of much more faith than Mr. Emerson." Many Thoreau scholars since have concurred that the eulogy was less than sympathetic to Thoreau's character, much less his literary legacy. Scholar Robert Sattelmeyer calls it "perhaps the most ambivalent eulogy in literary history," Emerson leaving the reader with "an insinuation that Thoreau's life was essentially a failure."

The written text of the eulogy, however, is almost certainly more impersonal than the original intimate church reading. For example, Emerson's so-called derision of Thoreau as nothing more than "captain of a huckleberry party" may have been seen as an affectionate remembrance when spoken among gathered family and friends who had walked with Thoreau on such excursions. Likewise, Emerson's comment that Thoreau had "graduated from Harvard College . . . without any literary distinction" was certainly meant ironically, given both

Thoreau's accomplishment with *Walden* (1854) and the fact that both Emerson and Thoreau questioned the value of a HARVARD COLLEGE education; indeed, Emerson goes on to note that "an iconoclast in literature, [Thoreau] seldom thanked colleges for their service to him, holding them in small esteem, whilst yet his debt to them was important." Emerson could have said the same about himself.

In his earlier essay "The POET" (1844), Emerson explained that the universe can be understood in constellations of three, "which reappear, under different names, in every system of thought, whether they be cause, operation, and effect; or, more poetically, Jove, Pluto, Neptune; or, theologically, the Father, the Spirit, and the Son; but which we will call here the Knower, the Doer, and the Sayer." He seems to have continued this theme in attempting to understand Henry David Thoreau, referring to him variously in the eulogy as "Henry," "Mr. Thoreau," or "Thoreau." "Henry" is the son, brother, and friend who grew to manhood among the scenes and neighbors of Concord. "Mr. Thoreau" was the writer, citizen, and reformer who "grew to be revered and admired by his townsmen," supported John Brown's abolitionist crusade, and wrote poetry and *Walden.* But it is "Thoreau" the hero, the prophet of nature, who provided an inspiration "by his holy living." This is the "Thoreau" whom Emerson not only eulogizes but also mythologies for future generations: "No truer American existed than Thoreau."

In eulogizing Thoreau as the greatest American hero in the same building where Thoreau had eulogized Brown the hero, Emerson strengthens the connection between the two men. The foundation of Emerson's heroic "Thoreau" lies in his relationship with the natural world: "Snakes coiled round his legs; the fishes swam into his hand and he took them out of the water; he pulled the woodchuck out of its hole by the tail, and took the foxes under his protection from the hunters." Interestingly, in his journal Emerson had also emphasized Brown's connection with the natural world: "He had three thousand sheep in Ohio, and would instantly detect strange sheep in his flock. . . . He always makes friends with his horse or mule."

Emerson muses that there was something greater about Thoreau; underlying his "simple and hidden life" was a "cardinal fact," namely, that he understood "the material world as a means and symbol." What Emerson most admires is Thoreau the Transcendentalist-poet, the interpreter of nature. This insight came naturally to Thoreau, and was "the muse and genius that ruled his opinions, conversation, studies, work, and course of life." Thoreau preached that "the best place for each is where he stands," and that the particulars of one place (just as the particulars of any singular fact in nature) represented the universal: "The pond was a small ocean; the Atlantic, a large Walden Pond."

Emerson reflects that "the country knows not yet, or in the least part, how great a son it has lost." By mingling the mythic in Thoreau's return to nature with the practical loss of him out of the world, Emerson laments not just the loss of a beloved if difficult friend but also a force that his war-torn and increasingly materialist country had desperately needed. Though Emerson would go on to promote Thoreau's writing for the rest of his life, the sad loss of what could have been if "our naturalist" had survived longer is the tragedy we must all lament. For both philosophical and personal reasons, then, Emerson shares that "It was a pleasure and a privilege to walk with him."

FURTHER READING

Richardson, Robert D. *Thoreau: A Life of the Mind.* Berkeley: University of California Press, 1986.

Sattelmeyer, Robert. "*Walden:* Climbing the Canon." In *More Day to Dawn: Thoreau's Walden for the Twenty-first Century,* edited by Sandra Harbert Petrulionis and Laura Dassow Walls. Boston: University of Massachusetts Press, 2007.

Smith, Harmon L. *My Friend, My Friend: The Story of Thoreau's Relationship with Emerson.* Amherst: University of Massachusetts Press, 1999.

Audrey Raden

"Threnody" (1847)

Emerson's poem "Threnody" is a remembrance of his firstborn child, Waldo, who died in January 1842 at age five of scarlet fever. Emerson probably began the poem soon after Waldo's death, but it was first published in *Poems* of 1847. The first half of the eight-stanza poem reveals the raw pain of Waldo's death, reflecting upon the boy's seemingly unnatural separation from the world. The second half of the poem turns to nature's processes of birth, death, and renewal in trying to understand how the child's death fits into nature's plan. In the final stanza Emerson tries to finally accept the inevitability of change and movement, understanding that childhood itself does not last forever and that the human form is only temporary.

"Threnody" is Emerson's effort to make sense of death, especially the seemingly senseless death of a child, in Transcendentalist terms. The poem is often read alongside the explorations of death and of grief in Emerson's essay "Experience" (from *Essays: Second Series* of 1844).

CRITICAL COMMENTARY

The first stanza contrasts the perpetual newness of nature—"Life, sunshine and desire"—with the loss in death. Even nature "cannot restore; . . . / . . . The darling who shall not return." The second stanza also contrasts the newness and youth of nature with this life cut short. In nature one finds "young pines and budding birches; / But finds not the budding man." The child's death is unnatural because it is a life not allowed to fully develop to its potential.

Waldo Emerson, first child of Ralph Waldo and Lidian Jackson Emerson, age five. Waldo died of scarlet fever just a few months after this photo was taken. *(Houghton Library, Harvard University)*

The third stanza moves from reflections on the child's separation from nature to his separation from the world and from other people. Emerson wonders why the father's "right" to his child has been taken away: "I had the right, few days ago, / Thy steps to watch, thy place to know; / How have I forfeited the right?" He longs for the child's presence in the household, and details how Waldo charmed not only his parents but other adults as well, the "fairest dames and bearded men" who visited the Emerson home and who "let the world's affairs go by" to take a moment to play with the child. Emerson also remembers Waldo among other children, taking his rightful place in "the school-march, each day's festival."

After recounting vivid and lively memories of Waldo's speech, personality, and actions, the fourth stanza presents contrasting images of stillness and quiet. The world seems to have stopped with the child's death, as Emerson details his toys and games frozen in time: "The painted sled stands where it stood; . . . / . . . His gathered sticks to stanch the wall." Everywhere Emerson looks around the family property he sees memories of the child's play, eerily observing even "the ominous hole he dug in the sand." But where the child's activities have ceased, nature continues on in her movement and cycles regardless of his absence: "The brook into the stream runs on; / But the deep-eyed boy is gone."

In the fifth stanza, Emerson recounts the day of the death itself through observations of the natural world. The day was ominously "shaded" and "dark with more clouds than tempests are." When the next day "dawned with needless glow," the father-poet feels a sense of injustice that nature should continue and wonders if there might not have been some way to save the innocent child: "Was there no star that could be sent, . . . / . . . No angel from the countless host . . . / . . . Could stoop to heal that only child." It seems that there should be a lesson in nature, but it is hard to understand.

Emerson has lost his "general hope" and is now questioning everything he thought he knew and understood. It seems especially unfair as, in the father's view, the child was destined for great things. Perhaps the world was not ready for his talents: "It was not ripe yet to sustain, / A genius of so fine a strain." Emerson concludes that perhaps the child was made for another era and would have "to wait an aeon to be born." While the child will live on in another form, the true loss is to those left behind. Emerson discusses how friends and family took the news of the death and a part of the father died as well: "The eager fate which carried thee / Took the larger part of me; / For this losing is true dying." After a long reflection on the child's life and death, the sixth short stanza is an interlude of anger and grief, almost as if, for a moment, Emerson will be unable to go on.

In the seventh stanza Emerson seeks to understand what lessons can be learned from Waldo's brief life. He concludes that, just because the child is gone, does not mean he is separated from those left behind: "'Tis not within the force of fate / The fate-conjoined to separate." He reflects on all that he taught the child and wonders, now, what lesson he is to learn. The concluding stanza is the longest section of the poem and reflects on Waldo's life as an example of the beauty of nature. Emerson acknowledges that nature is moving always onward and that even childhood is not meant to last forever. The laws of nature require constant movement, reflected in the poet's language of a nature that "radiates," "circulates," and "generates," while it is perpetually "pursuing" and "doing." Even in private grief one must look to the larger workings of nature and "see the genius of the whole." Unable to find consolation in traditional religious terms, Emerson is trying to make sense of the loss in Transcendentalist terms. The body is temporary, but the lessons of the child's life, or nature, are permanent: "Hearts are dust, hearts' loves remain."

FURTHER READING

Chapman, Mary. "The Economics of Loss: Emerson's 'Threnody.'" *American Transcendental Quarterly* (June 2002): 1–15.

Ellison, Julie. "Tears for Emerson: *Essays, Second Series.*" In *The Cambridge Companion to Ralph Waldo Emerson,* edited by Joel Porte and Saundra Morris, 140–161. Cambridge: Cambridge University Press, 1999.

"The Times"

See "INTRODUCTORY LECTURE ON THE TIMES."

"The Titmouse" (1867)

Emerson's poem "The Titmouse" was included in his last full-length collection of poetry, *MAY-DAY AND OTHER PIECES* (1867). The poem is based on an actual experience Emerson had during a winter walk in Walden Woods, although the bird he describes as a titmouse was actually (according to the noted ornithologist Peter Alden) a black-capped chickadee. The story of being so distracted by the bird's song that he loses his way and becomes chilled before finally making his way home becomes an allegory of death postponed. Published when Emerson was well into his 60s, the literary scholar Saundra Morris notes that "*May-Day*'s texts are preoccupied, even more than those of *Poems* [of 1847] with the challenges of controlling limitation and finding rejuvenation." Among the other poems in *May-Day* is the significant "TERMINUS," in which Emerson anticipates his loss of creativity and ends with the idea of sailing home to a safe harbor. "The Titmouse" is located early in the collection, between "MY GARDEN" and "SEA-SHORE," both of which contain the same elements as "Terminus." In "My Garden," unlike in his early *NATURE* (1836), Emerson laments that he has become incapable of "singing" the woods and that only eternal nature, and not finite man, is capable of singing her own song—the theme, also, of "SONG OF NATURE" (originally published in 1861, but also included in *May-Day*).

CRITICAL COMMENTARY

In the first quatrain of "The Titmouse" the poet reminds himself of his limitations as an older man:

"You shall not be overbold / When you deal with Arctic cold." Upon taking a winter walk he "found my lukewarm blood / Chilled wading in the snow-choked wood." The "lukewarm blood" is an internal response to the external reality of the cold and refers not only to aging and death but also to loss of faith in himself and in nature to restore him. At the end of the first stanza he longs to ride the wind currents like a bird—"Up and away for life! Be fleet!"—flying not just to physical safety but also to be lifted again into the realm of poetic power.

The next stanza begins with a premonition of death, both physical and spiritual, as "the frost-king" leaves him immobile—"my hands are stones, / Curdles the blood to the marble bones, / Tugs at the heart-strings, numbs the sense, / And hems in life with narrowing force." He is becoming frozen and losing his hold on life. He ends the stanza by imagining himself lying down in the snow "no ignoble shroud" and letting himself die into nature. But he hears nature calling him back in the song-poem of the bird, who acknowledges him and his predicament of age: "Fine afternoon, old passenger!"

The poet notes the "cheerful cry" of the bird, his "little savior." Here Emerson employs both the romantic sense of the poet's role in bringing cheer, or inspiration and encouragement, through his verses, and the religious reference of the "good news" or good cheer of the Christian Gospels. Emerson's bird is his "savior" and, like the Christian one, has the power to restore life. Emerson expands on the savior image when he says the bird "flew near, with soft wing grazed my hand," just as Jesus was believed to heal with a touch.

The bird also speaks with the voice of prophecy—"Hurling defiance at vast death"—the bird's song (nature) overpowering death. In the midst of all the cold of the poem Emerson introduces the imagery of fire and heat: "What fire burns in that little chest / So frolic, stout, and self possessed?" The poet's lukewarm blood is warmed by this fire, this inspiration, a prophecy of the eternal life-warmth of nature.

The bond between him and nature—"For well the soul, if stout within"—has made it possible for him to interpret the song, understanding the bird as the heroic avatar of winter. The bird has cheered the human poet enough to encourage him to continue on and go home, but not without a promise to return: "When here again thy pilgrim comes, / He shall bring store of seeds and crumbs." The poet has a new muse now, one much smaller and compact than that in "The SPHINX," which began his first collection of poems. Continuing the religious imagery, in the bird the aging poet has found his minister, his savior—"Henceforth I prize thy wiry chant / O'er all that mass and minister vaunt"—as well as his own song and a new entry into nature, which he had previously thought was only open to him through death.

FURTHER READING

Morris, Saundra. "'Metre-Making' Arguments: Emerson's Poems." In *The Cambridge Companion to Ralph Waldo Emerson,* edited by Joel Porte and Saundra Morris. New York: Cambridge University Press, 1999.

Audrey Raden

"To Ellen, at the South" (1843)

This poem, addressed to Emerson's first wife, Ellen Tucker Emerson, dates from April 1830. They had been married in September 1829 and had taken a trip to Philadelphia in mid-March of 1830; Emerson returned to BOSTON alone at the beginning of April, and the couple were separated until he returned to pick her up in mid-May. Ellen was already suffering from consumption, which would claim her life in February 1831 after only a year and a half of marriage. Although first published several years after her death, the poem was written during their brief marriage, at a time of geographical separation, and thus has a precious poignancy as a testament of Emerson's love for his young beautiful wife. After publication in the *DIAL* (January 1843) under the title of "To Eva at the South," it reappeared in *POEMS* (1847), and it was included with revisions under the title of "To Ellen, at the South" in EDWARD WALDO EMERSON's collection *Poems* (1884).

CRITICAL COMMENTARY

Emerson begins this most heartfelt of personal lyrics with reference to "the tune of the spring; / Every year plays it over / To the robin on the wing, and to the pausing lover." He is the pausing lover, and Ellen is the one for whom springtime 'tis a tune worth the knowing, / Though it change every minute." In this soft opening he expresses his own tender feeling for Ellen in her absence, his pining for her return. He continues the same theme by enlisting the services of the "nimble zephyr" that goes lightly "over ten thousand, thousand acres," where "the Flowers—tiny sect of Shakers— / Worship him ever." He bids his dear Ellen "hark to the winning sound! / They summon thee, dearest,— / Saying, 'We dress for thee the ground, / Nor yet thou appearest.'"

There is an EMILY DICKINSON quality to Emerson's imagery here, reminiscent of the way the flowers bow their heads to the hummingbird in "A Route of Evanescence." The pace is not as quick, but the flowers bowing their heads in worship express their love in this way and also their anxiety for Ellen's return from Philadelphia ("the South") to her husband's arms in Boston. Their anxiety concerns their evanescence: "O hasten; 'tis our time," they sing in the gentle breeze, "Ere yet the red Summer / Scorch our delicate prime." "O pride of they race!" they continue, "Sad, in sooth, it were to ours, / If our brief tribe miss thy face, / We poor New England flowers." Emerson has joined them in worship as they exclaim: "Fairest, choose the fairest members / Of our lithe society; June's glories and September's / Show our love and piety." They so urgently wish for Ellen to return to "command us all."

The final stanza repeats this precious sentiment voiced in the entreaties of the flowers of the north for Ellen's return: "O come, then, quickly come! / We are budding, we are blowing; / And the wind that we perfume / Sings a tune that's worth the knowing." The poignancy of this poem was undoubtedly not lost on Emerson when he revised it for publication in the years after Ellen's death. The poem reveals a mysterious foretelling of her death suggested by the seasonal urgency of the flowers to show their love and piety to her before the "red Summer" scorches their delicate prime, and that of Ellen and of the couple's relationship as well. Emerson's other love poems include "EROS," "GIVE ALL TO LOVE," "THINE EYES STILL SHINED," and "INITIAL, DAEMONIC, AND CELESTIAL LOVE."

David A. Dilworth

"The Tragic" (1844)

Emerson's essay "The Tragic" originally stems from the lecture course "Human Life," read in BOSTON (1839–40), was first published in the *DIAL* (April 1844), and was collected posthumously in *NATURAL HISTORY OF INTELLECT and Other Papers* (1893). It is the obvious predecessor and companion to "EXPERIENCE" of *ESSAYS: SECOND SERIES* (1844) and to the later "FATE" of *The CONDUCT OF LIFE* (1860). In his poetry as well is found this theme of the problem of evil in tension with the affirmation of life, as well as in later-phase works such as *LETTERS AND SOCIAL AIMS* (1876).

We should remember that Emerson, in addition to his own bouts with frail health and alarmingly poor eyesight, by the early 1840s had already weathered intense grief through the death of his first wife Ellen Tucker (1831), of his younger brothers EDWARD BLISS EMERSON (1834) and CHARLES CHAUNCY EMERSON (1836), and of his beloved son Waldo (1842). The essay should be read as a companion piece to his long poem "THRENODY" which was begun shortly after Waldo's death and published in *POEMS* (1847). These and other considerations add a poignant undertone to the essay, which provides access to the heart of Emerson's pondering of the meaning of life in the precarious and unstable world of nature.

SYNOPSIS

Emerson opens the essay by declaring, "He has seen but half the universe who never has been shown the house of Pain. As the salt sea covers more than two thirds of the surface of the globe, so sorrow encroaches in man on felicity." The first long paragraph is a veritable catalog of the "regrets and apprehensions" of human life. It ends with the remark that "no theory of life can have any right, which leaves out of account the values of vice, pain, disease, poverty, insecurity, disunion, fear and death."

He inquires into "the conspicuous tragic elements in human nature" and determines that "the bitterest . . . to be derived from an intellectual source is the belief in a brute Fate or Destiny," one in which the universe is indifferent if not also maladapted to human nature. This belief, he says, "lies at the foundation" of many ancient mythologies and "antique tragedy," but it has been progressively superseded by civilization and can no longer coexist given the rational reflections of a higher consciousness. These older stories and traditions, depending on the belief that "Destiny" is "an immense whim," has been displaced by "the doctrine of Philosophical Necessity," or "Optimism," which holds that "the suffering individual finds his good consulted in the good of all, of which he is a part." He contends that "reason and faith" have replaced the "paralyzing terror" of older traditions, taming "the tragic element," which previously "thwart[ed] the will of ignorant individuals."

After naming the "particular evils" that older societies explained as "Fate or Destiny"—"disease, want . . . famine, fever . . . madness and loss of friends"—Emerson explains that "the essence of tragedy" is a greater "Terror," which is "indefinite." This "Terror," however, resides in a certain "power of the imagination"—it is "the whisper overheard, the detected glance, the glare of malignity, ungrounded fears, suspicions, half-knowledge and mistakes." Those most susceptible to these fears are "imperfect characters," persons with "natures so doomed that no prosperity can soothe their ragged and disheveled desolation." From this he makes the astounding generalization that "all sorrow" is thus "superficial"; that "Tragedy is in the eye of the observer, and not in the heart of the sufferer . . . it is always another person who is tormented." Terror, or "panic," is thus "full of illusion." Whether "calamity" or "felicity," "the spirit is true to itself."

With this compensating thought, and in keeping with his insistence on the progressive achievements of human civilization, Emerson segues to a series of historical reflections. He first cites "the countenances of sublime tranquility [of] the Egyptian sphinxes" that have served as symbols for the human spirit for successive ages. The sphinxes, and other examples of ancient "sculpture," show no "emotion," no "joy or grief." To this he adds "the ideal beauty" of Greek statues and architecture, which idealized "serenity," which was also "true to human nature." Human life "demands of us . . . an equilibrium, a readiness, open eyes and ears, and free hands."

In nature, the tragic "is not beautiful," and it is as "guests in Nature,—not impassioned, but cool and disengaged." Extreme emotions, "all passion . . . belongs to the exterior life." "If a man is centred," he is not affected by the "perversity and profligacy" of society, for he understands it is part of nature's plan, "the simultaneous redress." This pragmatic consideration is one of the clearest statements of Emerson's logic of compensation. "Time [is] the consoler," it "dries the freshest tears" by bringing change, bringing something new in place of the tragic: "Nature will not sit still . . . new hopes spring, new affections twine, and the broken is whole again."

There is another positive aspect of the law of polarity that resides within the individual: "Temperament resists the impression of pain." Only the suffering is apparent to the outside observer, who cannot see "the self-adapting strength," "the mysterious counterbalance" nature supplies in individual cases. Emerson characteristically ends on a high note, musing that "the intellect is a consoler, which . . . converts the sufferer into a spectator and his pain into poetry."

CRITICAL COMMENTARY

"The Tragic" is one of the earliest expressions of Emerson's literary jousts with the physical and moral evils of life. It has deeply personal undertones in his own grieving over the death of family members and sets the precedent for, and is essentially continuous with, other "House of Pain" essays, including "Experience," "Fate," and other essays of his middle and late career.

In broad historical perspective, Emerson's cosmic optimism trumps the apparent evil of life, by reprising Heraclitean, PLATONIC, NEOPLATONIC, and Hindu conceptions of the Good and its higher ranking over Evil, conceived as the privation or absence of the Good. Despite the originality of his own thought, Emerson's spiritual faith transmits these older traditions of metaphysical affirmation. In his own time he endured the criticism of naysaying contemporaries (such as THOMAS CARLYLE, NATHANIEL HAWTHORNE, and HERMAN MELVILLE), but he remained committed to reaffirming the deeper spiritual optimism of the ages. Both contemporary and later skeptics would reject his signature doctrine of Transcendental idealism. Emerson's reply in "The Tragic" is, essentially, that we make our own reality; as he would put it in "Experience," also published in 1844: "Thus inevitably does the universe wear our color, and every object fall successively into the subject itself."

FURTHER READING

Arvin, Newton. "The House of Pain: Emerson and the Tragic Sense." *The Hudson Review* 12, no. 1 (Spring 1959): 37–58.

David A. Dilworth

"The Transcendentalist" (1843)

Emerson delivered his lecture "The Transcendentalist" in BOSTON as part of the winter 1841–42 series "The Times." The address was published in the *DIAL* (January 1843) and reprinted in *NATURE; ADDRESSES, AND LECTURES* (1849). In "The Transcendentalist" Emerson simplifies and historicizes the new movement: "What is popularly called Transcendentalism among us, is Idealism; Idealism as it appears in 1842." It is a "tendency to respect the intuitions" and had "deeply colored the conversation and poetry of the present day," as well as "the history of genius and of religion in these times," compelling Emerson to clarify what is meant by the term and the people who identify with it. Although he never embraced the label, he had clearly emerged as the major spokesperson of Transcendentalism. The essay seeks to explain the philosophical and social contours of the movement, but the primary focus, as the title implies, is on the individual believer or Transcendentalist as a type.

SYNOPSIS

Emerson begins the essay by asserting that Transcendentalism is "not new, but the very oldest of thoughts cast into the mould of these new times." All thought and all thinkers can be divided into materialists and idealists; the former "insists on facts, on history, on the force of circumstances, and the animal wants of man" compared to the idealist's belief in "the power of Thought and of Will, on inspiration, on miracle, on individual culture." And yet, the idealist "does not deny the sensuous fact" but sees it as the "completion of a spiritual fact."

The materialist considers only the "external world" while the idealist "has another measure, which is metaphysical . . . the *rank* which things themselves take in his consciousness"; that is, not what is it, but what is the meaning? For the idealist, "Mind is the only reality" and therefore he "does not respect" man-made institutions such as labor, property, government, or church. These are seen by the idealist only as "symbols" that reflect "the laws of being," not "the law of his mind."

All "ethics" come from this process of discerning the spiritual meaning of facts. This inquiry reveals the natural law of self-reliance: "Everything real is self-existent." Rather than being determined by our "circumstances," the idealist says, "I make my circumstance." Even "condition and economy" are only a reflection of "thought or motive," and the self is only a "thought which is called I," a "mould into which the world is poured like melted wax." The only rules that matter are those of the spirit, and the Transcendentalist, as an idealist, therefore believes himself to be both law and "Lawgiver."

As Transcendentalism is therefore only a "spiritual principle," originating from within the individual, "there is no such thing as a Transcendental *party* . . . there is no pure Transcendentalist." Only in nature do we find "something higher than our understanding," something transcendent, that is, instinct or intuition. When "the squirrel hoards nuts, and the bee gathers honey, without knowing what they do, and they are thus provided for without selfishness or disgrace," this is Transcendentalism. Only "Nature is transcendental," and it reveals a "life made of miracles."

Emerson places Transcendentalism in the context of Western intellectual history: "This way of thinking, falling on Roman times, made Stoic philosophers; falling on despotic times, made patriot Catos and Brutuses; falling on superstitious times, made prophets and apostles; on popish times, made protestants and ascetic monks, preachers of Faith against the preachers of Works; on prelatical times, made Puritans and Quakers; and falling on Unitarian and commercial times, makes the peculiar shades of Idealism which we know." The 19th-century form of idealism "acquired the name of Transcendental, from the use of that term by Immanuel Kant . . . who replied to the skeptical philosophy of Locke." Whereas JOHN LOCKE believed that all knowledge comes from "the senses," IMMANUEL KANT argued "that there was a very important class of ideas . . . which did not come by experience." So it is that any philosophy of "intuitive thought" is "popularly called at the present day *Transcendental.*"

Having explained the basic philosophy, Emerson turns to the "intelligent and religious persons" who now call themselves Transcendentalists. They have dedicated themselves to "a certain solitary and critical way of living," but without producing any "solid fruit." They live a "lofty dream" in which any physical labor "seems drudgery." The times inspire their hopefulness and these "seething brains, these admirable radicals, these unsocial worshippers, these talkers who talk the sun and moon away" are to be admired for their seeking. Society may find it "insulting" that the Transcendentalist "declareth all to be unfit to be his companions." This is not meant as an insult but is merely a "principle"; the Transcendentalist loves humanity but only rejects "common association."

Emerson ventures that society is uncomfortable with the Transcendentalist because "they make us feel the strange disappointment which overcasts every human youth. So many promising youths, and never a finished man!" This criticism is not unique to the Transcendentalists but pervades society: "Where are they who represented to the last generation that extravagant hope, which a few happy aspirants suggest to ours?" The Transcendentalists raise unanswerable questions and so, "by their unconcealed dissatisfaction, they expose our poverty, and the insignificance of man to man. . . . These exacting children advertise us of our wants."

Unable to find "their hope and religion" in society, the Transcendentalist turns instead to "a picture, a book, a favorite spot in the hills or the woods." Soon enough, these "seem real, and society the illusion." Admittedly, idealists "are not good citizens, not good members of society." They do not labor or join associations, "they do not even like to vote." The Transcendentalist rejects "what you call your fundamental institutions," whether "Abolition, Temperance, . . . Calvinism, or Unitarianism. . . . You make very free use of these words 'great' and 'holy,' but few things appear to them as such." The Transcendentalist finds the "courtesies" and "conventions" of society to have "a spirit of cowardly compromise" and declares that "unless the action is necessary, unless it is adequate, I do not wish to perform it." If the Transcendentalist has "doubts and objections" about his life and work, it comes from inside himself, not from a wish to fulfill society's expectations.

The Transcendentalist thus lives with a "double consciousness," feeling "that is to be done which he has not skill to do, or to be said which others can say better." The world of experience is "all buzz and din," while the world of the soul is "all infinitude and paradise," and the two are rarely if ever reconciled. The most the Transcendentalist can strive for is a life without "hypocrisy," that is, being true to oneself.

Emerson then turns to a more positive view of the Transcendentalists as "lovers and worshippers of Beauty." In fact, of "Truth, Goodness, and Beauty," they live most according to "Beauty." In this sense, the Transcendentalist fits in with his contemporaries because, while Beauty is *not* the guiding principle of "the old church" or of politics, it is the foundation of reform, of "the moral movements of the time": "the justice which is now claimed for the black, and the pauper, and the drunkard is for Beauty." These movements are guided by Beauty (synonymous, for Emerson, with balance or justice) because Good has a tendency to "dowdiness" and Truth can lead to "heartlessness."

Emerson acknowledges that the Transcendentalists do not have all the answers—"They are novices; they only show the road in which man should travel." Society should not denigrate "this class," for we need "bridges [and] ploughs" as well as "finer instruments." Emerson wonders if there might also "be room for . . . collectors of the heavenly spark with power to convey the electricity to others . . . rare and gifted men, to compare the points of our spiritual compass, and verify our bearings from superior chronometers." As it is, society operates on a "downward tendency." All talk is of politics and business and so, he pleads, "will you not tolerate one or two solitary voices in the land, speaking for thoughts and principles not marketable and perishable?"

CRITICAL COMMENTARY

Emerson begins the essay by defining idealism as a philosophy. He immediately diffuses criticism of the Transcendentalists, however, by asking whether there is so much difference between idealism and materialism, as even the materialist must admit, "we never go out of ourselves"—"What more could an idealist say?" In this sense, "every materialist will be an idealist; but an idealist can never go backward to be a materialist." The materialist thinks he "knows where he stands, and what he does"; the idealist-Transcendentalist is more comfortable with uncertainty.

For the Transcendentalist, the self is the only reality, the only authority; as Emerson explained in "SELF-RELIANCE" (1841), "Nothing is at last sacred but the integrity of your own mind." As he details throughout the essay, the Transcendentalist thus rejects all institutions, whether religious or social, and is guided only by an internal "private spirit." The Transcendentalist has "an invisible unsounded center in himself," and out of this self flows the "facts you call the world." This denial of "facts"—or, rather of a fact-based "world"—this belief in a completely "subjective or relative existence," leads to easy criticism of the Transcendentalists as "star-gazers and dreamers." In the essay "EXPERIENCE," Emerson would speak to this idea again (somewhat humorously): "Let us treat the men and women well: treat them as if they were real: perhaps they are."

Emerson defines Transcendentalism as both historically specific and universal; for example, the Buddhist whose "conviction that every good deed can by no possibility escape its reward . . . is a Transcendentalist." As part of a longer Western intellectual tradition, Transcendentalism is the idealist tendency happening upon "Unitarian and commercial times." Here Emerson emphasizes the distinctly American aspects of Transcendentalism as a response to specific religious and economic trends that privilege the individual.

Ultimately, Transcendentalism is merely an ideal, an aspiration. We have few examples "of a purely spiritual life" and there is "no pure Transcendentalist." Nature alone is transcendental and thus becomes our guide. The Transcendentalist is thus one who privileges spending time alone in nature, experiencing the human connection with nature. Emerson's *NATURE* (1836) served as his foundational statement on "the true position of nature in regard to man." The artist CHRISTOPHER PEARSE CRANCH caricatured some of Emerson's more extreme passages of his oneness with *Nature,* providing humorous drawings to accompany passages such as Emerson's enthusiastic "I expand and live in the warm day like corn and melons."

These Transcendentalists, "these few hermits" who seek only "fuller union with the surrounding system," are misunderstood and not appreciated. The Transcendentalist improves society by reaching toward something better and believing in humanity. Emerson admits that certain individuals "lay themselves open to criticism and to lampoons, and . . . ridiculous stories." He does not identify any of his Transcendentalist colleagues by name, but by 1841 (when the lecture was first given) a significant community had coalesced around Emerson in CONCORD, and the various failed social and educational experiments of these outsider figures, as well as their often obtuse writings, had exposed them to criticism.

The Transcendentalist offers hope to society, but, in return, society offers only customs, tradition, "routine," expectations, and work. He imagines a conversation between the Transcendentalists and their critics: "We are miserable with inaction . . . but we do not like your work . . . 'What will you do, then?' cries the world. / 'We will wait.' / 'How long?' / 'Until the Universe rises up and calls us to work.'" This is the Transcendentalist vocational dilemma that Emerson resolved for himself by becoming a successful lecturer and essayist but that plagued others, such as BRONSON ALCOTT, MARGARET FULLER, and HENRY DAVID THOREAU.

In this address, Emerson urges sympathy, not criticism, for these souls unable to reconcile their ideals with a world that defines selfhood purely in political or economic terms. "The Transcendentalist" is not an in-depth explanation of Emerson's philosophical idealism—for that, the reader could go directly to the source, in *Nature,* the ESSAYS (*FIRST SERIES* had been published by this date), or the "DIVINITY SCHOOL ADDRESS." In the end, it is merely a plea to make room for idealism in the marketplace of ideas.

"Two Rivers" (1858)

Emerson's poem "Two Rivers" describes the Musketaquit River, which flows through CONCORD, MASSACHUSETTS, and was part of Emerson's daily experience. Emerson also describes another river—the spiritual truth behind the fact of the actual river—in a symbolic way, to describe the pulse of life through every living thing. The poem was written between May and October 1857, and it was first published in the *ATLANTIC MONTHLY* in January 1858. A journal entry in the spring of 1840 is one possible source for the poem: "We see the river glide below us but we see not the river that glides over us & envelopes us in its floods." The first drafts of the poem appear in Emerson's journal in 1856. The poem appears in the "Nature" section of the book *MAY-DAY AND OTHER PIECES,* published in 1867, and it was collected in *SELECTED POEMS* (1876) and *Poems* (1884).

Emerson's "Two Rivers" makes an interesting companion piece to HENRY DAVID THOREAU's book, *A Week on the Concord and Merrimack Rivers* (1849). Thoreau records the strict natural details regarding his two rivers, allowing the beauty of his Concord setting to emerge organically from, and transcend, mere fact. Emerson, in his poem, attempts a similar reading of *his* two rivers—the actual river (the Musketaquit) and the unseen, "true" river.

CRITICAL COMMENTARY

Emerson uses the image of the Musketaquit, significant to Emerson in that using a specific river gives the poem a sense of place, to describe by analogy a "second" river—that "inundation sweet" that flows through all things. Emerson's "second" river might be thought of as an analogy for "second sight," or the ability of the poet to see beyond the facts of the world to perceive the spiritual truth that animates nature. This animating force is fluid and ever-changing; that is, it cannot be contained by man's laws. As opposed to the actual Musketaquit, this "stream . . . unbounded goes."

The poem is comprised of five self-contained stanzas; a "river" winds through each stanza; the lines are, for the most part, end-stopped, and each stanza closes with a period. As is typical of Emerson, the final stanza summarizes the theme of the poem; line 18, "Who drinks it shall not thirst again," refers to the Biblical verse of John 4:13, in which Jesus, speaking to the Samaritan woman at the well, tells her, "Whosoever drinketh of this water shall thirst again: but he that shall drink of the water I shall give him shall not thirst for ever." Indeed, the final line, "And ages drop in it like rain," suggests, even in the formal stanza setting, the timelessness of nature.

Bill Scalia

"Una" (1867)

Emerson's poem "Una" utilizes the image of the moon as the spirit of inspiration, a faithful companion to the poet. Emerson's traveler might be thought of as man in solitude, as he describes in *NATURE* (1836), with the eye of inspiration guiding him: "Standing on the bare ground,—my head bathed by the blithe air, and uplifted into infinite space,—allmean egotism vanishes. I become a transparent eye-ball; I am nothing; I see all; the currents of the Universal Being circulate through me; I am part or particle of God." The poem was drafted between November 1842 and March 1843 but was omitted from the 1847 volume *POEMS* (an indication of Emerson's struggle with the poem). "Una" first appeared in *MAY-DAY AND OTHER PIECES* (1867) and was collected by EDWARD WALDO EMERSON in *Complete Works* (1903–04).

CRITICAL COMMENTARY

In "Una," the moon is a constant reminder to the poet that inspiration, in the form of nature, is always present; the poet realizes that this presence depends on perception. The first four stanzas of the poem establish the fundamental connection for Emerson between nature and mind. The poem turns in stanza 5, however; when the poet is away from home (we may read home as center, or stability) the poet becomes "a thought" of the moon. That is, wherever the poet wanders, the moon is present. Nature never loses sight of its charge.

The poet's name resonates far from home, but at home he is "hidden and unknown"; what does Emerson mean with this seeming paradox? Emerson might be commenting on surface ("fame") versus depth ("hidden"). The poet at home (under the influence of spirit) is unknown in his solitude. This solitude is broken away from "home," where the influence is most perfect.

The poem is curious for Emerson in that its images do not resolve. Emerson is no mere sensualist, and he does not offer images for the sole sake of their beauty or pleasure. "Una" is a puzzle in this sense; Emerson's poetic powers weakened considerably late in his life, and "Una" is an example of a poem he just could not work to its final state. In his note on "Una" for *Complete Works,* Edward acknowledges the poem's problem: "It might be the sense of the poetical beauty refreshed in the poetical mind by new scenes and friends met in travel." Edward's tentative language implies much about the difficulty of this puzzling poem.

Bill Scalia

"Unity" (1847)

Emerson's poem "Unity" describes his continuing idea that the individual will must become subservient to (or, at least is expressed through) the "universal soul," an argument Emerson makes most clearly in his essay "The OVER-SOUL" (1841). Evidence from Emerson's journals suggests that he first drafted the poem "Unity" in late 1846 or early 1847. Emerson chose the poem, then untitled, to serve as motto for the essay "The Over-Soul" in the 1847 edition of *ESSAYS: FIRST SERIES* (the poem was not composed when *Essays* was originally published, in 1841). The poem was later collected, with the title "Unity," in *MAY-DAY AND OTHER PIECES* (1867), and it was reprinted in the posthumous *Poems* (1884) and in the *Complete Works* (1903).

CRITICAL COMMENTARY

The poem "Unity" is cast in 11 lines, discretely separated into three sections (three lines; three lines; five lines, as indicated by the punctuation of the lines). The first section states that, though "space is ample, east and west," "two cannot go abreast." *East* and *west* are terms used by Emerson to suggest an apparent opposition of the spiritual East and the rational West (as in his poem "EXPERIENCE" [1844]); though this space is wide, as the hyperbole of the riddle suggests, it is not wide enough to include both individual will and the universal soul. Emerson tells us, in "The Over-Soul," that the separation between will and soul is false: "Unity, that Over-soul, within which every man's particular being is contained and made one with all other" is its "inevitable nature," within which "private will is overpowered."

In the second section of the poem Emerson utilizes the symbol of the "masterful cuckoo," the bird that takes over the nest of another and "crowds every egg out of the nest . . . except its own." This symbol is most effective because Emerson does not labor over the significance, but he allows it to speak for itself (as opposed to the similar but less successful technique in the poem "LOVE AND THOUGHT" [1867]).

The final section of the poem contains five lines that bring together, in more prosaic terms—"A spell is laid on sod and stone, / Night and Day've been tampered with"—the first two sections of the poem. This last section, rather than relying on the riddle of the opening or the symbolism of the second section, instead tells us of the "power" of the universal soul, which "works its will on age and hour." Thus Emerson uses three means—riddle, symbolism, and finally, direct expression—to communicate the mystery, and significance, of the universal soul, which, as he expresses in "The Over-Soul," "is not an organ, but animates and exercises all organs . . . is not a faculty, but a light; is not the intellect or the will, but the master of the intellect and will."

Bill Scalia

"Uriel" (1847)

Emerson's poem "Uriel" was probably drafted in 1839 but was first published in *Poems* of 1847. In mythology as well as in literature (including in John Milton's *Paradise Lost*), Uriel is the god of fire or the Sun, a rebellious and misunderstood archangel. Emerson sets his story of an unresolved argument between Uriel and the other gods "in the ancient periods," but the poem is an allegory for his own experience in the aftermath of the "Divinity School Address," delivered in the summer of 1838. Son Edward Waldo Emerson later referred to the poem as "a celestial parable of the story of a crisis in its author's life": "The poem, when read with the history of the Divinity School Address, and its consequences, in mind, is seen to be an account of that event generalized and sublimed." Edward also noted that, in the essay on "Circles" (1841), Emerson had invoked the same language and theme of the poem, saying: "Beware when the great God lets loose a thinker on this planet."

"Uriel" is a commentary not only on Emerson's experience, but also on the challenge of Transcendentalism in general. A generation of Transcendentalist thinkers and writers were challenging not only the religious institutions but literary forms and social values as well. The writings of Margaret Fuller, Theodore Parker, Henry David Thoreau, and others proposed radical changes in the social, political, and theological order. In "Uriel," "the gods shook" amidst this collective rebellion.

CRITICAL COMMENTARY

The first stanza sets the story "in ancient periods" but also indicates that the issue is timeless, transcending the "calendar months and days" of "wild Time." The poem tells the story of "the lapse of Uriel, Which in Paradise befell." If Emerson is Uriel, then "Paradise" was Harvard College, where the poet "Sayd" "overheard the young gods talking." The poet "Sayd" (or "Saadi," as in his poem by that name) was another alterego of Emerson's, although here it could represent the Harvard faculty who worry over the students listening to Emerson's ideas, "the treason, too long pent." The students are debating the rigid "laws of form, and metre just," that is, the implications of Emerson's "treason" for literature and poetry, and they are considering now "what subsisteth, and what seems"—or, the difference between materialism and idealism.

In the poem, "One" (Emerson) has "defied" the "reverend use" of their gathering and brought "doubt" into their minds. Challenging their religion and their god, he has presented his own ideas as "divine"—a direct reference to Emerson's call in the "Divinity School Address" to be a "divine man." He has "stirr'd the devils everywhere" with his radical views: "Line in nature is not found; / Unit and universe are round; / In vain produced, all rays return." These ideas upset all boundaries, emphasizing there is no separation between man and nature, between man and god. Emerson's imagery of roundness or circles in this passage was one that resonated throughout his writings (in the essay "Circles" [1841], most clearly). Margaret Fuller's 1845 poem, "Double Triangle, Serpent and Rays" (printed in *Woman in the Nineteenth Century*), makes an interesting comparison to these lines in "Uriel," as Fuller's "Double Triangle" was encased in a "circle round" and her poem also took as its theme the elimination of social boundaries between "Male & female, black & white." Her poem also invokes "the diamond Sun," the illuminating center of the universe, the transcendental self, and, in Emerson's poem, Uriel the Sun-god.

In "Uriel," all previously held beliefs are turned upside down: "Evil will bless, and ice will burn." At this upset "a shudder ran around the sky;" and "the stern old war-gods," leaders of the Harvard and UNITARIAN establishments such as ANDREWS NORTON, "shook their heads." With Emerson's "rash word," "the balance-beam of Fate was bent" and no longer did the same truths hold. Even the boundary between heaven and hell, the very basis of their theology, is blurred: "The bounds of good and ill were rent; / Strong Hades could not keep his own, / But all slid to confusion."

In true Transcendentalist fashion, the controversy awakens a new sense of self: "A sad self-knowledge withering fell / On the beauty of Uriel." Self-knowledge is the goal, but in this case, it is reminiscent of the fall of Adam and Eve, as Emerson's eyes were opened to the fact of his own separation. He was once one of them—"In heaven once eminent, the god"—but now he is alone with his ideas—"Withdrew that hour into his cloud." He is unsure of his fate—"Whether doom'd to long gyration"—but realizes he has outgrown them, cast out "by knowledge grown too bright." He had been dismissed before, but "the fire-seed slept," that is, smoldering, but never extinguished. He continued in his work, "now and then, truth-speaking things," until his idealism put their religion to shame—"Shamed the angels' veiling wings."

Uriel/Emerson's philosophy of "the good of evil born" not only challenges the negative focus on evil and sin in religion (it was a phrase he used in the later essay, "Considerations by the Way" [1860] to explain evil as nature's balance to good) but also does double duty here as a reference to the positive lessons of this controversy. In "Uriel," he cannot entirely separate from or criticize them, because their institutions gave rise to his voice—"Came Uriel's voice of cherub scorn." This is a reminder that Uriel is an angel or "cherub," and that the critique comes from within. Emerson's words shamed the gods/teachers—"a blush tinged the upper sky"—and again blurred the boundaries between heaven and hell (upper and lower) in bringing a "blush" or tinge from below. The poem ends with an affirmation of the power of ideas, which have changed things irrevocably: "And the gods shook, they knew not why."

Emerson did not otherwise publicly respond to the intense criticism following the Divinity School Address. He only noted in his journal, "I fear it not." In the poem, Uriel/Emerson does not directly engage his critics but stands alone in a "sad self-knowledge, withering," while the truth stands for itself. Like the "great men" of Emerson's later *REPRESENTATIVE MEN* (1850), Uriel is not understood in his own time—he is a prophet, a visionary, whose poetic utterances threaten the existing order, even if "they knew not why." Identifying perhaps with the misunderstood visionary, the 20th-century poet Robert Frost deemed "Uriel" "the greatest Western poem yet" and explained to a correspondent his own withdrawal from political controversy by declaring, "I will take example of Uriel and withdraw into a cloud."

FURTHER READING

Keane, Patrick J. *Emerson, Romanticism, and Intuitive Reason: The Transatlantic "Light of All Our Day."* Columbia: University of Missouri Press, 2005.

Van Anglen, Kevin P. *The New England Milton: Literary Reception and Cultural Authority in the Early Republic.* Rev. ed. University Park: Pennsylvania State University Press, 2008.

"Uses of Great Men" (1850)

Emerson reworked the opening lecture from his 1845–46 series, "Uses of Great Men," into the introductory essay for *REPRESENTATIVE MEN* (1850). The introduction is followed by essays on six different "great men" in history: "PLATO; OR, THE PHILOSOPHER," "SWEDENBORG; OR, THE MYSTIC," "MONTAIGNE; OR, THE SKEPTIC," "SHAKSPEARE; OR, THE POET," "NAPOLEON; OR, THE MAN OF THE WORLD," and "GOETHE; OR, THE WRITER." In his earlier essay on "SPIRITUAL LAWS" (1841) Emerson notes, "The great man knew not that he was great. It took a century or two for that fact to appear. What he did, he did because he must; it was the most natural thing in the world." In "Uses of Great Men," Emerson explains his theory of biography, which is, namely, that what makes men great is not solely their individual characteristics or accomplishments but the extent to which those characteristics are universal and inspire greatness in others. Emerson's project is thus both a response and a challenge to friend THOMAS CARLYLE's book *On Heroes, Hero Worship and the Heroic in History* (1841).

SYNOPSIS

Emerson opens the essay by acknowledging, "It is natural to believe in great men." We name "our children and our lands" after them, we collect their works, we tell their stories. Life, in general, is a search for "the great"—great places, great people, even great "climates." Religion and fables all have in common their reliance upon great men, a tendency that forms the basis of "theism" (belief in a humanlike god). In social life, we attract and are attracted to greatness. Emerson defines a "great man" as one "who inhabits a higher sphere of thought" and lives his best self: "He is great who is what he is from nature, and who never reminds us of others." But a great man must also "be related to us"; that is, he must be recognizable, possessing universal traits. A great man may be "isolated" and apart from his own times, and only after some time passes is acknowledged as "effective, generative . . . fertile, magnetic," like a river or an apple seed.

There are "two kinds of use or service from superior men." The first use of great men is "direct giving . . . of material or metaphysical aid," such as through healing or prophecy. But such outward aid has no lasting effect. It is better to gain an "unfolding" or "discovery" of ourselves, rather than receive a "gift" that is "contrary to the law of the universe." The second use of great men, then, is "indirect service." Great men serve our "intellects" by what they "represent," rather than what they do.

Turning again to the comparison with nature, great men turn "raw material . . . to human use." Inventors, discoverers, and musicians are all connected to some part of nature. "A man is a centre of nature" through which nature flows and then relates outward. Nature awaits "a destined human deliverer" who can unlock its powers, but we must not limit ourselves to only "first advantages," or utilitarian uses, of nature. It is in the "higher advantages," such as "music, architecture, numbers, astronomy," that we see nature's inspiration. The sciences and arts consist of nature, plus "intellect," plus "will."

Nature attracts "some genius who occupies himself with one thing, all his life long." That genius must then be "translated" for others. In this manner, "unpublished nature will have its whole secret told." Each genius builds upon the next: "Every ship that comes to America got its chart from Columbus. Every novel is a debtor to Homer." We name these great men, but many more go unrecognized for their individual contributions: "Life is grit all around with a zodiac of sciences, the contributions of men who have perished to add their point of light to our sky."

We are wrong to passively accept the presence of greatness without making use of it: "We must not be sacks and stomachs." Instead, we must be going to the source of their greatness, "conversing with the same things," so that we might begin to think as they did: "We acquire very fast the habit of looking at things in the same light . . . we anticipate his thought." But why look for this "mental and moral force" from men of the past when "our own companions" have a more direct effect on us? We are overly enamored of "heroes of the day"—we want to see their bodies, their expressions in life. But, he argues, that force can be felt in literature as well. Shakespeare's name alone "suggests . . . purely intellectual benefits." We misplace our sense of greatness onto "medals [and] swords" of "senates and sovereigns" and "the power and beauty of the body," when we would gain a "higher benefit" from "intellectual feats." Emerson proposes a new "gymnasium" of the mind.

We must always be careful of "idolatry" and "oppression" under the ideas of great men. Religions, sects, and entire schools of thought are founded claiming the name of one man only, but true genius inspires not adoration but "new consciousness": "Rotation is the law of nature." When

"Nature removes a great man, people explore the horizon for a successor." There are no successors, there are only "ideas." We are too quick to let great men "know for us." We give them power, we erect statues and memorials.

But how to "measure" what true service or "benefit" great men can provide? Emerson uses the analogy of how, in his own time, men are always rushing off to business and watching the clock. "We live in a market" where children strive to be first, and "greatness" is a competition. Instead, wealth and immortality will come from learning some law or truth that cannot be measured. The greatest "heroes" serve others and do not seek personal gain and power. Great men raise up everyone: "With the great, our thoughts and manners easily become great." We need to transcend our own times and places to see what others are capable of. Great men "defend us from our contemporaries."

There is, again, a "limit to the use of heroes," and we must not become "underlings and intellectual suicides": "The best discovery the discoverer makes for himself." Nature's "law of individuality" ensures that the child will develop into his own person regardless of the efforts of the parents. And yet some people avoid the word "great," fearing it implies "caste" or "fate"; greatness implies there are others who are not great. But Emerson defends the usage, arguing that we cannot all "know the same things," so we should all be "teachers and pupils in turn," learning from each other's experiences and talents. But he also shifts the argument; rather than lament that all men are not great, we might raise the expectations of all by believing "there are no common men." The problem is not the existence (or absence) of greatness but the limitations, place upon ourselves.

Emerson is hopeful, however, that society is progressing; the era that prides itself on its own enlightenment "will one day be quoted, to prove its barbarism." We study individuals only to find it is the ideas that live on in other times. We are limited in our own greatness only by our "education" and "agency." Emerson ends on a poetic note, stating that our purpose, each of us, is "to tame the chaos . . . to scatter the seeds of science and of song."

CRITICAL COMMENTARY

In "Uses of Great Men," Emerson established the terms by which he would present and analyze the contribution of each of his representative men in the volume. He defined great men as those who turn the "raw material" of nature "to human use." We, in turn, are inspired by their ideas, creations, methods, or achievements. However, we also have our own "original relation to the universe" (as he phrased it in *NATURE* of 1836), and we have the ability to unlock nature's powers on our own. It is significant that, in a volume that focuses on men of the Western intellectual tradition, Emerson here calls upon a uniquely American greatness, giving as his examples of humanity harnessing nature's power and "secrets" our use of steam, iron, coal, cotton, or corn—all of which speak to the industrial, economic, but also scientific greatness of the United States in the 19th century. This was the theme as well of "The YOUNG AMERICAN" (1844), in which he articulated a vision of American genius tied to the availability of the land.

In "Uses of Great Men" he introduced the points that would echo throughout the essays on PLATO, EMANUEL SWEDENBORG, William Shakespeare, and the others. All of the figures in *Representative Men* are praised by Emerson as masters of synthesis, relying and building upon previous works and ideas. In selecting the order in which to present his representative men, he chose Plato as the first, identifying Plato as the foundation of all thought to follow. Yet, in "Uses of Great Men," even Plato is a student (of Socrates) and when we read Plato and "are exalted by his ideas, we do not owe this to Plato, but to the idea, to which, also, Plato was a debtor." This passage is reminiscent of "The AMERICAN SCHOLAR" (1837)—his earliest call for American genius and greatness—in which he warned against seeing greatness only in others, and trying to emulate that greatness rather than cultivating our own, reminding scholars that "Cicero, Locke, and Bacon were only young men in libraries, when they wrote these books."

Emerson thus spends a good portion of "Uses of Great Men" challenging the definition and idea of greatness. Throughout his works, as he explained also in "The American Scholar," he proudly declared "I embrace the common." He was (and his overviews of individual "great men" all eventually come to this point) a champion of the greatness of each individual. As he stated in "Uses of Great Men," "He is great who is what he is from nature, and who never reminds us of others." In the earlier essay "HEROISM" (1841), Emerson more fully developed his theory of genius and greatness within each of us, returning always to the foundational point restated throughout his writings: "Self-trust is the essence of heroism."

"Uses of Natural History" (1833)

Emerson delivered his lecture "Uses of Natural History" on November 5, 1833, for the Natural History Society at the Masonic Temple in BOSTON. He delivered the same lecture two years later, in November 1835, in Lowell, Massachusetts. The 1833 address was his first public lecture after deciding to leave the ministry in late 1832. In the intervening months he had traveled abroad for the first time, visiting Italy, Switzerland, England, Scotland, and France, and much of the lecture material comes from his journals of those visits. At the Cabinet of Natural History at the Jardin des Plantes in Paris in July 1833 he experienced an epiphany regarding man's relationship to nature and regarding his own vocation. He concluded, "The earth is a museum," and determined that "I will be a naturalist." In the "Language" section of *NATURE*, a few years later, he explained, "The use of natural history is to give us aid in supernatural history: the use of the outer creation, to give us language for the beings and changes of the inward creation." From this first lecture in 1833, then, to *Nature* and to his last public lectures in the 1870s on the *NATURAL HISTORY OF INTELLECT*, Emerson remained remarkably consistent in his ideas about nature and in his self-identification as, primarily, "a naturalist."

Perhaps because the ideas in "Uses of Natural History" influenced and were repeated throughout these other works, the lecture was not published during his lifetime. It has been collected in Bosco and Myerson's *The Selected Lectures of Ralph Waldo Emerson* (University of Georgia, 2005).

SYNOPSIS

In speaking before the Natural History Society, Emerson begins by admitting that his authority on the topic is of "inclination" rather than "ability." He then states, however, that "it seems to have been designed, if anything has, that men should be students of Natural History. Man is, by nature, a farmer, a hunter, a shepherd, and a fisherman, who are all practical naturalists and by their observations the true founders of all societies for the pursuit of science." Even men in "cities" and the "sedentary trades and professions" must have some knowledge of "the properties of water, of wood . . . of light, of heat, . . . of many insects, birds and beasts." If nothing else, the beauty of nature sparks our curiosity and is nature's way of encouraging our study of nature: "The earth is a museum, and the five senses a philosophical apparatus of such perfection." We are born scientists and nature gave us all the tools we need to understand the world.

Nature inspires culture and sentiments as well, such as the "love of country" that arises from the beautiful landscapes. Likewise, it is only in nature that an activity such as hunting takes on the tone of poetry—it does not have the same romance to chase down animals in the cities. Indeed, it is not the hunt, but "these scenes" of nature that a man loves. Beyond patriotism or hunting, though, Emerson asks, "what are the advantages" that will come "from the greater cultivation of Natural Science," admitting that we cannot yet know all the answers to this question: "I do not think we are yet masters of all the reasons that make this knowledge valuable to us."

He recounts his recent visit to "the Garden of Plants in Paris," which holds "the richest collection in the world of natural curiosities arranged for the most imposing effect." He describes the zoo, where "you walk among the animals of every country" all in one place, and the botanical collection as "a grammar of botany," "a natural alphabet," a "dictionary." In "the ornithological chambers" the "stuffed birds" seem out of literature rather than of nature. Again, Emerson's reference point is to the realm of imagination rather "than to a real tangible Scientific Collection." Finally, he visits the hall of "stuffed beasts" and then skeletons, a lesson in "comparative anatomy" of everything from a whale to the "highly developed skull of the Caucasian race of man." Here, with all of these specimens in one place, "The limits of the possible are enlarged, and the real is stranger than the imaginary. The universe is a more amazing puzzle than ever . . . I am moved by strange sympathies. I say I will listen to this invitation. I will be a Naturalist."

He then moves to the question of the "specific advantages" that come from the study of natural history. First, it is "serviceable to the health," both physical and mental. Whether gardening or bird watching or advancing science, the study of nature results in "active limbs and refreshed spirits," "sharpness of sight and bounding blood." Second, nature provides "the raw material out of which we construct our food, clothing, fuel, furniture, and arms." He laments modern modes of production that have caused us to forget the source for "the brasses, the silver, the iron, the gold . . . the glass, the cloth, the paints and dyes . . . fabrics, drugs," and so on that fill our homes. All of these require "the prospective power, the armed hand, the learned eye" of the naturalist, the scientist, the chemist, the engineer.

Having listed the practical uses of nature, the third "benefit" of studying natural history is "knowledge itself." To the person who asks why he should learn about "the Solar System" or "the faithful return of the seasons," Emerson responds, "Why, the good of knowing that fact. Is not that good enough?" He again uses the imagery of sight: "Every fact that is disclosed to us in natural history removes one scale more from the eye." When we think about geography and climate and the geometry of snowflakes, then the snow becomes more than a plaything or an impediment to trade: "The snowstorm becomes to your eye a philosophical experiment." So it is with coal, for understanding geology allows us to understand the history of the earth itself, where the coal comes from and how long it took to get to this present form, which has changed our society, mechanically, technologically, socially; such "knowledge will make the face of the earth significant to us." Knowledge of nature changes our perspective. "A lobster is monstrous to the eye the first time it is seen," but when we learn about each of its parts we then appreciate it "as perfect and suitable to his sea-house." Knowledge transforms everything in nature into "an object of some worth; perhaps of admiration."

The fourth reason for the study of natural history is "its salutary effect on the mind and character." When we admire "nature's workmanship," we are inspired ourselves to "work in her style." We get "all our ideas of sublimity and beauty" from nature. He gives the example of "The Earthworms," earth's "little gardeners and farmers," or "the economy of bees." Besides such practical examples, nature has a calming effect on the mind because it requires "discipline . . . patient, docile observation." Unlike society, which breeds conformity, nature inspires (requires even) "the peculiarities of original genius." Nature allows for "silence and solitude, and of constant familiarity with calm and great objects." Nature also "generates enthusiasm . . . the highest *state* of the character." It inspires an obsessive "interest in truth." The naturalist believes that "man has no nobler vocation than to watch and record the wonders that surround him." In Emerson's formulation here, there is no difference between the scientist-naturalist and the poet-philosopher; both are "observers" whose vocation it is to translate the language of nature.

This leads him to the fifth and "greatest office of natural science," that is, nature's ability "to explain man to himself." "The knowledge of all the facts of all the laws of nature will give man his true place in the system of being." But "the most mysterious and wonderful fact, after our own existence" is "the power of expression which belongs to external nature; or, that correspondence of the outward world to the inward world of thoughts and emotions." For example, "There is more beauty in the morning cloud" than the mere scientific fact. The cloud "reflects the aspects of mortal life, its epochs, and its fate." Just as "the whole of Nature is a metaphor or image of the human Mind" (here Emerson references EMANUEL SWEDENBORG), so it is that in science, "axioms" such as "A straight line is the shortest distance between two points" or "The whole is greater than its parts" or "Reaction is equal to action" all have "an ethical as well as a material sense"—"we repeat them because they are symbolical of moral truths." He continues with the metaphor of books and of reading nature: "I wish to learn this language—not that I may know a new grammar but that I may read the great book which is written in that tongue."

CRITICAL COMMENTARY

In this lecture Emerson began to outline the different "uses" of nature that would make up the chapters of the book, *Nature,* a few years later. Nature provides practical benefits, commodities, recreation, as well as reflection and, finally, spiritual understanding about humanity's "true place in the system of beings." This early lecture reveals Emerson's foundational interest in nature as metaphor or symbol, and in the role of the poet-naturalist in translating that language.

Emerson's visit to the Paris Gardens is a feast of the senses, but in particular of seeing. He presents the image of the eye so oft repeated later, in *Nature,* in "HISTORY," and other essays. The human eye is particularly equipped for "the perception of beauty," and he finds that "the eye is satisfied with seeing" the many specimens gathered together in the museum. On nature's ability to change our perceptions, he gives the example of a children's story titled "Eyes and No Eyes" (the original subtitle being, "or, the Art of Seeing"). Lastly, in comparing the scientist to the "traveller," whereas the latter sees only "a broken mountainside," the former, "his eye is reading as in a book the history of the globe." It is, Emerson notes, the greatest calamity for a scientist, such as Galileo was, to be "bereaved of sight."

Emerson's own perception of the museum experience was markedly different from that of HENRY DAVID THOREAU. Where Emerson finds the Paris nature specimens "a finer picture gallery than the Louvre," Thoreau would later write, "I hate museums. They are catacombs of Nature. They are preserved death." Scholar Laura Dassow Walls notes that "the contrast is revealing. Whereas the unnaturalness of the museum offended Thoreau, to Emerson it was in a sense more natural than even nature itself, more real than reality, since unlike in undisciplined wild nature, here every object was a 'specimen,' a 'proof-type,' purified to the *idea* of itself." In his journal Emerson noted, "How much finer things are in composition than alone. 'Tis wise in man to make Cabinets." For Emerson, the museum so perfectly reduced nature to its most basic forms, revealing a few laws, a system, rather than the chaotic and often unsatisfactory experience of actual nature. Emerson was invigorated by the chance to see specimens from around the globe gathered in one place, where he could observe each in relation to the others. This is quite different from his own perception of his friend, as Emerson noted in his eulogy "THOREAU," for whom there was no need to leave CONCORD, for "the pond was a small ocean; the Atlantic, a large Walden Pond." For Emerson, it is in the museum, not in Walden Woods, that "you are impressed with the inexhaustible gigantic riches of nature."

For Emerson, learning about nature is the very purpose of life. In the final lines of the lecture, Emerson notes "that all this outward universe shall one day disappear, when its whole sense hath been comprehended and engraved forever in the eternal thoughts of the human mind." It is nature that is temporal and temporary, while the human mind exists above and beyond nature. This is the universal mind of "History" that carries knowledge—about nature, about science—from one generation to the next.

FURTHER READING

Brown, Lee Rust. *The Emerson Museum: Practical Romanticism and the Pursuit of the Whole.* Cambridge, Mass.: Harvard University Press, 1997.

Walls, Laura Dassow. *Emerson's Life in Science: The Culture of Truth.* Ithaca, N.Y.: Cornell University Press, 2003.

"Voluntaries" (1863)

"Voluntaries" was one of Emerson's few poems responding to specific current events—in this case, the death in July 1863 of Colonel Robert Gould Shaw, leader of Massachusetts's first all-black regiment, and his volunteers who risked their lives to end slavery and preserve the Union. "Voluntaries" was first published in the *ATLANTIC MONTHLY* in October 1863, was circulated in antislavery papers, and was reprinted the following year in a memorial volume to Shaw. It was one of four poems included in Emerson's 1867 collection, *MAY-DAY AND OTHER PIECES*, which deals with the issues of slavery, ABOLITIONISM, and the Civil War (others are "FREEDOM," "ODE SUNG IN TOWN HALL, CONCORD, JULY 4, 1857," and "BOSTON HYMN," all of which were grouped together in *May-Day*). Some lines were added to the original poem for the *May-Day* collection and then later for its inclusion in *SELECTED POEMS* (1876).

CRITICAL COMMENTARY

The poem is divided into five parts or sections, of one or two stanzas each. The first section addresses the history of slavery, reaching back to Africa, "Where a captive sits in chains." The poem invokes the many sounds of slavery: the "low and mournful . . . strain," the "tones of penitence and pain," the "moanings" and "wailing song" of the slave and of the ocean that carries them from Africa to the Americas. The poem is itself a song of this sorrowful history, connecting slaves back to family and to the land itself; but, rather than the African land as their "sole estate," their only inheritance now is the song of slavery itself, "bequeathed—/ Hapless sire to hapless son." The images here are not just emotional but political as well. While U.S. law and government serve to protect private property, including slave property, the law also dictated that slavery was hereditary; slavery itself is therefore the only inheritance or "estate" that passes from African parents to children. Emerson, however, invokes this inheritance or legacy through the image of the father ("Hapless sire to hapless son") when, in fact, under American law, slave status passed from mother to child. In the poem, the relationship of the slave to the mother (and motherland) is one of physical and emotional separation: "Dragged from his mother's arms and breast," Emerson asks of the enslaved individual, "What his fault, or what his crime?" The African's only fault is a "heart too soft and will too weak," he is a "Dove," snatched by the greed of the European's "vulture's beak."

The remainder of the first section continues this contrast between the African family and American politics, as the "great men in the Senate" have their own legacy and inheritance in the founding of the United States. Unlike the "hapless" slave father, the "sage and hero" of this country successfully built "for their sons the State, / Which they shall rule with pride." Yet, given the opportunity, the founders "forbore to break the chain / Which bound the dusky tribe." Fearing that the southern states would not ratify the Constitution, they chose instead the "false peace" of compromise. "Destiny" warns of this decision, "'pang for pang your seed shall pay.'" Although addressed to the founders, these words invoke the hereditary nature of slavery, as well as bring the poem to the present crisis; the constitutional generation is long gone, but its "seed" being paid as "harvest-day" has come with Civil War, threatening the very "Union" they had tried to preserve. In this stanza, Emerson casts the Constitution in a different light, not as timeless principles, but as a historical decision implicated in the system of slavery, and the current threat of Civil War as atonement.

In the next section of the poem, however, there is hope, as "freedom all winged expands." Destiny "loves a poor and virtuous race" and so, although "long she loved the Northman well," it is Africa's time ("the offspring of the Sun") in history. The North refers not only to European Americans but also to New England in particular, the "colder zone" that is now overshadowed by a "dark sky" in the form of slavery. Emerson uses the image of "the snow-flake" as the North's "banner's star," an image used elsewhere, such as in the poem "Boston Hymn," in reference to the North. All is not politics, however, as there are forces beyond the "men of Northern brain," direct "avenues to God" behind the events now under way. Turning to the issue at hand of the volunteer black regiment, Emerson invokes the "generous chief" (Shaw) who will "lead him willing to be led" (the black soldiers) to fight for themselves, for their own freedom. In the short third section of the poem, Emerson praises the "heroic boys" who "hazard all in Freedom's fight." They stand out from the "fops and toys" of the age, giving up the "jolly games" and "youthful dames" of childhood for "famine, toil, and fray." Their actions are "messages" to America's "sloth and ease." They have responded to history: "When Duty whispers low, *Thou must,* / The youth replies, *I can.*"

Part four mentions twice the "inward sight" and "inward voice" of those who rise to meet this challenge of these "evil times." Surrounded by "the darkness and the dread," the volunteer soldier listens only to his own "rule and choice." "Walled with mortal terror round," he is guided by a higher "aim" and vision of the future, by "the sweet heaven his deed secures." This section of the poem mourns the dead and wounded, but acknowledges that "whoever fights, whoever falls" (including Shaw and his men) did not die in vain: "Justice conquers evermore" and "God . . . Crowns him victor glorified." Emerson is writing in 1863, only midway through the war, when the outcome of the war is still unsure, but he assures that the cause is just regardless of the overwhelming Union losses: "though he were ten times slain," and although the "poor foe" may be "self-assured that he prevails," Emerson assures that "the eternal scales" will ultimately restore the proper balance. "Blind with pride, and fooled by hate," the enemy may be winning battles but shall ultimately have a "speechless fate."

Having acknowledged the losses so far, and the difficulties of the battle still ahead, Emerson ends the poem in a hopeful tone. In the final stanza, victory is assured: "I see the wreath, I hear the songs / Lauding the Eternal Rights." Shaw is "the valiant chief" and the Confederates are "feigning dwarfs" who "crouch and creep." No matter that "the strong they slay," "Fate" assures that the heroes of this war are "gods" and all else "are ghosts besides," or figures of a dead past.

FURTHER READING

Cadava, Eduardo. "The Nature of War in Emerson's 'Boston Hymn.'" *Arizona Quarterly* 49, no. 3 (Autumn 1993): 21–58.

Morris, Saundra. 'Metre-Making' Arguments: Emerson's Poems." In *The Cambridge Companion to Ralph Waldo Emerson,* edited by Joel Porte and Saundra Morris. New York: Cambridge University Press, 1999.

"Waldeinsamkeit" (1857)

The term *waldeinsamkeit* was used by German romantics (a school Emerson knew well) to mean "forest solitude." One has only to think of Emerson's introduction to NATURE (1836) to understand the attraction of this term. The poem's speaker details his observations regarding the significance of solitude. Emerson's view on the divinity of nature—nature as a metaphor for the mind of God—is clearly expressed in this poem. Emerson first drafted "Waldeinsamkeit" in the summer of 1857, and he recorded the poem in the visitor's album at the Naushon Island estate of John Murray Forbes, in September 1858. The poem was first published (without Emerson's knowledge) in the ATLANTIC MONTHLY in October 1858 and later collected in the "Nature and Life" section of MAY-DAY AND OTHER PIECES (1867), in SELECTED POEMS (1876), and in *Poems* (1884).

CRITICAL COMMENTARY

"Waldeinsamkeit" is comprised of 13 stanzas, four lines each, set in alternating iambic tetrameter/trimeter. This form is popularly known as hymn stanza, and Emerson's readers would likely have understood the liturgical reference and implications. A significant aspect of Emerson's writing is his establishment of nature as a kind of Church, in keeping with the quasi-pantheism of the Transcendentalists; consider, for example, in *Nature,* Emerson finds "reason and faith," where "in these plantations of God, a decorum and sanctity reign"; and these lines from his poem, "The Apology" (1847): "Think me not unkind and rude / That I walk alone in grove and glen; / I go to the god of the wood / To fetch his word to men."

"Waldeinsamkeit" follows the poems "TWO RIVERS" and "SONG OF NATURE" in *May-Day,* and its placement is significant in that the poem follows a developing theme: recognizing, and utilizing, the divinity present throughout nature. Emerson's deism is clearly on display in this poem, but the attitude differs somewhat from "Two Rivers." In "Two Rivers," the speaker recognizes the divine force present in all things; in "Waldeinsamkeit" the speaker notes the *purpose* of this force: "Like God, it useth me" (line 4).

A familiar Emerson image appears in stanza 7, particularly in the last two lines of the stanza: "Through times that wear and forms that fade / Immortal youth returns." Emerson writes, in chapter I of *Nature,* "To go into solitude, a man needs to retire as much from his chamber as from society," and later, "In the woods too, a man casts off his years, as the snake his slough, and at what period soever of his life, is always a child. In the woods is perpetual youth." The power of the eternal God, nature, the speaker's "loyal friend," belies time and form. This is apparent in stanza 11: "Leave another's eyes and fetch your own / to brave the landscape's locks." Man's correspondence with nature is felt (intuited), not learned.

Bill Scalia

"Wealth" (1860)

The original date of composition of this poem "Wealth" has not been determined, but Emerson appended it as the motto of his essay of the same name in *The* CONDUCT OF LIFE (1860) and later collected it in SELECTED POEMS (1876). "Wealth" plays out two of Emerson's central philosophical tenets, his sense of mankind's destined arrival in the evolutionary process and the affinity of man's still emerging mind with the laws of the universe. The principal motif of this poem, then, harkens all the way back to the opening motto of his first work, NATURE (1836), in which Emerson wrote: "A subtle chain of countless rings / The next unto the farthest brings; / The eye reads omens where it goes, / And speaks all languages the rose; / And, striving to be man, the worm / Mounts through all the spires of form." *Nature*'s motto provides the clearest evidence that Emerson heartily endorsed the theory of evolution a quarter century before Charles Darwin's *Origin of Species* (1859). Along with "Wealth," these mottoes sound the keynote of terrestrial evolution leading up to man, "the coming king," as Emerson expressed it in "FATE" (also of 1860), another key essay roughly contemporaneous with the appearance of Darwin's work.

CRITICAL COMMENTARY

The poem opens with ruminations on the once "lifeless ball" of the planet over which "hung idle stars and suns." It asks, "What god the element obeyed?" as the primeval winds bore "the puny seeds of power," with the stupendous result that "the primal pioneer" came "to build in matter home for mind." It goes on to detail symbolic stages in this evolutionary spiral, across "creeping centuries." Thus "the leaves of ages" strew matted thickets for "the granite slab to clothe and hide, / Ere wheat can wave its golden pride." "Dizzy eons dim and mute" passed before "copper and iron, lead and gold" could take their places in the rocky faults; and how many uncountable races perished "to pave / The planet with a floor of lime?" Similarly, "Ferns and palms were pressed / Under the tumbling mountain's breast" in order to form "the safe herbal of the coal." And yet, all this quarry still remained "waste and worthless, till / Arrives the wise selecting will, / And, out of slime and chaos, Wit / Draws the threads of fair and fit."

With the advent of human intelligence, there were newer manifestations of life and creativity: "Then temples rose, and towns, and marts, / The shop of toil, and the hall of arts." Next, humans began to explore—"Then flew the sails across the sea"—and harnessed the power of nature—"the rivers," the wind, and "strong-shouldered steam." "Then docks were built, and crops were stored, / And ingots added to the hoard." In effect, the poem encapsulates mankind's history, moving from ages of agriculture to those of exploration and international trade.

In all this cosmogony, "remembering Matter pays her debt." In this metaphor connected to the theme of wealth is Emerson's perspective of mankind's destined arrival in the evolutionary process. Matter fulfills its appointed role, still providing "electric thrills and ties of Law, / Which bind the strength of Nature wild / To the conscience of a child." Here is Emerson's ubiquitous theme of the affinity or correspondences of even small, childlike man's mind with the powerful forces of nature.

As Emerson wrote in the prose version of "Wealth," man's privilege consists in his creative intelligence: "The forces and resistances are Nature's, but the mind acts in bringing things from where they abound to where they are wanted; in wise combining, in directing the practice of the useful arts, and in the creation of finer values, by fine art, by Eloquence, by song, or the reproductions of memory." The real wealth of the planet now consists in man's mental progress that is carrying on the work of natural evolution. Mankind's ability to discover the laws of nature presupposes that nature and man continue to evolve together. The poem "Wealth" is a profound anticipation of the implications of this insight.

David A. Dilworth

"Wealth" (1860)

Emerson delivered a series of lectures "The Conduct of Life" at Pittsburgh, Pennsylvania, in the spring of 1851. The introductory lecture was entitled "Laws of Success," and this was followed by "Wealth," "Economy," "Culture," and "Worship," all of which were reworked into essays for *The* CONDUCT OF *LIFE* (1860). Just as "POWER" was the companion essay to "FATE" in the volume, "Power" and "Wealth" can be read together as forming a new pair devoted to his celebration of human potency and potential in the context of mankind's discovery of his productive affinity with the laws of nature.

Emerson noted in the preceding essay, "Power," that some, but not all, of the essays in *The Conduct of Life* were primarily mundane in focus. Ostensibly "Wealth" and "CULTURE" developed such worldly trajectories, while "WORSHIP," "BEAUTY," and the final sentences of the capping essay "ILLUSIONS" articulated ranges of the higher spiritual consciousness. But these form a continuum, low and high degrees in the soul's discovery of its many-faceted powers. The essay on "Wealth" provides balanced reflections on "how to live," on spiritual wealth, given mankind's quest for and production of material wealth.

SYNOPSIS

Emerson begins by observing that "every man is a consumer, and ought to be a producer." There is a correspondence between thought and all production; because a "better order is equivalent to vast amounts of brute labor. The forces and resistances are Nature's, but the mind acts in bringing things from where they abound to where they are wanted."

"Wealth requires," he continues, "besides the crust of bread and the roof,—the freedom of the city, the freedom of the earth, travelling, machinery, the benefits of science, music, and the fine arts, the best culture, and the best company." In this context, political economy has a moral aspect, "inasmuch as it is a point of virtue that a man's independence be secured" by his own work in the world: "He is no whole man until he knows how to earn a blameless livelihood." The reverse of this coin is that "poverty demoralizes," enslaves a man to his debts, and makes him vulnerable to the cruel immorality of a "barbarous" society.

Accordingly, Emerson writes, "Men of sense esteem wealth to be the assimilation of nature to themselves, the converting of the sap and juices of the planet to the incarnation and nurtriment of their design. Power is what they want,—not candy;—power to execute their design, power to give legs and feet, form an actuality to their thought, which, to a clear-sighted man, appears the end for which the Universe exists." The same transforming power that Emerson had assigned to the regenerative power of poetry he now credits to the strenuous kinds of wealth producing labor required to harness nature for the accumulative enhancement of civilization: "This *speculative* genius is the madness of few for the gain of the world." Not everyone possesses this power, as "commerce is a game of skill, which every man cannot play, which few men can play well." But it is such individualism of those who play the game well that has driven social economic progress: "An infinite number of shrewd men, in infinite years, have arrived at certain best and shortest ways of doing, and this accumulated skill in arts, cultures, harvestings, curings, manufactures, navigations, exchanges, constitutes the worth of our world to-day." Thus the generations derive their "common wealth" from the aspirations and accomplishments of the prosperous individuals who "can animate all their possessions" toward wealth creation.

Emerson goes on to recognize that "the socialism of our day has done good service in setting men on thinking how certain civilizing benefits, now only enjoyed by the opulent, can be enjoyed by all." But while conceding the moral idealism of socialism, Emerson remains firmly within the Lockean (see JOHN LOCKE), and laissez-faire capitalist, camp. As an application of his logic of compensation or balance in nature, he emphasizes that wealth brings with it its own "checks and balances." The law of political economy is "non-interference" in the marketplace: "The only safe rule is found in the self-adjusting meter of demand and supply. Do not legislate. Meddle, and you snap the sinews with your sumptuary laws." This principle, according to Emerson, works "throughout nature," for "the interest of petty economy is this symbolization of the great economy; the way in which a house, and a private man's methods, tally with the solar system."

Drawing these various threads together, Emerson now lays down certain axioms relevant to wealth getting: "The first of these measures is that each man's expense of labor must proceed from his character." It is all a matter of a man finding his vocation, and of doing his unique work: "The crime which bankrupts men and states, is, job-work;—declining from your main design, to serve a turn here or there." It follows that "society can never prosper, but must always be bankrupt, until every man does that which he was created to do."

"The second rule of wealth is to spend after your genius, *and by system*." In this context Emerson praises the New England farms of his day, which were largely self-subsistent: "A farm is a good thing, when it begins and ends with itself, and does not need a salary, or a shop, to eke it out." But this principle of self-reliance has to be squared with man's desire to be rich and to participate in the resources and rewards of higher civilization.

The third rule of economic health and the wisdom of living, he continues, is found "in the custom of the country," which often reveals the most efficient and practical methods for doing things: "Nature has her own best mode of doing each thing, and she has somewhere told it plainly, if we will keep our eyes and ears open." A fourth axiom is that of consistency of application: "Look for seed of the same kind as you sow: and not to hope to buy one kind with another kind." So it is that "friendship buys friendship; justice, justice; military merit, military success. Good husbandry finds wife, children, and household. The good merchant large gains, ships, stocks, and money. The good poet fame, and literary credit; but not either, the other."

At the conclusion of this essay Emerson declares, "I have not at all completed my design." Having discussed practical methods and nature's laws for producing wealth, it is now time to look "into the interior recesses." As it is in the world of business, so it is in "philosophy," so that "there is nothing in the world, which is not repeated in [the human] body," and "there is nothing in his body, which is not repeated as in a celestial sphere in his mind." All things are interrelated and the "body is a sort of miniature or summary of the world." Man, then, is not only a capitalist in an economic sense, but he is always so in a much more significant moral sense. His real capital is mental, and "the bread he eats is first strength and animal spirits: it becomes, in higher laboratories, imagery and thought; and in still higher results, courage and endurance. This is the right compound interest; this is capital doubled, quadrupled, centupled; man raised to his highest power."

CRITICAL COMMENTARY

The essay ends on this note of ascent and charge of evolution, the higher striving of the human soul toward a more prosperous life: "The true thrift is always to spend on the higher plane; to invest and invest, with keener avarice, that he may spend in spiritual creation, and not in augmenting animal existence." Mankind is not enriched through material or animal pursuits. It is a matter of going forward, striving for the highest life, the fulfillment of our evolutionary destiny in the growth of the spiritual life. Here Emerson does not entirely depart from his earlier romanticism of the Transcendentalist individual who participates in ever-expanding circles of the moral universe; but, at the same time, he now incorporates productive labor as one of nature's laws, which also lead to the progress of civilization.

In contrast to HENRY DAVID THOREAU, who was revising *Walden; or, Life in the Woods* in 1854 in the time frame between the first appearance of "Wealth" as a lecture in 1851 and its release for publication in *The Conduct of Life* in 1860, Emerson represented and celebrated the bourgeoning civilization of mid-19th-century America. His thesis turned Thoreau's monkish philosophy of thrift on its head, maintaining that man "is born to be rich." He questions whether any man will truly "content himself with a hut and a handful of dried pease?" concluding that man is happiest when he expands his possibilities, rather than limiting them, and "finds his well-being in the use of his planet, and of more planets than his own."

As in his later essay "FARMING" in *SOCIETY AND SOLITUDE* (1870), the self-reliant individuals who harness the forces of nature remain Emerson's emblems of the production of human wealth. "Wealth" brilliantly articulates one concrete application of *The Conduct of Life*'s opening essays on "Fate" and "Power." Reminiscent of Aristotle and Locke, it conceives of the production of wealth as a function of mankind's natural and moral natures—as a necessary component in the full "pursuit of happiness" of the citizen and the state. It is also one of many great essays in which Emerson broke with his Puritan past. The trajectory of wealth concretizes man's destiny to embody natural power on a plentiful but precarious planet.

David A. Dilworth

"Woman" (1855)

On September 20, 1855, Emerson spoke at the New England Women's Rights Convention held in BOSTON. At least part of the address was first published many years later under the title "Woman" in the *Woman's Journal* in 1881. "Woman" was included in its entirety in the posthumous *Miscellanies* (1884) and as part of the *Complete Works* (1903–04) compiled and edited by his son EDWARD WALDO EMERSON.

Ralph Waldo Emerson had been invited to speak at women's rights conventions in both 1850 and 1851, but he declined, finally agreeing to the request by Paulina Wright Davis to appear at the 1855 meeting. Other speakers at the event included representatives of ABOLITIONISM, such as Wendell Phillips and THOMAS WENTWORTH HIGGINSON, and the prominent women's rights activists Lucy Stone, Susan B. Anthony, and Transcendentalist feminist CAROLINE DALL. Emerson's speech was filled with qualifications and limits on full support for the women's cause, prompting Dall to write to him after the convention that, based on the newspaper reports of the address, it was not clear "whether you were for us or against us." Regardless of this critique, after 1855 women's rights leaders claimed Emerson as a friend of the cause.

SYNOPSIS

Emerson's address opens with the reflection that "woman is the power of civilization," and that if women are given the vote, they will "civilize" the political process, just as their presence civilizes in other arenas. Emerson trusts in women's superior instincts, conceding, "any remarkable opinion or movement shared by women will be the first sign of revolution." In terms of their roles in society, "Man is the will, and woman the sentiment"; "in this ship of humanity," man is "the rudder" and woman "the sail." If women move away from their natural sphere, participating in an "art or trade," it is only ever as a matter of necessity, never "a primary object." Emerson declares "there is usually no employment or career which they will not . . . quit for a suitable marriage." He twice quotes Plato's view that women "are the same as men in faculty, only in less degree."

He then focuses on women's professions, pointing out that "in no art or science, not in painting, poetry, or music, have women produced a masterpiece." Women do, however, excel in "conversation," which, according to Emerson, is "better" than any of these other areas or pursuits, as conversation "is our account of ourselves." He cites SAMUEL TAYLOR COLERIDGE and others on women as civilizers, saying women are only truly "disfranchised" when they are "out of place." He goes so far as to say that the women's "convention should be holden in the sculpture gallery," an environment more fitting for women than the lecture hall. After praising woman's superior nature, he concedes that the law of "nature" demands that every "gift" has a "drawback"—for all of woman's strengths and influence, the drawback or "penalty" is that she is "more vulnerable, more infirm, more mortal than men."

In the next section Emerson uses religious imagery to compare women to Eve, who was the model for "humility." In love, women see "nobleness," whereas men ask of love only "usefulness and advantages." Women have "a divining power," and they understand "at first sight the characters of those with whom they converse." This power comes, in part, from "their sequestration from affairs." He gives an example of a woman he knows (identified by some scholars as an allusion to his aunt MARY MOODY EMERSON) who was not just religious but was herself "a Bible, miscellaneous in parts, but one in Spirit . . . chapters of prophecy, promises, and covenants of love, that make foolish the wisdom of the world." To Emerson, these parts make the ideal woman.

Emerson identifies "three or four instrumentalities" that illuminate woman's "strength" as well as her "faults." Religion reveals woman's "importance" through examples such as "the deification of woman in the Catholic Church," but also the "equality in the sexes" in sects such as the Quakers and Shakers. A second model for understanding women's roles is seen in the French salons and a third, grounded in the metaphysical, comes from "the doctrine of Swedenborg," which showed the "difference of sex to run through nature and through thought." Lastly, he acknowledges that the antislavery movement was responsible for a radical change in women's roles. The movement has "given woman a feeling a public duty, and an added self-respect," so that she is now "urging . . . her rights of all kinds." Emerson acknowledges that women are now demanding the right "to one half of the world," and he lists the demands of the new women's movement, such as education, employment, property, equality in marriage, access to professions, and, finally, the vote.

In the next section Emerson differentiates his arguments against an organized reform movement from those who oppose women's rights in principle. He argues that it is a "cheap wit" who believes that women "have not a sufficient moral or intellectual force" or "who believe women to be incapable of anything but to cook; incapable of interest in affairs." This is not Emerson's belief, although he still maintains that women "are victims of their finer temperament" and, in particular, that they must devote at least "twenty years" to "maternity," a fact that makes them less capable of participating in public affairs.

Emerson admits that arguments for specific rights cannot be denied, but he comes to his own conclusion that "the best women do not wish these things." He believes the movement is propelled by a few "people who intellectually seek" these rights, but without "the support or sympathy of the truest women." For example, he is concerned about those who would reform or change marriage laws, believing instead that marriage "as it exists in America, England, and Germany" is still "the best solution" to "woman's problem." Likewise, he agrees that the question of the vote is not a matter of women's competency, and it would be "absurdity" to deny the principle of woman suffrage; he concedes, "certainly all my points would be sooner carried in the state, if women voted." The question, for Emerson, is "why need you vote?" He feels it makes more sense to focus on questions of "religion, customs, laws," and "new career" options for women and that, if these avenues are opened to women, "votes will follow."

Yet Emerson returns to his main objection to the women's movement: "I do not think it yet appears that women wish this equal share in public affairs." Emerson advocates access to education and property rights before women can determine for themselves "whether they wish a voice in making the laws that are to govern them." He cautions against "expediency" on this issue and reiterates the belief that a "true woman" influences "the lawgiver," rather than seeking to be the lawgiver herself. "Woman should find in man her guardian," who will be "prompted to accomplish" that which her "heart is prompted to desire."

CRITICAL COMMENTARY

In "Woman," Emerson argues that women exert a positive influence over men, society, and politics through their superior moral sensibility and intuition. This influence was more important than direct participation in politics or business, and he believes that "the best women" did not desire the vote. Throughout the speech, he reiterated the feeling that the women's rights movement was propelled by only a few women acting on principle (and with the general principle of women's equality he did not disagree), but that the majority of American women did not join this call, and therefore the movement was not truly representative of women's desires.

Between the 1830s and 1850s other Transcendentalists were increasingly connected with the cause of women's rights. In 1839 MARGARET FULLER began her series of Conversations for women, promoting women's education and self-development, and in 1843, Fuller published an article in the *DIAL* magazine titled "The Great Lawsuit. Man versus Men. Woman versus Women." The main argument of "The Great Lawsuit" (as indicated by the subtitle) was that limited social roles for both men and women prevented the full development of individuals, both male and female. Fuller expanded the article and the idea into the 1845 book *Woman in the Nineteenth Century,* the first full-length feminist text published in the United States. The male Transcendentalists such as AMOS BRONSON ALCOTT, Thomas Wentworth Higginson, and THEODORE PARKER also publicly supported both the abolitionist and the women's movement by the 1850s. These activities by his colleagues, his close friendship with Fuller, and his role in publishing her memoirs after her death in 1850 probably explain the assumption by women's rights activists that Emerson could speak on their behalf.

Emerson, however, was always reluctant to identify with any one group or cause, maintaining, as he did throughout his writings, that reform must come from within, as a matter of individual conscience and development. While he was increasingly drawn out to speak on the issue of slavery, "Woman" was his only public address (and only published essay) on the topic of women's rights. He did reflect privately in his journals, letters, and conversations on woman's position with individuals such as Fuller, his aunt Mary Moody Emerson, and his wife LIDIAN JACKSON EMERSON. Even when confronted with examples of female genius, Emerson still saw woman's primary role not as personal or intellectual but as social, as wives, mothers or "muses." Despite his conservative view of women's natural sphere of influence centered in the home and family, in his journal in 1843 he had also conceded that "man can never tell woman what her duties are."

Emerson's main critique throughout the address was not with the principle of women's equality but with participation in an organized reform movement. He believed, throughout his writings on reform (such as in "MAN THE REFORMER" [1841] and "NEW ENGLAND REFORMERS" [1844]), in the natural progression of society and in the "levelling circumstance" of nature. In "COMPENSATION" (1841) he explained that nature eventually balances out any inequalities: "Every crime is punished, every virtue rewarded, every wrong redressed." Likewise, in his essay on "HEROISM" (1841), he called upon women who are faced with "a new and unattempted problem to solve" to rely upon their own inner resources, to "accept the hint of each new experience, search in turn all the objects that solicit her eye," and make her own path. Despite his qualified views on all questions of reform, in 1869 Emerson was elected a vice president of the New England Woman Suffrage Association. His was not necessarily an active role but rather a position biographer Robert Richardson explains as "ceremonial or conferred with an eye to publicity."

FURTHER READING

Cole, Phyllis. "The New Movement's Tide: Emerson and Women's Rights." In *Emerson Bicentennial Essays,* edited by Ronald A. Bosco and Joel Myerson. Boston: Massachusetts Historical Society, 2006.

Garvey, T. Gregory, ed. *The Emerson Dilemma: Essays on Emerson and Social Reform.* Athens: University of Georgia Press, 2001.

Gougeon, Len. "Emerson and the Woman Question: The Evolution of His Thought." *NEQ* 71 (1998): 570–592.

"Woodnotes" I and II (1840–41)

Four hundred lines in length, Emerson's "Woodnotes" spanned two of the early issues of the Transcendentalist literary journal the *DIAL*, of October 1840 and October 1841. Emerson included it in *POEMS* (1847) and in abridged form in *SELECTED POEMS* (1876); it was restored to its original length for the posthumously published *Poems* (1884). "Woodnotes" was the poetic Magna Carta of Transcendentalism. It poeticized the theme of his inaugural work *NATURE* (1836) and such ensuing essays of spiritual naturalism as "The METHOD OF NATURE" (1841) and the later essay "NATURE" of *ESSAYS: SECOND SERIES* (1844). The poem also reinforced the affirmations of many of his other nature poems such as "The WORLD-SOUL," "The HUMBLE-BEE," "The SNOW-STORM," "The RHODORA," "MONADNOC," and "TWO RIVERS," all of which extolled the inspirations of nature in the human soul.

CRITICAL COMMENTARY

"Woodnotes I" captures countless layers of remembrance of Emerson listening to the soothing music of the wind in the stately white pine—Emerson's favorite tree with which he often communed in his own pine grove by Walden Pond. He bequeathed this central trope of the "forest seer, / Minstrel of the natural year" to the Transcendentalist movement, which explored new paths of individual spirituality apart from the orthodox religious establishments of the day.

The poem begins with Emerson's description of the poet who is out of sorts with the "money-loving herd" of commercial times but thoroughly at home in nature where "the pine tree tosses its cones / To the song of its waterfall tones." The knowledge he gains in his conversations with the pine tree seems fantastic to the rest of men, as does his "pondering shadows, colours, clouds, / Grass-buds, and caterpillar-shrouds. / Boughs on which the wild bees settle, / Tints that spot the violet's petal, / Why Nature loves the number five." His pine tree teaches him to contemplate such refreshing revelations, indeed to be "lover of all things alive," "wonderer at all he meets," and indeed "wonderer chiefly at himself."

On "one of the charmed days, / When the genius of God doth flow," the musing poet realizes that "he was the heart of all the scene." His face is known to hill and cloud, as "the likeness of their own; / They knew by secret sympathy / The public child of earth and sky." In such lines Emerson reinforces his conception of the correspondences of man and nature that make the poet's life in metaphor possible: "For Nature ever faithful is / To such as trust her faithfulness." The forest, he intuits, shall never betray her poet-lover.

In "Woodnotes II," the pine tree repeatedly identifies itself as "the giver of honour." It is "old as Jove, / Old as Love," coeval with the mountains old, the waters cold, the moon and the stars. With this pedigree it delivers a moral lesson in rejection of material consumption. It says that "the rough and bearded forester / Is better than the lord . . . The lord is the peasant that was, / The peasant the lord that shall be; / The lord is hay, the peasant grass, / One dry, and one the living tree."

As a "prophetic wind" shakes its lithesome boughs, the pine tree goes on further to describe the message of its musical sounds. Its mystic song is "the chronicle of art," telling "the sweet genesis of things, / Of tendency through endless ages." "The rushing metamorphosis, / Dissolving all that fixture is, / Melts things that seem to be to things that seem, / And solid nature to a dream." But this "chorus of ancient Causes" only the pure ear can hear. "The rune that it rehearses / Understands the universe," so that the slightest breeze in its boughs "brings again the Pentecost." It invites the poet to learn its fatal song, its lofty rhymes, "of things with things, of times with times, / Primal chimes of sun and shade, / Of sound and echo, Man and maid."

The very antidote to all "bankruptcy" and vice, the pine tree promises to the solitary forest-loving poet with "visions sublime." Once he turns his back on all the mundane world's merchandise, its "churches" and "charities," and abstains from "peacock wit," "pedant lore," and "wormy pages," he will enjoy "the primal mind / That flows in streams, that breathes in wind." He will "outsee seers, and outwit sages." He will learn what the bird sings when it flies gaily forth.

The pine tree concludes with another metaphysical lesson, saying that "all the forms are fugitive, / But the substances survive. Ever fresh the broad creation, / A divine improvisation, / From the heart of God proceeds, / A single will, a million deeds." "Once slept the world an egg of stone," until God commanded motion, "and the vast mass became vast ocean." This God is the "eternal Pan" of nature. "Like wave or flame," it forever escapes "into new forms, / Of gem, and air, of plants, and worms." Pan, this great god of metamorphosisis, the "Maker and original," pours out his " . . . wine unto every race and age." "The world is the ring of his spells, / And the play of his miracles." "Pleaseth him, the Eternal Child, / To play his sweet will, glad and wild." Thus, "as the bee through the garden ranges, / From world to world the godhead changes."

Emerson ends the pine tree's paeon to Pan in tones that precede his later Hindu- and Sufi-inspired poem "BRAHMA" (published in 1857). His pine tree declares that "if you seek him in globe and galaxy, / He hides in pure transparency"; and "if you ask for him in fountains and in fires, / He is the essence that inquires." Pan is "the axis of the star," "the sparkle of the spar," "the heart of every creature," "the meaning of every feature," and "his mind is the sky, / Than all it holds more deep, more high."

"Woodnotes" I and II together reinforce Emerson's mystical religiosity of nature articulated in his early prose works of the same period. It struck against the commercialized masses and the exhausted dogmas of the establishment churches, while suggesting another access to the spiritual life through the refreshing vigor of the forest. As well as any of his writings, it emphasizes the Transcendentalist belief in man's affinity with nature and the pursuit of truth through the process of growth and change.

FURTHER READING

Tuerk, Richard. "Emerson's 'Woodnotes' poems." *ATQ* 6, no. 4 (December 1992): 295.

David A. Dilworth

"Works and Days" (1870)

Emerson borrowed the title of this essay appearing in SOCIETY AND SOLITUDE of 1870 from Hesiod's poem "Works and Days," while otherwise developing "a lesson to this day and hour." He first read it in 1857 and then included it as the second lecture in the course "Natural Method of Mental Philosophy" in the spring of 1858. Just before this, in November of 1857, Emerson published a companion poem, "DAYS," together with "BRAHMA," both of which express Oriental overtones concerning the illusions of objective time that pervade the essay. The structural movement of this essay is from *works* to *days*. Emerson first takes up *works*, here referring to the external works of the burgeoning 19th-century products of material science and industry, that he will later contrast with the inner, qualitative *days* of the person of enlightened character.

SYNOPSIS

He begins the essay by waxing eloquent on the mechanical and technological miracles of his 19th century. It is, he says, "the age of tools," and tools are an extension of man: "The human body is the magazine of inventions, the patent office, where are the models from which every hint was taken. All the tools and engines on earth are only extensions of its limbs and senses." He extends this consideration with a theme of human progress, such that the new age of "steam and galvanism, sulphuric ether and ocean telegraphs, photograph and spectroscope" both elicits our pity for our less tool-advanced forefathers and "opens great gates for a future, promising to make the world plastic and to lift human life out its beggary to a godlike ease and power."

But with this consideration Emerson also details the questionable properties of technological modernization. "Machinery is aggressive"—it mechanizes its users, ties them to habits of repetition—and it is "doubtful" if all this technological innovation has "lightened the day's toil of one human being." Rather, "the machine unmakes the man. Now that the machine is so perfect, the engineer is nobody." And this is true across the board of human activities, as modern newspapers dumb the reader down, "politics were never more corrupt and brutal," and trade, viewed as the crowning achievement of modernization, "ends in shameful defaulting, bubble and bankruptcy, all over the world." As for the worth of man, "we cannot assume the mechanical skill and chemical resources as the measure of worth." Emerson argues that "'tis too plain that with the material power the moral progress has not kept pace. . . . Works and days were offered us, and we took works."

Emerson therefore concludes, "let us try another gauge." As already celebrated in the old mythologies, it is the *day* that holds divine power. Emerson touches upon Hesiod's "Works and Days" in this context as suggesting the title of his own essay. It is a poem, he says, "full of economies for Grecian life" but may be "adapted to all meridians by adding the ethics of works and of days." He returns to his own agenda in further remarking that Hesiod "has not pushed his study of days into such inquiry and analysis as they invite."

Emerson celebrates the spiritual potentials of the day—"how the day fits itself to the mind, winds itself round it like a fine drapery, clothing all its fancies!" He gives the example of the "dignity" we give to holidays or days of special memories—Election Day, the Fourth of July, Thanksgiving, and Christmas as well as important school days, graduation, and even the Sabbath. These days "are the carnival of the year," "days when the great are near us." But every day, every "blue sky," reveals nature's glory: "The miracle is hurled into every beggar's hands . . . Nature could no further go." Every day's blue sky signifies "the face of the world," captured in part by the "Latin word, with its delicate future tense,—*natura, about to be born,* or what German philosophy denotes as a *becoming.*" Only "the Greek *Kosmos*" fully "expresses that power" in nature "which seems to work for beauty alone."

Metaphysically considered, modern man is merely repeating the experiences of people in ancient times: "An everlasting Now reigns in Nature, which hangs the same roses on our bushes which charmed the Roman and the Chaldean in their hanging-gardens." But caught up in the day-to-day, it is "the deep to-day which all men scorn; the rich poverty which men hate; the populous, all-loving solitude which men quit for the tattle of towns." The reverse of this coin is that idolizing the past is an "illusion" given that "the deeds of our ancestors" were accomplished in the creative strength of *their* days, while we feel "there is not enough time for our work." Another "illusion," therefore, is the sense that a longer period of time—"a year, a decade, a century"—is more "valuable" than today. But "God works in moments," as in the French proverb "*En peu d'heure Dieu labeure.*" The "measure of a man," then, is this "apprehension of a day," this ability to value, utilize, and "recommend to me the space between sun and sun."

In the end, it is the self-reliant individual who appreciates the gifts of days, fusing "the moment and character." This is the real "progress of every earnest mind; from the works of man and the activity of the hands to a delight in the faculties which rule them . . . to a wise wonder at this mystic element of time in which he is conditioned." We must reconcile "the amount of production *per* hour to the finer economy which respects the quality of what is done." The "roots" of our work and ourselves "are in eternity, not in time." This realization "is the only definition we have of freedom and power."

CRITICAL COMMENTARY

"Works and Days" reaffirms the romantic prioritization of humanity's spiritual destiny over its material accomplishments. In the context of Emerson's own burgeoning 19th-century technological culture, it is a call for the application of human power to moral ends. It contrasts the illusions of pride of accomplishment in external works with the qualitative inner life of the soul. To underline the metaphysics of the "deep to-day" to which most men are oblivious, Emerson writes, "He lurks, he hides,—he who is success, reality, joy, and power." As EDWARD WALDO EMERSON comments in his notes to this sentence in the Centenary Edition, the *he* here resonates with a parallel usage in the closing lines of "WOODNOTES II." *He* is the pantheistic thread lacing through all of his poetry. "Works and Days" expresses the net effect of all of these poems in drawing the conclusion that one of the root illusions of our lives is that "the present hour is not the critical, decisive hour."

In thus reprising the concluding sentiment of "ILLUSIONS" (1860), "Works and Days" repeats his central metaphysical binary of identity and metamorphosis or change. The latter functions as "Maia, the illusory energy" of life that "lends all its force to hide the values of present time." Emerson's insistence on the creative potential of the day also traces back to his poem "Days," and in the ensuing essay "Works and Days" he combines this focus on the eternal present with his increasingly Eastern-inspired sense of the illusions of time. But he also blends this Oriental influence in a wider generalization, recollecting that variations on "the masquerading Days" occur in Norse as well as Hindu legends, in Greek and Christian symbolisms, "in the maxim of Aristotle and Lucretius," and in the writings of EMANUEL SWEDENBORG.

In addition to the lines of his poem "Days," the Riverside edition of "Works and Days" is prefaced with the lines: "This passing moment is an edifice / Which the Omnipotent cannot rebuild." In the essay Emerson speaks of "the irrecoverable years," which weave "their blue glory between to-day and us." These passing hours have the capacity to "glitter and draw us as the wildest romance and the homes of beauty and poetry." One can think here of WALLACE STEVENS's poems, "Of Bright & Blue Birds & The Gala Sun," "Woman in Sunshine," "Bouquet of Roses in Sunlight," "Credences of Summer," and "Things of August," among many other Stevens's poems of Emersonian inspiration that feature the luminous day-life of the soul.

David A. Dilworth

"The World-Soul" (1847)

Emerson wrote the poem "The World-Soul" sometime between 1843 and 1845. MARGARET FULLER published some of its lines in the *New York Daily Tribune* in 1845, and the entire poem first appeared in the *Diadem*, a Philadelphia publication, in 1847 and then in Emerson's first poetry collection, *POEMS* (1847); it was reprinted in *POETRY COLLECTION* (1876). The title of the poem reflects the influence of WILLIAM WORDSWORTH, but it derives ultimately from Emerson's keen interest in NEOPLATONISM as expressed in many of his prose and poetic writings. The primary themes concern the cycles of the seasons, youth and old age, the indestructibility of our essential nature, and the oneness of our spiritual identity in the world-soul. The poem has a particular poignancy in having been written soon after the death of his son Waldo in 1842.

Neoplatonic philosopher Plotinus conceived the world-soul as the third aspect of the divine nature, namely, as an "emanation" from the One or Good to the Divine Intellect and thence to the world-soul. Emerson here expands on this mystical framework for understanding degrees or levels of spiritual consciousness. The poem first describes the soul's downward *plunge* into vice and folly and then its possibilities of upward *ascent* toward an *identification* with the world-soul. The world-soul thus stands in for "The OVER-SOUL" of the earlier essay of that name, while also speaking to the idea of polarities or balance articulated in the essay "COMPENSATION" (both of *ESSAYS: FIRST SERIES* [1841]).

CRITICAL COMMENTARY

The poem begins by giving "thanks to the morning light, / Thanks to the foaming sea, / To the uplands of New-Hampshire, / To the green-haired forest free," associating these manifestations of pristine nature with "each man of courage," with "maids of holy mind," and with "the boy with his games undaunted" (obliquely referring to his son Waldo). Swinging then to the negative pole of human activity, Emerson catalogs the "cities of proud hotels," the baseness of their politics and letters, the ensnarements of their "trade and the streets."

But characteristically, against this litany of human plots and failures, Emerson returns to a positive formulation in his "evil is good in the making" (as he later articulated it in "Considerations by the Way" of 1860). Ever the Transcendental optimist, he affirms that our saving "angel" always sits among us in some disguise, "in a stranger's form, / Or woman's pleading eyes; / Or only a flashing sunbeam / In at the window-pane," or in some piece of music with "its beautiful disdain."

This saving grace is the world-soul's own ubiquitous presence. It penetrates into "cellars" and the "factory"; it signals us by "yon ridge of the purple landscape," and "yon sky between the walls." It is only that its haunting presences are lost on egocentric men, who "cannot learn the cipher / That's writ upon our cell." As in the poem "The SPHINX" (1847), humans are locked within their self-made chaos and "no one has found the key" to the "mystery" of life. Almighty "trade" continues to "sow cities / Like shells along the shore," and to spawn "towns the prairie broad" with their connecting "railways ironed o'er." But again, despite these mundane endeavors, "still, still the secret presses." The world-soul ever lures our higher consciousness with "the crimson morning" that "flames into / The fopperies of the town," and by the noon sun that "shines heartily" overhead, and by the night stars that "weave eternal rings." These lines echoed those of *NATURE* (1836), in which "these delicately emerging stars, with their private and ineffable glances, . . . eloquent of secret promises."

These intuitions of our higher consciousness let us understand our condition as they, too, "take their shape and sun-colour / From him that sends the dream." The world-soul is such a spiritual force and destiny, which "shoots his thought, by hidden nerves, / Through the solid realm." And this energetic genius of nature is never thwarted: "The seeds of land and sea / Are the atoms of his body bright, / And his behest obey." It "serveth the servant," and loves the brave; it "kills the cripple and the sick, / And straight begins again." Ever changing, it overrides the "old world," fashioning a fairer world complete. It is the "unimagined good of men," which "forbids to despair"—lines embodying Emerson's principal life-affirming theme that threads through all of his writings.

The final stanza of "The World-Soul" refers to his own aging and mortality and reads in its entirety:

> Spring still makes spring in the mind,
> When sixty years are told;
> Love wakes anew this throbbing heart,
> And we are never old.
> Over the winter glaciers,
> I see the summer glow,
> And, through the wild-piled snowdrift,
> The warm rosebuds below.

This poem of mystical contemplation on human identity has an added significance in having been written soon after the death of his beloved five-year-old son, Waldo, and is thus a powerful precedent to his lament for Waldo in "THRENODY" (1847). It also reverberates with two key Transcendentalist essays, "The METHOD OF NATURE" (first delivered as a lecture in 1841) and "NATURE" (1844), which theorized the inner nature of the world, and with many of his poems, notably the near contemporary "WOODNOTES" (1847). Emerson gradually expanded this concept of the world-soul, blending in Hindu and Sufi connotations with the Neoplatonic influences, yet making it his own unique Transcendentalist formulation on the spiritual and moral realization of the individual.

David A. Dilworth

"Worship" (1860)

Emerson's poem "Worship" warns against mistaking the objects of worship for the truth they represent. In keeping with this ongoing Emersonian theme, the poem advises us to see the truth behind the facts; that is, to read images, icons, ideas (the "facts" of nature) as externalizations of the *truth* of nature.

A principal source for the poem is the *Vishnu Purana,* the primary sacred text of the Vaishnava branch of Hinduism, which Emerson read in 1845.

The date indicates that the poem may have been drafted as early as 1845, though Emerson's usual practice was to draft mottoes close to the time of the accompanying essay's publication. The poem was therefore first published as the motto for the essay "WORSHIP" in *The* CONDUCT OF LIFE (1860). A fair copy of the poem was published, in facsimile form, in the book *Autograph Leaves of Our Country's Authors* (published in Baltimore, 1864). It was collected in MAY-DAY AND OTHER PIECES (1867), SELECTED POEMS (1876), and *Poems* (1884).

CRITICAL COMMENTARY

The *Vishnu Purana* is part of a chronology of Hindu narratives describing the creation of the current universe to its destruction; the chronology covers time periods as long as 100 trillion years. The poem "Worship" deals with the idea of fate, especially in this context. The poem consists of 23 lines (10 rhymed couplets and a tercet). The first half of the poem consists of a compact chronology in the manner of the *Purana,* but also resembling classical theogony. The second half of the poem concerns the significance of these events, or the truth *behind* the myths.

If "fate" is a determinable pattern in time (always in retrospect), then Emerson represents, through his example of Jove, one example of what we might think of as fate. However, Emerson warns us against mistaking the pattern (fate) for actual worship. Thus line 11, "This is he men miscall Fate / Threading dark ways, arriving late." Jove is an expression, or metaphor, for human qualities; when we see Jove, we see, in a figurative way, ourselves:

He is the oldest, and best known,
More near than aught thou call'st thy own,
Yet, greeted in another's eyes,
Disconcerts with glad surprise.

Emerson's concern in the poem is in keeping with his attitude toward orthodoxy (see, for example, the "DIVINITY SCHOOL ADDRESS," "The AMERICAN SCHOLAR," and the letters to his Second Church congregation regarding "The LORD'S SUPPER"). The tercet that ends the poem summarizes this thinking:

Draw, if thou canst, the mystic line
Severing rightly his from thine,
Which is human, which divine.

The danger is twofold: If we mistake the object for the truth, we "miscall" our worship; also, perhaps more significantly, we fail to see the divine in ourselves.

Bill Scalia

"Worship" (1860)

Emerson's essay "Worship" was written in the 1850s and first published in *The* CONDUCT OF LIFE in 1860. "Worship," even more than "POWER," follows up on the mature religiosity of his essay "FATE." It affirms the human potential for achieving one's own "original relation to the universe"—a central theme of his writing going back to NATURE (1836) and the "DIVINITY SCHOOL ADDRESS" (1838). Here he boldly claims, "The decline of the influence of Calvin, or Fenelon, or Wesley, or Channing, need give us no uneasiness." "God," he says, "builds his sanctuary in the private heart on the ruins of churches and religions." Such antinomian pronouncements continued to provoke a backlash of criticism from the prominent preachers of his time.

Emerson acknowledges that such previous essays in *The Conduct of Life* as "Fate," "Power," "WEALTH," "CULTURE," and "BEHAVIOR" have been "on too low a platform." The present subject of "Worship" is meant to set these essays within the higher registers of his mature thought.

SYNOPSIS

The essay takes as its point of departure a rejection of religious skepticism. Emerson affirms that he has "no infirmity of faith" and is "sure that a certain truth will be said" through him. His words should therefore not threaten, for "a just thinker will allow a full swing to his skepticism. I dip my pen at the blackest ink, because I am not afraid of falling into the inkpot." He therefore insists on balancing the roughest and ugliest facts of life—the "corrupt society [that] stated itself out in passions, in war, in trade, in the love of power and pleasure, in hunger and need, in tyrannies, literatures, and arts"—with the counterstatement of his own deep-seated conviction about the possibility of an authentic personal religious life.

Emerson's faith is comprehensive. He writes that "we are born loyal," that is, loyal to the universe. The whole creation, he says, "coheres in a perfect ball" and "a man bears beliefs, as a tree bears apples." In this context Emerson goes on to state that, while the previous chapters of *The Conduct of Life* have dealt with "some particulars of the question of culture," the "flowering and completion" of culture is seen in "Religion, or Worship." With regard to the degree of genuine worship in his own day, he observes, there is and will always be some religion and worship, "though they cannot arise above the historical state of the votary." His own generation now lives in a transition period in which sincere persons are justified in loosening their ties from the religions of the past: "The stern old faiths have all pulverized."

For one thing, he notes, the "fatal . . . divorce between religion and morality" in the churches is contemporary proof that "the old faiths which comforted nations have spent their force." Emerson here critiques the current crop of "know-nothing religions, or churches that proscribe intellect; scortatory religions; slave-holding and slave-trading religions," as evidence that the established churches have lost their souls. Religion has been replaced by "faith" in science, "machinery," and materialism. (His European admirer FRIEDRICH NIETZSCHE was to pick up on just these Emersonian reflections in his proclamation of the "death of God.")

"Worship" goes on to reprise Emerson's doctrine of the over-soul and ethics of self-reliance by emphasizing a person's intimate but at the same time public relation to the universe: "We believe that holiness confers a certain insight, because not by our private, but by our public force, can we share and know the nature of things." Religion and morality are indivisible, and there is also "an intimate interdependence of intellect and morals . . . [an] alliance of mind and heart." The physical laws are themselves tropes of the spirit; they are so many "declarations of the soul." Even "the primordial atoms are prefigured and predetermined to moral issues, are in search of justice, and ultimate right is done."

Here Emerson goes on to blend this sense of worship with the historic antecedents of Heraclitean, Hindu, and Buddhist ideas. It is through such a perennial metaphysical framework that Emerson expands his theme of loyalty to the moral universe grounded in the bedrock of self-reliance. Moral "remuneration," he says, is not the wages of "money, or office, or fame." The "happy" and successful man looks "not into the market, nor into opinion, nor into patronage" for validation. Rather, his own "work is victory," and he need only satisfy his own self: "You want but one verdict: if you have your own, you are secure of the rest." It is the same deeply grounded religious and moral instinct that guides us through "misfortunes" and indeed teaches us "that adversity is the prosperity of the great."

At the end of this essay Emerson takes up the theme of the immortality of the soul, concluding that the "well employed" soul "is incurious" about life beyond this world: "'Tis a higher thing to confide, that, if it is best we should live, we shall live,—'tis higher to have this conviction." Once again, Emerson's religiosity, his faith in the moral universe, coincides with his principle of uniquely personal performance: "You must do your work, before you shall be released." As far as the questions of the spiritual "government of the Universe" and of immortality, he quotes Roman emperor Marcus Aurelius: "'It is pleasant to die if there be gods; and sad to live, if there be none.'"

"The last lesson of life," Emerson declares, "is a voluntary obedience, a necessitated freedom." Such a religion of submission to the higher power of nature is the true worship: "Man is made of the same atoms as the world is, he shares the same impressions, predispositions, and destiny. When his mind is illuminated, when his heart is kind, he throws himself joyfully into the sublime order, and does, with knowledge, what the stones do by structure." In a direct challenge to the idea of Jesus as mediator, Emerson's cosmic worship is one of self-reliance. It "shall send man home to his central solitude . . . he shall walk with no companion. . . . He needs only his own verdict."

CRITICAL COMMENTARY

Just as he was to do in the final words of "ILLUSIONS"—the concluding essay of *The Conduct of Life*—Emerson ended "Worship" on the NEOPLATONIC note of *solus cum solo,* alone with the alone. He blended this with strains of Heraclitean, Hindu, and Buddhist thought, reading the universe in terms of moral cause and effect. With his poem "BRAHMA" (1857), which was contemporaneously budding in his mind, Emerson grappled with reality manifesting itself through the unification of *Purusha* (spirit) and *Prakriti* (matter). He explored this framework for understanding the moral dimensions of human conduct as well in the essays "COMPENSATION," "SPIRITUAL LAWS," "EXPERIENCE," "Fate," "Power," "HEROISM," and many other contexts.

Emerson had addressed the question of immortality in former contexts as well, most notably in the "Divinity School Address" of 1838, in which he argued that the idea of an afterlife was not an original teaching of Jesus but only the dogma of his followers. In "Worship" he pays homage to JOHANN WOLFGANG VON GOETHE who, it was reported, speculated in his old age on *entelechy,* or a driving force or spirit toward self-realization. Here Emerson reprises the sentiment of Goethe on the question: "Higher than the question of our duration is the question of our deserving. Immortality will come to such as are fit for it, and he who would be a great soul in future, must be a great soul now." In "Immortality," from *LETTERS AND SOCIAL AIMS* (1876), he was to pursue these considerations with extended reference to the Hindu scriptures.

"Worship" was a prism through which these central Emersonian themes were refracted in *The Conduct of Life* in 1860. It is a representative expression of Emerson's multifaceted moral theory of personal, social, and cosmic progress. In this same blend of the religious and the ethical dimensions of human nature, he ingeniously affirms that "work is victory," that is, one's unique work, consciously dedicated to the public and cosmic good, is the highest example of religious worship. Emerson's literary genius was to conjoin the idea of authentic personal worship with a new "American" religiosity that challenged both the church and the secular establishments of his day, which (in retrospect) settled his place as one of the preeminent religious and moral thinkers of his time. As a key expression of Emerson's mature thought, "Worship" presaged such later works of the 1870s as "POETRY AND IMAGINATION" and *NATURAL HISTORY OF INTELLECT,* which declared that both poetry and science were expressions of man's religious and moral affinities with the laws of the world.

David A. Dilworth

"The Young American" (1844)

Emerson's "The Young American, A Lecture read before the Mercantile Library Association, Boston, February 7, 1844" was later published in *NATURE; ADDRESSES, AND LECTURES* (1849). In this lecture, Emerson identifies the most salient fact of American identity as the availability of land in the West and the spread of commerce as the basis of the economy. He looks to these features of American development as the sources of a new American culture, away from European influence, as he had discussed earlier in "The AMERICAN SCHOLAR" (1837). "The Young American" was delivered at the peak of Emerson's own engagement with issues of reform including ABOLITIONISM. In 1844 alone he produced four major political statements, not only "The Young American," but also "NEW ENGLAND REFORMERS" and "POLITICS" (both published in *ESSAYS: SECOND SERIES*), and "EMANCIPATION OF THE NEGROES IN THE BRITISH WEST INDIES."

SYNOPSIS

In "The Young American," Emerson determines that America is "beginning to assert itself" and the influence of "Europe is receding." America is advancing in education, politics, and "internal improvements" such as transportation. Our "rage for road building," in particular, is necessary for creating a more "national" system and identity, and minimizing "local peculiarities and hostilities" across such vast geographical space.

Emerson identifies several aspects of American political, economic, and cultural development. First, he affirms that the building of an infrastructure and settlement of the West have changed "time" in this country, speeding up activity in agriculture, mining, and other pursuits. The railroad has become the "surveyor's line," marking out the line of settlement, which Emerson predicts will soon reach across the continent: "The bountiful continent is ours, state on state, and territory on territory, to the waves of the Pacific sea."

But this project, this responsibility "requires an education and a sentiment" different from that in the East. Now "every American should be educated with a view to the values of land," whether in "engineering," "architecture," "agriculture," "minerals," or "timber-lands." It is the land that feeds our minds and bodies in America and "brings us into just relations with men and things." The opening of the West has resulted in a generation of "young men who withdraw from cities" and business to "cultivate the soil."

This shift in the focus of the economy has also had an effect on American culture. The availability of "cheap land" "invites to the arts of agriculture, of gardening, and domestic architecture." But we move too quickly and are too spread out in "distant tracts" to create the same types of architecture and "public gardens" as those in Europe. Instead, our private "lands and dwellings . . . [are] poverty-stricken, and the buildings plain and poor." If American aesthetics are lacking, the positive side is that a connection to the land "generates the feeling of patriotism." European culture is still more important and influential "in the Atlantic states," where the emphasis is "commercial" rather than agricultural, but Emerson is hopeful that a new "American genius" will soon rise out of the influence of the "rocky West."

The position of America—situated "betwixt the two oceans"—and the availability of land, will only increase our political and economic power. The main problem with this always forward-looking tendency is a lack of concern with the present age: "We build railroads, we know not for what or for whom; but one thing is certain, that we who build will receive the very smallest share of benefit." This "patriarchal form of government," of one generation ruling in the interests of the future, can be dangerous, as children may have a "difference of opinion." This is true of the feudal system, which was characterized by "petulance and tyranny," but the new era is characterized by "Trade," which emphasizes the role of the individual and will "make the governments insignificant." The down side is that trade puts "everything into market, talent, beauty, virtue, and man himself."

Still, trade is only temporary and will eventually be replaced by another system. There are "signs" of the new system in reforms that seek a new role for government, in the call for widespread education, regulation of labor, and promotion of "the agricultural life." Emerson is not himself convinced that farming is the best model as, indeed, there are numerous farmers who perform endless "drudgery" and still end up "bankrupt, like the merchant." The "communists" ought instead to approach agriculture as a "science." He praises the "noble thought" of the followers of CHARLES FOURIER, whose communities are "founded in love, and in labor," but economically it does not make sense: "It has turned out cheaper to make calico by companies . . . and to bake bread by companies."

The communal experiments made other "abundant mistakes." For example, it is not fair to pay the same rate for all jobs, nor to expect all members would spend their money in a way that benefited the entire community. Emerson points out that the women in these communities object to the idea of "a common table, and a common nursery, &c., setting a higher value on the private family with poverty, than on an association with wealth." Still, the communities must be commended for seeking "an equal and thorough education" for all members: "This is the value of the Communities; not what they have done, but the revolution which they indicate as on the way."

What is needed is better government, leaders as "*land*-lords, who understand the land and its uses." He goes so far as to propose that government become a "private" system, subject to the market: "It would be an easy extension of our commercial system, to pay a private emperor a fee for services, as we pay an architect, an engineer, or a lawyer."

We could hire individuals with "a talent for righting wrong, for administering difficult affairs, for counseling poor farmers how to turn their estates to good husbandry," and so on: "We must have kings . . . only let us have the real instead of the titular. Let us have our leading and our inspiration from the best." Who are to be these leaders?: "I call upon you, young men, to obey your heart, and be the nobility of this land." The "Young American" has a special calling in the world "to stand for the interests of general justice and humanity"—to reveal "the secret of heroism, that 'Man alone / Can perform the impossible?'"

Emerson clarifies that he would not "throw stumbling-blocks in the way of the abolitionists, the philanthropist," but only that we should mind "our own affairs, our own genius," instead. America has a "short history, and unsettled wilderness" and cannot be compared to the "antiquated" ways of Europe. Europe has many problems that the younger America will avoid, such as the "tithes," the restrictions on the press, the rampant "pauperism," and the "aristocracy." Most significantly, Europe lacks land and space. America itself, just like the "Young American" to whom he speaks, is "slight and new; but youth is a fault of which we shall daily mend." All that is needed is "a new order," and he ends the essay by urging, "let us live in America," and we shall build "a new and more excellent social state than history has recorded."

CRITICAL COMMENTARY

The essay is as much about "The Young American" as about a young America: "It is the country of the Future. . . . it is a country of beginnings, of projects, of designs, and expectations." With youth comes promise, but also inexperience. The *land* itself, however, on which America's promise will be played out, "is as old as the Flood." "The Young American" is Emerson's statement of Manifest Destiny: "The bountiful continent is ours, state on state, and territory on territory, to the waves of the Pacific sea."

The main problem or obstacle in the essay is that the particular geographical situation of America requires that the "laws and institutions" of the current generation "exist on some scale of proportion to the majesty of nature." This concern that America was not yet living up to the potential of its landscape was one that he had articulated in earlier works, such as "The American Scholar" (1837) and "LITERARY ETHICS" (1838). As early as 1836 he had written in his journal, "'twas pity that in this Titanic continent where nature is so grand, Genius should be so tame."

Whereas "The American Scholar," however, focused on the specific role of the scholar or poet-writer, "The Young American" focuses on the role of the land itself, and on the people in general, in shaping American culture. The address is ultimately Emerson's reconciliation of American industrial power—of capitalism—with her moral and intellectual destiny. Our duty as Americans is "not to block improvement." Whereas "The American Scholar" calls the thinker to direct action, "The Young American" calls reformers to stay out of the way. Here he celebrates the natural progression or evolution of society, rather than the interference of forced revolution. The use of the word *revolution* calls to mind his general view on reform, as articulated in "MAN THE REFORMER" (1841), for example, to pursue only cultivation of the self and "let our affection flow out to our fellows; it would operate in a day the greatest of all revolutions."

Land is the basis of the American economy and political system, and Emerson alludes to the struggle over the West as both the source of national unity and a threat to "the Union of these States." By 1844 northern and southern states and congressmen were in a protracted battle over the fate of slavery in (and therefore political control of) the West. Emerson, however, seeks to shift the terms of the debate, from acting as if we depended upon that Union to realizing that the Union depends on us, as individuals, for its strength. He declares confidently that if the Union should fall apart, we would "combine in a new and better constitution." For now he trusts in the markets, saying that trade is "the principle of Liberty . . . it makes peace and keeps peace, and it will abolish slavery."

A significant portion of "The Young American" addresses the question of UTOPIAN communities as a model for use of the land. Although he does not mention BROOK FARM by name, at the time of this lecture the community had just adopted FOURIERISM as a plan for organizing labor according to the talents of each member. While Emerson referred to Brook Farm elsewhere as "a noble . . . experiment of better living," here he details the "abundant mistakes," both economic and spiritual, in trying to force individuals to live according to communal rules. He rearticulates his view on reform that would echo throughout his writings—that "the private mind" is the only "balance to a corrupt society." Trusting the private mind means trusting nature. We must not look to politics or government, which depends "on the silly die." Instead, there is "an organic simplicity and liberty, which, when it loses its balance, redresses itself presently."

Part III

Related People, Places, and Topics

abolitionism Throughout the 1840s and 1850s Ralph Waldo Emerson spoke publicly against slavery on numerous occasions and published several essays on the topic. Most of the Transcendentalists participated in the abolitionist movement in some way, whether by attending conventions and meetings, giving public addresses, supporting antislavery political candidates, or writing for and reading abolitionist papers. Emerson, however, resisted joining any antislavery organization, rejecting the idea of single-issue reform in favor of reform of the self. This argument echoes in his many writings and lectures on a variety of reform topics, not only abolitionism, but education, UTOPIANISM, and women's rights as well.

Many within Emerson's immediate circle were drawn into the abolitionist movement. LIDIAN JACKSON EMERSON had met with the sisters Sarah and Angelina Grimké on their antislavery speaking tour in 1837, and HENRY DAVID THOREAU's mother and other CONCORD women were active in female antislavery societies. BRONSON ALCOTT and his wife, Abigail May Alcott, boycotted the use of slave-produced items, such as cotton, at their utopian community, Fruitlands. THEODORE PARKER was head of a BOSTON Vigilance Committee to assist fugitive slaves unjustly captured under the Fugitive Slave Act in the 1850s, and in 1854 Emerson was among those outraged over the case of Anthony Burns, an alleged fugitive slave who was arrested and put on trial in Boston. Emerson was also closely associated with the reformers and intellectuals known as the "Secret Six" who secretly supported and funded the 1859 crusade of the radical abolitionist JOHN BROWN in his attempted slave revolt at Harpers Ferry, Virginia. Thoreau had lectured in opposition to the Fugitive Slave Act in his "Slavery in Massachusetts" (1854) and was one of the most ardent public supporters of John Brown and his cause, hailing Brown as a martyr in "A Plea for Captain John Brown" and other addresses.

Although Emerson once claimed, "I do not often speak to public questions," he did, in fact, give several public lectures on the topic of slavery, as well as publishing essays and poems on the subject. In addition to "THE FUGITIVE SLAVE LAW" address (1851), which was reprinted throughout the decade, he spoke on the anniversary of the "EMANCIPATION OF THE NEGROES IN THE BRITISH WEST INDIES" (1844), gave a lecture on "AMERICAN SLAVERY" (1855), and delivered a mid–Civil War address, "FORTUNE OF THE REPUBLIC" (1863) to support President Lincoln's dual goals of preserving the Union and the complete abolition of slavery in the United States.

While Emerson was often critical of reform organizations and of individual reformers in essays such as "MAN THE REFORMER" (1841) and "NEW ENGLAND REFORMERS" (1844), he appeared at local antislavery meetings in Dedham, Worcester, Concord, and Boston, and wrote letters and addresses responding to specific national controversies in the 1850s and 1860s, such as events in the Kansas-Nebraska territory and the John Brown case. Emerson also published several poems dealing with the topics of slavery, emancipation, and the Civil War, four of which were grouped together in the postwar 1867 collection, *MAY-DAY AND OTHER PIECES:* "FREEDOM," "ODE SUNG IN TOWN HALL, CONCORD, JULY 4, 1857," "BOSTON HYMN" (a poem he read publicly in 1863 in celebration of Abraham Lincoln's Emancipation Proclamation), and "VOLUNTARIES" (to honor the black troops who fought in the war). An earlier commentary on abolitionism, "ODE, INSCRIBED TO W. H. CHANNING," had been included in his first collection of *POEMS* (1847).

Recent scholars have contended that Emerson's earliest biographers consciously downplayed his reform commitments in favor of promoting his image as a detached genteel philosopher, concerned more with the idealized life of the mind than with the political and social issues of his day. But his contemporaries knew him as a man deeply concerned with the spiritual costs of slavery, yet hopeful that the nation would eventually be set upon the right course. Many of his antislavery writings have only recently been recovered and made available in print, showing Emerson's steady engagement with abolitionism from the late 1830s through the era of the Civil War.

Further Reading

Gougeon, Len. *Virtue's Hero: Emerson, Antislavery, and Reform.* Athens: University of Georgia Press, 1990.

Gougeon, Len, and Joel Myerson, eds. *Emerson's Anti-Slavery Writings.* New Haven, Conn.: Yale University Press, 1995.

Alcott, Amos Bronson (1799–1888) The educator, UTOPIAN reformer, and Transcendentalist poet Amos Bronson Alcott first heard Ralph Waldo Emerson speak in BOSTON, MASSACHUSETTS, as early as 1828, but the two did not meet until several years later. Alcott was born in Connecticut. His father was a farmer and could not afford to send his son to school. Bronson Alcott was entirely self-educated and worked for some years as a peddler, traveling throughout the southern states, before deciding to become a teacher in Connecticut, Massachusetts, and then Pennsylvania. He was married to Abigail May (sister of UNITARIAN minister SAMUEL JOSEPH MAY) in 1830, and the couple had four daughters—Anna Bronson, Louisa May, Elizabeth Sewall, and Abigail May—who served as the model for LOUISA MAY ALCOTT's best-selling novel, *Little Women* (1868).

Amos Bronson Alcott

Bronson Alcott read and was influenced by many of the same romantic and idealist European writers and philosophers as Emerson, such as THOMAS CARLYLE, SAMUEL TAYLOR COLERIDGE, IMMANUEL KANT, and EMANUEL SWEDENBORG. Alcott was most interested in applying new theories of education to the teaching of young children; he returned to Boston in 1834 to open the Temple School with his assistant ELIZABETH PALMER PEABODY. In the fall of 1835 Alcott began regularly visiting Emerson in CONCORD, and the two men began a lifelong friendship. Emerson recorded that he found Alcott "a wise man, simple, superior to display." The Alcotts eventually moved to Concord, and Emerson had an enormous influence on the young Louisa May Alcott, who later referred to him as "the god of my idolatry." Emerson also assisted Bronson Alcott financially at times, including sponsoring a trip to England in the early 1840s for Alcott to meet with social and educational reformers there.

Soon after their first meeting, Emerson and Alcott were among the founding members of the TRANSCENDENTAL CLUB in 1836. Out of those meetings, Alcott and Emerson, along with MARGARET FULLER and GEORGE RIPLEY, launched the *DIAL* literary magazine as a forum for the "new school" of Transcendentalism. Alcott published his "Orphic Sayings" in the *Dial,* obscure philosophical musings that came to represent the excesses of Transcendentalism to its critics. Emerson continued to read, edit, and defend Alcott. The same year that the Transcendental Club was formed, Alcott was embroiled in controversy over the publication of his *Conversations with Children on the Gospels.* The book revealed Alcott's experimental teaching methods with young children and earned him even more criticism and, eventually, the loss of his school, but Emerson and other Transcendentalists stood by Alcott. The book also revealed the affinity between Emerson and Alcott, in their rejection of traditional institutions of learning and their emphasis instead on self-education.

Alcott's reform activities were focused on educational and communitarian experiments. He became immersed in utopianism through the community at BROOK FARM and, in 1843, moved his family to and lead the short-lived community at Fruitlands, which he founded with CHARLES LANE. In the early 1840s Emerson ranked Alcott among the men doing the most to bring about societal change through the establishment of alternative communities. He praised "Fourier, Owen, Alcott, and Channing" as men who "would rewrite institutions and destroy drudgery." Emerson, however, was more grounded in his comfortable domestic life, in his writing and lecturing schedule, and ultimately in his belief in individual reform, and never joined the communities himself.

Alcott had a lifelong interest in alternative education for adults as well as children. In the 1840s he led a series of Conversations attended by many in the Transcendentalist community. After the Civil War he joined the Free Religious Association, a forum for the discussion of comparative religion, and in the 1870s he founded the CONCORD SCHOOL OF PHILOSOPHY AND LITERATURE. The Concord School was the realization of Alcott's dream to bring together the best minds of the era to discuss philosophy, literature, and education. Many of the Transcendentalists lectured at or attended the Concord School, including Emerson, and the 1882 summer meeting was a memorial session dedicated to the legacy and influence of the sage of Concord. The school ended after Alcott's death in 1888.

Amos Bronson Alcott was ultimately known more as a reformer than as a poet or writer, although he published dozens of books and pamphlets across genres of philosophy, poetry, and autobiography over the course of six decades.

Further Reading

Dahlstrand, Frederick. *Amos Bronson Alcott: An Intellectual Biography.* East Brunswick, N.J.: Associated University Presses, 1982.

Matteson, John. *Eden's Outcasts: The Story of Louisa May Alcott and Her Father.* New York: W.W. Norton, 2007.

Alcott, Louisa May (1832–1888) The novelist Louisa May Alcott, author of the best-selling children's book, *Little Women* (1868), was the daughter of the Transcendentalist reformer AMOS BRONSON ALCOTT and Abigail May Alcott. While Louisa May Alcott never identified as a Transcendentalist, she grew up in CONCORD, MASSACHUSETTS, in the midst of Transcendentalist activity. She was subject to her father's educational and philosophical experiments, and when she was 10 years old, her family lived at the UTOPIAN community at Fruitlands, founded by her father and CHARLES LANE. This experience she satirized in the later short story, "Transcendental Wild Oats," published in 1873. She mined her childhood, as well, growing up in a household of four sisters, for *Little Women.*

Alcott's real-life childhood included hiking in the woods with teacher HENRY DAVID THOREAU and friendships with the Emerson daughters; Alcott dedicated an early book of children's stories to ELLEN EMERSON. Alcott was taught at home primarily by her father, Bronson Alcott, who observed all of his daughters' intellectual and social development closely as subjects for his educational theories. Her education was supplemented by being allowed to browse the shelves of Ralph Waldo Emerson's study, where she remembered reading works by William Shakespeare, Dante, JOHANN WOLFGANG VON GOETHE, and THOMAS CARLYLE. Despite these idealized memories, life in the Alcott home was often harsh, as the family suffered financial hardships throughout most of Louisa May Alcott's young life, due to Bronson Alcott's choice to forego regular employment. Emerson at times assisted the family financially, until Louisa May became the family breadwinner with her published short stories and novels.

Her novels were always autobiographical in some sense and included caricatures of Concord figures, such as Thoreau (in the character of Mr. Hyde in *Little Men,* 1871) and THEODORE PARKER (in the novel *Work,* 1873). She always had the highest regard for Emerson and "his cheerful philosophy." She remembered many aspects of life in the Emerson household. In May 1882 she published a short essay, "Reminiscence of Ralph Waldo Emerson," after his death. The article began, "I count it the greatest honor and happiness of my life to have known Mr. Emerson." In assessing his literary legacy, she concluded that "Emerson wrote essays more helpful than most sermons; lectures

The Alcott family at Orchard House, Concord, Massachusetts, located just down the road from the Emerson household *(Louisa May Alcott Memorial Association)*

which created the lyceum; poems full of power and sweetness."

Louisa May Alcott never married and lived with her parents at Orchard House in Concord, and then on her own in BOSTON. Born on her father's birthday in 1832, she died just two days after him in 1888 and is buried in the family plot at Sleepy Hollow Cemetery in Concord.

Further Reading

Matteson, John. *Eden's Outcasts: The Story of Louisa May Alcott and Her Father.* New York: W.W. Norton, 2007.

Atlantic Monthly (1857–) The *Atlantic Monthly: A Magazine of Literature, Art, and Politics* began publication in November 1857 and continues today as the *Atlantic.* Emerson was among those who met in BOSTON, MASSACHUSETTS—writers, editors, and intellectuals such as JAMES ELLIOT CABOT, HENRY WADSWORTH LONGFELLOW, JAMES RUSSELL LOWELL, and OLIVER WENDELL HOLMES, all also members of the SATURDAY CLUB—to discuss the need for a new journal of ideas and literary culture. Emerson's work appeared in the very first issue—an essay ("ILLUSIONS") and four poems ("BRAHMA," "DAYS," "The Rommany Girl," and "THE CHARTIST'S COMPLAINT"). Emerson remained closely associated with the magazine during its first several decades and worked with its first three editors: Lowell (editor from 1857 to 1861), James T. Fields (1861–71), and William Dean Howells (1871–81). At a time when the magazine paid an average of $6 a page for an essay or prose form, by the 1850s and '60s Emerson could command $10 a page.

Lowell was the first editor of the magazine that its founders, as Emerson noted in his journal, hoped would serve an important role as cultural arbiter, printing only "pieces of permanent worth." This self-conscious cultural and intellectual role was recalled by fellow Transcendentalist THOMAS WENTWORTH HIGGINSON in his later memoirs, when he noted of the founders and contributors of the early *Atlantic Monthly*, including Emerson: "That New England was appointed to guide the nation, to civilize it, to humanize it, none of them doubted." The paper was not only a literary forum for friends of Emerson; through the *Atlantic Monthly* he entered into a conversation with and enjoyed a wider readership among his contemporaries on political and social issues of the day. The journal was also an important forum for Emerson during the Civil War, when his address on "The President's Proclamation" (Abraham Lincoln's Emancipation Proclamation) was published in the November 1862 issue and his poem on the topic, "BOSTON HYMN," appeared in February 1863; later that year, in the October issue, his poem "VOLUNTARIES" was published as well.

The magazine quickly rose to be one of the most influential cultural forums of the mid-19th century and published some of the most important voices of the day. Although its writers and editors (including Emerson) spoke out against slavery, the editors declared in the first issue that the magazine would not be explicitly political and would "be the organ of no party or clique, but will honestly endeavor to be the exponent of what its conductors believe to be the American idea. It will deal frankly with persons and with parties, endeavoring always to keep in view that moral element which transcends all persons and parties, and which alone makes the basis of a true and lasting prosperity."

Long after his death, the *Atlantic Monthly* claimed Emerson as one of the paper's foundational figures and as representative, along with NATHANIEL HAWTHORNE, WALT WHITMAN, Longfellow, HENRY JAMES, and others, of the best of American culture in the mid-19th century. In 1903 and in 2003 the magazine celebrated the centennial, and then bicentennial, of Emerson's birth with tribute articles.

Further Reading

Asarnow, Jenny. "Flashbacks: Ralph Waldo Emerson. The Sage and the Magazine." *The Atlantic Online* (December 23, 2003). http://www.theatlantic.com/unbound/flashbks/emerson.htm (accessed October 3, 2007).

Sedgwick, Ellery. *The Atlantic Monthly, 1857–1909: Yankee Humanism at High Tide and Ebb.* Amherst: University of Massachusetts Press, 1994.

Bancroft, George (1800–1891) George Bancroft was an eminent historian, statesman, and friend of Ralph Waldo Emerson. He was born in Worcester, Massachusetts and studied at HARVARD COLLEGE and in Göttingen, Germany. After his return to America he delivered sermons in UNITARIAN churches. Emerson saw the young Bancroft preaching at the New South Church in BOSTON in 1822 and referred to him in his journal as "an infant Hercules." In 1824 Bancroft founded an innovative school in Northampton, Massachusetts. In 1834 he published the first volume of his *History of the United States,* which he continued writing until the final volume was released in 1874.

Bancroft developed a friendship with Emerson during the 1830s. Bancroft's interests, social sphere, and philosophical outlook overlapped with those of Emerson and other Transcendentalists. Like Emerson, he looked to German idealist philosophy and to English romanticism as a corrective to the Lockean empiricism then prevalent among the Boston Unitarian establishment. They also shared an interest in American history, and Bancroft drew upon Emerson's 1835 discourse on the history of CONCORD for his own work. Emerson read Bancroft's *History of the United States* with great interest, as is evidenced in numerous journal entries.

Unlike Emerson, Bancroft's political outlook corresponded well with one of the two major American political parties of the 1830s and '40s. During Andrew Jackson's second term Bancroft committed himself to the Democratic Party. He was inspired by the idea that in politics the "voice of the people" would always be proven right. He was made Collector of the Port of Boston by Jackson's successor, Martin Van Buren, and ran for governor of Massachusetts in 1842. When the expansionist Democrat James Polk took office as president in 1845, Bancroft was made Secretary of the Navy. Bancroft ordered some of the military operations that provoked the Mexican War in 1846, a war Emerson strongly opposed. In the same year Bancroft was made ambassador to Britain and moved to

London with his wife, Elizabeth, a childhood friend of Emerson's wife LIDIAN JACKSON EMERSON from Plymouth, Massachusetts.

Despite political differences, Bancroft and Emerson rekindled a friendship in London during Emerson's 1847–48 lecture tour. As ambassador, Bancroft had become personally acquainted with numerous prominent political and intellectual figures in London and was eager to introduce Emerson into their exclusive company. The Bancrofts threw a party in Emerson's honor in London in 1848 and arranged meetings for him with Samuel Rogers, Thomas Macaulay, Richard Monckton Milnes, and other scientists, scholars, and politicians. Bancroft supported the French Revolution of 1848 and placed Emerson in contact with the American ambassador to France, Richard Rush, who provided him an entry pass to the debates of France's new National Assembly.

After his return to America in 1849 Bancroft continued writing history. From 1867 to 1874 he served as minister to Berlin and witnessed the unification of Germany. He died a celebrated figure in Washington in 1891.

Further Reading

Handlin, Lilian. *George Bancroft: The Intellectual as Democrat.* New York: Harper and Row, 1984.

Daniel Robert Koch

Bartol, Cyrus Augustus (1813–1900) Cyrus Bartol was a graduate of HARVARD Divinity School and a UNITARIAN minister who became a founding member of the TRANSCENDENTAL CLUB in 1836. Bartol had attended lectures by Ralph Waldo Emerson and ultimately defended Emerson against critics of his 1838 "DIVINITY SCHOOL ADDRESS." Bartol was more conservative in his own views than either Emerson or the radical Unitarian THEODORE PARKER, who also ended up at the center of theological controversy after publication of his 1841 *Discourse on the Transient and Permanent in Christianity.* Both Emerson and Parker advocated a personal religion that was not dependent on a belief in the existence of God or in the divinity of Christ. Bartol disagreed with this idea, but he defended Emerson's right to speak and Parker's right to continue preaching. In a review of Emerson's 1847 collection *POEMS,* Bartol was critical that Emerson did not acknowledge Christianity or the relationship between God and man as a source of inspiration; indeed, for Emerson, God and man were the same.

Bartol explained his own position in his *Discourse on the Christian Spirit and Life* (1850). Bartol maintained a belief in the divinity of Christ, while some Transcendentalists such as Emerson saw Jesus only as a "divine man." Using Emerson's own language for understanding the historical Jesus, Bartol countered that Jesus was "not, in the phrase of the day, a 'representative man,' but representative of deity . . . He transcends all our transcendentalism." While Bartol therefore did not entirely accept the Emersonian rejection of Christianity and organized religion, by the 1860s he had, like many Transcendentalists, moved away from the Unitarian Church and become interested in comparative religion and free thought. He helped found the Free Religious Association and the RADICAL CLUB, two Transcendentalist-inspired groups, and in 1872 he published an essay on "Transcendentalism" that defended idealism as a philosophy. Lastly, a profile of Emerson was included in Bartol's 1880 collection of essays on influential literary figures, *Principles and Portraits.* Bartol joined again with many Transcendentalist colleagues at AMOS BRONSON ALCOTT'S CONCORD SCHOOL OF PHILOSOPHY AND LITERATURE in the 1870s and 1880s, where he lectured on the ideas and influence of individuals such as William Shakespeare, JOHANN WOLFGANG VON GOETHE, and, of course, Ralph Waldo Emerson.

Further Reading

Heath, William G. "Cyrus Bartol's Transcendentalism." *Studies in the American Renaissance* (1979): 399–408.

Boston, Massachusetts Although known as the sage of CONCORD, the town of his ancestors and where he spent most of his adult life, and educated in CAMBRIDGE (home of HARVARD COLLEGE), Ralph Waldo Emerson was actually born in Boston, Massachusetts, about 15 miles from Concord. Reformers and literary figures congregated around Emerson in Concord, and yet Boston was the more urban center of 19th-century Transcendentalism and New England literary culture in general. It was in Boston that MARGARET FULLER held her Conversations for women at ELIZABETH PALMER PEABODY's West Street bookstore, and BRONSON ALCOTT began his controversial Temple School. The Transcendentalist-UNITARIAN connection extended from the Reverend WILLIAM ELLERY CHANNING's Federal Street Church at the turn of the 19th century through Emerson's years as minister of the Second Street Church (where his father, WILLIAM EMERSON, had served), to THEODORE PARKER preaching to thousands at his new Twenty-Eighth Congregational Society, which met in Boston's Music Hall. Emerson and others of the Transcendentalist literary circle were among those Massachusetts elites that came to be referred to as "Boston Brahmins"; so tied was 19th-century Boston to the Transcendentalist movement that Charles Dickens once remarked, "If I were a Bostonian, I think I would be a Transcendentalist."

Boston has loomed large in New England—indeed, American—literary and political culture. It was founded in 1630 as the first settlement of the Puritans, their "City on a Hill" or shining example to the rest of the world, and became the colonial and eventually state capital. In the 1770s Boston was the hotbed of Patriot activity that sparked the American Revolution, from the Boston Massacre to the Boston Tea Party to Paul Revere's ride from Boston to Lexington and Concord. This Puritan and revolutionary heritage combined to secure the city's reputation for rebellion, new ideas, and nonconformity for centuries to come. By 1720 the population had swelled to 12,000, making Boston America's largest city, but the population grew slowly over the next decades and by the time of the signing of the Declaration of Independence in 1776 the city of 16,000 people had been surpassed in population by New York (25,000) and Philadelphia (40,000), which would become the new nation's capital and cultural center.

In the early 1800s Boston was still New England's most important port city and harbor, bringing in goods and emigrants from Europe and around the world, and the Industrial Revolution and cotton industry of New England swelled Boston's population to around 70,000 by the 1830s, when Transcendentalism emerged. Boston's population continued to grow tremendously through Emerson's lifetime, and the city saw increased diversity with the large Irish immigration of the 1840s. Emerson was born in 1803 into a city of about 25,000; by the time of his death in 1882, the city was home to more than 360,000 people.

In addition to lecturing often and regularly in Boston, Emerson wrote about Boston as the city of his birth and was perpetually tied to Boston's cultural, literary, and political happenings. After 1850 Boston was an important stop on the Underground Railroad and an important site for battles over slavery and the Fugitive Slave Law, which outraged many Northern citizens and cities with arrests of alleged and escaped slaves. With such public fugitive slave cases as Shadrach Minkins in 1851 and Anthony Burns in 1854, Emerson was among those Bostonians who felt their city had been turned into the slave master's "hound." In his earlier poem, "ODE, INSCRIBED TO W. H. CHANNING" (1847), Emerson made reference to "Boston Bay and Bunker Hill" as revolutionary sites in the context of lamenting Boston's 19th-century ties to the slave economy and politics.

Emerson addressed this legacy of Boston as the founding city of freedom and as a site of political and social reform in other poems as well. The poem "BOSTON HYMN" was written in response to Abraham Lincoln's Emancipation Proclamation, effective January 1, 1863. The later poem, "BOSTON" (published in 1876) was read at Faneuil Hall on December 16, 1873, the centennial of the Boston Tea Party, and opens with a Latin phrase, *Sicut patribus, sit Deus nobis,* or "God be with us, as he was with our fathers," the official city seal or motto of Boston.

Further Reading

Felton, R. Todd. *A Journey into the Transcendentalists' New England.* Berkeley, Calif.: Roaring Forties Press, 2006.

Von Frank, Albert J. *The Trials of Anthony Burns: Freedom and Slavery in Emerson's Boston.* Cambridge, Mass.: Harvard University Press, 1998.

Brook Farm In 1841 GEORGE RIPLEY and SOPHIA RIPLEY, along with Charles Dana, established the UTOPIAN socialist community of Brook Farm on nearly 200 acres in West Roxbury, Massachusetts, eight miles outside of BOSTON, "to combine the thinker and the worker . . . to guarantee the highest mental freedom . . . to do away the necessity of menial services, by opening the benefits of education and the profits of labor to all; and thus to prepare a society of liberal, intelligent, and cultivated persons."

Perhaps the most famous of the numerous utopian experiments of the early 19th-century, Brook Farm is frequently linked with Emerson, HENRY DAVID THOREAU, BRONSON ALCOTT, and MARGARET FULLER, although none of these individuals joined the community. Brook Farm's most famous member was NATHANIEL HAWTHORNE, who initially found his agrarian duties exhilarating but soon discovered they interfered with his writing. *Blithedale Romance* (1852) provides a fictional account of Hawthorne's experiences with Brook Farm.

Almost none of the Brook Farmers had farming experience. The land had been used for a dairy farm and was composed of rocky, sandy soil; the necessary improvements to successfully farm the area were out of reach of the community. The Brook Farm constitution of 1844 acknowledged that "the first few years must be passed in constant and unwearied labor," but it also asserted that "every step has strengthened the faith with which we set out." Eventually the Brook Farmers formally adopted the policies of French socialist Charles Fourier, some of which were informally observed before the official conversion. Ripley and Dana hoped that the clearly defined structure of FOURIERISM, in addition to the larger public recognition it would bring, would enable the community to achieve self-sufficiency; however, other members feared that the rigidity of Fourierism would diminish the individual's freedom within the community. A smallpox outbreak in late 1845 created additional problems, but the final blow was the devastation by fire of the Phalanstery, a newly constructed building intended to be the center of the community, which left the farmers nearly $7,000 in debt. Later Ripley sold most of his personal library to help cover the debt.

Although the Brook Farmers never prospered, the community attracted hundreds of members and thousands of visitors over the years. Numerous building and farming projects were successfully undertaken. The largest source of revenue was the Brook Farm school, which served all ages and provided equal education for women. The school gained wide acclaim and was even recommended by HARVARD COLLEGE for college preparatory coursework. The community published the *Harbinger*, a weekly magazine devoted to social and political issues of the day. Contributors included JAMES RUSSELL LOWELL, JOHN GREENLEAF WHITTIER, and Horace Greeley, and Ripley maintained the *Harbinger* even after Brook Farm dissolved.

Emerson later wrote, "It was a noble and generous movement in the projectors, to try an experiment of better living. They had the feeling that our ways of living were too conventional and expensive, not allowing each to do what he had a talent for, and not permitting men to combine cultivation of mind and heart with a reasonable amount of daily labor. At the same time, it was an attempt to lift others with themselves, and to share the advantages they should attain." Still, Emerson was critical of the idea of "association," and of Brook Farm in particular, in addresses such as "NEW ENGLAND REFORMERS" (1844).

After the community was abandoned, the farm and lands were eventually sold and became a training base during the Civil War. Toward the end of the century, an orphanage was established on the grounds, which operated for nearly 100 years. Today the land remains undeveloped, and no extensive archaeological studies have been completed.

Further Reading

Delano, Sterling. *Brook Farm: The Dark Side of Utopia.* Cambridge, Mass.: Belknap Press of Harvard University, 2004.

Swift, Lindsay. *Brook Farm: Its Members, Scholars, and Visitors.* New York: Macmillan Press, 1900.

Kari Miller

Brown, John (1800–1859) John Brown became a martyr to the cause of ABOLITIONISM on the eve of the Civil War, when he armed slaves and raided the federal arsenal at Harpers Ferry, Virginia, on October 16, 1859. Brown was born in Connecticut and his grandfather had served as a captain in the Revolutionary War. Brown's family moved to western Ohio in 1805, and as a young man he studied briefly for the ministry. In his early adulthood he worked various farming and manual labor jobs in Massachusetts, Pennsylvania, and Ohio. At the age of 49 he settled his family in a black community at North Elba, New York. In 1855 he went to Kansas Territory, which was then the scene of violent skirmishes between free-state and pro-slavery factions. After the so-called Pottawatomie Creek massacre, which killed five free-soil advocates, Brown led four of his sons and three others in a bloody retaliation against five pro-slavery settlers.

As a radical abolitionist, by 1858 he had gained the financial support of the "Secret Six," comprised of New England reformers, including Transcendentalists THOMAS WENTWORTH HIGGINSON, THEODORE PARKER, and FRANKLIN BENJAMIN SANBORN, along with Samuel Gridley Howe, Gerritt Smith, and George Luther Stearns. In the summer of 1859 Brown set in motion a plan to organize an armed antislavery revolt. A small band of 16 white men and five black men gathered in a rented farmhouse in Virginia and then seized a federal armory and rounded up 60 hostages. Overpowered by a small force of U.S. Marines, led by Colonel Robert E. Lee, 10 of Brown's followers, including two of his sons, were killed; six others were later captured and executed. Brown was tried for murder, slave insurrection, and treason against the Commonwealth of Virginia, and hung on December 2, 1859. At his trial Brown declared: "I am too young to understand that God is any respecter of persons. I believe that to have interfered as I have done . . . in behalf of His despised poor, was not wrong but right."

Brown had impressed Emerson when he earlier visited CONCORD, MASSACHUSETTS, to speak at an antislavery gathering, but Emerson did not personally know in advance of Brown's Virginia plot. Emerson delivered a series of lectures in BOSTON in November 1859 while Brown was under sentence, calling Brown "a new saint awaiting his martyrdom," and another address at Salem on January 6, 1860, in which he denounced the pro-slavery politicians of the North who complained about lingering sympathy for Brown: "The sentiment of mercy is the natural recoil which the laws of the universe provide to protect mankind from destruction by savage passions. . . . For the arch-abolitionist, older than Brown, and older than the Shenandoah Mountains, is Love, whose other name is Justice, which was before Alfred, before Lycurgus, before slavery, and will be after it."

Emerson's original lecture on Brown underwent various revisions until the local and topical references were generalized into the essay published 11 years later as "COURAGE" (1870). Other Transcendentalists also contributed to the public discussion and martyrdom of Brown, including HENRY DAVID THOREAU, LOUISA MAY ALCOTT, and Lydia Maria Child, who, with Emerson, contributed to James Redpath's collection of essays, *Echoes of Harper's Ferry* (1860). Thoreau did the most to express the moral and religious significance of Brown's action in his three published essays in defense of Brown—"A Plea for Captain John Brown" and "Martyrdom of John Brown," both in 1859, and "The Last Days of John Brown" in 1860.

Further Reading

Renehan, Edward J., Jr. *The Secret Six: The True Tale of the Men Who Conspired with John Brown.* New York: Crown, 1995.

David A. Dilworth

Brownson, Orestes Augustus (1803–1876) The minister, lecturer, writer, and editor Orestes Brownson was one of the key figures in the Transcendentalist controversy when it began in the 1830s. Brownson was a self-educated man who became a UNITARIAN minister. Along with Ralph Waldo Emerson and other BOSTON intellectuals, Brownson was one of the original members of the TRANSCENDENTAL CLUB, which first met in 1836; at least one early meeting, on the topic of the "Education of Humanity," was held at Brownson's home. Brownson was particularly interested in questions of theological and social reform, and his early critique of Unitarianism, *New Views of Christianity, Society, and the Church,* was published in 1836, the same year as Emerson's *NATURE.* Brownson increasingly distanced himself from Emerson, however, who was moving completely away from Christianity and organized religion, and also from radical Unitarians such as THEODORE PARKER. When Emerson became the target of harsh criticism and charges of heresy after his 1838 "DIVINITY SCHOOL ADDRESS," Brownson shared in the condemnation of Transcendentalism as irreligious, but at the same time he defended Emerson's right to speak his mind.

Brownson began his own church, the Society for Christian Union and Progress, and his theology was based not only on his Transcendentalist critique but also on his readings in French socialism and theories on labor and the working classes. Between 1838 and 1842 he edited the *Boston Quarterly Review,* announcing his mission "to christianize democracy and democratize the church." The *Boston Quarterly Review* promised to be an important literary forum for the Transcendentalist movement, and Brownson invited many of the more reform-minded writers to contribute, such as MARGARET FULLER, Theodore Parker, ELIZABETH PALMER PEABODY, and GEORGE RIPLEY. As Brownson began to more openly criticize Transcendentalism, however, Emerson, Fuller, Ripley, and BRONSON ALCOTT were among those who saw the need for their own paper, leading to the founding of the *DIAL* magazine in 1840.

Although Brownson was part of the early Transcendentalist critique of Unitarianism, he became one of the earliest and most outspoken critics of the new philosophy. Transcendentalism came to be defined through Emerson's focus on the self and individual reform, while Brownson was among those who sought to "change the system." As Brownson explained in his 1840 essay on "The Laboring Classes," rather than cultivating only the self, he sought a solution in anticapitalism and alternative social and labor arrangements such as BROOK FARM, where Brownson's son briefly resided. Emerson was aware of Brownson's critique of Transcendentalism, and named Brownson as one of the "young people" (an interesting reference since Brownson and Emerson were, in fact, born in the same year) who "think that the vice of the age is to exaggerate individualism" and seek, instead, communal or alternative ways to organize society. Emerson rejected such reforms in favor of man's "obedience to his own genius."

Brownson finally publicly decried Transcendentalism with an 1845 essay entitled, "Transcendentalism, or the Latest Form of Infidelity." He reviewed Emerson's *POEMS* of 1847 as "hymns to the devil." Brownson declared that "Protestantism ends in Transcendentalism" and, having rejected both, he converted to Catholicism. For the remainder of the century, he focused on economic and labor reform and on Catholic apologetics, publishing a Catholic intellectual journal, *Brownson's Quarterly Review,* for more than 20 years.

Further Reading

Carey, Patrick W. *Orestes A. Brownson: American Religious Weathervane.* Grand Rapids, Mich.: William B. Eerdmans Publishing, 2004.

Power, Edward J. *Religion and the Public Schools in Nineteenth-Century America: The Contribution of Orestes A. Brownson.* New York: Paulist Press, 1996.

Cabot, James Elliot (1821–1903) James Elliot Cabot was Ralph Waldo Emerson's literary executor, assisting Emerson and ELLEN EMERSON in editing and publishing *LETTERS AND SOCIAL AIMS* (1876). He is best known for the publication of the Riverside Edition of *The Works of Ralph Waldo Emerson* (12 volumes published between 1883 and 1893). Cabot was a native of BOSTON who graduated from HARVARD COLLEGE in 1840 and Harvard Law School in 1845. He was less interested in the law, however, than in studying German philosophy, and worked various jobs to support his literary and scholarly interests, including working with his brother, an architect, and accompanying Harvard naturalist Louis Agassiz on a geological expedition. Cabot himself admitted that he "was something of a transcendentalist" and held a certain "contempt for the working-day world."

Cabot was introduced to Emerson's writing through reading issues of the Transcendentalist journal, the *DIAL,* while studying in Germany.

After returning to the United States, Cabot began corresponding with Emerson and published an essay on IMMANUEL KANT in the last issue of the *Dial* (April 1844). Cabot went on to lecture and publish widely on philosophical topics and co-edited another paper, the *Massachusetts Quarterly Review*, with THEODORE PARKER. He was a member, with Emerson, of the TOWN AND COUNTRY CLUB and the SATURDAY CLUB and published articles in the *ATLANTIC MONTHLY*. In the early 1870s, both Cabot and Emerson were part of a lecture series at Harvard, the result of which was Emerson's work on the *NATURAL HISTORY OF INTELLECT*, which Cabot collected and published in 1893. Cabot also wrote an 1887 *Memoir of Ralph Waldo Emerson*, which relied upon previously unpublished journals and correspondence. As Emerson's friend and literary executor, Cabot had a central role in establishing the importance of both Emerson and Transcendentalism in the American literary canon.

Further Reading

Myerson, Joel. *The New England Transcendentalists and the Dial: A History of the Magazine and Its Contributors*. London and Toronto: Associated University Presses, 1980.

Simmons, Nancy Craig. "Arranging the Sibylline Leaves: James Elliot Cabot's Work as Emerson's Literary Executor." *Studies in the American Renaissance* (1983): 335–389.

Cambridge, Massachusetts Many of the Transcendentalists were educated at HARVARD COLLEGE and Divinity School in Cambridge, Massachusetts. Ralph Waldo Emerson and three of his brothers attended Harvard, as did HENRY DAVID THOREAU and all of the Transcendentalists who had been trained as UNITARIAN ministers. Emerson delivered two of his most important and controversial early addresses to Harvard audiences in Cambridge, "THE AMERICAN SCHOLAR" (1837) and the "DIVINITY SCHOOL ADDRESS" (1838). Emerson's CONCORD (about 12 miles from Cambridge) became the new hub of intellectual and literary activity for those who separated (either voluntarily or involuntarily) from Cambridge's Unitarian community surrounding Harvard. Emerson is still remembered in Cambridge with several markers, including a plaque noting the location of his address at the Divinity Hall chapel, and Emerson Hall at Harvard Yard, which opened in 1900. HENRY WADSWORTH LONGFELLOW lived in Cambridge, as did many friends and relatives of the Boston and Concord Transcendentalists. Cambridge is also the location of Mount Auburn Cemetery, where many notable 19th-century figures were laid to rest, including a monument to MARGARET FULLER.

Cambridge is located just across the Charles River from BOSTON and was founded by the original Massachusetts Bay Colony settlers in 1630 as Newetowne. Harvard College was founded in 1636, and its first president had been educated at Cambridge University in England, the inspiration for the town's name change in 1638. Originally part of Boston proper, the West Boston Bridge connected Boston and Cambridge in 1792, facilitating quicker travel between the two. Cambridge was incorporated as its own city in 1846.

Cambridge has gone through various stages in its history, with emphasis at different times on its farming and then industrial economies, but it returned to its roots and remains today an educational and intellectual center, home not only to Harvard University and Radcliffe College (founded in 1879 as a women's "annex" to Harvard, and fully integrated with Harvard as an affiliated Institute for Advanced Study only in 1999), but also the Massachusetts Institute of Technology (MIT; founded in Boston in 1861 and moved to Cambridge in 1916) and other schools and colleges.

Further Reading

Felton, R. Todd. *A Journey into the Transcendentalists' New England*. Berkeley, Calif.: Roaring Forties Press, 2006.

Carlyle, Thomas (1795–1881) The Scottish writer Thomas Carlyle was a contemporary of the American Transcendentalists and introduced them to many of the German idealist philosophers that would come to define the movement. He produced English-language translations of German works and literary reviews such as "State of German Literature" (1827), "Signs of the Times" (1829), and

"Characteristics" (1831), all of which were read by Ralph Waldo Emerson and other Transcendentalists. Emerson first met Carlyle (they would meet in person three times) and his wife, Jane Welsh Carlyle, while touring England in 1833, and the two began a personal and professional correspondence that would last for decades. It was Emerson who arranged for the publication of American editions of Carlyle's works.

Carlyle's translations and biographies of German idealists such as JOHANN WOLFGANG VON GOETHE and FRIEDRICH VON SCHILLER made available the ideas that formed the core of American Transcendentalist philosophy. Carlyle's own work also greatly influenced Emerson's view of the interconnectedness of all things in the universe and of the individual mind as the source of all knowledge. When Carlyle sent Emerson a copy of his book *The French Revolution* in 1836, Emerson replied, "You have broken away from all books, and written a mind." Carlyle's emphasis on the unity of all things in nature was in line with Emerson's developing ideas in his poetry of this period and in his writing of *NATURE,* published in 1836. In *Sartor Resartus* (first published in installments in 1833–34) Carlyle also explained his belief in "harmonious self-development by cultivating the special, not the vague or general capabilities which are innate in us." It is no wonder that Emerson's biographer, Robert D. Richardson, identified Emerson's reading of Carlyle as a clear "call-to-arms of transcendentalism."

Carlyle's biographical studies and his 1841 *On Heroes, Hero-Worship and the Heroic in History* not only inspired Emerson by example, but also Carlyle personally urged Emerson to "take an American hero, one whom you really love, and give us a history of him." Emerson subsequently prepared a series of lectures on "great men" (although no "American hero" among them) that became the essays in his 1850 collection, *REPRESENTATIVE MEN.* The book was in many ways a response to and argument with Carlyle's *On Heroes,* although their general views of what Emerson called the "USES OF GREAT MEN" were similar. Carlyle wrote that "all things that we see standing accomplished in the world are properly the outer material result, the practical realization and embodiment, of thoughts that dwelt in the Great Men sent into the world." Thomas Carlyle was one of the "representative" Englishmen Emerson discussed in his 1856 book, *ENGLISH TRAITS.*

Carlyle's reviews of Emerson were mixed. After Emerson sent him a copy of his 1847 *POEMS,* Carlyle responded that he found in his friend's poetry "a real satisfaction and some tone of the Eternal Melodies sounding, afar off, ever and anon, in my ear!" He continued, with somewhat reserved but playful praise of Emerson's overall project: "A grand View of the Universe, everywhere the sound (unhappily *faroff* as it were) of a valiant, genuine Human Soul: this, even under rhyme, is a satisfaction worth struggling for . . . I wish you would become *concrete,* and write in prose the straightest way; but under any form I must put up with you; that is my lot." In the end, Carlyle praised Emerson for breaking from the "dreadful incubus of *Tradition.*" Carlyle heaped clearer praise on Emerson's 1870 book, *SOCIETY AND SOLITUDE,* considering it a work of "such brevity, simplicity, softness, homely grace; with such penetrating meaning . . . as *silent electricity* goes."

His contemporary JAMES FREEMAN CLARKE, himself a scholar of the German philosophers, later reflected that Carlyle provided for his generation "new and profound views of familiar truths, which seemed to open a vista for endless reflection." And one of the earliest historians of the movement, OCTAVIUS BROOKS FROTHINGHAM, wrote in 1876 that "Carlyle was the high priest of the new philosophy" of Transcendentalism.

Further Reading

Allen, Gay Wilson. *Waldo Emerson.* New York: Viking Press, 1981.

Harris, Kenneth Marc. *Carlyle and Emerson: Their Long Debate.* Cambridge, Mass.: Harvard University Press, 1978.

Weisbuch, Robert. *Atlantic Double-Cross: American Literature and British Influence in the Age of Emerson.* Chicago: University of Chicago Press, 1986.

Channing, Edward Tyrrel (1790–1856) Edward Tyrrel Channing joined the HARVARD COLLEGE faculty as Boylston Professor of Rhetoric and Oratory in 1819, filling a position once held by none other than John Quincy Adams. Channing was a lawyer, a former editor of the *North American Review,* and the younger brother of the influential UNITARIAN minister and Emerson mentor WILLIAM ELLERY CHANNING. As a Harvard professor, Edward Channing had a significant influence on the development of New England literary culture in the 1820s, '30s, and '40s, as among his students were many of the emerging generation of Transcendentalists, including Emerson, JAMES FREEMAN CLARKE, and HENRY DAVID THOREAU, all of whom benefited not only from Channing's oratorical model but also from regular critiques of their writing.

Many of Channing's ideas about the role of American writers and about public speaking were echoed in Emerson's later works. Channing warned his students against "constant association with great writers," encouraging them instead to write freely in their own voice. This may have influenced Emerson's own approach to "great writers" and other "great men," which was not to copy their ideas but to understand men of conviction who spoke to their own times. Channing's lecture "The Orator and His Times" connected great speakers to their own times and urging not emulation but originality in new American voices. These ideas certainly inspired not only Emerson's own call to "The AMERICAN SCHOLAR" (and Channing was present as the address was delivered in August 1837) but also Emerson's later essays in *REPRESENTATIVE MEN* (1850), including the introductory piece "USES OF GREAT MEN." Channing's words and influence were also reflected in Emerson's own quest as an American writer and thinker and in the public speaker he would become.

Further Reading

Howe, Daniel Walker. *The Unitarian Conscience: Harvard Moral Philosophy, 1805–1861.* Cambridge, Mass.: Harvard University Press, 1970.

Channing, William Ellery (1780–1842) The Reverend William Ellery Channing was the greatly admired theologian of UNITARIANISM in the early 19th century. Upon his death, Emerson called him "the star of the American church." Although Channing himself never associated with Transcendentalism, in his various essays and sermons he in fact articulated what would become core Transcendentalist concepts such as self-culture, humanistic religion, and individual reform, leading some scholars to identify him as a "pre-Transcendentalist." His younger brother, EDWARD TYRREL CHANNING, was the HARVARD COLLEGE professor of rhetoric when Emerson attended, but William Ellery Channing had an even more profound influence on Emerson and on the development of Transcendentalism as a minister, writer, and reformer.

Channing became minister of the Federal Street Church in BOSTON in 1803, but it was his 1819 sermon preached in Baltimore, "Unitarian Christianity," that established him as the leader of a new kind of rational, practical, and socially concerned Unitarianism in the United States. In his sermons and writings, Channing emphasized a highly individualized and rational approach to spirituality and morality. He taught that the Bible's "meaning is to be sought in the same manner as that of other books." In his 1821 sermon, "Evidences of Revealed Religion," however, Channing defined the limits of that rationalism by retaining a belief in Jesus's miracles as supernatural events, a belief Emerson would ultimately reject.

Channing's 1828 sermon, "Likeness to God," argued that the goal of human spiritual life is to become more godlike, to become "a bright image of God," and in "Self Culture" (1838) he explained that self-knowledge was the route to spiritual growth as well as social and cultural reform. All of these ideas were combined in Emerson's radical appreciation of the divinity of man (and more grounded assessment of the humanity of Christ) in his 1838 "DIVINITY SCHOOL ADDRESS" and in "SELF-RELIANCE" of 1841.

Channing was also an early voice against slavery in the United States, and his particular emphasis on individual moral reform and on Christ as a model of human behavior influenced Emerson's approach to the issue. Channing's main work on the topic was his essay *Slavery* (1835). Channing's explanation that slavery prevents the full development of the individual slaves as human beings became the primary argument of many Transcendentalists, including Emerson. It was not only on issues of reform and human rights that Channing moved beyond the pulpit, as he also published literary criticism and reviews. His 1830 essay "The Importance and Means of a National Literature" was a precursor to Emerson's call in "THE AMERICAN SCHOLAR" (1837). By the mid-1830s Emerson had cut his ties with the Unitarian Church and with Harvard, yet Channing's influence would continue to echo in Emerson's humanistic emphasis on reform and on the spiritual rewards of self-education.

Further Reading

Delbanco, Andrew. *William Ellery Channing: An Essay on the Liberal Spirit in America.* Cambridge, Mass.: Harvard University Press, 1981.

Howe, Daniel Walker. *The Unitarian Conscience: Harvard Moral Philosophy, 1805–1861.* Cambridge, Mass.: Harvard University Press, 1970.

Channing, (William) Ellery (1817–1901) William Ellery Channing, the younger (known by the name "Ellery"), was the nephew of the UNITARIAN minister WILLIAM ELLERY CHANNING, who influenced the spiritual, political, and literary style of Ralph Waldo Emerson. Ellery Channing's other uncles included the American romantic landscape artist Washington Allston and the HARVARD COLLEGE professor of rhetoric and oratory EDWARD TYRREL CHANNING. Ellery Channing eventually married MARGARET FULLER's sister, Ellen, and the couple settled in CONCORD, MASSACHUSETTS, where Channing befriended many within the Transcendentalist circle, including Emerson and HENRY DAVID THOREAU.

Ellery Channing was a poet and was among the group of young writers whose talent Emerson sought to encourage and develop in the 1840s. Emerson profiled Channing's work in an 1840 essay on "New Poetry" in the Transcendentalist literary journal the DIAL. As editors of the *Dial,* both Emerson and Fuller regularly published Channing's poems in the journal between 1841 and 1844. Channing also had one essay, "The Youth of the Poet and Painter," published in the *Dial* and went on to produce seven books of poetry between 1843 and 1888. In his role as mentor, Emerson helped negotiate the publication of at least one of Channing's books, and his 1871 collection, *The Wanderer,* included an introduction by Emerson. After Channing's death, his friend, editor and literary journalist FRANKLIN BENJAMIN SANBORN, published a comprehensive collection of Channing's *Poems of Sixty-Five Years* (1902).

Despite his prolific publication record, Ellery Channing has never received critical notice as a significant Transcendentalist poet. He was characterized by one contemporary critic as "a feeble and diluted copy of Emerson," and even Emerson, who admittedly saw most writers as works in progress, remarked that Channing's "rhymes" were only "very nearly poetry."

Ellery Channing was especially close friends with Henry David Thoreau and is best remembered as an editor and biographer of Thoreau. Channing accompanied Thoreau on several wilderness expeditions and walking tours and is often assumed to be responsible for suggesting the idea to Thoreau that he build a cabin at Walden Pond; in return, Channing is the anonymous "Poet" referred to in Thoreau's resulting book, *Walden* (1854). After Thoreau's death, Channing worked with Sophia Thoreau to assemble and edit her brother's journals and notes for the posthumous publications, *Cape Cod* (1865) and *A Yankee in Canada* (1866). Channing also published several articles and, ultimately, a biography, *Thoreau, The Poet-Naturalist* (1873), which includes some of Channing's own poetry or "Memorial Verses" in honor of Thoreau. Other personal memories of Thoreau were published as a series of "Reminiscences of Thoreau" in the *Boston Commonwealth* magazine beginning in 1862 and "Days and Nights in Concord" in *Scribner's Monthly* in 1878.

Further Reading

Hudspeth, Robert N. *Ellery Channing.* New York: Twayne, 1973.

Myerson, Joel. *The New England Transcendentalists and the Dial: A History of the Magazine and Its Contributors.* London and Toronto: Associated University Presses, 1980.

Channing, William Henry (1810–1884) The transcendentalist reformer, editor, and UNITARIAN minister William Henry Channing (known by the name "Henry") was the nephew of Emerson's mentor, the Reverend WILLIAM ELLERY CHANNING. Henry Channing was also the nephew of the reformer-abolitionist THOMAS WENTWORTH HIGGINSON. Like Emerson, Channing was a graduate of HARVARD COLLEGE Divinity School and, at LIDIAN JACKSON EMERSON's request, was called upon to christen some of the Emerson children. Channing held a post as a minister in Cincinnati, Ohio, for several years but eventually returned to BOSTON. Channing later spent time as a minister in England and, during the Civil War, served as chaplain of the House of Representatives in the U.S. Congress.

In Ohio, Henry Channing was coeditor with JAMES FREEMAN CLARKE of the early Transcendentalist journal the *WESTERN MESSENGER*; after that paper ended in 1841 he contributed essays to the Boston-based *DIAL*, edited by Emerson and MARGARET FULLER. Channing was an active social reformer, participating in ABOLITIONISM and UTOPIAN reform, and particularly visible in the women's rights movement of the 1840s and 1850s. He was the subject of Emerson's 1847 poem "ODE, INSCRIBED TO W. H. CHANNING," which provides a contrast between the two men's approaches to reform and antislavery by explaining Emerson's reluctance to join Channing in public reform activities and organizations. In his journal Emerson referred to Channing as one of "the young people" who felt "that the vice of the age is to exaggerate individualism" and who sought instead to "rewrite institutions" and build a new human community.

Channing never joined the community at BROOK FARM that attracted so many among the Transcendentalists, but he was actively involved in the experiment. He was particularly interested in the utopian socialist ideas of French thinker Charles FOURIER and edited the New York–based Fourierist journal the *Present*. In 1847, Channing founded the Boston Religious Union of Associationists, and he later edited another utopian reform paper, *Spirit of the Age*.

Perhaps Henry Channing's greatest Transcendentalist legacy is the publication of biographical studies of two other major Transcendentalist figures with whom he was particularly close. He published the three-volume *Memoir of William Ellery Channing* (1848), and he coedited with James Freeman Clarke and Ralph Waldo Emerson the two-volume *MEMOIRS OF MARGARET FULLER OSSOLI* (1852). It was Henry Channing who accompanied HENRY DAVID THOREAU to the site of the shipwreck where Fuller had died in the summer of 1850. In his section of *Memoirs*, Channing included information and interviews about the shipwreck and about Fuller's and her family's last days on board the ship. Another Transcendentalist colleague, OCTAVIUS BROOKS FROTHINGHAM, in turn published *Memoirs of William Henry Channing* in 1886.

Further Reading

Habich, Robert. *Transcendentalism and the Western Messenger: A History of the Magazine and Its Contributors, 1835–1841*. London and Cranbury, N.J.: Associated University Presses, 1985.

Myerson, Joel. *The New England Transcendentalists and the Dial: A History of the Magazine and Its Contributors*. London and Toronto: Associated University Presses, 1980.

Clarke, James Freeman (1810–1888) The UNITARIAN minister, writer, and editor James Freeman Clarke was one of the central figures in the early Transcendentalist movement of the 1830s and 1840s. Like Emerson, Clarke was a graduate of HARVARD COLLEGE and was influenced in his formative years by European thinkers such as THOMAS CARLYLE, SAMUEL TAYLOR COLERIDGE, JOHANN WOLFGANG VON GOETHE, and IMMANUEL KANT. Upon reading these works, Clarke later explained in his *Autobiography*, he "discovered that I was born a transcendentalist."

Clarke was one of the founding members of the TRANSCENDENTAL CLUB, which began in 1836 and was regularly attended by Clarke, Emerson, BRONSON ALCOTT, GEORGE RIPLEY, CONVERS FRANCIS, ORESTES BROWNSON, and others. Another club, the Aesthetic Club, drew on the same circle for members and met at Clarke's home. In 1835 he founded the *WESTERN MESSENGER*, a magazine that predated the BOSTON-based *DIAL* by several years and was thus the first Transcendentalist journal. The *Western Messenger* was a forum for liberal UNITARIANISM and included items related to literature, philosophy, and social reform, including ABOLITIONISM. Clarke personally invited Emerson to submit writings, and many of Emerson's earliest poems were published in the *Western Messenger.*

James Freeman Clarke was one of Emerson's personal friends who attended the "DIVINITY SCHOOL ADDRESS" in the summer of 1838. Unlike Emerson, Clarke did not reject organized religion in favor of Transcendentalism, but he defended both Emerson and, later, THEODORE PARKER against critics of their challenges to Christianity. Clarke spent most of his career as minister of the liberal Church of the Disciples, which he founded in Boston in 1841, and was a Christian Transcendentalist who, in his later years, promoted the idea of a "universal religion." Among his most well-known works are the two-volume *Ten Great Religions: An Essay in Comparative Theology* (1871, 1883) and *Events and Epochs in Religious History* (1881). Beginning in the 1870s he taught the first courses in comparative religious studies at Harvard Divinity School.

Clarke was an especially close friend of MARGARET FULLER (who was, in fact, a distant cousin), who also befriended his sister, artist Sarah Freeman Clarke. James Freeman Clarke and Fuller studied and translated German writers together; they were among the few people in America at that time reading Goethe in the original German. It was Clarke who ultimately urged Emerson in the study of German theology and spiritualism. In addition to his own poems, translations, sermons, and other published works, Clarke also was coauthor with Emerson and WILLIAM HENRY CHANNING of the MEMOIRS OF MARGARET FULLER OSSOLI (1852), after Fuller's untimely death in 1850. Many years later, in 1882, Clarke delivered Emerson's funeral address.

Further Reading

Habich, Robert. *Transcendentalism and the Western Messenger: A History of the Magazine and Its Contributors, 1835–1841.* London and Cranbury, N.J.: Associated University Presses, 1985.

Coleridge, Samuel Taylor (1772–1834) The English writer and poet Samuel Taylor Coleridge was one of the most important contemporary influences on Emerson and the American Transcendentalists. Along with his friend, WILLIAM WORDSWORTH, Coleridge was one of the founders of the English romantic movement. His most famous poems were *The Rime of the Ancient Mariner* (1798) and *Kubla Khan* (1816). Coleridge's poetry of nature and his use of simple language to convey spiritual truths influenced a generation of poets, including Emerson. Coleridge was responsible, along with THOMAS CARLYLE and FREDERIC HENRY HEDGE, for introducing the ideas of German thinkers such as FRIEDRICH SCHELLING and IMMANUEL KANT to the English-speaking world. Coleridge's book, *Aids to Reflection,* was published in the United States in 1829 with an extensive introduction by James Marsh. Emerson read Marsh's edition as well as Hedge's 1833 review of "Coleridge's Literary Character" in the *Christian Examiner;* Emerson praised Hedge's articles on Coleridge as "the best pieces that have appeared in the Examiner." Many contemporaries as well as later scholars traced the origins of the American Transcendentalist movement to Hedge's 1833 review, the very appearance of which was evidence already of the interest in romanticism and idealism among New England intellectuals.

The *Christian Examiner* followed up on Hedge's articles with a series on Coleridge and other idealist philosophers such as Kant, Schelling, Johann Gottlieb Fichte, and EMANUEL SWEDENBORG, all of whom would greatly influence Emerson in the development of his own philosophy of the relationship of the individual mind to nature. Coleridge's introduction of Kant and these other thinkers opened the way to the Transcendentalist critique of the rationalist empiricism of JOHN LOCKE and other ENLIGHTENMENT thinkers. Transcendentalism emphasized instead the supremacy of subjective experience, utilizing from Coleridge the idea that while the physical senses could be appreciated through "Understanding," or something outside of ourselves, there was another spiritual or mental dimension of "Reason," or intuition. In Coleridge's use of the term, "Reason" was not seen as logic or rationality but as a fixed but subjective consciousness, always within us. As Emerson explained it in his great essay on subjectivity, "EXPERIENCE"

(1844), while life seems chaotic and random, there "is that in us which changes not" and that is "the consciousness in each man." This belief in the power of intuition, of the subjective self, as the source of knowledge, of morality, of spirituality, was the very foundation of Emerson's Transcendentalist philosophy. As Emerson said of the inspiration he found in Coleridge, "What a living soul, what a universal knowledge."

Emerson met Coleridge in England in 1833 and was somewhat disappointed to find the aging thinker more interested in debating the relative merits of UNITARIANISM (which Emerson had recently renounced) and of WILLIAM ELLERY CHANNING than of philosophical ideas. Emerson continued to read Coleridge, however. In 1835 he was reading Coleridge's *Biographia Literaria,* in which Emerson would find confirmation for the Transcendentalist tenet to "know thyself" as the foundation of literary and moral culture. Other Transcendentalists would continue to acknowledge the influence of Coleridge on American philosophy of the 19th century. In his 1876 history of the movement, *Transcendentalism in New England,* OCTAVIUS BROOKS FROTHINGHAM concluded that "the prophet of the new philosophy in England was Samuel Taylor Coleridge; in the early part of the present century, perhaps the most conspicuous figure in our literary world."

Further Reading

Richardson, Robert D. *Emerson: The Mind on Fire.* Berkeley: University of California, 1995.

Concord Lyceum Integral to understanding American Transcendentalism are the reforms that swept the nation in response to the depredations of the Industrial Revolution. Major among them was the lyceum movement, which democratically hoped to educate all Americans, but especially those who worked in factories or labored on farms. The Transcendentalists locked into this concept early because of its importance to self-culture and to the idea that an individual's development of the intellect brings a closer understanding of the universe. Therefore, many Transcendentalists spoke in public halls and private parlors lecturing on current topics and their philosophy. Perhaps the best known of the lecturers is Ralph Waldo Emerson, who offered his wisdom across the nation and in England. However, nowhere was he more associated with the lyceum, a term for a place of learning and discussion, than in CONCORD, MASSACHUSETTS.

The Concord Lyceum was founded and privately managed by Rev. EZRA RIPLEY, Emerson's step-grandfather, and others in 1828. Although Emerson saw Ripley as old-fashioned and the last of the old order, he agreed with the younger UNITARIAN ministers who emphasized self-culture as the discovery of God's voice within the individual that could be promoted through education and higher thinking. Meetings were initially held in the hall over the Concord Academy and were well attended. Lecturers were paid for their expenses, including stage fare for those from BOSTON, and given room and board while in town. Many of the speakers were from Concord or neighboring towns and, therefore, spoke gratuitously.

Emerson was not only a member of the Concord Lyceum but also an enthusiastic supporter of the idea. He was often available at the last minute to replace speakers and to preview his new essays or present old ones for discussion. His fame and ease as a lecturer and educator allowed Emerson to make a career of public speaking. Inspired by Transcendentalism and stimulated by education and discussion, the Lyceum was active for 50 years and persists, through various incarnations, today. In an address celebrating the 50th anniversary of the Concord Lyceum in 1879, Judge Ebenezer Rockwood Hoar attributed the success of the Concord Lyceum to its townspeople and its strong community spirit. He also praised those Transcendentalists who had spoken to the Lyceum audiences, including HENRY DAVID THOREAU who had given 19 lectures. However, his greatest honors went to Emerson, whom he described as "the education of the town" and the voice of his generation. Ralph Waldo Emerson gave his 100th lecture at the Concord Lyceum in February 1880.

Further Reading

Jarvis, Edward. *Traditions and Reminiscences of Concord, Massachusetts 1779–1878,* edited by Sarah Chapin. Amherst: University of Massachusetts Press, 1993.

Wilson, Leslie Perrin. *In History's Embrace: Past and Present in Concord, Massachusetts.* Hollis, N.H.: Hollis Publishing, 2007.

Barbara Downs Wojtusik

Concord, Massachusetts Concord, Massachusetts, was founded by Peter Bulkeley, a paternal ancestor of Ralph Waldo Emerson. Bulkeley was expelled from his ministerial duties in Odell, Bedfordshire, England, because of his nonconformist Puritan preaching. In 1635, when he arrived in the New World, Bulkeley purchased land from the Musketaquid tribe and founded Concord as the first inland Puritan settlement in America. A church was established in 1636, and Bulkeley became its first minister, a position he maintained for 22 years. During his tenure, he became most notable for presiding over the heresy trial of Anne Hutchinson. Bulkeley's daughter Elizabeth married Reverend Joseph Emerson—hence, the legacy of Emerson ministers began.

Peter Bulkeley's great-grandson, William Emerson (grandfather of Ralph Waldo Emerson), was minister of the First Parish Church of Concord at the onset of the American Revolution. He was an ardent Patriot, although his wife, Phebe Bliss, whose father had been Emerson's predecessor, was from a Tory family whose two brothers fled Concord for BOSTON and later Canada to become officers in the British army. William Emerson, however, was appointed chaplain of the Minutemen, the rebel militia, by the Massachusetts Provincial Congress. Prior to the war, Reverend Emerson had built the OLD MANSE, overlooking the North Bridge, as a home for his family. Although he is said to have watched the battle at the bridge from the Manse, local accounts state that William Emerson was the first Concordian to respond and to muster in the village center. Reverend Emerson accompanied the Minutemen into battle as their spiritual leader and died soon after from dysentery. Upon the death of Rev. William Emerson, the people of Concord hired EZRA RIPLEY as their minister. Ripley later married his predecessor's widow and lived in the Manse for many years.

Ralph Waldo Emerson's father, also named WILLIAM EMERSON, was born at the Old Manse, and

Daniel Chester French's 1914 statue of Emerson, displayed in the Concord Free Public Library. A few years later, French would complete his most famous marble statue, the Lincoln Memorial in Washington, D.C. *(Concord Free Public Library)*

the young Waldo Emerson often stayed there with his grandmother and his step-grandfather, especially after his father's death. Rev. Ezra Ripley took pride in teaching the young Emerson Concord history and the family's place in it, and in introducing Waldo to the wonders of nature. In 1834, after the death of both his first wife, Ellen Tucker Emerson, and his brother EDWARD BLISS EMERSON, Ralph Waldo Emerson and his mother, RUTH HASKINS EMERSON, moved into the Old Manse. Emerson had recently given up the ministry and had begun a new career as lecturer. At the Old Manse he was able to complete *NATURE* (1836), the founding book of Transcendentalism. In 1835 Emerson established himself as a permanent Concordian when he brought his second wife, Lydia Jackson (LIDIAN JACKSON EMERSON) of Plymouth, to Concord and purchased the "Bush" home on the Cambridge Turnpike. That same year Emerson gave the keynote speech at the bicentennial celebration of the town of Concord.

In 1837 the people of Concord requested that Emerson write a poem for the dedication of the Battle Monument near the North Bridge, and Emerson complied with the "CONCORD HYMN." As a citizen of Concord, Emerson taught Sunday school, became a member of the school and library committees, attended town meetings, and spoke often at the CONCORD LYCEUM. A Transcendentalist literary community soon converged around Emerson in Concord, including native Concordian HENRY DAVID THOREAU, AMOS BRONSON ALCOTT and family (including daughter LOUISA MAY ALCOTT), and NATHANIEL HAWTHORNE and his wife, SOPHIA PEABODY HAWTHORNE.

In 1872 a fire threatened to destroy the Emerson home and its contents. The people of Concord rallied and successfully rescued Emerson's books and papers from the burning home. As the house was unlivable, members of the community took in the family and raised money to send Emerson and his daughter ELLEN EMERSON on an extended trip abroad while the home was being restored. Upon their return to Concord, Emerson and his daughter were surprised by a cheering crowd, schoolchildren, local dignitaries, and ringing bells, and a band playing "Home Sweet Home." Throughout the rest of his life, when his literary fame brought a steady stream of visitors to Concord, the townspeople of Concord vigorously protected Emerson's privacy and his dignity. Upon his death in 1882 Emerson was interred among his fellow Concordians in Sleepy Hollow Cemetery, which had often been a favorite picnic spot of the Transcendentalists. In 1855 the land had been converted into a garden cemetery while still maintaining the natural contour of the land and its native plants and trees and, in fact, Emerson gave an address at the park's dedication. Thus, Emerson remains in Concord in an area that reflects the Transcendentalist tenet of nature as tranquillity and a home for the soul.

Further Reading

Gross, Robert A. *The Minutemen and Their World.* New York: Hill and Wang, 1976.

Wilson, Leslie Perrin. *In History's Embrace: Past and Present in Concord, Massachusetts.* Hollis, N.H.: Hollis Publishing, 2007.

Barbara Downs Wojtusik

Concord School of Philosophy and Literature

The Concord School of Philosophy and Literature was a summer program of lectures and conversations held between 1879 and 1888 in CONCORD, MASSACHUSETTS. The Concord School was organized by the reformer AMOS BRONSON ALCOTT and met in a building known as the Hillside Chapel next door to the Alcotts' family home Orchard House. Alcott was assisted in establishing the school primarily by his St. Louis friend and America's premier Hegelian philosopher, William Torrey Harris; in addition, FRANKLIN BENJAMIN SANBORN served as secretary. The Concord School became a meeting place for late-century Transcendentalists, and its speakers included a who's who of both first- and second-generation Transcendentalists. In addition to Alcott and Sanborn, other lecturers included CYRUS BARTOL, WILLIAM HENRY CHANNING, Ednah Dow Cheney, Ralph Waldo Emerson, FREDERIC HENRY HEDGE, THOMAS WENTWORTH HIGGINSON, Julia Ward Howe, ELIZABETH PALMER PEABODY, and David Wasson, as well as many other prominent American intellectuals, including visiting lecturers from several universities, such as HARVARD COLLEGE's Benjamin Peirce (father of Pragmatist CHARLES SANDERS PEIRCE).

Three volumes of Concord School lectures were published. The first was collected by a journalist, Raymond Bridgman, who had attended and reported on the school; his volume, *Concord Lectures on Philosophy: Comprising Outlines of All the Lectures at the Concord Summer School of Philosophy in 1882,* was published in 1883. This volume includes several of the commemorative lectures given on Emerson at the first meeting after his death in May 1882; but in 1884 a complete session was devoted to Emerson, the lectures for which were collected by Sanborn as *The Genius and Character of Emerson,* published in 1885. The Emerson volume includes a complete listing of lectures given in the first six years of the school's existence, from 1879 to 1884. Emerson is listed in the "Second Year's Programme" (that would be 1880) as giving the lecture "Aristocracy." The third volume of lectures from the school is from the 1885 summer series dedicated to the ideas of JOHANN WOLFGANG VON GOETHE; this volume, also edited by Sanborn, was published in 1886 as *The Life and Genius of Goethe.*

The founders and organizers made it clear there was no specific school of thought to be presented at the meetings, but the intention was only to provide an alternative forum for the best American minds and ideas. The introduction to Bridgman's *Concord Lectures on Philosophy,* however, noted that "the lecturers generally agree in an utter repudiation of materialism and in maintaining the existence of a personal, self-conscious, spiritual cause above the material universe." Still, "each lecturer is responsible for his opinions only." In other words, the school was infused with the still-lingering spirit of Emersonian Transcendentalism. In the face of new scientific approaches to knowledge and ideas in the late 19th century (a newspaper report on the school's proceeding noted a discussion on "the influence of Mill, Spencer, and Darwin"), participants at the Concord School believed in the continued relevance of intuition and "self culture," in "the supremacy of mind." This was exemplified in their numerous lectures on PLATONISM and on the German idealists IMMANUEL KANT, FRIEDRICH SCHELLING, ARTHUR SCHOPENHAUER, and, most notably, on Goethe. Other lecture titles (besides the entire session devoted to Goethe) that indicate the philosophical commitments of the group include "Philosophy of the Bhagavad Ghita" (by William Torrey Harris), "Hebrew, Greek, Persian and Christian Oracles" (by Franklin Benjamin Sanborn), and a lecture on "Nature" (by Ednah Dow Cheney, and which makes reference to writings in the *DIAL* some 40 years earlier).

The Concord School ceased to meet after the death of founder Bronson Alcott in 1888.

Further Reading

Dahlstrand, Frederick. *Amos Bronson Alcott: An Intellectual Biography.* East Brunswick, N.J.: Associated University Press, 1982.

Wayne, Tiffany K. *Woman Thinking: Feminism and Transcendentalism in 19th-Century America.* Lanham, Md.: Lexington Books, 2005. (*See* chapter 5, "The Concord School of Philosophy and the Feminization of Transcendentalism after the Civil War.")

Cousin, Victor (1782–1867) The French philosopher Victor Cousin was a contemporary of Ralph Waldo Emerson, and it was primarily through Cousin that the American Transcendentalists were introduced to German idealist philosophers such as IMMANUEL KANT. Emerson was most interested in Cousin's eclecticism and approach to the history of philosophy. He read Cousin's *Cours de l'histoire de la philosophie* in 1831, in which Cousin identified four distinct "systems" of philosophy: sensationism, idealism, scepticism, and mysticism. These were also phases within the history or development of ideas, and it was Cousin who sparked Emerson's interest in Indian philosophy, in particular the Bhagavad Gita, as representative of mystical philosophy.

As the Emerson biographer Robert D. Richardson notes, Emerson had previously considered Indian spirituality as "superstition," but after reading Victor Cousin, Emerson began to see "the Bhagavad Gita as a scripture of equal standing with the Gospels." Cousin explained the Hindu belief that "a perpetual and eternal energy has created all which you see and renews it without cessation," an idea that greatly influenced Emerson's concept of "THE OVER-SOUL" and found expression directly in poems such as "BRAHMA." From Cousin, Emerson also adapted an approach to the history of ideas through a study of "great men." Cousin looked to individuals as "representations of nations, epochs, of humanity, of nature, and of universal order." This became Emerson's project in his 1850 collection of essays, *REPRESENTATIVE MEN.*

Other Transcendentalists also read Cousin, and GEORGE RIPLEY, for example, translated Cousin's writings for his *Philosophical Miscellanies from the French of Cousin, Jouffroy, and Benjamin Constant*

(1838). Ripley's project, as well as Emerson's, and indeed Transcendentalism in general, was modeled in many ways on Cousin's eclectic or synthetic approach to philosophy, on taking the best of each tradition and on finding new uses for old ideas.

Further Reading

Leighton, Walter L. *French Philosophers and New England Transcendentalism.* New York: Greenwood Press, 1968.

Richardson, Robert D., Jr. *Emerson: The Mind on Fire.* Berkeley: University of California Press, 1995.

Cranch, Christopher Pearse (1813–1892) Christopher Pearse Cranch was a UNITARIAN minister, artist, and one of the few Transcendentalist poets. As a sometime writer and editor of the movement's first journal, the *WESTERN MESSENGER,* Cranch (and coeditor JAMES FREEMAN CLARKE) helped spread the ideas of Ralph Waldo Emerson and New England Transcendentalism into Kentucky and later, Ohio, where the paper was published. Cranch eventually returned to Massachusetts and attended meetings of the TRANSCENDENTAL CLUB (founded in 1836) and published several of his poems in the BOSTON-based *DIAL* magazine, edited by Emerson and MARGARET FULLER. Cranch was a supporter of and visitor to the UTOPIAN community at BROOK FARM, and his writings also appeared in the community's newspaper, the *Harbinger.* Cranch was among those friends and supporters who publicly defended Emerson in the wake of controversy after the "DIVINITY SCHOOL ADDRESS" (1838), and Cranch's first published collection of *Poems* (1844) was dedicated to Emerson. In addition to an 1841 essay on "Transcendentalism" for the *Western Messenger,* Cranch wrote two later essays on Emerson: "Ralph Waldo Emerson" (*Unitarian Review,* 1883) and "Emerson's Limitations as a Poet" (New York *Critic,* 1892).

Cranch was perhaps best-known, however, for his caricatures of Emerson's friend's Transcendentalist writings. Cranch's most famous drawing shows Emerson as a walking or "transparent eyeball," taken from a line in *NATURE* (1836): "Standing on the bare ground,-my head bathed by the blithe air, & uplifted into infinite space,-all mean egotism vanishes. I become a transparent Eyeball." Other Cranch drawings spoofed the Transcendentalist emphasis on humanity's relationship to nature, portraying vegetables and plants with human faces, and the appeal of idealist philosophizing over actual work, such as a caricature featuring a reader of the *Dial* dreamily lounging while a woman serves him refreshments, accompanied by a verse from CAROLINE STURGIS TAPPAN's poem "Life" (published in the *Dial* of October 1840): "Why for work art thou striving, / Why seek'st thou for aught? / To the soul that is living / All things shall be brought."

Most of Cranch's drawings were done only for private amusement and shared with friends among the Transcendentalist circle, but a collection was finally published in the 1950s. His most significant collection of poetry was *The Bird and the Bell,* published in 1875. Cranch also authored and illustrated several children's fantasy books, including *The Last of the Huggermuggers* (1856) and *Kobboltozo* (1857), which have been recently reprinted.

Further Reading

Cranch, Leonora Scott, ed. *The Life and Letters of Christopher Pearse Cranch, by His Daughter Leonora Scott Cranch.* Reprint, New York: AMS Press, 1969.

Miller, DeWolfe F. *Christopher Pearse Cranch and His Caricatures of New England Transcendentalism.* Cambridge, Mass.: Harvard University Press, 1951.

Curtis, George William (1824–1892) George William Curtis, born in Providence, Rhode Island, was a prominent author, editor, and lecturer. He first became popular at mid-century by penning a string of breezy, light-hearted travel books and novels, among them *Nile Notes of a Howadji* (1851), *Lotus-Eating: A Summer Book* (1852), *Potiphar Papers* (1853), and *Prue and I* (1856). In the 1860s he was an editor for *Harper's Monthly* and *Harper's Weekly,* contributing columns that were widely read and very influential in the forming of public opinion. He became increasingly passionate, in these columns, about social and political reform. In 1871 President Ulysses S. Grant appointed him as chair of a commission to report on civil service reform; later, he served as president of the National Civil Service Reform League and of the New York Civil Service Reform Association. Near the end of his life, Curtis was also one of the founders of the New York City Board of Education and a regent of the State University of New York.

As a young man, Curtis was heavily influenced by Ralph Waldo Emerson and Transcendentalism. After reading Emerson's works and hearing him lecture in Providence, Curtis (along with his older brother Burrill) joined the UTOPIAN community at BROOK FARM, just outside of BOSTON. The brothers were not actual members of the community, but they attended the school there in hopes of being close to Emerson, GEORGE RIPLEY, and other leaders of the Transcendentalist movement, and in hopes of realizing Emerson's call for an education that was more closely tied to nature. Curtis eventually left Brook Farm in 1844, after a two-year stay, because he disagreed with the FOURIERIST direction that the community was taking; but for another two years, he and Burrill boarded with farmers in CONCORD in order to be near Emerson. George Curtis emerged as one of Emerson's youngest and most avid disciples in the 1840s, and published a poem in the *DIAL* (July 1843) under Emerson's editorship.

According to early biographer John Chadwick, Emerson's influence on Curtis was "more practical than speculative. The doctrine of the Oversoul might be so high that he could not attain to it; but the summons to simplicity, to sincerity, to independence, to a preference for the light within his own clear breast to any other, however vaunted as from heaven, was perfectly comprehensible—easily understood, if not as easily obeyed." Curtis never forgot Emerson's lessons about self-reliance, independence, and the positive impact that a single individual can have on society. These ideas appear again and again in Curtis's later writings, and his commitment to these ideals led to his work in the fight against slavery and in instituting civil service reform.

Although he acquired (in Chadwick's words) "a frank distaste" for "what was merely peculiar and eccentric in the Transcendentalist Movement," Curtis remained a lifelong Emerson devotee, and he had much to do with the good press that Emerson received in his troubled later years. In 1880, for instance, Curtis wrote in the *Literary World:* "Those who have felt throughout their lives the purifying and elevating and liberalizing power, and who have seen in his inspiring career the perfect sanity of true genius, can never think without affectionate reverence of Ralph Waldo Emerson." As early as the 1850s Curtis had published brief anecdotal pieces on both Emerson and NATHANIEL HAWTHORNE, biographies that were reprinted separately in 1896.

Further Reading

Chadwick, John White. *George William Curtis.* New York: Harper and Brothers, 1893.

Milne, Gordon. *George William Curtis and the Genteel Tradition.* Bloomington: Indiana University Press, 1956.

Mark Sullivan

Dall, Caroline Wells Healey (1822–1912) The daughter of a UNITARIAN merchant in BOSTON, Caroline Dall first heard both Ralph Waldo Emerson and THEODORE PARKER lecture while she was still a teenager. She became interested in the "new thought" of the emerging Transcendentalist movement and, after befriending ELIZABETH PALMER PEABODY (who, according to Dall, "would dearly love to make a transcendentalist of me—if she could"), attended Conversations with both MARGARET FULLER and BRONSON ALCOTT; she later published her account of Fuller's talks as *Margaret and Her Friends* (1895), which mentions Emerson's participation at such gatherings. In 1841 Dall recorded in her journal reading Emerson's recently published *ESSAYS: FIRST SERIES*. She felt that the essay "on Compensation is the finest thing upon the subject—which I ever read, ditto to that upon History—but the views advanced in that upon self reliance—are extravagant and unsafe."

Despite her early reservations (feeling she had too much "common sense" to become a Transcendentalist), Dall retained close ties to the movement, both socially and philosophically, and, in her later years, described herself as "a Transcendentalist of the Old New England sort." She became one of the movement's first historians with her 1897 text, *Transcendentalism in New England.*

Dall's history paid particular attention to the role and influence of women within the movement. She herself had been inspired by Transcendentalism's call for self-development and maintained, through the end of the century, that the "Transcendental movement" was defined by "its agitation for the rights of woman and the enlargement of her duties." Dall was active in the women's rights cause for several decades, beginning as coeditor of the *Una,* which became a forum for an explicitly Transcendentalist perspective on women's rights and for memorializing Fuller, who died prematurely in July 1850, just three months before the first national women's rights movement meeting, held in Worcester, Massachusetts.

Dall was vice president and speaker at the New England Women's Rights Convention held in Boston in September 1855, an event at which Emerson delivered "WOMAN," his only public address on the topic of women's rights. Dall praised him in her journal, saying Emerson "seemed to lure the Conservatives on over his flowers, till all of a sudden their feet were pierced with the thorns of reform." The following week she wrote to Emerson, thanking him for the speech but admitting that some of the newspaper reports of his lecture made it unclear "whether you were for us or against us." Through the years she continued to attend Emerson's lectures, remarking of an 1858 lecture, "I never enjoyed an hour so much it was full, full to the brim of thought"; she recorded, proudly, that Emerson told her, "you have a great cause & a sure one!" In 1867 Dall published one of the most forceful mid-century feminist treatises, *The College, the Market, and the Court; or, Woman's Relation to Education, Labor, and Law.* The book had a clear Transcendentalist message with its emphasis on women's right to self-culture, or, what she termed, "unrestricted mental culture."

Dall also published widely on topics related to theology and religious reform. She felt that had she been a man, she would have pursued a career as a minister. Many of her most important mentors were male preachers such as her close friends CYRUS BARTOL and Theodore Parker. Dall was well-regarded within Unitarian circles, and her essay, Nazareth, was included along with writings by the Reverend WILLIAM ELLERY CHANNING, JAMES FREEMAN CLARKE, FREDERIC HENRY HEDGE, Parker, and even Emerson's "DIVINITY SCHOOL ADDRESS" in a 1905 collection of "Tracts" available from the American Unitarian Association.

Further Reading

Deese, Helen, ed. *Daughter of Boston: The Extraordinary Diary of a Nineteenth-Century Woman, Caroline Healey Dall.* Boston: Beacon Press, 2005.

Wayne, Tiffany K. *Woman Thinking: Feminism and Transcendentalism in Nineteenth-Century America.* Lanham, Md.: Lexington Books, 2005.

Dial, The (Boston, 1840–1844) The *Dial* was a BOSTON-based literary journal founded by Ralph Waldo Emerson, MARGARET FULLER, BRONSON ALCOTT, and GEORGE RIPLEY in 1840. That year the TRANSCENDENTAL CLUB held its final meeting, and members of the circle were seeking a new forum for their ideas and continued conversations. The first issue of the quarterly magazine was published in July 1840, and the last appeared in April 1844. At its peak the magazine enjoyed 300 subscribers, and it was the most important forum for the writings of the Transcendentalists during this era. The magazine was edited first by Fuller, then Emerson, both of whom were committed to nurturing new talent and voices in essays, poetry, and book reviews. As the editors noted in the inaugural issue, the *Dial* was envisioned as "one cheerful rational voice amidst the din of mourners and polemics." The idea for the *Dial* was modeled on European literary magazines that the Transcendentalists subscribed to and read. There had also already been an American experiment with *WESTERN MESSENGER,* edited by JAMES FREEMAN CLARKE, CHRISTOPHER PEARSE CRANCH, and WILLIAM HENRY CHANNING between 1835 and 1841.

Emerson took over editorship in 1842 and oversaw the last two years of publication (HENRY DAVID THOREAU, who had worked as an editorial assistant for Emerson, was guest editor for one issue in April 1843). Emerson committed almost all of his time to the magazine during these years, soliciting his friends, favorite writers, and protégées as contributors. He reprinted in the *Dial* several of his own lectures, such as "INTRODUCTORY LECTURE ON THE TIMES," "The CONSERVATIVE," "MAN THE REFORMER," and "The TRANSCENDENTALIST," as well as numerous poems, including "SAADI" and "BLIGHT" (nearly half of Emerson's published writing between 1842 and 1844 appears in the pages of the *Dial*; *see* Joel Myerson for complete listing). Emerson also published essays by others on social reform topics (SOPHIA RIPLEY, ELIZABETH PALMER PEABODY, and Bronson Alcott's colleague, CHARLES LANE, all contributed pieces on reform), reports of lectures and conventions attended, and book reviews of both American and European texts. Perhaps his greatest distinction as editor was that Emerson used the *Dial* to promote the cultural work of the poet, including the poems of many young people he had personally selected as the best emerging American voices, including Thoreau, CAROLINE STURGIS TAPPAN, JONES VERY, and many others.

One of the innovations that Emerson brought to the *Dial* was a series he coedited with Thoreau entitled "Ethnical Scriptures," which featured analysis and excerpts of a different religious text in each designated issue. Included in this series were passages from Hindu texts (July 1842 and January 1843), from Confucianism (April 1843), from Persian prophets (July 1843), from the Chinese *Four Books* (October 1843), and from Buddhism (January 1844). Both Emerson and Thoreau had a special interest in Eastern religions and philosophy during this period, as reflected in Emerson's writings and poetry such as "BRAHMA" and "Saadi." As Emerson noted in his introduction to the series in the *Dial*, "Each nation has its bible more or less pure . . . None has yet been willing or able in a wise and devout spirit to collate its own worth with those of other nations, and sinking the civil-historical and the ritual portions, to bring together the grand expressions of the moral sentiment in different ages and races."

The *Dial* was not only Emerson's forum but also included the first publication of some of the most important early Transcendentalist essays. Thoreau's "Natural History of Massachusetts" first appeared in the *Dial* (July 1842), as did Margaret Fuller's "The Great Lawsuit. Man versus Men. Woman versus Women" (July 1843), which Fuller later revised and expanded into the book, *Woman in the Nineteenth Century* (1845). Bronson Alcott became somewhat famous (and caricatured) for his *Dial* contributions in the form of the "Orphic Sayings," poetic utterances of mystical thought.

Emerson ultimately determined that the *Dial*'s "writers were its chief readers" and that the project had become too time-consuming and too expensive to maintain; the magazine was ended in 1844. Inspired by the earlier Transcendentalists, UNITARIAN minister Moncure Conway established a new *Dial* journal in 1860, based in Cincinnati, Ohio.

Further Reading

Myerson, Joel. *The New England Transcendentalists and the Dial: A History of the Magazine and Its Contributors.* London and Toronto: Associated University Presses, 1980.

Richardson, Robert D., Jr. *Emerson: The Mind on Fire.* Berkeley: University of California Press, 1995.

Dickinson, Emily (1830–1886) Although not directly involved with the community, Emily Dickinson is generally associated with Emerson and the Transcendentalist movement of the mid-19th century and engaged in the same philosophical concerns and literary themes such as individualism, romanticism, nature, and experimentation with genre. Dickinson lived in Amherst, Massachusetts, and did not leave her father's house and grounds for 25 years; the Transcendentalists of CONCORD and BOSTON produced no other poets of her caliber or productivity. In assessing her place in literary history, she has been compared to William Shakespeare and is arguably the English language's greatest female poet.

Emerson lectured in Amherst in 1857 and stayed at the home of Emily's brother, Austin Dickinson, who was a leading lawyer and treasurer of Amherst College. Austin Dickinson's property abutted on Emily's father's, and at the reception given for Emerson there, it is likely that Emily was present, though there is no record of a direct encounter with Emerson. At a later time, in 1869, she was invited to attend a reading by Emerson in Boston, to be followed by a meeting with him at a women's club. She never responded to the invitation.

Regardless of whether they ever actually met, there was a close spiritual affinity between Dickinson and Emerson—perhaps almost as close, though differently, as that between Emerson and WALT WHITMAN. Dickinson had a copy of Emerson's *POEMS* (1847), and she explored the dimensions of Transcendentalist subjectivity in her own private and different way. Her poetry is replete with Emersonian themes, such as solitary self-reliance and the immortality of artistic achievement. Poems redolent with Emerson's sense of self-reliant genius include "God made a little Gentian," "On a Columnar Self," "This Consciousness that is aware," "Exhilaration—is within," and "The Heart is the Capitol of the Mind," among many others. "Dare you see a Soul at the White Heat?" is one such example of a personalized variation on Emerson's theme of the interior life of the poetic genius, ". . . the finer Forge / That soundless tugs—within."

Dickinson's "I taste a liquor never brewed" echoes Emerson's "wine which never grew / In the belly of the grape" from his poem "BACCHUS," and her "His oriental heresies / Exhilarate the Bee," "The Bumble Bee's Religion," and "Bees are black, with Gilt Surcingles" inevitably take us back to Emerson's fascination with "The HUMBLE-BEE," a poem to which she alluded three times in her letters.

Many of Dickinson's poems fall into a related Transcendentalist category of self-awareness of her creative power. "I dwell in Possibility———," "The Brain is wider than the Sky," "Beauty crowds me till I die," and "It is a lonesome Glee" are just a sampling of Dickinson poems that have their theoretical correlates in Emerson's prose and poetry. Some of Dickinson's best poems describe an Emersonian sense of affinity with nature's forms, processes, and regenerative powers. The incomparable one in this category is her poem on the hummingbird, "A Route of Evanescence," but others include "I watched the Moon around the House," "My faith is larger than the Hills," "It bloomed a dropt, a Single Noon," and "The most triumphant Bird I ever knew or met," and an infinitely longer list than can be named here. Among Dickinson's greatest poems are "Farther to Summer than the Birds," "Safe in their Alabaster Chambers," "These are the Days the Birds come back," and "I'll tell you how the Sun rose." They blend the various Transcendentalist categories indicated above and are supreme poetic achievements of the romantic sublime also found in Emerson's authoritative prose and original poetry.

The only words of Emerson that Dickinson directly quoted in her letters were "the tumultuous privacy of storm" from his poem "The SNOW-STORM." It is not clear whether, as a superior poet, she considered it one of his best poetic lines or whether she quoted it because it suited her own psychology. Either way, it is clear that Dickinson amplified Emerson's spirit in her own creative *poesis*.

Further Reading

Leiter, Sharon. *Critical Companion to Emily Dickinson.* New York: Facts On File, 2007.

Tufariello, Catherine. "'The Remembering Wine': Emerson's Influence on Whitman and Dickinson." In *The Cambridge Companion to Ralph Waldo Emerson,* edited by Joel Porte and Saundra Morris, 162–191. New York: Cambridge University Press, 1999.

David A. Dilworth

Dwight, John Sullivan (1813–1893) John Sullivan Dwight began his career as a UNITARIAN minister but eventually dedicated himself to reform, music criticism, and writing and editing *Dwight's Journal of Music. A Paper of Art and Literature* for more than 30 years. As a graduate of HARVARD COLLEGE Divinity School, Dwight had connections within Unitarian and Transcendentalist circles before he met Ralph Waldo Emerson. At Harvard Dwight became friends with artist and musician CHRISTOPHER PEARSE CRANCH and reformer and minister THEODORE PARKER. Dwight thus shared many of the theological, literary, and aesthetic values of the Transcendentalist circle. In the 1830s and 1840s, Dwight attended meetings of the TRANSCENDENTAL CLUB, participated in BRONSON

ALCOTT's Conversations, and was a member of the SATURDAY CLUB; through any of these activities he would have come into contact with Emerson.

In 1836, the same year the Transcendental Club was formed and the year Emerson's *NATURE* was published, Dwight published his essay "The Proper Character of Poetry and Music for Public Worship" in the *Christian Examiner* (November 1836). In 1839 he contributed an edition of *Select Minor Poems, Translated from the German of Goethe and Schiller* for GEORGE RIPLEY's multivolume series, *Specimens of Foreign Standard Literature,* which represented the range of intellectual and literary influences on the Transcendentalists. Dwight ultimately published three pieces in the *DIAL* while the paper was edited by MARGARET FULLER: "The Religion of Beauty" (in the inaugural issue of July 1840) and "Ideals of Every-Day Life" (published in two parts, January 1841 and April 1841). Dwight joined the UTOPIAN community at BROOK FARM and lived there for at least three years, entertaining visitors with his music, lecturing on education, and writing essays for the FOURIERIST paper, the *Harbinger.*

In 1852 he founded his own paper, *Dwight's Journal of Music,* which was published until 1881. As one of the earliest and longest-living music appreciation and criticism journals, *Dwight's Journal of Music* provides important insights into music criticism, theory, tastes, and education in 19th-century America—a time when no colleges offered formal music study and music appreciation was still an amateur affair. Dwight's project was also one of connecting music and philosophy by promoting music as a source of beauty and truth, in the same way that the Transcendentalist-romantics looked to art or poetry. This perspective can be seen in the titles of his lectures, such as "Music a Means of Culture" and "The Intellectual Influence of Music," both of which were published in the ATLANTIC MONTHLY in 1870. Emerson paid less attention to music as a separate art form, although he applied his concept of beauty to various forms of artistic expression, including music. In *Nature* (1836), Emerson explained that "the poet, the painter, the sculptor, the musician, the architect, seek each to concentrate this radiance of the world on one point, and each in his several work to satisfy the love of beauty which stimulates him to produce."

Further Reading

Grant, Mark N. *Maestros of the Pen: A History of Classical Music Criticism in America.* Boston: Northeastern University Press, 1998.

Myerson, Joel. *The New England Transcendentalists and the Dial: A History of the Magazine and Its Contributors.* London and Toronto: Associated University Presses, 1980.

Saloman, Ora Frishberg. *Beethoven's Symphonies and J. S. Dwight: The Birth of American Music Criticism.* Boston: Northeastern University Press, 1995.

Emerson, Charles Chauncy (1808–1836) Charles Chauncy Emerson was Ralph Waldo Emerson's youngest brother, the fifth surviving son in the Emerson family, which included WILLIAM EMERSON, Ralph Waldo, EDWARD BLISS EMERSON, ROBERT BULKELEY EMERSON, and Charles; the first-born son, John Clarke, died in early childhood the year before Charles was born. In many ways, Emerson was closest to his youngest brother, Charles, only five years his junior. Their father, Rev. WILLIAM EMERSON, died in 1811, when Waldo was only eight years old, and eldest brother William attended HARVARD COLLEGE and then worked as a schoolteacher to help put Waldo, Edward, and then Charles through school. Charles was valedictorian and gave the graduation speech when he left Harvard, a speech that Emerson reviewed and critiqued for him. Charles enrolled at Harvard Law School and planned to practice law in CONCORD, MASSACHUSETTS.

In 1833 Charles became engaged to ELIZABETH HOAR and, during their engagement, lived briefly with Waldo and LIDIAN JACKSON EMERSON, who planned to build rooms onto their home for Charles and Elizabeth after their marriage. Unfortunately, the couple never married as Charles died from tuberculosis in May 1836 at only 28 years of age. Elizabeth Hoar never married but remained close to the Emerson family and to Ralph Waldo Emerson in particular, who treated her as a sister.

Charles Chauncy Emerson was a favorite of aunt MARY MOODY EMERSON and regularly corresponded with her, as did his older brother. Aunt Mary expected all of the Emerson boys to become ministers, and while Waldo followed that path only to reject the ministry later, Charles early on explained his decision to study the law instead, saying "I greatly distrust my fitness for the sacred office . . . my mind is of a very secondary order." In the 1830s Charles became interested in the new ideas of Transcendentalism but died before the movement fully emerged; it is not clear that he would have fully accepted what became the cornerstone of his brother's philosophy of self-reliance. In 1831 Charles recorded his thoughts in his diary: "When we look at the world from Self as center, nothing can be more perplexed." Still, Ralph Waldo Emerson regularly discussed his ideas with his brother and felt that he and Charles were so close that they "made but one man together."

Emerson had hoped to publish a volume of his brother's journal manuscripts but was unable to collect enough that was finished and publishable. Later, as editor of the *Dial* magazine, he published some of Charles's writings as "Notes from the Journal of a Scholar" in the first issue (July 1840) and published several of his poems as well. Emerson himself reflected on his childhood with his brothers in the poem "DIRGE," published in POEMS (1847).

Further Reading

Bosco, Ronald A., and Joel Myerson, eds. *The Emerson Brothers: A Fraternal Biography in Letters.* New York: Oxford University Press, 2005.

Cole, Phyllis. *Mary Moody Emerson and the Origins of Transcendentalism: A Family History.* New York: Oxford University Press, 1998.

Myerson, Joel. *The New England Transcendentalists and the Dial: A History of the Magazine and Its Contributors.* London and Toronto: Associated University Presses, 1980.

Emerson, Edith (1841–1929) Edith Emerson was the third child, and second daughter, born to Ralph Waldo and LIDIAN JACKSON EMERSON. Upon Edith's birth, Emerson wrote to his brother WILLIAM EMERSON to announce the event, gushing about his expanding family:

> born unto this house this day at 5 o clock this afternoon; it is a meek little girl which I have just seen . . . But there is nothing in her aspect to contradict the hope we feel that she has come for a blessing to our little company. Lidian is very well and finds herself suddenly recovered from a host of ails which she suffered from this morning. Waldo is quite deeply happy with this fair unexpected apparition & cannot peep & see it enough. Ellen has retired to bed unconscious of the fact & of all her rich gain in this companion. Shall I be discontented who had dreamed of a young poet that should come? I am quite too much affected with wonder & peace at what I have and behold & understand nothing of, to quarrel with it that it is not different.

When Edith was just two months old, her five-year-old brother, Waldo, died of scarlet fever.

Unlike the other surviving siblings (ELLEN EMERSON and younger brother, EDWARD WALDO EMERSON), Edith Emerson did not remain in CONCORD, much to her parents' dismay. In 1865 she married William Hathaway Forbes, a graduate of HARVARD COLLEGE who had fought in the Civil War before joining his wealthy father's railroad company. He later became president of the American Bell Telephone Company. Edith and William lived in Milton, Massachusetts, and eventually had eight children, the first of whom was named Ralph Emerson Forbes, after his maternal grandfather; six of Edith's children lived to adulthood. Edith, her husband, and her father-in-law, John Murray Forbes, all accompanied Emerson on a trip to California in 1871, during which he visited Yosemite and met naturalist John Muir. In 1874 Edith assisted her sister, Ellen, in helping their father prepare the manuscript for his collection of favorite poems, PARNASSUS (1874).

Further Reading

Bosco, Ronald, and Joel Myerson, eds. *Emerson in His Own Time: A Biographical Chronicle of His Life, Drawn from Recollections, Interviews, and Memoirs by Family, Friends, and Associates.* Iowa City: University of Iowa Press, 2003.

Emerson, Ellen Tucker. *The Life of Lidian Jackson Emerson,* edited by Delores Bird Carpenter. Boston: Twayne, 1980.

Emerson, Edward Bliss (1805–1834) Ralph Waldo Emerson's next youngest brother, Edward Bliss Emerson, was the fifth child of WILLIAM EMERSON and RUTH HASKINS EMERSON and one of the five Emerson brothers who lived to adulthood. Despite his closeness in age to Ralph Waldo, less is known about Edward than any other of the brothers, besides ROBERT BULKELEY EMERSON, who remained in a childlike state throughout his life.

Older brother WILLIAM EMERSON worked as a schoolteacher to put both Ralph Waldo and Edward through college, and Edward graduated from HARVARD COLLEGE in 1824 at the top of his class, giving the class oration with French Revolution hero, Lafayette, in the audience. All who knew the Emerson family felt Edward held the most promise, and he was certainly the most ambitious and most driven of the brothers. Waldo recorded that his brother "lived, acted, and spoke with preternatural energy." For his part, Edward once warned younger brother, CHARLES CHAUNCY EMERSON, never to accept second best in school, for "the poor number two who flattered himself, with the idea of having but *one* above him," would soon find himself out in the larger world where he "finds a thousand" better than him.

Edward studied law with Daniel Webster (famed Massachusetts senator who would anger Ralph Waldo Emerson and others when he supported the Fugitive Slave Act in 1850) while teaching for extra money on the side. The pressure, combined with chronically poor health, would eventually get to Edward. In 1828 he wrote to Charles in a tone of resignation, "I read no law, no letters. I have ceased to resist God and Nature." He subsequently suffered a mental collapse, and the family was forced to have him briefly institutionalized at McLean's Asylum in Charlestown, Massachusetts (where brother Bulkeley stayed on occasion as well). Edward traveled to Virginia, to Europe, and then to Puerto Rico, all in pursuit of rest and a healthier climate, but to no avail. Charles (also suffering from tuberculosis) also traveled to Puerto Rico but returned home temporarily relieved of his symptoms. Edward stayed on and got a job as a clerk for the U.S. consulate in San Juan, but he died there in October 1834.

Ralph Waldo Emerson was in New York when he heard the news of Edward's death several weeks later. Edward was the first of the adult brothers to die, and the news affected Emerson deeply. He wrote, "I am bereaved of part of myself." Edward's body was returned to Emerson, and his brother was buried in Sleepy Hollow Cemetery in CONCORD, MASSACHUSETTS. Edward's death, in some ways, drew Waldo closer to his next youngest brother, Charles. Unfortunately, Charles also died of tuberculosis, less than two years later, in May 1836.

Emerson published Edward's poem, "The Last Farewell," in the first issue of the *DIAL* (July 1840). He subsequently included the poem in both *MAY-DAY AND OTHER PIECES* (1867) and in his collection of favorite poems and poets, *PARNASSUS* (1874). Emerson himself wrote two poems memorializing his brother—"DIRGE," published in *POEMS* (1847), remembers the shared childhood of the "five rosy boys," and "IN MEMORIAM E.B.E.," which was published in *May-Day*.

Further Reading

Bosco, Ronald A., and Joel Myerson, eds. *The Emerson Brothers: A Fraternal Biography in Letters.* New York: Oxford University Press, 2006.

Emerson, Edward Waldo (1844–1930) Edward Waldo Emerson was the fourth and last child, and only surviving son, of Ralph Waldo and LIDIAN JACKSON EMERSON. He was born in 1844, two years after the tragic death of their first son, Waldo, at age five, and during the same summer that Ralph Waldo Emerson purchased what he termed "a pretty pasture and wood-lot" at Walden Pond. All of the Emerson children were fond of and often under the tutelage of HENRY DAVID THOREAU, and Edward also attended a school run by FRANKLIN BENJAMIN SANBORN in CONCORD, MASSACHUSETTS.

Edward went on to graduate from HARVARD COLLEGE in 1866, and attended medical school in England before enrolling at Harvard Medical School, from which he graduated in 1874. He set up a medical practice in Concord and in 1874 married fellow Concordian Annie Shepard Keyes, with whom he had seven children, only four of whom survived to adulthood. Edward Emerson was active

Emerson in his 70s with son, Edward Emerson, and grandson, Charles L. Emerson (1876–80) *(Concord Free Public Library)*

in local Concord politics and cultural projects, serving as superintendent of schools, on the Board of Health, the cemetery and library committees, and was a founding member of the Concord Antiquarian Society.

All three of the adult Emerson children—Edward, EDITH EMERSON, and ELLEN EMERSON—assisted their father in his later years as his memory and health failed. They appeared with him in public and helped prepare some of his final works for publication in the 1870s. After Ralph Waldo Emerson's death in 1882, Edward left medicine to write and edit his father's works. He published a personal memoir, *Emerson in Concord* (1889), and edited the multivolume Centenary Edition of his father's writings, *Complete Works* (published in 1903–04), to which scholars still refer for the annotations and insights into Emerson's writing process and personal life. Edward also edited and published some of his father's correspondence and several volumes (coedited with nephew Waldo Emerson Forbes, son of Edith) of the *Journals of Ralph Waldo Emerson* (1909–14). Edward Emerson also published early biographies and personal reminiscences of other major Transcendentalists, including *Life and Letters of Charles Russell Lowell* (1907), a biography of *Ebenezer Rockwood Hoar* (1911), *Henry David Thoreau as Remembered by a Young Friend* (1917), and *Early Years of the Saturday Club, 1855–1870* (1918).

Further Reading

Emerson, Ellen Tucker. *The Life of Lidian Jackson Emerson,* edited Delores Bird Carpenter. Boston: Twayne, 1980.

Richardson, Robert D., Jr. *Emerson: The Mind on Fire.* Berkeley: University of California Press, 1995.

Emerson, Ellen Tucker (1839–1909) Ellen Emerson was the second child and eldest daughter of Ralph Waldo and LIDIAN JACKSON EMERSON. Emerson considered it a gift from his wife that the child was named after his first wife, Ellen Tucker Emerson, who had died in 1831 after only a year of marriage. He recorded in his journal that "Lidian, who magnanimously makes my gods her gods, calls the babe Ellen. I can hardly ask more for thee my babe, than that name implies. Be that vision & remain with us, & after us." Daughter Ellen never married but remained at her family home in CONCORD her entire life. She served on the Concord School Committee and taught Sunday school at the First Parish Church.

In later years, Ellen became her busy but aging father's secretary, handling his correspondence as well as his financial affairs. She also did much of the housekeeping as her mother, Lidian, was often plagued with ill health. After a devastating fire at the Emerson family home, Ellen made the arrangements for and accompanied her father on a trip to England in 1872—where her father met again with his friend THOMAS CARLYLE—and then on an extended journey through Europe (France and Italy) and on to Egypt (from December 1872 to February 1873), where they were able to visit archaeological and historical sites. As Emerson's physical health and memory declined, Ellen

Ellen Emerson, oldest daughter of Ralph Waldo Emerson *(Houghton Library, Harvard University)*

accompanied him to public events and helped him with his lecture notes. At what was likely his last public appearance, an 1881 memorial for Carlyle, Ellen sat nearby and mouthed the words for him to say.

Ellen Emerson assisted her father in compiling and publishing the book LETTERS AND SOCIAL AIMS (1876), and after his death, she joined with literary executor JAMES ELLIOT CABOT in editing her father's papers for publication. She also wrote a manuscript biography of her mother, *The Life of Lidian Jackson Emerson,* which remained unpublished until 1980. Like the edited works and reminiscences published by her brother, EDWARD WALDO EMERSON, Ellen Emerson's biography provides a unique inside perspective on the Emerson household and on Ralph Waldo Emerson's later career. Besides the biography of her mother, Ellen's record of the Emerson family and of life in Concord during the time of Transcendentalism remains mostly in unpublished journals and letters. It was she who recorded her father's last words and days at home before his death in April 1882.

Further Reading

Emerson, Ellen Tucker. *The Life of Lidian Jackson Emerson,* edited by Delores Bird Carpenter. Boston: Twayne, 1980.

Thomas, Joseph M. "Late Emerson: *Selected Poems* and the 'Emerson Factory,'" *ELH (English Literary History)* 65, no. 4 (1998): 971–994.

Emerson, Lidian Jackson (1802–1892) Lydia Jackson married Ralph Waldo Emerson in September 1835 and became known, at Emerson's request, as Lidian. He wrote to a cousin that "the philistines baptized her Lydia, but her name is Lidian," and he sometimes referred to her as "my Lydian Queen" or simply "Queenie." She always referred to her husband as "Mr. Emerson." Although she had heard him preach in 1830 (at which time he was still married to Ellen Tucker), the two formally met in 1834 when Emerson was a guest preacher in her Plymouth, Massachusetts, congregation. It was said that a friend remarked that Lydia was hearing someone else preach her own ideas, so closely aligned were she and Emerson spiritually and intellectually. He proposed a year later, explaining, "I am persuaded that I address one so in love with what I love . . . that an affection founded on such a basis cannot alter."

Lidian Emerson shared with her husband an intellectual interest in the writings of EMANUEL SWEDENBORG and in the idea "that each individual should consider himself as but a part of a great whole." Like Emerson, she rejected the orthodox Christianity of their Puritan heritage, but she never completely accepted UNITARIANISM or the radical philosophy of, as she termed it, these "Transcendental Times." She maintained a personal belief in the God of the Bible, a belief that "Mr. Emerson" respected and often deferred to. He accepted her criticisms of his ideas, some of which she lightheartedly recorded in a "Transcendental Bible," a satirical look at Transcendentalism as a new religion. She criticized both the "egotistical" aspects of a philosophy of the self ("Great souls are self-sustained and stand ever erect, saying only to the prostrate sufferer 'Get up, and stop your complaining'") and its shortcomings compared to Christianity ("Never speak of the hope of Immortality" and "Loathe and shun the sick. They are in bad taste, and may untune us for writing the poem floating through our mind").

In many ways, Lidian's marriage to Ralph Waldo Emerson was always overshadowed by the memory of his first wife, Ellen Tucker Emerson, who died of tuberculosis after less than two years of marriage. Everyone in the household spoke openly about the loss of Ellen, and it was a gesture of her love that Lidian chose to name their first daughter ELLEN TUCKER EMERSON. Upon the child's birth, Emerson wrote in his journal, "Lidian, who magnanimously makes my gods her gods, calls the babe Ellen." She ultimately bore four children: Waldo (who died of scarlet fever at age five), Ellen, EDITH EMERSON, and EDWARD WALDO EMERSON. Lidian had difficult pregnancies and was physically ill or weak most of her adult life. The death of little Waldo in 1842 was a devastating blow from which neither parent ever fully recovered, but there were other strains on the marriage, most notably Emerson's deep friendships with other women, such as MARGARET FULLER and poet CAROLINE STURGIS TAPPAN, who were often invited guests in the Emerson home. For her part, Lidian and the children were particularly close to HENRY DAVID THOREAU, who stayed at the Emerson home when Emerson was away on lecture or travel tours.

Various strains and tensions within the marriage ultimately led Ralph Waldo Emerson to reflect philosophically on the institution. Beginning in the 1840s, Emerson wrote in several instances that he did not believe in marriage as a permanent state, noting in his journal that "it is not in the plan or prospect of the soul, this fast union of one to one," and that "plainly marriage should be a temporary relation, it should have its natural birth, climax and decay, without violence of any kind,—violence to bind or violence to rend." In his journal of 1850, however, he felt marriage "the perfection love aimed at, ignorant of what it sought." Regardless, the couple remained married for nearly 50 years, and Lidian headed a lively household that incorporated not only her own family and extended family but also her husband's numerous friends and admirers streaming through their CONCORD home.

Lidian was strong-minded in her own views and their daughter, Ellen, recalled heated debates in the Emerson home about reform issues, such as ABOLITIONISM and women's rights; on the latter, Lidian strongly supported the cause while her husband (who articulated his views in the 1855 address "WOMAN") was less eager to concede that women should have the right to vote. Lidian hosted reform meetings in her home and joined organizations such as the Women's Anti-Slavery Association of Concord, of which Henry David Thoreau's mother, Cynthia Thoreau, was also a member. Lidian once draped the Emersons' front gate with black cloth in an antislavery protest against the celebration of July 4 in a country where all were not free. She met with and was greatly influenced by the sisters Sarah and Angelina Grimké when they came to Concord in 1837 after the controversial publication of their letters on women's duty to speak out against slavery.

Lidian Emerson outlived her husband by a decade and died at home in Concord with children Ellen and Edward by her side.

Further Reading

Carpenter, Delores Bird. *The Selected Letters of Lidian Jackson Emerson.* Columbia: University of Missouri Press, 1987.

Emerson, Ellen Tucker. *The Life of Lidian Jackson Emerson,* edited by Delores Bird Carpenter. Boston: Twayne, 1980.

Emerson, Mary Moody (1774–1863) Mary Moody Emerson was known by many as Ralph Waldo Emerson's eccentric and fiercely independent paternal aunt, and her intellectual and philosophical influence on her famous nephew has long been recognized. Mary's few published writings, along with her correspondence and copious diaries, indicate that she was a precursor of romantic consciousness and the source of many Transcendentalist concepts. Her belief in living a life of solitude and drawing on nature and the imagination to develop a closer relationship with God influenced not only her nephew but also other acquaintances like HENRY DAVID THOREAU, ELIZABETH PALMER PEABODY, and WILLIAM ELLERY CHANNING.

Mary Moody Emerson, born August 25, 1774, was the fourth child of Rev. William Emerson and Phebe Bliss Emerson. After her father died of a fever while serving in the Revolutionary army in 1776, Mary was sent to Malden to live with her widowed grandmother and two aunts. She spent most of her adult life in Maine before returning to the OLD MANSE in CONCORD after the death of her favorite brother, WILLIAM EMERSON, in 1811 to educate and care for his children, including Ralph Waldo Emerson, who at the time was not quite eight years old. As an aunt, Mary sought to embed in Waldo and his brothers a respect for their ancestors and to educate them in philosophy, theology, and literature, focusing on authors like Milton, Antoninus, and Plato. When her nephews were older and her assistance was no longer needed, she traveled throughout Connecticut and Maine, but Emerson frequently engaged in philosophical discussions with his Aunt Mary through letters for the better part of his young adulthood. Though their relationship became more strained after Emerson's Transcendentalist break from the UNITARIAN Church, they remained in occasional contact until her death on May 1, 1863.

Notorious for her fascination with death, which she indulged by dressing in funeral shrouds and having her bed made up to resemble a coffin, Mary Moody Emerson was widely read in ENLIGHTENMENT thought and familiar with many of the people Emerson later identified as originators of Transcendentalism. She did what she could, given the restrictions placed upon women at the time, to become an active part of the movement. From 1804 to 1805 she wrote articles for BOSTON's first literary review, the *Monthly Anthology and Boston Review*, under the pseudonym "Constance," many of which contain key ideas later associated with Transcendentalism, such as the importance of nature and imagination.

Mary's philosophical beliefs stressed the importance of intuition, personal discipline, independent thought, and self-reliance. Although she was religiously devout, she firmly believed that the individual was responsible for developing a relationship with God and that priests and churches were not always necessary for doing so. She once wrote to Emerson, "In intire [*sic*] solitude, minds become oblivious to care & find in the uniform & constant miracle of nature, revelation alter [*sic*] & priest." Emerson clearly took Mary's teachings to heart. His letters indicate that as a young man he spent a week in the country with his brother WILLIAM EMERSON (the third) hoping to experience the sort of inspirational breakthrough once explained to him by his Aunt Mary, but he was disappointed when he experienced only a fraction of the elation she described. In another letter to a HARVARD COLLEGE classmate, Emerson wrote that he was seeking an acquaintance with nature because his aunt "was anxious that her nephew might hold high & reverential notions regarding it as the temple where God & the Mind are to be studied & adored & where the fiery soul can begin a premature communication with other worlds."

When Emerson entered the ministry in the late 1820s, Aunt Mary shared with him excerpts from her journals (or "almanack"), and he incorporated into his sermons many of her ideas about an internal, natural religion that stressed a direct and personal relationship with God. Emerson so admired his aunt's writings that for years he copied her letters and journal passages into his own journals, attributing them to "Tnamurya" (an anagram for "Aunt Mary"); as late as 1870, at the age of 67, he was still reading and re-reading her writings, and he placed many phrases from them in his essays and poems. In his journals, he named her as one of his 10 most influential "friends," included her among "great men of the American past," and occasionally characterized her as a muse, oracle, and prophetess. Emerson's affection and respect for Mary are abundantly clear in his writings about her, particularly "Amita," a eulogy read before the New England Women's Club in Boston in 1869.

Further Reading

Cole, Phyllis. *Mary Moody Emerson and the Origins of Transcendentalism: A Family History*. New York: Oxford University Press, 1998.

Wendy Commons

Emerson, Robert Bulkeley (1807–1859) Younger brother of Ralph Waldo Emerson, Robert Bulkeley Emerson was the sixth child of WILLIAM EMERSON and RUTH HASKINS EMERSON, and one of the five Emerson brothers to live to adulthood. Born between EDWARD BLISS EMERSON and CHARLES CHAUNCY EMERSON, he was called "Bulkeley" by the family, which was itself an ancestral name going back to Peter Bulkeley, founder of CONCORD, MASSACHUSETTS. Robert Bulkeley Emerson remained mentally a child and required lifelong care until his death at age 52. There is little precise information about his symptoms and behavior, and so the exact nature of his condition is unknown, whether he was mentally retarded or suffered a milder form of mental illness. What is known is that Bulkeley was usually cared for by family members, although he periodically had to be institutionalized at McLean's Asylum in Charlestown, Massachusetts (where Edward Bliss Emerson also stayed when he suffered a mental breakdown and where poet and friend of Ralph Waldo Emerson, JONES VERY, also stayed on occasion). Bulkeley also came for extended visits to the home of Waldo and LIDIAN JACKSON EMERSON in Concord and was sometimes able to perform day labor for families that would board him.

Little else is known about Bulkeley, except for occasional affectionate inquiries about his care and "infirmities" in the letters of the other Emerson brothers. When Bulkeley died in 1859 Emerson asked HENRY DAVID THOREAU to arrange the funeral. Bulkeley was buried at Sleepy Hollow Cemetery in Concord, and Emerson reported to older brother WILLIAM EMERSON that "it did not seem so odious to be laid down there under the oak trees in as perfect an innocency as was Bulkeley's," who was "clean of all vices."

Further Reading

Bosco, Ronald A., and Joel Myerson, eds. *The Emerson Brothers: A Fraternal Biography in Letters.* New York: Oxford University Press, 2006.

Reiss, Benjamin. *Theaters of Madness: Insane Asylums and Nineteenth-Century American Culture.* Chicago: University of Chicago Press, 2008. (*See* chapter 4, "Emerson's Close Encounters with Madness.")

Emerson, Ruth Haskins (1768–1853) The mother of Ralph Waldo Emerson, Ruth Haskins was the daughter of Hannah Upham and successful BOSTON merchant John Haskins. She married Rev. WILLIAM EMERSON in 1796 and gave birth to eight children, five of whom lived to adulthood: Phebe (1798–1800), John Clarke (1799–1807), WILLIAM EMERSON, Ralph Waldo, EDWARD BLISS EMERSON, ROBERT BULKELEY EMERSON, CHARLES CHAUNCY EMERSON, and Mary Caroline (1811–1814). When Ruth was widowed in 1811, she was left to care for and educate six children still under the age of 10. She took in boarders to support the family and was assisted in raising the children by her unmarried sister-in-law, MARY MOODY EMERSON.

In 1826 Ruth brought the family to CONCORD to live at the OLD MANSE, the home of Rev. EZRA RIPLEY and Phebe Bliss Emerson, her mother-in-law. In 1835 Ralph Waldo Emerson married LYDIA JACKSON (LIDIAN JACKSON EMERSON) and purchased their own Concord home called "Bush"; his mother came to live with them until her death at age 85.

Upon her death in late 1853 Ralph Waldo Emerson wrote an obituary and sent it to Nathaniel Frothingham, his father's successor as minister at First Church in Boston. Emerson commented on how his mother's long life had spanned the generations and history: "I have been in the habit of esteeming her manners & character the fruit of a past age. She was born a subject of King George, had lived through the whole existence of the Republic, remembered & described with interesting details the appearance of Washington at the Assemblies in Boston after the war, when every lady wore his name on her scarf; & had derived from that period her punctilious courtesy extended to every person, and continued to the last hour of her life." He ended by noting her greatest legacy, according to friends: "She got the children educated."

Further Reading

Cole, Phyllis. *Mary Moody Emerson and the Origins of Transcendentalism: A Family History.* New York: Oxford University Press, 1998.

Emerson, William (1769–1811) Rev. William Emerson was Ralph Waldo Emerson's father. A native of CONCORD, MASSACHUSETTS, his own father, also named William Emerson, was a minister during the Revolutionary War and built a house in Concord (later known as the OLD MANSE) on a site near the North Bridge, where the first battle of the Revolution would be fought. The elder William Emerson was a chaplain to the Continental Army and died in 1776, when young William was only seven years old. William's mother, Phebe Bliss Emerson, married another minister, EZRA RIPLEY, who then lived at the Old Manse and become Ralph Waldo Emerson's step-grandfather.

William Emerson attended HARVARD COLLEGE, graduating in 1789, and became minister of First Church in BOSTON. In 1796 he married RUTH HASKINS (EMERSON), with whom he had eight children—six sons and two daughters. Only the five middle sons survived into adulthood: WILLIAM EMERSON (the third), Ralph Waldo, EDWARD BLISS EMERSON, ROBERT BULKELEY EMERSON, and CHARLES CHAUNCY EMERSON.

William Emerson was one of the first of the new breed of UNITARIAN ministers, and also a man of letters, involved in intellectual life through founding several social and literary groups, such as the Philosophical Society, the Boston Athenaeum, and the Anthology Club. He was an editor and writer for the latter's publication, the *Monthly Anthology,* which eventually became the *North American Review,* an important periodical during Ralph Waldo Emerson's own Unitarian-Transcendentalist times. Ralph Waldo Emerson had few memories of his father (he was only eight when William Emerson died in 1811), but he later assessed his father's intellectual legacy, noting, "His literary merits really are that he fostered the Anthology & the Athenaeum. These things ripened into Buckminster, Channing & Everett."

Although he died when his children were all still quite young, William Emerson had been committed to their spiritual and literary education. The boys were raised and educated through the efforts of their mother and their aunt, William's sister, MARY MOODY EMERSON, although Waldo recalled curiously that the women did little to foster his father's legacy: "I have never heard any sentence or sentiment of his repeated by Mother or Aunt."

Further Reading

Cole, Phyllis. *Mary Moody Emerson and the Origins of Transcendentalism: A Family History.* New York: Oxford University Press, 1998.

———. "Emerson Father and Son: A Precedent for 'The American Scholar.'" *NEQ* 78 (2005): 101–124.

Emerson, William (1801–1868) William Emerson (the third) was the older brother of Ralph Waldo Emerson. He was the third child and second son born to RUTH HASKINS EMERSON and WILLIAM EMERSON (the father), and was the oldest of those who survived to adulthood: William, Ralph Waldo, EDWARD BLISS EMERSON, ROBERT BULKELEY EMERSON, and CHARLES CHAUNCY EMERSON. As their father died while the boys were still young, William helped take responsibility for raising his brothers. After his own graduation from HARVARD COLLEGE in 1818, he went to work as a schoolteacher to help pay the college expenses of three of his younger brothers, including Waldo.

William went on to study theology at the University of Göttingen in Germany and was an important early intellectual influence on Waldo as well. In Germany William met with the German idealist philosopher JOHANN WOLFGANG VON GOETHE, who would become one of the most important influences on American Transcendentalism. He reported back to his younger brother on lectures he attended and recommended that Waldo read not only Goethe but also other thinkers such as Johann Gottfried Herder and FRIEDRICH SCHLEIERMACHER, which he promptly did. As early as 1824 William was coming to conclusions that would later echo in Ralph Waldo Emerson's addresses on the nature of God and on the individual's relationship to the divine. William once wrote to brother Edward that, "I do not find it needful to seek for proofs of the being and omnipresence of God in my metaphysical subtleties, for I find them in my own thoughts, in my own moral history." This sentiment would be the predominant theme in Ralph Waldo Emerson's later "DIVINITY SCHOOL ADDRESS" (1838), as well as in other writings.

William's philosophical studies, however, led him away from his original plan to become a minister and away from Christianity in general, a path Waldo would follow as well. William studied the law instead, but the two brothers continued to discuss theology and literature. One point they agreed upon was the lack of meaning in the ritual of communion in the church, an issue that resulted in Ralph Waldo Emerson's controversial sermon on "The LORD'S SUPPER" in September 1832, an address that served as his own resignation from the ministry. He confided to a sympathetic William a few months later that "the severing of our strained cord that bound me to the church is a mutual relief."

In 1833 William married Susan Haven, and they had three children. William was a lawyer and judge in New York City, and their family lived primarily on Staten Island. Ralph Waldo Emerson was visiting there with him when his brother died in 1868. His body was removed to CONCORD, MASSACHUSETTS, where he was buried at Sleepy Hollow Cemetery.

Further Reading

Bosco, Ronald A., and Joel Myerson, eds. *The Emerson Brothers: A Fraternal Biography in Letters.* New York: Oxford University Press, 2005.

Enlightenment The Enlightenment is the term commonly applied to the period in European and colonial American history beginning approximately in 1650 and ending with the outbreak of the French Revolution in 1789. Another name given to the period is the "Age of Reason," because leading cultural and political figures of the era maintained as a fundamental tenet that reason (meaning scientific and mathematical principles as well as syllogistic forms) could and should be employed to gain a deeper understanding of the natural world and, more importantly, to organize society in accordance with natural laws.

The foremost spokesmen for Enlightenment principles were the French philosopher-writers (philosophes), such as Voltaire, Diderot, Condorcet, d'Alembert, Montesquieu, and Rousseau. Drawing upon the rationalist doctrine of René Descartes, the mechanistic physics of Isaac Newton, and the empiricism and political writings of JOHN LOCKE, the philosophes in their works criticized the irrational dogmatism they perceived in Catholicism and the tyranny of "divine-right" absolutism. From a positive standpoint, they began to promote the application of reason to government, universal respect for human rights (especially individual liberty), and the inevitability of human progress. These values spread throughout Europe among the literary and political elite. In Britain, philosophers such as David Hume reflected the spread of the Enlightenment to Scotland, which in turn had a noticeable impact on American students such as Benjamin Franklin and Thomas Jefferson. Lockean and French Enlightenment ideas found their way into the basic ideology of the American revolutionaries and are reflected in important passages of founding documents, such as the Declaration of Independence and the Constitution of 1787.

The Enlightenment contributed in particular to the New England culture of the late 18th and early 19th centuries through its emphases on individualism and religious skepticism. Newtonian mechanics provided the underpinning for Deism, a religious doctrine centered on the view that God was not personally involved in nature but rather created the universe and allowed it to run in accordance with immutable natural laws. Deists disavowed the concept of divine "miraculous" intervention into human affairs, or special revelation. Such revisionist thinking about the nature of God and the place of man in nature helped create the cultural environment capable of producing UNITARIANISM, the liberal Christianity of early-19th-century New England.

Transcendentalists, while breaking away from the structure of Unitarianism in many cases, took the individualist theme to new levels by rejecting the authority of tradition. Rather than denying religion entirely, Ralph Waldo Emerson and his contemporaries generally sought to embrace a universal spiritual and intellectual experience founded in Kantian ethics ("transcendental idealism") and exemplified in the writings not only of classical and modern European philosophers but of Asian sages also. Thus, while continuing to promote basic Enlightenment principles of individual liberty, equality, and democracy, Emerson and the Transcendentalists generally rejected Enlightenment rationalism in favor of a more romantic viewpoint. In practical terms, Emerson and other Transcendentalists such as MARGARET FULLER, HENRY DAVID THOREAU, BRONSON ALCOTT, and GEORGE RIPLEY drew at least indirectly from the cultural background of the Enlightenment in their participation in reform programs in education, women's rights, and ABOLITIONISM.

James Brent

Fourier / Fourierism / Fourierist Several of the Transcendentalists adopted the UTOPIAN socialist ideas of Francois Marie Charles Fourier (1772–1837), who came from a business family in Besançon, France. Fourier elaborated a theory for the reconstruction of society based on a rejection of capitalism. Harkening back to the ideas of Rousseau's *Origin of Inequality,* Fourier developed a romanticized theory of the natural passions by the free expression of which people would attain personal morality rather than the corrupting social morality. By the time of his death Fourierist communities had sprung up in eastern Europe, South America, France, and the United States. His economic ideas were brought to New England in the 1830s by Albert Brisbane who, after meeting Fourier in Paris, expounded his ideas in Horace Greeley's *New York Tribune,* while translating several of his works into English.

Fourier's economic model centered on his concept of the "phalanx," a cooperative community comprised of approximately 400 families of four members each, for a total of 1,600 living in a *phalanstère* or common building. The members were to engage in large-scale but intensive agriculture, with manufacturing having only a secondary role. The separate phalanxes were to engage in a system of barter through public service clearinghouses operating without the middleman's profit taking. The phalanx was to be physically arranged to provide for a community center, public schooling, library, hotel services, shopping, public health facility, a trade clearinghouse, a bank, and social insurance office.

The early Transcendentalists were drawn to Fourier's premise that in giving free rein to the gamut of the natural passions, people's activities would spontaneously be distributed into the full range of types of work needed by society. Fourier's ideas impacted (WILLIAM) ELLERY CHANNING (the younger), GEORGE RIPLEY, ELIZABETH PALMER PEABODY, and even the independent-minded theologian-reformer HENRY JAMES, SR. Fourierist-inspired communities sprang up in New Jersey, Massachusetts, and Wisconsin, eventually contributing to the background of American labor unionism as well.

The former UNITARIAN minister George Ripley founded the utopian community of BROOK FARM on a nearly 200-acre site in West Roxbury, Massachusetts, in 1841. The original charter was based on the Transcendentalist principles of self-culture and self-reliance, but after reading Fourier and meeting Brisbane, Ripley and others reorganized it on Fourierist lines beginning in 1844–45. The stated goal was to effect a natural union between intellectual and manual labor to promote both individual and social development, but the Fourierist regimen eventually overwhelmed the expression of individual pursuits. After a fire destroyed the building of a large phalanstery or dormitory, Brook Farm closed in 1846.

Though she never lived at Brook Farm, Elizabeth Palmer Peabody promoted a species of Fourierism in the *DIAL,* combining it with her own views of Christian Transcendentalism. She rejected Fourier's unconventional ideas regarding marriage and sexuality, arguing that Fourier's socialism was compatible with Christian morality and the Christian ideal of marriage. MARGARET FULLER, in her *Woman in the Nineteenth Century* (1845), also discussed Fourier, drawn to his ideas of radical social and sexual equality.

Emerson often visited but demurred from endorsing the Fourierist socialism of Brook Farm, which he later parodied as "arcadian fanaticism" and "a perpetual picnic, a French Revolution in small, an Age of Reason in a patty-pan." His essays "WEALTH" in *THE CONDUCT OF LIFE* (1860) and "FARMING" in *SOCIETY AND SOLITUDE* (1870) included later reflections on the chasm between its "unnatural" communitarian ideals and their practical execution. Emerson in general avoided organized reform movements, and regarded communal living as stifling to individual creativity. NATHANIEL HAWTHORNE had originally joined Brook Farm but soon came to the same conclusion and ended up caricaturing the community in his novel *The Blithedale Romance* (1852).

Further Reading

Beecher, Jonathan. *Charles Fourier: The Visionary and His World.* Berkeley: University of California Press, 1986.

David A. Dilworth

Francis, Convers (1795–1863) Convers Francis was a UNITARIAN clergyman, scholar, biographer, and historian. He studied at HARVARD Divinity School, was ordained in 1819, served as minister at Watertown, Massachusetts, until 1842, then held the post of Parkman Professor of Pulpit Eloquence at Harvard for the rest of his life. He was a scholar of German philosophy and biblical criticism, publishing several early articles in the Unitarian press. These ideas put him in association with many of the emerging Transcendentalists, and Francis was one of the original (and oldest) members of the TRANSCENDENTAL CLUB. That same year that the Transcendental Club was organized, 1836, Emerson published *NATURE*, the foundational statement of Transcendentalist philosophy, and Francis published his *Christianity as a Purely Internal Principle.*

Francis was, however, ultimately a more moderate Unitarian than radicals such as Emerson, THEODORE PARKER, or GEORGE RIPLEY, all of whom Francis still defended against critics of the new thought. He regularly attended Emerson's lectures, including the "DIVINITY SCHOOL ADDRESS" of 1838, and defended Emerson against Unitarian critics. Immediately after Emerson's address, Francis reported to FREDERIC HENRY HEDGE that "the discourse was full of divine life,—and was a true word from a true soul. I did not agree with him in some of his positions, & think perhaps he did not make the peculiar significance of Jesus so prominent as he ought . . . The discourse gave dire offence to the rulers at Cambridge." In a subsequent letter, once the criticism from "the rulers at Cambridge" (most notably ANDREWS NORTON) became public, Francis determined that the response was "wholly disproportionate to the occasion." Francis also said of Emerson that "he is a true godful man; though in his love for the ideal he disregards too much the actual." And yet Francis's sympathies with the intellectual inquiries of the Transcendentalists were such that he also defended former student Theodore Parker a few years later when Parker's *Discourse on the Transient and Permanent in Christianity* led some Unitarians to attempt to ban Parker from the pulpit.

Convers Francis was also a supporter of ABOLITIONISM, and his sister was Lydia Maria Child, a participant in MARGARET FULLER's Conversations for women and an author, reformer, and editor of the *National Anti-Slavery Standard.* As a liberal Unitarian Francis was an important teacher to a new generation at Harvard and in the pulpit, mentoring the younger Transcendentalists, such as CAROLINE DALL and OCTAVIUS BROOKS FROTHINGHAM.

Frothingham, Octavius Brooks (1822–1895) Octavius Brooks Frothingham was a second-generation Transcendentalist whose 1876 book, *Transcendentalism in New England,* was the first history of the movement. Frothingham was a HARVARD COLLEGE graduate and was one of the youngest members of the TRANSCENDENTAL CLUB. He was the son of conservative UNITARIAN minister, Nathaniel Langdon Frothingham, who had succeeded Ralph Waldo Emerson's father, WILLIAM EMERSON, as pastor at First Church in BOSTON. Nathaniel Frothingham had also been a part of the Unitarian establishment that tried (unsuccessfully) to remove THEODORE PARKER from the pulpit in light of Parker's radical Transcendentalist views in *A Discourse on the Transient and Permanent in Christianity* (1841). Octavius Brooks Frothingham later acknowledged his father's role in the 19th-century Unitarian Church with his 1890 history of *Boston Unitarianism 1820–1850: A Study of the Life and Works of Nathaniel Langdon Frothingham.*

Octavius Brooks Frothingham was also a reformer and an advocate of ABOLITIONISM. He spoke out in the case of fugitive slave Anthony Burns in 1854 and, in particular, called upon "the Christian Church universal of this country," which, in his opinion, "is blind and indifferent to the most hideous Institution now existing under the sun; an institution which, on an enormous scale, outrages human rights and crushes human nature." Frothingham preached in Boston and Salem, before moving to New Jersey, and then New York, where he finally split from the Unitarianism of his father and established his own nondenominational Independent Liberal Church for "thinking people" of any faith or persuasion. His church drew some of the largest crowds in New York and led to the founding of the Free Religious Association in 1867. Not only was Octavius Brooks Frothingham mentored by Theodore Parker, and identified more with the radical Transcendentalists than the Unitarianism of his father, but also he became the first president of the Free Religious Association, which included Ralph Waldo Emerson among its guest speakers. In 1873 Frothingham published the book *The Religion of Humanity*, which incorporated Transcendentalism as well as other philosophical and scientific theories that had an influence on Frothingham.

In *Transcendentalism in New England: A History* (1876), Frothingham traced the beginnings of the movement in German philosophy and biblical criticism, in French philosophy, and in the English romantics. Then, in a format similar to that of Emerson in *REPRESENTATIVE MEN* (1850), he devoted a chapter each to Emerson (whom he termed "The Seer" of the movement), AMOS BRONSON ALCOTT ("The Mystic"), MARGARET FULLER ("The Critic"), Theodore Parker ("The Preacher"), and GEORGE RIPLEY ("The Man of Letters"). Frothingham's other published works on the Transcendentalists include *Life of Theodore Parker* (1874), the biography *George Ripley* (1883), and *Memoir of William Henry Channing* (1886).

Further Reading

Caruthers, J. Wade. *Octavius Brooks Frothingham, Gentle Radical.* Tuscaloosa: University of Alabama Press, 1977.

Fuller, (Sarah) Margaret (1810–1850) The journalist, author, and reformer Margaret Fuller was one of Ralph Waldo Emerson's closest confidantes within the Transcendentalist circle. She was also the most vocal female and feminist voice of the early movement. Born in CAMBRIDGE, MASSACHUSETTS, her father, Timothy Fuller, was a graduate of HARVARD COLLEGE, a prominent lawyer, and a state and then U.S. congressman. As the oldest child, Margaret Fuller received a thorough classical education from her father. With few professional opportunities for a woman of her education, she turned first to schoolteaching and then to writing and translation work. She taught at AMOS BRONSON ALCOTT's Temple School in BOSTON, where she came to know ELIZABETH PALMER PEABODY. She taught briefly in Rhode Island before returning to Boston and initiating a series of Conversations for women held at Peabody's home and bookstore. The Conversations were meant to allow women to ask for themselves, "What were we born to do? How shall we do it?" and were attended by many in the emerging Transcendentalist movement, including SOPHIA RIPLEY and CAROLINE STURGIS TAPPAN; an 1841 coed session was attended by Emerson.

Fuller had known of Emerson's work before meeting him in CONCORD in 1836. She remained in Cambridge but regularly visited the Emerson home for extended visits, and the two formed an intense friendship. Her sister, Ellen, eventually married (WILLIAM) ELLERY CHANNING, the younger. Fuller was one of the few in that circle, along with friend JAMES FREEMAN CLARKE, who read German philosophy in the original, and she published several books and translations of the works of JOHANN WOLFGANG VON GOETHE. She was one of the few women involved in the TRANSCENDENTAL CLUB beginning in 1836 and in 1840 helped found the *DIAL* magazine with Emerson and GEORGE RIPLEY. Fuller served as editor for the first two years of the paper's existence (1840–42), and Emerson, the last two years (1842–44). She also wrote for the paper, including book reviews, poems, and essays. Her essay on women's rights, "The Great Lawsuit. Man versus Men. Woman versus Women," appeared in the July 1843 issue of the *Dial.* She later revised the essay into the first full-length American feminist book, *Woman in the Nineteenth Century* (1845).

By the time *Woman in the Nineteenth Century* was published, Fuller had moved to New York and was hired by Horace Greeley as the first book

Margaret Fuller in the 1840s

reviewer for the *New York Tribune* and eventually its first female editor. The *Tribune* gave her a wider audience and a chance to pursue a wider agenda beyond the literary and philosophical focus of the *Dial,* and her *Tribune* essays and reviews tackled political and social reform topics such as ABOLITIONISM, education, prison reform, and women's rights. She traveled to Europe in 1846 as a foreign correspondent for the paper and reported first-hand on the Italian Revolution through her "dispatches" published in the *Tribune.*

While in Italy, Fuller met and later married an Italian revolutionary named Giovanni Ossoli and, in September 1848, gave birth to a son. Fuller was returning to the United States with Ossoli and their child when their ship ran aground off the coast of Fire Island, New York, on July 18, 1850. Emerson dispatched HENRY DAVID THOREAU to the site hoping to recover her belongings, including a manuscript history of the revolution that her friends believed her to have been writing at the time of her death; neither a manuscript nor Fuller's body was ever recovered. Fuller's death affected Emerson profoundly; he wrote in his journal, "I have lost my audience. I hurry now to my work admonished that I have few days left." He also reflected in his journal: "For her opulent mind the day was never long enough to exhaust, and I who have known her intimately for ten years from July 1836 till August 1846 when she left this country never saw her without some surprise at her new powers."

Almost immediately after her death a memorial volume was begun, to be edited by Emerson, Clarke, and WILLIAM HENRY CHANNING. Their book, *MEMOIRS OF MARGARET FULLER OSSOLI,* was published in 1852.

Further Reading

Capper, Charles. *Margaret Fuller: An American Romantic Life.* Vol. 1, *The Private Years.* New York: Oxford University Press, 1992.

———. *Margaret Fuller: An American Romantic Life.* Vol. 2, *The Public Years.* New York: Oxford University Press, 2007.

Furness, William Henry (1802–1896) William Henry Furness was a childhood friend and schoolmate of Ralph Waldo Emerson, and at Boston Latin School the two once collaborated on a poem. Furness attended HARVARD Divinity School and became a minister in Philadelphia, where Emerson was a guest preacher while visiting. As a minister Furness was at the center of the 1830s debate between liberal and radical UNITARIANS that led to the emergence of the Transcendentalist movement. At the center of that debate was the question of the divinity of Christ and the nature (whether supernatural or not) of the miracles detailed in the New Testament. In 1836, a seminal year for Transcendentalism with the publication of Emerson's *NATURE* and the founding of the TRANSCENDENTAL CLUB, Furness published his *Remarks on the Four Gospels.* Furness came down on the radical side of the debate in arguing that the miracles could be explained within the laws of nature. He followed up with an article on "The Miracles of Jesus" published in the *Christian Examiner* (July 1837). He was thus among the first and most outspoken of the Transcendentalists to take up the question of Christ's miracles, arguing that they were not necessary to prove Christ's divinity or the truth of his message—rather the truth of the message was revealed to the extent that it fit with our own individual sense of moral truth. Furness argued that the miracles themselves were not necessarily supernatural occurrences but perhaps were just unexplainable, given the limits of humankind's understanding and knowledge.

Furness echoed Emerson in his focus on the miracles in nature, concluding that "the existence of the merest atom, when we duly consider it, is an unspeakable miracle." Furness also mused that "the restoration of a dead man to life is not the least more wonderful than the birth of a human being." This was precisely Emerson's view and language on the miracle of everyday life, as articulated first in *Nature* and then in the "DIVINITY SCHOOL ADDRESS" (1838), in which Emerson stated that the miracles as performed by Christ were elevated by the church, wrongly, above the miracle of "the blowing clover and the falling rain."

Furness was thus among those radical Unitarians (a group that included Emerson, GEORGE RIPLEY, THEODORE PARKER, and others) whose views were attacked in the press by the conservative ANDREWS NORTON and others. Furness responded and expanded on his views with *Jesus and His Biographers* (1838). Like several other Transcendentalists, Furness was particularly interested in the works of German idealist philosophers and was trained in the German language so that he translated their texts into English in *Prose Writers of Germany* (1848). Furness also shared a commitment to reform and became active in ABOLITIONISM, opposing the Fugitive Slave Law of 1850 and, along with many other Bostonians (including Emerson and HENRY DAVID THOREAU), was moved by the actions and trial of JOHN BROWN for his raid on Harpers Ferry. Furness wrote a hymn, "Song of Old John Brown," which Emerson called "the most effective song that theme has found."

Upon Emerson's death Furness traveled from Philadelphia to give a private service for the family. In 1910 Furness's son, Horace Howard Furness, published a collection of correspondence between Furness and Emerson as *Records of a Lifelong Friendship, 1807–1882*.

Further Reading

Gougeon, Len. *Virtue's Hero: Emerson, Antislavery, and Reform*. Athens: University of Georgia Press, 1990.

Hoffmann, R. Joseph. "William Henry Furness: The Transcendentalist Defense of the Gospels." *New England Quarterly* 56, no. 2 (June 1983): 238–260.

Goethe, Johann Wolfgang von (1749–1832) The German philosopher and dramatist Johann Wolfgang von Goethe was one of the most important intellectual influences on Emerson and the American Transcendentalists. Goethe was part of the early turn to romanticism, and Transcendentalist interest in Goethe was intense by the early 1830s. Emerson lectured on Goethe and included "GOETHE; OR, THE WRITER" as one of his essays in *REPRESENTATIVE MEN* (1850). Perhaps what most appealed to Emerson was that Goethe was a great synthesizer of other ideas from philosophy, from nature, and so on. In all of his "representative men," Emerson emphasized the idea that genius is not original but synthetic, and that true genius lies in making the best use of the ideas of others (see "USES OF GREAT MEN," the introductory essay for *Representative Men*). Goethe himself wrote that "every one of my writings has been furnished to me by a thousand different persons, a thousand different things." This was the very nature of genius that Emerson saw not only in Goethe but also in his other representative men (as in "SWEDENBORG; OR, THE MYSTIC" and "SHAKSPEARE; OR, THE POET"). Indeed, it was what Emerson sought to do in his own work.

As a writer, Emerson was also particularly interested in Goethe's ability to cross genres; as Emerson noted in the essay on Goethe, he was a writer of "histories, mythologies, philosophies, sciences, and national literatures." In other contexts, Emerson was particularly drawn to Goethe as a botanist, corresponding to Emerson's own developing ideas about science and nature; in this respect, his own philosophy grew out of his readings in Goethe and in EMANUEL SWEDENBORG. As an interpreter of nature, Emerson was influenced by Goethe's ability to "see connection where the multitude see fragments." Emerson's own poem on the interconnectedness of all things in nature, "EACH AND ALL" (1839), was directly inspired by Goethe's similarly-titled poem, "Eins und Alles" ("One and All").

Emerson biographer Robert Richardson notes that "the effect of Goethe on Emerson is nearly impossible to overestimate" and that "Goethe laid down fundamental lessons that over the years became part of Emerson's own bedrock." The single concept that spoke most directly to the concerns of the Transcendentalists, however, was Goethe's idea of "self-culture," the inspiration for Emersonian "SELF-RELIANCE" in its many forms—as self-culture, self-development, self-education, and self-knowledge. Emerson wrote in his journal that "self-cultivation is yet the moral of all that Goethe has written." The very title of Goethe's own autobiography, *Truth and Poetry, From My Own Life,* summed up the Emersonian project of self-examination and the self as the source of universal meaning.

Besides Emerson, Goethe exerted an enormous influence on other Transcendentalists, notably MARGARET FULLER who, with JAMES FREEMAN CLARKE, was one of the few people to read Goethe in the original German. THOMAS CARLYLE translated some of Goethe's writings beginning in the 1820s, but it was Fuller who almost single-handedly brought Goethe to America with her translations of his plays and writings. Interested in the nature and character of genius, especially in this near contemporary, the Transcendentalists mined Goethe's life as well as his philosophy—and Fuller also made available Goethe's correspondence with Bettina von Arnim (as well as translating one of von Arnim's novels) and a translation of Johann Peter Eckermann's *Conversations with Goethe in the Last Years of His Life.* When she died in 1850, Fuller also left an unfinished biography of Goethe. In her feminist treatise, *Woman in the Nineteenth Century* (1845), Fuller explained the attraction to Goethe as one of three "prophets of the coming age" (the other two being Charles FOURIER and Emanuel Swedenborg). Fuller saw the implications for women of Goethe's philosophy of "pure self-subsistence, and a free development of any powers with which they may be gifted by nature as much for them as for men."

The Transcendentalists remained consistently interested in Goethe's idea of "self-culture" throughout the 19th century. Several speakers chose Goethe as the subject of their lectures at BRONSON ALCOTT's later CONCORD SCHOOL OF PHILOSOPHY AND LITERATURE, which met between 1879 and 1888. Indeed, during those 10 years of summer session, only two seasons were devoted to individual thinkers: the 1882 session on Emerson and the entire 1885 session devoted to the *Life and Genius of Goethe* (collected and published by FRANKLIN BENJAMIN SANBORN in 1886).

Further Reading

Cromphout, Gustaaf Van. *Emerson's Modernity and the Example of Goethe.* Columbia: University of Missouri Press, 1990.

Zwarg, Christina. *Feminist Conversations: Fuller, Emerson, and the Play of Reading.* Ithaca, N.Y.: Cornell University Press, 1995.

Harvard College Harvard College (now Harvard University) is the oldest college in the United States. Harvard is located in CAMBRIDGE, MASSACHUSETTS, and was founded as "New College" in 1636 by the first Puritan settlers of the Massachusetts Bay Colony as an institution primarily for the training of Puritan ministers. The importance Puritans placed on educating their own ministers, indeed on education in general, is evident by the fact that Harvard was founded just six years after the first settlers arrived in 1630. Harvard retained its connection to the Calvinist heritage of Puritanism until the faculty became influenced by liberal Christianity, or UNITARIANISM, in the early 19th century. Although training for the ministry was the original purpose of Harvard College, it became one of the most important American institutions of higher learning in general; the Divinity School became a separate program beginning in 1819, serving as the training ground for Unitarian ministers throughout the 19th century.

And yet Harvard of the early 19th century was still small and local. At the time Emerson attended, Harvard graduated fewer students than Yale in Connecticut or Dartmouth in New Hampshire, and had fewer than a dozen faculty members. Drawing its student body primarily from BOSTON, Cambridge, and the surrounding suburbs (including CONCORD), many Transcendentalist writers and thinkers were educated at Harvard—not only Emerson, but also JAMES FREEMAN CLARKE, FREDERIC HENRY HEDGE,

THEODORE PARKER, GEORGE RIPLEY, HENRY DAVID THOREAU, and numerous others. Four out of the five Emerson brothers graduated from Harvard. Older brother WILLIAM EMERSON graduated in 1818 and Waldo in 1821; they, in turn, worked to pay for the education of their younger brothers, EDWARD BLISS EMERSON and CHARLES CHAUNCY EMERSON, who graduated in 1824 and 1828, respectively. Not finding his calling in school teaching, Ralph Waldo Emerson returned to Harvard Divinity School and was ordained as a Unitarian minister in 1829.

In the early 1830s the faculty and program of the Divinity School, and Harvard College in general, became the target of criticism by many of the new Transcendentalists. Emerson's 1838 "DIVINITY SCHOOL ADDRESS" caused a public controversy by criticizing the faculty, rigid educational methods, and organized religion in general, which all emphasized book-based learning and rituals over spirituality and a personal relationship with the universe. Emerson did not speak at Harvard again for 30 years. His own son, EDWARD WALDO EMERSON, also attended Harvard after the Civil War, graduating from Harvard medical school in 1874.

By the mid-1800s a Harvard education had become synonymous with elite social status and connections, and with the Boston Brahmin class in particular. Originally a state-funded university, 19th-century Harvard was now private. By the time Emerson graduated from Harvard, the school was still relatively small but was on the verge of the most expansive growth in its history. Charles William Eliot (cousin of CHARLES ELIOT NORTON) became president in 1869 and served until 1909, the longest-serving president in the school's history. Eliot reorganized the undergraduate and graduate programs, adding electives, a greater emphasis on research, and a new lecture series, which included lectures by Emerson in 1870 and 1871 that became the basis for his later *NATURAL HISTORY OF INTELLECT*.

A notable exception to a Harvard education among Emerson's friends and among the Transcendentalists was, of course, MARGARET FULLER. Fuller's father, brother, and most of her male friends attended Harvard; in the 1830s she petitioned for and became one of the few women to have library reading privileges. Harvard graduated its first African-American student in 1870, and in 1879 Radcliffe College was opened as a women's "annex" to Harvard; it was not until the 1940s that women could attend regular Harvard classes with the male students. In 2007 Harvard appointed its first female president, American historian Drew Gilpin Faust.

Further Reading

Story, Ronald. *The Forging of an Aristocracy: Harvard and the Boston Upper Class, 1800–1870*. Middletown, Conn.: Wesleyan University Press, 1981.

Hawthorne, Nathaniel (1804–1864) The New England-born writer Nathaniel Hawthorne added the letter *w* to his last name to escape his ancestral connection with the Salem witch trial judge, John Hathorne. Ironically, Hawthorne's life and writings inexorably connect him to Salem, Massachusetts, the city of his birth, and Puritanism, the religion of his ancestors. A childhood injury, whether real or imagined, confined a youthful Nathaniel Hawthorne to bed where he read and dreamt, planned his future, and honed his skills as a young writer of essays, poetry, short stories, and contributor of news articles for the short-lived *Spectator*.

Hawthorne's lifetime of financial difficulties began with his father's death in 1808. Hawthorne, his mother, and his sisters depended on the generosity of his maternal Manning relatives during his youth and college years at Bowdoin College. The years of financial struggle lessened with Hawthorne's appointments to the BOSTON Customs House and, later, as surveyor for the District of Salem and Beverly and revenue inspector for the Port of Salem. This work, however, denied Hawthorne sufficient time for his writing. An 1853 appointment as U.S. consul at Liverpool, England, by friend and fellow Bowdoin alumnus, President Franklin Pierce, gave him four years of sufficient income to permit a tour of Europe and to purchase his only home, the former BRONSON ALCOTT family residence in CONCORD, MASSACHUSETTS, renamed the Wayside.

Hawthorne's dark, magnetic good looks drew people to him. His shyness kept them at a distance. Women were attracted to him and solicited both literary and financial support on his behalf. It is possible that the memories of his childhood convalescence found a kindred spirit in his selection of SOPHIA PEABODY (HAWTHORNE) for his wife over her elder, healthier, and more independent sister, ELIZABETH PALMER PEABODY. The Peabody sisters were members of Concord's Transcendentalist movement, and Hawthorne joined the UTOPIAN community at BROOK FARM in 1841 more to save money for his impending marriage to Sophia than from strong intellectual convictions. He stayed less than a year, but the experience contributed to the content of his novel, *The Blithedale Romance* (1852).

In 1842 Elizabeth Peabody persuaded Ralph Waldo Emerson to offer the Emerson family home at the OLD MANSE to the newly wedded Hawthornes. Initially Emerson was not taken with either Hawthorne or his literary talent, but Hawthorne had strong advocates in Peabody and in fellow Transcendentalist MARGARET FULLER, who went to great lengths to extol both his virtue and literary talent to Emerson. EDWARD WALDO EMERSON would later write that his father came to appreciate Hawthorne's personality, but he found Hawthorne's works suffocating because of its excessive emphasis on Puritan guilt, sin, and evil. Emerson's 1864 letter of condolence to Hawthorne's widow expressed great sadness that he could no longer develop what might have been a great friendship. It is clear that Emerson came to admire Nathaniel Hawthorne and his publications, even perceiving himself as a mentor, but Hawthorne's shyness, hermitlike existence, and frequent employment away from Concord prevented what might have been a closer relationship between the two men.

Nathaniel Hawthorne's friendships numbered some of America's most legendary 19th-century writers. Among them, besides Emerson, were Concord authors HENRY DAVID THOREAU, Bronson Alcott, and his daughter, novelist LOUISA MAY ALCOTT. Poet HENRY WADSWORTH LONGFELLOW, a fellow Bowdoin College alumnus, poet OLIVER WENDELL HOLMES, *ATLANTIC MONTHLY* publisher and bookseller James T. Fields, and *Graham Magazine* and *Literary World* literary critic Edwin Percy Whipple were among Hawthorne's friends who later served as his pallbearers. Hawthorne's two-year friendship and mentoring of HERMAN MELVILLE influenced Melville's writing style in his masterpiece, *Moby-Dick* (1851). Edgar Allan Poe criticized Hawthorne's *Twice-Told Tales* and *Mosses from an Old Manse,* while novelist HENRY JAMES and poet JOHN GREENLEAF WHITTIER praised his collective body of work.

The dark struggles in Hawthorne's novels, *The Scarlet Letter* (1851) and *The House of Seven Gables* (1851), perhaps mirrored his own strivings to understand human nature and relationships, to achieve financial and familial security, and to secure the success he believed to be a birthright. Hawthorne's unexpected 1864 death while traveling through New Hampshire ended a writing career that described a historically emerging and conflicted American character and an American dream fraught with demons, constantly changing, and forever elusive—themes that would torment and challenge future generations of American writers.

Further Reading

Bosco, Ronald A., and Jillmarie Murphy. *Hawthorne in His Own Time.* Iowa City: University of Iowa Press, 2007.

Marshall, Megan. *The Peabody Sisters: Three Women Who Ignited American Romanticism.* Boston and New York: Houghton Mifflin, 2005.

Wineapple, Brenda. *Hawthorne: A Life.* New York: Alfred A. Knopf, 2003.

William A. Paquette

Hawthorne, Sophia Peabody (1809–1871) Sophia Peabody Hawthorne, while best known as the wife of author NATHANIEL HAWTHORNE, was an artist and writer in her own right. She was born in Salem, Massachusetts, in 1809 to Elizabeth Palmer and Nathaniel Peabody. As the sister of the publisher, author, and editor ELIZABETH PALMER PEABODY, she had an early introduction to Transcendentalist thought. By the 1830s, Sophia Peabody, who attended one of Ralph Waldo Emerson's early sermons while visiting BOSTON in 1828, was so effusive in her praise of Emerson that her sister Mary teasingly accused her of blasphemy.

Emerson encouraged Sophia Peabody's work as an artist. Despite ongoing health problems, she studied with some of the country's best-known painters, including Chester Harding, Washington Allston, and Thomas Doughty. She often worked as a copyist, although Emerson, along with Allston, urged her to create original paintings. In 1840 she sculpted a bas-relief of CHARLES CHAUNCY EMERSON, Emerson's younger brother who had died in 1836. Emerson, pleased with the result, praised it in letters to MARGARET FULLER and to brother WILLIAM EMERSON, as well as to Peabody herself. Beyond his praise and encouragement, Emerson and Peabody shared similar ideas about the artistic process, about which they corresponded. They believed nature provides the spark of inspiration in the painter, and it is the painter's role to find and portray the beauty in what may seem an uninspiring, everyday setting.

Sophia Peabody and her sister Mary, who would later marry education reformer Horace Mann, spent 18 months in Cuba beginning in December 1833. Sophia wrote long, detailed letters of her experiences to her family, which were widely circulated. Sister Elizabeth prepared portions of the letters to be published in the *ATLANTIC MONTHLY*, but Sophia was embarrassed that so many had already read her private sentiments and blocked the publication. They were eventually published as the *Cuba Journal* in 1985.

Sophia Peabody married writer Nathaniel Hawthorne in 1842. They moved to CONCORD, MASSACHUSETTS, where Emerson arranged for them to live in the OLD MANSE. Sophia stopped painting in 1844, the year her first daughter, Una, was born. The Hawthornes had two more children, Julian in 1846 and Rose in 1851.

From 1853 though 1857 the family lived in Liverpool, England, where Nathaniel Hawthorne served as American consul. In 1858 they traveled through Italy. Elizabeth Peabody and James T. Fields suggested that Sophia Hawthorne publish her diaries of her stay in Europe and contribute to the *Atlantic Monthly*, but Sophia refused the offers. After her husband's death in 1864 left her struggling financially, she changed her mind. Sophia serialized *Notes on Italy and England* in *Putnam's* magazine in 1869 and published it as a book the following year in the United States. While the market was flooded with travel memoirs, fewer than 50 had been written by women at the time Sophia's appeared. She also edited three volumes of her husband's journals for publication, the first, *Passages from the American Notebooks*, appearing in 1868. Sophia Peabody Hawthorne died in England in 1871 and was buried in Kensal Green Cemetery in London. In 2006 her remains were moved and interred next to her husband in Sleepy Hollow Cemetery in Concord, Massachusetts.

Further Reading

Hall, Julie E. "'Coming to Europe,' Coming to Authorship: Sophia Hawthorne and Her *Notes in England and Italy*." *Legacy* 19, no. 2 (2002): 137–151.

Marshall, Megan. *The Peabody Sisters: Three Women Who Ignited American Romanticism*. Boston: Houghton Mifflin, 2005.

Valenti, Patricia Dunlavy. *Sophia Peabody Hawthorne. A Life*. Vol. 1, *1809–1847*. Columbia: University of Missouri Press, 2004.

Kate Culkin

Hedge, Frederic Henry (1805–1890) A native of CAMBRIDGE, MASSACHUSETTS, Frederic Henry Hedge was a roommate of Ralph Waldo Emerson at HARVARD Divinity School and remained an intellectual companion of Emerson throughout his life. The son of a Harvard professor of logic and two years younger than Emerson, at the age of 13 Hedge had gone to Germany, where he studied four years at a gymnasium; his lifelong interest in German philosophy earned him the nickname "Germanicus Hedge" in college. He returned to Cambridge in 1822 and entered the junior class at Harvard, where his classmates included Emerson's younger brother, EDWARD BLISS EMERSON. From there Hedge went on to the Divinity School, taking a degree in 1829. He became a UNITARIAN minister in West Cambridge, and later in Rhode Island and Maine.

Hedge regularly attended the TRANSCENDENTAL CLUB that was founded in 1836. Some people called it "Hedge's Club" because of his intellectual influence and because meetings were scheduled around

Hedge's visits from Maine. Although serving as a minister in Bangor, Maine, during these early years of the Transcendental movement, Hedge remained a peripheral member of the Boston and CONCORD-based circle. Unlike many of his more radical colleagues, he never abandoned his Christian faith and ministry and in the early 1860s served a term as president of the American Unitarian Association.

Hedge's early articles in the *Christian Examiner* in 1833 and 1834 on SAMUEL TAYLOR COLERIDGE and EMANUEL SWEDENBORG powerfully impacted the young Ralph Waldo Emerson. Hedge considered Coleridge, a close companion of WILLIAM WORDSWORTH, to be an intellect of the highest order, a profound thinker and a powerful writer, but not a great poet or critic. He lamented that Coleridge never gave a thorough interpretation of IMMANUEL KANT and the German idealists, and Hedge undertook to provide a summary himself in a series of articles. Unlike most of the Transcendentalists (including Emerson), Hedge was able to read Kant, Johann Gottlieb Fichte, and FRIEDRICH SCHELLING in the original German, and thus boldly mapped Kant's self-described "Copernican revolution" in philosophy. Hedge summarized the key point of the speculations of Kant and his followers as a new emphasis on "the interior consciousness, distinguished from the common consciousness, by its being an active and not passive state."

As there were no English translations of Schelling's works available at the time when Emerson and other American Transcendentalists were writing, Hedge's 1833 review of Coleridge played the key role of transmitting his ideas to the early wave of American Transcendentalists. JAMES ELLIOT CABOT provided Emerson with an English translation of some of Schelling's essays before publishing one of Schelling's lectures in Hedge's 1848 collection, *The Prose Writers of Germany*.

In 1858 Hedge returned to Massachusetts, embarking on a career as Harvard professor of church history and German literature, while continuing to move within the inner circles of Transcendentalism. He was a member of the SATURDAY CLUB, the RADICAL CLUB, and participated in BRONSON ALCOTT's later CONCORD SCHOOL OF PHILOSOPHY AND LITERATURE. In 1870, the new president of Harvard, Charles William Eliot (cousin of Harvard art history professor, CHARLES ELIOT NORTON), was reorganizing graduate education and turned the existing program of university lectures into two yearlong series of lectures. There were seven lecture courses in the philosophy series; besides Emerson, who lectured on the Natural History of Intellect (collected and published posthumously in 1893; see *NATURAL HISTORY OF THE INTELLECT*), the other lecturers were Hedge, Cabot, Francis Bowen, John Fiske, CHARLES SANDERS PEIRCE, and George Fisher. The American pragmatist philosopher Peirce's most important metaphysical essay, "The Law of Mind" (1892), begins by referring to the influence on his own thought of Schelling, "Concord transcendentalism," and Emerson and Hedge.

David A. Dilworth

Hegel, Georg Wilhelm Friedrich (1770–1831) Georg Wilhelm Friedrich Hegel was a fellow student of FRIEDRICH SCHELLING at the university of Tübingen and became an influential professor of philosophy at the universities of Heidelberg and then of Berlin. Hegel's difficult *The Phenomenology of Mind* appeared in 1806, followed by numerous other works, including *The Science of Logic* (1812), *The Philosophy of History* (1818), and *The Philosophy of Right* (1821). Hegel was at one time the neighbor of JOHANN WOLFGANG VON GOETHE, who regarded him cordially but rejected what he called the "dialectical disease" of Hegel's system that culminated in the overarching tenet that "the real is rational and the rational is the real."

Hegel's first book concerned the differences between his post-Kantian predecessors, Johann Gottlieb Fichte and Schelling, with Schelling postulating the emergence of spirit or mind out of inanimate nature, which then reached its highest revelations in human artistic creativity. Hegel offered instead the ideas of Absolute Idealism, in which *Geist* (or spirit) achieved subjective self-awareness, and of Zeitgeist, in which individual creativity is folded into "the spirit of the times" as part of the larger unfolding of history. Nature and history were thus the autobiography of the spirit, an idea that certainly resonated in Emerson. For

Hegel, however, this led to his rejection of liberal individualism and his endorsement of the constitutional monarchy of the Prussian state so that, in its own historical unfolding, Hegel's moral and political philosophy influenced various nationalist theories, including both Nazism and communism. Among his contemporaries, ARTHUR SCHOPENHAUER and Soren Kierkegaard roundly rejected Hegel's totalizing rationalism; in the next generation, FRIEDRICH NIETZSCHE, strongly influenced by the Emersonian alternative, also denounced Hegel.

Glimmerings of Hegel's ideas came to the early Transcendentalists through the writings of FREDERIC HENRY HEDGE, THOMAS CARLYLE, and others; but his influence spread in America only after the Civil War, chiefly through the activities of William Torrey Harris, founder of the St. Louis Philosophical Society in 1866 and its organ, the *Journal of Speculative Philosophy*. In 1878 Harris brought his Hegelian ideas to his numerous lectures at BRONSON ALCOTT'S CONCORD SCHOOL OF PHILOSOPHY AND LITERATURE, which met every summer between 1879 and 1888. Harris went on to publish some of those lectures in *Hegel's Logic: A Book on the Genesis of the Categories of the Mind* (1890).

Although this American interest in Hegel in the post–Civil War era for the most part bypassed Emerson (who was more influenced by Hegel's neighbor, Goethe), the divine universal presence of Emerson's earlier *NATURE* (1836) and "THE OVER-SOUL" (1841) superficially resembled Hegel's concept of the unitary *Geist*. Their differences, however, were more pronounced. As opposed to Hegel's rationale for change as a dialectical process between opposing forces, Emerson's philosophy was based on the more affirmative law of correspondences in nature, as articulated in the 1841 essay "*Compensation.*" Emerson's is the law of "Evil will bless, and ice will burn" (from the poem, "URIEL," 1847) and of his later binary of "FATE" and "POWER" in *The* CONDUCT OF LIFE (1860). Emerson's ethics of self-reliance was a version of this logic that promoted liberal democratic individualism, especially in terms of creative genius, in effect repudiating the collective morality and politics of Hegel.

At the turn of the 20th century, Hegelianism was eventually rejected by the new wave of empirically based Darwinists and philosophical Pragmatists led by CHARLES SANDERS PEIRCE and WILLIAM JAMES, both of whom reworked the anti-Hegelian thrust of Emerson's metaphysical framework and his spirit of romantic individualism.

David A. Dilworth

Higginson, Thomas Wentworth (1823–1911) Thomas Wentworth Higginson is known primarily as the first publisher of EMILY DICKINSON'S poetry, but the bulk of his career was spent as a UNITARIAN minister, writer and editor, advocate of ABOLITIONISM and a reformer, and a lesser-known member of the New England Transcendentalists. Higginson served Unitarian congregations in Newburyport and Worcester, Massachusetts, and was greatly influenced by the work of Ralph Waldo Emerson. He also campaigned passionately against slavery and in support of women's rights and lived an "activist's life."

Higginson had been influenced by earlier abolitionist writings, but following passage of the Fugitive Slave Act in 1850, Higginson joined the BOSTON Vigilance Committee and worked with THEODORE PARKER and others to rescue fugitive slave Thomas Sims in 1851 and Anthony Burns in 1854. During the Civil War he served as colonel of the 1st South Carolina Volunteers, the first black regiment in the war and the subject of his narrative, *Army Life in a Black Regiment* (1870). While the regiment never engaged in a major battle, the 1st South Carolina helped prepare the way for the renowned 54th Massachusetts—Higginson led his men on a small, but well publicized, expedition along the St. Marys River between Georgia and Florida and later participated in the capture of Jacksonville.

Higginson also played an important role in the movement for women's equality and, with Lucy Stone and others, founded the American Woman Suffrage Association and coedited the organization's journal for 14 years. He went on to publish several books on women's equality, including *Woman and Her Wishes* (1853), *Common Sense about Women* (1881), *Women and Men* (1888), and *Women and the Alphabet* (1900). Higginson published two novels—*Malbone: An Oldport Romance*

(1869) and *Oldport Days* (1873)—as well as poetry and essays and served as the poetry editor of the *Nation* for 26 years.

Higginson was a well-known literary critic for the ATLANTIC MONTHLY and in 1862 his essay "Letter to a Young Contributor" prompted Emily Dickinson to write him directly to ask him if her verse was "alive," thus beginning a 23-year correspondence. Higginson warned her against publishing her poetry, however, due to her unconventional style; after her death, he worked with Mabel Loomis Todd in publishing Dickinson's poetry, unfortunately editing it to conform to more conventional punctuation and style.

Higginson had attended lectures by Ralph Waldo Emerson, even before he entered college, and as a young minister he was influenced by Transcendentalism, or what he called the "newness." He credited Emerson for his new thinking on the role of the writer in American society and submitted—and had rejected—several poems to the Transcendentalist journal the DIAL. Higginson identified Emerson as a part of the "*Atlantic* circle," a group of writers who contributed to the *Atlantic Monthly*, where Higginson served as editor. Following the Civil War, Higginson joined the Free Religion Association, formed by Transcendentalists (including Emerson) and radical Unitarians to support "pure religion" and the "scientific study of theology." Emerson was present at the group's first meeting, and Higginson later served as its president. In 1900 Higginson published *Contemporaries*, in which he recorded his own observations of the writers he had known; his entry on Emerson was the first among them.

Further Reading

Meyer, Howard N. *Colonel of the Black Regiment: The Life of Thomas Wentworth Higginson.* New York: W.W. Norton, 1967.

———, ed. *The Magnificent Activist: The Writings of Thomas Wentworth Higginson.* New York: Da Capo Press, 2000.

Wineapple, Brenda. *White Heat: The Friendship of Emily Dickinson and Thomas Wentworth Higginson.* New York: Knopf, 2008.

Jane E. Rosecrans

Hoar, Elizabeth (1814–1878) Elizabeth Sherman Hoar was Ralph Waldo Emerson's fellow intellectual and a close friend of the Emerson family. She came from a prestigious CONCORD family, and her father was the notorious judge Samuel Hoar, who later became a Massachusetts state senator and U.S. congressman. Elizabeth attended and graduated from the Concord Academy, a private school cofounded by her father in 1822, where she received the same training in the classics as boys preparing for HARVARD COLLEGE. A proficient Greek scholar who was trained in several other languages, Elizabeth was both well-educated and deeply religious.

In 1833 Elizabeth became engaged to CHARLES CHAUNCY EMERSON, Ralph Waldo Emerson's youngest brother. Charles managed Samuel Hoar's law office during his term in Congress beginning in 1835. The two made plans to marry in September of 1836, but Charles died of tuberculosis the preceding May. Elizabeth never married and reportedly wore black for 20 years in mourning for Charles. Emerson bonded with Elizabeth while the two were grieving Charles's death, and they remained close thereafter. She was treated as part of the Emerson family; Emerson's mother RUTH HASKINS EMERSON and aunt MARY MOODY EMERSON formed close relationships with her, the Emerson children called her Aunt Lizzie, and Emerson himself referred to her as his "sister." Elizabeth grew particularly fond of Emerson's wife LIDIAN JACKSON EMERSON; she helped nurse her and managed the Emerson household during her illness.

Along with Emerson, Elizabeth Hoar associated with many important Transcendentalists living in and near Concord, Massachusetts. She held among her closest associates notable figures and families such as the Alcotts, the Channings, the Hawthornes, the Peabody sisters, SARAH ALDEN BRADFORD RIPLEY, CAROLINE STURGIS TAPPAN, Anna Ward, Sarah Freeman Clarke, and MARGARET FULLER. She was also a good friend of the Thoreaus; she and her brothers had once been schoolmates of HENRY DAVID THOREAU, and after his death she assisted Sophia Thoreau and (WILLIAM) ELLERY CHANNING in creating a posthumous collection of his works. Elizabeth became an esteemed member of the TRANSCENDENTAL CLUB; she, Margaret

Fuller, and SOPHIA RIPLEY were among the few women in attendance at the group's first meetings. She also regularly attended Margaret Fuller's Conversations and BRONSON ALCOTT's later Conversations, and she contributed to and prepared copy for the *DIAL* during Emerson's tenure as editor. She also translated the private correspondence of Fuller and Giovanni Ossoli, her Italian husband, from Italian to English and contributed an account of the life of Sarah Alden Bradford Ripley for the 1876 book *Women in Our First Century*.

Emerson had immense respect for Hoar's intellect and generosity and referred to her as "Elizabeth the Wise." In a poem he wrote about her, he proclaimed, "My sister is a Greek in mind & face . . . no judge or scribe / Could vie with her unerring estimate." When his daughter ELLEN EMERSON asked him whether she should study Greek, Emerson said yes and cited Aunt Lizzie as an example of an intelligent woman with a "Greek mind." He listed her as "an influence I cannot spare" and part of his essential "platoon" with the likes of Alcott, Thoreau, and Fuller.

Further Reading

Bosco, Ronald A., and Joel Myerson, eds. *Emerson in His Own Time: A Biographical Chronicle of His Life, Drawn from Recollections, Interviews, and Memoirs by Family, Friends, and Associates*. Iowa City: University of Iowa Press, 2003.

Cole, Phyllis. "'Men and Women Conversing': The Emersons in 1837." In *Emersonian Circles: Essays in Honor of Joel Myerson*, edited by Joel Myerson, Wesley T. Mott, and Robert E. Burkholder, 129–159. Rochester, N.Y.: University of Rochester, 1997.

Robbins, Paula. *The Royal Family of Concord: Samuel, Elizabeth, and Rockwood Hoar and Their Friendship with Ralph Waldo Emerson*. Bloomington, Ind.: Xlibris Corporation, 2003.

Wendy Commons

Holmes, Oliver Wendell (1809–1894) The son of a minister, Oliver Wendell Holmes was born in CAMBRIDGE, MASSACHUSETTS. He was the father of Oliver Wendell Holmes, Jr., a Supreme Court justice. Holmes, Sr., became a physician and HARVARD COLLEGE professor of anatomy and physiology but was also a poet and writer. He was the author of the first biography of *Ralph Waldo Emerson*, published in 1884, just two years after Emerson's death.

Holmes had been in attendance at Emerson's 1837 address "The AMERICAN SCHOLAR" and later declared the speech our "intellectual Declaration of Independence." Holmes knew Emerson as a fellow member of the SATURDAY CLUB. He published a poem on the club in the *ATLANTIC MONTHLY* (which he also helped found) and was among the generation of new American poets that included HENRY WADSWORTH LONGFELLOW, JAMES RUSSELL LOWELL, and JOHN GREENLEAF WHITTIER. In August 1858 Holmes accompanied Emerson and other members of the Adirondack Club on a wilderness expedition, the subject of Emerson's poem, "The ADIRONDACS." It was Holmes (in an 1860 *Atlantic Monthly* story) who termed his generation of Boston-area elites with ties to the Puritan founders, which included both Holmes and Emerson, the "Boston Brahmins."

As a biographer and contemporary of Emerson, Holmes had an important role in preserving Emerson's memory and reputation for future readers. Many at the time were surprised that Holmes would write the biography of Emerson, as the two men were not particularly close friends nor did they share the same ideas, particularly about reform. Holmes (whose cousin was prominent abolitionist Wendell Phillips) was a unionist, but he was critical of ABOLITIONISM and held prejudices about the superiority of the white race that upset many abolitionists. Later scholars, as well, would be critical of the portrait of Emerson provided by Holmes, particularly his omission of Emerson's numerous antislavery speeches. Holmes wrote that Emerson had never been "hand in hand with the Abolitionists . . . he seems to have formed a party by himself." While true in a philosophical sense, it was counter to what many knew of Emerson's antislavery commitment; many radical abolitionists, in fact, had considered Emerson a firm supporter of the cause.

Holmes made important contributions as a doctor, publishing an important treatise, *The Contagiousness of Puerperal Fever* (1843), which was one of the earliest understandings of germ theory and infection, in this case, in regard to one of the leading causes of death of women during childbirth. As a result of his insights on this issue, many doctors and midwives changed their practices, and some historians have noted that the death rate from puerperal fever began to decrease in New England. Holmes is also credited with coining the term "anesthesia" for a colleague's pathbreaking use of ether during surgery.

As a member of Boston's elite and as a Harvard professor, Holmes was acquainted with many in the Transcendentalist circle. He did not, however, seem to share the Transcendentalist philosophy, although he did share an interest in poetry and literary criticism. Holmes published three novels and a collection of essays, *The Autocrat of the Breakfast Table* (1858), as well as contributing poems and essays to the *Atlantic Monthly*. His best-known poem, "Old Ironsides" (1830), was a patriotic tribute to the USS *Constitution*, a War of 1812 ship that was scheduled to be scrapped but ultimately, in part due to Holmes's tribute, was saved.

Further Reading

Gibian, Peter. *Oliver Wendell Holmes and the Culture of Conversation.* New York: Cambridge University Press, 2001.

Gougeon, Len. *Virtue's Hero: Emerson, Antislavery, and Reform.* Athens: University of Georgia Press, 1990.

Menand, Louis. *The Metaphysical Club.* New York: Farrar, Straus and Giroux, 2001.

Hooper, Ellen Sturgis (1812–1848) Ellen Sturgis Hooper was considered to be one of the most talented poets of American Transcendentalism. She was born in BOSTON, the second child and the eldest daughter of the six children born to Elizabeth Davis, a *Mayflower* descendant, and William Sturgis, a self-made China-trade shipping tycoon who by 1825 was the wealthiest man in Boston. As a Boston socialite, Ellen Sturgis was provided an excellent education and was free to amuse herself with intellectual endeavors. She attended reading parties led by ELIZABETH PALMER PEABODY and conversations with MARGARET FULLER. She attended Ralph Waldo Emerson's lectures in Boston, and the Sturgis family often entertained the Emersons. In 1837, despite already suffering from consumption, Ellen Sturgis married Dr. Robert William Hooper and bore three children between 1838 and 1843. The youngest child, Clover, later became the wife of writer and historian Henry Adams.

With the introduction of the DIAL in 1840, Hooper was asked by Emerson and Fuller to submit poetry and published her most famous poem, "I slept and dreamed that life was Beauty." Eventually, 11 of her poems were published in the *Dial*, and several others were published privately, including in Elizabeth Peabody's short-lived magazine, *Aesthetic Papers* (1849). HENRY DAVID THOREAU used the last stanza of her poem, "The Wood Fire," which originally appeared in the *Dial*, in the "House-Warming" chapter of *Walden; or, Life in the Woods* (1854). Emerson included her poems "Wayfarers" and "The Chimney-Sweep" as "Sweep Ho!" and "The Nobly Born" in *PARNASSUS*, the collection of his favorite poems published in 1874.

Perhaps in an attempt to distract Hooper from her illness and maternal cares, Margaret Fuller and Ellen's sister, the poet CAROLINE STURGIS TAPPAN, urged her association with the Transcendentalists. Like Emerson, in particular in his essay "EXPERIENCE" (1844), Hooper's poetry yearns for the ideal but is very aware of the mundane. She was a poet living in a world of housewifery, anger, hard work, and sickness—trying to unite with the divine spirit of nature and its eternal source. Her poetry connects with the search within "Experience" for the explanations of death and grieving in the universal order and the ability to transcend the pain of human emotion. Although Ellen Hooper's poems are ultimately more Transcendental by association than by theme, she was greatly revered by the Transcendentalists. Her early death at the age of 36 enshrined her, in the memories of her associates, as a Transcendental angel.

Further Reading

Kaledin, Eugenia. *The Education of Mrs. Henry Adams.* Philadelphia: Temple University Press, 1981.

Myerson, Joel. *The New England Transcendentalists and the Dial.* Rutherford, N.J.: Farleigh Dickinson University Press, 1980.

Barbara Downs Wojtusik

James, Henry, Jr. (1843–1916) The novelist Henry James, Jr., was the younger brother of psychologist-philosopher WILLIAM JAMES and son of HENRY JAMES, SR., theologian and lifelong friend of Emerson and the Transcendentalists. The father shepherded the two brothers and three other siblings around Europe, affording them privileged educations in private tutorial settings. Henry Jr. briefly attended HARVARD COLLEGE intending to study the law, but left to pursue a literary career. In his adult years Henry Jr. was considered "countryless," leaving America to travel in Europe and eventually settling in London. Near the end of his life he became a British citizen and, for his pro-British war writings, received the Order of Merit from King George V. In the course of his 50-year expatriate career he wrote more than 20 novels, a dozen plays, and numerous short stories, volumes of travel writing, and literary criticism, establishing himself as the leading cosmopolitan writer of his era and enjoying status in England as a literary lion. William James characterized his brother, who never married, as "caring for very little but his writing," although "full of dutifulness and affection for all gentle things."

Henry James became known, in particular, for his literary realism in transatlantic novels of ironic encounters between the New World and the Old. Headquartered in London, James established a protective distance from his American origins, while his major novels portrayed a naive innocence of the New World as against the corruption and wisdom of the Old. When the Old and New worlds clashed, his sympathies were decidely with the Old. His novels portrayed the passing of the generations while forecasting America's coming moral problems as it grew into a world power in the 20th century. His early short stories concerned the problems of growing up in the Civil War era in America, and his "character novels," such as *Daisy Miller* (1879), *The Portrait of a Lady* (1881), *The Bostonians* (1886), *The Princess Casamassima* (1886), *The Tragic Muse* (1890), *The Ambassadors* (1901), *The Wings of a Dove* (1902), and *The Golden Bowl* (1903), offered satirical commentary on the lifestyles and mindsets of upper-class Americans, both at home and abroad.

The Bostonians, in particular, caricatured the earlier generation of New England Transcendentalists, as "not so much interesting themselves as interesting because for a season Emerson thought them so." Published after Emerson's death, the novel critiqued the Bostonian's efforts for social reform; in another context, James dismissed people like THOMAS WENTWORTH HIGGINSON (biographer of MARGARET FULLER and leader of the first black regiment during the Civil War) as drawn to "agitations on behalf of everything, almost, but especially of the negroes and the ladies."

James continued his critique of Emerson in a review article of JAMES ELLIOT CABOT's two-volume *Memoir of Ralph Waldo Emerson* (1887). This piece, later appearing in *Critical Portraits* (1888), effectively extended the theme of *The Bostonians,* repeating a contemporary criticism of Emerson's cosmic optimism: "There he could dwell with ripe unconsciousness of evil which is one of the most beautiful signs by which we know him. His early writings are full of quaint animadversion upon the vices of the place and time, but there is something charmingly vague, light and general in the arraignment." James goes on to say: "We feel that his first impressions were gathered in a community from which misery and extravagance, and either extreme, of any sort, were equally absent." In the sociological observations of a novelist, James thus glossed over Emerson's own literature of personal grief as expressed in such essays as "The TRAGIC," "EXPERIENCE," and "FATE," and in poems memorializing the death of his first wife, his two younger brothers, and his five-year-old son Waldo, as well as Emerson's commitments (like Higginson) to ABOLITIONISM and other critical issues.

James's *Critical Portraits* also expressed personal reminiscences of Emerson. He remembers his attendance at Emerson's reading in 1863 of "BOSTON HYMN" to celebrate the Emancipation Proclamation, and he places himself with Emerson in Europe on two occasions in 1872, when the two men walked together through the Louvre and the Vatican. All of James's literary reminiscences corroborated his portrait of Emerson's personality as muted and mild, and yet he conceded a lasting influence, noting that "the impression that he serves . . . will not wear out" and "we cannot afford to drop him."

David A. Dilworth

James, Henry, Sr. (1811–1882) Henry James, Sr., the father of psychologist WILLIAM JAMES, novelist HENRY JAMES, and diarist Alice James, was born in 1811 in Albany, New York, the son of an Irish immigrant. James's father, William, had amassed a considerable fortune by the time Henry was a young adult. James spent much of his youth rebelling against his father's strict Presbyterianism, leading a somewhat dissolute lifestyle; his share of his father's estate left him an annual income of $10,000 for life. While in Albany, James enjoyed outdoor sports, and during one such outing in 1823 he burned his leg so badly it had to be amputated above the knee. The two years James spent recovering from this accident led him to confront God seriously for the first time; he spent much of his recuperative time in reflection and meditation.

James entered Union College in Schenectady in 1828 and reverted to his previous undisciplined lifestyle. He graduated in 1830 and, to appease his father, attempted to study law. However, he soon broke off his study and, seeking to understand his misgivings over religion, entered Princeton Theological Seminary in 1835. However, James left Princeton in order to deal with a newly formed sense of intense religious guilt. James married in 1840, and he and his wife Mary took a home in Washington Square in New York. He met Ralph Waldo Emerson in New York in 1842 and established a lifelong friendship.

In 1844 James suffered a mental breakdown, attributed to anxiety and guilt. At this time he believed he had an experience that EMANUEL SWEDENBORG termed a *vastation.* Swedenborg's theory of vastation—that the process for spiritual regeneration (awakening, purgation, and illumination) was necessary for the rebirth of man into the secret of divine creation—consumed James. While recovering, he explored the breadth of Swedenborg's works, later claiming that in Swedenborg he found the truth he already knew in his heart. This truth, in part, was the realization that "God's great work was wrought not only in the minds of individuals here and there, as my theology taught me, but in the very stuff of human nature itself, in the very commonest affections and appetites and passions of universal man."

Captivated, James spent the rest of his life devoted to the study of Swedenborg. Like many other 19th-century New Englanders, he also became interested in the French social reformer Charles FOURIER. Fourier claimed that all human impulses were good, and that a communal society would be better served in a formal, disciplined arrangement by which the moral impetus served all. James's marriage of Fourierist reform and Swedenborgian theology corresponded with the founding of such communal experiments as GEORGE RIPLEY's BROOK FARM and BRONSON ALCOTT's Fruitlands. James's significant writings in this period include *The Social Significance of Our Institutions* (1861) and *The Secret of Swedenborg, Being an Elucidation of His Doctrine of the Divine Natural Humanity* (1869). James's last book, published in 1879, was titled *Society, the Redeemed Form of Man, and the Earnest of God's Omnipotence in Human Nature;* the title alone attests to James's sincerity.

Henry James, Sr., became something of a literary celebrity in his later years. Through his friendship with Emerson, James came to know the Transcendentalists, who eagerly shared his thinking. James was an elder statesman in New England literary and spiritual circles, known for his writings (particularly those on Swedenborg) and warm, affectionate nature. Henry James, Sr., died in BOSTON in 1882. *The Literary Remains of Henry James,* a book of James's last writings, was edited and published by his son William James in 1885.

Further Reading

Lewis, R. W. B. *The Jameses: A Family Narrative.* New York: Farrar, Straus and Giroux, 1991.

Matthiessen, F. O. *The James Family, Including Selections from the Writings of Henry James, Senior, William, Henry, & Alice James.* New York: Knopf, 1947.

Bill Scalia

James, William (1842–1910) Still heralded as America's most innovative psychologist as well as one of its greatest academic philosophers, William James was by one year the elder brother of novelist HENRY JAMES, JR., and the two brothers were equally famous during their lifetimes. William, it was said, wrote philosophy like a novelist, and Henry Jr. wrote novels like a philosopher. Along with three other siblings, the James brothers grew up in a tight-knit family dominated by their father, HENRY JAMES, SR., a voluble and idiosyncratic theologian-reformer who was drawn to the mystical philosophy of EMANUEL SWEDENBORG and the UTOPIAN ideals of Charles FOURIER. The James children enjoyed the advantages of private tutors as their wealthy father moved them throughout England and the Continent.

After starting out as an artist, the young William was persuaded by his father to pursue a scientific career. He studied medicine at HARVARD COLLEGE before accompanying Louis Agassiz on a zoological expedition to South America in 1865–66. Returning to become a lecturer on physiology and psychology at Harvard, in 1890 he completed a monumental 12-year effort, his two-volume *The Principles of Psychology,* still the classic in its field. James went on to write many moralistic essays on "the energies of men" and "the strenuous life," and his *Will to Believe, and Other Essays in Popular Philosophy* (1897) revealed the influence of Emerson on James's principles of moral conduct. In 1898 James published *Talks to Teachers: and to Students on Some of Life's Ideals,* and he championed intuitional belief in his *The Varieties of Religious Experience* (1902). He went on to argue for the meaning of truth in terms of "subjective cash-value" in his *Pragmatism* (1907). While acknowledging his good friend CHARLES SANDERS PEIRCE as the actual founder of Pragmatism, James promoted the idea of immediately lived experience and social commitment.

Henry Sr. was a longstanding friend of Emerson and others among the Transcendentalists, and the young William James revered the older philosopher. William gave a brilliant eulogy at the centenary celebration of Emerson's birth in CONCORD on May 25, 1903. On Emerson's spirit he wrote, "as long as our English language lasts men's hearts will be cheered and their souls strengthened and liberated by the noble and musical pages with which you have enriched it." In this address William James described Emerson's basic philosophy—his self-reliant individualism based on the immediate presence of God in the receptive human heart and in nature. James went on to emphasize what his own philosophy would also celebrate—Emerson's sense of creative moments "suffused with absolute radiance," which are connected with the moral sentiment and the sense in which individuals thus act "as symbolic mouthpieces of the Universe's meaning."

James's own work reflected Emerson's philosophy in many ways. He famously resolved the issue of free will in making his first act one of believing in free will. But throughout his writings he offered a retrenched doctrine of Emersonian optimism and idealism under the name of "meliorism," not only as a psychological but as a theistic and cosmological position as well. Building on earlier characterizations of the immanent in his *Principles of Psychology,* he developed a unique ontology of a "world of pure experience," which is prior to the subject-object distinction that we have in direct experience. Distinguishing this "radical empiricism" from "ordinary empiricism" of the earlier British schools, James theorized the role of the human mind in this world of pure experience.

In all of these works James remained within the general orbit of Emerson's legacy. Emerson's individualism, and the importance of human power expressed in "POWER" in *The* CONDUCT OF LIFE (1860), prominently resurfaced in James's philosophy. But James, with his predominantly empiricist bent, diverged from Emerson's metaphysics of a universal identity—as well as from Peirce and from other contemporary philosophers such as Harvard colleague and proponent of GEORG HEGEL, Josiah Royce, and British idealist F. H. Bradley. In his later-phase writings such as *Essays in Radical Empiricism* (essays dating from 1904–05 but published posthumously in 1912), *A Pluralistic Universe* (1909), and *The Meaning of Truth: A Sequel to Pragmatism* (1909), James argued in his own way for a radical sense of the "each-form" of "pure experience," while, unlike Emerson and the others, eschewing any "Absolute" in the "all-form." In his last speculations, collected in *Some Problems of Philosophy: A Beginning of an Introduction to Phi-*

losophy (published posthumously in 1911), James was experimenting with metaphysical over beliefs similar to those of Emerson and Peirce that went beyond radical empiricism and pragmatics.

David A. Dilworth

Kant, Immanuel (1724–1804) The German philosopher Immanuel Kant was one of the most important thinkers of the late ENLIGHTENMENT era and paved the way for romantic philosophy of the next generation. After an already distinguished career he entered into his most important work at the relatively late age of 67. Between 1781 and 1790 Kant wrote his three groundbreaking *Critiques* (of Pure Reason, Practical Reason, and Reflective Judgment, respectively). This self-named "Copernican revolution" in philosophy was an attempt to overthrow the dogmatic empiricism of rationalist philosophy in favor of a Transcendental idealism emphasizing the a priori, or intuitive, faculties that situate the source of knowledge outside of sensual experience. Kant's "critical philosophy" ultimately influenced all the schools of philosophy that came after him, offering an alternative source of moral, cognitive, and aesthetic knowledge. Significantly for Emerson, Kant set the stage for his own break from the rationalist religion of UNITARIANISM and the subsequent development of his American Transcendentalist philosophy.

Emerson first encountered Kant and the post-Kantian German idealists (such as Johann Gottlieb Fichte, FRIEDRICH SCHELLING, and GEORG HEGEL) through the writings of his HARVARD Divinity School colleague FREDERIC HENRY HEDGE. Hedge's 1830s writings in the *Christian Examiner* conveyed the key strain of Kant's contribution in his speculations on "the interior consciousness, distinguished from the common consciousness, by its being an active and not passive state." The "passive state" referred to the British empiricists' (including JOHN LOCKE, whose idea of the individual self made possible Kant's later critiques) emphasis on the role of experience in shaping the self.

Although Emerson incorporated Kantian idealism from his very first writings, such as *NATURE* (1836), he gave perhaps the clearest definition of Kant's influence on his own philosophy in "The TRANSCENDENTALIST" (1843), in which he explained,

> the Idealism of the present day acquired the name of Transcendental, from the use of that term by Immanuel Kant, of Konigsberg, who replied to the skeptical philosophy of Locke, which insisted that there was nothing in the intellect which was not previously in the experience of the senses, by showing that there was a very important class of ideas, or imperative forms, which did not come by experience, but through which experience was acquired; that these were intuitions of the mind itself; and he denominated them *Transcendental* forms.

Emerson's reading of Kant was mediated through the writings of not only Hedge but also SAMUEL TAYLOR COLERIDGE and THOMAS CARLYLE. He also read the works of Kant's contemporaries, JOHANN WOLFGANG VON GOETHE and FRIEDRICH VON SCHILLER through the English-language translations of MARGARET FULLER and others among the American Transcendentalists.

But it was ultimately Emerson's own post-Kantian philosophy—through his widely read prose and poetry and through his extensive activity on the lyceum lecture circuit—that became the chief conduit for the 19th-century American reception and understanding of Kant's ideas and influence. Emerson's many writings conveyed the Kantian legacy of the autonomy of the mind and of another layer of understanding or consciousness beyond the material world of experience. Emerson's later writings, such as "POETRY AND IMAGINATION" (1876) and *NATURAL HISTORY OF INTELLECT* (based on his 1870 lectures), carried on the basic idealist tenets of Kant in emphasizing the natural affinities of the human mind with the laws of nature.

Adding to Kant's basic idea of "intuition" over what Emerson termed "tuition," or education, Emerson combined Kant with insights from Coleridge, EMANUEL SWEDENBORG, and the larger school of German idealists to form the central tenets of American Transcendentalism in the 19th century. The next generation of American philosophers, such as CHARLES SANDERS PEIRCE, WILLIAM

JAMES, Josiah Royce, and John Dewey, all drew from this Emersonian post-Kantian legacy.

David A. Dilworth

Lane, Charles (1800–1870) Charles Lane was an English writer, social reformer, and a cofounder of the Fruitlands UTOPIAN community. Before becoming known to Ralph Waldo Emerson in the early 1840s Lane worked in journalism and was editor of the *London Mercantile Price-Current.* He became interested in the work of James Pierrepont Greaves, an influential London reformer who had learned of BRONSON ALCOTT's works through Harriet Martineau and founded "Alcott House," a school and community based on Alcott's education principles at Ham Common in the London suburb of Richmond-upon-Thames in 1838. Lane was working at Alcott House in 1842 when Alcott visited England. Along with an Alcott House colleague, Lane edited the *Healthian,* a monthly periodical that advocated an ascetic vegetarian diet and cold-water cures. Alcott sent some of Lane's writings to Emerson from England. Emerson reviewed these favorably in his article "English Reformers," which was published in the DIAL in October 1842.

Lane followed Alcott to America with his son and contributed several articles to the *Dial.* He purchased a farm in Harvard, Massachusetts, which became the site of the Fruitlands community that he cofounded with Alcott in 1843. Fruitlands was an attempt to elevate life to the ideal by abstaining from artificial contaminants in food, abolishing abusive labor practices, sharing property, and achieving purity in spiritual life. Membership in Fruitlands grew to 14, but Alcott and Lane were unsuccessful in recruiting Emerson. Lane's asceticism, coldness, and insistent, preachy attitude were problematic for Emerson, who quipped in his journal that Alcott and Lane "are always feeling of their shoulders to find if their wings are sprouting." Besides feeling a personal repulsion to Lane, Emerson, though interested in the experiment, saw Fruitlands as unworkable. Not enough food was produced to survive the winter, and the venture failed within one year. For these reasons, Lane was also not liked by Abigail May Alcott or by LOUISA MAY ALCOTT, who later caricatured Lane and the Fruitlands experiment in her 1873 short story, "Transcendental Wild Oats."

After the collapse of Fruitlands in 1844 Lane joined a local Shaker community, attracted by their values of celibacy and communal property. He was obliged to sign over legal guardianship of his son William to the Church Family Trustees upon joining. In the following year Lane realized he had made a mistake, left the Shakers, and returned to England. He was forced to leave his son with the community and became involved in an anguishing transatlantic custody battle, which Emerson knew of through correspondence. Emerson acted sympathetically on Lane's behalf in effecting the sale of the Fruitlands farm and assuring that Lane received payment. Emerson delivered money when he met Lane in London in 1847 before embarking on his British lecture tour. He visited again with Lane in Ham Common during his travels. Lane's son was able to return to England in 1848. In that year Lane informed Emerson in a letter that he had abandoned his ascetic path. He later returned to journalism, remarried, and had four more children in England.

Further Reading

Brewer, Priscilla J. "Emerson, Lane, and the Shakers: A Case of Converging Ideologies." *New England Quarterly* 59, no. 4 (1982): 254–275.

Francis, Richard. *Transcendental Utopias: Individual and Community at Brook Farm, Fruitlands, and Walden.* Ithaca, N.Y.: Cornell University Press, 1997.

Daniel Robert Koch

Locke, John (1632–1704) Emerson's relation to the 17th-century British philosopher John Locke is multifaceted. Locke was a key figure in the philosophical and political tradition that spread from his own generation to ENLIGHTENMENT thinkers and American political founders in the mid-18th century, and was subsequently challenged by the idealist philosophy of IMMANUEL KANT and SAMUEL TAYLOR COLERIDGE, which so directly impacted Emerson. Locke was influenced by the scientific revolution initiated by Copernicus, Kepler, and Galileo and inspired to raise crucial questions as to the origin of human knowledge and social life. His scientific rationalism as applied to the individual as a social and political being thus opened the door to skepticism and idealism, both of which were significant aspects of Emerson's American Transcendentalism of the 19th century.

Emerson endorsed Locke's social contract concerning individual liberty, democratic government, and "natural rights" as the basis of equality under the law. Key aspects of Locke's *Essay Concerning Human Understanding* (1690) entered into Emerson's writings. Locke's "historical, plain method," in which there are no innate ideas, reemerges in Emerson's own naturalistic temper, notably in the cumulative project on *NATURAL HISTORY OF INTELLECT* (published posthumously in 1893). But he departed from Locke in also absorbing Transcendentalist accounts of the superiority of the intuitive mind in PLATONISM and NEOPLATONISM, and in Kant, Coleridge, and FRIEDRICH SCHELLING. Whereas from these sources Emerson developed a philosophy of the universal connection between all things in nature, for Locke universal ideas are only abstract *names* we impose on the real essence of physical *things*, the latter being the source of knowledge. Locke downplayed the relationship between subjective and objective experience, concluding "there is no true science of bodies, much less of spirits."

Locke contributed another set of ideas that entered into Emerson's idealist expansion of such materialism (as Emerson explained most clearly in "The TRANSCENDENTALIST" of 1843). Locke's *Second Treatise of Government* (also 1690) introduced a naturalistic discourse on human "power" that impacted America's founding political fathers as well as American philosophy. Locke distinguished between active and passive power, aligning active power with God's will and the "idea of power" with the human will, or mind. Power, of course, became one of the master-concepts of Emerson throughout his career, from *NATURE* (1836) to the essays on "FATE," "POWER," and "ILLUSIONS" (among others) in *The CONDUCT OF LIFE* (1860), as well as the essays in *SOCIETY AND SOLITUDE* (1870). Emerson received and transformed from JOHANN WOLFGANG VON GOETHE, Kant, Coleridge, and the English romantic poets, a reworking of Locke's "idea of power" in ways that contested Locke's nominalism, or emphasis on the unreality of abstract concepts. Emerson's "NOMINALIST AND REALIST" (1844) offered a balanced account of the relative claims of each side, a problem he bequeathed to the American pragmatists, such as CHARLES SANDERS PEIRCE and WILLIAM JAMES. FRIEDRICH NIETZSCHE was also indebted to Emerson for his own master-concept of "the will to power," which was blended with the ideas of Goethe and of ARTHUR SCHOPENHAUER from his own native German tradition.

Emerson reworked the Lockean framework, distilling the concepts of individual liberty, power, and work for his own democratic individualism in Transcendentalism. His essay "POLITICS" (1844) is only one of many variations on the theme of moral character emerging from individual imagination and intellectual expression. His descriptions of the active "power" of the human mind, governed by the same universal laws of nature, was explored as well in "The METHOD OF NATURE" (1849). In the new American "religion" of Transcendentalism, Emerson was indebted to, but moved beyond, his British predecessor's 17th-century Protestant ethic and empiricism.

David A. Dilworth

Longfellow, Henry Wadsworth (1807–1882) Henry Wadsworth Longfellow was the most popular American poet of the 19th century. Many of his poems have become part of the American literary canon; among them are "The Song of Hiawatha," "Evangeline," "The Courtship of Miles Standish," "The Children's Hour," and "Paul Revere's Ride." Longfellow was also noted as a professor of modern languages at Bowdoin and HARVARD Colleges, and as the first American to translate Dante Alighieri's *The Divine Comedy* into English. His home in CAMBRIDGE, MASSACHUSETTS—Craigie House—was a focal point of American intellectual and cultural life for several decades at mid-century.

Scholars have debated vigorously as to whether Longfellow and Ralph Waldo Emerson were close friends. The two corresponded with one another, belonged to the same clubs, and visited each other

Henry Wadsworth Longfellow (top), Ralph Waldo Emerson (right), and Nathaniel Hawthorne (left), portraits by Eastman Johnson, 1846

on occasion. In public, each praised the other's work graciously; in private, however, they sometimes sniped at each other, as when Emerson wrote to Longfellow shortly after the publication of "The Song of Hiawatha": "I have always one foremost satisfaction in reading your books—that I am safe." Longfellow, for his part, once wrote to his father that Emerson's *ESSAYS: FIRST SERIES* of 1841 was "full of sublime prose-poetry, magnificent absurdities, and simple truths" but not worth sending on by mail to the elder Longfellow. Longfellow's most famous private assessment of Emerson came in 1849: "Emerson is like a beautiful portico, in a lovely scene of nature. We stand expectant, waiting for the High-Priest to come forth; and lo, there comes a gentle wind from the portal, . . . and we ask, 'When will the High-Priest come forth and reveal to us the truth?' and the disciples say, 'He has already gone forth, and is yonder in the meadows.' 'And the truth he was to reveal?' 'It is Nature; nothing more.'"

One might suspect, from the above quotes, that these two literary giants felt somewhat threatened or overshadowed by one another's presence on the Cambridge-CONCORD literary scene. Jealousy certainly seems to be behind this passage from Emerson's journal, dated around 1853: "If Socrates were here, we could go & talk with him; but Longfellow we cannot go and talk with; there is a palace, & servants, & a row of bottles of different coloured wines, & wine glasses, & fine coats."

On a deeper level, though, the two men seemed to have inspired each other to greater heights in their work. At the very least, they helped each other sort out their beliefs and how to express those beliefs in writing. Longfellow, for example, was never fond of Transcendentalism, finding it a bit too abstract and idealizing; so he made it a point to be more concrete, or descriptive, in his poetry. Emerson, for his part, was disturbed by what he saw as too much sentimentality in Longfellow's work, so he made it his business to offset the romanticism that still pervaded American literature.

Near the end of their long lives, Longfellow and Emerson seemed to appreciate each other much more than they had for years. Emerson included one of Longfellow's poems in his 1874 poetry anthology, *PARNASSUS*. After attending Longfellow's funeral in 1882 Emerson remarked, "the gentleman we have just been burying was a sweet and beautiful soul."

Further Reading

Calhoun, Charles C. *Longfellow: A Rediscovered Life.* Boston: Beacon Press, 2004.

Gale, Robert L. *A Henry Wadsworth Longfellow Companion.* Westport, Conn., and London: Greenwood Press, 2003.

Mark Sullivan

Lowell, James Russell (1819–1891) James Russell Lowell was a good friend and promoter of Ralph Waldo Emerson. Lowell was an influential poet, literary critic, and editor, as well as a professor of literature at HARVARD COLLEGE for 20 years. As a member of the SATURDAY CLUB (founded in 1854) and for four years the editor of the *ATLANTIC MONTHLY* (which began in 1857), Lowell was involved in the careers of nearly every major author of the 19th century. Lowell was born and died at Elmwood, the family estate in CAMBRIDGE, MASSACHUSETTS, of a distinguished family that, in the 20th century, included the poets Amy Lowell and Robert Lowell. Though he himself was class poet, James Russell Lowell graduated with difficulty from Harvard in 1838. He took a Harvard Law School degree in 1840, though never practiced as an attorney and chose to pursue a literary career instead.

During his senior year of college Lowell traveled to CONCORD to meet Emerson. While never a theoretical or practical Transcendentalist, he had a love of nature and also shared Emerson's views on the poet as a prophet and critic of society. He was an early participant in ABOLITIONISM, and his wife, Maria White, was also an ardent abolitionist. White was also a gifted poet and inspired Lowell's 1841 collection of poems, *A Year's Life*. That same year he published his sonnet "To a Voice Heard on Mount Auburn," in the January 1841 issue of the DIAL, following with another set of poems in the January 1842 issue. He also contributed to the *Harbinger*, the paper of the BROOK FARM community and in 1843 coedited the *Pioneer*, which during its short life featured the works of NATHANIEL HAWTHORNE and JOHN GREENLEAF WHITTIER, as well as writings by Transcendentalists such as JOHN SULLIVAN DWIGHT, ELIZABETH PALMER PEABODY, and JONES VERY.

In 1845 Lowell published *Conversations on Some Old Poets*, which combined literary criticism with politics. He eventually published about 50 antislavery articles in various journals, and in 1846 he began serializing his *Biglow Papers* (collected in book form in 1848), written in a New England dialect and satirizing the Mexican War. In 1848 he published *A Fable for Critics*, a book-length satirical poem that urged writers to "forget Europe entirely" and appreciate native poets such as Whittier. While celebrating Emerson's genius, *A Fable for Critics* disdainfully caricatured HENRY DAVID THOREAU, AMOS BRONSON ALCOTT, MARGARET FULLER, THEODORE PARKER, and other Transcendentalists as pseudo-intellectuals who did not think for themselves. Fuller returned the favor, calling Lowell's poetry stereotyped and shallow, a view of his verse that has tended to stick.

Intellectually, between 1850 and 1867 Lowell concentrated on national issues. After another year of study in Germany and Italy, in 1855 he succeeded the poet HENRY WADSWORTH LONGFELLOW as Harvard professor of modern languages. For 20 years in this capacity he echoed Emerson in promoting America as a potential source of great poetry. In his own second series of *Biglow Papers* in 1867 he promoted the American scene and vernacular, while championing liberty over the threat of political disunion. After the Civil War, Lowell's thought focused on the Emersonian ethics of self-reliance as exemplified in traditional literary archetypes. As coeditor, with CHARLES ELIOT NORTON, of the *North American Review* between 1864 and 1872, he published critical essays on Dante, Chaucer, Spenser, Shakespeare, Milton, WILLIAM WORDSWORTH, THOMAS CARLYLE, and Emerson. Taking a page from Emerson, he looked to these authors for evidences of "clarified experience" that taught the value of personal character as the antidote to national greed. Always a promoter of Emerson's literary career, he reflected on Emerson's importance as a lecturer in the book *My Study Windows* (1871) and dedicated his most significant collection of literary essays, *Among My Books: Second Series* (1876), to Emerson.

After receiving honorary degrees from both Oxford and Cambridge universities, Lowell resigned from Harvard, although he continued teaching for several years. He served for eight years as U.S. ambassador to Spain and England. After his death in 1891, HENRY JAMES, JR., wrote two eulogistic essays on Lowell, and his editor later named Lowell "the most representative of man's artistic experience through the ages yet attained in America." Sixteen volumes of his collected works were published in 1904.

David A. Dilworth

May, Samuel Joseph (1797–1871) Samuel Joseph May, a UNITARIAN minister, committed himself to a wide range of reforms, including ABOLITIONISM, temperance, nonresistance, and education. Born in BOSTON, MASSACHUSETTS, he was the son of Dorothy Sewall and Colonel Joseph May, a merchant. After attending HARVARD COLLEGE and Divinity School, he married Lucretia Flagge Coffin in 1825; the couple had four children. He served as the pastor to congregations in Brooklyn, Connecticut, and South Scituate (now Norwall), Massachusetts, before moving to Syracuse, New York, to take the ministry of the Church of the Messiah in 1845.

Although May originally supported the American Colonization Society, hearing a speech by William Lloyd Garrison in 1830 converted him to immediate abolitionism. Emerson was one of only two ministers who offered May a place to speak on the subject in Boston, although Emerson did not yet share May's abolitionist fervor. On May 29, 1831, Samuel May gave a sermon entitled *Discourse on Slavery in The United States* from the pulpit of Emerson's Second Unitarian Church. May would go on to help found the American Anti-Slavery Society, encourage Rev. WILLIAM ELLERY CHANNING's involvement in abolition, and, in 1836, publish *Slavery and the Constitution.* In 1844 both Emerson and May spoke at the celebration of "EMANCIPATION OF THE NEGROES IN THE BRITISH WEST INDIES," an event sponsored by the CONCORD Female Anti-Slavery Society and marking a new level of commitment to the cause by Emerson.

Samuel May's relationship with the educator BRONSON ALCOTT, who married May's sister, Abigail, in 1830, tied him to Emerson's town of Concord and its reform movements. May and Alcott shared an interest in educational reform, and through Alcott May learned about the theories of Swiss educator Johann Pestalozzi. May often provided financial support to the constantly struggling Alcotts, including help in underwriting Alcott's UTOPIAN community at Fruitlands. As the experiment fell apart, a frustrated May refused to honor the note he had signed for the Fruitlands property; Emerson eventually assumed responsibility for the note, saving May from possibly serious financial trouble.

May's reform interests stretched far and wide. He helped Horace Mann launch the normal school system of teacher education, served as president of the Normal School of Lexington, Massachusetts, and helped establish a public—and desegregated—school system in Syracuse. In 1846 he published *The Rights and Conditions of Women,* based on a sermon the year before; his interest in women's rights was sparked, in part, by his belief that enfranchised women would support causes such as temperance and nonresistance. His own commitment to nonresistance was tested as the fight for abolition dragged on, a moral conflict about which he corresponded with Emerson. Outraged by the Fugitive Slave Law, May helped plan the rescue of Jerry McHenry in Syracuse, during which a marshal was injured; afterward Emerson teased him about the nonresistant who gave speeches that drove men to violence. May eventually accepted the need for the Civil War, during which he participated in relief efforts for the freedmen and argued for African Americans to be recognized as full citizens of the United States. May died following a stroke he suffered in Syracuse.

Further Reading

Yacovone, Donald. *Samuel Joseph May and the Dilemmas of the Liberal Persuasion, 1797–1871.* Philadelphia: Temple University Press, 1991.

Kate Culkin

Melville, Herman (1819–1891) Herman Melville, born in New York, was forced to sea by the first 25 years of a life full of family struggles. After a brief trip to Liverpool as a cabin boy (experiences related in the 1848 novel *Redburn*), the young man signed on to the *Acushnet,* for a whaling voyage to the South Seas. At the Marquesa Islands, Melville and a companion jumped ship and lived with the Typee natives for three weeks. From there, he sailed across the Pacific, landing at Tahiti and then the Sandwich Islands, finally returning to BOSTON in 1842 on a U.S. Navy frigate. These years provided a lifetime of writing material that would be complemented only by his intellectual development.

By 1847 Melville had encountered the thought of Ralph Waldo Emerson who was lecturing widely in New England and whose works such as *NATURE* (1836) and "SELF-RELIANCE" (1841), were at the heart of the intellectual climate of the day. In 1849 Melville wrote to his editor, Edward Duyckinck, about hearing Emerson speak and reading some of his key essays. He describes Emerson as "a great man" yet with flaws, including a lack of passionate feelings and a tendency toward abstraction. Though Melville was stimulated by "the deep diving" of Emerson, he could never square his own experiences in a Calvinistic Dutch household and as a common sailor with the sublime optimism of Emerson. In the summer of 1850, Melville developed an intense friendship with NATHANIEL HAWTHORNE while both were living in western Massachusetts. This friendship confirmed Melville's intuition of the darker energies attested to by traditional theologies of evil and original sin.

Critics agree that ironic reflections upon the Transcendental spirit can be found throughout the text of Melville's 1851 masterpiece, *Moby-Dick*. For example, the chapter "The Masthead" warns against losing one's identity in the mystical sea, "the visible image of the deep, blue invisible soul." Death awaits the Platonist when reality intrudes. The Transcendental impulse is found again, in Ahab's obsessive need for a direct experience of the inscrutable forces of life itself. For Ahab, the forces beneath the appearances are hostile and need to be confronted with defiance. The Ishmaelian consciousness is more nuanced. In the chapter on "The Whiteness of the Whale," he reflects on the possibility that beneath the sublime beauty of the universe is "the nothingness of atheism." Ishmael better reflects the struggles of Melville to reconcile his Emersonian tendencies with his own Calvinistic views.

After the relative failure of *Moby-Dick* and the total failure of *Pierre* (1852), Melville plunged into a depression that left him on the verge of a breakdown. During this period, he wrote *The Confidence Man* (1857) in which we see his most satiric portrait of Emerson as the confidence man, a hypocrite and a poseur named Mark Winsome. Melville critics see Winsome as a damning portrait of Emerson—two-thirds Yankee businessman and one-third charlatan. However, scholars have also pointed to a series of richly ambiguous marginalia in Melville's own copies of Emerson's *ESSAYS: FIRST SERIES* (1841) and *ESSAYS: SECOND SERIES* (1844), which capture Melville's conflicting judgments about Emerson. For example, Emerson in "Prudence" writes, "The drover, the sailor, buffets it [the storm] all day, and his health renews itself as vigorous a pulse under the sleet, as under the sun of June." Melville comments, "To one who has weathered Cape Horn as a common sailor what stuff all this is."

The Civil War changed forever American intellectual life, and did so for Melville. In 1866 he acquired a job at the New York Custom House and, for the next 20 years, quietly kept writing, his mind still struggling with the problems of free will, determinism, evil, providence. A new dose of Emersonian thought mediated through the German philosophers touched Melville in these later years and the inspired vision of Emerson reverberated throughout all of his works. Melville died in 1891 and the contradictory readings of his posthumously published *Billy Budd* make it clear that Melville never reached a resolution about Emerson's musings on the universe, but that he struggled with those ideas until the very end.

Further Reading

Delbanco, Andrew. *Melville: His World and Work*. New York: Knopf, 2005.

Leyda, Jay, ed. *The Melville Log: A Documentary Life of Herman Melville*. New York: Harcourt, Brace, 1951.

Hank Galmish

Neoplatonic / Neoplatonism Neoplatonism significantly figured in Emerson's thought, beginning with his citation of Plotinus (204–269 C.E.) on the title page of his maiden work, *NATURE* (1836): "Nature is but an image or imitation of wisdom, the last thing of the soul; nature being a thing which doth only do, but not know." Emerson further formulated his metaphysical conceptions of nature in essays such as "The OVER-SOUL" and his idea of unity in variety in such Neoplatonic language. In due course he blended Neoplatonism with his readings of EMANUEL SWEDENBORG, FRIEDRICH SCHELLING, and Hindu, Buddhist, and Sufi texts. Emerson's mystical individualism attests to a pervading incorporation of Neoplatonic themes in Emerson's synthesis of religious, metaphysical, and poetical ideas.

Plotinus was the last of the great Greek philosophers. He transformed the philosophy of Plato into a pronounced mystical strain, thereafter, the Christian West absorbed his mysticism in two main trajectories, stemming from the Greek Patristic writers, on the one hand, and from the Latin legacy of St. Augustine, on the other. The traditions of Neoplatonism subsequently flowered in Renaissance mystics such as Meister Eckhart and Jacob Boehme; they resurfaced in Swedenborg, the German idealists, and the British romantics (such as WILLIAM WORDSWORTH), through whom they became available to American Transcendentalist writers of the 19th century. As religious thinkers concerned with emancipating themselves from their Puritan and then UNITARIAN heritages, the Transcendentalists absorbed the pre-Christian PLATONISM and combined it with currents of eastern mystical thought.

Plotinus's *Enneads* reworked Platonism by placing Plato's eternal Forms or Ideas on an intermediate level between the Divine Mind (called *Nous*) and the contemplation of a higher level called the One or Good. The One or Good diffuses itself into the Forms or Ideas, which in turn radiate downward in the unitary world-soul. Reflective human souls, fleeing the world of appearances, are engaged in an attempted ascent toward the Divine Intelligence, ultimately seeking a mystical union with the One. The human soul thus experiences the tension of both the downward drag into endless multiplicity, on the one hand, and the upward pull of its higher striving toward unity on the other.

Emerson transcribed this Neoplatonic mystical drama into his own doctrine of individual spiritual transparency. He was most likely introduced to Neoplatonism through 18th-century English translations as well as through summaries in VICTOR COUSIN's *Introduction to the History of Philosophy*, translated into English in 1832. This was the time when he was also impacted by the ideas of SAMUEL TAYLOR COLERIDGE and of Neoplatonic strains in Wordsworth and Schelling, among others. Emerson aligned Coleridge's binary of "intuition" and "tuition" with the Neoplatonic tension between the soul's lower and higher destinies. Though "there is a crack in every thing God has made," as Emerson says in his essay "COMPENSATION" (1841), there is no crack in the soul, and there is no end to the higher circles of spiritual consciousness attained in the quest for union with the One or "The Over-Soul."

Emerson expressed the productive power of nature (with Wordsworthian overtones) in "The WORLD-SOUL," "WOODNOTES," and many of his other poems to exhibit the same theme of the fusion of the soul with nature, an idea explored as well in prose essays such as "The METHOD OF NATURE" and "NOMINALIST AND REALIST," among others. Fused with Swedenborg's doctrine of moral and physical "correspondences"—which itself had its provenance in Plato and in Plotinus—Emerson developed his career-long principle of the affinity of the human mind with the laws of physical nature.

Neoplatonism stood for the mystical end of Platonism. Emerson, from his inaugural work *Nature*, and then in "SPIRITUAL LAWS," "CIRCLES," "NATURE," "The Method of Nature," and other early essays, aligned his religious, intellectual, and poetic resources with the Neoplatonic frame of reference. The exigencies of his own emancipation from his Puritan heritage served to liberate Neoplatonism from its associations with Christian theology, allowing it to have a new "naturalistic" life in 19th-century Transcendentalist thought. Neoplatonic mysticism, in its turn, served to suffuse the Transcendentalist sense of nature with the profoundest idealistic overtones. Broadly conceived, this marriage of Neoplatonism and Transcendentalism constituted the new religion of America, the religion of the romantic sublime.

David A. Dilworth

Nietzsche, Friedrich (1844–1900) Emerson's greatest European disciple was the German philosopher Friedrich Nietzsche, whose career partially overlapped with Emerson's later years. Nietzsche's first philosophical essay, "History and Fate," combined the title and themes of Emerson's essays "HISTORY" (1841) and "FATE" (1860). From there Nietzsche approvingly cited Emerson more than 40 times in his writings—noteworthy, considering Nietzsche's critical disdain for most other philosophers. In addition to a running commentary of journal entries on Emerson, Nietzsche kept a marked-up German copy of Emerson's essays (*Versuche*) in his travel bag. But the external signs of their relation are inadequate to estimate the degree to which Nietzsche's thought depended upon Emerson's foundational ideas. This is also true of the other major influence on Nietzsche, the philosophy of ARTHUR SCHOPENHAUER, which, though eventually rejected by Nietzsche, left a deep-seated mark on Nietzsche's overall philosophy of life. In effect, Nietzsche's thought is built upon the ostensibly contradictory influences of these two figures.

Some of Nietzsche's most conspicuous philosophical themes have their provenance in Emerson's prose and poetic writings. The "God Is Dead" theme with which he has become popularly associated has its theoretical foundation in Schopenhauer, but the idea also drew from the philosophical and practical example of Emerson's "DIVINITY SCHOOL ADDRESS" of 1838, which was followed by decades of Emerson's declaration of the exhausted nature of religious doctrine and institutions. Nietzsche tied the death of God and the bankruptcy of Christian morality to the advent of the nihilistic worldview of modern scientific progress, whereas Emerson's rejection of religion more positively embraced the new world of scientific intelligence together with a broad front of idealistic metaphysical concepts that Nietzsche attacked. But the net effect of both their philosophies was to undermine the authority of the dogmatic traditions. Nietzsche followed Emerson's suit, as well, in preaching his own version of moral authenticity of the self-reliant individual who eschews the herd mentality.

Nietzsche's call for a new basis of values looked to the god Dionysius as symbol of this new morality in *Beyond Good and Evil* (1886). Here Nietzsche drew from Emerson's own central imagery of "BACCHUS," the god of wine, which Emerson featured in his 1846 poem. Emerson returned to the wine god as symbol of the mystical and poetical life in the imagery of "FROM THE PERSIAN OF HAFIZ" (1847) and in the essays "POETRY AND IMAGINATION" and "PERSIAN POETRY" (both in *LETTERS AND SOCIAL AIMS*, 1876). Nietzsche's image of the intoxicated Dionysius and his dictum that life can be justified only in aesthetic terms derives in great part from Emerson's influence here. Nietzsche seems also to have taken the title of one of his works, *The Gay Science* (1882), from the phrase "Poetry is the *gai science*" appearing in Emerson's "Poetry and Imagination."

In *The CONDUCT OF LIFE* (1860) and *SOCIETY AND SOLITUDE* (1870) Emerson wrote a number of essays extolling the pursuit of physical health and happiness by living and working in accordance with nature, apart from the false expectations of society. He articulated the tension between the twin forces of "fate," standing for the laws of physical nature, on the one hand, and "power," representing human imagination, intellect, and will, on the other—all in the optimistic tone of Transcendentalism. Nietzsche's signature concept of "the will to power" essentially reprised Emerson's binary of fate and power, while also taking over the American's own signature affirmation of life (Nietzsche's "affirmation of all becoming"). Despite their social criticism in different contexts, both philosophers were profoundly positive humanists, heralding the coming of a future race in prophetic terms.

Emerson's *The Conduct of Life* contains essays on "Fate," "POWER," "WEALTH," "BEHAVIOR," "CULTURE," "WORSHIP," and "ILLUSIONS" that catalog themes that Nietzsche developed for his own purposes. Conspicuously, Nietzsche's concept of "*amor fati*" traces back to Emerson's concluding theme of building an altar to the "Blessed Unity" articulated in "Fate" and played out in poems of personal grief and resignation such as "THRENODY." Energetic "power" and "expression" in the face of life's resistances, as well as a suspicion of society's demands and, ultimately, one's own self-deceptions, occupy both authors in various ways. Nietzsche echoed Emerson in describing an antagonistic universe in which there are natural hierarchies of power, temperament, moral character, and aesthetic sensibilities.

Further Reading

Mikics, David. *The Romance of Individualism in Emerson and Nietzsche.* Athens: Ohio University Press, 2003.

David A. Dilworth

Norton, Andrews (1786–1853) Andrews Norton was, along with WILLIAM ELLERY CHANNING, one of the founders of American UNITARIANISM in the early 19th century. He was a professor of theology at HARVARD Divinity School and became one of the most vocal critics of the emerging Transcendentalist movement, and of Ralph Waldo Emerson, in particular. In 1836 a series of articles and books by former Divinity School graduates, including Emerson, ORESTES BROWNSON, CONVERS FRANCIS, WILLIAM HENRY FURNESS, and GEORGE RIPLEY, prompted a response from Norton that set off a debate within Unitarianism that led to the Transcendentalist split.

Norton was upset with the interest these younger thinkers had in questioning not only the doctrines and rituals of Christianity (as in Emerson's sermon on "The LORD'S SUPPER" of 1832) but also their rejection of Christ's miracles as supernatural events. For radicals such as Emerson and Ripley, the miracles of the New Testament were merely metaphorical, and Emerson, especially as he would articulate in *NATURE* of 1836, posited that no "miracles" can take place outside of the laws of nature—that nature itself is the miracle. For Norton and other conservative Unitarians, without the supernatural miracles as evidence of the divinity of Christ, there was no basis for Christianity. Emerson did not publicly respond to Norton, but Norton and Ripley embarked on a series of heated public exchanges in the Unitarian press.

When Emerson delivered his "DIVINITY SCHOOL ADDRESS" at Harvard in 1838, Norton was further incensed at this attack on the professors and institution that trained Emerson. Norton again publicly criticized Emerson and predicted that Emerson's ideas "could have a disastrous effect upon the religion and moral state of the community," calling the address not only a rejection of Christianity but also "a general attack upon the Clergy." Besides publishing his criticisms in magazine articles, Norton now responded with a book stating his views, *Discourse on the Latest Form of Infidelity* (1839). Emerson, again, chose not to publicly engage Norton in this debate, but he did not speak at Harvard again for 30 years. Emerson's poem "URIEL," published in 1847, is an allegory of this conflict between "the stern old war-gods" of Harvard and the "truth-speaking" Uriel.

The attacks from Norton prompted, in part, the founding of the TRANSCENDENTAL CLUB in 1836 as a forum for those interested in the "new school in literature and religion." After his retirement from Harvard, Norton continued his defense of the divinity of Christ with his three-volume theological work, *Evidences of the Genuineness of the Gospels*, published between 1837 and 1844. His son, CHARLES ELIOT NORTON, was later a friend and supporter of Emerson.

Further Reading

Wright, Conrad Edick, ed. *American Unitarianism, 1805–1865.* Boston: Massachusetts Historical Society and Northeastern University Press, 1989.

Norton, Charles Eliot (1827–1908) Charles Eliot Norton was a Bostonian of many scholarly and literary interests. Although he is not particularly well-known today, his accomplishments were many. He was the first professor of art history in the United States (he taught at HARVARD University from 1875 to 1898) and was the first president of the Archaeological Institute of America (1879 to 1890). Norton founded the Dante Society in 1881 and was one of its first presidents, along with HENRY WADSWORTH LONGFELLOW and JAMES RUSSELL LOWELL. He had cofounded an informal Dante Club as early as 1861 (*The Dante Club* made famous in Matthew Pearl's 2003 novel of the same title) in an effort to educate Americans not only about Dante but also about Italian Renaissance culture in general.

Norton was an author, his most memorable books being *Notes of Travel and Study in Italy* (1859) and *An Historical Study of Church-Building in the Middle Ages: Venice, Siena, and Florence* (1880). He was also a prolific editor, working for the *North American Review* from 1864 to 1868 and later editing for publication the correspondence of many of his associates, among them Ralph Waldo Emerson, THOMAS CARLYLE, James Russell Lowell, GEORGE WILLIAM CURTIS, and John Ruskin. Along with Emerson and others, Norton was also a member of the SATURDAY CLUB.

Norton's relationship with Emerson was a long and complicated one, with many twists and turns. It began inauspiciously, with Charles's father ANDREWS NORTON, a UNITARIAN theologian, denouncing Emerson and Transcendentalism in the 1830s as "the latest form of infidelity." Charles, in spite of his father's antipathy toward Emerson (an antipathy that lasted until Andrews Norton died in 1853), gradually became interested in Emerson's ideas. At first he saw Emerson's writings as "cold and heartless"; but after meeting Emerson, he came to sympathize with the latter's (and the general Transcendentalist) view that each person experiences the world in a unique way, and has his or her own unique religious experience that may not have much to do with any organized religion or philosophical view.

After the Civil War, Norton was even more supportive of Emerson's ideas. He wrote several articles in the *Nation* and *North American Review* that credited Emerson (and the Transcendentalist movement in general) with forcing Americans to reflect more deeply on themselves and on their future during the 1830s and 1840s. According to Norton, it was largely because of Emerson that the young men of the northern states had finally developed enough "moral energy" to take up arms and rid the country of slavery. Soon, in Norton's view, the arts and culture would flourish in America because it had become a better place morally. When the promise of the Reconstruction period failed to materialize, and the arts did not seem to blossom in the United States, Norton was disappointed, and he began to see Emerson's "inveterate and persistent" optimism as dangerous if taken up by the whole nation. That optimism could turn into "a fatalistic indifference to moral considerations, and to personal responsibilities," as Norton confided to his journal in 1873.

At Emerson's passing in 1882, Norton wrote to a friend that Emerson was "not one of the Universal men in a large sense; but a man of some universal sympathies and relations curiously and instructively hampered by local, provincial bonds." Yet he agreed to edit several volumes of Emerson's correspondence for publication and was unfailingly discreet and complimentary of Emerson in those efforts. It is very much due to Charles Eliot Norton that Emerson was so popular and highly respected in the United States in the late 19th and early 20th centuries.

Further Reading

Dowling, Linda. *Charles Eliot Norton: The Art of Reform in Nineteenth-Century America.* Hanover and London: University Press of New England, 2007.

Turner, James. *The Liberal Education of Charles Eliot Norton.* Baltimore and London: Johns Hopkins University Press, 1999.

Mark Sullivan

Old Manse On November 15, 1834, Emerson wrote in his journal, "Hail to the quiet fields of my fathers! Not wholly unattended by supernatural friendship & favor let me come hither. Bless my purposes as they are simple and virtuous." Emerson wrote these words from his desk upstairs at the Old Manse, the CONCORD, MASSACHUSETTS, home of his step-grandfather, Rev. EZRA RIPLEY; here Emerson would begin work on his seminal Transcendentalist text, *NATURE* (1836). "Manse" was an English word for the parsonage, or home, of a minister, and the Concord home was christened "The Old Manse" with the publication of NATHANIEL HAWTHORNE's short-story collection, *Mosses from an Old Manse,* in the late 1840s.

After the death of his first wife in 1831, and his resignation from Boston's Second Church the following year, Emerson sent his mother and brother to Dr. Ripley's home in Concord and left for an 18-month tour of Europe. Upon his return, he took up residence in the Manse and began his career as a lecturer and writer in Concord. Until the purchase of his own home the following year, Emerson had not been a regular resident of Concord, having been born, raised, and schooled in BOSTON. He was, however, a frequent visitor, especially after his father, William Emerson, died in 1811, and his mother, RUTH HASKINS EMERSON, struggling to raise her five boys, frequently sent them to stay at the Manse, often accompanied by Aunt MARY MOODY EMERSON.

William Emerson, Ralph Waldo's grandfather, was minister at Concord's First Parish Church and in 1770 borrowed £100 from the church to buy the land and then build the Manse. From the back of the house the occupants could see Old North Bridge, where British soldiers marched into Concord on the day of the first battle of the Revolutionary War. William Emerson served as a chaplain during the war and died of camp fever in 1776. His wife, Phebe Bliss Emerson, inherited one-third of the house and outbuildings, with the rest going to their only son, William, with small amounts for daughters and future grandsons. She rented a room in her third of the house to the new minister, young Ezra Ripley, and they soon married, despite her being 10 years his senior. In the 1780s and '90s Ripley bought out the shares of his stepchildren, and thus the Manse no longer officially belonged to the Emerson family. As the descendant of seven generations of Concord ministers, going back to the town's founding in 1635, Emerson always considered the Manse (and Concord) his ancestral home.

Throughout the 19th century the Old Manse was open to the Ralph Waldo Emerson family. When the Emerson home caught fire and was badly damaged in 1872, Waldo, LIDIAN JACKSON EMERSON, and their daughter ELLEN EMERSON moved into temporary quarters at the Manse. After the stress of the fire, Emerson and daughter Ellen embarked on a recuperative trip to Europe and Egypt, leaving Lidian to stay at the Manse "quite happily." Emerson always acknowledged the personal significance of the Manse to his life in Concord. In September 1838 he recorded in his journal of a Sabbath evening visit: "I went at sundown to the top of Dr. Ripley's hill & renewed my vows to the Genius of that place."

After the death of Ezra Ripley in 1841, the Manse was rented to Nathaniel Hawthorne and his new bride SOPHIA PEABODY HAWTHORNE; they lived there from 1842 to 1845. As a wedding gift, and also due to his attachment to the house, Emerson paid HENRY DAVID THOREAU to plant an extensive vegetable garden for the newlyweds. After the Hawthornes moved to Salem, Rev. SAMUEL RIPLEY and his brilliant wife SARAH ALDEN BRADFORD RIPLEY moved into the family home. Samuel died in 1867, and Sarah inherited the house and property in its entirety. Upon her death in 1895, the property went to her daughter, and members of the Ripley family lived in the Old Manse until 1939, when they sold it to the Massachusetts Trustees of Reservations. The Old Manse became a National Historic Landmark in 1966.

Further Reading

"The Old Manse." The Trustees of Reservations Web site. Available online. URL: http://thetrustees.org/places-to-visit/greater-boston/old-manse.html. Accessed April 1, 2010.

Audrey Raden

Parker, Theodore (1810–1860) The reformer, promoter of ABOLITIONISM, and UNITARIAN minister Theodore Parker began his career as a schoolteacher, but graduated from HARVARD Divinity School in 1836 and became a central figure in the early Transcendentalist controversy. A native of Lexington, Massachusetts, Parker was lecturing in nearby CONCORD in 1836 when he met Emerson for the first time. That same year, Parker began attending meetings of the new TRANSCENDENTAL CLUB.

Parker's recent biographer concedes that while interactions between Parker and Emerson were, in Emerson's words, "quite accidental," Emerson had an enormous impact on Parker, who played a significant role in the continued theological debates among the Transcendentalists. While Emerson was among those who left the Unitarian ministry as a protest of conscience and became the spokesperson for a secular philosophy, Parker remained a significant voice within radical Unitarian theology from a Transcendentalist perspective. Considered, along with WILLIAM ELLERY CHANNING, to be one of the most influential Unitarian ministers of the 19th century, he was a religious mentor for others within the movement who retained their ties to liberal Christianity, such as CAROLINE DALL, ELIZABETH PALMER PEABODY, OCTAVIUS BROOKS FROTHINGHAM (who published an 1874 biography of Parker), and THOMAS WENTWORTH HIGGINSON.

Both Parker and Emerson were interested in religious reform but, whereas Emerson's "DIVINITY SCHOOL ADDRESS" of 1838 (which Parker attended) was a scathing critique of Unitarianism and marked

Emerson's rejection of organized religion, Parker's sermons on "The State of the Church" and "The Duties of these Irreligious Times" called for a new approach to religion and spirituality from within the church. Parker's most Transcendental and controversial statement on the issue was his "South Boston Sermon," published in 1841 as *A Discourse on the Transient and Permanent in Christianity.* The *Discourse* created almost as much controversy and criticism as Emerson's "Divinity School Address" a few years earlier. Parker, like Emerson, questioned the divinity of Jesus Christ and the supernatural nature of the miracles, by looking at Jesus as a historical figure and criticizing dogmatic institutions and teachings. The sermon clearly aligned Parker with Emersonian Transcendentalism and led some to call, unsuccessfully, for Parker's removal from the ministry. Many of his Unitarian colleagues and friends (such as CONVERS FRANCIS) broke ties with Parker over the address and subsequently banned him from preaching in their pulpits.

Parker did not go as far as Emerson, however, and, rather than rejecting religion, went on to found his own wildly popular Twenty-Eighth Congregational Society, which became the largest church in BOSTON for a time; worshippers at Parker's church included prominent reformers William Lloyd Garrison and Elizabeth Cady Stanton, and novelist and daughter of Transcendentalism, LOUISA MAY ALCOTT. Parker followed up on the theological controversy with another series of lectures and sermons published in 1842 as *A Discourse of Matters Pertaining to Religion.* He further aligned himself with the Transcendentalist controversy and with Emerson in the early 1840s by publishing numerous essays, poems, and sermons in the *DIAL,* first under the editorship of MARGARET FULLER and later under Emerson. The first issue of the *Dial* in July 1840 included Parker's essay "The Divine Presence in Nature and in the Soul."

Theodore Parker remained a minister, but he was also a popular lecturer on theological as well as political and social reform. He founded his own literary and reform journal, the *Massachusetts Quarterly Review* (1847–50), supported women's rights, and was an active abolitionist. He was chairman of the Boston Vigilance Committee, which opposed the federal Fugitive Slave Act of 1850 and encouraged citizens in the Northern states to ignore the law by assisting fugitive slaves. In 1854 Parker was jailed (but never charged) for encouraging public protest in the Boston case of the arrest and return of an alleged fugitive, Anthony Burns. In 1859 Parker, like Emerson and HENRY DAVID THOREAU, defended white abolitionist and revolutionary JOHN BROWN. Parker died in Europe in 1860.

Further Reading

Grodzins, Dean. *American Heretic: Theodore Parker and Transcendentalism.* Chapel Hill: University of North Carolina Press, 2002.

Peabody, Elizabeth Palmer (1804–1894) The reformer, author, and publisher Elizabeth Palmer Peabody first met Ralph Waldo Emerson when she employed him as a Greek tutor in BOSTON in the 1820s. The two formed a close friendship based on intellectual like-mindedness, and Peabody was at the center of Transcendentalist activities for more than 60 years. Peabody never married and was the older sister of Mary Peabody and SOPHIA PEABODY HAWTHORNE, wife of the novelist NATHANIEL HAWTHORNE. Elizabeth Peabody was a protégée of the UNITARIAN minister WILLIAM ELLERY CHANNING and, like Emerson, was interested in questions of spirituality, historical Christianity, and self-education. She had helped run a school with her mother and sisters and was committed to education in all its forms. She assisted BRONSON ALCOTT with his controversial Temple School in Boston, about which she published her notes as *Record of a School* (1835). Her interest in education extended throughout the century, and she is best-known today as the founder of the first public kindergarten in the United States in 1860 and as a writer and editor of the journal *Kindergarten Messenger.*

Peabody spent extended periods in the Emerson household in CONCORD, was close friends with LIDIAN JACKSON EMERSON, and recorded her accompaniment of Emerson on his "daily walk and conversation" in those days. For one 1836 journal entry Peabody recorded that she and Emerson "looked for the Gothic architecture, or rather it showed itself to us, the low Saxon Arch, and the painted Gothic window, formed by the naked branches against the sunset sky"—the exact imagery and analogy that Emerson used in his poem "The SNOW-STORM" and in his essay "HISTORY" (both published in 1841).

Peabody assisted Emerson in organizing his manuscripts and lectures—helping him, as she phrased it, "discipline himself to integrate his thoughts" and improve his "carrying power with the masses." She assisted him in having his lectures published, in the role of agent and then as a publisher herself. In 1840 Peabody opened the West Street bookstore and library at her home in Boston, an invaluable resource for the emerging Transcendentalist literary community. Peabody's store made available many translated works of prose and poetry for the first time and was Emerson's own source for several volumes during these years; one friend referred to the store as a "Transcendental exchange." Peabody published six issues of the *DIAL*, in which some of her own essays on UTOPIAN reform and BROOK FARM were printed, such as "A Glimpse of Christ's Idea of Society" (October 1841), "Plan of the West Roxbury Community" (January 1842), and "Fourierism" (April 1844). Emerson named Peabody as one of the "young people" (even though she was, in fact, a year younger than Emerson) interested in communitarian reform as a way to "rewrite institutions," noting in his journal that "Brownson, Channing, Greene, Peabody, and possibly Bancroft think that the vice of the age is to exaggerate individualism."

Peabody also hosted several of MARGARET FULLER's Conversations for women in her bookstore-parlor, as well as the final 1840 meeting of the TRANSCENDENTAL CLUB. She was responsible for introducing many promising young people to Transcendentalism and to Emerson, including the women's rights activist CAROLINE DALL and the poet JONES VERY. In 1849 Peabody edited and published a collection entitled *Aesthetic Papers*, which printed for the first time HENRY DAVID THOREAU's essay "Resistance to Civil Government" (later known as "Civil Disobedience"). She also encouraged the literary career of her friend and then brother-in-law Nathaniel Hawthorne, publishing some of his early children's stories under her own press.

In the 1870s and 1880s Peabody lectured at the CONCORD SCHOOL OF PHILOSOPHY AND LITERATURE, organized by her lifelong friend and colleague Bronson Alcott. Living to almost age 90, Peabody was one of the longest-living of Emerson's generation of Transcendentalists and one of the most active in the movement throughout the century.

Further Reading

Marshall, Megan. *The Peabody Sisters: Three Women Who Ignited American Romanticism.* Boston: Houghton Mifflin, 2005.

Ronda, Bruce A. *Elizabeth Palmer Peabody: A Reformer on Her Own Terms.* Cambridge, Mass.: Harvard University Press, 1999.

Peirce, Charles Sanders (1839–1914) Charles Sanders Peirce was the founder of Pragmatism, which he later called Pragmaticism to distinguish his philosophy from the popularized version of his close friend, HARVARD COLLEGE psychologist and philosopher WILLIAM JAMES. In his most important metaphysical essay, "The Law of Mind," Peirce acknowledged the influence on his thought by theologian HENRY JAMES, SR., and by Ralph Waldo Emerson and CONCORD Transcendentalism during his younger years. Peirce's father, Benjamin, occupied the chair of mathematics and astronomy at Harvard and was, with Emerson, a charter member of the monthly SATURDAY CLUB, founded in BOSTON in 1856.

After graduating at the age of 20 from Harvard with a degree in chemistry, Charles Peirce eventually developed expertise across the mathematical, logical, and hard and soft sciences. During his lifetime he published prolifically on topics ranging from astronomy, mathematics, chemistry, geodesy, surveying techniques, cartography, lexicography, economic theory, and the history of science and philosophy. He was a lifelong student of medicine, a prolific book reviewer, dramatist, actor, short story writer, and inventor. Except for a brief tenure teaching logic at Johns Hopkins University, Peirce's own career as a writer and thinker took place primarily outside of the university. His chief employment was as a government surveyor and physicist, and he represented the United States at several international scientific conferences.

Peirce grew up amidst a generation of Boston Brahmins and CAMBRIDGE intellectuals whose lives had been impacted by Ralph Waldo Emerson, who, in his later years, was a welcome visitor in both the Peirce and James families. Though more diffused, Peirce became Emerson's greatest philosophical disciple (even greater than FRIEDRICH NIETZSCHE) of the next generation, and Peirce's master concepts of Fallibilism, Abduction, Synechism, and Objective Idealism were formed out of Emerson's Transcendentalist-idealism in novel ways. Although a professional scientist, ultimately Peirce's chief genius was philosophical; he was particularly interested in IMMANUEL KANT and, partly through Emerson and FREDERIC HENRY HEDGE, was also influenced by the writings of FRIEDRICH SCHELLING and GEORG HEGEL.

Peirce began the mature phase of his metaphysical speculations with "A Guess at the Riddle" (1878–88), which directly referenced Emerson's popular poem "The SPHINX" (1841). In his 1892 essay "The Law of Mind" Peirce developed his theory of spontaneous variation in nature, which he classified under the category of "Firstness," corresponding in significant ways to what Emerson understood as intuition or instinct. In a playful fashion, Peirce acknowledged that his system had its roots in Emerson's Transcendentalism: "I may mention, for the benefit of those who are curious in studying mental biographies, that I was born and reared in the neighbourhood of Concord—I mean in Cambridge—at the time when Emerson, Hedge, and their friends were disseminating the ideas that they had caught from Schelling, and Schelling from Plotinus, from Boehm, and from God knows what minds stricken with the monstrous monism of the East." He went on to joke that he was "not conscious of having contracted any of the virus" of "Concord transcendentalism," but it was "probable that . . . some benignant form of the disease was implanted in my soul."

Indeed, several years earlier, in 1870, Peirce had shared a lecture series with Emerson and Hedge at Harvard. Emerson's 16 lectures in that series became his *NATURAL HISTORY OF INTELLECT* (published posthumously in 1893), a compositely edited collection of the most important philosophical work of Emerson's later career. As Peirce was then contemporaneously acquainted with Emerson's lectures, it is likely that, consciously or unconsciously, Emerson influenced Peirce's explanation in "The Law of Mind" that "all the regularities of nature and of mind are regarded as products of growth," and that "matter" is "mere specialized and partially deadened mind."

Peirce's "Firstness" also corresponded with Emerson's principle expressed in "The OVER-SOUL," which emphasized the correlations between nature and the human mind, and the poetic and scientific transformation of the former into the latter. As a logician and more systematic philosopher, however, Peirce's sprawling texts differed markedly from the rhetorical-poetic masterpieces of Emerson. Emerson analogized where Peirce analyzed. Nevertheless, Peirce's ideas were fundamentally in line with, and anticipated by, his predecessor Emerson, and he gracefully acknowledged that influence.

Further Reading

Brent, Joseph. *Charles Sanders Peirce: A Life.* Rev. ed. Bloomington: Indiana University Press, 1998.

Peirce, Charles Sanders. *The Essential Peirce,* 2 vols., edited by Nathan Houser and Christian Kloesel. Bloomington: Indiana University Press, 1992 and 1998.

David A. Dilworth

Platonic / Platonism In "PLATO; OR, THE PHILOSOPHER," positioned as the first essay in his collection *REPRESENTATIVE MEN* (1850), Emerson declared: "Out of Plato come all things that are still written and debated among men of thought." "Plato is philosophy, and philosophy, Plato," he continued, "neither Saxon nor Roman have availed to add any idea to his categories." In due course Plato's philosophy was the prism through which were refracted the systems of Aristotle, Plotinus, the Christian Neoplatonists (*see* NEOPLATONIC / NEOPLATONISM), Dante and St. Thomas, the Cambridge Platonists and Berkeley, Descartes and Leibniz, IMMANUEL KANT and the German Idealists, and then the American Transcendentalists.

Eloquently writing of "Plato's range"—his "broad humanity" that transcends all sectional lines—

Emerson noted that "Plato seems, to a reader in New England, an American genius." Plato in fact deeply appealed to other Transcendentalists, such as AMOS BRONSON ALCOTT and GEORGE RIPLEY, and it was Emerson's own writings, beginning with *NATURE* (1836), that were responsible for the deep currents of Platonism in 19th-century American Transcendentalism.

Emerson concluded his essay on Plato by observing that Plato influenced and transcended any philosophical system, before or after: "He has clapped copyright on the world." So, Emerson admits, Platonism itself can hardly be defined: "The acutest German, the lovingest disciple, could never tell what Platonism was; indeed, admirable texts can be quoted on both sides of every great question from him." Plato's lack of system, then, was both praiseworthy and the sole defect of Plato, according to Emerson, as his writings lack "the vital authority" of "prophets" and "sermons," that is, of religion.

Emerson's own writings defied systemization, emulating Plato's broad metaphysical principles, such as the "world of becoming," which resurfaces in Emerson's sense of the "evanescence and lubricity of all objects" ("EXPERIENCE," in *ESSAYS: SECOND SERIES* [1844]), and his attempt to balance the idea of metamorphosis, or change, in nature against the idea of a core, stable identity forms the basis of "INTELLECT" (1841) and the later "ILLUSIONS" (1860). Indeed, that binary is front and center throughout Emerson's prose and poetry. He reprises Plato's sense of persuasion over force in his own dialectic of "FATE" and "POWER" in the essays of *The CONDUCT OF LIFE* (1860). Emerson's evolutionary optimism, an understanding of the connection between the human mind and the laws of nature that also drew on his readings of EMANUEL SWEDENBORG, JOHANN WOLFGANG VON GOETHE, and FRIEDRICH SCHELLING, is another variation on Plato's worldview.

In his own Transcendentalism-idealism, Emerson thoroughly absorbed Plato's philosophy of absolutes, while simultaneously promoting poetic intuition as the chief access to the over-soul (of his 1841 essay "The OVER-SOUL"). Furthermore, Emerson's ethics of self-reliant democratic individualism were in decisive contrast to Plato's communitarian politics. In his own work, then, Emerson revised Platonism on a more universal and liberating plane. Plato's writings displayed a kind of spiritual clairvoyance reprised in Emerson's signature image of the "transparent eyeball" and other expressions that situated knowledge of universal laws within the subjective standpoint of the individual.

In Plato's *Dialogues,* Socrates consults the Delphic oracle, through whom the highest wisdom of the gods is revealed (much like "The SPHINX" in Emerson's poem). Plato himself frequently speaks in a mythic voice that reveals a higher, spiritual truth concerning a realm of being that "eternally is" in contrast to the shifting world of natural phenomena that are "always becoming and never are." This is the realm of the ideas or forms, and it is the goal of the self-guided soul to move beyond the understanding of the senses toward Plato's over-arching idea of the good or beautiful. This governing principle resurfaces as the principle of justice in the *Republic,* as psychological and aesthetic integrity in the *Symposium* and *Phaedrus,* and as cosmological order in the *Timaeus.*

Emerson employed Platonism, as a way to interpret experience and nature, in his poetic sensibility as well. In the chapter on "Literature" in *ENGLISH TRAITS* (1856) he explained: "Whoever discredits analogy, and requires heaps of facts, before any theories can be attempted, has no poetic power, and nothing original or beautiful will be produced by him. John Locke is as surely the influx of decomposition and of prose, as Bacon and the Platonists, of growth . . . 'Tis quite certain that Spencer, Burns, Byron and Wordsworth will be Platonists, and that the dull men will be Lockists."

In the next generation CHARLES SANDERS PEIRCE expressed his indebtedness to Emerson's "Concord transcendentalism" by acknowledging Emerson's influence in his key chapter "The Law of Mind" in 1892 and further developing the idealistic worldview of Platonism through his own idea of "concrete reasonableness."

David A. Dilworth

Radical Club Ralph Waldo Emerson was a member of, and frequent lecturer at, the informally organized Radical Club, founded in BOSTON by the minister CYRUS BARTOL in 1867 and continuing until 1880. The Radical Club was an offshoot of the Free Religious Association, both of which drew their post–Civil War membership from those associated with Transcendentalism and with radical UNITARIANISM. Among Emerson's circle of friends, attendees at the Radical Club included BRONSON ALCOTT, WILLIAM HENRY CHANNING, JAMES FREEMAN CLARKE, CHRISTOPHER PEARSE CRANCH, JOHN SULLIVAN DWIGHT, FREDERIC HENRY HEDGE, THOMAS WENTWORTH HIGGINSON, ELIZABETH PALMER PEABODY, and JOHN WEISS, among others. The Radical Club was committed to a free and open discussion of spiritual topics, both within and outside of particular religious traditions. As founder Bartol explained in his book *Radical Problems* (1872), the Radical Club "denies to affirm, clears the way to travel, vetoes less than it signs, and tears down to build."

There is no formal record of the Radical Club, but the most comprehensive contemporary account is Mrs. John T. (Mary Elizabeth Fiske) Sargent's *Sketches and Reminiscences of the Radical Club of Boston* (1880). Sargent (at whose home the club often met) recorded many of Emerson's responses to lectures by other members and gives an account of an 1873 "reception" for Emerson, noting that, "while the genius of Ralph Waldo Emerson belongs to the whole world he is essentially the property of Boston." Besides regular club members, the reception was attended by prominent reformers and literary figures, including JOHN GREENLEAF WHITTIER, HENRY WADSWORTH LONGFELLOW, and abolitionist Wendell Phillips. Sargent reprinted Emerson's poem "BOSTON" and at least one Emerson club lecture on "Religion" (May 1867).

In her *Reminiscences* (1899), attendee Julia Ward Howe reported that, as the club attracted more well-known members, accounts of the meetings were deemed of interest to the general public and were reported in such widely read papers as the *New York Tribune.* According to Howe, "Mr. Emerson objected strongly to newspaper reports of the sittings of the Radical Club." Emerson feared that the publicity "interfered with the freedom of the occasion," and, according to Howe, "When this objection failed to prevail, he withdrew from the club almost entirely, and was never more heard among its speakers."

Ripley, Ezra (1751–1841) Ezra Ripley was Ralph Waldo Emerson's step-grandfather and a CONCORD minister for 63 years. Ripley was born in Connecticut but educated at HARVARD COLLEGE in CAMBRIDGE, MASSACHUSETTS. After his graduation in 1776 he moved to Concord and was ordained as minister of the First Parish Church in 1778; he served there until his death in 1841. In 1780 he married Phebe Bliss Emerson, widow of Rev. William Emerson, his predecessor at First Church and grandfather of Ralph Waldo Emerson. Ezra Ripley moved into the Emerson family homestead at the OLD MANSE in Concord and raised William Emerson's children as well as three children he fathered with Phebe Bliss Emerson. Young Ralph Waldo and his brothers were frequent visitors to the Ripley home in Concord, as their own mother, RUTH HASKINS EMERSON, was widowed and arranging for the education of five sons. Emerson returned again to stay with his grandparents in Concord in 1835, writing part of his work on *NATURE* (1836) in the upstairs study of the Old Manse.

Ezra Ripley was thus still a prominent citizen of Concord when Ralph Waldo Emerson settled there as an adult, and he relayed to Emerson much about Concord's people and history. Theologically, Ripley was a conservative Congregationalist minister who was older and more traditional than the new, liberal UNITARIANS and not affiliated with Transcendentalism. Many years after Ripley's death, Ralph Waldo Emerson published a reminiscence of his step-grandfather in the *ATLANTIC MONTHLY*, placing Ripley in the history of the church as a man "identified with the ideas and forms of the New England Church, which expired about the same time with him."

Ripley, George (1802–1880) Born in 1802, George Ripley was raised an orthodox Congregationalist. After graduating from HARVARD Divinity School with high honors, he entered the UNITARIAN ministry as pastor of BOSTON's Purchase Street Church in 1826. One year later, he married the educated and cultured SOPHIA WILLARD DANA (RIPLEY). Although well-respected and admired by his congregation and the public as a religious leader, Ripley was not content in his position. During his early years in the ministry, he embarked on an extensive study of German philosophy. In 1836, the TRANSCENDENTAL CLUB formed with Ripley, Emerson, ORESTES BROWNSON, BRONSON ALCOTT, FREDERIC HENRY HEDGE, and THEODORE PARKER among the original members. The primary intent of the loosely organized group was to discuss the current unsatisfactory state of theology and philosophy, and what possible reform might be achieved. Several meetings were hosted at the Ripley home. Later Ripley served as assistant editor of the *DIAL*, under MARGARET FULLER.

Ripley's studies in German philosophy, participation in the Transcendental Club, and his increasing frustration with Unitarian colleagues led him to publish *Discourses on the Philosophy of Religion* in 1836, the same year Emerson's *NATURE* appeared. Ripley's text stressed individual intuition and the presence of the divine in every man. In outrage, ANDREWS NORTON, professor at Harvard, publicly challenged Ripley to defend his views in the *Boston Daily Advertiser*. Ripley responded, succinctly stating that he believed Lockean (*see* JOHN LOCKE) philosophy to be "superficial, irreligious, and false in its primary elements." The two would debate in print several more times over the years; Ripley also defended Emerson against Norton's public attack on the "DIVINITY SCHOOL ADDRESS" in 1838.

In August of 1840, Ripley, Theodore Parker, and Bronson Alcott attended the Christian Union Convention in Groton, a gathering organized to "protest against all creeds and sects." Also in attendance was Adin Ballou, who was in the process of outlining plans for his Hopedale community. Ripley and Ballou discussed collaborating on a new community, yet differed on the issue of religious exclusivity. Unlike Ballou, George and Sophia Ripley envisioned a nonsectarian community; their goal was to "meet in the church on the broadest ground of spiritual equality." Alcott later went on to found the utopian community at Fruitlands. Within two months of the convention, at the age of 38 and after 15 years in the ministry, Ripley submitted his letter of resignation to the Purchase Street Church, with Sophia's support. Emerson praised the move and wrote that it "cannot be without an important sequel." That sequel was the utopian community of BROOK FARM, nearly 200 acres in West Roxbury, eight miles outside of Boston, to which the Ripleys moved in the spring of 1841.

Ripley's enthusiasm for the project caused Emerson no small amount of disquietude. In a letter to Emerson, Ripley detailed his ideal of a community that would "be a place for improving the race of men that lived on it." Upon receipt of the letter, Emerson spent more than a month in soul-searching debate on the topic of community but ultimately declined the invitation to join, primarily on the grounds that he "must assume his own vows." Both Ripley and Alcott believed that life in an ideal community would allow the individual to reach his full potential; Emerson and HENRY DAVID THOREAU were skeptical. Emerson believed that "a man is stronger than a city; that his solitude is more prevalent and beneficent than the concert of crowds"; this decision would later form the basis of his 1841 essay "SELF-RELIANCE." Emerson also saw some of the potential flaws in Ripley's plans, particularly the equal payment plans, which did in fact contribute to problems amongst the Brook Farmers.

Nevertheless, Brook Farm lasted for seven years, during which time the members were plagued with financial woes, a smallpox outbreak, and a devastating fire that resulted in crushing debt. And yet, during the community's short lifetime, it attracted hundreds of members and several thousand annual visitors; the Brook Farm school was widely celebrated and even recommended by Harvard as a preparatory school; and the *Harbinger*, its weekly magazine that focused on social and political issues, achieved modest success as a publication, with contributors such as JAMES RUSSELL LOWELL, JOHN GREENLEAF WHITTIER, and Horace Greeley.

After the sale of Brook Farm, the Ripleys moved to New York, where George accepted Margaret Fuller's former position as editor for the *New York Tribune* under his friend Horace Greeley. He helped to found *Harper's New Monthly Magazine* one year later, and with Charles Dana edited the 16-volume *New American Cyclopaedia*, a project that finally enabled him to pay off the Brook Farm debt. In his career as literary critic, Ripley finally found his calling. Ripley's articles and reviews were often syndicated; in particular, he received widespread acclaim for his review of Darwin's *On the Origin of Species.* After Sophia's death in 1861, Ripley married Augusta Schlossberger in 1865. He spent the remainder of his life in New York as an editor with the *New York Tribune.*

Further Reading

Crowe, Charles. *George Ripley: Transcendentalist and Utopian Socialist.* Athens: University of Georgia Press, 1967.

Kari Miller

Ripley, Samuel (1783–1847) Samuel Ripley was a "newer breed" UNITARIAN minister of the generation before Emerson. He was Emerson's half-uncle, the son of Emerson's paternal grandmother, Phebe Bliss Emerson, and her second husband, minister EZRA RIPLEY, who still embraced the conservative orthodoxy of 18th-century Puritanism. Together with his highly educated wife, SARAH ALDEN BRADFORD RIPLEY, Samuel Ripley ran a respected boy's school to prepare young men for HARVARD COLLEGE. Ralph Waldo Emerson worked as a tutor there while a student at Harvard, as did his brothers, and Emerson preached his first sermon, "Pray without Ceasing," in his uncle's congregation in Waltham, Massachusetts, in the fall of 1826.

Samuel Ripley was not a Transcendentalist but remained a supporter of many of the radical figures of the movement when they were under fire from the Unitarian establishment in the 1830s. Although alarmed by certain controversial elements of his nephew's 1838 "DIVINITY SCHOOL ADDRESS," Ripley kept his pulpit open to him and extended a similar welcome to THEODORE PARKER when he was shut out of other Unitarian churches after 1841. Samuel Ripley also defended Emerson's cousin, GEORGE RIPLEY, against the attacks of fellow minister ANDREWS NORTON over the "miracles controversy," which pitted the Unitarians against the Transcendentalists over the supernatural character of Christ's miracles.

Samuel Ripley retired in 1846 to his childhood home at the OLD MANSE in CONCORD, the 22-acre homestead where Emerson had lived with his mother, RUTH HASKINS EMERSON, in 1834–35 and NATHANIEL HAWTHORNE and SOPHIA PEABODY HAWTHORNE had lived between 1842 and 1844. It was here at the Old Manse that Samuel and Sarah Ripley regularly entertained many of the Transcendentalist circle until Samuel's unexpected death by heart attack at age 64.

David A. Dilworth

Ripley, Sarah Alden Bradford (1793–1867) Sarah Alden Bradford Ripley was the wife of Ralph Waldo Emerson's half-uncle, the UNITARIAN minister SAMUEL RIPLEY, and was a friend of many among the Transcendentalists. She entertained family, friends, and leading intellectuals of the day at her home in Waltham, Massachusetts, and later at the family homestead in CONCORD, the OLD MANSE, where she lived from 1846 until her death in 1867. Sarah Bradford and Samuel Ripley were married in 1818 and had nine children, seven of whom survived childhood. She and her minister husband operated a boy's school to prepare young men for HARVARD COLLEGE, where Emerson and his brothers also had jobs as tutors. She was one of the few women who attended the meetings of the TRANSCENDENTAL CLUB, especially those held at the Emerson home in Concord, although neither she nor Samuel Ripley ever identified as Transcendentalists.

Sarah Alden Bradford descended from prominent pilgrim families, and her parents were members of the First Church of BOSTON, whose minister was WILLIAM EMERSON, father of Ralph Waldo. Her father was a Boston-based sea captain in the Mediterranean trade, and her mother became an invalid with tuberculosis. By the time she was 14, Sarah had major responsibility for the household and her six younger sisters and brothers, but she seized every opportunity for study. She learned Latin along with her brothers and taught herself Greek; her father brought books home from his travels, and soon Sarah was reading French and Italian works as well. Independently she took up physics, chemistry, and botany, the latter as a lifelong study. When her brothers entered Harvard College, she devoured their books and thus gave herself a college education. She tutored the youngest members of the family at home and began reading the new German biblical criticism and trading thoughts on theology with MARY MOODY EMERSON, the young Emerson boys' brilliant and opinionated aunt and Sarah's self-appointed mentor. The president of Harvard, Edward Everett, was so impressed with her that he once admitted she could have been on the faculty if women were allowed.

Her friend ELIZABETH HOAR later wrote a memorial entry on "Mrs. Samuel Ripley" for the 1876 book *Worthy Women in Our First Century;* the volume reprints numerous letters from Sarah Alden Bradford Ripley to Mary Moody Emerson and a young Ralph Waldo Emerson, as well as reminiscences by FREDERIC HENRY HEDGE and Ralph Waldo Emerson's obituary of Ripley after her death in 1867.

Further Reading

Goodwin, Joan W. *The Remarkable Mrs. Ripley: The Life of Sarah Alden Bradford Ripley.* Boston: Northeastern University Press, 1998.

David A. Dilworth

Ripley, Sophia Willard Dana (1803–1861) Sophia Dana was born into an illustrious BOSTON Brahmin family. Her ancestors included a signer of the Declaration of Independence, a Revolutionary War hero, and a president of HARVARD COLLEGE. Sophia was considered one of the best-educated women of her time. Unfortunately, her father depleted the family fortune, and financial difficulties caused Sophia and her mother to have to establish a school in CAMBRIDGE where they educated sons of many prominent families. The school was successful, and Sophia was remembered by her former students for her intelligence and erudition.

In 1827 Sophia Dana married GEORGE RIPLEY, the liberal UNITARIAN minister of the Boston Purchase Street Church. He and other like-minded thinkers eventually established the TRANSCENDENTAL CLUB, the first group to be identified with an American Transcendentalist movement. The meetings were often held at the Ripley home with Sophia in attendance. Sophia Ripley participated in most of the activities of Transcendentalism, including regularly attending MARGARET FULLER's Conversations and contributing three articles to the *DIAL*. Her best remembered piece, "Woman," began as a topic for discussion at the Conversations. In it Sophia promotes the Transcendental tenets of self-reliance and self-culture, particularly for women. Her interests in scholarship, education, and Transcendentalism made her a valuable partner to George Ripley. Together in 1841 they founded BROOK FARM, the UTOPIAN community dedicated to the Transcendental ideals of plain living and high thinking.

Even as Sophia Ripley prepared for the establishment of the "Brook Farm Institute of Agriculture and Education," she continued to assist with the publication of the *Dial* by proofreading Emerson's essays, and she assisted her husband in writing sermons. However, her duties multiplied with the opening of Brook Farm. Education was paramount to the institution, and Sophia was primarily in charge of this aspect. Her 10-hour days also included administrative duties, ironing, and even the task of caring for a young leper. Meanwhile, she taught Greek and Latin, translated French philosophy, and gave various other courses, including one on Dante thought to be the first such course in America. Sophia Ripley was an unfaltering advocate of Brook Farm from its inception in 1840 until its collapse in 1847. A series of catastrophes added to its demise, but the school was always considered one of the community's few successes.

Once again after the financial disaster of Brook Farm, Sophia relied on her education. She and George moved to Long Island, New York, while George attempted to secure a job in New York City. In the meantime, Sophia supported the family by teaching. Although she had been considering it previously, in 1849 Sophia formally announced her conversion to Catholicism. A group of other Transcendentalists had also converted over the years, including ORESTES BROWNSON, but Sophia's decision attracted considerable attention. A well-known woman from a liberal, Protestant, Brahmin family had joined a church consisting mainly of poor, uneducated Irish immigrants. Ironically, upon her premature death in 1861, her funeral services were held in the Purchase Street Church, where she and George had begun their married life, but which had since become a Catholic church.

Further Reading

Delano, Sterling. *Brook Farm: The Dark Side of Utopia.* Cambridge, Mass.: Harvard University Press, 2004.

Raymond, Henrietta Dana. *Sophia Willard Dana Ripley: Co-Founder of Brook Farm.* Portsmouth, N.H.: P. E. Randall, 1994.

Swift, Lindsay. *Brook Farm: Its Members, Scholars, and Visitors.* 1900. Reprint, New York: Citadel Press, 1973.

Barbara Downs Wojtusik

Sanborn, Franklin Benjamin (1831–1917) Franklin Benjamin Sanborn was a teacher, journalist, social reformer, founder of the American Social Science Association, and early biographer of prominent Transcendentalists, including Ralph Waldo Emerson, HENRY DAVID THOREAU, and AMOS BRONSON ALCOTT. As a younger Transcendentalist, Sanborn was one of the few who were not also UNITARIAN ministers. Sanborn had grown up amidst the fervor of Transcendentalism; in 1851, while a student at HARVARD COLLEGE, Sanborn descended on the home of Ralph Waldo Emerson, intending to introduce himself to the man whose works he had come to idolize. Though the front door was open, Sanborn did not meet Emerson that day, waiting another two years before introducing himself—a meeting during which Emerson told the young man that he hoped to see a "good crop of mystics" emerge from Harvard. Later, Sanborn would consult "the oracle" as he referred to Emerson, and he would open a small school in CONCORD, MASSACHUSETTS, under Emerson's patronage.

By far, Sanborn's greatest reform passion was ABOLITIONISM. At the age of nine, he announced to his family that he had determined that slavery was wrong and in 1851 heard his first abolitionist speeches, by THEODORE PARKER and Wendell Phillips. Sanborn met JOHN BROWN in 1857 and worked for "Free Kansas," Brown's program to defend the territory against pro-slavery advances. Later he served as an important conduit between Brown and abolitionist sympathizers in Concord, including Emerson, Thoreau, and Parker. Sanborn became a member of the "secret six," a small group who had knowledge of the overall details and had directed elements of the final stages of Brown's plan to raid the arsenal at Harpers Ferry, Virginia. Following the failure at Harpers Ferry, Sanborn left the country for Canada as a known coconspirator, whose writing had been found among Brown's papers. Emerson urged Sanborn to return to Concord and plead Brown's case, but Sanborn returned only after learning that none of the six would be tried for treason.

Following his return, Sanborn became the epicenter of a series of dramatic events, later described by Abbie May, the youngest Alcott daughter, as the "Sanborn kidnapping." Sanborn had received a summons to testify in Washington, D.C., before the Senate committee investigating the events of Harpers Ferry, but Sanborn ignored the summons, and on the evening of April 3, 1860, four federal marshals appeared at his door to apprehend him. According to his own account, Sanborn claims to have used his 6-foot-5-inch frame to physically resist the "four rascals." Before long, the entire town of Concord was involved in the melee, the news having been spread by the townswomen. Thanks to legal maneuverings, Sanborn was released and the following day appeared before the state supreme court in BOSTON, where the warrant was dismissed and Sanborn was returned to Concord a hero.

Sanborn was involved in other social reforms and in 1865 founded the American Social Science Association in order to forward reform in the treatment of prisoners and the mentally ill and to advocate for the poor. Sanborn served as editor of the Boston *Commonwealth* (1863–67), editor of the *Journal of Social Science* (1867–97), and was a correspondent for the Springfield *Republican* (1868–1914). In the 1870s and 1880s he was heavily involved in Bronson Alcott's CONCORD SCHOOL OF PHILOSOPHY AND LITERATURE and edited two volumes of lectures from those meetings. As a chronicler of the Transcendentalists, he also wrote biographies of *Thoreau* (1872), *Emerson* (1895),

Hawthorne (1908), and coauthored (with William Torrey Harris) *A. Bronson Alcott: His Life and Philosophy* (1893). Sanborn's *Recollections of Seventy Years* (1909) includes many reminiscences of the Transcendentalists in Concord. Sanborn died in 1917, on the cusp of World War I, and was buried at Sleepy Hollow Cemetery in Concord.

Jane E. Rosecrans

Saturday Club The Saturday Club was a BOSTON-based social and literary club founded in 1854 and whose original members included Emerson, HARVARD COLLEGE professors Louis Agassiz and Benjamin Peirce (father of philosopher CHARLES SANDERS PEIRCE of the next generation), BRONSON ALCOTT, JAMES FREEMAN CLARKE, JOHN SULLIVAN DWIGHT, NATHANIEL HAWTHORNE, OLIVER WENDELL HOLMES, HENRY WADSWORTH LONGFELLOW, editor JAMES RUSSELL LOWELL, HENRY DAVID THOREAU, and JOHN GREENLEAF WHITTIER, among other prominent Bostonians. Later members included HENRY JAMES, JR., and WILLIAM JAMES, as well as Emerson's own son, EDWARD WALDO EMERSON.

The group (which continued well into the 20th century) met one Saturday per month, with its meeting times originally coinciding with Emerson's periodic visits to take care of publishing business in Boston. This monthly trip usually included dining with friends, and the Saturday Club was born. Club members soon became interested in launching a new literary magazine to represent New England and were responsible for founding the *ATLANTIC MONTHLY* just a few years later in 1857.

The Saturday Club had no single philosophical bent, although membership overlapped with and was drawn from other Transcendentalist gatherings. Many of the same individuals had been members years earlier of the TRANSCENDENTAL CLUB and the TOWN AND COUNTRY CLUB. As Edward Emerson would later note, "Certain foreshadowings of our Club appear by 1836." It was also from the Saturday Club that the Adirondack Club emerged with, again, many of the same members. An 1858 Adirondack Club camping trip was the subject of Emerson's poem "The ADIRONDACS."

Oliver Wendell Holmes wrote a poem, "At the Saturday Club," which appeared in the *Atlantic Monthly* of January 1884. The poem included commentary on individual members, including Emerson, of whom Holmes wrote, "Ask you what name this prisoned spirit bears / While with ourselves this fleeting breath it shares? / Till angels greet him with a sweeter one / In Heaven, on earth we call him EMERSON." Holmes also noted of the "lofty" ideals of club members, that "Lofty, but narrow; jealous passers-by / Say Boston always held her head too high."

One hundred years of the Saturday Club have been recorded in three volumes: Edward Waldo Emerson's *Early Years of the Saturday Club, 1855–1870* (1918); M. A. DeWolfe Howe's *Later Years of the Saturday Club, 1870–1920* (1927); and Edward Waldo Forbes's (grandson of Emerson and son of EDITH EMERSON) *The Saturday Club: A Century Completed, 1920–1956* (1958).

Schelling, Friedrich (1775–1854) Friedrich Wilhelm Joseph von Schelling was a German philosopher whose ideas greatly impacted Emerson and the Transcendentalists at the very beginning of the movement. FREDERIC HENRY HEDGE spent fours years in Germany, returning to the United States to write articles in 1833 and 1834 in the *Christian Examiner* on Schelling and the other post-Kantian German Idealists, as well as on SAMUEL TAYLOR COLERIDGE and EMANUEL SWEDENBORG, articles that powerfully impacted the young Emerson just as he was making his break from UNITARIANISM. Hedge (who went on to play a leading role in the TRANSCENDENTAL CLUB of 1836) wrote of IMMANUEL KANT and his followers, including Schelling, that they promoted "the interior consciousness, distinguished from the common consciousness, by its being an active and not passive state."

Schelling, the son of a Lutheran minister who became a professor of Oriental languages, was academically brilliant as a child. In his teens he absorbed the philosophies of Spinoza, Kant, and Fichte, and at the age of 23 he was appointed professor of philosophy at the university in Jena in Thuringia, then the most prestigious educational center in the German states. Beginning with *Of the Ego as Principle of Philosophy* (1795), his system underwent a series of metamorphoses, as expressed in 15 books, including *Ideas toward a Philosophy of Nature* (1797), *System of Transcendental Idealism* (1800), and *Philosophical Inquiries into the Nature of Human Freedom* (1809). He continued to write and lecture until shortly before his death at the age of nearly 80.

The Transcendentalists gained access to Schelling's ideas either through Hedge's articles or by traveling to the German states and personally hearing Schelling lecture. A young American, Charles Stearns Wheeler, who worked on a multivolume series of THOMAS CARLYLE's writings published in 1838–39, traveled with JAMES ELLIOT CABOT and JOHN WEISS to the Continent; they attended Schelling's lectures, and Wheeler sent notes on these lectures back to Emerson, who published them in the *DIAL* in 1843. Cabot provided Emerson with early English translations of some of Schelling's essays before publishing one of Schelling's lectures in Hedge's 1848 collection, *The Prose Writers of Germany*.

Schelling's *Ideas toward a Philosophy of Nature* became his most influential "romantic" philosophical work. Schelling argued for an evolutionary philosophy of spirit in which objective nature was the one and total reality. From a pristine nature develop perpetually changing and ascendant forms of plants, animals, and humans. Schelling posited that mankind is matter having achieved spiritual form within the ongoing creative process of nature's inner striving, the *natura naturans*—a concept that reappeared in Schelling's contemporary ARTHUR SCHOPENHAUER and in Emerson's essay "NATURE" (1844). It is especially through artistic creativity, Schelling argued, that mankind represents the culmination of nature's process of spiritualization.

Schelling's ideas, including his romanticism of nature, influenced his contemporaries, including his personal friend JOHANN WOLFGANG VON GOETHE, Coleridge, Schopenhauer, composer Carl Maria von Weber, and the poets Hölderlin and Novalis. Goethe and Coleridge, in particular, would influence the American Transcendentalists and, beginning with *NATURE* (1836), Schelling's ideas surfaced ubiquitously in Emerson's prose and poetic writings. For example, Emerson's central and abiding insistence on the affinity of nature and spirit comes directly from Schelling who, in *Ideas toward a Philosophy of Nature,* wrote, "Nature is visible Spirit; Spirit is invisible Nature." In Emerson's theory of the intuitive revelations of the poetic genius, and in his concept of nature's culmination in human consciousness, he shared with Schelling the idea that matter was merely a form of mind. In Emerson's Transcendentalism, however, Schelling's concepts were poetically blended with PLATONISM, NEOPLATONISM, Swedenborg, and the Hindus as well. Schelling's influence continued into the next generation with CHARLES SANDERS PEIRCE who, in his 1892 essay "The Law of Mind," explicitly acknowledged his debt to Schelling via Hedge and Emerson.

David A. Dilworth

Schiller, (Johann Christoph) Friedrich von (1759–1805) Johann Christoph Friedrich von Schiller was a dramatist, poet, historian, and aesthetician and is regarded, along with his colleague JOHANN WOLFGANG VON GOETHE, as one of the greatest German literary figures of his time. His early dramas were concerned with social and political oppression, and later ones—such as *Maria Stuart* (1801) and *Wilhelm Tell* (1804)—addressed spiritual freedom liberated from the claims of the world and depicted man as participating in an eternal moral order. His histories of the revolt of the Netherlands (1788) and of the Thirty Years' War (1791–93) led to a professorship of history at the University of Jena in 1790. These historiographical writings also provided background material for his greatest drama, the *Wallenstein* trilogy (1800), which was translated and highly praised by SAMUEL TAYLOR COLERIDGE as "not unlike Shakespeare's historical plays—a species by itself." In his poetry and philosophical treatises Schiller reflected his encounter with the ideas of his contemporaries Johann Gottlieb Fichte and IMMANUEL KANT.

Kant's *Critique of Practical Reason* (1787) and *Critique of Judgment* (1790) both articulated Transcendental dimensions of freedom as over and against the determined world of the senses and its scientific understanding elaborated in his *Critique of Pure Reason* (1781). Schiller's influential *Letters on the Aesthetic Education of Man* exploited Kant's third *Critique* by prioritizing the "play impulse," which accounts for our judgments of taste with respect to beauty in nature and in the fine arts. Schiller placed such aesthetic experience as occupying an intermediate region between sensuous nature and ethical or logical form. Accordingly he argued that aesthetic appreciation must precede political, moral, and scientific education, being the only viable means to reconcile the inner antagonisms between sense and intellect, nature and freedom, in the decadent modern world.

Together with Goethe, Schiller's work and thought greatly impacted the American Transcendentalists. Emerson read THOMAS CARLYLE's *Life of Schiller* (published in 1825), and Emerson's entire philosophy ultimately incorporated Goethe and Schiller's aesthetic ideals and priorities. Like Schiller, Emerson retained Kant's idea of the reciprocal relationship between sensuous matter and intellectual and moral formation; at the same time he blended in FRIEDRICH SCHELLING's sense of the spiritual evolution of form out of matter from an original force in nature. Emerson's idea of "intuition" was thus an aesthetic naturalism at the basis of which functioned Schiller's "play impulse," implicated in Emerson's ideas of nature and those expressed in "The WORLD-SOUL" and "The OVER-SOUL."

Interest in Schiller was promoted as well by Emerson's Transcendentalist colleagues JAMES FREEMAN CLARKE, JOHN SULLIVAN DWIGHT, MARGARET FULLER, FREDERIC HENRY HEDGE, and Charles Timothy Brooks. Dwight contributed translations of Schiller and Goethe's poems in GEORGE RIPLEY's 14-volume *Specimens of Foreign Standard Literature;* Fuller translated and wrote critical studies of Goethe and Schiller; Hedge wrote on many of the German authors, literary and philosophical, for the *Christian Examiner;* and Brooks produced translations of two of Schiller's poems for the April 1844 issue of the *DIAL*. Interest in Goethe and Schiller continued after the Civil War, as for example in CYRUS BARTOL's lecture on the two German authors at AMOS BRONSON ALCOTT's CONCORD SCHOOL OF PHILOSOPHY AND LITERATURE, founded in 1879.

Schiller's philosophical influence extended into the next generation to CHARLES SANDERS PEIRCE, who translated Emerson's ideas into his own metaphysical concepts in such essays as "A Guess at the Riddle" (1887–88) and "The Law of Mind" (1892). Peirce directly conceptualized an aesthetic ideal prior to the ethical and logical domains of human inquiry and built in Schiller's concept of the "play impulse" *(Spieltrieb)* as the source of all forms of creative thought—scientific, poetical, and religious.

David A. Dilworth

Schlegel, August Wilhelm von (1767–1845)
August Wilhelm von Schlegel was a contemporary of JOHANN WOLFGANG VON GOETHE, FRIEDRICH VON SCHILLER, FRIEDRICH SCHELLING, ARTHUR SCHOPENHAUER, and other shapers of German idealism and romanticism. Schlegel contributed to Schiller's periodical *Die Horen* in 1796; afterward, with his brother Friedrich Schlegel he founded the influential journal *Athenäun,* which also published FRIEDRICH SCHLEIERMACHER in its pages. As professor at the University of Jena from 1798, August Schlegel wrote essays promoting Goethe and embarked on his own magnum opus of a poetical translation of the works of William Shakespeare. The work included 17 plays translated by Schlegel himself, with others completed under the direction of his colleague Johann Ludwig Tieck; the Schlegel Shakespeare translations are still a standard text in Germany. In his lectures on literature and art Schlegel promoted Shakespeare and Dante while rejecting the values of the modern European ENLIGHTENMENT. He also published translations of Italian, Spanish, and Portuguese romance literatures.

Schlegel was a traveling companion of Madame Germaine de Staël in the early 1800s, and her writings also influenced the Transcendentalists. Her German history, *De l'Allemagne* (1810), incorporated many of Schlegel's core romantic values of intuition and individualism. Her work (and her life) was of particular interest among the Transcendentalists, and Emerson read her as early as the 1820s. MARGARET FULLER was one of the few American Transcendentalists to read Schlegel in the original German; Emerson read him in translation, including an 1833 edition of Schlegel's *Lectures on Dramatic Art and Literature*. The Americans had their own access to Shakespeare in English but were influenced by Schlegel's organic theory, which emphasized the creative genius as "representing" specific cultural circumstances as well as universal characteristic of human nature. In his *REPRESENTATIVE MEN* (1850) Emerson subsequently featured essays on "SHAKSPEARE; OR, THE POET" and "GOETHE; OR, THE WRITER." Schlegel's theory of art, which prioritized the poetic or artistic life over the theoretical, moral, and political dimensions, is broadly present in Emerson's writings.

Schlegel became a professor of literature at Bonn University in 1818, where he became the first German specialist in Sanskrit language and literature. His pioneering work in this area included a scholarly three-volume work, *Indische Bibliothek* (1820–30), the printing of the Bhagavad Gita in Sanskrit with a Latin translation (1823), and a printing of the *Ramayana* (1829–46). This work impacted Schopenhauer and, together with Emerson, the two became the chief philosophical conduits for the reception of Hindu ideas in 19th-century Europe and America, respectively.

David A. Dilworth

Schleiermacher, Friedrich Daniel Ernst (1768–1834) Friedrich Schleiermacher emerged as one of the most influential thinkers of 19th-century Protestantism. The American Transcendentalists Emerson and GEORGE RIPLEY, who were both breaking from their UNITARIAN background, became the chief early conduits for Schleiermacher's ideas, which they blended with similar currents of idealist and romantic thought from EMANUEL SWEDENBORG, JOHANN WOLFGANG VON GOETHE, FRIEDRICH SCHILLER, AUGUST SCHLEGEL, and others. Emerson first learned of Schleiermacher from his older brother, WILLIAM EMERSON, who studied in Germany and sent back reports of Schleiermacher's mystical theology. FREDERIC HENRY HEDGE and JAMES FREEMAN CLARKE also encouraged Emerson to study Schleiermacher in tandem with other German philosophers at a time when Emerson was making his own break from Unitarianism.

George Ripley ultimately became Schleiermacher's greatest exponent and translator and drew attention to his thought through a running debate with the Transcendentalist critic ANDREWS NORTON who denounced Schleiermacher as "the German pantheist." For his part, Ripley, impacted by Schleiermacher, rejected rational explanations of the Bible and hewed to the German's view that religious truth and experience can be found only in personal feeling. Paralleling Ripley's position, as articulated in his collection of sermons, *Discourses on the Philosophy of Religion: Addressed to Those Who Wish to Believe* (1836), Emerson, from his earliest writings such as *NATURE* (1836) and the "DIVINITY SCHOOL ADDRESS" (1838), rejected a dependence on tradition and rational theological interpretation in favor of his view of the divinity within. Schleiermacher's inward-focused spirituality also surfaced in other Transcendentalist writings of 1836, notably WILLIAM HENRY FURNESS's *Remarks on the Four Gospels* and ORESTES BROWNSON's *New Views of Christianity, Society, and the Church.*

His family expected him to be a pastor in the Moravian Church, but Schleiermacher became a student of IMMANUEL KANT, then of Spinoza, Plato, and Fichte, ultimately rejecting the establishment teachings of the church. Still, he became a professor of theology while joining the circle of the German romantics and becoming a close friend of Schlegel, with whom he embarked on a translation of Plato. In 1799 Schleiermacher anonymously published *On Religion: Speeches to Its Cultured Despisers*, which maintained that religion is independent of knowledge and morality; he developed his ideas about ethics in *Soliloquies* (1800) and in *Outlines of a Critique of Previous Ethical Theory* (1803). His *Brief Outline of Theological Studies* (1811) was an encyclopedia of theological disciplines expressing his core philosophical tenets and reflected the influence of Schelling. Schleiermacher's chief theological work, *The Christian Faith* (1821–22), became the basis for evangelical theology in the 19th century.

Schleiermacher expressed his metaphysics of knowledge in a work, *Dialectic,* which remained unfinished at his death. He viewed knowledge as arising out of the conflict of our sensible and rational natures, the reconciliation of which is always only approximate; consequently, knowledge of God always falls short. Transcending rational explanation, then, God is understood as immanently present and accessible through personal religious feeling. Schleiermacher's work contributed to Ripley, Emerson, and other ex-Unitarian Transcendentalists a romantic framework in which to discuss spirituality independently of Christian doctrine and tradition. Emerson, in particular, reconfigured Schleiermacher's idea of immediate intuitive awareness of the divine in essays such as "The OVER-SOUL" and "SELF-RELIANCE" (both of 1841).

David A. Dilworth

Schopenhauer, Arthur (1788–1860) The German philosopher Arthur Schopenhauer was among the first to contend that the universe is not a rational place. His doctoral dissertation, *The Fourfold Root of the Principle of Sufficient Reason* (1814), and his philosophical classic, *The World as Will and Representation* (1818), combined fundamental ideas of both Plato and IMMANUEL KANT. Two of his most famous essays on "human will" were published together as *Two Fundamental Problems of Ethics* (1841). Schopenhauer's family expected him to be a merchant, and he learned to speak German, French, and English. He was, however, more interested in the life of a scholar than in business. His mother was a writer who ran a literary salon in the early 1800s and was a friend of JOHANN WOLFGANG VON GOETHE. The young Schopenhauer studied at Göttingen and at the University of Berlin where he later lectured alongside GEORG HEGEL.

Almost nothing was heard of Schopenhauer in America, however, until after his death. The first biographies were published in the 1870s, and translations of his most important work in the 1880s, which means it is unlikely Emerson ever read Schopenhauer directly. Emerson quoted the German philosopher in an 1864 journal entry after reading a "lively article" on him: "Schopenhauer said. . . 'An impersonal God is a word void of sense, invented by professors of philosophy to satisfy fools and hack-drivers. . . . My great discovery is to show how, at the bottom of all things, there is only one identical force, always equal, and ever the same, which slumbers in plants, awakens in animals, but finds its consciousness only in man—the Will.'" This particular passage shows Emerson initially forming a positive consideration of Schopenhauer.

The only extended reference to Schopenhauer in Emerson's published works appears in LETTERS AND SOCIAL AIMS (1876), in which Emerson resumes his discussion of faith in the "affirmative power" over loss and evil inscribed in "The TRAGIC," "EXPERIENCE," and "FATE," among other writings. In "Resources" from *Letters and Social Aims,* Emerson writes:

> A Schopenhauer, with logic and learning and wit, teaching pessimism,—teaching that this is the worst of all possible worlds, and inferring that sleep is better than waking, and death than sleep,—all the talent in the world cannot save him from being odious. But if instead of these negatives you give me affirmatives,—if you tell me that there is always life for the living; that what man has done man can do; that this world belongs to the energetic; that there is always a way to everything desirable; that every man is provided, in the new bias of his faculty, with a key to Nature, and that man only rightly knows himself as far as he has experimented on things,—I am invigorated, put into genial and working temper; the horizon opens, and we are full of good-will and gratitude to the Cause of Causes.

This passage denounces Schopenhauer's pessimism (who himself argued against the "optimistic" rationalism of Hegel, among others), and yet it is not necessarily an accurate representation of his work to say that it has neither virtue or genius, considering that the second half of his classic work, *The World as Will and Representation,* is devoted to his metaphysics of art and genius and of morals.

Elsewhere in *Letters and Social Aims,* Emerson categorizes Schopenhauer along with Kant, FRIED-

RICH SCHELLING, FRIEDRICH SCHLEIERMACHER, and Hegel as constituting a "metaphysical age" of reason in Germany. The essay on "Immortality" of the same volume includes the prose version of Emerson's earlier poem "BRAHMA," declaring, "The soul is not born: it does not die: it was not produced from any one. Nor was any produced from it. Unborn, eternal, it is not slain, though the body is slain." Such declarations of identity are found in Schopenhauer, who was the chief European conduit of Hindu and Buddhist philosophy in the 19th century. Schopenhauer's essay "The Indestructibility of Our Essential Nature" coincides with Emerson's "Immortality," and the former's "pessimism" turns out to be similar to Emerson's sense of the illusions of life. The two chief influences on FRIEDRICH NIETZSCHE were, notably, Emerson and Schopenhauer, attesting to the affinity between the two philosophers.

David A. Dilworth

Secret Six *See* BROWN, JOHN.

Stevens, Wallace (1879–1955) Wallace Stevens's poetry and prose show the influences of English romanticism, modernist art, and French symbolism while even more conspicuously carrying forward the legacy of Emerson's literary and philosophical Transcendentalism. Stevens grew up in Pennsylvania, attended HARVARD for three years, and took a law degree at New York University. While a student at Harvard, his mother gave him a 12-volume set of the complete works of Ralph Waldo Emerson. He was also influenced by WILLIAM JAMES and FRIEDRICH NIETZSCHE, but literary scholar Joseph Carroll concludes that "Emerson exercises a deeper conceptual influence on Stevens' poetic cosmology than any other writer, and Emerson provides the most incisive formulations of the ideas that govern that cosmology."

Stevens never gave up practicing law, but he began to gain public recognition as a writer when he contributed four poems to an issue of *Poetry* in 1914; and his first small collection, *Harmonium,* was published in 1923 when Stevens was already 44 years old. In 1949 he received the Bollingen Prize in Poetry of the Yale University Library, followed in 1951 by the National Book Award. Stevens published several other volumes of poetry, and *The Collected Poems of Wallace Stevens* won another National Book Award as well as a Pulitzer Prize in 1955, the year of his death. He lectured at major universities in his later career and collected his prose essays in *The Necessary Angel: Essays on Reality and the Imagination* in 1951.

Stevens's poetry is of commonplace experience and of *poesis*—that is, the activity of the poetic mind in all aspects of life. He strove for a "pure poetry" emerging from a creative atmosphere outside of the realm of politics. The earlier phases of Stevens's career reflected Emerson's influence concerning the poet's transformation of the external world into an expression of the spirit, as Emerson explored in *NATURE* (1836), "The POET" (1841), and in many other contexts. This essential aspect of Stevens's idealism was evident in an early poem, "Tea at the Palaz of Hoon," in which he writes, "Out of my mind the golden ointment rained, / And my ears made the blooming hymns they heard. / I was myself the compass of that sea."

One of the later poems of which Stevens himself was particularly fond was his "Large Red Man Reading," in which Stevens speaks of the souls that thought they had gone to heaven only to find it a frozen wasteland. He laughed, as he sat there "reading,"

> . . . from out of the purple tabulae,
> The outlines of being and its expressings, the
> syllables of its law:
> *Poesis, poesis,* the literal characters, the vatic
> lines,
>
> Which in those ears and in those thin, those
> spended hearts,
> Took on color, took on shape and the size of
> things as they are
> And spoke the feelings for them, which was
> what they had lacked.

"The purple tabulae" signified the revelations of the poetic imagination, a direct allusion to Emerson's great poem of the romantic sublime, "BACCHUS," which ended with the lines:

Refresh the faded tints,
Recut the aged prints,
And write my old adventure with the pen
Which on the first day drew,
Upon the tablets blue,
The dancing Pleiads and eternal men.

In another instance of conscious reverberation, Stevens's "The River of Rivers in Connecticut" reprises the theme of Emerson's "TWO RIVERS."

The later phase of Stevens's career reveals an increasingly meditative mindset and further allusions to the tenets of Transcendental idealism. His Emersonian "Primitive Like an Orb," for example, with its "essential poem at the centre of things," and his "Final Soliloquy of an Interior Paramour," which put forth the idea that "God and the imagination are one," both resonate with Emerson's doctrine expressed in "The OVER-SOUL." As with EMILY DICKINSON and WALT WHITMAN in the 19th century, Wallace Stevens carried the spiritual influence of Emerson into the 20th century.

Further Reading

Carroll, Joseph. "Stevens and Romanticism." In *The Cambridge Companion to Wallace Stevens,* edited by John N. Serio, 87–102. New York: Cambridge University Press, 2007.

David A. Dilworth

Swedenborg, Emanuel (1688–1772) / **Swedenborgianism** Swedish mystic and philosopher Emanuel Swedenborg exercised an abiding influence on Emerson and the Transcendentalists. His ideas were introduced to early-19th-century America by Sampson Reed. A young Emerson was initially impressed by Reed's Swedenborgian "Oration on Genius" (1821) and his book *Observations on the Growth of the Mind* (1826). Reed wrote continuously on Swedenborg in the *New Jerusalem Magazine,* which he cofounded in 1827. In "The POET" (1844), Emerson wrote: "Swedenborg of all men in recent ages, stands eminently for the translator of nature into thought." He lectured on Swedenborg beginning in 1845, and *REPRESENTATIVE MEN* (1850) included Emerson's essay on "SWEDENBORG; OR, THE MYSTIC." Other Transcendentalists inspired by Swedenborg included AMOS BRONSON ALCOTT and MARGARET FULLER, who named Swedenborg as one of the "prophets of the coming age."

Swedenborg was one of the outstanding scientific and philosophical polymaths of the Western tradition. Born in Stockholm and educated at Uppsala University, Swedenborg traveled extensively in England, Holland, France, and Germany, gaining proficiency in mathematics and astronomy. From an early period he showed inventive and mechanical genius. He published a scientific periodical and in 1716 began a 30-year career as an official in Sweden's metal-mining industry. In 1718 he published the first book on algebra in the Swedish language; he followed this with work propounding a geometrical explanation of chemistry and physics, and ultimately engaged in anatomical and physiological studies as well.

In tandem with these scientific pursuits, Swedenborg experienced a mystical revelation that led him to a philosophy of an infinite God as the unitary power and inner life of all creation; this idea he combined with Christian theology to conclude that all created things are effects of specific aspects of divine love and wisdom. From this formulation came his theory of "correspondences"—that is, that every physical fact symbolizes a spiritual fact, the outward form being a manifestation of the inward experience. He wrote prodigiously on this theme, producing multiple volumes of essays leading up to his most popular work, *On Heaven and Hell* (1758), itself followed by several more theological volumes on the symbolic universe. Swedenborg's universe, then, was a unique combination of his scientific training and Christian upbringing but had its precedents in NEOPLATONISM; his work "corresponded" as well in significant aspects with that of his near predecessors, Spinoza (1632–77) and Leibniz (1646–1716).

Emerson explicitly echoed Swedenborg's doctrine of spiritual correspondences in his own philosophy of the relationship between the human mind and nature, and of nature as an inexhaustible universe of symbols. This was the very foundation of Emerson's inaugural work, *NATURE* (1836), in which the philosopher finds all "currents of the Universal Being circulate through me; I am part or particle of God."

From Swedenborg came this concept of spiritual clairvoyance, in which the whole of nature is a symbol of Spirit. Emerson continued this idea throughout his early works, "THE OVER-SOUL" and "The METHOD OF NATURE" (both of 1841), the latter containing the Swedenborgian concept of the *natura naturans,* or inner creative presence, of the universe.

In "Swedenborg; or, the Mystic," Emerson extolled Swedenborg as an "ecstatic" who anticipated the metaphysical connection between the spiritual and the new scientific universe, which he, Emerson, expounded to the end of his own career. Emerson came to criticize Swedenborg's reliance upon Christian forms and allegories, but it is clear that Swedenborg infused Emerson's work from the first writings in *Nature* through to his theories of the unity of poetic and scientific imagination that came to full fruition in "POETRY AND IMAGINATION" (1876) and *NATURAL HISTORY OF INTELLECT* (which began as lectures in the 1870s).

David A. Dilworth

Tappan, Caroline Sturgis (1819–1888) Caroline Sturgis Tappan is best known for her association with many 19th-century luminaries among the Transcendentalists. She was a pupil of, and later became best friend to, MARGARET FULLER. She boarded with NATHANIEL HAWTHORNE and SOPHIA PEABODY HAWTHORNE at the OLD MANSE and later rented her "Little Red House" at Tanglewood to them. She went boating with HENRY DAVID THOREAU, was a confidante to HENRY JAMES, SR., and is mentioned affectionally by HENRY JAMES, JR., in *Notes of a Son and Brother.* She had poetry published in the Transcendentalist literary journal the *DIAL* and, with the help of Lydia Maria Child, published children's books. However, her most prominent connection was her nearly 50-year friendship with Ralph Waldo Emerson.

In 1834 and 1835, Emerson gave a series of lectures in CONCORD, Plymouth, and primarily BOSTON, MASSACHUSETTS. Emerson and his soon-to-be-wife, Lydia Jackson (*see* LIDIAN JACKSON EMERSON), attended a party in the home of the William Sturgis family after a Boston lecture; Jackson and Caroline's mother, Elizabeth Davis Sturgis, had grown up together in Plymouth. In attendance was the 16-year-old Caroline, whose father, a partner in a shipping firm that dominated the China trade, was one of the wealthiest men in Boston. His riches did not, however, ensure Caroline of a happy childhood. After the only male of the six Sturgis children died in a boating accident at age 16, her father would never again allow the son's name to be mentioned. Her mother suffered from bouts of depression that resulted in Elizabeth Sturgis leaving her husband and children to live with her sister on Cape Cod. Hence, Caroline began her "gypsy" existence, moving constantly to live with assorted friends and relatives.

During this period, Margaret Fuller became Caroline Sturgis's mentor. When Fuller first went to Concord to visit Emerson in 1836, she brought Sturgis with her, initiating her into what Lidian Emerson referred to as the "Transcendental Times." Sturgis had included some of her poems in letters to Fuller and Emerson, which they both admired very much, and they asked both Caroline and her older sister, ELLEN STURGIS HOOPER, to contribute to the *Dial* when it was founded in 1840. Emerson selected 11 of Caroline's poems for the second issue, and several more poems were published in subsequent volumes. Sturgis felt there was an exceptional bond between herself and Emerson and shared his Transcendental beliefs: "Where we differ in nature from Margaret & others, is that we unfold from within, while they seek without." Emerson considered her a delight and a source of inspiration, even referring to her as his "Ideal Friend."

Even though the intensity and passion of the friends' letters and conversations decreased over the years, the tie remained between Sturgis and Emerson. Emerson combated Sturgis's loneliness and homelessness by arranging for her to meet William Aspinwall Tappan, whom she eventually and unhappily married. She entered New York society, traveled much in Europe while taking extraordinary photographs, sketched, raised two daughters, campaigned for women's rights, and produced children's literature, all the while remaining devoted friends with Emerson. In 1850 Emerson consulted her before agreeing to coauthor the *MEMOIRS OF MARGARET FULLER OSSOLI.* In 1868 Tappan asked

Emerson's assistance in publishing her poems urging women's suffrage. Later she arranged for Emerson and JAMES ELLIOT CABOT to meet, and Cabot became Emerson's literary executor. In 1872 Tappan contributed $5,000 to the fund to rebuild Emerson's house after it was damaged by fire. Until 1880 Tappan spent most of her time in Europe but continued her correspondence with Emerson until his death in 1882. Caroline Sturgis Tappan died in 1888, and the Tappan papers were bequeathed to the Houghton Library at HARVARD; many of her letters are included in the Emerson collection there, simply marked, "Mr. Emerson's friend Tappan."

Further Reading

Carpenter, Delores Bird, ed. *The Selected Letters of Lidian Jackson Emerson.* Columbia: University of Missouri Press, 1987.

Barbara Downs Wojtusik

Thoreau, Henry David (1817–1862) A native of CONCORD, MASSACHUSETTS, Henry David Thoreau enjoyed a more than 30-year friendship with his neighbor and mentor, Ralph Waldo Emerson. Thoreau was still a student at HARVARD COLLEGE when he first met Emerson early in 1835. Emerson delivered "The AMERICAN SCHOLAR" address to Thoreau's graduating class in August 1837, after which Thoreau returned to his hometown permanently. He lived for a time with the Emerson family and stayed with LIDIAN JACKSON EMERSON and the children when Emerson was away on lecture tours and travel. At Emerson's urging, Thoreau began keeping a journal of his readings and observations on the natural world.

Thoreau worked briefly in Concord as a schoolteacher but quit over the required disciplinary measures. He sought another teaching position but eventually found work as a land surveyor. In his later elegy of his friend, "THOREAU" (1862), Emerson observed that this particular work Thoreau did not mind, as he had great knowledge of Concord and the surrounding areas and the work kept him in contact with nature.

Thoreau attended meetings of the TRANSCENDENTAL CLUB beginning in 1836 and his prose and poetry were published in the *DIAL,* including the poem "Sympathy," his essay on the "Natural History of Massachusetts," and a special selection of "Ethnical Scriptures" from various religious traditions, which he prepared with Emerson. Thoreau himself edited one volume of the paper in 1843.

In 1842, just a few weeks after Emerson's son Waldo died from scarlet fever, Thoreau's brother, John Thoreau, cut himself while shaving and died suddenly from lockjaw. His journals from an 1839 excursion with his brother led to the publication of Thoreau's first book, *A Week on the Concord and Merrimack Rivers,* published 10 years later in 1849. Also in 1849, ELIZABETH PALMER PEABODY published Thoreau's essay "Resistance to Civil Government" in her collection of *Aesthetic Papers.* The essay, an account of his experience of being jailed for nonpayment of taxes, was later reprinted as "Civil Disobedience" and has inspired nonviolent resistance movements in the United States and beyond to this day.

On July 4, 1845, Thoreau moved into a cabin he built in Walden Woods, on land owned by Emerson. Thus began a two-year experiment in self-reliance that he recorded in his most famous work, *Walden; or, Life in the Woods,* published in 1854. Thoreau explained, "I went to the woods because I wished to live deliberately, to front only the essential facts of life, and see if I could not learn what it had to teach, and not, when I came to die, discover that I had not lived." The book became a statement of practical Transcendentalism, of Emersonian "SELF-RELIANCE" to the extreme, a model of simple living, of economy, and of ecological awareness. Thoreau's experiment brought him immortal literary fame, but many at the time misunderstood Thoreau as the hermit philosopher. In 1852 Emerson, however, recorded in his journal a list of friends, "a few persons who give flesh to what were else mere thoughts." Among these, Emerson praised Thoreau for giving him "my own ethics. He is far more real, & daily practically obeying them, than I; and fortifies my memory at all times with an affirmative experience which refuses to be set aside."

Thoreau and his family were committed to ABOLITIONISM and, along with the AMOS BRONSON ALCOTT family and FRANKLIN BENJAMIN SANBORN,

Walden Pond *(Photo by Tiffany K. Wayne)*

among others, assisted fugitive slaves through Concord. Thoreau was among the first to speak publicly in support of JOHN BROWN, after the radical abolitionist was captured and sentenced to hang, resulting in his forceful antislavery address, "A Plea for Captain John Brown" (1859).

A Week and *Walden* were the only two books Thoreau published in his lifetime, although he also published several essays in the ATLANTIC MONTHLY and in the antislavery press. Thoreau died in 1862 at the age of 44 of tuberculosis, a disease he had battled for years. Many of his works were collected and published posthumously by friends and family, including his poetry and journals, and his other significant writings as a reformer and naturalist, with *The Maine Woods* (1864), *Cape Cod* (1865), *A Yankee in Canada, with Anti-Slavery and Reform Papers* (1866), and numerous other volumes. Emerson's elegy, "Thoreau," provides detail not only on Thoreau's life in Concord but also on his predicted literary and intellectual legacy. Thoreau's close friend (WILLIAM) ELLERY CHANNING published the first biography, *Thoreau the Poet-Naturalist,* in 1873.

Further Reading

Richardson, Robert D. *Henry Thoreau: A Life of the Mind.* Berkeley: University of California Press, 1986.

Robinson, David M. *Natural Life: Thoreau's Worldly Transcendentalism.* Ithaca, N.Y.: Cornell University Press, 2004.

Smith, Harmon L. *My Friend, My Friend: The Story of Thoreau's Relationship with Emerson.* Amherst: University of Massachusetts Press, 2001.

Town and Country Club The short-lived Town and Country Club was founded by Transcendentalist philosopher, poet, teacher, reformer, and writer AMOS BRONSON ALCOTT in 1849 to bring together BOSTON "town" intellectuals and their "country" counterparts, such as Ralph Waldo Emerson who resided in the western suburb of CONCORD. Emerson aided Alcott in establishing the club, which was an outgrowth of a recent series of Conversations on the great philosophical and historical issues of the day—which Alcott had organized in his Boston Temple School and later took on the road in his western lecture tours. Many of the first participants in the Town and Country Club had been members of the earlier TRANSCENDENTAL CLUB of 1836–40 and had attended Alcott's conversations, which, during the height of their popularity between 1848 and 1853, regularly convened crowds of 50 or more people.

Alcott's Town and Country Club was organized along more formal lines, with a constitution, rules, and membership fees. In addition to Emerson, attendees included JAMES ELLIOT CABOT, JAMES FREEMAN CLARKE, JOHN SULLIVAN DWIGHT, JAMES RUSSELL LOWELL, THEODORE PARKER, HENRY DAVID THOREAU, and JOHN WEISS. The club attracted more than 100 members, but a controversy developed over the admission of females, with Alcott, William Lloyd Garrison, and THOMAS WENTWORTH HIGGINSON favoring their admittance and other more conservative members, including Emerson, dissenting out of fear it would become a "ladies club." These tensions, as well as concerns over the club's growing size and the financial burdens of holding regular meetings, led to the disbanding of the Town and Country Club in May 1850.

David A. Dilworth

Transcendental Club The Transcendental Club was a gathering of "like-minded" individuals that met regularly in the BOSTON area between 1836 and 1840. The club brought together individuals interested in discussing "deeper and broader views" of theology and culture and, in particular, those engaged in the new Transcendentalist movement against the conservative culture of both HARVARD COLLEGE and the UNITARIAN establishment. Emerson's later literary executor and biographer JAMES ELLIOT CABOT described the group as "the occasional meetings of a changing body of liberal thinkers, agreeing in nothing but their liberality." The group was referred to by several names, including the "symposium," "the Aesthetic Club," or, more often, "Hedge's Club," due to the role of FREDERIC HENRY HEDGE in establishing the group and because meetings were often scheduled around Hedge's visits to Massachusetts from his home in Bangor, Maine. Attendees included at one time or another nearly every major figure associated with the Transcendentalist movement. Emerson, Hedge, and GEORGE RIPLEY were the primary founders, and regular attendees included AMOS BRONSON ALCOTT, CYRUS BARTOL, ORESTES BROWNSON, JAMES FREEMAN CLARKE, CHRISTOPHER PEARSE CRANCH, JOHN SULLIVAN DWIGHT, CONVERS FRANCIS, MARGARET FULLER, ELIZABETH HOAR, THEODORE PARKER, ELIZABETH PALMER PEABODY, SARAH ALDEN BRADFORD RIPLEY, SOPHIA RIPLEY, HENRY DAVID THOREAU, and JONES VERY, among others; GEORGE BANCROFT and WILLIAM ELLERY CHANNING were among those who visited the club at least once but were not specifically associated with Transcendentalism.

The first meeting of the club, in September 1836, coincided with the publication of Emerson's *NATURE* (1836). Several other volumes representing the new thought were published that year—including Brownson's *New Views of Christianity, Society, and the Church,* Francis's *Christianity as a Purely Internal Principle,* WILLIAM HENRY FURNESS's *Remarks on the Four Gospels*—provoking response and criticism from conservative Unitarians such as ANDREWS NORTON. All Transcendentalists may not have thought alike, but the Transcendental Club provided a sense of community and point of affinity for those launching a more sophisticated intellectual response to, as Hedge put it, the "rigid, cautious, circumspect, conservative tang in the very air of Cambridge."

The club had no regular meeting date, but met five or six times a year if possible, and no regular meeting place, alternating among the homes of Alcott, Bartol, Brownson, Emerson, or other members. Although the club had no predetermined list of topics (nor was any topic off-limit), the meetings often centered on a single theme for discussion. A sampling of meeting topics shows the club's broad-ranging intellectual, literary, and theological concerns on themes that would define the emerging Transcendentalist movement in its many forms. Specific topics included "American Genius—the causes which hinder its growth, and give us no first rate productions," "Education of Humanity," "What is the essence of Religion as distinct from morality?" "Does the species advance beyond the individual?" (held at Emerson's house in the summer of 1837), "Is Mysticism an element of Christianity?" "On the character and genius of Goethe," "Pantheism," and "The Inspiration of the Prophet and Bard, the nature of Poetry, and the causes of sterility of poetic Inspiration in our Age and country" (also held at Emerson's house, in May 1840).

The Transcendental Club was one of only three major organized public expressions of the early movement—the others being the creation of a paper, the *DIAL*, and the UTOPIAN community at BROOK FARM, established in 1841. In late 1839 the group began considering the need for their own journal or magazine; the *Dial* published its first issue in July 1840 with Margaret Fuller as editor. Just a few months later, in September 1840, the Transcendental Club held its last meeting.

Further Reading

Myerson, Joel. "A Calendar of Transcendental Club Meetings." *American Literature* 44, no. 2 (May 1972): 197–207.

Richardson, Robert D. *Emerson: The Mind on Fire.* Berkeley: University of California Press, 1995.

Unitarian / Unitarianism American Unitarianism of the 18th and 19th centuries originated in two geographical locations and produced two very different forms of Unitarianism. Philadelphia Unitarianism was largely influenced by the English "dissenters," while New England Unitarianism emerged from Congregationalism and was initially labeled "Unitarian" as an accusation, a term the new denomination eventually embraced. It is from New England Unitarianism that Transcendentalism emerged.

By the end of the 18th century, many of the largest churches in New England had grown more theologically liberal, particularly in asserting the freedom of the human will, and rejected as nonbiblical such doctrines as original sin, the depravity of the human race, predestination, and the Holy Trinity. They also adopted doctrines affirming the goodness of humanity and the potential for human beings to evolve spiritually, morally, and intellectually.

What has come to be known as the "Unitarian controversy" erupted in the early decades of the 19th century in response to this increasing theological liberalism. Calvinist ministers ceased exchanging their pulpits with liberals, new organizations were formed to which liberals were not invited, and a schism between Calvinists and liberals was clearly under way. WILLIAM ELLERY CHANNING, who was to become the early leader of the new denomination, preferred the term "liberal Christian" to "Unitarian," but by 1819, the year Channing delivered his sermon "Unitarian Christianity," he had clearly accepted the new label.

Just on the heels of this controversy, however, emerged another, more radical development—the rise of Transcendentalism. The vast majority of early Transcendentalists were Unitarian ministers, and Transcendentalism might best be understood as the natural progression of the theological debate begun by early Unitarians such as Channing. For these ministers, Unitarianism had become too much a religion of rational empiricism (which the Unitarians had embraced in their schism with the Calvinists), and they argued that subjective intuition was an equally compelling source for truth.

This tension between the young Transcendentalist radicals and the Unitarian establishment developed into the movement we now know as Transcendentalism. The immediate debate concerned the question of miracles as performed by Jesus as proof of God's existence, a position rejected by the Transcendentalists because it signaled a separation between divinity and humanity. In 1838 Emerson delivered his controversial "DIVINITY SCHOOL ADDRESS," in which he charged that "the word Miracle, as pronounced by Christian churches, gives a false impression; it is Monster." The Unitarian ANDREWS NORTON, who had earlier done battle with the Calvinists, now blasted the Transcendentalists, accusing them of a heresy that "strikes at the root of faith in Christianity."

Emerson descended from a long line of ministers; his father WILLIAM EMERSON had served as the Unitarian minister of First Church in BOSTON, and the Emerson family attended Channing's church. Emerson was ordained into the ministry in 1829 and served as minister of Second Church in Boston until his resignation in 1832. The controversy generated by Emerson's "Divinity School Address" has often been caricatured as a battle between the radical Transcendentalists and the "orthodox" Unitarians. Although some Unitarians attacked Emerson, others defended him, including GEORGE RIPLEY and THEODORE PARKER. While Emerson may have resigned his ministry, he never gave up his profession. He continued to preach at Unitarian churches as a guest minister through 1839, served as the regular minister at the Unitarian church in East Lexington, and came close to accepting a permanent position as minister of the Unitarian church in New Bedford, Massachusetts. As the regular minister of the Unitarian church in East Lexington, Emerson sometimes read from the lectures he was delivering in Boston in place of sermons and later commented in a letter to THOMAS CARLYLE that the platform of the lecture hall had become the "new Pulpit." Emerson preached periodically in the 1840s, and as late as 1863 preached in Theodore Parker's church following Lincoln's signing of the Emancipation Proclamation.

Despite his many criticisms of Unitarianism, Emerson continued to think of the denomination as the best place for "the new religion" he envisioned. In 1841 he wrote, "I think the Unitarian Church like the Lyceum as yet an open & uncommitted organ free to admit the ministrations of any inspired man that shall pass by."

Further Reading

Cooke, George Willis. *Unitarianism in America: A History of Its Origin and Development.* Boston: American Unitarian Association, 1902.

Howe, Daniel Walker. *The Unitarian Conscience: Harvard Moral Philosophy, 1805–1861.* Middletown, Conn.: Wesleyan University Press, 1988.

Robinson, David. *Apostle of Culture: Emerson as Preacher and Lecturer.* Philadelphia: University of Pennsylvania Press, 1982.

Jane E. Rosecrans

utopian / utopianism The term "Utopia" was first used by Sir Thomas More, an English statesman, in his imaginative work of that title, which was published in 1516. More envisioned an island society in the Atlantic in which a perfect order and harmony existed, religious principle prevailed, and private property no longer existed. More was later sentenced to death by Henry VIII, but his work had a lasting influence. The utopian genre continued to evolve during the Elizabethan era and the ENLIGHTENMENT. The idea of a society that, through its own initiatives and strivings, can achieve perfection inspired the Jacobins in the French Revolution. One motivation for the "Reign of Terror" (1793–94) was a belief that enemies and saboteurs of the harmonious vision must be weeded out. Utopian visions were later used as fuel for other types of political movements and ideologies.

The 19th-century United States witnessed the greatest wave of peaceful utopian experiments the world had yet seen. Robert Owen reorganized a mill community in New Lanark, Scotland, according to his utopian vision by instituting profit-sharing and funding education. The experiment was successful, and in 1825 he began work in a new community at New Harmony, Indiana. The utopian impulse grew in America, inspired in part by the works of Owen and the French theorist Charles FOURIER, and mixed with the religious energies of the Second Great Awakening. Scores of religious and secular communities were founded in America in the second third of the 19th century. Most were short-lived, but several, including the Oneida community, the Mormon settlements in Utah and elsewhere, and the Zoar community in Ohio, had long-term success and lasting significance.

Some Transcendentalists were attracted to the idea of utopian communities as a way in which to live without implicating themselves in the injustices they saw as inherent in contemporary society. Goods produced through slavery or unfair labor practices, a production economy that encroached on the spiritual life, and for some even the slaughter of animals and the use of money, were modern conventions that they rejected. Utopian communities were seen not simply as an escape but also as a chance to show society by example that a greater harmony and happiness would result if the fundamental structure of social interaction were improved. The utopias with which Emerson was most intimately familiar were Fruitlands, a farm community cofounded by his friend and colleague BRONSON ALCOTT and the English reformer CHARLES LANE in Harvard, Massachusetts, and the BROOK FARM utopia in West Roxbury, Massachusetts, founded by GEORGE RIPLEY and SOPHIA RIPLEY. Brook Farm was founded in 1841. In 1845 it organized itself as a Fourierist phalanx. Fruitlands was founded in 1843. Its founders placed high emphasis on ascetic purity in food and spiritual life.

Both communities tried unsuccessfully to convince Emerson to join. In writings like "NEW ENGLAND REFORMERS" (1844) and "The YOUNG AMERICAN" (1844) Emerson salutes the motivations of utopian reformers, casting them in a positive light as people working actively to create a better world. However, he doubted the efficacy of the experiments. He saw communal life as unnatural and as detrimental to the formation of heroic individuals. Both Brook Farm and Fruitlands had a short lifespan. The former was forced to disband after its main barn burned in 1846. Fruitlands was defunct after 1844, when food shortages and internal tensions led to its collapse.

Further Reading

Delano, Sterling. *Brook Farm: The Dark Side of Utopia.* Cambridge, Mass.: Belknap Press of Harvard University, 2004.

Guarneri, Carl. *The Utopian Alternative: Fourierism in Nineteenth-Century America.* Ithaca, N.Y.: Cornell University Press, 1994.

Daniel Robert Koch

Very, Jones (1813–1880) The historian Perry Miller writes that the precepts of the Transcendentalist theory of genius "practically demanded one or two mad poets." Contemporary E. A. Silsbee wrote that Jones Very "moved in Salem like Dante among the Florentines: a man who had seen God." Very fulfilled the notion of the poet as a vehicle for the spirit (which the Transcendentalists referred to as "genius"), sacrificing himself in the process; his sonnets from 1837–39 remain among the best in American letters.

Jones Very was born in Salem, Massachusetts, in 1813. His exposure to religious variety and culture began early; his mother, Lydia, was an avowed atheist. His father, a sea captain, took the young Very on trips to Russia and Europe, perhaps inspiring Jones's exoticism. Very entered HARVARD COLLEGE in 1833, at age 20, and graduated second in his class. His religious feeling deepened while at Harvard; Very entered the Divinity School in the fall of 1836 (the same year Emerson published his first book, *NATURE*) and became a tutor in Greek at Harvard.

When Very first encountered Emerson's *Nature* in 1836 he was electrified by its ideas regarding poetry, especially Emerson's emphasis of intuition over reason, spontaneity over mere form, and openness to the direct influence of the Holy Spirit. Very began to receive pronouncements directly from the Holy Spirit in 1837. Under the spell of religious ecstasy, he began writing essays and poems, working exclusively in the sonnet format. Very took Emerson's precepts as a manifesto for a new kind of poetic ideal; he came to believe himself to be the "new born bard of the Holy Ghost" Emerson would call for in his "DIVINITY SCHOOL ADDRESS" in 1838. Very believed, as did Emerson, that God was the source of the poet's inspiration; however, Very also believed that true religious experience required complete denial of will and surrender of all conscious thought.

In 1837, convinced he was in God's care, Very delivered an address titled "Why There Cannot be Another Epic Poem." The address focused on Very's belief in an inward, Christian-seeking for truth as opposed to the external, objective world of the classical epic form. His essays on "Shakespeare," and "Hamlet" brought him to Emerson's attention, who was much taken with Very's enthusiasm and literary insight. After reading a sample of Very's poetry, particularly the poems "Enoch" and "In Him We Live," Emerson arranged for Very to bring out a book of poetry and essays, which finally appeared in 1839.

In 1838 Very's position at Harvard was jeopardized by accusations that he was insane. He was subsequently dismissed from the Harvard faculty but continued to write and speak under the influence of the Holy Spirit. He had made the mistake of trying to baptize several Salem ministers, who had Very committed to the McLean Asylum, where Emerson came to his aid; said Emerson, "such a mind cannot be lost." Upon release from a one-month stay at McLean's, Very returned to Salem and soon after visited Emerson in CONCORD. His mission was to see to the rebirth of the Emerson family. Very believed that the Second Advent referred to the releasing of Christ, who is in all men. Very believed that if Emerson followed his directives (following John the Baptist's model, as Very interpreted it), even Emerson could be reborn. While BRONSON ALCOTT stated that Very was "insane with God—diswitted in the contemplation of the holiness of divinity," Emerson, along with (WILLIAM) ELLERY CHANNING, was less unfavorable regarding Very's mental condition, considering his insanity superficial and less than divinely inspired.

In 1840 Very's religious ecstasy began to wane, though he continued to write poetry. However, the poems written after 1840 are marked by a more mechanical style, losing the subtlety of his earlier verse. Very was ordained to preach in 1843 and held several UNITARIAN pastorates. He lived his later years in seclusion in Salem and died in 1880.

Further Reading

Reiss, Benjamin. *Theaters of Madness: Insane Asylums and Nineteenth-Century American Culture.* Chicago: University of Chicago, 2008. (*See* chapter 4, "Emerson's Close Encounters with Madness.")

Very, Jones. *Jones Very: The Complete Poems,* edited by Helen R. Deese. Athens: University of Georgia Press, 1993.

Bill Scalia

Weiss, John (1818–1879) John Weiss, Jr., of Jewish ancestry hailing from Worcester, Massachusetts, was a HARVARD Divinity School colleague of HENRY DAVID THOREAU. After spending several months absorbing German idealism at the University of Heidelberg, he became a UNITARIAN minister. He took over the pulpit of friend CONVERS FRANCIS in Watertown, Massachusetts, for four years until he was forced to resign due to his radical ABOLITIONISM. Weiss wrote articles on religious philosophy and on the relation of religion and science for the *Boston Quarterly,* the *Massachusetts Quarterly,* the *Christian Examiner,* the ATLANTIC MONTHLY, and the *Radical,* to which he also contributed poetry. He was active in the early phase of Transcendentalism in the 1830s and 1840s, promoting the philosophies of Johann Gottlieb Fichte, FRIEDRICH SCHELLING, FRIEDRICH VON SCHILLER, and IMMANUEL KANT. In the post–Civil War era he was a member of the TOWN AND COUNTRY CLUB, the RADICAL CLUB, and helped found the Free Religious Association in 1867. In addition to his numerous essays and published sermons, he wrote a two-volume biographical study of his abolitionist mentor, the radical Unitarian minister THEODORE PARKER, *The Life and Correspondence of Theodore Parker* (1864).

OCTAVIUS BROOKS FROTHINGHAM, in his 1876 *Transcendentalism in New England: A History,* wrote of Weiss's work: "The volume entitled *American Religion,* published in 1871, shows the power of [Weiss's] spiritual philosophy to extract noble meanings from the circumstances of the New World. Weiss treads the border-land between religion and science, recognizing the claims of both, and bringing to their adjustment as fine intellectual scales as any of his contemporaries." His method, according to Frothingham, was "purely poetic, imaginative." Weiss called it "theistic naturalism," advocating the interrelationship between the human spirit and nature, while also promoting the idea of America religiosity as a "new world" experiment in which every person could have his own religious consciousness in a spiritual democracy free of the "old world" priestcraft. Like Emerson, he stressed the divine immanence as a ubiquitous presence revealed in personal intuition and held to Emerson's tenet of the affinity of the human mind and the universe.

David A. Dilworth

Western Messenger (1835–1841) The *Western Messenger* was a Transcendentalist literary journal that preceded and outlasted, but overlapped with, the BOSTON-based *DIAL* (1840–44), although the latter is often the only acknowledged periodical of the movement. The *Western Messenger* was founded and edited by JAMES FREEMAN CLARKE, a close friend of Emerson and of MARGARET FULLER, and coedited at different times by CHRISTOPHER PEARSE CRANCH and WILLIAM HENRY CHANNING. The *Western Messenger, Devoted to Religion, Life, and Literature* (as its masthead announced) had a more specifically UNITARIAN purpose and audience, and had financial support from the Western Unitarian Association and American Unitarian Association. Eventually the paper moved toward a more literary and Transcendentalist emphasis, and many of the early Transcendentalists who would later found and write for the *Dial* were first published in the *Western Messenger*—these included Emerson and Fuller, but also AMOS BRONSON ALCOTT, FREDERIC HENRY HEDGE, THEODORE PARKER, ELIZABETH PALMER PEABODY, and poets CAROLINE STURGIS TAPPAN and JONES VERY.

The paper was published out of Louisville, Kentucky, and then out of Cincinnati, Ohio, but contemporaries recognized the *Western Messenger* as a Transcendentalist paper; or, as one critic so perceptively concluded, it was "essentially an eastern messenger, the organ of New England liberalism in the Valley of the Ohio." Others saw it primarily as another forum for Ralph Waldo Emerson whose popularity would soon be facilitated by a successful career as a lecturer in the western states. Among entries in the *Western Messenger* related to Emerson's early career were favorable reviews of, and even reprinted passages from, *NATURE* (1836), an obituary for Emerson's brother, CHARLES CHAUNCY EMERSON, reviews of "The AMERICAN SCHOLAR" (1837) and the "DIVINITY SCHOOL ADDRESS" (1838), an article on "R. W. Emerson and the New School," and an 1840 essay on "Transcendentalism" by Cranch. Some of Emerson's poems that appeared in the *Western Messenger* included "EACH AND ALL," "The HUMBLE-BEE," and "The RHODORA," all of 1839.

Back in New England, many associated with or interested in Transcendentalism subscribed to the paper, and in fact, it may have inspired the idea and need for a Boston-based journal for Transcendentalist ideas. Historian Clarence L. F. Gohdes determined that "the reader of *The Dial* and *The Western Messenger* finds scarcely any type of material which is not common to both journals."

Further Reading

Gohdes, Clarence L. F. *The Periodicals of American Transcendentalism*. Durham, N.C.: Duke University Press, 1931.

Habich, Robert. *Transcendentalism and the Western Messenger: A History of the Magazine and Its Contributors, 1835–1841*. London and Cranbury, N.J.: Associated University Presses, 1985.

Whitman, Walt (1819–1892) In "The POET" (1844) Emerson wrote of "the ideal American poet" as having not yet arrived: "We have yet had no genius in America . . . Yet America is a poem in our eyes; its ample geography dazzles the imagination, and it will not wait long for metres." Shortly thereafter Emerson published his own first volume of POEMS (1847). Emerson, however, never claimed that his own poems fulfilled his call—"I look in vain for the poet whom I describe"—and when he selected his "representative" poet of 1850, he still looked to the past, as evidenced by "SHAKSPEARE; OR, THE POET." In entirely different venues, it was Emerson's contemporaries, EMILY DICKINSON and Walt Whitman, who would be known as the great American poets of the 19th century.

Emerson played a significant role in promoting Whitman's work. On receiving the first edition of *Leaves of Grass* from Whitman in the summer of 1855, Emerson wrote a letter of congratulatory praise: "I find it the most extraordinary piece of wit and wisdom that America has yet contributed." He went on to muse, "I rubbed my eyes a little, to see if this sunbeam were no illusion," and assured Whitman, "I greet you at the beginning of a great career." Whitman shrewdly parlayed this letter from the most eminent literary figure of the day into an advertisement for *Leaves of Grass*. Emerson subsequently regretted the endorsement, particularly due to the erotic content of Whitman's poetry, for which Emerson personally chided the poet when they met a few years later. While Whitman anonymously advertised *himself* as "an American bard at last!" Emerson did not include Whitman in his later anthology of favorite poets, *PARNASSUS* (1874).

Scholars are still attempting to unravel the complicated relationship between the two contemporary geniuses, Emerson and Whitman. The Long Island–born Whitman had worked as a journeyman printer, editor, grammar school teacher, and a sentimental temperance novelist, and honed his sharp observations of the varieties of human nature in his newspaper career. He attended an Emerson lecture on a version of "The Poet" in New York City in March 1842 and reported on the lecture a few days later in the newspaper *Aurora,* describing the lecture as "one of the richest and most beautiful compositions, both for its matter and style, we have ever heard anywhere, at any time." Thirteen years later Whitman finally burst onto the literary scene with his own *Leaves of Grass*. In later correspondence he remembered of this time in his life, "I was simmering, simmering, simmering; Emerson brought me to a boil."

Walt Whitman, 1854 *(Courtesy of Library of Congress)*

Later Whitman insisted he had not read Emerson's prose before composing *Leaves of Grass*—a denial that may be on a par with Emily Dickinson's own disingenuous disclaimer that she had never read the scurrilous Whitman. But the preface alone of the first edition of *Leaves of Grass* entirely expressed Emerson's vision of the American poet, dealing with American themes, and echoed Emerson's own epigrammatical style and forceful prose of lived experience, from the most Transcendentalist "Song of Myself" to "A Song for Occupations," "To Think of Time," "I Sing the Body Electric," "I Hear America Singing," "Song of the Answer," "A Boston Ballad," "There Was a Child Went Forth," "Crossing Brooklyn Ferry," "Out of the Cradle Endlessly Rocking," "As I Ebb'd with the Ocean of Life," "Who Learns My Lessons Complete," and "Great Are the Myths," to name just a few.

These were Emersonian poems of self-reliance, in both a personal and cosmic sense, which played out the life-affirming themes of Emerson's principles from his essay "The OVER-SOUL," "SELF-RELIANCE," "CIRCLES," and "SPIRITUAL LAWS," and echoed in his own poems, such as "The WORLD-SOUL," "WOODNOTES," "The SPHINX," "BACCHUS," "MERLIN," and many others. In these works Emerson explained the poetic spirit in nature and its relationship to everyday life, cataloging life and death, male and female, rich and poor, white and black, cities, occupations, farms, frontiers, landscapes, love, and the peaceful lives of animals—all of which was transmuted in Whitman's poetry.

Whitman also penned prose works of philosophical as well as literary value, notably *Democratic Vistas* (1871) and *Specimen Days* (1882); and his "A Backward Glance O'er Travel'd Roads" (1888) ranks with the original preface to *Leaves of Grass* for its theoretical poetics and overall philosophy of life. Walt Whitman and Emily Dickinson in the 19th century, and WALLACE STEVENS and Robert Frost among others in the 20th century, were American poets of the first rank, and each of these aligned with Emerson's prophetic manifesto in "The Poet" of 1844. Each contributed highly individualized poetic legacies that are at the same time noticeably philosophical. While diverging in their idiosyncratic geniuses, they collectively forged a tradition of variations on Emerson's Transcendentalist vision.

Further Reading

Reynolds, David S. *Walt Whitman.* New York: Oxford University Press, 2005.

David A. Dilworth

Whittier, John Greenleaf (1807–1892) John Greenleaf Whittier, a Quaker poet, editor, and reformer, played a critical role in the American ABOLITIONISM. Born in 1807 in Haverhill, Massachusetts, Whittier was a controversial figure due to his reform activities, although after the Civil War he became a beloved American writer. He was frustrated at Emerson's slow embrace of the antislavery movement but rejoiced when the poet philosopher did finally speak out on the cause, and Emerson's influence is clear in Whittier's own work.

In 1826 Whittier's first published poem, "The Exile's Departure," attracted the attention of William Lloyd Garrison, who encouraged him to pursue a formal education. After completing his studies in 1829 at the Haverhill Academy, Whittier held a series of editing positions and published his first book, *Legends of New England in Prose and Verse* (1831). Whittier helped to draft the American Anti-Slavery Standard Declaration of Sentiments, published the pamphlet, *Justice and Expediency; or, Slavery Considered with a View to Its Rightful and Effectual Remedy, Abolition,* in 1833, and in 1836 became a secretary of the Anti-Slavery Society. He also served in the Massachusetts legislature in 1835–36. Although he regularly published abolitionist verse, collected in *Voices of Freedom* (1846), the author believed it to be of lesser artistic value than his other work. His dedication to abolition cost him dearly. Many periodicals refused to publish him, his political ambitions were curbed, and more than once, he was pelted by rocks thrown by violent antiabolitionist mobs. Despite his friendship with Garrison, Whittier moved away from immediate abolitionism and moral suasion, helping to found the Liberty Party in 1839.

Whittier was thrilled when Emerson, whom he considered America's finest poet, delivered his speech "EMANCIPATION OF THE NEGROES IN THE BRITISH WEST INDIES" in August 1844. In response, the following month Whittier wrote a piece for the *Middlesex Standard,* a Liberty Party newspaper that he edited, celebrating Emerson for his stance. The *Emancipator* published a letter from Whittier to Emerson that included a call to action for anyone with antislavery leanings in 1845. Both men were horrified by the Compromise of 1850, especially the Fugitive Slave Act, and were outraged by Massachusetts senator Daniel Webster's support of it. As sectional tensions grew, the men continued to correspond, discussing political parties and abolition.

Whittier, in ill health, began to withdraw from public life in the 1840s, moving to Amesbury, Massachusetts. He invited Emerson to speak at the Amesbury Lyceum in 1852 and 1853; during those visits Emerson helped introduce Whittier to the literature of the Far East, a subject of increasing interest to Whittier as he grew older. The frequent appearance of his work in the *ATLANTIC MONTHLY,* which Emerson helped to found in 1857, boosted Whittier's reputation as a poet; he, in addition, attended many of the planning sessions for the first issue. Emerson's influence on Whittier's work is most clearly seen in Whittier's most famous poem, "Snow-Bound" (1866), which echoes Emerson's "The SNOW-STORM" (1841). The success of the poem ensured Whittier's financial security in his later years. He died in 1892 in Hampton Falls, New Hampshire.

Further Reading

Pickard, John B. *The Letters of John Greenleaf Whittier.* Cambridge, Mass.: Harvard University Press, 1975.
Pollard, John A. *John Greenleaf Whittier, Friend of Man.* Boston: Houghton Mifflin, 1949.
Wagenknecht, Edward. *John Greenleaf Whittier: A Portrait in Paradox.* New York: Oxford University Press, 1967.

Kate Culkin

women's rights *See* "WOMAN."

Wordsworth, William (1770–1850) William Wordsworth, along with SAMUEL TAYLOR COLERIDGE, helped launch the romantic movement in English literature with the 1798 publication of *Lyrical Ballads.* The revolutionary collection, beginning with Coleridge's "The Rime of the Ancient Mariner" and concluding with Wordsworth's "Tintern Abbey," broke with the poetical decorum of the 18th century. In the 1802 "Preface to *Lyrical Ballads,*" Wordsworth aptly described the original collection of 23 poems, for which he wrote all but four, as "an experiment." Unlike his neoclassical predecessors, Wordsworth chose incidents from "common life," and he described them with common language. He was the quintessential romantic poet—a "man speaking to men" about powerful emotion, "recollected in tranquility."

By the 1830s Wordsworth was, in biographer Stephen Gill's words, a "national monument," a literary legend. Rydal Mount, his home in the Lake District, became a stopping point for a steady stream of visitors wishing to pay their respects. In 1833, 30-year-old Ralph Waldo Emerson, having resigned his UNITARIAN ministry in BOSTON the previous year, decided to travel abroad. He met Wordsworth on August 28, 1833, at Rydal Mount. In *ENGLISH TRAITS* (1856) Emerson described Wordsworth as "a plain, elderly, white-haired man, not prepossessing, and disfigured by green goggles." Wordsworth, suffering from inflammation of the eye, spoke at length on his two favorite topics, politics and education, and encouraged Emerson and his fellow Americans "to cultivate the moral, the conservative." Emerson later wrote that he was "surprised by the hard limits" of Wordsworth's thought and the narrowness of his "very English mind." He concluded that "off his own beat," Wordsworth's "opinions were of no value."

As they walked in the gardens, Wordsworth offered to recite three sonnets he had recently composed. At first, as he recounted in *English Traits,* Emerson found the spectacle amusing and nearly laughed at the "old Wordsworth, standing apart, and reciting . . . like a schoolboy." His mood quickly changed, however, when Wordsworth's words proved "more *beautiful* than any of his printed poems," as Emerson explained in his journal. Years later Emerson would comment that "you would scarcely believe that some of the best poetry of this century could come from Wordsworth, after seeing him,—such a simple man, and with such strange notions."

Emerson returned to Rydal Mount in March 1848, 15 years after his initial visit. As before, he arrived unannounced, not knowing that Wordsworth was still grieving the loss of his daughter Dora who had died the previous year. He found Wordsworth asleep on the sofa. Unaware initially of his guest's identity, the groggy Wordsworth was "a little short and surly." After listening to Wordsworth disparage the French, the Scotchman, the *Edinburgh Review,* and THOMAS CARLYLE, to name a few, Emerson confided in his journal that he found Wordsworth a "bitter old Englishman." Later, however, when Emerson recounted the details of his last visit in *English Traits,* he paid homage to the "revolution he [Wordsworth] had wrought." Through Wordsworth's "courage," "new means were employed, and new realms added to the empire of the muse."

Further Reading

Bosco, Ronald, and Joel Myerson, eds. *Emerson in His Own Time: A Biographical Chronicle of His Life, Drawn from Recollections, Interviews, and Memoirs by Family, Friends, and Associates.* Iowa City: University of Iowa Press, 2003.
Gill, Stephen. *William Wordsworth: A Life.* New York: Oxford University Press, 1989.

Beth Jensen

PART IV

Appendixes

Chronology of Ralph Waldo Emerson's Life and Times

1768
November 9: Ruth Haskins (Emerson's mother) born in Boston, Massachusetts

1769
May 6: William Emerson (father) born in Concord, Massachusetts

1770
March 5: Boston Massacre—conflict between colonists and British soldiers leads to five civilian deaths
Emerson family home, the "Old Manse," built in Concord

1773
December 16: Boston Tea Party—colonists protesting British taxation destroy shiploads of tea in Boston Harbor (100 years later Emerson would read his memorial poem "Boston")

1774
August 25: Mary Moody Emerson (paternal aunt) born in Concord

1775
April 19: British soldiers are met at Old North Bridge in Concord during first battles of the American Revolution (the subject of Emerson's poem "Concord Hymn")

1776
July 4: Continental Congress adopts Declaration of Independence
October 20: William Emerson (grandfather) dies in Vermont while serving as chaplain for Patriot army

1780
November 16: Phebe Bliss Emerson (grandmother) marries Rev. Ezra Ripley, William Emerson's successor in Concord church

1781
Immanuel Kant's *Critique of Pure Reason* published

1788
February: Massachusetts is sixth state to ratify U.S. Constitution; new federal government begins operation in early 1789

1789
William Emerson (father) graduates from Harvard College

1796
October 25: William Emerson and Ruth Haskins (parents), are married
John Adams of Quincy, Massachusetts, elected second president of the United States

1798
February 9: Phebe Ripley Emerson (sister) born

1799
November 28: John Clarke Emerson (brother) born
William Emerson (father) becomes pastor of First Church, Boston

1800

September 28: Phebe Ripley Emerson (sister) dies at age two

1801

July 31: William Emerson (brother) born

1802

September 20: Lydia Jackson born

1803

May 25: Ralph Waldo Emerson born in Boston, Massachusetts, the fourth child of William and Ruth Emerson

The *Monthly Anthology* founded; William Emerson (father) a founding editor and contributor

The Louisiana Purchase more than doubles the geographical size of the United States

1805

April 17: Edward Bliss Emerson (brother) born

Boston Athenaeum founded

1807

April 11: Robert Bulkeley Emerson (brother) born

April 26: John Clarke Emerson (brother) dies at age seven

International slave trade abolished

1808

November 27: Charles Chauncy Emerson (brother) born

1811

February 26: Mary Caroline Emerson (sister) born

May 12: Rev. William Emerson (father) dies of a stomach tumor at age 42

1812–1817

Emerson attends Boston Latin School

1813

The *Christian Disciple* (later, *Christian Examiner*) established, cofounded by Rev. William Ellery Channing

1814

April 14: Mary Caroline Emerson (sister) dies at age three

First American textile mill operates in Waltham, Massachusetts

1815

North American Review established

1817

July 12: Henry David Thoreau born in Concord, Massachusetts

October: Emerson enters Harvard College

Edward Everett is first American to receive Ph.D. at University of Göttingen in Germany

Samuel Taylor Coleridge's *Biographia Literaria* published

American Colonization Society founded with plan to send freed African Americans to Liberia, Africa

1818–1821

August 29: Emerson teaches school, including at brother William's school for young ladies

1820

Missouri Compromise seeks to balance number of slave and free states in the United States; Maine separates from Massachusetts to become new state

1821

August 29: Emerson graduates from Harvard College

The *Christian Register* established

1822

November: Emerson publishes first article, "Thoughts on the Religion of the Middle Ages," in the *Christian Disciple* and in *Theological Review*

1823

December 23: Emerson takes over teaching at William's school

1824

Emerson quits schoolteaching and begins theological studies

1825

February: Emerson enters Harvard Divinity School, but problems with vision force him to take a leave from studies and begin teaching again

February 16: grandmother, Phebe Bliss Emerson (b. 1741), dies in Concord

Brother William returns from Germany and decides against entering the ministry

American Unitarian Association established

Robert Owen founds New Harmony (first secular utopian community in America) in Indiana

Erie Canal opens

1826

July 4: former presidents John Adams and Thomas Jefferson both die on 50th anniversary of signing of Declaration of Independence

August 2: Emerson attends memorial services for the presidents at Faneuil Hall in Boston

October 15: Emerson preaches first sermon, "Pray without Ceasing," in Samuel Ripley's pulpit in Waltham

November: bothered by lung problems, Emerson travels to South Carolina and Florida to restore health

First lyceum in America established at Millbury, Massachusetts

1827

June 3: Emerson returns to Boston from Southern trip

December 25: Emerson meets Ellen Louisa Tucker while preaching in Concord, New Hampshire

Daniel Webster elected U.S. senator from Massachusetts

First African-American newspaper, *Freedom's Journal,* founded

1828

July 2: brother Edward suffers mental collapse and is admitted to McLean Asylum for several months

December 17: Emerson is engaged to Ellen Tucker

Noah Webster's *American Dictionary of the English Language* published

1829

January: Emerson becomes junior pastor at Second Church, Boston; becomes chaplain of state senate, a position once held by his father

March 11: Emerson ordained at Second Church; promoted to pastor in July

September 30: Emerson marries Ellen Tucker in Concord, New Hampshire

Concord (Mass.) Lyceum established

James Marsh publishes American edition of Samuel Taylor Coleridge's *Aids to Reflection*

1830

December: brother Edward travels to Puerto Rico for his health

Charles Lyell's *Principles of Geology* is published; both Emerson and Thoreau are influenced by idea that the Earth itself has a history

President Andrew Jackson's Indian Removal Act passed by Congress

1831

February 8: wife Ellen Tucker Emerson dies of tuberculosis at the age of 19

December: brother Charles travels to Puerto Rico to restore health and to be with Edward

Nat Turner leads slave uprising in Virginia, killing 60 whites

William Lloyd Garrison begins publication of radical abolitionist paper, the *Liberator,* in Boston

1832

March: Emerson visits Ellen's tomb and opens coffin

September 19: Emerson delivers sermon "The Lord's Supper"

October: brother Edward travels to Puerto Rico again

December 22: Emerson sends official letter of resignation to Second Church

December 25: Emerson embarks on first trip to Europe; meets Coleridge, Wordsworth, and Carlyle

New England Anti-Slavery Society founded in Boston

1833

October 7: Emerson returns to Boston after nine-month trip through Europe

November 5: Emerson, after leaving ministry, delivers first public lecture "The Uses of Natural History" at Masonic Temple, Boston

Frederic Henry Hedge publishes article "Coleridge's Literary Character" in the *Christian Examiner*

1834

March: Emerson meets Lydia Jackson in Plymouth

May: Emerson receives first portion of Ellen Tucker Emerson's settled estate

October 1: brother Edward Bliss Emerson dies of tuberculosis in Puerto Rico at age 29

October 9: Emerson moves to Concord, Mass., to stay with family at the Old Manse

Bronson Alcott establishes experimental Temple School with Elizabeth Palmer Peabody as assistant

1835

January 24: Emerson is engaged to Lydia Jackson

January 29: Emerson begins lecture series "Biography" in Boston

September 12: Emerson delivers "Historical Discourse" on Concord's 200-year history

September 14: Ralph Waldo Emerson marries Lydia Jackson, whom he then calls Lidian; they move into Coolidge house (renamed "Bush") in Concord, Mass., which Emerson had purchased for $3,500

November: Emerson begins winter lecture series "English Literature" in Boston

The *Western Messenger* established with James Freeman Clarke as founding editor

1836

May 9: brother Charles Chauncy Emerson dies of tuberculosis in New York at age 27

July: Margaret Fuller visits Concord and stays with the Emersons for three weeks

September 9: Emerson's first book, *Nature,* published

September 19: first meeting of the Transcendental Club

October 30: Emerson's first child, Waldo, born

December 8: Emerson begins winter lecture series "Philosophy of History" in Boston

American edition of Thomas Carlyle's *Sartor Resartus* published with preface by Emerson

William Henry Furness's *Remarks on the Four Gospels* published

Orestes Brownson's *New Views of Christianity, Society, and the Church* published

George Ripley's *Discourses on the Philosophy of Religion* published

Convers Francis's *Christianity as a Purely Internal Principle* published

1837

July 4: Emerson's poem "Concord Hymn" (written the previous year) sung at Concord Fourth of July celebration and subsequently printed and published in newspapers

July: Emerson receives second installment from Ellen's settled estate

August 30: Henry Thoreau graduates from Harvard

August 31: Emerson delivers "The American Scholar" address for Harvard's Phi Beta Kappa graduation ceremony

September: abolitionists Sarah and Angelina Grimke lecture in Concord and visit the Emersons

November: Emerson delivers first antislavery address at church in Concord, in response to death of antislavery newspaper editor, Elijah Lovejoy, in Illinois

December 6: Emerson begins winter lecture series "Human Culture" in Boston

Massachusetts Board of Education formed

Thomas Carlyle's *The French Revolution* published

Nathaniel Hawthorne's *Twice-Told Tales* published

Andrews Norton's *Evidences of the Genuineness of the Gospel* published

1838

February: Emerson requests removal from guest preaching at East Lexington church

April 6: General Winfield Scott given orders to forcibly remove remaining Native Americans from southeastern states

April 22: Emerson speaks at Concord meeting to oppose removal of Cherokee and other tribes

April 23: Emerson writes open letter to President Martin Van Buren to protest Indian removal; letter is subsequently published in various newspapers

July 15: Emerson delivers "Divinity School Address" at Harvard

July 24: Emerson delivers address on "Literary Ethics" at Dartmouth College

December: final removal of Cherokees along "Trail of Tears" from Georgia to Indian territory in present-day Oklahoma

First volume of George Ripley's 14-volume *Specimens of Foreign Standard Literature* published

American edition of Thomas Carlyle's *Critical and Miscellaneous Essays* published, edited by Emerson

Boston Quarterly Review established by Orestes Brownson

Andrews Norton's "The New School in Literature and Religion" published

1839

February 24: Emerson's second child, daughter Ellen, born

December 4: Emerson begins winter lecture series "The Present Age" in Boston

Margaret Fuller begins Conversations for women

Jones Very's *Essays and Poems* published, edited by Emerson

Andrews Norton's *A Discourse on the Latest Form of Infidelity* published, a criticism of Emerson and of Transcendentalism; Orestes Brownson and George Ripley among those who respond in writing to Norton

1840

March 20: Emerson begins lecture series "Human Life" in Providence, Rhode Island

July 1: first issue of the *Dial* magazine published (Margaret Fuller as editor)

September 2: Emerson attends final meeting of the Transcendental Club

November: Emerson attends Chardon Street Convention of reformers and abolitionists

Elizabeth Palmer Peabody opens bookstore and publishing house in Boston

Alcott family moves to Concord

1841

March 19: Emerson's *Essays: First Series* published

May 19: Theodore Parker delivers *A Discourse on the Transient and Permanent in Christianity* sermon in Boston; resulting controversy leads to calls for Parker to leave ministry

April: Brook Farm community founded by George and Sophia Ripley in West Roxbury, Massachusetts

August 11: Emerson delivers "The Method of Nature" address at Waterville College, Maine

September 21: Emerson's step-grandfather Rev. Ezra Ripley (b. 1751) dies; Emerson's memorial sermons are published

November 22: Emerson's third child, daughter Edith, born

December 2: Emerson begins winter lecture series "The Times"

Henry David Thoreau moves into Emerson household

Thomas Carlyle's *On Heroes and Hero-Worship* published

New York Tribune begins publication, founded and edited by Horace Greeley

1842

January 11: John Thoreau, older brother of Henry David Thoreau, dies at age 26 of lockjaw

January 27: Emerson's son Waldo dies of scarlet fever at age five

February: Emerson travels to New York to lecture

March: Emerson takes over editorship of the *Dial*

July: newlyweds Nathaniel and Sophia Peabody Hawthorne move into Emerson family home, the Old Manse, in Concord; they live there until 1845

October 2: Rev. William Ellery Channing (b. 1780) dies

Henry Wadsworth Longfellow publishes *Poems of Slavery*

1843

January 10: Emerson begins lecture series "New England" in Baltimore

January: Bronson Alcott jailed for refusing to pay poll tax

May: American edition of Carlyle's *Past and Present* published, edited and with preface by Emerson

Bronson Alcott travels to England to meet with reformers with financial assistance from Emerson

Fruitlands utopian community established by Bronson Alcott and Charles Lane (disbands in 1844)

1844

April 8: final issue of the *Dial* published
July 10: Emerson's fourth and last child, son Edward, born
August 1: Emerson delivers "Emancipation of the Negroes in the British West Indies" address in Concord
September: Emerson purchases 14 acres at Walden Pond
October 19: Emerson's *Essays: Second Series* published
Samuel Morse sends first message via telegraph

1845

April 1: the Alcott family moves into "Hillside" house in Concord with financial assistance from Emerson
July 4: Henry David Thoreau moves into cabin at Walden Pond
December 2: Emerson purchases additional 41 acres at Walden Pond
December 31: Emerson begins winter lecture series "Representative Men" in Concord
Emerson turns down offer to lecture at New Bedford Lyceum because blacks are denied membership
Margaret Fuller's *Woman in the Nineteenth Century* published
The *Harbinger* (journal of the Brook Farm community) established
Edgar Allan Poe's *The Raven and Other Poems* published

1846

December 25: Emerson's first collection of *Poems* published
Emerson attends meeting of the Concord Anti-Slavery Society
Margaret Fuller leaves for Europe as foreign correspondent for *New York Tribune*
Margaret Fuller's *Papers on Literature and Art* published
Nathaniel Hawthorne's *Mosses from an Old Manse* published
Henry Thoreau jailed for refusal to pay taxes

1846–1848

Mexican War

1847

September: Thoreau leaves Walden Pond; stays with Lidian and children during Emerson's absence in Europe
October 5: Emerson leaves for second trip to Europe for English lecture tour; meets Carlyle, Wordsworth, and others
Main building at Brook Farm burns and community disbands
Massachusetts Quarterly Review established by Theodore Parker

1848

June 6: Emerson begins lecture series "Mind and Manners in the Nineteenth Century" in London
July 27: Emerson returns to America from Europe
Margaret Fuller travels to Italy and reports back as foreign correspondent for *New York Tribune*
James Russell Lowell's *A Fable for Critics* published
First women's rights convention held at Seneca Falls, New York
New York State passes Married Woman's Property Act

1849

February 1: Emerson begins lecture series "English Traits" in Chelmsford, Massachusetts
March 20: first meeting of the Town and Country Club
September 11: Emerson's *Nature; Addresses, and Lectures* published; includes reprint of *Nature,* as well as key lectures given between 1837 and 1844
Elizabeth Palmer Peabody's *Aesthetic Papers* published; includes first printing of Thoreau's "Resistance to Civil Government" (later known as "Civil Disobedience")
Henry David Thoreau's *A Week on the Concord and Merrimack Rivers* published
Spirit of the Age established by William Henry Channing
"Gold rush" sends thousands of speculators and settlers westward to California

1850

January 1: Emerson's *Representative Men* published

May–June: Emerson's first midwestern lecture tour to Ohio and other locations

July 19: Margaret Fuller (b. 1810) dies in shipwreck on return from Europe

October: first national women's rights convention held in Worcester, Massachusetts; Emerson declines invitation to speak

October: former slave and radical abolitionist Frederick Douglass speaks in Boston, inspiring creation of the Boston Vigilance Committee to assist fugitive slaves

Nathaniel Hawthorne's *The Scarlet Letter* published

Harper's Monthly Magazine established

Fugitive Slave Law passed by U.S. Congress; as part of "Compromise" of 1850, California admitted as a free state and slave trade banned in Washington, D.C.

1851

February: Shadrach Minkins arrested in Boston as an alleged fugitive slave; later rescued by the Boston Vigilance Committee and aided in an escape to Canada

March: Emerson begins lecture series "The Conduct of Life" in Pittsburgh

May 3: Emerson delivers "Fugitive Slave Law Address" in Concord

December 22: Emerson begins winter lecture series "The Conduct of Life" in Boston and New York

Nathaniel Hawthorne's *The House of the Seven Gables* published

Herman Melville's *Moby-Dick* published

New York Times begins publication

1852

February 14: Memoirs of Margaret Fuller Ossoli published, coedited by Emerson, William Henry Channing, and James Freeman Clarke

April: Emerson lectures in Montreal, Canada

June: the Hawthornes return to Concord after living in Salem and Lenox; they buy Alcott home at "Hillside" and rename it "Wayside"

November–February 1853: Emerson on midwestern lecture tour

Nathaniel Hawthorne's *The Blithedale Romance* published

Harriet Beecher Stowe's *Uncle Tom's Cabin* published

1853

November 16: Emerson's mother Ruth Haskins Emerson dies in Concord at age 85

The *Una* established, a women's rights periodical, founded and edited by Transcendentalist feminists Paulina Wright Davis and Caroline Dall

Putnam's Monthly Magazine established

1854

January–February: Emerson on midwestern lecture tour

January 3: Emerson begins lecture series on "Topics of Modern Times" in Philadelphia

March 7: Emerson delivers second "Fugitive Slave Law Address" in New York

August 15: Emerson delivers commencement address at Williams College

December 16: first meeting of the Saturday Club

December: Emerson meets Walt Whitman in New York

Henry David Thoreau's *Walden; or, Life in the Woods* published

Louisa May Alcott's *Flower Fables* published, a collection of children's stories dedicated to Ellen Emerson

Kansas-Nebraska Act overrides earlier Missouri Compromise by allowing "popular sovereignty" on question of whether territories will be slave or free, setting off a wave of violence known as "Bleeding Kansas" between pro-slavery and antislavery groups in the area

Republican Party created as a "free labor" and antislavery party

Massachusetts grants married women's property rights

1855

August 8: Emerson delivers commencement address at Amherst College

September 20: Emerson delivers address at women's rights convention in Boston (later published as "Woman")

September 29: Emerson delivers address at dedication of Sleepy Hollow Cemetery in Concord

Franklin Benjamin Sanborn founds Concord Academy, where Emerson children will attend

Walt Whitman's *Leaves of Grass* published

Evert and George Duyckinck publish their *Cyclopaedia of American Literature* with entries on Emerson, Hawthorne, Thoreau, and others of their circle, establishing their place as important 19th-century literary figures

1856

August 6: Emerson's *English Traits* published

1857

January–February: Emerson on midwestern lecture tour

July: Emerson moves coffins of mother Ruth and son Waldo to new family plot at Sleepy Hollow Cemetery

The Alcotts return to Concord after living in Boston and Connecticut; buy house next door to the Hawthornes and name it "Orchard House"

Atlantic Monthly established with James Russell Lowell as founding editor

Harper's Weekly established

Transatlantic cable laid between New York and London, a technological event Emerson mentions in poem "The Adirondacs"

1858

March: Emerson begins lecture series "The Natural Method of Mental Philosophy" in Boston

August: Emerson goes on camping trip to Adirondack Mountains with other members of the Adirondack Club

George Ripley's first volume of *New American Cyclopaedia* published

1859

May 27: Emerson's brother Robert Bulkeley Emerson dies at age 52

October 16: John Brown leads raid on federal arsenal at Harpers Ferry, West Virginia

October 30: Henry David Thoreau delivers "A Plea for Captain John Brown" in Concord

December 2: John Brown executed in Charles Town, Virginia

December 4: Emerson delivers lecture for John Brown memorial service in Boston

Charles Darwin's *On the Origin of Species* published

1860

January–February: Emerson on midwestern lecture tour

May 10: Theodore Parker (b. 1810) dies in Europe; Emerson's "Tribute to Theodore Parker" is published

November 6: Abraham Lincoln elected 16th president of the United States

December 8: Emerson's *The Conduct of Life* published

December 20: South Carolina votes to secede from the United States

Elizabeth Palmer Peabody establishes first English-language kindergarten in the United States, in Boston

Nathaniel Hawthorne's *The Marble Faun* published

1861

January–June: 11 more states secede from the Union, forming the Confederate States of America

April 2: Emerson begins lecture series "Life and Literature" in Boston

April 12: shots fired on federal forces at Fort Sumter, South Carolina, signaling start of American Civil War

July: Emerson's son Edward Waldo Emerson enters Harvard

President Lincoln makes first transcontinental telegraph communication

1862

May 6: Henry David Thoreau dies of tuberculosis at age 44

August: Emerson's eulogy "Thoreau" published in *Atlantic Monthly*

November: Emerson's essay "The President's Proclamation" published in *Atlantic Monthly*

Emerson delivers lecture "American Civilization" in Washington, D.C., and meets President Lincoln

Several of Thoreau's essays published posthumously in *Atlantic Monthly*

Homestead Act encourages western settlement

1863

January–February: Emerson on midwestern lecture tour

January 1: Emerson reads poem "Boston Hymn," in Music Hall on date Emancipation Proclamation goes into effect

May 1: Emerson's aunt Mary Moody Emerson dies in New York at age 88; buried at Sleepy Hollow Cemetery in Concord

July: violence erupts and draft offices burned in New York City in protest against a Union army draft

October 10: Thoreau's *Excursions* published, edited by Emerson

November 27: Emerson begins winter lecture series "American Life" in Boston

December 1: Emerson delivers "Fortune of the Republic" address in Boston

Louisa May Alcott publishes *Hospital Sketches,* a novel of her experiences as a Civil War nurse

1864

May 19: Nathaniel Hawthorne (b. 1804) dies in New Hampshire; buried in Sleepy Hollow Cemetery in Concord

Emerson elected to new American Academy of Arts and Science

Thoreau's *The Maine Woods* published

1865

January–February: Emerson on midwestern lecture tour

April 9: General Robert E. Lee, commander of the Confederate army, surrenders at Appomattox, Virginia, ending the Civil War after four years of fighting and more than 600,000 dead

April 14: President Abraham Lincoln assassinated

April 19: Emerson delivers address at Lincoln memorial services in Concord

July 22: Thoreau's *Letters to Various Persons* published, edited by Emerson

October 3: Emerson's daughter Edith Emerson marries William Hathaway Forbes

Henry David Thoreau's *Cape Cod* published posthumously

Walt Whitman's *Drum Taps* collection of Civil War poems is published

Thirteenth Amendment to the Constitution ends slavery in the United States

Ku Klux Klan is founded by former Confederate soldiers in attempt to restore white supremacy in the South

1866

January–February: Emerson on midwestern lecture tour

April: Emerson begins lecture series "Philosophy for the People" in Boston

June: two-volume edition of Emerson's *Complete Works* published in England

July 10: Emerson's first grandchild, Ralph Emerson Forbes, born

July 18: Emerson awarded honorary law doctorate from Harvard

1867

January–March: Emerson on midwestern lecture tour

April 29: Emerson's second collection of poems, *May-Day and Other Pieces,* published

July: Emerson appointed overseer of Harvard University; delivers commencement address "The Progress of Culture"

December–January 1868: Emerson on midwestern lecture tour

Free Religious Association founded; Emerson delivers address at inaugural meeting

Radical Club founded

1868

September 13: Emerson's brother William Emerson dies in New York at age 67

Louisa May Alcott's *Little Women* is published

Fourteenth Amendment to the U.S. Constitution redefines national citizenship to include former slaves

1869

March 1: Emerson reads "Amita," a biography of aunt Mary Moody Emerson, at the New England Women's Club

Transcontinental railroad completed

Wyoming Territory grants woman suffrage

1870

March 5: Emerson's *Society and Solitude* published

April 26: Emerson begins lecture series "Natural History of Intellect" at Harvard

Fifteenth Amendment to the U.S. Constitution establishes voting rights for African-American men

1871

April–May: Emerson travels to California, meets John Muir

November–December: Emerson on midwestern lecture tour

1872

January: Emerson delivers address "What Books to Read" at Howard University in Washington, D.C.

July 24: Emerson family home at "Bush" burns; friends raise money to help Emerson rebuild

October 23: Emerson leaves for Europe and also Egypt with daughter Ellen; meets Carlyle for last time

1873

May 26: Emerson returns from trip abroad; entire town of Concord comes out to welcome him home

October 1: Emerson delivers address at opening of the Concord Free Public Library

December 16: Emerson reads poem "Boston" at Faneuil Hall on centennial of Boston Tea Party

Louisa May Alcott's "Transcendental Wild Oats" published (a satire of Transcendentalist idealism)

1874

September 19: Emerson's son Edward Waldo Emerson marries Annie Shepard Keyes

December 14: Emerson's selection of poems, *Parnassus*, published

1875

April 19: Emerson speaks at centennial celebration of Revolutionary War battle in Concord

December 15: Emerson's *Letters and Social Aims* published

Mark Twain's *The Adventures of Tom Sawyer* published

1876

June: Emerson travels south to speak at University of Virginia

November 8: Emerson delivers address at centennial celebration of Boston Latin School

November: Selected Poems published

Octavius Brooks Frothingham's *Transcendentalism in New England: A History* published

1879

Concord School of Philosophy and Literature founded by Bronson Alcott (meets every summer until 1888)

1880

February 4: Emerson delivers "Historic Notes of Life and Letters in New England" as 100th lecture at Concord Lyceum

July 4: George Ripley (b. 1802) dies in New York

July: Emerson delivers lecture "Aristocracy" at Concord School of Philosophy

Elizabeth Palmer Peabody's *Reminiscences of Rev. Wm. Ellery Channing* published

1881

February 5: Thomas Carlyle (b. 1795) dies

February 10: Emerson reads tribute to Carlyle at Massachusetts Historical Society, his last public address

September: Walt Whitman visits Emerson in Concord

1882

March: Emerson attends funeral for Henry Wadsworth Longfellow in Cambridge

April 27: Ralph Waldo Emerson dies of pneumonia at age 78 in Concord; buried at Sleepy Hollow Cemetery

Concord School of Philosophy summer session dedicated to *The Genius and Character of Emerson*

Moncure Conway's *Emerson at Home and Abroad* published

Franklin Benjamin Sanborn's *Henry D. Thoreau* published

1883

James Elliot Cabot begins publication of Riverside Edition of Emerson's *Complete Works* (12 vol-

umes, 1883–93), including publication of many previously uncollected pieces
Correspondence of Carlyle and Emerson published, edited by Charles Eliot Norton
Julia Ward Howe's *Margaret Fuller* published

1884
Thomas Wentworth Higginson's *Margaret Fuller Ossoli* published

1885
Oliver Wendell Holmes's biography of *Ralph Waldo Emerson* published

1886
Henry James's *The Bostonians* published

1887
James Elliot Cabot's two-volume *A Memoir of Ralph Waldo Emerson* published

1888
March 4: Bronson Alcott (b. 1799) dies in Boston
March 6: Louisa May Alcott (b. 1823) dies in Boston

1890
Henry Salt's *The Life of Henry David Thoreau* published
Forced removal of Lakota Sioux at Wounded Knee, South Dakota

1892
March 26: Walt Whitman (b. 1819) dies
November 13: Lidian Emerson dies at age 90
Franklin Benjamin Sanborn publishes Emerson-Thoreau correspondence in *Atlantic Monthly*
Journalist Ida B. Wells begins antilynching campaign

1893
James Elliot Cabot collects and publishes Emerson's lectures on *Natural History of the Intellect and Other Papers,* as final volume of *Complete Works*
Colorado voters approve woman suffrage

1894
January 3: Elizabeth Palmer Peabody (b. 1804) dies

1896
Idaho voters approve woman suffrage and Utah admitted as state with woman suffrage
Supreme Court ruling in *Plessy v. Ferguson* allows racial segregation under doctrine of "separate but equal"

1897
Caroline Dall's *Transcendentalism in New England* published

1898
Franklin Benjamin Sanborn publishes collection of lectures from the Concord School of Philosophy on *The Genius and Character of Emerson*

1903
Son Edward Waldo Emerson publishes centenary edition of *The Complete Works of Ralph Waldo Emerson* (12 volumes, with annotations)

1909
January 14: Emerson's daughter Ellen Tucker Emerson dies at age 70

1909–1910
Emerson's son Edward Waldo Emerson and grandson Waldo Emerson Forbes publish 10 volumes of Emerson's *Journals*

1920
Nineteenth Amendment to the U.S. Constitution guarantees women's right to vote

1929
November 20: Emerson's daughter Edith Emerson Forbes dies at age 88

1930
January 27: Emerson's son Edward Waldo Emerson dies at age 85

Bibliography of Emerson's Works

Major Works Published in Emerson's Lifetime

Nature. Boston: James Munroe, 1836.

Essays [First Series]. Boston: James Munroe, 1841; Rev. ed., 1847.

Essays: Second Series. Boston: James Munroe, 1844.

Poems. Boston: James Munroe, 1847.

Nature; Addresses, and Lectures. Boston: James Munroe, 1849.

Representative Men: Seven Lectures. Boston: Phillips, Sampson, 1850.

Memoirs of Margaret Fuller Ossoli, 2 vols. Edited by William Henry Channing, James Freeman Clarke, and Ralph Waldo Emerson. Boston: Phillips, Sampson, 1852.

English Traits. Boston: Phillips, Sampson, 1856.

The Conduct of Life. Boston: Ticknor & Fields, 1860.

May-Day and Other Pieces. Boston: Ticknor & Fields, 1867.

Society and Solitude. Boston: Fields, Osgood, 1870.

Parnassus. Boston: Osgood, 1875.

Selected Poems. Boston: Osgood, 1876.

Letters and Social Aims. Boston: Osgood, 1876.

Collections of Emerson's Works, Journals, Letters, and Related Primary Sources

American editions. The following are listed chronologically.

The Prose Works of Ralph Waldo Emerson. 3 vols. Boston: Fields, Osgood, 1870; Houghton, Osgood, 1879.

Emerson's Complete Works, Riverside Edition. 12 vols. Edited by J. E. Cabot. Boston and New York: Houghton, Mifflin, 1883–93. [Nine vols. of previously published works, plus *Lectures and Biographical Sketches* (vol. 10), 1884; *Miscellanies* (vol. 11), 1884; and *Natural History of Intellect and Other Papers* (vol. 12), 1893.]

The Correspondence of Thomas Carlyle and Ralph Waldo Emerson: 1834–1872. 2 vols. Edited by Charles Eliot Norton. Boston: James Osgood, 1883; Boston: Ticknor, 1886.

Two Unpublished Essays. The Character of Socrates: The Present State of Ethical Philosophy. Edited by Edward Everett Hale. Boston and New York: Lamson, Wolffe, 1896.

A *Correspondence between John Sterling and Ralph Waldo Emerson.* Edited by Edward Waldo Emerson. Boston and New York: Houghton, Mifflin, 1897.

Letters from Ralph Waldo Emerson to a Friend [Samuel Gray Ward], *1838–1853.* Edited by Charles Eliot Norton. Boston and New York: Houghton, Mifflin, 1899.

Correspondence between Ralph Waldo Emerson and Herman Grimm. Edited by Frederick William Holls. Boston and New York: Houghton, Mifflin, 1903.

Complete Works of Ralph Waldo Emerson, Centenary Edition. 12 vols. Edited by Edward Waldo Emerson. Boston and New York: Houghton, Mifflin, 1903–04.

The Journals of Ralph Waldo Emerson. 10 vols. Edited by Edward Waldo Emerson and Waldo Emerson Forbes. Boston and New York: Houghton, Mifflin, 1909–14.

Records of a Lifelong Friendship, 1807–1882: Ralph Waldo Emerson and William Henry Furness. Edited by Horace Howard Furness. Boston and New York: Houghton, Mifflin, 1910.

Uncollected Writings: Essays, Addresses, Poems, Reviews and Letters. Edited by Charles C. Bigelow. New York: Lamb Publishing, 1912.

Uncollected Lectures. Edited by Clarence Gohdes. New York: William Edwin Rudge, 1932.

Emerson-Clough Letters. Edited by Howard F. Lowry and Ralph Leslie Rusk. Cleveland, Ohio: Rowfant Club, 1934.

Young Emerson Speaks: Unpublished Discourses on Many Subjects. Edited by Arthur Cushman McGiffert, Jr. Boston: Houghton, Mifflin, 1938.

The Letters of Ralph Waldo Emerson. 10 vols. Edited by Ralph L. Rusk and Eleanor Tilton. New York: Columbia University Press, 1939; 1990–1995.

The Early Lectures of Ralph Waldo Emerson. 3 vols. Edited by Robert E. Spiller, Stephen E. Whicher, and Wallace E. Williams. Cambridge, Mass.: Harvard University Press, 1959–72.

Dante's Vita Nuova: Translated by Ralph Waldo Emerson. Edited by J. Chesly Mathews. Boston: Ralph Waldo Emerson Memorial Association. Rev. ed., Chapel Hill: University of North Carolina Press, 1960.

The Journals and Miscellaneous Notebooks of Ralph Waldo Emerson. 16 vols. Edited by William H. Gilman et al. Cambridge, Mass.: Harvard University Press, 1960–83.

The Dial: A Magazine for Literature, Philosophy, and Religion [1840–44]. Reprint, New York: Russell and Russell, 1961.

One First Love: The Letters of Ellen Louisa Tucker to Ralph Waldo Emerson. Edited by Edith W. Gregg. Cambridge, Mass.: Harvard University Press, 1962.

The Correspondence of Emerson and Carlyle. Edited by Joseph Slater. New York and London: Columbia University Press, 1964.

The Collected Works of Ralph Waldo Emerson. 8 vols. to date. Edited by Alfred R. Ferguson, Joseph Slater, Douglas Emory Wilson et al. Cambridge, Mass.: Harvard University Press, 1971– .

The Letters of Ellen Tucker Emerson. 2 vols. Edited by Edith Gregg. Kent, Ohio: Kent State University Press, 1982.

The Poetry Notebooks of Ralph Waldo Emerson. Edited by Ralph H. Orth, Albert J. von Frank, Linda Allardt, and David W. Hill. Columbia: University of Missouri Press, 1986.

The Selected Letters of Lidian Jackson Emerson. Edited by Delores Bird Carpenter. Columbia: University of Missouri Press, 1987.

The Complete Sermons of Ralph Waldo Emerson. 4 vols. Edited by Albert J. von Frank et al. Columbia: University of Missouri Press, 1989–92.

The Topical Notebooks of Ralph Waldo Emerson. 3 vols. Edited by Ralph H. Orth et al. Columbia: University of Missouri Press, 1990–94.

Emerson: Essays and Lectures. Edited by Joel Porte. New York: Library of America, 1993.

Emerson: Collected Poems and Translations. Edited by Harold Bloom and Paul Kane. New York: Library of America, 1994.

Emerson's Antislavery Writings. Edited by Len Gougeon and Joel Myerson. New Haven, Conn.: Yale University Press, 1995.

The Selected Letters of Ralph Waldo Emerson. Edited by Joel Myerson. New York: Columbia University Press, 1997.

Transcendentalism: A Reader. Edited by Joel Myerson. New York: Oxford University Press, 2000.

Emerson's Prose and Poetry: A Norton Critical Edition. Edited by Saundra Morris and Joel Porte. New York: W.W. Norton, 2001.

The Later Lectures of Ralph Waldo Emerson, 1843–1871. 2 vols. Edited by Ronald Bosco and Joel Myerson. Athens: University of Georgia Press, 2001.

The Spiritual Emerson: Essential Writings. Edited by David M. Robinson. Boston: Beacon Press, 2003.

Emerson in His Own Time: A Biographical Chronicle of His Life, Drawn from Recollections, Interviews, and Memoirs by Family, Friends, and Associates. Edited by Ronald A. Bosco and Joel Myerson. Iowa City: University of Iowa Press, 2003.

The Political Emerson: Essential Essays on Politics and Social Reform. Edited by David M. Robinson. Boston: Beacon Press, 2004.

The Emerson Brothers: A Fraternal Biography in Letters. Edited by Ronald A. Bosco and Joel Myerson. New York: Oxford University Press, 2005.

The Essential Transcendentalists. Edited by Richard G. Geldard. New York: Tarcher, 2005.

The American Transcendentalists: Essential Writings. Edited by Lawrence Buell. New York: Random House/Modern Library, 2006.

Bibliography of Secondary Sources

Bibliographies and Reference Guides

Barton, William, Jr. *A Calendar to the Complete Edition of the Sermons of Ralph Waldo Emerson.* Memphis, Tenn.: Bee Books, 1977.

Bryer, Jackson R., and Robert A. Rees. *A Checklist of Emerson Criticism, 1951–1961.* Hartford, Conn.: Transcendental Books, 1964.

Burkholder, Robert E. "Ralph Waldo Emerson." In *The Transcendentalists: A Review of Research and Criticism,* edited by Joel Myerson, 135–167. New York: Modern Language Association, 1984.

Burkholder, Robert E., and Joel Myerson. *Emerson: An Annotated Secondary Bibliography.* Pittsburgh: University of Pittsburgh Press, 1985.

———. *Ralph Waldo Emerson: An Annotated Bibliography of Criticism, 1980–1991.* Westport, Conn.: Greenwood Press, 1994.

Cameron, Kenneth W. *Ralph Waldo Emerson's Reading.* Raleigh, N.C.: Thistle Press, 1941. (*Note:* Readers are directed to the numerous collections of primary source material and indexes related to Emerson and the Transcendentalists compiled by Kenneth Walter Cameron, many published under the Transcendental Books imprint of Hartford, Connecticut.)

Carpenter, Frederick Ives. *Emerson Handbook.* New York: Hendricks House, 1953.

Charvat, William. *Emerson's American Lecture Engagements. A Chronological List.* New York: New York Public Library, 1961.

Cooke, George Willis. *A Bibliography of Ralph Waldo Emerson.* Boston and New York: Houghton, Mifflin, 1908.

Harding, Walter. *Emerson's Library.* Charlottesville: University Press of Virginia, 1967.

Hubbell, George Sheldon. *A Concordance to the Poems of Ralph Waldo Emerson.* New York: H.W. Wilson, 1932.

Ihrig, Mary Alice. *Emerson's Transcendental Vocabulary: A Concordance.* New York: Garland, 1981.

Konvitz, Milton R. *The Recognition of Ralph Waldo Emerson: Selected Criticism Since 1837.* Ann Arbor: University of Michigan Press, 1972.

Myerson, Joel. "A Calendar of Transcendental Club Meetings." *American Literature* 44, no. 2 (May 1972): 197–207.

———, ed. *Emerson and Thoreau: The Contemporary Reviews.* Cambridge: Cambridge University Press, 1992.

———. *Ralph Waldo Emerson: A Descriptive Bibliography.* Pittsburgh: University of Pittsburgh Press, 1982.

———, ed. *The Transcendentalists: A Review of Research and Criticism.* New York: Modern Language Association, 1984.

Ralph Waldo Emerson Society. "Annual Bibliographies." 1991–present. Available online. URL: http://www.cas.sc.edu/engl/emerson/AboutEmerson/AnnualBibliographies.html. Accessed October 1, 2009.

Stovall, Floyd. "Ralph Waldo Emerson." In *Eight American Authors,* edited by Floyd Stovall et al., 37–83. New York: Modern Language Association, 1956. Rev. ed., 1971.

Von Frank, Albert J. *An Emerson Chronology.* New York: G.K. Hall, 1994.

Selected Biographies and Reminiscences of Emerson

The following are listed chronologically.

Searle, January [George Searle Phillips]. *Emerson, His Life and Writings*. London: Holyoake & Co., 1855.

Alcott, Amos Bronson. *Emerson*. Cambridge, Mass.: 1865. Reprinted as *Ralph Waldo Emerson: Philosopher and Seer.* Boston: Cupples and Hurd, 1888.

Alcott, A. Bronson. *Concord Days*. Boston: Roberts Bros., 1872.

Cooke, George Willis. *Ralph Waldo Emerson; His Life, Writings, and Philosophy*. Boston: Osgood, 1881.

Guernsey, Alfred Hudson. *Ralph Waldo Emerson; Philosopher and Poet*. New York: Appleton, 1881.

Conway, Moncure Daniel. *Emerson at Home and Abroad*. Boston: Osgood, 1882.

Ireland, Alexander. *Ralph Waldo Emerson: His Life, Genius, and Writings*. London: Simpkin, Marshall, 1882.

———. *In Memoriam. Ralph Waldo Emerson: Recollections of His Visits to England in 1833, 1847–8, 1872–3, and Extracts from Unpublished Letters*. London: Simpkin, Marshall, 1882.

Thayer, James B. *A Western Journey with Mr. Emerson.* Boston: Little, Brown, 1884.

Sanborn, F. B., ed. *The Genius and Character of Emerson. Lectures at the Concord School of Philosophy.* Boston: Osgood, 1885.

Holmes, Oliver Wendell. *Ralph Waldo Emerson*. Boston and New York: Houghton, Mifflin, 1885.

Dana, William Franklin. *The Optimism of Ralph Waldo Emerson*. Boston: Cupples, Upham & Co., 1886.

Cabot, James Elliot. *A Memoir of Ralph Waldo Emerson*. 2 vols. Boston and New York: Houghton, Mifflin, 1887–89.

Emerson, Edward Waldo. *Emerson in Concord. A Memoir.* Boston: Houghton, Mifflin, 1888.

Higginson, Thomas Wentworth. *Contemporaries*. Boston: Houghton, Mifflin, 1899.

Woodbury, Charles J. *Talks with Ralph Waldo Emerson.* London: Baker & Taylor, 1890.

Forster, Joseph. *Four Great Teachers: John Ruskin, Thomas Carlyle, Ralph Waldo Emerson, and Robert Browning.* New York: Scribner & Welford, 1890.

Albee, John. *Remembrances of Emerson*. New York: Cooke, 1901.

Sanborn, Franklin Benjamin. *Ralph Waldo Emerson.* Boston: Small, Maynard, 1901.

———. *The Personality of Emerson*. Boston: Charles Goodspeed, 1903.

Mead, Edwin Doak. *The Influence of Emerson*. Boston: American Unitarian Association, 1903.

Cary, Elisabeth Luther. *Emerson, Poet and Thinker.* New York: G.P. Putnam's Sons, 1904.

Woodberry, George Edward. *Ralph Waldo Emerson.* New York: Macmillan, 1907.

Firkins, Oscar W. *Ralph Waldo Emerson*. Boston: Houghton, Mifflin, 1915.

Snider, Denton J. *A Biography of Ralph Waldo Emerson.* St. Louis: William Harvey Miner, 1921.

Brooks, Van Wyck. *The Life of Emerson*. New York: Dutton, 1932.

Scudder, Townsend. *The Lonely Wayfaring Man: Emerson and Some Englishmen*. New York: Oxford University Press, 1936.

Rusk, Ralph L. *The Life of Ralph Waldo Emerson*. New York: Scribner, 1949.

Pommer, Henry F. *Emerson's First Marriage*. Carbondale: Southern Illinois University Press, 1967.

Bode, Carl. *Ralph Waldo Emerson; A Profile*. New York: Hill and Wang, 1969.

Porte, Joel. *Representative Man: Ralph Waldo Emerson in His Time*. New York: Oxford University Press, 1979.

Allen, Gay Wilson. *Waldo Emerson: A Biography*. New York: Viking, 1981.

Yannella, Donald. *Ralph Waldo Emerson*. Boston: Twayne, 1982.

McAleer, John. *Ralph Waldo Emerson: Days of Encounter.* Boston: Little, Brown, 1984.

Richardson, Robert D. *Emerson: The Mind on Fire*. Berkeley: University of California Press, 1995.

Buell, Lawrence. *Emerson*. Cambridge, Mass.: Harvard University Press, 2003.

Selected Books and Articles about Emerson and Transcendentalism

Acharya, Shanta. *The Influence of Indian Thought on Ralph Waldo Emerson*. Lewiston, N.Y.: Edwin Mellen Press, 2001.

Arvin, Newton. "The House of Pain: Emerson and the Tragic Sense." *The Hudson Review* 12, no. 1 (Spring 1959): 37–58.

Asarnow, Jenny. "Flashbacks: Ralph Waldo Emerson. The Sage and the Magazine." *The Atlantic Online* (December 23, 2003). Available online. URL: http://www.theatlantic.com/unbound/flashbks/emerson.htm. Accessed October 3, 2007.

Baker, Carlos, with James Mellow. *Emerson among the Eccentrics: A Group Portrait.* New York: Viking, 1996.

Bean, Judith Mattson. "Texts from Conversation: Margaret Fuller's Influence on Emerson." *Studies in the American Renaissance* (1994): 227–244.

Beecher, Jonathan. *Charles Fourier: The Visionary and His World.* Berkeley: University of California Press, 1986.

Bercovitch, Sacvan, ed. *The Cambridge History of American Literature.* Vol. 2: *1820–1865.* New York: Cambridge University Press, 1995.

Bode, Carl. *The American Lyceum: Town Meeting of the Mind.* Carbondale: Southern Illinois University Press, 1968.

Bloom, Harold, ed. *Ralph Waldo Emerson.* Modern Critical Views Series. New York: Chelsea House, 1985. Rev. ed., 2006.

Bosco, Ronald A. "His Lectures Were Poetry, His Teaching the Music of the Spheres: Annie Adams Fields and Francis Greenwood Peabody on Emerson's 'Natural History of the Intellect' University Lectures at Harvard in 1870." *Harvard Library Bulletin* 8, no. 2 (Summer 1997): 1–79.

———. "'Poetry for the World of Readers' and 'Poetry for Bards Proper': Poetic Theory and Textual Integrity in Emerson's *Parnassus.*" In *Studies in the American Renaissance,* edited by Joel Myerson, 257–312. Charlottesville: University of Virginia Press, 1989.

———. "'What poems are many private lives': Emerson Writing the American Plutarch." *Studies in the Literary Imagination* 27, no. 1 (Spring 1994): 103–129.

Bosco, Ronald A., and Jillmarie Murphy. *Hawthorne in His Own Time.* Iowa City: University of Iowa Press, 2007.

Bosco, Ronald A., and Joel Myerson, eds. *Emerson Bicentennial Essays.* Boston: Massachusetts Historical Society; Charlottesville: University of Virginia Press, 2006.

Brent, Joseph. *Charles Sanders Peirce: A Life.* Bloomington: Indiana University Press, 1993. Rev. ed., 1998.

Brewer, Priscilla J. "Emerson, Lane, and the Shakers: A Case of Converging Ideologies." *New England Quarterly* 59, no. 4 (1982): 254–275.

Bridgman, Richard. "From Greenough to 'Nowhere': Emerson's *English Traits.*" *New England Quarterly* 59, no. 4 (1986): 469–485.

Broaddus, Dorothy C. *Genteel Rhetoric: Writing High Culture in Nineteenth-Century Boston.* Columbia: University of South Carolina Press, 1999.

Brock, Erland, ed. *Swedenborg and His Influence.* Bryn Athyn, Pa.: Academy of the New Church, 1988.

Brodwin, Stanley. "Emerson's Version of Plotinus: The Flight to Beauty." *Journal of the History of Ideas* 35, no. 3 (1974): 477.

Brooks, Paul. *The People of Concord: One Year in the Flowering of New England.* Chester, Conn.: Globe Pequot Press, 1990.

Brown, Lee Rust. *The Emerson Museum: Practical Romanticism and the Pursuit of the Whole.* Cambridge, Mass.: Harvard University Press, 1997.

Buckley, Thomas L. "The Bostonian Cult of Classicism: The Reception of Goethe and Schiller in the Literary Reviews of the *North American Review, Christian Examiner,* and the *Dial,* 1817–1865." In *The Fortunes of German Writers in America: Studies in Literary Reception,* edited by Wolfgang Elfe, James Hardin, and Gunther Holst, 27–40. Columbia: University of South Carolina Press, 1992.

Buell, Lawrence. "The American Transcendentalist Poets." In *The Columbia History of American Poetry: The 19th Century,* edited by Jay Parini, 97–119. New York: Columbia University Press, 1995.

———. *Literary Transcendentalism: Style and Vision in the American Renaissance.* Ithaca, N.Y.: Cornell University Press, 1973.

———, ed. *Ralph Waldo Emerson: A Collection of Critical Essays.* Englewood Cliffs, N.J.: Prentice Hall, 1993.

Burkholder, Robert. "The Contemporary Reception of English Traits." In *Emerson Centenary Essays,* edited by Joel Myerson, 156–172. Carbondale: Southern Illinois University Press, 1982.

Burkholder, Robert, and Joel Myerson, eds. *Critical Essays on Waldo Emerson.* Boston: G.K. Hall, 1983.

Burkholder, Robert E. "(Re)Visiting 'The Adirondacs': Emerson's Confrontation with Wild Nature." In *Emerson Bicentennial Essays,* edited by Ronald A.

Bosco and Joel Myerson, 247–269. Boston: Massachusetts Historical Society; Charlottesville: University of Virginia Press, 2006.

Burkholder, Robert E., and Wesley T. Mott, eds. *Emersonian Circles: Essays in Honor of Joel Myerson*. Rochester, N.Y.: University of Rochester Press, 1997.

Cadava, Eduardo. "The Nature of War in Emerson's 'Boston Hymn.'" *Arizona Quarterly* 49, no. 3 (Autumn 1993): 21–58.

———. *Emerson and the Climates of History*. Stanford, Calif.: Stanford University Press, 1997.

Cady, Edwin H., and Louis J. Budd, eds. *On Emerson: The Best from American Literature*. Durham, N.C.: Duke University Press, 1988.

Cain, William E., ed. *A Historical Guide to Henry David Thoreau*. New York: Oxford University Press, 2000.

Calhoun, Charles C. *Longfellow: A Rediscovered Life*. Boston: Beacon Press, 2004.

Capper, Charles. *Margaret Fuller: An American Romantic Life*. Vol. 1: *The Private Years*. New York: Oxford University Press, 1992.

———. *Margaret Fuller: An American Romantic Life*. Vol. 2: *The Public Years*. New York: Oxford University Press, 2007.

Capper, Charles, and Conrad Edick Wright, eds. *Transient and Permanent: The Transcendentalist Movement and Its Contexts*. Boston: Massachusetts Historical Society, 1999.

Carey, Patrick W. *Orestes A. Brownson: American Religious Weathervane*. Grand Rapids, Mich.: William B. Eerdmans Publishing, 2004.

Carpenter, Delores Bird. "Lidian Emerson's 'Transcendental Bible.'" *Studies in the American Renaissance* (1980): 91–95.

Carpenter, Frederic Ives. *Emerson and Asia*. Cambridge, Mass.: Harvard University Press, 1930.

Carroll, Joseph. "Stevens and Romanticism." In *The Cambridge Companion to Wallace Stevens*, edited by John N. Serio, 87–102. New York: Cambridge University Press, 2007.

Caruthers, J. Wade. *Octavius Brooks Frothingham, Gentle Radical*. University: University of Alabama Press, 1977.

Castillo, Susan. "'The Best of Nations'? Race and Imperial Destinies in Emerson's *English Traits*." *Yearbook of English Studies* 34 (2004): 200–211.

Cavanaugh, Cynthia A. "The Aeolian Harp: Beauty and Unity in the Poetry and Prose of Ralph Waldo Emerson." *Rocky Mountain Review* (Spring 2002): 25–35.

Cavell, Stanley. *Conditions Handsome and Unhandsome: The Constitution of Emersonian Perfectionism*. Chicago: University of Chicago Press, 1990.

Cavell, Stanley, and David J. Hodge. *Emerson's Transcendental Etudes*. Stanford, Calif.: Stanford University Press, 2003.

Cayton, Mary Kupiec. *Emerson's Emergence: Self and Society in the Transformation of New England, 1800–1845*. Chapel Hill: University of North Carolina Press, 1989.

Chadwick, John White. *George William Curtis*. New York: Harper and Brothers, 1893.

Chapman, Mary. "The Economics of Loss: Emerson's 'Threnody.'" *American Transcendental Quarterly* 16 (2002): 73–87.

Chevigny, Bell Gale. *The Woman and the Myth: Margaret Fuller's Life and Writing*. New York: The Feminist Press, 1976.

Cheyfitz, Eric. *The Trans-Parent: Sexual Politics in the Language of Emerson*. Baltimore: Johns Hopkins University Press, 1981.

Christy, Arthur. *The Orient in American Transcendentalism: A Study of Emerson, Thoreau, and Alcott*. New York: Columbia University Press, 1932.

Cole, Phyllis. "Emerson, England, and Fate." In *Emerson: Prophesy, Metamorphosis, and Influence*, edited by David Levin, 83–105. New York: Columbia University Press, 1975.

———. "Emerson Father and Son: A Precedent for 'The American Scholar.'" *NEQ* 78 (2005): 101–124.

———. *Mary Moody Emerson and the Origins of Transcendentalism: A Family History*. New York: Oxford University Press, 1998.

———. "'Men and Women Conversing': The Emersons in 1837." In *Emersonian Circles: Essays in Honor of Joel Myerson*, edited by Joel Myerson, Wesley T. Mott, and Robert E. Burkholder, 127–159. Rochester, N.Y.: University of Rochester Press, 1997.

———. "The New Movement's Tide: Emerson and Women's Rights." In *Emerson Bicentennial Essays*, edited by Ronald A. Bosco and Joel Myerson,

117–152. Boston: Massachusetts Historical Society; Charlottesville: University of Virginia Press, 2006.

Collison, Gary. "Emerson and Antislavery." In *A Historical Guide to Ralph Waldo Emerson,* edited by Joel Myerson, 179–209. New York and Oxford: Oxford University Press, 2000.

———. *Shadrach Minkins: From Fugitive Slave to Citizen.* Cambridge, Mass.: Harvard University Press, 1998.

Cooke, George Willis. *Unitarianism in America: A History of Its Origin and Development.* Boston: American Unitarian Association, 1902.

Crain, Caleb. *American Sympathy: Men, Friendship, and Literature in the New Nation.* New Haven, Conn.: Yale University Press, 2001.

Cranch, Leonora Scott, ed. *The Life and Letters of Christopher Pearse Cranch, by his Daughter Leonora Scott Cranch.* Reprint. New York: AMS Press, 1969.

Crowe, Charles. *George Ripley: Transcendentalist and Utopian Socialist.* Athens: University of Georgia Press, 1967.

Dahlstrand, Frederick. *Amos Bronson Alcott: An Intellectual Biography.* East Brunswick, N.J.: Associated University Presses, 1982.

———. "Science, Religion, and the Transcendentalist Response to a Changing America." *Studies in the American Renaissance* (1988): 1–25.

Dameron, J. Lasley. "Emerson's 'Each and All' and Goethe's 'Eins und Alles.'" *English Studies* 67, no. 4 (August 1986): 327–330.

Deese, Helen. "'A Liberal Education': Caroline Healey Dall and Emerson." In *Emersonian Circles: Essays in Honor of Joel Myerson,* edited by Robert E. Burkholder and Wesley T. Mott, 237–260. New York: University of Rochester Press, 1997.

———, ed. *Daughter of Boston: The Extraordinary Diary of a Nineteenth-Century Woman, Caroline Healey Dall.* Boston: Beacon Press, 2005.

De Groot, Jean, ed. *Nature in American Philosophy.* Washington, D.C.: Catholic University of America Press, 2004.

Delano, Sterling. *Brook Farm: The Dark Side of Utopia.* Cambridge, Mass.: Harvard University Press, 2004.

———. *The Harbinger and New England Transcendentalism: A Portrait of Associationism in America.* London: Associated University Presses, 1983.

Delbanco, Andrew. *Melville: His World and Work.* Knopf, 2005.

———. *William Ellery Channing: An Essay on the Liberal Spirit in America.* Cambridge, Mass.: Harvard University Press, 1981.

DeVoll, Matthew W. "Emerson and Dreams: Toward a Natural History of Intellect." *ATQ* 18 (2004): 69–87.

Donadio, Stephen, Stephen Railton, and Ormond Seavey. *Emerson and His Legacy: Essays in Honor of Quentin Anderson.* Carbondale: Southern Illinois University Press, 1986.

Dowling, Linda. *Charles Eliot Norton: The Art of Reform in Nineteenth-Century America.* Hanover, N.H., and London: University Press of New England, 2007.

Edmundson, Mark. *Towards Reading Freud: Self-Creation in Milton, Wordsworth, Emerson, and Sigmund Freud.* Chicago: University of Chicago Press, 2007.

Elfe, Wolfgang, James Hardin, and Gunther Holst, eds. *The Fortunes of German Writers in America: Studies in Literary Reception.* Columbia: University of South Carolina Press, 1992.

Ellison, Julie. "Tears for Emerson: *Essays, Second Series.*" In *The Cambridge Companion to Ralph Waldo Emerson,* edited by Joel Porte and Saundra Morris, 140–161. New York: Cambridge University Press, 1999.

Ellison, Julie K. *Emerson's Romantic Style.* Princeton, N.J.: Princeton University Press, 1984.

Emerson, Ellen Tucker. *The Life of Lidian Jackson Emerson,* edited by Delores Bird Carpenter. Boston: Twayne Publishers, 1980.

Engstrom, Sallee Fox. *The Infinitude of the Private Man: Emerson's Presence in Western New York, 1851–1861.* New York: Peter Lang, 1997.

Felton, R. Todd. *A Journey into the Transcendentalists' New England.* Berkeley, Calif.: Roaring Forties Press, 2006.

Field, Peter S. *Ralph Waldo Emerson: The Making of a Democratic Intellectual.* Lanham, Md.: Rowman & Littlefield, 2002.

Field, Susan. "Open to Influence: Ralph Waldo Emerson and Audre Lorde on Loss." *ATQ* 19 (2005): 5–22.

———. *The Romance of Desire: Emerson's Commitment to Incompletion.* Rutherford, N.J.: Fairleigh Dickinson, 1997.

Francis, Richard. *Transcendental Utopias: Individual and Community at Brook Farm, Fruitlands, and Walden.* Ithaca, N.Y.: Cornell University Press, 1997.

Francis, Richard Lee. "The Poet and Experience: *Essays: Second Series.*" In *Emerson Centenary Essays,* edited by Joel Myerson, 93–106. Carbondale: Southern Illinois University Press, 1982.

Fresonke, Kris. *West of Emerson: The Design of Manifest Destiny.* Berkeley: University of California Press, 2003.

Frothingham, Octavius Brooks. *Transcendentalism in New England.* New York: G.P. Putnam, 1876.

Fuller, Randall. *Emerson's Ghosts: Literature, Politics, and the Making of Americanists.* New York: Oxford University Press, 2007.

Gabriel, Ralph Henry. *The Course of American Democratic Thought.* Westport, Conn.: Greenwood Press, 1986.

Gale, Robert L. *A Henry Wadsworth Longfellow Companion.* Westport, Conn.: Greenwood Press, 2003.

Garvey, T. Gregory, ed. *The Emerson Dilemma: Essays on Emerson and Social Reform.* Athens: University of Georgia Press, 2001.

———. "Emerson, Garrison, and the Anti-Slavery Society." In *Emerson Bicentennial Essays,* edited by Ronald A. Bosco and Joel Myerson, 153–182. Boston: Massachusetts Historical Society; Charlottesville: University Press of Virginia, 2006.

Gatta, John. *Making Nature Sacred: Literature, Religion, and Environment in America from the Puritans to the Present.* New York: Oxford University Press, 2004.

Geldard, Richard. *God in Concord: Ralph Waldo Emerson's Awakening to the Infinite.* Burdett, N.Y.: Larson, 1998.

Gelpi, Donald L. *Endless Seeker: The Religious Quest of Ralph Waldo Emerson.* Lanham, Md.: University Press of America, 1991.

Gibian, Peter. *Oliver Wendell Holmes and the Culture of Conversation.* New York: Cambridge University Press, 2001.

Gill, Stephen. *William Wordsworth: A Life.* New York: Oxford University Press, 1989.

Goetzmann, William, ed. *The American Hegelians: An Intellectual Episode in the History of Western America.* New York: Knopf, 1973.

Gohdes, Clarence. *The Periodicals of American Transcendentalism.* Durham, N.C.: Duke University Press, 1931.

Goodwin, Joan W. *The Remarkable Mrs. Ripley: The Life of Sarah Alden Bradford Ripley.* Boston: Northeastern University Press, 1998.

Goto, Shoji, and Phyllis Cole. *The Philosophy of Emerson and Thoreau: Orientals Meet Occidentals.* Lewiston, N.Y.: Mellen, 2007.

Gougeon, Len. *Emerson and Eros: The Making of a Cultural Hero.* Albany: State University of New York, 2007.

———. "Emerson and the British: Challenging the Limits of Liberty." *REAL: Yearbook of Research in English and American Literature* 22 (2006): 179–213.

———. "Emerson and the Woman Question: The Evolution of His Thought." *New England Quarterly* 71, no. 4 (December 1998): 570–592.

———. *Virtue's Hero: Emerson, Antislavery, and Reform.* Athens: University of Georgia, 1990.

Grant, Mark N. *Maestros of the Pen: A History of Classical Music Criticism in America.* Boston: Northeastern University Press, 1998.

Gravil, Richard. *Romantic Dialogues: Anglo-American Continuities, 1776–1862.* New York: St. Martin's, 2000.

Green, Judith Kent. "A Tentative Transcendentalist in the Ohio Valley: Samuel Osgood and the *Western Messenger.*" *Studies in the American Renaissance* (1987): 79–92.

Grodzins, Dean David. *American Heretic: Theodore Parker and Transcendentalism.* Chapel Hill: University of North Carolina Press, 2002.

Gross, Robert A. *The Minutemen and Their World.* New York: Hill and Wang, 1976.

Grossman, Jay. *Reconstituting the American Renaissance: Emerson, Whitman, and the Politics of Representation.* Durham, N.C.: Duke University Press, 2003.

Grossman, Richard, ed. *The Tao of Emerson: The Wisdom of the Tao Te Ching as Found in the Words of Ralph Waldo Emerson.* New York: Modern Library, 2007.

Guarneri, Carl. *The Utopian Alternative: Fourierism in Nineteenth Century America.* Ithaca, N.Y.: Cornell University Press, 1991.

Gura, Philip. *The Wisdom of Words: Language, Theology, and Literature in the New England Renaissance.*

Middletown, Conn.: Wesleyan University Press, 1981.

Gura, Philip F. *American Transcendentalism: A History.* New York: Hill and Wang, 2007.

Gura, Philip F., and Joel Myerson, eds. *Critical Essays on American Transcendentalism.* Boston: G.K. Hall, 1982.

Guthrie, James R. *Above Time: Emerson's and Thoreau's Temporal Revolutions.* Columbia: University of Missouri Press, 2001.

Habich, Robert D. *Transcendentalism and the Western Messenger: A History of the Magazine and Its Contributors, 1835–1841.* Rutherford, N.J.: Farleigh Dickinson University Press, 1985.

Hall, Julie E. "'Coming to Europe,' Coming to Authorship: Sophia Hawthorne and Her *Notes in England and Italy.*" *Legacy* 19, no. 2 (2002): 137–151.

Handlin, Lilian. *George Bancroft: The Intellectual as Democrat.* New York: Harper and Row, 1984.

Hankins, Barry. *The Second Great Awakening and the Transcendentalists.* Westport, Conn.: Greenwood Press, 2004.

Hankins, Thomas L., and Robert J. Silverman. *Instruments and the Imagination.* Princeton University Press, 1999. (*See* chapter 5, "The Aeolian Harp and the Romantic Quest of Nature.")

Harris, Kenneth Marc. *Carlyle and Emerson: Their Long Debate.* Cambridge, Mass.: Harvard University Press, 1978.

Harris, Mark W. *Historical Dictionary of Unitarian Universalism.* Lanham, Md.: Scarecrow Press, 2004.

Haskell, Thomas L. *The Emergence of Professional Social Science: The American Social Science Association and the Nineteenth-Century Crisis of Authority.* Champaign: University of Illinois, 1977.

Heath, William G. "Cyrus Bartol's Transcendentalism." *Studies in the American Renaissance* (1979): 399–408.

Hodge, David Justin. *On Emerson.* Belmont, Calif.: Thomson/Wadsworth, 2002.

Hoffmann, R. Joseph. "William Henry Furness: The Transcendentalist Defense of the Gospels." *New England Quarterly* 56, no. 2 (June 1983): 238–260.

Hopkins, Vivian C. *Spires of Form: A Study of Emerson's Aesthetic Theory.* New York: Russell & Russell, 1965.

Howe, Daniel Walker. *Making the American Self: Jonathan Edwards to Abraham Lincoln.* Cambridge, Mass.: Harvard University Press, 1997.

———. *The Unitarian Conscience: Harvard Moral Philosophy, 1805–1861.* Cambridge, Mass.: Harvard University Press, 1970.

Hudnut, Robert K. *The Aesthetics of Ralph Waldo Emerson: The Materials and Methods of His Poetry.* Lewiston, N.Y.: Edwin Mellen Press, 1996.

Hudspeth, Robert N. "'Born with Knives in Their Brain': Recent Writings on American Transcendentalism." *MHR* 7 (2005): 120–131.

———. *Ellery Channing.* New York: Twayne, 1973.

———. "Later Emerson: 'Intellect' and The Conduct of Life." In *Emerson Bicentennial Essays,* edited by Ronald A. Bosco and Joel Myerson, 405–431. Massachusetts Historical Society; Charlottesville: University of Virginia Press, 2006.

Jackson, Carl T. *The Oriental Religions and American Thought: 19th-Century Explorations.* Westport, Conn.: Greenwood Press, 1981.

Jarvis, Edward. *Traditions and Reminiscences of Concord, Massachusetts 1779–1878,* edited by Sarah Chapin. University of Massachusetts Press, 1993.

Johnson, Glenn M. "Emerson's Essay 'Immortality': The Problem of Authorship." In *On Emerson: The Best from American Literature,* edited by Edwin Harrison Cady and Louis J. Budd, 245–262. Durham, N.C.: Duke University Press, 1988.

Johnson, Linck C. "'Liberty Is Never Cheap': Emerson, 'The Fugitive Slave Law,' and the Antislavery Lecture Series at the Broadway Tabernacle." *NEQ* 76 (2003): 550–592.

Kaledin, Eugenia. *The Education of Mrs. Henry Adams.* Philadelphia: Temple University Press, 1981.

Kateb, George. *Emerson and Self-Reliance.* Lanham, Md.: Rowman & Littlefield, 1995. Rev. ed., 2002.

Keane, Patrick J. *Emerson, Romanticism, and Intuitive Reason: The Transatlantic "Light of All Our Day."* Columbia: University of Missouri Press, 2005.

Kirklighter, Cristina, and Gail Y. Okawa. *Traversing the Democratic Borders of the Essay.* State University of New York Press, 2002. (*See* chapter 3: "Essaying an American Democratic Identity in Emerson and Thoreau.")

Knight, Denise D. *Writers of the American Renaissance: An A-to-Z Guide.* Westport, Conn.: Greenwood Publishing Group, 2003.

Konvitz, Milton R., and Stephen E. Whicher, eds. *Emerson: A Collection of Critical Essays.* Englewood Cliffs, N.J.: Prentice-Hall, 1962.

LeBeau, Bryan F. *Frederic Henry Hedge: Nineteenth Century American Transcendentalist.* Allison Park, Pa.: Pickwick Publications, 1985.

Lee, Maurice S. *Slavery, Philosophy, and American Literature, 1830–1860.* New York: Cambridge, 2005.

Leighton, Walter L. *French Philosophers and New England Transcendentalism.* New York: Greenwood Press, 1968.

Leiter, Sharon. *Critical Companion to Emily Dickinson.* New York: Facts On File, 2007.

Leland, Charles. "A Defense of 'Brahma.'" In *Critical Essays on Waldo Emerson,* edited by Robert Burkholder and Joel Myerson, 164–169. Boston: G.K. Hall, 1983.

Levin, David, ed. *Emerson: Prophesy, Metamorphosis, and Influence.* New York: Columbia University Press, 1975.

Levin, Jonathan. *The Poetics of Transition: Emerson, Pragmatism, and American Literary Modernism.* Durham, N.C.: Duke University Press, 1999.

Lewis, R. W. B. *The Jameses: A Family Narrative.* New York: Farrar, Straus and Giroux, 1991.

Leyda, Jay, ed. *The Melville Log: A Documentary Life of Herman Melville.* Harcourt, Brace, 1951.

Lopez, Michael. "*The Conduct of Life:* Emerson's Anatomy of Power." In *The Cambridge Companion to Ralph Waldo Emerson,* edited by Joel Porte and Saundra Morris, 243–366. New York: Cambridge University Press, 1999.

———. *Emerson and Power: Creative Antagonism in the Nineteenth Century.* Dekalb: Northern Illinois University Press, 1996.

Loving, Jerome. *Emerson, Whitman, and the American Muse.* Chapel Hill: University of North Carolina Press, 1982.

Lundin, Roger. *From Nature to Experience: The American Search for Authority.* Lanham, Md.: Rowman & Littlefield, 2005.

Maibor, Carolyn. *Labor Pains: Emerson, Hawthorne, and Alcott on Work and the Woman Question.* New York: Routledge, 2004.

Makarushka, Irene S. *Religious Imagination and Language in Emerson and Nietzsche.* New York: St. Martin's, 1994.

Marchi, Dudley M. *Montaigne among the Moderns: Receptions of the Essais.* New York: Berghahn Books, 1994. (*See* chapter 2, "Emerson and Nietzsche: Between Innovation and Repetition.")

Mariani, Giorgio, et al., eds. *Emerson at 200: Proceedings of the International Bicentennial Conference.* Rome: Aracne, 2004.

Marovitz, Sanford E. "Emerson's Shakespeare: From Scorn to Apotheosis." In *Emerson Centenary Essays,* edited by Joel Myerson, 122–155. Carbondale: Southern Illinois University Press, 1982.

Marshall, Megan. *The Peabody Sisters: Three Women Who Ignited American Romanticism.* Boston: Houghton Mifflin, 2005.

Matteson, John. *Eden's Outcasts: The Story of Louisa May Alcott and Her Father.* W.W. Norton, 2007.

Matthiessen, F. O. *American Renaissance: Art and Expression in the Age of Emerson and Whitman.* New York: Oxford University Press, 1941.

———. *The James Family, Including Selections from the Writings of Henry James, Senior, William, Henry, and Alice James.* New York: Knopf, 1947.

Maynard, W. Barksdale. *Walden Pond: A History.* New York: Oxford University Press, 2004.

McFarland, Philip. *Hawthorne in Concord.* New York: Grove Press, 2004.

McMillin, T. S. *Our Preposterous Use of Literature: Emerson and the Nature of Reading.* Urbana: University of Illinois Press, 2000.

McMurry, Andrew. *Environmental Renaissance: Emerson, Thoreau and the Systems of Nature.* Athens: University of Georgia Press, 2003.

McNulty, John Bard. "Emerson's Friends and the Essay on Friendship." *New England Quarterly* 19, no. 3 (September 1946): 390–394.

Meehan, Sean Ross. *Mediating American Autobiography: Photography in Emerson, Thoreau, Douglass, and Whitman.* Columbia: University of Missouri Press, 2008.

Menand, Louis. *The Metaphysical Club.* New York: Farrar, Straus and Giroux, 2001.

Meyer, Howard N. *Colonel of the Black Regiment: The Life of Thomas Wentworth Higginson.* New York: W.W. Norton, 1967.

———, ed. *The Magnificent Activist: The Writings of Thomas Wentworth Higginson.* New York: Da Capo Press, 2000.

Mikics, David. *The Romance of Individualism in Emerson and Nietzsche.* Athens: Ohio University Press, 2003.

Miller, DeWolfe F. *Christopher Pearse Cranch and His Caricatures of New England Transcendentalism.* Cambridge, Mass.: Harvard University Press, 1951.

Miller, Norman. "Emerson's 'Each and All' Concept: A Reexamination." In *Critical Essays on Ralph Waldo Emerson,* edited by Robert Burkholder and Joel Myerson, 346–354. Boston: G.K. Hall, 1983.

Milne, Gordon. *George William Curtis and the Genteel Tradition.* Bloomington: Indiana University Press, 1956.

Mitchell, Charles E. *Individualism and Its Discontents: Appropriations of Emerson, 1880–1950.* Amherst: University of Massachusetts Press, 1997.

Morris, Saundra. "'Metre-Making' Arguments: Emerson's Poems." In *The Cambridge Companion to Ralph Waldo Emerson,* edited by Joel Porte and Saundra Morris, 218–243. New York: Cambridge University Press, 1999.

———. "The Threshold Poem, Emerson, and 'The Sphinx.'" *AL* 69 (1997): 547–570.

Mott, Wesley T., ed. *Biographical Dictionary of Transcendentalism.* Westport, Conn.: Greenwood Press, 1996.

———. *Encyclopedia of Transcendentalism.* Westport, Conn.: Greenwood Press, 1996.

———. *"The Strains of Eloquence": Emerson and His Sermons.* University Park: Pennsylvania State University Press, 1989.

Mott, Wesley T., and Robert E. Burkholder, eds. *Emersonian Circles: Essays in Honor of Joel Myerson.* Rochester, N.Y.: University of Rochester Press, 1997.

Myerson, Joel, ed. *The Cambridge Companion to Henry David Thoreau.* New York: Cambridge University Press, 1995.

———. *Historical Guide to Ralph Waldo Emerson.* New York: Oxford University Press, 2000.

———. *The New England Transcendentalists and the Dial: A History of the Magazine and Its Contributors.* London and Toronto: Associated University Presses, 1980.

New, Elisa. *The Regenerate Lyric: Theology and Innovation in American Poetry.* New York: Cambridge University Press, 1993.

Newfield, Christopher. *The Emerson Effect: Individualism and Submission in America.* Chicago: University of Chicago Press, 1996.

Newman, Lance. *Our Common Dwelling: Henry Thoreau, Transcendentalism, and the Class Politics of Nature.* New York: Palgrave, 2005.

Nicoloff, Philip. *Emerson on Race and History: An Examination of English Traits.* New York: Columbia University Press, 1964.

Niemeyer, Mark. "Emerson's Napoleon; or, the French Emperor as (American) Democrat and Businessman." *Sources* 18, no. 1–2 (Spring, 2005): 29–41.

O'Keefe, Richard R. "Emerson's 'Montaigne; or, the Skeptic': Biography as Autobiography." *Essays in Literature* 23, no. 2 (Fall 1996): 206–217.

———. "'Experience': Emerson on Death." *American Transcendental Quarterly* 9, no. 2 (June 1995): 119–129.

———. *Mythic Archetypes in Ralph Waldo Emerson: A Blakean Reading.* Kent, Ohio: Kent State University Press, 1995.

———. "The Rats in the Wall: Animals in Emerson's 'History.'" *American Transcendental Quarterly* 10, no. 2 (June 1996): 111–121.

Ostrander, Gilbert M. *Republic of Letters: The American Intellectual Community, 1776–1865.* Madison, Wisc.: Madison House, 1999.

Packer, Barbara L. *Emerson's Fall: A New Interpretation of the Major Essays.* New York: Continuum, 1982.

———. "History and Form in Emerson's 'Fate.'" In *Emerson Bicentennial Essays,* edited by Ronald A. Bosco and Joel Myerson, 432–452. Boston: Massachusetts Historical Society; Charlottesville: University of Virginia Press, 2006.

———. *The Transcendentalists.* Athens: University of Georgia Press, 2007.

Patterson, Anita Haya. *From Emerson to King: Democracy, Race, and the Politics of Protest.* New York: Oxford University Press, 1997.

Petrulionis, Sandra H. *To Set This World Right: The Antislavery Movement in Thoreau's Concord.* Ithaca, N.Y.: Cornell University Press, 2006.

Pickard, John B. *The Letters of John Greenleaf Whittier.* Cambridge, Mass.: Harvard University Press, 1975.

Pochmann, Henry A. *New England Transcendentalism and St. Louis Hegelianism.* New York: Haskell House, 1970.

Pollard, John A. *John Greenleaf Whittier, Friend of Man.* Boston: Houghton Mifflin, 1949.

Pommer, Henry F. *Emerson's First Marriage.* Carbondale: Southern Illinois University Press, 1967.

Porte, Joel. *Consciousness and Culture: Emerson and Thoreau Reviewed.* New Haven, Conn.: Yale University Press, 2004.

———. *Emerson and Thoreau: Transcendentalists in Conflict.* Middletown, Conn.: Wesleyan University Press, 1966.

Porte, Joel, and Saundra Morris, eds. *The Cambridge Companion to Ralph Waldo Emerson.* New York: Cambridge University Press, 1999.

Power, Edward J. *Religion and the Public Schools in Nineteenth-Century America: The Contribution of Orestes A. Brownson.* New York: Paulist Press, 1996.

Raymond, Henrietta Dana. *Sophia Willard Dana Ripley: Co-Founder of Brook Farm.* Portsmouth, N.H.: P. E. Randall, 1994.

Reiss, Benjamin. *Theaters of Madness: Insane Asylums and Nineteenth-Century American Culture.* Chicago: University of Chicago Press, 2008. (*See* chapter 4, "Emerson's Close Encounters with Madness.")

Renehan, Edward J., Jr. *The Secret Six: The True Tale of the Men Who Conspired with John Brown.* New York: Crown, 1995.

Reynolds, David S. *John Brown, Abolitionist.* New York: Knopf, 2005.

———. *Walt Whitman.* New York: Oxford University Press, 2005.

Richardson, Robert D. *Emerson: The Mind on Fire.* Berkeley: University of California Press, 1995.

———. *First We Read, Then We Write: Emerson on the Creative Process.* Iowa City: University of Iowa Press, 2009.

———. *Henry Thoreau: A Life of the Mind.* Berkeley: University of California Press, 1986.

Richardson, Todd H. "Publishing the Cause of Suffrage: The *Woman's Journal*'s Appropriation of Ralph Waldo Emerson in Postbellum America." *NEQ* 79, no. 4 (December 2006): 578–608.

Robbins, Paula. *The Royal Family of Concord: Samuel, Elizabeth, and Rockwood Hoar and Their Friendship With Ralph Waldo Emerson.* Bloomington, Ind.: Xlibris Corporation, 2003.

Roberson, Susan L. *Emerson in His Sermons.* Columbia: University of Missouri Press, 1995.

Robinson, David. *Apostle of Culture: Emerson as Preacher and Lecturer.* Philadelphia: University of Pennsylvania Press, 1982.

———. *Emerson and the Conduct of Life: Pragmatism and Ethical Purpose in the Later Work.* New York: Cambridge University Press, 1993.

———. "The Method of Nature and Emerson's Period of Crisis." In *Emerson Centenary Essays,* edited by Joel Myerson, 74–92. Carbondale: Southern Illinois University Press, 1982.

———. *Natural Life: Thoreau's Worldly Transcendentalism.* Ithaca, N.Y.: Cornell University Press, 2004.

———. "Why Emerson Matters." *Journal of Unitarian Universalist History* 23 (2003): 49–63.

Rohler, Lloyd. *Ralph Waldo Emerson: Preacher and Lecturer.* Westport, Conn.: Greenwood, 1995.

Ronda, Bruce. *Elizabeth Palmer Peabody: A Reformer on Her Own Terms.* Cambridge, Mass.: Harvard University Press, 1999.

Rose, Anne C. *Transcendentalism as a Social Movement, 1830–1850.* New Haven, Conn.: Yale University Press, 1981.

Rosenwald, Lawrence. *Emerson and the Art of the Diary.* New York: Oxford University Press, 1988.

Rowe, John Carlos. *At Emerson's Tomb: The Politics of Classic American Literature.* New York: Columbia University Press, 1997.

Rudy, John G. *Emerson and Zen Buddhism.* Lewiston, N.Y.: Edwin Mellen, 2001.

Ryan, Barbara. "Emerson's 'Domestic and Social' Experiments: Service, Slavery, and the Unhired Man." *American Literature* 66, no. 3 (September 1994): 485–508.

Sacks, Kenneth S. *Understanding Emerson: "The American Scholar" and His Struggle for Self-Reliance.* Princeton, N.J.: Princeton University Press, 2003.

Saito, Naoko. *The Gleam of Light: Moral Perfectionism and Education in Dewey and Emerson.* New York: Fordham University Press, 2005.

Saloman, Ora Frishberg. *Beethoven's Symphonies and J. S. Dwight: The Birth of American Music Criticism.* Boston: Northeastern University Press, 1995.

Sattelmeyer, Robert. "*Walden:* Climbing the Canon." In *More Day to Dawn: Thoreau's Walden for the Twenty-first Century,* edited by Sandra Harbert Petrolionis and Laura Dassow Walls, 11–27. Boston: University of Massachusetts Press, 2007.

Scalia, Bill, ed. *Ralph Waldo Emerson.* Bloom's Classic Critical Views Series. New York: Chelsea House, 2007.

Schirmeister, Pamela. *Less Legible Meanings: Between Poetry and Philosophy in the Work of Emerson.* Stanford, Calif.: Stanford University Press, 1999.

Schmidt, Leigh Eric. *Restless Souls: The Making of American Spirituality From Emerson to Oprah.* New York: HarperSanFrancisco, 2005.

Schreiner, Samuel A., Jr. *The Concord Quartet: Alcott, Emerson, Hawthorne, Thoreau, and the Friendship That Freed the American Mind.* Hoboken, N.J.: Wiley, 2006.

Scudder, Townsend. "Emerson's British Lecture Tour, 1847–1848: Part II: Emerson as a Lecturer and the Reception of the Lectures." *American Literature* 7, no. 2 (1935): 166–180.

Sealts, Merton M., Jr. *Emerson on the Scholar.* Columbia: University of Missouri Press, 1992.

Sealts, Merton M., and Alfred R. Ferguson. *Emerson's Nature: Origin, Growth, Meaning.* Carbondale: Southern Illinois University Press, 1979.

Sedgwick, Ellery. *The Atlantic Monthly, 1857–1909: Yankee Humanism at High Tide and Ebb.* Amherst: University of Massachusetts Press, 1994.

Selinger, Eric Murphy. "'Too Pathetic, Too Pitiable': Emerson's Lessons in Love's Philosophy." *ESQ: A Journal of the American Renaissance* 40, no. 2 (1994): 139–182.

Shklar, Judith N. "Emerson and the Inhibitions of Democracy." *Political Theory* 18, no. 4 (November 1990): 601–614.

Simmons, Nancy Craig. "Arranging the Sibylline Leaves: James Elliot Cabot's Work as Emerson's Literary Executor." *Studies in the American Renaissance* (1983): 335–389.

———. "Emerson and His Audiences: The New England Lectures, 1843–1844." In *Emerson Bicentennial Essays,* edited by Ronald A. Bosco and Joel Myerson, 51–85. Boston: Massachusetts Historical Society; Charlottesville: University of Virginia Press, 2006.

Smith, Harmon L. *My Friend, My Friend: The Story of Thoreau's Relationship with Emerson.* Amherst: University of Massachusetts Press, 1999.

Sowder, William J. *Emerson's Impact on the British Isles and Canada.* Charlottesville: University Press of Virginia, 1966.

Specq, François. "Emerson's Rhetoric of Empowerment in 'Address to the Citizens of Concord on the Fugitive Slave Law' (1851)." In *Ralph Waldo Emerson dans ses texts: rhétorique et philosophie,* edited by Philippe Jaworski and François Brunet, 115–129. Paris: Institut d'Études Anglophones, Université Paris VII, 2004.

Stack, George J. *Nietzsche and Emerson: An Elective Affinity.* Athens: Ohio University Press, 1992.

Stadler, Gustavus. *Troubling Minds: The Cultural Politics of Genius in the United States, 1840–1890.* Minneapolis: University of Minnesota Press, 2006.

Steele, Jeffrey. *The Representation of the Self in the American Renaissance.* Chapel Hill: University of North Carolina Press, 1987.

———. "Transcendental Friendship: Emerson, Fuller, and Thoreau." In *The Cambridge Companion to Ralph Waldo Emerson,* edited by Joel Porte and Saundra Morris, 121–139. New York: Cambridge University Press, 1999.

Steinman, Lisa M. *Masters of Repetition: Poetry, Culture, and Work in Thomson, Wordsworth, Shelley, and Emerson.* New York: St. Martin's Press, 1998.

Stiles, Bradley J. *Emerson's Contemporaries and Kerouac's Crowd: A Problem of Self-Location.* Madison, N.J.: Fairleigh Dickinson, 2003.

Stoehr, Taylor. *Nay-Saying in Concord: Emerson, Alcott, Thoreau.* Hamden, Conn.: Archon Books, 1979.

Story, Ronald. *The Forging of an Aristocracy: Harvard and the Boston Upper Class, 1800–1870.* Middletown, Conn.: Wesleyan University Press, 1981.

Sudol, Ronald A. "'The Adirondacs' and Technology." In *Emerson Centenary Essays,* edited by Joel Myerson, 173–179. Carbondale: Southern Illinois University Press, 1982.

Swift, Lindsay. *Brook Farm: Its Members, Scholars, and Visitors.* 1900. Reprint, New York: Citadel Press, 1973.

Teichgraeber, Richard F., III, *Sublime Thoughts/Penny Wisdom: Situating Emerson and Thoreau in the American Market.* Baltimore: Johns Hopkins University Press, 1995.

Thomas, Joseph M. "Late Emerson: *Selected Poems* and the 'Emerson Factory.'" *ELH* 65, no. 4 (1998): 971–994.

Tuerk, Richard. "Emerson and the Wasting of Beauty: 'The Rhodora.'" *ATQ* 4 (March 1990): 5–11.

———. "Emerson's 'Woodnotes' poems." *ATQ* 6, no. 4 (December 1992): 295.

Tufariello, Catherine. "'The Remembering Wine': Emerson's Influence on Whitman and Dickinson." In *The Cambridge Companion to Ralph Waldo Emerson,* edited by Joel Porte and Saundra Morris, 162–191. New York: Cambridge University Press, 1999.

Turner, James. *The Liberal Education of Charles Eliot Norton.* Baltimore and London: Johns Hopkins University Press, 1999.

Valenti, Patricia Dunlavy. *Sophia Peabody Hawthorne. A Life.* Vol. 1: *1809–1847.* Columbia: University of Missouri Press, 2004.

Van Anglen, Kevin P. *The New England Milton: Literary Reception and Cultural Authority in the Early Republic.* Rev. ed. University Park: Pennsylvania State University Press, 2008.

Van Cromphout, Gustaaf. *Emerson's Ethics.* Columbia: University of Missouri Press, 1999.

———. *Emerson's Modernity and the Example of Goethe.* Columbia: University of Missouri Press, 1990.

Van Leer, David. *Emerson's Epistemology: The Argument of the Essays.* New York: Cambridge University Press, 1986.

Vásquez, Mark G. *Authority and Reform: Religious and Educational Discourses in Nineteenth-Century New England Literature.* Knoxville: University of Tennessee Press, 2003.

Versluis, Arthur. *American Transcendentalism and Asian Religions.* New York: Oxford University Press, 1993.

Vogel, Stanley M. *German Literary Influences on the American Transcendentalists.* New Haven, Conn.: Yale University Press, 1955.

Von Frank, Albert J. "Essays: First Series (1841)." In *The Cambridge Companion to Ralph Waldo Emerson,* edited by Joel Porte and Saundra Morris, 106–120. New York: Cambridge University Press, 1999.

———. *The Trials of Anthony Burns: Freedom and Slavery in Emerson's Boston.* Cambridge, Mass.: Harvard University Press, 1998.

Wagenknecht, Edward. *John Greenleaf Whittier: A Portrait in Paradox.* New York: Oxford University Press, 1967.

Waggoner, Hyatt. *Emerson as Poet.* Princeton, N.J.: Princeton University Press, 1974.

Walls, Laura Dassow. *Emerson's Life in Science: The Culture of Truth.* Ithaca, N.Y.: Cornell University Press, 2003.

———. *Seeing New Worlds: Henry David Thoreau and Nineteenth-Century Natural Science.* Madison: University of Wisconsin Press, 1995.

Warren, James Perrin. *Culture of Eloquence: Oratory and Reform in Antebellum America.* University Park: Pennsylvania State University Press, 1999.

Wayne, Tiffany K. *Encyclopedia of Transcendentalism.* New York: Facts On File, 2006.

———. *Woman Thinking: Feminism and Transcendentalism in Nineteenth-Century America.* Lanham, Md.: Lexington Books, 2005.

Weisbuch, Robert. *Atlantic Double-Cross: American Literature and British Influence in the Age of Emerson.* Chicago: University of Chicago Press, 1986.

———. "Postcolonial Emerson and the Erasure of Europe." In *The Cambridge Companion to Ralph Waldo Emerson,* edited by Joel Porte and Saundra Morris, 192–217. New York: Cambridge University Press, 1999.

West, Michael. *Transcendental Wordplay: America's Romantic Punsters and the Search for the Language of Nature.* Athens: Ohio University Press, 2000.

Whicher, Stephen E. *Freedom and Fate: An Inner Life of Ralph Waldo Emerson.* Rev. ed. Philadelphia: University of Pennsylvania Press, 1971.

Wider, Sarah A. *The Critical Reception of Emerson: Unsettling All Things.* Rochester, N.Y.: Camden House, 2000.

———. "Only the Hearer Quotes Well: Emerson and His Audiences." *Journal of Unitarian Universalist History* 23 (2003): 29–40.

Williams, John B. *White Fire: The Influence of Emerson on Melville.* Long Beach: California State University Press, 1991.

Wilson, Eric. *Emerson's Sublime Science.* New York: Macmillan, 1999.

Wilson, Leslie Perrin. *In History's Embrace: Past and Present in Concord, Massachusetts.* Hollis, N.H.: Hollis Publishing, 2007.

Wineapple, Brenda. *Hawthorne: A Life.* New York: Knopf, 2003.

———. *White Heat: The Friendship of Emily Dickinson and Thomas Wentworth Higginson.* New York: Knopf, 2008.

Wittenberg, David. *Philosophy, Revision, Critique: Rereading Practices in Heidegger, Nietzsche, and Emerson.* Stanford, Calif.: Stanford University Press, 2001.

Worley, Sam McGuire. *Emerson, Thoreau, and the Role of Cultural Critique.* Albany: State University of New York Press, 2001.

Wright, Conrad Edick, ed. *American Unitarianism: 1805–1865.* Boston: Northeastern University Press, 1989.

Wynkoop, William M. *Three Children of the Universe: Emerson's View of Shakespeare, Bacon, and Milton.* The Hague: Mouton, 1966.

Yacovone, Donald. *Samuel Joseph May and the Dilemmas of the Liberal Persuasion, 1797–1871.* Philadelphia: Temple University Press, 1991.

Yannella, Donald. *Ralph Waldo Emerson.* Boston: Twayne, 1982.

Zwarg, Christina. *Feminist Conversations: Fuller, Emerson, and the Play of Reading.* Ithaca, N.Y.: Cornell University Press, 1995.

Internet Resources

Emerson, Edward Waldo, ed. *The Complete Works of Ralph Waldo Emerson.* Centenary Edition. University of Michigan Digital Library. URL: http://quod.lib.umich.edu/e/emerson/. Accessed April 24, 2009.

"Emerson in Concord: An Exhibition in Celebration of the 200th Anniversary of the Birth of Ralph Waldo Emerson." Concord Free Public Library, 2003. URL: http://www.concordlibrary.org/scollect/Emerson_Celebration/Table_of_contents.html. Accessed April 24, 2009.

Lewis, Jone Johnson. "Ralph Waldo Emerson (1803–1882), Guide to Resources on Transcendentalism and Emerson." URL: http://www.transcendentalists.com/1emerson.html. Accessed April 24, 2009.

"The Life and Works of Ralph Waldo Emerson." Ralph Waldo Emerson Institute. URL: http://www.rwe.org/resources. Accessed April 24, 2009.

Ralph Waldo Emerson Society. University of South Carolina. URL: http://www.cas.sc.edu/engl/emerson/. Accessed April 24, 2009.

"Ralph Waldo Emerson Texts." Emerson Central. URL: http://www.emersoncentral.com/. Accessed April 24, 2009.

Reuben, Paul. "Ralph Waldo Emerson (1803–1882)." PAL: Perspectives in American Literature—A Research and Reference Guide. California State University. Stanislaus. URL: http://www.csustan.edu/english/reuben/pal/chap4/emerson.html. Accessed April 24, 2009.

Schulman, Frank. "Ralph Waldo Emerson." Dictionary of Unitarian and Universalist Biography, Unitarian Universalist Historical Society (UUHS). URL: http://www25-temp.uua.org/uuhs/duub/articles/ralphwaldoemerson.html. Accessed April 24, 2009.

Woodlief, Ann M. "American Transcendentalism Web." Virginia Commonwealth University. URL: http://www.vcu.edu/engweb/transcendentalism/index.html. Accessed April 24, 2009.

List of Works Included in This Volume, by Date and by Format

By Date (of first publication)

1832 "The Lord's Supper"
1833 "Uses of Natural History"
1836 *Nature*
1837 "The American Scholar"
1838 "Divinity School Address"
"Literary Ethics"
1839 "Each and All"
"The Humble-Bee"
"The Rhodora"
1840 "Woodnotes" I and II
1841 *Essays: First Series*
"Art"
"Circles"
"Compensation" (poem)
"Compensation"
"Friendship" (poem)
"Friendship"
"Heroism"
"History"
"Intellect"
"Love"
"The Over-Soul"
"Self-Reliance"
"Spiritual Laws"
"Introductory Lecture on the Times"
"Man the Reformer"
"The Method of Nature"
"The Snow-Storm"
"The Sphinx"
1842 "The Conservative"
"Saadi"
1843 "Ode to Beauty"
"To Ellen, at the South"
"The Transcendentalist"
1844 *Essays: Second Series*
"Character"
"Experience" (poem)
"Experience"
"Manners"
"Nature"
"New England Reformers"
"Nominalist and Realist"
"The Poet"
"Politics" (poem)
"Politics"
"Blight"
"Emancipation of the Negroes in the British West Indies"
"Eros"
"The Tragic"
"The Young American"
1845 "Dirge"
1847 *Poems*
"Astræa"
"Bacchus"
"From the Persian of Hafiz"
"Give All to Love"
"Hamatreya"
"Hymn, Sung at the Completion of the Concord Monument"
"Initial, Daemonic, and Celestial Love"
"Merlin, I and II"
"Mithridates"
"Monadnoc"
"Ode, Inscribed to W. H. Channing"
"Thine Eyes Still Shined"
"Threnody"

"Uriel"
"The World-Soul
"Heroism" (poem)
"Spiritual Laws" (poem)
"Unity"
1849 *Nature; Addresses, and Lectures*
1850 *Representative Men*
"Goethe; or, the Writer"
"Montaigne; or, the Skeptic"
"Napoleon; or, the Man of the World"
"Plato; or, the Philosopher"
"Shakspeare; or, the Poet"
"Swedenborg; or, the Mystic"
"Uses of Great Men"
1851 "The Fugitive Slave Law"
1852 *Memoirs of Margaret Fuller Ossoli*
1854 "Freedom"
1855 "American Slavery"
"Woman"
1856 *English Traits*
1857 "Brahma"
"The Chartist's Complaint"
"Days"
"Waldeinsamkeit"
1858 "Two Rivers"
1860 *The Conduct of Life*
"Beauty"
"Behavior"
"Culture" (poem)
"Culture"
"Fate"
"Illusions"
"Manners" (poem)
"Power"
"Wealth" (poem)
"Wealth"
"Worship" (poem)
"Worship"
1861 "Song of Nature"
1862 "Thoreau"
1863 "Boston Hymn"
"Fortune of the Republic"
"Voluntaries"
1864 "Sea-Shore"
1866 "My Garden"
1867 *May-Day and Other Pieces*
"The Adirondacs"
"Art"
"Beauty"
"Character"
"In Memoriam, E.B.E."
"Love and Thought"
"May-Day"
"Nature"
"Ode Sung in the Town Hall, Concord, July 4, 1857"
"Solution"
"Terminus"
"The Titmouse"
"Una"
1870 *Society and Solitude*
"Art"
"Books"
"Civilization"
"Courage"
"Domestic Life"
"Eloquence"
"Farming"
"Old Age"
"Society and Solitude"
"Success"
"Works and Days"
1874 *Parnassus*
1876 *Selected Poems*
"Boston"
"The Harp"
"Maiden Speech of the Aeolian Harp"
Letters and Social Aims
"Persian Poetry"
"Poetry and Imagination"
1893 *Natural History of Intellect*

By Format

Books

Conduct of Life, The
English Traits
Essays: First Series
Essays: Second Series
Letters and Social Aims
May-Day and Other Pieces
Memoirs of Margaret Fuller Ossoli
Natural History of Intellect
Nature
Nature; Addresses, and Lectures

Parnassus
Poems
Representative Men
Selected Poems
Society and Solitude

Essays

"Art" (*Essays: First Series*)
"Art" (*Society and Solitude*)
"Beauty" (*The Conduct of Life*)
"Behavior" (*The Conduct of Life*)
"Books" (*Society and Solitude*)
"Character" (*Essays: Second Series*)
"Circles" (*Essays: First Series*)
"Civilization" (*Society and Solitude*)
"Compensation" (*Essays: First Series*)
"Courage" (*Society and Solitude*)
"Culture" (*The Conduct of Life*)
"Domestic Life" (*Society and Solitude*)
"Eloquence" (*Society and Solitude*)
"Experience" (*Essays: Second Series*)
"Farming" (*Society and Solitude*)
"Fate" (*The Conduct of Life*)
"Friendship" (*Essays: First Series*)
"Goethe; or, the Writer" (*Representative Men*)
"Heroism" (*Essays: First Series*)
"History" (*Essays: First Series*)
"Illusions" (*The Conduct of Life*)
"Intellect" (*Essays: First Series*)
"Love" (*Essays: First Series*)
"Manners" (*Essays: Second Series*)
"Montaigne; or, the Skeptic" (*Representative Men*)
"Napoleon; or, the Man of the World" (*Representative Men*)
"Nature" (*Essays: Second Series*)
"New England Reformers" (*Essays: Second Series*)
"Nominalist and Realist" (*Essays: Second Series*)
"Old Age" (*Society and Solitude*)
"The Over-Soul" (*Essays: First Series*)
"Persian Poetry" (*Letters and Social Aims*)
"Plato; or, the Philosopher" (*Representative Men*)
"The Poet" (*Essays: Second Series*)
"Poetry and Imagination" (*Letters and Social Aims*)
"Politics" (*Essays: Second Series*)
"Power" (*The Conduct of Life*)
"Self-Reliance" (*Essays: First Series*)
"Shakspeare; or, the Poet" (*Representative Men*)
"Society and Solitude" (*Society and Solitude*)
"Spiritual Laws" (*Essays: First Series*)
"Success" (*Society and Solitude*)
"Swedenborg; or, the Mystic" (*Representative Men*)
"Uses of Great Men" (*Representative Men*)
"Wealth" (*The Conduct of Life*)
"Works and Days" (*Society and Solitude*)
"Worship" (*The Conduct of Life*)

Lectures and Sermons

"The American Scholar"
"American Slavery"
"The Conservative"
"Divinity School Address"
"Emancipation of the Negroes in the British West Indies"
"Fortune of the Republic"
"The Fugitive Slave Law"
"Introductory Lecture on the Times"
"Literary Ethics"
"The Lord's Supper"
"Man the Reformer"
"The Method of Nature"
"Thoreau"
"The Tragic"
"The Transcendentalist"
"Uses of Natural History"
"Woman"
"The Young American"

Poems

"The Adirondacs"
"Art"
"Astræa"
"Bacchus"
"Beauty"
"Blight"
"Boston"
"Boston Hymn"
"Brahma"
"Character"
"The Chartist's Complaint"
"Compensation"
"Culture"
"Days"
"Dirge"
"Each and All"

"Eros"
"Experience"
"Freedom"
"Friendship"
"From the Persian of Hafiz"
"Give All to Love"
"Hamatreya"
"The Harp"
"Heroism"
"The Humble-Bee"
"Hymn, Sung at the Completion of the Concord Monument, April 19, 1836"
"Initial, Daemonic, and Celestial Love"
"In Memoriam E.B.E."
"Love and Thought"
"Maiden Speech of the Aeolian Harp"
"Manners"
"May-Day"
"Merlin, I and II"
"Mithridates"
"Monadnoc"
"My Garden"
"Nature"
"Ode, Inscribed to W. H. Channing"
"Ode Sung in the Town Hall, Concord, July 4, 1857"
"Ode to Beauty"
"Politics"
"The Rhodora"
"Saadi"
"Sea-Shore"
"The Snow-Storm"
"Solution"
"Song of Nature"
"The Sphinx"
"Spiritual Laws"
"Terminus"
"Thine Eyes Still Shined"
"Threnody"
"The Titmouse"
"To Ellen, at the South"
"Two Rivers"
"Una"
"Unity"
"Uriel"
"Voluntaries"
"Waldeinsamkeit"
"Wealth"
"Woodnotes," I and II
"The World-Soul"
"Worship"

About the Contributors

Note: Unsigned entries in this volume were written by the editor, Tiffany K. Wayne.

James A. Brent is an associate professor of history and political science at Arkansas State University–Beebe, where he teaches survey classes in history and U.S. government and, in addition to other duties, serves as cosponsor of the ASU-Beebe Debate Club. He is also district coordinator for National History Day in his local area. Dr. Brent is a member of the Southern Historical Association, Society for Historians of the Early American Republic, the Arkansas Political Science Association, and the Association of Arkansas College History Teachers.

Wendy Commons lives near Dallas, Texas, where she teaches at a local community college (Collin College). She is currently working on her Ph.D. in rhetoric at Texas Woman's University.

Kate Culkin is associate professor of history at Bronx Community College. She was the associate editor of the Harriet Jacobs Family Papers and is currently completing a biography of the 19th-century American sculptor Harriet Hosmer.

David A. Dilworth is professor of philosophy at State University of New York, Stony Brook. He holds degrees in philosophy from Fordham University (1963) and in East Asian languages and cultures from Columbia University (1970). He has specialized in modern Japanese philosophy while also ranging more widely in the history of ideas, East and West, with special interest in classical American philosophy and the American Transcendentalist tradition. He is the author of *Philosophy in World Perspective: A Comparative Hermeneutic of the Major Theories* (1989) and translator and coeditor of *Sourcebook for Modern Japanese Philosophy: Selected Documents* (1998).

Hank Galmish is a tenured English professor at Green River Community College in Auburn, Washington, where he has taught for the past 20 years. He teaches a variety of courses, including American literature and Irish literature, and has published articles on Herman Melville, the iconography of the Green Man in literature, and Somerset Maugham. He is an active member of the Community College Humanities Association, the Pacific Northwest Scholars Association, and the Melville Society.

Len Gougeon is a Distinguished University Fellow and professor of American literature at the University of Scranton in Pennsylvania. A past president of the Ralph Waldo Emerson Society, he is the author of *Virtue's Hero: Emerson, Antislavery, and Reform* (1990, 2010) and coeditor (with Joel Myerson) of *Emerson's Antislavery Writings* (1995, 2001). His most recent book is *Emerson & Eros: The Making of a Cultural Hero* (2007). He was the 2008 recipient of the Ralph Waldo Emerson Society's Distinguished Achievement Award and is currently at work on a study of the political and cultural impact of the Civil War on relations between New England and British writers.

Nicholas Guardiano is an adjunct lecturer of history and philosophy at CUNY York College and a Ph.D. student of philosophy at Southern Illinois University, Carbondale. He received a master's in philosophy from The New School for Social Research, with a thesis entitled "The Correspondence between Art and Nature: Emersonian Aesthetics." His scholarly interests primarily include Emerson, Schopenhauer, Proust, Wallace Stevens, aesthetics, and nature.

Beth Jensen is professor of English at Georgia Perimeter College. She has published a book, *Leaving the M/other: Whitman, Kristeva, and Leaves of Grass* (2002), as well as several articles on Dickinson and Whitman. She is currently working on a book about Whitman, Grant, and the American Renaissance.

Michael Jonik is a Ph.D. candidate in English at the State University of New York, Albany. His dissertation, *The Place of the Mind: Form, Perception, and Experience in Eighteenth and Nineteenth-Century American Literature and Thought,* focuses on the use of natural science and philosophy in the work of Edwards, Emerson, Thoreau, and Melville. He is the 2008 recipient of the Emerson Society Research Grant for his work on Emerson's *Natural History of Intellect* and has published on Melville, Charles Olson, and the relationship between science, literature, and philosophy in American intellectual history. He is currently beginning a longer project devoted to Emerson's later thinking.

Daniel Robert Koch is affiliated with the University of Oxford where he recently completed doctoral studies in history. He is currently working on a book on Emerson and Europe.

Roger Lopez is a Ph.D. candidate in philosophy at the State University of New York, Stony Brook. His dissertation title is "Between Emerson and Unamuno: The Ethics of Solitude and the Value of Society for the Individual." His article, "La presencia de Platón en la filosofía del amor quijotesco," is forthcoming in the proceedings of the I Simposio Internacional de Estudios Cruzados Sobre la Modernidad: "Unamuno y Nosotros."

Kari Miller is an assistant professor of English at Georgia Perimeter College. She has a master's degree in English education from Florida State University and has completed postgraduate work at Valdosta State University. She is an active member of the Community College Humanities Association (CCHA) and participated in a CCHA-NEH summer workshop on Transcendental Concord in 2008.

William A. Paquette is a professor of history at Tidewater Community College, Virginia. He has published more than 125 articles in journals and encyclopedias and written six books. He currently serves as governor of the Virginia Mayflower Society and is education chairman for the General Society of Mayflower Descendants. Dr. Paquette is annually listed in *Who's Who in Education, Who's Who in America,* and *Who's Who in the World.* He has been awarded 11 National Endowment for the Humanities grants.

Audrey Raden is a Ph.D. candidate at the CUNY Graduate School, writing, under the direction of David S. Reynolds, a dissertation entitled "'Were I Not Here': Thoreau's Anticipation of Death." She has presented papers and participated in panel discussions at the MLA, ALA, and the Thoreau Society Annual Gathering. She has taught Transcendentalism, the American Renaissance, and American and British Literature at Brooklyn College and CUNY–Hunter College for more than 11 years and is a published poet.

Jane E. Rosecrans is professor of English at J. Sargeant Reynolds Community College in Richmond, Virginia, where she teaches American literature, women's literature, world literature, the Bible as literature, world religions, and religion in America. She is chair of *Collegium,* an organization for religious liberal scholars, and a member of the history section. She is currently pursuing an M.A. in theological studies at Union Presbyterian

Seminary, where she has done advanced work on the Transcendentalist interest in Eastern religion. Her 2005 sermon, "Transcendentalism for the New Age," is available online through the American Transcendentalism Web. She has most recently presented work on the relationship between the Transcendentalists, the peace and abolition movements, and the Civil War.

Bill Scalia has published essays on religion and film in *Religion and Literature* and *Literature/Film Quarterly*. He has recently edited the anthology *Bloom's Classic Critical Views: Ralph Waldo Emerson* and is currently completing a book on Emersonian aesthetics. Dr. Scalia teaches writing and literature at St. Mary's Seminary and University in Baltimore, Maryland.

Mark Sullivan is the director of the art history program at Villanova University in Pennsylvania and has published widely on the Hudson River School of artists. He is now concentrating on Transcendentalism and its influence on the visual arts in America. His latest book project is a study of the many portraits of Thoreau that have been done since the publication of *Walden* in 1854.

Charlene Williams is an associate professor of English at Ocean County College in Toms River, New Jersey, where she teaches British literature, American literature, and has developed a special annual workshop on Henry David Thoreau. She has also developed courses on literature and the fine arts in the 19th century, a project she worked on as part of an NEH summer program on Transcendental Concord in 2008. Williams is a member of the Community College Humanities Association (CCHA) and the Thoreau Society.

Barbara Downs Wojtusik has recently retired after teaching high school English in the Bristol, Connecticut, public schools. Wojtusik has pursued research on Transcendentalism through grants from the National Endowment for the Humanities, Reader's Digest Teacher/Scholar program, and the Peterson Fellowship of the American Antiquarian Society. Her research culminated in conference papers presented at the National Conference of Teachers of English, the Northeast Modern Language Association, and the Central New York Conference on Language and Literature. Her publications include entries in *Dictionary of Literary Biography*, *American National Biography*, and *The Encyclopedia of Transcendentalism*. Wojtusik is a charter member of the current Emerson Society and served on the board of directors of the Thoreau Society for several years.

MaryCatherine Youmell is currently a Ph.D. candidate at Boston University, with interests including ethics, narrative, and the history of philosophy. She holds a master's degree in philosophy from The New School for Social Research. Her thesis is "Mourning and Ethical Subjectivity: The Demanding Experience of Loss in Judith Butler, Ralph Waldo Emerson, and Emmanuel Levinas."

INDEX

Boldface entries and page numbers indicate major treatment of a topic. *Italic* page numbers denote photos or illustrations.

A

D

E

O

P

T

U

V